The Quest for the Christ Child

in the Later Middle Ages

THE MIDDLE AGES SERIES

Ruth Mazo Karras, Series Editor
Edward Peters, Founding Editor

A complete list of books in the series is available from the publisher.

# THE QUEST FOR
# THE CHRIST CHILD
# IN THE LATER
# MIDDLE AGES

Mary Dzon

**PENN**

UNIVERSITY OF PENNSYLVANIA PRESS

PHILADELPHIA

Published by
University of Pennsylvania Press
Philadelphia, Pennsylvania 19104-4112
www.upenn.edu/pennpress

Printed in the United States of America on acid-free paper
10 9 8 7 6 5 4 3 2 1

A Cataloging-in-Publication record is available from the
Library of Congress
ISBN 978-0-8122-4884-5

In loving memory of Christine T. Dzon

*Coram patre Deus par patri lusit ab aevo,*
*Coram matre nova tempore lusit homo.*
  —Alexander Neckam, *De laudibus*
                      *divinae sapientiae*

# CONTENTS

# ABBREVIATIONS

| | |
|---|---|
| AASS | *Acta Sanctorum*, 69 vols. (Paris, 1863–1940) |
| Add | Additional |
| BL | British Library |
| BnF | Bibliothèque nationale de France |
| CCCM | Corpus Christianorum, Continuatio Mediaevalis |
| CCSA | Corpus Christianorum, Series Apocryphorum |
| CCSL | Corpus Christianorum, Series Latina |
| CF | Cistercian Fathers |
| CS | Cistercian Studies |
| CSEL | Corpus Scriptorum Ecclesiasticorum Latinorum |
| DS | *Dictionnaire de spiritualité ascetique et mystique, doctrine et histoire*, ed. Marcel Viller, 17 vols. (Paris: G. Beauchesne et ses fils, 1937–1995) |
| EETS | Early English Text Society |
| o.s. | Original Series |
| e.s. | Extra Series |
| s.s. | Supplementary Series |
| FAED | *Francis of Assisi: Early Documents*, edited by Regis J. Armstrong, J.A. Wayne Hellmann, and William J. Short, 4 vols. including the index (New York: New City Press, 1999–2002) |
| FC | Fathers of the Church |
| FF | *Fontes Franciscani*, edited by Enrico Menestò and Stefano Brufani (Assisi: Edizioni Porziuncola, 1995) |
| GL | *Golden Legend* |
| LA | *Legenda aurea* |
| MED | *Middle English Dictionary*, ed. Hans Kurath et al. (Ann Arbor: University of Michigan Press, 1952–2001) |
| MGH | Monumenta Germaniae Historica |

OED      *Oxford English Dictionary*, ed. J. A. Simpson and E. S. C. Weiner,
            2nd ed. (Oxford: Oxford University Press, 1989)
PG       *Patrologia Graeca*, ed. J.-P. Migne, 161 vols. (Paris, 1857–66)
PL       *Patrologia Latina*, ed. J.-P. Migne, 221 vols. (Paris, 1844–64)
PMLA     Publications of the Modern Language Association
RS       Rolls Series
SC       Sources Chrétiennes
SFSS     Samlingar utgivna av Svenska Fornskrifsällskapet (Swedish
            Medieval Texts' Society Series)
ST       *Summa theologiae*

The Quest for the Christ Child

in the Later Middle Ages

# Introduction

## Recovering Christ-Child Images

I will rise, and will go about the city: in the streets and the broad
ways I will seek him whom my soul loveth: I sought him, and I
found him not. (Song of Songs 3:2)

## Medieval Christians' Desire to Know About Jesus' Childhood

In *The Book of Margery Kempe*, the story of a fifteenth-century English woman
who, desiring a more spiritual way of life, parted from her husband to go
on pilgrimages, we learn about how she wandered along the streets of Rome
in hopes of stumbling upon Jesus, come to earth again, as a handsome man
or as a darling baby boy. Margery would apparently have been pleased just to
find a male who resembled and thus reminded her of her divine beloved. While
her rather frantic and unconventional search for Jesus attracted attention and
in many cases scorn from her fellow Christians in England and abroad, she
was nevertheless a product of the religiosity of her times, not least in her devotion to the baby Jesus.[1]

As many scholars have observed, in the high Middle Ages (basically, the
period stretching from the eleventh century and into the thirteenth) a new
emphasis was placed upon the humanity of Christ, particularly the sufferings
he endured in his Passion. Men and women living under religious vows, as
well as the laity, began to concentrate more closely on the historical life of
Jesus, especially his dramatic death—a trend that intensified toward the end
of the medieval period. Through meditation on the events of Christ's human

existence, often with the aid of devotional books and images, Christians sought to gain a deeper understanding of the God-man who came to earth to redeem sinful humanity. The liturgical year, like the Creeds, had for centuries called Christians' attention to the two main events of Christ's life—his birth (at Christmastime) and the sufferings that culminated in his salvific death (in Holy Week). Yet it took roughly a millennium (from the time of Christ) before Europeans sought a deeper, more intimate—and, in many cases, intense—relationship with the God of love who became a little baby, lived, worked, and pursued his ministry within a Jewish community, and then suffered a brutal and ignominious death.[2] Even medieval religious writers who stressed that the ultimate goal of the spiritual life was union with the deity, a pure spirit, often encouraged Christians to become more familiar with Jesus in his sacred humanity; by virtue of his concreteness, God the Son was accessible to an array of people at different levels of the spiritual life.[3] While reflection upon the life of Christ was intended to produce feelings of compassion, love, and gratitude, it also provided an exemplar that ideally guided Christians' actions.[4] The high Middle Ages witnessed new religious movements that strove to return to the *vita apostolica* practiced by Jesus' first disciples, as described in the New Testament, and epitomized by Christ himself—a man detached from worldly things, who ministered to those in need and preached salvation, before suffering on the cross.[5] By the later medieval period, Christ the Almighty, whose divine retribution at the Last Judgment traditionally instilled fear, became for Christians a human being to be imitated and loved, on account of his labors and sacrifices on their behalf, as well as his innate goodness. Nonetheless, believers did not lose sight of Jesus' divinity, as we shall see when considering the figure of the Christ Child in the later Middle Ages (generally speaking, the thirteenth through fifteenth centuries).

A desire to know more about Christ's humanity undoubtedly impelled medieval Christians to seek greater knowledge of the events that constituted his life, in its various stages. In other words, curiosity about Christ, linked with a desire to be like him and to share in his sufferings, was a factor in the development of christocentric piety. Significantly, biblical exegetes began to pay more attention to the *series narrationis* of the biblical text at about the same time that the literary form of the romance emerged in Western Europe—a genre that focuses on an individual's experiences over time, or at least on the most exciting and memorable incidents.[6] It was thus natural for Christians to desire a more detailed, if not fully sequential account of Jesus' life. Scripture, however, says very little about Jesus' birth, even less about the marriage of his parents, and almost nothing about his childhood and adolescence. Only two of the four Gospels tell us something about the beginning of Christ's life. The Gospel of Luke (chapter 2) recounts Jesus' birth, the visit of the shepherds, the Child's circumcision, and his Presentation in the Temple; it then skips to the time when Jesus stayed behind in Jerusalem at the age of twelve. The Gospel of Matthew, the only other canonical gospel that discusses Jesus' early life, tells (in chapter 2) how the Magi visited the Christ Child and paid him homage, after which Herod ordered the slaughter of the Innocents. To avoid the mortal blow intended for the baby Jesus, the Holy Family fled into Egypt, where, according to Matthew, they lived for an unspecified duration of time, and then later returned to Judea after Herod's death. The Gospels of Mark and John simply skip over Jesus' infancy and childhood, basically beginning with Jesus' public debut at his baptism (which John, for his part, recounts after his famous prologue about the Incarnation of the divine Word). The "hidden" years of Christ's childhood, which remained a mystery to Christians due to the discontinuity of the Gospel narratives of Luke and Matthew and the complete silence of the other two, obviously posed a problem for Christians who wished to reflect upon the humanity of Christ in all of its stages and aspects.

This book will explore some of the ways in which medieval people tried to make inroads into the early period of Christ's life, which encompasses his infancy, childhood, adolescence, and youth, prior to his public ministry (as presented in the canonical gospels). Although the highly influential early medieval encyclopedist Isidore of Seville demarcated and defined these first four ages of the human life cycle (the first two of which last seven years, the third fourteen years, and the fourth more than twenty years!), medieval authors were not always so precise and not always consistent in their use of terminology pertaining to the stages of human life.[7] In this study I will focus on medieval depictions and discussions of the young and (more frequently) the very young Jesus; I will often refer to Christ's hidden years as his "childhood," broadly construed, though by the phrase "Christ Child" I usually have in mind a younger, preadolescent Jesus (which, in terms of the New Testament's presentation of him, means Jesus before or during the Finding in the Temple episode).

How did medieval people deal with the difficult situation of wanting to know more about Christ's childhood yet lacking ample information, it seemed, from the Bible as well as the liturgy? One approach was for Christians to turn to ancient apocryphal legends about the Christ Child and his family, or, if they were already familiar with some of them, to further their knowledge of such lore. Besides providing many interesting details, these legends laid claim to some authority, which stemmed from their supposedly being written by those who knew the Child (and his parents or the Jewish community in which they lived); at the very least, these stories derived credibility from purportedly being woven from the narratives of reliable witnesses.[8] Crafted as historical accounts written by reputable authors, these narratives seem to have had a popular appeal. Yet as victims of their own success, it seems, within a few centuries of their composition they suffered the fate of being listed in the so-called Gelasian Decree (sixth century) among the many "apocryphal" books that the Church rejected, largely because of the perceived uncertainty surrounding their authorship. In other words, they were not accepted as being part of the official canon of biblical writings and could not be read in church.[9] Even though they lacked the indubitable authority of the inspired Scriptures and aroused ecclesiastical suspicion, these apocryphal infancy texts were still considered valuable as sources of information about the births and childhoods of both Mary and Jesus.[10] Christians' willingness, in the later medieval period as well as earlier, to give credence to numerous details from the apocryphal infancy narratives is understandable considering that believers, many of whom were not literate, did not rely solely on Scripture and on official Latin texts and ecclesiastical teachings for the contents of their faith, but also looked to oral traditions and vernacular culture.

There were other possible approaches if one wished to know more about the Christ Child and his parents but did not wish to resort to apocryphal legends, which indeed had a certain aura of dubiousness about them. Focusing on reliable, biblical texts, one could seek greater knowledge of the early stages of Christ's life through careful study of Scripture, by linking together passages that directly deal with the Christ Child with verses from different parts of the Bible that seemed applicable to him. Medieval Christian scholars viewed many passages from the Hebrew Scriptures as prophecies of, or encoded references to, the child Jesus, and such typological readings were transmitted to broader audiences.[11] Another approach, one that seems to have yielded a more diverse outcome, was the retrospective application of the New Testament's presentation of the adult Christ to Jesus' boyhood, according to the common view that famous or saintly people were biographically consistent over the course of their lifetime. So, for example, if Jesus when he was a preacher spoke of himself as "meek and humble of heart" (Matt. 11:29), then it only stands to reason that the child Jesus would have been like that, too. On the other hand, the adult Jesus' conflicts with the Jewish authorities suggested to some medieval Christians that he likely experienced opposition from Jewish elders (or those who were to become such) early on: just as he healed a blind man on the Sabbath using moistened clay (John 9:1–15), so also in his childhood, one might have reasoned, he fashioned clay birds at a riverside in violation of the Jewish day of rest.[12] Related to this notion of biographical consistency is the popular belief that people destined for greatness give signs of this early on, as baby Hercules famously did when he killed the snake insidiously placed in his cradle.[13] Yet not everyone was willing to take a more fanciful approach to Jesus' childhood, or, on the other hand, had the training and leisure to study the Bible's numerous (both clear and subtle) references to Christ as a way to discover something about his childhood. A conservative yet still somewhat creative approach was for a Christian to meditate prayerfully on scenes or episodes from Jesus' early life, which are mentioned in the canonical gospels and commemorated in the liturgy, using his or her imagination to yield further details, which, if not completely accurate in a historical sense, were at least conducive to devotion. One could also aspire to supernatural communication with Jesus and Mary themselves, who might graciously reveal information about Christ's childhood or help one reenvision it, as it transpired long ago within the household of the Holy Family and the village in which they lived—details that would have otherwise remained hidden. In short, medieval Christians who wished to gain a greater imaginary hold on the early part of Jesus' life clearly had a variety of approaches at their disposal; besides turning to the apocrypha, they could study Scripture, pray and meditate, and also think of Jesus' youth in terms of more contemporary constructs (such as late medieval ideals of masculinity).

## A Shift in Medieval Christians' Response to the Divine Child

In the patristic and early medieval periods, religious writers focused not so much on the early events of Christ's life as a way to draw Christians closer to Jesus, but on the paradox of the Incarnation—of God condescending to become a human being—surely a great cause for wonderment.[14] How was it possible for Mary's womb to contain the Lord of the universe, who is "the wondrous sphere that knows no bounds, that has its centre everywhere and whose circumference is not in any place"?[15] Another paradox frequently propounded by early writers was the transformation of the Eternal Word into an *infans*—literally, one who does not speak.[16] While Christians during the first fifteen hundred years of the Church continuously wondered at God's becoming a child and the paradoxes that followed thereon, it seems generally to be the case that, starting around the late eleventh century, more attention was paid to Jesus' humanity per se—that is, not simply as a way to highlight the contrast between Christ's divine and human natures. The experience of wonder arguably shifted in emphasis, with less weight being given to the intellectual stupefaction resulting from the awareness of paradox and more to the delight produced by the approachability of a God who became a lowly infant and simple child.[17] In one of his Christmas homilies, the eleventh-century Italian monk and reformer Peter Damian, who is sometimes seen as a herald of the new concentration on Christ's humanity, evinces the emotion of wonder as he calls attention to the Christ Child's humanity, yet, at the same time, he does not seem to foster an emotional or imaginative interaction with the baby Jesus. Damian thus seems to stand at the end of a long tradition of Christ-directed piety:

> Who would not be astounded that he who is not held in by the vastness of heaven is laid in a narrow manger? He who clothes his elect with the stole of immortality does not despise being covered by base rags. He who is the food of angels reclined on the straw of beasts. He who quells the storms of the sea . . . awaits the precious drops of milk from the Virgin's breast. . . . The little infant who is tightly bound in a child's swaddling clothes by his mother is the immense one who, with his Father, governs the rights of all things. O how great were the castellated palaces of the world's kings . . . and yet he who chose the manger as the crib of his Nativity despised all those things. . . . He wished to be cast down so that he might carry us to the heights; he became a poor person in this world, so that he might present us partakers of his riches. Dearly beloved brothers, ponder the humility of our Redeemer with all the contemplation of your soul.[18]

Damian in this passage is concerned with eliciting a response of loving gratitude and joy based upon an intellectual and imaginative realization of what the Incarnation really means: Christ deigned to become a poor and powerless child so that he might generously share his divine wealth with lowly human beings. Who would have thought of such a thing!

In the following century, the eloquent Cistercian abbot Bernard of Clairvaux, in one of his sermons for the Vigil of Christmas, claimed that the belief
that God united himself with humanity and that a virgin became a mother
was itself a cause of wonder, since it entailed the coupling of faith and the
human heart, which, by implication, is naturally inclined to disbelieve the
pairing of polar opposites. Bernard uses striking language to speak of these
three conjunctions, stating, for example: "Majesty compressed himself to join
to our dust (*limo nostro*, literally, 'our mud') the best thing he had, which is
himself. . . . Nothing is more sublime than God, nothing is lower than dust—
and yet God descended into dust with great condescension . . . a mystery as
ineffable as it is incomprehensible."[19] Further in the sermon, Bernard recon-
siders the wonder implicated in belief in the Incarnation, asking rhetorically:
"Are we to believe then that the one who is laid in the manger, who cries in his
cradle, who suffers all the indignities children have to suffer, who is scourged,
who is spat upon, who is crucified . . . is the high and immeasurable God?"[20]
Though Bernard here briefly mentions concrete aspects of Christ's babyhood,
he does not urge his audience to savor such homely details. Elsewhere, in a
sermon for Christmas day, he leads his reader to a more personal reflection on
the lowliness of Christ's Nativity: "I recognize as mine the time and place of
his birth, the tenderness of the infant body, the crying and tears of the baby. . . .
These things are mine . . . they are set before me, they are set out for me to
imitate."[21] In this passage, while he praises God's wisdom, Bernard focuses
on the example of asceticism provided by the infant Word; God did not
become human by assuming the form of a strong man—in the view of many,
the most impressive type of human being—but "became flesh, weak flesh,
infant flesh, tender flesh, powerless flesh, flesh incapable of any work, of any
effort."[22] The helplessness of the baby Jesus, lying in the manger, underscores
the weakness of all human flesh, including that of monks who were supposed
to discipline their body continually, in order to overcome pride and subdue
fleshly desires.

Though Bernard approaches his subject rhetorically rather than scholas-
tically, he shares a sentiment with high-medieval intellectuals who wondered
at the tenderness of infants' bodies. I refer here to how some scholars pondered why God, the author of nature, made it much easier for the babies of
animals to move about on their own and seek food. The new Aristotelianism
that partially prompted such questions may very well have led to greater reflection on the human nature of Jesus, who was thought to have truly passed

through the early stages of the human life cycle. In other words, Jesus was believed to have experienced what other babies, children, and adolescents experienced—to be like us in all things but sin (Heb. 4:15).[23] Another possibility was that Jesus simply gave the appearance that he was developing, as he non-dramatically bided his time until undertaking his adult mission.

Thus far, I have sketched out a broad picture of how Christians roughly in the first millennium and a half of the Christian era regarded the God-Man who, among other surprising things, had chosen to begin his earthly existence as a little child. The desire to know more about the Savior was probably always present among Christians. But as the centuries passed, believers felt a greater urge to delve into the human aspects of Christ's existence, to imagine what it was like for Jesus to have been a helpless baby and then a growing boy. Although acknowledgement of the union of the two natures in Christ must have always been a cause of wonderment, Christians in the later Middle Ages seem to have approached this mystery on a more personal level, reflecting, for instance, on how the lowliness of their own humanity was willingly assumed by the Son of God. Yet as we shall see, though God became more approachable, especially in his childhood form, Christians continued to reverence his mighty power and mysterious transcendence, which were recognized even in the boy Jesus.

## Previous Scholarship Pertaining to the Medieval Christ Child

Although scholars focusing on Mary or the adult Jesus occasionally mention the child Jesus, there has been no broad-reaching, single-authored study of this figure specifically in the medieval period, as William MacLehose has observed.[24] This is the case, despite the fact that the Christ Child was the object of intense devotion in the later Middle Ages, and was a pervasive presence throughout medieval society. Scholars can find traces of the Christ Child's influence even in areas where we might not expect to encounter evidence of the power and allure of Jesus as an infant or boy, such as papal politics, the crusade movement, intercultural relations, and the dynamics within local communities and domestic settings.[25] While people looked for and esteemed the traces of Jesus' early years on earth, often traveling great distances and enduring many hardships in order to make contact with the remnants of his historical past,[26] medieval Christians acted as if Jesus still existed as a child and was accessible to them in their own settings—at home, in the convent, and in the nearby parish church. Writers and artists frequently spoke of and represented the Christ Child in their works, ostensibly with the goal of linking Christians with Jesus' past and also of underscoring the living reality of Christ as a child with whom they could engage in the present. Ironically, the widespread presence of the Christ-Child figure within medieval culture may largely explain why he has not received a tremendous amount of critical attention from modern scholars, who may acknowledge his importance but consider it a constant and steady feature rather than a crucial factor within, or indication of, a particular medieval cultural setting.

The following brief overview of some of the scholarship on the medieval cult of the Christ Child will suggest further hypotheses as to why this area of research has not flourished more bountifully. To start with the more recent: *The Christ Child in Medieval Culture*, a 2012 essay collection I coedited with Theresa Kenney, focuses on later medieval sources, both textual and visual. In that book, which brought together scholars from a range of disciplines, Kenney and I sought to orient future scholarship in the field by exploring some of the key aspects of the Christ Child's cult. The study was divided into three parts: "The Christ Child as Sacrifice," "The Christ Child and Feminine Spirituality," and, last, "The Question of the Christ Child's Development." Of these groupings, the third cluster of essays relates most closely to this current book, though the authors of those pieces did not intend to treat the issue of Christ's childhood development systematically, with an eye to understanding the interrelationship of various sources. That part of the book simply offered three essays that dealt with the implications of medieval belief in Jesus as a real child, both physically and psychologically. From that section, Pamela Sheingorn's chapter on two medieval Italian textual reworkings of the apocryphal legends about Jesus' childhood, in my opinion, complements the present study particularly well. Sheingorn takes a microcosmic view of the apocryphal infancy tradition, focusing on two illustrated manuscripts (which contain related but substantially different narratives), whereas my approach to the apocryphal legends in this book is much more general. As I explain below, here I am interested in demonstrating the broad influence of the apocryphal tradition on later medieval culture. Hence it follows that although I mention (specifically in Chapter 3) some of the medieval manuscripts containing apocryphal infancy texts and illustrations, space does not permit me to focus on particular texts or manuscripts in great detail. In the Appendix, though, I offer a summary of the chapters in William Caxton's *Infantia salvatoris*, which is fairly representative of the Latin narratives about Christ's childhood circulating in the later Middle Ages.

Previous studies on the medieval Christ Child (that is, prior to the 2012 essay collection) tended to concentrate on two interrelated facets of the cult: first, the association of the child Jesus with the Eucharist, specifically the numerous cases in which he is said or shown to inhere in the consecrated host in a veiled manner, sometimes becoming visible to those who look upon the sacrament; and, second, his occasional appearance to and interaction with holy men and women generally considered mystics. The first approach is well illustrated by Leah Sinanoglou Marcus's 1973 *Speculum* article "The Christ Child as Sacrifice: A Medieval Tradition and the Corpus Christi Plays," which discusses conflations of the Eucharist and the Christ Child that we commonly find in late medieval drama and other sources, such as contemporaneous and earlier homilies. This classic essay has frequently been cited by medievalists and other scholars, not only because of its superb insights and impressive range, but also because other treatments of the child Jesus (in English and other languages) have been lacking.[27] Caroline Walker Bynum's numerous studies on medieval holy women constitute the prime example of the second, related category. Bynum frequently mentions the appearance of Jesus in the host, especially as he is savored by medieval holy women, who in a sense consume him, while denying themselves earthly food. Their gusto in relishing the baby Jesus may be summed up in an exclamation from a German nun whom Bynum quotes more than once: "If I had you, I'd eat you up, I love you so much!"[28] Bynum also cites various instances of holy women enacting what were considered maternal roles and sentiments vis-à-vis the Christ Child, either meditatively, through the use of props, or with the Child himself, mystically reincarnated, so to speak, in their midst. Countering the pejorative view of some modern critics that such women were simply expressing their repressed femininity, for example, by naively playing with Christ-Child dolls or cradles, Bynum argues that such behavior, which was inextricably tied to the medieval discourse of women's rootedness in the body, was consciously chosen and even enjoyed by women as an active mode of spirituality which they themselves could direct and excel at.

While the studies of both Bynum and Marcus are tremendously valuable, an accidental result of their successes has been that scholarship in the area of the medieval Christ Child has tended not to expand into other areas. In my view, when those of us whose work occasionally touches upon the medieval Christ Child cite such studies and then move on, without trying to learn more about medieval views of Jesus' childhood, we run the risk of accepting a partial picture in place of a broader, more detailed landscape. A student of medieval culture in search of a summary of the medieval Christ Child prior to the 2012 collection may, understandably, have concluded that the child Jesus was simply a Eucharistic phenomenon or an important feature of female piety—the particular focus of women religious whose opportunities within the church were indeed limited. While the figure of the child Jesus certainly seems to have been appropriated differently by different genders,[29] in my view, it is incorrect to regard him as mainly falling within the devotional purview of medieval women, a point supported by an observation made by Peter Dinzelbacher years ago in discussing christocentric piety among high-medieval mystics.[30] So, we need to look more broadly at medieval sources touching or focusing on the Christ Child that were produced by, and for, men and women (and even possibly for children), examining different kinds of texts, images, and objects, not just those dealing with the Eucharist or centering around people regarded as saintly. Keeping the big picture in mind, we need to consider the Christ Child from various angles and the early part of his human life in relation to his adulthood and divinity, without limiting ourselves to a particular aspect of his personage or behavior, in isolation from the rest of his identity.[31]

The continuing influence of the apocryphal legends about Jesus' infancy and childhood into the Middle Ages, and the role played by other imaginative texts, has, in my view, been obscured by the heavy emphasis of scholarship on mystical and Eucharistic encounters with Jesus. While these are certainly key pieces in the puzzle, they cannot stand alone as embodiments of medieval piety toward the Christ Child. Indeed, I suspect that the shortness and unpredictability of such supernatural encounters may, at least at times, have been frustrating to medieval Christians who wanted to enter more deeply into the mysteries of Jesus' childhood—to advance along the quest for deeper knowledge of the divine child. When Jesus appears in the host as an infant or slightly older boy, the description we get of him usually emphasizes his amazing beauty, but it is nevertheless often tantalizingly nondescript; concomitantly, the duration of the vision or heavenly visitation is usually very short. Moreover, such mystical experiences were regarded as gifts rather than as something one could willfully lay claim to, though they could definitely be prepared for, especially by pious meditational reading, interaction with related artworks, pilgrimage to shrines, and attentive participation in the liturgy.

Margery Kempe, whom I mentioned earlier, felt the frustration of not having her wishes for a mystical experience with the child Jesus come true. Once when she saw some Italian women with babes in arms, who turned out to be, not surprisingly, just ordinary human infants, her "mende [was] so raveschyd into the childhod of Crist, for desir that sche had for to see hym, that sche mith not beryn [endure] it."[32] Nor did Margery, despite her imitation of earlier holy women, ever see the baby Jesus in the host, as he is said to have appeared to many female saints. Even though it may have seemed like a disappointment to her, Margery could still return to the devotional books she had access to back in England, which likely included a version of St. Birgitta of Sweden's revelations, which, as we shall see, shed much light on the Christ Child. And if Margery was curious and persistent enough, she could have learned of the apocryphal tales of Jesus' childhood, which at that time circulated in English and were also rendered artistically.

One of the reasons that medievalists have not pressed very far beyond such previous studies,[33] extremely worthwhile and indeed essential though they are, is that the attention of scholars interested in medieval religiosity has been directed elsewhere. That is, recent studies on medieval devotion to the humanity of Christ have focused almost exclusively on the Passion of Christ and medieval Christians' sacramental access to it through the Eucharist—the figure of the suffering Jesus, who, driven by love and exhausted from physical abuse, hangs on the cross, offering his body both as a propitiatory sacrifice and as spiritually nourishing food.[34] Without a doubt, medievalists' focus on the Man of Sorrows is both understandable and justifiable, given the centrality of this figure in the later Middle Ages.[35] One valuable area of contribution within this latter field has been the recent work done on the anti-Judaic aspects of medieval treatments of the Passion and their unfortunate social consequences.[36] Equally important has been the recent scholarship on devotion to the Virgin Mary in the medieval period, which has tended to focus on medieval approaches to the compassion she felt on Calvary or tales of her miraculous interventions in medieval people's lives. In their concern about the undeniable historical meaning and importance of Mary, these studies often gesture at, if not actually grapple with, contemporary feminist/gender issues.[37] Such contemporary concerns have probably resulted in more attention being paid to the medieval Virgin Mary than to the medieval Christ Child, even though interest in historical or other types of childhood studies has grown over the last fifty years or so. Still, medievalists do not seem to have felt a strong exigency to explore the medieval Christ Child more thoroughly. This deficiency largely accounts for the synthetic and interdisciplinary nature of the present study, which (though limited in scope) aims to bring together and explore some of the ways in which medieval Christians imagined Jesus in the early part of this life.

To be sure, we would have a much better understanding of medieval piety if we knew what it was about the figure of Mary that inspired, among many other things, a young man to wed himself to her, solemnizing the dedication of his heart to this lovely lady by placing a ring around the finger of her effigy. The Praemonstratensian canon Hermann-Joseph of Steinfeld (d. 1241) indeed performed this ritualistic and deeply meaningful gesture in his youth, if we can believe his hagiographer.[38] Yet Hermann-Joseph also played with the Christ Child when he was a boy, having been invited to do so by Mary (who supposedly communicated with the pious youth through a statue of the Virgin and Child). As we shall see, in the later Middle Ages, many people interacted with the child Jesus, sometimes on a one-on-one basis. An animated statue of the Virgin and Child comes into play in another tale, a Miracle of the Virgin found in a thirteenth-century manuscript: when a nun was at prayer, the Christ Child spoke to her and instructed her sometimes to say "Ave benigne Deus" to him (by implication not simply the "Ave Maria" to his mother).[39] Although medieval Christians sometimes seem to have focused on either Mary or the Christ Child, these figures were thought to be inextricably intertwined on account of their perpetual maternal-filial relationship.[40] Arguments in favor of Mary's bodily Assumption in fact drew attention to her loving care of and constant companionship with her son during his lifetime, implying that it would be impossible for Jesus not to reciprocate his mother's love by having her beside him in heaven.[41] That Mary and Jesus are closely linked by an enduring bond is likewise conveyed by an *exemplum* recounted in the *Legenda aurea* of Jacobus de Voragine, an immensely popular collection of saints' lives from the thirteenth century: a woman who wanted to liberate her imprisoned son devised a novel yet effective plan. She detached an image of the baby Jesus from a statue of the Virgin and Child, took the effigy home with her, and locked it in a cupboard in order to force Mary to help her regain her son. This the Virgin promptly did, in order to recover her own beloved child.[42]

To sum up: in this section I have shown how there has previously been no broad-ranging study of the child Jesus as a focus of devotion and curiosity specifically in the Middle Ages, though a number of studies dealing with related aspects of medieval piety (and Christianity more generally) have explored important aspects of the medieval Christ-Child cult. Scholars interested in the ideas and social realities surrounding childhood in the Middle Ages have also touched upon this central figure within medieval culture.[43]

## Studying the Christ Child and Medieval Childhood

At the outset, it is worthwhile stating my view that, given the inherently theological character of medieval images of and legends about Christ, they seem to have only a limited capacity to shed light upon medieval childhood (a difficult, though rewarding area of research, due to the relative scarcity of medieval sources focusing on children or childhood). Nevertheless, studying the medieval Christ Child can give us some indication of how medieval adults thought of and treated children.[44] An example of this occurs in the vita of Ida of Louvain, a thirteenth-century Cistercian nun, which tells of a vision that Ida had one night, in which a lovely-looking boy Jesus, wearing a full-length seamless tunic, appeared to her sister who had badly mistreated her that very day. Climbing onto her bed, he proceeded to "overpower her with his punching fists and kicking feet." He also "added bold outspoken words, in which he took her to task for the stupidity and wickedness behind her upbraiding of her sister [Ida]," who was accustomed to caring for him.[45] This vita provides another naturalistic view of Christ as a normal human child (though in a more positive sense), in its account of Ida's vision of being privileged to assist St. Elizabeth, Jesus' aunt, in bathing him. First the women arranged the bathtub and the other things that were needed: "Then Elizabeth, along with Ida, carefully sat the Infant in the lukewarm water to be bathed. Seated there, this Choicest of Children cupped his hands and clapped on the water—as playing children will do. He toyed with the waves he stirred and he splashed [water onto] the floor all around."[46] Commenting on this passage, social historian David Herlihy remarks that "the male author of this life had clearly observed babies in the bath, and noted the delight which real mothers took in washing their infants."[47]

Just as sources dealing with the Christ Child have the potential to reveal medieval perceptions of children and attitudes toward childhood, so the study of medieval childhood helps situate medieval representations of the boy Jesus within the broader culture. For instance, knowing that swaddled babies, in medieval art, look very similar to deceased infants (who are similarly shrouded) helps us appreciate why the Christ Child in Nativity scenes is frequently depicted tightly swaddled, lying on a block-like, almost tomb-like manger. Such images represent the newborn Jesus as a sacrificial offering, placed, as it were, upon the altar at Mass. The Infant's swaddling clothes, with their connotations of burial, foreshadow the adult Christ's shroud and thus his future death, an association with perhaps more poignancy for medieval viewers, who dealt with deceased infants much more regularly than we do.[48] To take another example, one from day-to-day life: knowledge that medieval mothers were often responsible for the education and formation of young children infuses greater realism into medieval images of Mary interacting with Jesus, as if to instill in him basic skills or knowledge about the world around him, if not also to confer with him regarding his future mission.[49] Medieval sources probably had an even more powerful effect on their audiences when they involved a reversal of cultural norms; for example, some medieval texts and images suggest that the child Jesus actually instructed his mother about the suffering that lay ahead for both of them.

Other scholars have recognized the connection between medieval childhood and the medieval Christ Child as interrelated phenomena. In a wide-ranging essay on medieval childhood, originally published in 1978, David Herlihy argued that the urbanization of Western Europe in the eleventh and twelfth centuries and the dangers posed to children's lives from contemporary social upheavals resulted in a greater "willingness on the part of society to invest substantially in [children's] welfare [and] education."[50] Herlihy provides some evidence for adults' concern that their children acquire marketable skills within the new urban economy, and also some indication of adults' (presumably new or newly reflected upon) understanding of the particular nature of children. While noting that monks in the earlier Middle Ages, according to the sources, tended to praise children's virtues and treat them humanely, Herlihy claims that the Cistercians in the twelfth century started a new trend of idealizing childhood, which later appealed to the laity, who sometimes felt burdened by materialism—an idea that complements my suggestion below that medieval adults desired somehow to reappropriate the simplicity of childhood. Herlihy boldly proposes that the "widespread devotion to the Child Jesus," which developed from the twelfth century onward, and was strongly promoted by the Cistercians and Franciscans, stemmed from the appeal of childhood itself—an intriguing hypothesis that, intuitively, seems to have a good deal of truth to it.[51]

While investigations that consider the synergy among ideas about and images of childhood on the one hand and of the Christ Child on the other are definitely valuable, I would stress the importance of keeping in mind the diversity that existed within the latter category—a multiplicity that reflects the inherent difficulty medieval people faced when pondering the deity's having become a child. Not only was God challenging (indeed impossible) for medieval Christian adults to comprehend, but so, too, it appears, was the very nature of a child. Studying the medieval Christ Child sheds light on this mystery, as medieval people perceived it—something that the other sources examined by social historians do not often convey, even though they may indicate parents' emotional investment in their offspring, for example.[52]

## Adding More to the Mix: Appealing Images of the Child, Yet None Completely Authoritative or Fully Satisfactory

Herlihy's hypotheses that the emergence of a new urban economy led to a greater concern for and awareness of children, and that the idealization of children helped to relieve the stresses of day-to-day life for medieval adults, are certainly plausible. Yet his explanation for the new European interest in the Christ Child seems reductionistic. In sum, Herlihy says that what lay and religious people of the later Middle Ages most admired about the Christ Child was his childlikeness.[53] Although a number of medieval sources call attention to the ways in which Jesus embodies the positive, natural virtues of children,[54] most of the texts and images examined in this present study do not have this emphasis. Herlihy rightfully draws our attention to the successful efforts of the Cistercians and Franciscans to promote devotion to the child Jesus, but the members of these two groups did not simply portray the boy Jesus as a sweet and charming child, worthy of love and emulation on a basic human level. There were other ways in which the Child was presented and regarded, by various groups and individuals, in the high and later Middle Ages.

As we shall see in Chapter 2, for the twelfth-century Cistercian Aelred of Rievaulx, the Christ Child is the mystical bridegroom for whom the soul yearns and toward whom it makes progress, especially by retracing the key events of Christ's early life. While Aelred, in one section of his well-known treatise on the twelve-year-old Jesus, sketches a picture of Christ as a charming child, he clearly wants his reader to go beyond such a conceptualization and visualization by developing spiritually, specifically through the cultivation of the virtues. In this treatise, Aelred also speaks derogatorily of the Jews, ostensibly to present a stark alternative: allegorizing the story in Luke about the loss of the twelve-year-old Jesus, he says that the Jews (represented in this episode by Jesus' parents) have great difficulty finding the Messiah. By implication, Aelred's monastic reader should do what it takes to avoid losing Jesus, and thus avoid the grief experienced by Jesus' parents and the other members of the Jewish community who knew him. So, while Aelred deserves credit for laying important groundwork for greater reflection on Christ's childhood in the later medieval period, his main goal was clearly not to promote a fundamentally sentimental approach to the boy Jesus; his treatment of the Christ Child is definitely more complex. Such complexity exists among Franciscan sources as well. As I show in the latter part of Chapter 2, Francis of Assisi had, and promoted, a more affective response to the infant Jesus, whom he regarded as a poor boy worthy of tremendous compassion. Yet for the Italian saint and his Franciscan followers the Child was not merely a darling *bambino* who captured their hearts. Much of their attention focused on the suffering that Jesus embraced at birth and throughout his life, which revealed the heights of divine love and was worthy of radical reciprocation. Moreover, the love of the Father who gave his Son to the world to redeem humankind—long ago in Bethlehem and in the present, on the altar at every Mass—was considered a cause of great rejoicing and also a mystery to be profoundly revered.

While it is true that the Cistercians and Franciscans invigorated the cult of the Christ Child for the later medieval period, as Herlihy emphasized, there were many Christians not belonging to or affiliated with these groups who fostered greater attention and a more intense response to the child Jesus—numerous men and women who in varying ways contributed to the historical cult of the Christ Child but who, for lack of space, cannot be featured here in detail (or, in some cases, mentioned at all). In terms of iconography, there was a range of images of the Christ Child in circulation; the "new picture of the Child Jesus," whose humility and gentleness were attractive to medieval adults, did not simply supplant the old apocryphal portrayal of an "all-knowing and all-powerful" Christ Child, as Herlihy's brief comments about the apocrypha seem to imply.[55] The two main types of images he speaks of should, instead, be thought of as having competed with each other and, in many cases, overlapped with each other, as well as with other images. To be sure, in the medieval period there were not simply two types of Christ-Child figures, which were basically diametrically opposed, though it may be helpful to think of broad categories.

When we consider medieval iconography, we certainly perceive a difference between, on the one hand, the older Romanesque depiction of a hieratic, stern-looking Christ Child seated upon his mother's lap, like a priestly or regal figure wielding influence from a throne, and, on the other hand, the more human Virgin and Child of Gothic art, who tenderly and playfully interact with each other. On the basis of the emergence of the latter, more approachable image, Philippe Ariès claimed that the seeds of the discovery of childhood in Western culture were sown in the later Middle Ages, when artists began to portray the child Jesus more realistically. Although it took a long time for this trend of realism "to extend beyond the frontiers of religious iconography," he considered it "nonetheless true that the group of the Virgin and Child changed in character and became more and more profane: the picture of a scene of everyday life."[56] Though Ariès's unsubstantiated (and rather ambiguous) remark that medieval society lacked a "sentiment de l'enfance" has rightfully been dismissed,[57] he should surely be given credit for noting that a discovery of the Christ Child, so to speak, occurred in the later Middle Ages. A new outlook and sensibility did indeed arise, in the sense that the boy Jesus became the object of fresh attention and zeal, and that the implications of his having been a real child were pondered with new interest and open-mindedness.[58]

A little more than a decade after the appearance of Ariès's book on the history of childhood, Leah Sinanoglou Marcus provided a brief though cogent overview of the medieval Christ Child as background for her literary study of Early Modern childhood. Despite the fact that her summary is quite insightful and still useful, it might lead one to think that a sentimental (fundamentally Franciscan) view of the Child predominated in the later Middle Ages:

> From the beginning of the thirteenth century, the childhood of
> Jesus was portrayed with increasing frequency and realism. Latin
> nativity hymns from the fourth to the twelfth centuries are nearly
> all abstract treatments of doctrine just as visual depictions of the
> Christ Child from that period display him with hieratic formalism
> as the grave Incarnation of Divine Wisdom or the sacrificial Victim
> of the mass. But in the vernacular carols of the Franciscan Jaco-
> pone da Todi (1228–1306) the new affective spirit bursts forth. Jesus
> is "our sweet little brother," called by the endearing diminutives
> "Bambolino" and "Jesulino."

Figure 1. The boy Jesus reverenced as king by other boys, in an illustrated *Vita rhythmica* manuscript. London, British Library, Add. 29434, fol. 57v (fifteenth century?). By permission of the British Library Board.

Drawing a sharp contrast between a more intellectualized and a more affective Christ Child, Marcus sums up the emergence of a new image of Jesus by
saying that, in the later Middle Ages, "the Infant Jesus leapt out of his Byzantine impassivity and became recognizably infantile, laughing, sucking the pap,
or playing with fruit and toys."[59] A new iconography definitely emerged, yet
the older images did not simply disappear. While Marcus's succinct account
of the later medieval Christ Child is impressive, it involves some exaggeration
and oversimplification (Jacopone is surely not conventional).[60] Images of a jocund Christ Child who noticeably laughs or even smiles are actually difficult
to find.[61] And evidence is lacking that Francis himself referred to Jesus as "our
sweet little brother," though the sources definitely indicate that the saint was
deeply touched by the humility and lowliness that God manifested in becoming a human child. Significantly, in the twelfth- to fifteenth-century Latin
and Middle English texts that I concentrate on in this study Jesus is not referred to endearingly, as far as I am aware, as "little brother." This is not to
deny, however, that some medieval authors, reflecting on mankind's new familial relationship with God made possible through Mary's divine motherhood, spoke of Jesus as our "brother."[62] In contrast to sources that call attention
to the deity's approachability on account of the Incarnation, the late medieval redactions of the apocrypha recount how Jesus' childhood friends and
the adults with whom he came into contact often called him "Lord."[63] Such
reverence can extend even further: in an illustrated late medieval manuscript
that retells a number of the apocryphal infancy legends, the boy Jesus is shown
seated on a throne and reverently crowned by two boys, while a number of
other boys who surround him kneel in obeisance (London, British Library,
Add. 29434, fol. 57v; fig. 1).[64]


## Proceeding from, Rather than Searching for Origins

This book, which gratefully acknowledges the contributions of previous related scholarship, which I have sought to synthesize and build upon, takes the
mid-twelfth century as its starting point; it by no means aims to provide an
encompassing history of the ideas, images, and emotions surrounding the
Christ Child over the course of the first millennium and a half of Western
Christianity, or even during the European Middle Ages. While some medievalists may choose to concentrate on the crucial turning points in medieval

culture or to sort out which historical personages were most instrumental in the emergence of new developments, that is not my approach here, mainly because I am ultimately interested in the medieval reception of the apocryphal Christ Child and the relationship of the apocryphal legends to other roughly contemporary sources. I begin, in a sense, in medias res with well-known Cistercian and Franciscan saints and other figures, without giving a great deal of attention to their precursors or contemporaries, such as the numerous holy women and men who likewise embraced christocentric piety and *imitatio Christi*, and showed a notable degree of interest in Jesus as an infant, child, or youth.[65] I have purposefully limited my focus to the later medieval period because of the abundance and richness of the relevant sources dating from this time. As a result, I survey in this book a range of texts from the high and later Middle Ages that attempt to provide a fuller picture of the child Jesus—texts that for the most part seem intended to help their readers progress along the quest of finding the "hidden" Christ Child, and also acknowledge the impossibility of completing that quest on earth.[66] I primarily examine works that may be broadly classified as devotional literature,[67] periodically mentioning medieval exegetical, theological, liturgical, dramatic, and lyrical texts; this book thus encompasses various types of religious literature pertaining to the Christ Child, with special attention paid to works whose readership extended beyond those who were highly educated. While I give priority to late medieval redactions of the apocryphal infancy legends, I intentionally focus on an assortment of sources, both medieval and patristic, that originated from different parts of Europe, as well as the Eastern Mediterranean.[68] This study also explores, though to a lesser extent, related visual sources, and other forms of material culture, such as relics and the physical aspects of pilgrimage. My overarching goal is to provide a broad conceptual and categorical map that will amply illustrate the influence of the apocrypha on later medieval writers who attempted to reconstruct Jesus' early years in diverse ways—a wide-ranging yet focused picture that will help frame future studies. Therefore, none of my primary sources are treated exhaustively, neither those I explore in detail, nor those I mention briefly, mainly for comparison's sake. My aim is to argue for intertextuality—or, more specifically, a synergy among sources—rather than to produce a comprehensive and meticulous cultural history of the Christ Child throughout the Middle Ages. Nevertheless, what I offer covers much literary and intellectual territory. It is my wish that the broad argument of this book and the numerous details contained therein will serve as a guide to other scholars, especially given the lack of previous work in this field.

## A Study of Different Identities for the Child Jesus—Commonly Linked with the Apocrypha

To recap and forecast the major threads of this study: in a general sense, the present book shows Christians' tendency in the later Middle Ages to regard the Christ Child as an individual with whom they could communicate, in whose experiences they could share, and whose historical interactions with others (such as his family members and neighbors) they hoped they could better understand and profit from spiritually. My exploration of the Child's cult illustrates Christians' desire to make progress on a quest for deeper spirituality and greater knowledge of the God-man, Jesus Christ, through the use of various texts, objects, and artworks that shed light on the hidden years of Jesus' youth. As we shall see, certain aspects of late medieval culture were incorporated (probably unconsciously) into diverse imaginative attempts to reconstruct Christ's childhood and youth. This imaginative appropriation is readily apparent in the case of the early Franciscans, who thought of the child Jesus as a pauper like themselves. One can also sense that, within late medieval culture, parallels were perceived between the infant Jesus and the supernatural beings of medieval folklore: incubi, changelings, and demons who appear in human form.[69]

At the same time that writers added color to their portrayals of the young Jesus by incorporating new details that stemmed from the constructs and objects with which they themselves were familiar, they relied upon ancient traditions of both a popular and theological nature. These include the belief that Christ was, at least in a non-physical sense, a perfect person from the beginning of his life,[70] an idea which, on the face of it, seems at odds with Luke's remark (2:52) that Jesus progressed as he grew up (increasing "in wisdom, and age, and grace with God and men"). The view that the Christ Child was perfect—a human fully developed psychologically, due to his divinity—can be perceived in the fourteenth-century *Meditationes vitae Christi* and in other sources. As Jaime Vidal points out, we might assume that the Christ Child of this Franciscan-authored devotional text (whom the reader is invited to embrace lovingly and relate to in other tender ways) is simply a literary version of contemporary Gothic depictions of Jesus as a recognizably human child.

Yet the case is more complex: the Christ Child of the *Meditationes vitae Christi* is not simply a charming and loveable boy. Insofar as he is also endowed with uncannily mature characteristics, the Christ Child of the *Meditationes* can be said to resemble Romanesque-Byzantine portrayals of the child Jesus:[71] the Romanesque image of a little man, seated on his mother's lap, as if on a throne,[72] or the Byzantine image of "Christ Emmanuel," a depiction of a serious and wise-looking Boy, portrayed in isolation from his mother.[73]

In the *Meditationes vitae Christi*, we do indeed find a less childlike, if not completely hieratic, Christ Child in the account of the Epiphany, where Jesus "watches [the kings] benignly, with maturity and gravity, as though He understood them." After they lay their gifts at and kissed his feet, the "wisdom-filled boy (*puer sapientissimus*) also stretched out his hand to them to be kissed, to give them greater solace, and to strengthen them in his love. He made the sign (of the cross) and blessed them as well."[74] As Burrow remarks in his study on the importance of gestures in later medieval literature, "to kiss someone's hand, leg, or foot evidently humbles the kisser and signifies respect."[75] Yet the regal and gracious Jesus depicted here seems concerned, not just with the respect he deserves, but also with his visitors' well-being, in a way allowing himself to be kissed as "a sign of Catholic unity, as . . . when a guest is received."[76] Even more friendly interaction between the infant king and the Magi can be seen in a fourteenth-century fresco depicting the Adoration in the Monastery of the Sacro Speco of St. Benedict in Subiaco (fig. 2), in which the baby Jesus places his hand on the eldest king's snow-white head, the latter's crown having been removed. Here, as in other devotional works, the old man is shown kissing the Infant's bare feet, a demonstrative act of reverence and supplication.[77] Regardless of what exactly the baby Jesus is said or seen to do in numerous Epiphany scenes, "the image of a mere baby receiving the homage of grown men . . . forcefully expresses the transcendent standing of the incarnate God in his relation to human hierarchies. . . . Old men submit to infants."[78] In short, medieval texts and images that focus on the Epiphany often underscore the paradoxicality that medieval Christians perceived in the Christ Child.

While the child Jesus throughout the medieval period was regarded by orthodox Christians as both God and man, there are differences—both striking and subtle—in how he is portrayed. Such differences give us some indications of how artists, writers, thinkers, and more ordinary people viewed the relationship between Christ's two natures. To be sure, Christians' attempt to understand the so-called hypostatic union was, to say the least, challenging. Traditionally, it has been considered erroneous to think that Jesus' two natures

Figure 2. The ministration of the midwives; the adoration of the Magi. Fresco attributed to the Master Trecentesco of Sacro Speco School, Monastero di San Benedetto, Subiaco (fourteenth century). By permission of Bridgeman Images.

were blended or otherwise modified by their intimate association within the person of Jesus Christ. Joseph Ratzinger recently reiterated this idea, in a book on the canonical infancy narratives, where, at one point, he discounts the idea that Greco-Roman myths offer parallels to Jesus' virgin birth. Restating traditional doctrine, Ratzinger forcefully emphasizes that "in the Gospel accounts, the oneness of the one God and the infinite distance between God and creature is fully preserved. There is no mixture, no demi-god."[79] Despite this perennial orthodox teaching, medieval Christians, as we shall see, sometimes verged on getting things wrong: coming close to or apparently detracting from (if not wholly discounting) the perfect divinity of Christ, by laying too much stress on the naturalness of his humanity, or, on the other hand, exaggerating his divinity to such an extent that his humanity was regarded as a mere act, which gave outsiders the wrong impression about his identity (specifically, by suggesting that he was not truly human).

Though it is difficult to sort out all the various cultural components that contributed to a given medieval representation of the Christ Child or the Virgin Mary, the following study of select religious texts dealing with these figures suggests that the apocryphal narratives, which earnestly explore the duality of Christ's identity, had a significant influence upon other later medieval writers' attempts at reconstructing Jesus' hidden years. Originally composed in the Early Christian period, these legends were revived and elaborated in the high and later Middle Ages, when they appeared in new Latin redactions and in vernacular translations. With varying degrees of frequency, depending on the particular tale, these legends were also depicted in Western art, even though many of these legends were without any (or hardly any) biblical basis.

Artistic renderings of the apocryphal childhood of Jesus took a number of forms. Sometimes they helped fill out a sequence of images devoted to Christ's childhood or were part of a cycle covering the span of Jesus' life, thus providing a visual narrative paralleling the written accounts offered by devotional literature. Sometimes artistic scenes based upon the apocrypha were deftly mixed with more conventional images derived from Scripture, sometimes they themselves formed visual sequences depicting apocryphal legends. Artistically rendered in various ways, on the walls and ceilings of churches, as well as in Books of Hours and in illuminated manuscripts (occasionally as illustrations accompanying apocryphal texts), images of the apocryphal Jesus were viewed by both private and public audiences and were in no way limited to those who intentionally sought alternative Christologies.[80] Some of the legends were loosely tied to Scripture (such as the story about the Child's destruction of the idols in Egypt, which was linked with Isaiah 19:1). Legends that ended up being depicted very frequently acquired quasi-canonical status, such as the latter tale and the belief that an ox and an ass were present at the Christ Child's manger. A number of apocryphal or legendary details crept into standard scenes, like the representation of the midwives who were summoned to assist Mary at Jesus' birth and arrived belatedly. In artworks these women are often shown helping her with childcare, often by bathing the baby Jesus. They clearly have a central place in a fourteenth-century fresco of the Nativity in the monastery of the Sacro Speco: while one of these handmaidens prepares a bath, the other zealously extends her arms, reverently covered with a cloth, in order to receive the baby Jesus from his mother Mary (fig. 2). The cloth covering the woman's hands and arms indicates her recognition of the divinity of the Child, whom she is privileged to attend.

In contrast, tales about the miracles that Christ supposedly worked as he was growing up, which were frowned upon by a number of medieval churchmen, were visually rendered much more rarely. In Chapter 3 I examine opposition to such legends on the part of the famous thirteenth-century Dominican theologian Thomas Aquinas. Despite the reasonableness of Aquinas's arguments against Jesus' childhood miracles, stories about them were nevertheless popular since they appealed to both lay and clerical audiences, who regarded such material as both entertaining and devotional. In addition to providing diversion for their audiences, such legends would have been welcomed as sources of information about the unknown period of Jesus' youth, even if this material were only piecemeal or hypothetical.

Given the widespread popularity of such apocryphal stories, it is fair to suppose that late medieval writers were familiar with these accounts. The controversy surrounding the apocryphal legends may have actually drawn people's attention to them, as well as impelled others to seek information from more reliable sources or to exercise their own creativity in dealing with Christ's childhood. Chapter 4 considers the revelations of the fourteenth-century mystic Birgitta of Sweden concerning the Nativity and the family life of Jesus at Nazareth, some of which seem to respond to apocryphal traditions about Christ's infancy and childhood (for example, by implicitly denying that midwives assisted Mary in attending to her newborn, a detail derived from early apocryphal narratives). Although this study could have focused on many other mystics from the later Middle Ages,[81] I have chosen Birgitta since she provides an interesting perspective as a laywoman who gave birth to and cared for a number of children, and also because her revelations about the Virgin and Child are so numerous and frequently include the theme of Mary's compassion, a common feature of late medieval piety. In addition, Birgitta was a popular saint throughout Europe and had a definite impact on late medieval English devotional culture, to which I give some priority in this study. Readers of this book who are interested in other mystics who had a special devotion to the Christ Child are invited to pursue some of my references and those of other scholars. Along similar lines, I do not explore representations of the child Jesus in a wide range of Middle English literary texts, but only mention (apart from the Middle English poems on Christ's apocryphal childhood, which I examine in some detail) a sampling of Middle English works that deal with the beginning of Jesus' life. These include a few Middle English lyrics, some late medieval biblical plays, and also *Mandeville's Travels*. Elsewhere, I explore how Christ's youth is handled in the well-known and highly regarded Middle English poem *Piers Plowman*, in which William Langland depicts the young Christ as a knight in training eager to fight against the devil in a tournament. By insisting on the Child's having restrained himself from exercising his divine power for many years, and by exaggerating Jesus' youthfulness at the wedding feast of Cana, Langland's poem arguably addresses issues that are raised by the apocrypha.[82]

The interaction among the sources I examine in this book is complex, because we are not just dealing with the intertexuality of apocryphal and other written narratives; we must also consider the (in many cases mutual) influences wielded by oral tales, visual representations, and the popular traditions surrounding actual and imaginary places and objects. I move into less strictly textual domain in the latter part of Chapter 4, where I briefly deal with the legend that Mary made Jesus' seamless tunic when he was still a boy and that it increased in size as he grew up. This legend was associated with a particular place, the Priory of Sainte-Marie in Argenteuil, which, from the middle of the twelfth century, claimed to have the relic of Jesus' tunic. A distant yet important source for this legend was the apocryphal version of the Annunciation, which describes Mary as spinning thread when she conceived Jesus in her womb—a detail commonly depicted in Byzantine art.[83] Since the notion of Mary as a textile worker was probably transmitted in multiple ways and also broadly reflects the social conditions of women in the pre-modern world, I would not venture to propose only one source—the apocrypha—for the legend that the Virgin made the seamless tunic at the beginning of Christ's life. Nevertheless, the apocrypha clearly played a role in the spinning of this pious yarn, so to speak.[84]

On the whole, my study indicates that the apocryphal infancy legends were sources of both information and inspiration for writers (and artists) of the later medieval period. There were a variety of possible responses to the apocryphal material: some people apparently took these legends seriously, while others seem to have regarded them lightheartedly, or at least tolerated them as pious fiction. Still others—we may infer—tried to counteract them by offering alternative views of Jesus' childhood. Even when they met with disapproval, the apocryphal legends had the effect of drawing attention to the vexed questions of whether Jesus behaved in a normal fashion during his boyhood and whether he developed gradually like other human children.[85]

## The Appeal of Jesus—a Real Child Who Is Nonetheless Divine

As I have already suggested, one of the reasons why the Christ Child appealed to medieval Christians was that they perceived a surprising, inexplicable, and

delightful conundrum resulting from God's assumption of the form and characteristics of a little boy. Another ostensible reason was that, by becoming an
infant and child, the deity became more approachable while still wielding a
powerful influence upon people's lives. The extremely popular *Legenda aurea*
illustrates this principle in its chapter on Christmas, in which we hear that
"a fallen woman, finally repenting of her sins, despaired of pardon. Thinking of
the Last Judgment she considered herself worthy of hell; turning her mind to
heaven she thought of herself as unclean; dwelling on the Lord's passion, she
knew she had been ungrateful. But then she thought to herself that children
are more ready to be kind, so she appealed to Christ in the name of his childhood, and a voice told her that she had won forgiveness."[86] Although Christ
of course passed beyond childhood during his life on earth, he was regarded
as, somehow, a perpetual child in heaven who was always willing to grant
forgiveness and offer his love.[87] Bernard of Clairvaux went so far as to de-
clare that "contact with [Jesus'] childhood is the only remedy for human
sinfulness."[88] This presupposes that Christ's childhood is still a reality and
within reach, an idea that complements Jesus' stipulation in the Bible that, in
order to enter into heaven, one must embrace childhood (Matt. 18:3). The
fourteenth-century Englishman Henry of Lancaster, in fact, explicitly claims
that Jesus continues to be a child in heaven, because Christ is always ready to
forgive.[89] The underlying assumption that children are naturally forgiving (and,
in a negative sense, inconstant, or—stated more neutrally—malleable in their
interactions with other people) is reflected in a number of medieval sources.
The thirteenth-century Franciscan encyclopedist Bartholomaeus Anglicus, for
instance, notes (in the words of his fourteenth-century translator): "For
mouynge of hete of fleisch and of humours þey ben eþeliche and sone wrooþ
and sone iplesed and forȝeuen sone" (Because of the mobility of heat, of flesh,
and of the humors, they are easily and quickly angered and readily pleased and
quickly forgive).[90] In the same chapter, which is devoted to the characteristics
of children, Bartholomaeus explains, citing the (folk) etymology given by
Isidore of Seville, that the Latin word for children (*pueri*) comes from the
Latin adjective "purus" ("pure"). This attribute obviously refers to children's
sexual inactivity (their being pristine) and is grounded in the tenderness of their
newly molded flesh, but it also seems to encompass their simplicity of character and light-heartedness.[91] Describing children as pure also speaks to their
mental and moral status, specifically the belief that young children are not
yet capable of willingly choosing evil.[92] In the aforesaid chapter on children,
Bartholmaeus goes on to say that, before puberty, "children ben neisch of

fleisch, lethy and pliant of body, abel and liȝt to meuynge, witty to lerne car-
oles, and wiþoute busines, and þey lede here lif wiþoute care and business. . . .
And þey loven an appil more þan gold" (children are tender of flesh, flexible
and malleable in body, agile and nimble for movement, keen to learn carols
[or dances], and do not engage in serious tasks, and they lead their life without care and anxiety. . . . And they love an apple more than gold).[93] Medieval
adults' desire to recover purity through repentance and spiritual cleansing
and also to return, more generally, to the more carefree way of life exemplified by children (if not, more spiritually, to acquire a childlike trust and dependency on their divine Father),[94] probably helps explain to a large extent
the attraction that the child Jesus held for medieval Christians.[95] Believers
seem to have taken to heart Christ's famous words: "unless you be converted,
and become as little children, you shall not enter into the kingdom of heaven"
(Matt. 18:3–4).

Nostalgia of an escapist sort, rather than a healthy desire for personal reformation, may sometimes have instilled the urge to find a lost childhood. More
specifically, medieval Christians may have chosen to reflect upon Jesus' childhood in order to ignore, at least temporarily, the negative aspects of their own
lives or to avoid thinking about the suffering Jesus endured as an adult. In
the Life of Blessed Margaret of Faenza (d. 1330), a Vallombrosan nun, we learn
that she spent a good deal of time, "perfecting her meditations on the childhood of the Savior." She experienced such "marvelously sweet things (*mirabi-
les dulcedines*) during them" that "she did not care to pass onto Christ's later
life (*ad altiora conscendere*, literally, "to climb to higher things")."[96] Perhaps
feeling somewhat offended by the way she ignored his adulthood, Jesus finally told her that it was "not right to wish to taste only the honey and not
the gall (*de melle meo . . . & non de felle*)." Margaret henceforth concentrated
completely on the Passion, with great intensity, apparently exchanging all the
honey for gall (though Christ's rhyming of words suggests that sweetness and
bitterness may go hand in hand). Other evidence suggests that at least some
medieval people perceived a danger in fascination with Christ's childhood.
Once Humiliana de' Cerchi (d. 1246), a Franciscan tertiary, was subjected to
an illusion by the devil, who, "understanding her desires, showed her the figure of Our Lady and the child Jesus, radiant of face and raiment," yet the
pious widow saw through this demonic trick, which interestingly reveals the
imaginative seductiveness, for some, of the Mother-and-Child duo.[97]

Although Christ had acquired the characteristics of ordinary children by
the later Middle Ages,[98] in contemporaneous sources he often seems distant

and aloof, and occasionally imperious, so we would be wise to avoid the over-generalization that, at that time, the figure of a formidable Christ, such as the exacting Judge of the eerie *Dies irae* hymn, was completely superseded by the suffering Savior on the cross, as well as the gentle Child who is perpetually open to reconciliation.[99] All three manifestations of the Son of God are in fact referred to—in quick succession, suggestive of a conflation—in a much earlier passage by St. Jerome, with which medieval scholars well read in patristic writings would have been familiar. Intending to convince his friend Heliodorus of the superiority of the anchoritic way of life, Jerome concludes his letter to him by reminding him that the God who will come to judge him and the whole human race is he who was a lowly man and a child who suffered during life, implying that Christ will show mercy to those who are likewise simple, humble, and patient.[100] Given the many aspects of Christ's persona—the different forms he assumes at the various stages of his earthly life, and in his current and future state of glory, forms which are able to coexist by virtue of his divinity—it is not surprising that medieval Christians imagined the child Jesus as a multifaceted and rather unpredictable personage. In an *exemplum* found in an early fifteenth-century collection of religious tales, "evidently compiled by a Franciscan in northern Italy," the Christ Child (perhaps to be expected of one who is "purus") is initially ill-disposed toward a prostitute who prays to him, but is then mollified by his merciful mother.[101] In the famous early thirteenth-century collection of tales by the Cistercian Caesarius of Heisterbach, the *Dialogus miraculorum*, we learn, along similar lines, that the Christ Child turned his face away from a priest who presumed to consecrate the Eucharist unworthily.[102] So the boy Jesus was not always imagined as a sweet and gentle child. He could express his displeasure in even more dramatic ways, as we have seen in an anecdote from the vita of Ida of Louvain, in which the Christ Child lashed out in a sort of temper tantrum at Ida's sister, in defense of his beloved.

The Christ Child is, however, more often shown to be mysterious and elusive than retributive. In a didactic dialogue text transmitted in various medieval languages, the Child appears to the Emperor Hadrian; without at first identifying himself, he instructs the emperor in the central tenets of the Christian faith, and then disappears, immediately after revealing who he is.[103] The Child likewise vanishes shortly after he appears to the boy Edmund of Abingdon (d. 1240), telling him that he was always beside him during his studies, and that he will continue to be with him.[104] In his mystical dealings with the fourteenth-century Dominican nun Margaret Ebner, who cared for the infant Jesus as for a real child, Christ made a point of emphasizing his ability to leave her at will.[105] In speaking of similar tales included in the so-called Sister Books that record the experiences and imaginary world of late medieval German nuns, Richard Kieckhefer remarks that "the theme of divine presence is expressed in these stories with something of the teasing playfulness associated with the Bridegroom in the Song of Songs."[106] While Kieckhefer's comment is applicable in this more general discussion of the Child who often seems to be a flirtatious and inaccessible lover, I would stress the playful paradoxicality of a divine child who seems almost to play a game of "hide-and-seek" with his devotees.[107] Along similar lines, in the vita of the Augustinian nun Clare of Montefalco by Berengario di Donadio, we learn that when she was still a child but had already entered the convent, the Virgin Mary appeared to her many times: "in her mantle the Virgin was [leading] the Child Jesus, who seemed to be the same age as Clare. Urged by his Mother, the Child Jesus [at times] approached Clare [on foot], took her hand, and filled her with wonderful consolations." Yet Jesus made it clear to her that he was not accessible for play as she had assumed he would be, as someone her own age. "Seeing him thus with her own eyes, Clare wanted to take hold of him and play with him, but the Child eluded her and returned to his mother, leaving Clare in a state of deep desire."[108] Perhaps seeking to get at the ultimate untouchability of the child Jesus that stems from his divine majesty, an early fourteenth-century fresco based upon this episode depicts the young Clare kneeling before the child Jesus. Standing erect on his own two feet and partly sheltered by his mother's mantle, the divine child blesses his young devotee (Master of St. Clare, Church of St. Clare, Chapel of the Holy Cross, Montefalco, c. 1333; fig. 3).

In the later Middle Ages, Christ not only at times suddenly absented himself from his devotees, but also often appeared all at once, showing himself to be engaged in an activity or in a form that caused surprise.[109] Vito of Cortona, the Franciscan biographer of the devout Florentine widow Humiliana de' Cerchi (d. 1246), recounts how Jesus once visited her as a four-year-old boy, playing in her room—a discovery that produced some flirtatious banter: "O sweet love! Dear boy! Don't you know how to do anything except play?" Right after recounting this incident, the hagiographer casts a shroud of mystery on Humiliana's interactions with the Christ Child, commenting: "There are several things about the child Jesus which we will not put down in writing lest we should relate uncertainties." While Vito may seem dismissive of such mystical encounters, his further remark suggests that Humiliana herself chose not to disclose such intimate experiences: "We have also heard it said that she

Figure 3. The boy Jesus appears to Chiara of Montefalco in her girlhood. Fresco by the Master of St. Clare, Chapel of the Holy Cross, Church of St. Clare, Montefalco (fourteenth century). By permission of De Agostini Picture Library/Art Resource, NY.

kissed his feet; and we believe it, because she received many more things from Jesus than can be related and she concealed more than she declared."[110] Explicitly calling Humiliana an "enclosed garden" (*hortus conclusus*, Sg. 4:12), her reticent biographer delicately preserves the mysterious character of Jesus' apparitions to, and interactions with, the holy woman—thus in a way imitating John the Evangelist, who opted to leave much about Jesus' life unspoken (John 21:25). Whereas Humiliana did not expect to find Jesus playing in her room, the Dominican tertiary Osanna of Mantua (d. 1505) must have been startled to an even greater extent when, in a vision, she saw the Christ Child bearing a crown of thorns on his head and a large cross on his shoulders.[111] These examples show that the Christ Child was present to medieval Christians under many guises, and that he remained mysterious to them, despite their confidence in being able to gain an increasing knowledge of and greater familiarity with him. Thus, even when the Child became more humanized in the later Middle Ages, he still maintained his mystique, often to the frustration of his devotees as well as to writers and artists who had little authoritative material to work with (yet, positively, much creative space at their disposal). Furthermore, the Child sometimes made known his superiority in ways that took people aback.

The medieval tendency to ascribe a surprise element to the Christ Child is clearly seen in the Life of St. Christopher that was extremely popular in the later Middle Ages: a giant with a "fearsome visage," Christopher set out to find "the greatest prince in the world," but after he realized that the powerful king he initially hoped to serve was not the mightiest lord of all, and that neither was the devil, he continued his search. He then came across a hermit, who instructed him in the Christian faith and assigned him a task suitable to one his size: ferrying people across a tempestuous river. After a while, the giant was graced with a mysterious visitation by the child Jesus, when Christopher answered the repeated plea for transportation from what looked like an ordinary child, standing on the riverbank. As he carried the child across the treacherous water, the giant felt his little burden on his shoulders become extremely heavy. This prompted him to remark, after he had completed his task: "My boy, you put me in great danger, and you weighed so much that if I had the whole world on my back I could not have felt a heavier burden!" Rather than thank the giant for the transportation he had been given, the Child informed him that he had just borne the Creator of the world, and his king, on his shoulders. As if the Boy's almost unbearable weight were not proof enough of his almighty power, the Christ Child promised to work a miracle (in a short time, the blossoming of Christopher's staff, as soon as it was implanted in the ground).[112] Then he disappeared.[113]

In this story, the giant is transformed from being a coarse fellow who seeks to advance his own interest into a humble servant who is aware of his own weakness and later embraces martyrdom. By accepting the task to care for the unknown child, he literally accepts Christ himself (Matt. 18:5), encountering him personally in an embodied form—one of ostensible human weakness. Note too that, in this story, the child Jesus does not comfort the future saint by allowing him to experience the tenderness of his boyhood; instead, he tangibly demonstrates his power—both to acknowledge Christopher's faithful, vassal-like service and to teach him the paradoxicality of the Son of God, about whom the giant had already heard.[114] The tale, which stresses who Jesus is rather than his lovability (that is, his essence rather than his appealing qualities), reflects, in an analogous way, the shift that occurred in medieval Christians' stance toward the divine child in the high Middle Ages: from then on, they encountered the Christ Child more personally, while continuing to acknowledge his Lordship.


## A Child with Different Personae, Yet Always Lovable Lord and Savior

One of the most important goals of this book is to show that at the same time that medieval culture increasingly emphasized Jesus' humanity—his entrance into a human family and his assumption of the human condition—it never lost sight of his unique status as the Lord and Savior of humankind and as the divine Son of God. The frequent association of the infant Jesus with the Passion—the historical sacrifice on Calvary presented anew in the Mass—underscored the Christ Child's vulnerability and selflessness as well as his transcendence of human time and unique propitiatory power, hence his divinity. Indeed, many medieval texts and images concerned with Jesus' childhood convey the message that his salvific mission was his raison d'être and that he had knowledge of his work of redemption—and was even eager for it—from his earliest years. Mary thus makes her son's seamless tunic when he is still a boy, not only because it is her maternal duty to clothe her child, but also because Jesus is definitely headed for the Passion, where his clothes will be rudely stripped from him and irreverently gambled for by uncouth partici-

Figure 4. The boy Jesus holding a Eucharistic host and chalice. Venice, Biblioteca Nazionale Marciana, cod. lat. cl. III, 111 (=2116): *Missale Sancti Marci*, fol. 177v (fourteenth century). By permission of the Ministero dei Beni e delle Attività Culturali e del Turismo—Biblioteca Nazionale Marciana.

pants in his execution. From a broad perspective, Jesus' wearing of the same garment in his boyhood and at the Crucifixion signifies his ontological oneness as the Savior, who is both priest and victim,[115] especially considering that the Jewish high priest was thought to wear a seamless tunic.[116] Such a conceptualization of a priestly Jesus is dramatically underscored in a miniature from the fourteenth-century *Missale* for the Basilica of San Marco in Venice (Venice, Biblioteca Nazionale Marciana, cod. lat. cl. III, III, fol. 177v; fig. 4). Here a young Jesus positioned frontally stands alone before billowy clouds of Eucharistic hosts, holding a large host in one hand and a chalice in the other, like a priest displaying the consecrated elements at the climax of the Mass, except that here the priest and the sacrificial victim are truly one and the same.[117]

Although much further work on the medieval Christ Child needs to be done, especially on sources from the earlier medieval period, my multifaceted research thus far seems to indicate more continuity than abrupt change with regard to images and conceptualizations of the Christ Child from the late antique and medieval periods.[118] Devotion toward the personages, places, and objects associated with Jesus' birth and early life was often reinvigorated and elaborated, rather than completely invented out of whole cloth in the later Middle Ages. This can be seen, for example, in devotion to the manger, which was originally an object in the Holy Land venerated as a relic, as indicated, for example, by St. Jerome, who tells how St. Paula reverently visited the crib in Bethlehem. Privileged to be in the presence of the sacred object, Paula was prompted to "behold with the eyes of faith the infant Lord wrapped in swaddling clothes and crying in the manger."[119] For pious Christians who lived during the many centuries of Late Antiquity and the Middle Ages who, for reasons of practicality, where unable to go to the Holy Land, the manger was an object they could wistfully imagine. The crusade movement and the more frequent undertaking of pilgrimages to the Holy Land beginning in the high Middle Ages probably intensified Christians' attraction to the mysterious food bin that served as a crib for the infant God, as well as other objects and sites associated with the events of Christ's earthly existence. In the early twelfth century, Bernard of Clairvaux remarked offhand, when speaking of the Holy Sepulcher in Jerusalem, that "people are more moved by the remembrance of [Christ's] death than of his life."[120] Along similar lines, Jerusalem (specifically, Mount Calvary) was considered the exact center of the world—not Bethlehem, for all its importance in being the spot where God initiated his plan for the redemption.[121] Yet all the places in the Holy Land—where Christ was born, lived, suffered, and died—were highly venerated. Moreover, one could make a mental as well as physical pilgrimage to the places and objects that had been physically touched by Christ. At the turn of the thirteenth century, Mary of Oignies envisioned Jesus as a poor boy lying in the manger,[122] but it was St. Francis of Assisi who a little later popularized the crèche as a paraliturgical object, one that could be seen and touched by ordinary people in medieval villages and towns, as well as by those fortunate enough to visit or live within the great city of Rome, which was thought to possess remnants of the actual crib.

The basin in which the baby Jesus had been bathed was likewise highly valued by the Christ Child's devotees. Writing about half a century after the death of Agnes of Montepulciano (d. 1317), a Dominican nun considered a saint, Raymond of Capua tells how she "desired with great affection to visit the lands across the sea, where our Savior was conceived, born, lived, and suffered for our salvation." Although the Lord denied the nun's request for distant travel, he provided some consolation through an angel, who brought her a clod of soil from beneath the cross, moistened by Jesus' blood, and "a piece of that basin in which our Savior was placed in his tender age and bathed in the manner of little ones."[123] Centuries earlier, Arculf, a Frankish bishop who visited the Holy Land, saw a stone that was hollowed out by the water "in which the little body of the Lord was first washed"—the bath-water that was poured over a wall after it had been used. According to Adomnán (d. 704), the abbot of Iona who wrote a description of the Holy Land based upon Arculf's travels, this stone in Bethlehem "has ever since been full of the purest water, without any diminution"[124]—a wonder well-matched by the continuous stream of pilgrims who visited the places where Jesus himself had lived and died.[125] Such passages referring to the bathing of the Christ Child indicate that, throughout the Middle Ages, Christians imaginatively harkened back to the milestone events and also the everyday occurrences of Jesus' childhood.[126]

Whereas Herlihy offered an economic and social explanation for the new interest in the Christ Child, Marcus suggested that the new cult of the child Jesus was (in part) a European reaction against scholasticism—an effort to return to the simplicity of childhood.[127] Rather than see the new devotion to the Christ Child as primarily stemming from social and economic conditions or as an inverse response to the highly intellectualized climate of the time— that is, mainly as a defensive measure—I prefer to view it as a natural outgrowth, to a large extent, of the increasing emphasis placed upon Christ's humanity—on God's having assumed the lowliness, deficiencies, and even miseries of the human condition, including the common characteristics of childhood. Numerous sources indicate that Christians in the later Middle Ages delighted in the paradox that ensued from having as their Lord a God who had become and, in some way, was still a child. Believers were probably drawn to their Savior even further, when they reflected that he began to save them from the very beginning of his life. The greater interest given to the Virgin, and the continual role she was believed to play in human salvation over the course of the centuries, undoubtedly also led medieval Christians to focus more intensely on the early stages of Jesus' life, which he intimately shared with Mary (and also with Joseph, whose prerogatives had attracted the attention of the devout by the later Middle Ages).[128]

As I have argued above, there were a host of competing and overlapping images of the Christ Child in the later Middle Ages, a multiplicity that stemmed from a number of causes, most prominent of which was the difficulty of imagining the presence of divinity, the summation of perfection, adhering in a human child, which to medieval adults bespoke development and change. The apocryphal childhood legends explored this paradoxical situation in a dramatic manner, showing the tension that could arise when a young Jesus not shy about his divine lordship interacted with those around him. Raising a number of theological issues, such legends likely inspired medieval Christians to reflect more deeply upon Christ's early years. Whatever approach they took, medieval Christians in search of the near but elusive child-God likely felt that the issue of Christ's childhood, which the canonical gospel writers probably bypassed for a very good reason, was always open to further exploration.

Before turning to an examination of apocryphal infancy gospels and Birgittine materials pertaining to Mary's relationship with her son Jesus, this study will consider well-known Cistercian and Franciscan treatments of Christ's childhood,[129] which create an important backdrop for the other (generally later) materials discussed below. The twelfth- and thirteenth-century religious figures with whom I begin strove to make the child Jesus, who for centuries had lurked in the background of European culture, come to the fore. The Bible rather than the apocrypha was their main inspiration, yet they did not completely ignore extra-scriptural details that seemed useful in promoting devotion to the Christ Child among their fellow Christians.

# The Christ Child in Two Treatises of Aelred of Rievaulx and in Early Franciscan Sources

In one of his numerous sermons on the Song of Songs, the renowned Cistercian abbot Bernard of Clairvaux (d. 1153) invites his audience to imagine "how Mary's husband Joseph would often take him [the Christ Child] on his knees and smile as he played with him." This particular sermon, which momentarily turns to a scene of domestic intimacy, focuses on the verse "A bundle of Myrrh is my beloved to me, he shall abide between my breasts" (Sg. 1:12); it is specifically the word *fasciculus* ("little bundle") that prompts Bernard to think of the infant Jesus. Myrrh, the bitter herb mentioned in the verse, recalls Jesus' sufferings, which, according to Bernard, were manifest first in "the privations of his infancy," and then in "the hardships he endured in preaching, the fatigues of his journeys, the long watches in prayer, the temptations when he fasted, his tears of compassion, the heckling when he addressed the people, and finally the dangers from traitors in the brotherhood, the insults, the spitting, the blows, the mockery, the scorn, the nails and similar torments that are multiplied in the Gospels."[1] Bernard mentions Christ's infancy only briefly within this increasingly dramatic sequence,[2] concentrating instead on the Passion, the climax of Christ's life, which was recounted in the Gospels with considerable detail and elaborated even further in medieval devotional texts and images. Bernard advises his fellow monks to keep the recollection of Jesus' life and death as a "delectable bunch" between their breasts; they are to have it before their mind's eye, especially when they experience difficulties. It is near the end of this short sermon where Bernard introduces the aforementioned image of Joseph bouncing the infant Jesus on his knees.[3] Yet he finally closes not with this charming vignette, but with a more abstract reference to

Christ as the "Church's bridegroom." This implies that the members of the Church, especially the individual monk who hears or reads the sermon, are to seek mystical union with Christ—an intimate relationship with the God-man that is both fostered by and transcends meditation on the events of Jesus' earthly existence.

Although it may seem strange that Bernard associates the infant Jesus with the bridegroom desired by the bride in the Song of Songs, other medieval Christians commonly thought of the Christ Child in this way. As Ann Astell remarks, in medieval texts in which the bride is interpreted as the Virgin Mary, the groom "assumes the striking form of an Infant Boy nursing at her breasts."[4] The Christ Child was not simply the beloved of the Virgin Mary, but also the spouse desired by Christians who sought a deeper spirituality. Such imagery is reflected in the vita for the Beguine Mary of Oignies (d. 1213) authored by Jacques de Vitry: "Sometimes it seemed to her that she held him [God] tightly between her breasts like a clinging baby for three or more days and she would hide him there lest he be seen by others and at other times she would play with him, kissing him (*osculando ludebat*) as if he were a child." Mary's biographer also notes that: "Once when she had lain continuously in bed for three days and had been sweetly resting with her Bridegroom, the days slipped by most stealthily because her joy was so great and so sweet."[5] In this chapter from Mary of Oignies's vita, Jacques clearly has in mind the verse from the Song of Songs about the spouse having myrrh between her breasts, since he specifically says that the divine child who visited Mary and caused her such delight was nestled between her breasts (*inter ubera commorantem*; cf. Sg. 1:12).

Bernard's disciple Aelred of Rievaulx (d. 1167), who served for twenty years as abbot of an influential Cistercian monastery in Yorkshire, Rievaulx Abbey, also uses language and imagery from the Song of Songs when speaking of the Christ Child, as we shall see in considering two of his devotional treatises that deal with Jesus' youth. An examination of these works shows that the figure of the Christ Child was employed by Aelred not simply in a sentimental way, that is, with the single goal of having his reader meditate upon and delight in the lovableness of the young Jesus, imaginatively re-presented in the here and now. The Cistercian abbot's agenda is rather more complex, at least in the case of the treatise directed at a male reader, the *De Jesu puero duodenni* (*On Jesus at the Age of Twelve*). Yet in both cases, Aelred seeks to capture his reader's attention by focusing on the divine child, whom one could imaginatively see and touch. In differing degrees, Aelred moves beyond the historical details of Jesus' life, prompting his reader to engage in more abstract levels of thinking and to undergo an inner reformation—to undertake, more broadly speaking, a spiritual quest that would culminate in an ineffable experience of the divine.

This chapter will focus on two works of Aelred of Rievaulx and on thirteenth-century texts by and about St. Francis and his disciple St. Clare, because scholars have traditionally (and rightfully so in my view) given the Cistercians and Franciscans major credit for initiating a new type of devotion to the child Jesus that became widespread in the later Middle Ages, an affective piety that was focused on the Christ Child's hardships as well as his attractiveness and sweetness as a tender child. Yet, as we shall see, the Cistercian abbot Aelred focuses only to a small degree on the human qualities of Christ's boyhood, preferring in his now famous treatise on the twelve-year-old Jesus to draw the attention of his monastic male reader to the process of conversion and spiritual development that he himself must undergo, a transformation that should parallel the Christ Child's birth and growth throughout the life cycle. While Aelred's other work to be considered below, a letter addressed to his sister, who was an anchoress, appeals more to the senses in the relatively short section on the historical life of Christ that is relevant here, the recluse is encouraged not just to imagine what the human Jesus was like at different stages of his life, but also to reflect deeply on her own status as a bride of Christ, who has turned from this world so as to prepare herself better for the next, in which the union with her beloved will finally be realized. To become more familiar with Christ in the here and now and also to make herself more worthy of being his bride, the anchoress is to imagine herself interacting with Jesus as did his mother and his other female followers featured in the canonical gospels. The recluse is also to imitate Jesus in the way he lived his life, as a poor and humble man, detached from the power structures and, to some extent, social obligations of this world (like reproduction and child-rearing). Just as such Cistercian works do much, in a literary way, with the relatively few details from the canonical gospels dealing with Christ's early life, so do the early Franciscan sources succeed in making the child Jesus who is hidden in the Bible come to the fore. Whereas the Cistercians' approach was more inward, that of the Franciscans was more performative and tangible (in the sense of being focused on real objects like the manger), yet in both cases audiences were encouraged to imitate and have a greater love for the lowly and tender Child who was born in Bethlehem and grew up in obscurity in Nazareth, in a loving and humble family that focused on the basics of everyday life. Significantly, both Francis and Clare, the founders of the first and second orders of Franciscans (the Friars Minor and the Poor Clares) had consciously turned away from the comfortable lifestyles that they could easily have enjoyed as adults (because of their families' wealth and social standing) and, instead, embraced a life of total poverty. This may help explain why Christ's lifelong scantiness of clothing and nakedness had an extremely strong hold on the Franciscans' imagination from the very beginning of the movement.

## The Christ Child in Aelred's *De Jesu puero duodenni*

Aelred of Rievaulx's treatise *De Jesu puero duodenni*, written sometime between 1153 and 1157, is the first meditational text produced in the West that concentrates on the boy Jesus.[6] A clarification is in order, however, considering that the apocryphal *Infancy Gospel of Thomas*, which was originally composed in the second century in Greek and later translated into medieval Latin, was the first text that ever focused on the boy Jesus, covering as it does select events from the fifth to twelfth year of his childhood. Although these two texts center upon the same biblical personage, they are quite different in terms of their content and aims. At the end of his treatise, Aelred tells his addressee, a monk named Ivo from Wardon (a daughterhouse of Rievaulx), that he has given him seeds of meditation (*meditationum semina*), as the monk had earlier requested.[7] By leaving his treatise open-ended and inviting his reader to personalize it, Aelred encourages the individual meditator's appropriation of his text. In contrast, the anonymous author of the *Infancy Gospel of Thomas* seems primarily concerned with filling in the gaps left in the canonical gospels' account of Jesus' early life by recounting exceptionally remarkable events. Though the anonymous author compensates for only some of these lacunae, the reader is not invited to extend the work imaginatively further. Another crucial difference is that, instead of providing mundane or intimate details about Jesus' childhood that would arouse the reader's piety by increasing his or her yearning for Christ, as do Aelred's treatise and other medieval texts, the apocryphal narrative focuses on the Boy's mighty deeds and his precocious wisdom, which are displayed repeatedly during Jesus' partially reconstructed childhood.

While the anonymous author of the *Infancy Gospel of Thomas* may have primarily intended his narrative to be informational (that is, by recounting some of the most notable things that supposedly occurred during Jesus' childhood), by the later Middle Ages the *Infancy Gospel of Thomas* in Latin and its offshoots clearly took on the character of a devotional narrative. By this I mean that it was considered conducive to increasing one's reverence for the God-man, who, according to the text, had assumed the form of an extremely gifted and exceptional child. The devotional character of medieval redactions of the *Infancy Gospel of Thomas* is suggested by their survival in a number of manuscripts from monastic libraries and other indications of its being read by Christians intensely focused on their spiritual life, such as the work's inclusion among the treasured devotional books of the pious dowager Cecily Neville (d. 1495).[8] Though both the *Infancy Gospel of Thomas* and Aelred's treatise may have been read in a devotional and meditative manner in the later Middle Ages, the overall thrust of these texts is quite different, as I have already indicated. Aelred, who focuses on a specific episode from the Gospel of Luke (the twelve-year-old Jesus' staying behind in the Temple), is mainly concerned with helping his reader make progress in the spiritual life, through becoming more virtuous and Christ-like and by deepening his relationship with his spiritual bridegroom. In contrast, the original author of the *Infancy Gospel of Thomas* and also the medieval redactors of apocryphal tales of Jesus' childhood appear uninterested in promoting the reader's contemplative union with Christ; instead, their ostensible aim is to impress the reader with the Boy's powerful deeds and uncanny wisdom, more than anything else.[9]

In what follows, I provide an overview of Aelred's treatise *De Jesu puero duodenni*, focusing on specific passages in order to show that it concentrates only to a small extent on the historical aspects of Christ's childhood (specifically the literal details having to do with Jesus' staying behind in the Temple, mentioned by Luke), compared to its repeated emphasis on the monastic reader's spiritual development. Aelred clearly believes that the latter process rests on an experiential encounter with Christ—an imaginative experience of the incarnate God with one's inner senses, paired with appropriate emotional responses. Modern readers might at first approach Aelred's text as a spiritual classic or even as a creative work, an early example of historical fiction, without realizing that it is grounded in the traditional routine of monastic life. The fact that Aelred is commenting on a certain *lectio evangelica*, as he says early on in his treatise, means that the biblical text in question is one which the entire community of monks would have heard, "sung or read," within the liturgy.[10] Individual monks may have also read and meditated on the text from Luke (2:41–52) in their *lectio divina* (that is, their personal spiritual reading).

Aelred's treatise is based upon the assumption that the individual monk's task is to achieve greater knowledge about Christ's childhood through private prayer, in other words, through intimate communication with Christ that occurs within the monk's soul. Aelred regards his book as an aid to such prayer, rather than as an authoritative source of hidden knowledge about Christ's boyhood, as, for example, the apocryphal infancy gospels claimed to be. In other words, Aelred's book is not meant to provide all the answers, as it were, but rather to serve as a springboard for further reflection and contemplation.

At the beginning of the text, Aelred reminds his addressee Ivo that he requested plausible hypotheses as to what the twelve-year-old Jesus was doing during the three days when he was intentionally apart from his parents, after they left Jerusalem. Yet Aelred does not pretend to provide easy solutions. As if privy to the monk's inward thoughts, the Cistercian abbot says that he is aware "with what familiarity . . . you are wont to ask these very questions of Jesus himself in your holy prayers, when you have before the eyes of your heart the sweet likeness of that dear boy, when with a certain spiritual imagination you reproduce the features of that most beautiful face; when you rejoice in the gaze of those most charming and gentle eyes bent upon you."[11] Aelred thus suggests that Ivo has already made some inroads regarding the questions that are of concern to him or has at least revealed his inquisitiveness. While the abbot encourages the monk's imaginative recovery of Christ's youth, he also recommends that the monk not press too hard at trying to attain knowledge of Jesus' hidden years, but rather respect the secret details of Christ's life— the choice that Jesus apparently made to hide the events of his childhood from future generations.[12] On one occasion Aelred explicitly warns Ivo: "when you [are] alone with [him]," be careful lest Christ "charge you with presumption in your questioning and . . . bridle your curiosity."[13] Aelred's comment here is reflective of medieval clerics' view of curiosity as a vice when it entailed an excessive desire for knowledge.[14] Those who propagated apocryphal legends about Jesus' childhood may, in fact, have been thought to cater to it, by prying into territory that was scripturally unknown and then speaking about it as if authoritatively.[15] It is possible, though, that in the aforementioned passage, in which Aelred warns his friend against having an inordinate desire to know about the Savior's youth, Aelred may simply be cautioning Ivo about plying Jesus with too many questions, particularly those that are of a factual nature and specifically concerned with details about his childhood.

Aelred himself, toward the beginning of the treatise, asks the boy Jesus a number of questions on behalf of Ivo. He later returns to some of these when he focuses on the historical aspects of the Temple episode, which constitutes the first main section of his treatise. Early on, Aelred questions Jesus with an anxious tone, which could perhaps express despair at getting concrete answers, as well as sincere solicitousness concerning the Christ Child's physical well-being when he had detached himself from his parents: "O dear boy, where were you? Where were you hiding? Who gave you shelter? Whose company did you enjoy? Was it in heaven or on earth, or in some house that you spent the time? Or did you go off with some boys your own age into a hidden place (*secreto loco*) and regale them with mysteries (*secretorum mysteria profundebas*), in accordance with those words of yours in the Gospel: 'Allow the children to come to me'" (Lk. 18:16, Matt. 19:14).[16] Anselm Hoste remarks that, in this treatise, Aelred makes his reader *sicut praesens* in the life of Christ,[17] yet when Aelred (on behalf of his reader) asks Jesus and later his mother questions like these concerning the Temple incident, such inquiries could be retrospective, as if the monk were conversing with Jesus and Mary in the reader's present, rather than with them in the midst of the episode, as it unfolds, or immediately after it occurs. The past tense of the verbs in the queries cited above supports this alternative view, though Aelred's addressing Jesus as a "dear boy" does seem to indicate that he is speaking to Jesus of the historical past (imaginatively re-presented).[18] Be that as it may, it is clear that Aelred wants the reader of his text to replay the past in his memory and to insert himself in the course of events as if he were in the thick of their unfolding—to act as if such occurrences really matter in the here and now, to the reader who is imaginatively close to Jesus.

Aelred's supposition in the above-cited passage that the Christ Child may have gone off with other children seems logical, considering that children are, and were, known to prefer the company of those their own age. Commenting on the biblical verse from Luke in which Christ essentially identifies himself with a young child (Lk. 9:47–48), the thirteenth-century Dominican exegete Hugh of Saint-Cher noted children's natural affinity for each other: "they love each other."[19] As we shall see in the following chapter, the idea that the boy Jesus would have enjoyed being with his peers (and they with him) is highlighted in the *Infancy Gospel of Thomas* and medieval texts derived from it, in which Jesus is repeatedly described as playing with other boys, usually outdoors.

The attention that Aelred's treatise calls to children, here and elsewhere, arguably stems from his view that the boys who were privileged to interact with the twelve-year-old Jesus metaphorically represent monks, who, like Ivo, have chosen to enter a "hidden place" to gain access to Christ's mysteries. Bernard of Clairvaux had earlier said that monastic life is characterized by three main features, one of which is hiddenness, a state that enables the monk to commune privately with his Lord.[20] Thus, when Aelred speaks of boys going off with Jesus to a "hidden place," he may very well have in mind the monastery, an environment chosen as conducive to acquiring greater intimacy with Christ, through meditation on the various stages of his life as well as other monastic practices. The fact that Cistercian communities did not accept child oblates (as did the Benedictines and other related groups) may, paradoxically, have given the monks more of an opportunity to envision themselves as children (and also parents) in a metaphorical sense.[21] Aelred's famous lament for his beloved friend and fellow monk Simon, found in his *De speculo caritatis* (*Mirror of Charity*), illustrates the abbot's view of the monastery as a place where boys, as it were, are spiritually gathered around the child Jesus. Speaking, at one point, of a monk dear to his heart, Aelred tells how the "tender and delicate boy" Simon (*puerum tenerum et delicatum*) entered monastic life at a young age, running after the boy Jesus, who exuded "the scent of his perfumes" (Sg. 1:3). Aelred admires Simon for turning aside from his noble family and entering the abbey at Rievaulx in order to pursue his spiritual quest for Jesus. It was there that Simon succeeded in imitating the Christ Child, who "show[ed] him the manger of his poverty, the resting place of his humility, [and] the chamber of his charity decked with blossoms of his grace."[22] Like the bride in the Song of Songs, Simon yearned for the bridegroom of his soul, Jesus, and succeeded in interacting with him in the privacy of the cloister.

It should come as no surprise that Aelred, a disciple of Bernard of Clairvaux, alludes to the Song of Songs throughout the *De Jesu puero duodenni*, to speak of the soul's search for Christ and to convey its delight in his spiritual presence. To give another example of how this poetical book from Scripture (a love song) permeates Aelred's text: Aelred tells his reader to visualize how the people traveling with the boy Jesus to the Temple in Jerusalem reached out and seized him: "Old men kiss him, young men embrace him, boys wait upon him. . . . Each of them, I think, declares in his inmost heart: 'Let him kiss me with the kiss of his mouth' (Sg. 1:1). And to the boys who long for his presence . . . it is easy to apply the words: 'Who will grant me to have you as my brother, sucking my mother's breasts, to find you outside and kiss you?' (Sg. 8:1)."[23] Toward the end of the treatise, Aelred again quotes this verse from the Song of Songs when speaking of Ivo's "longing for one kiss and one touch of [Jesus'] dear lips." Aelred assures Ivo that when he sighs for Christ as for a brother, "Then certainly he will come to you with all the fragrance of ointments and perfumes."[24] The abbot's repeated emphasis on fragrance emanating from Christ, a detail which appeared in the above-cited passage from the *Mirror of Charity*, is clearly based upon the olfactory imagery in the Song of Songs. The sensuousness of this latter text, in my view, helps explain why Aelred, at one point, asks the boy Jesus who bathed and anointed him when he was separated from his parents for three days. Without explicitly claiming that this image has homosexual connotations, Brian Patrick McGuire suggests as much when, referring to this passage, he speaks of "Aelred's fantasy about a massage for Jesus."[25] If we keep in mind, though, that Aelred's treatise is mainly concerned with the monk's spiritual relationship with Christ and that Aelred constantly employs language and images from the Song of Songs, then the sensuousness of such passages will seem less startling and will less plausibly be read as a clear indication of Aelred's putative homosexuality.[26] Aelred's concern about the Christ Child's hygiene may stem, in part, from the maternal care toward monks that he himself was accustomed to exercise as abbot.[27] It also suggests his identification with Mary in her search for Christ, insofar as she is envisioned in that episode as the bride par excellence yearning for the bridegroom, and also imagined as a solicitous mother. In this treatise, Ivo and the other monks are invited to identify with her. Toward the end of this work, when speaking of the rewards of the spiritual life, Aelred tells his monastic reader that he will eventually be able to utter the words that Mary herself said when she finally found her twelve-year-old son in the Temple: "Then there are embraces, then there are kisses, then: 'I have found him whom my soul loves, I have held him fast and will not let him go'" (Sg. 3:4).[28]

Having discussed the overall orientation of the *De Jesu puero duodenni*—the way it encourages the monastic reader to envision himself as seeking the most beloved of boys, as did the Christ Child's family, friends, and neighbors—I will now flesh out the treatise's contents more precisely in order to show that it places greater emphasis upon spiritual growth than upon the actual or hypothetical details of the Temple episode. Aelred gives his treatise a tripartite structure, dividing it into sequential considerations of the historical, allegorical, and moral senses of the biblical anecdote about the twelve-year-old Jesus. Numerically speaking, only the first ten of the text's thirty-two sections (according to how its modern editors have divided it) are devoted to what the Christ Child did during his three-day sojourn in Jerusalem or to the issue of his subsequent advancement "in wisdom, and age, and grace" when he returned to Nazareth (Lk. 2:52). In other words, less than a third of the treatise is concerned with the historical (or broader, Christological) sense of the biblical account about the twelve-year-old Jesus' staying behind in the

Temple.[29] That Aelred is more interested in the episode's moral sense is indicated by the fact that his treatise culminates in this mode of interpretation,
and also by his reference to the theme of the soul's infancy and development
in sections that are ostensibly devoted to the historical and allegorical interpretations of the aforesaid biblical episode. For instance, early on, in the first
(that is, historical) section of the treatise, after remarking that the boy Jesus
did not come into the Temple "as a teacher, but as a boy who learns . . . [and]
does not withdraw from the control of his parents" (a comment that, incidentally, undermines the potential view of Jesus as a disobedient and disrespectful
child), Aelred suddenly reflects upon his own past sinful behavior, likening
himself to the Prodigal Son (Lk. 15:11–32) who, through folly, soon found
himself without food. In need of bread like the Prodigal Son, Aelred eventually came to his senses and returned to Bethlehem, a town whose name means
"House of Bread." There, on the altar in the Church, he found the Eucharist,
which is none other than the Christ Child in the manger, and fed thereon.[30]
Aelred then offers a moral reading of his own behavior and of the beasts
widely thought to have been gathered around the manger at the first Christmas: "This is the beginning of conversion, a spiritual birth as it were, that we
should model ourselves on the Child, take upon ourselves the marks of poverty, and becoming like animals before you, Lord, enjoy the delights of your
presence."[31] Aelred clearly regards Bethlehem as a symbol of Christians' spiritual birth. Proceeding along these tropological lines further, he explains that
the Infant's hiding of himself in Egypt (a dangerous place that nevertheless
served as a safe haven for the child Jesus and his family) signifies the soul's
temptation, and that the Boy's subsequent upbringing in Nazareth (a name
meaning "flower") represents the soul's growth, or blossoming, in virtue. "For
just as the Lord Jesus is born and conceived in us, so he grows and is nour-
ished in us, until we come to perfect manhood, that maturity which is pro-
portioned to the complete growth of Christ" (Eph. 4:13).[32] Aelred here assumes
his reader is aware of how "scripture speaks of two sorts of age," as Origen
put it: "One is the age of the body, which is not subject to our power but to
the law of nature. The other is the age of the soul, which is properly under our
control. If we will it, we grow daily in this age."[33] In other words, the monk
whom Aelred is addressing must consciously pursue spiritual development. By
thus encouraging his reader to imitate the Christ Child by being spiritually
reborn and developing after his pattern, Aelred, as abbot and spiritual guide,
can be said to labor like a mother so that Christ might be formed in the monks
entrusted to his care (cf. Gal. 4:19). After this digression about his own spiri-

tuality, which leads to his offering of moral advice, Aelred returns to a consideration of what transpired while the boy Jesus stayed behind in Jerusalem.

At the beginning of the second part of the work, in which he offers what he sees as the obvious allegorical meaning of the text (namely, that Christ's parents in searching for him represent the Jews in search of the Messiah), Aelred reiterates the idea that the events of Christ's early life (his birth, his persecution by Herod, and his upbringing at Nazareth) signify the monk's spiritual progress.[34] Later on, in the third main section, when he centers his attention on the moral sense, Aelred uses a striking metaphor when he speaks of how the monk experiences "the infancy of the new way of life" (*novae conversationis . . . infantia*) at Bethlehem. Elaborating on a point he made earlier, Aelred explains that the monk imitates the poverty of Christ's birth by renouncing the world and, in addition, acquires wealth at Nazareth by growing in virtues. He goes further, pointing out that Christ's "going up" to Jerusalem with his parents signifies the soul's eventual ascent to contemplation and that his "going down" to Nazareth with his parents means that a monk (especially an abbot charged with the responsibility of pastoral care) should turn aside from the heights of prayer when duty calls.[35]

Whereas up until this point Aelred had spoken of the soul's imitation of the child Jesus in an analogous sense, here he says, more literally, that the characteristics of infants are worthy of emulation: an infant, since it has "not yet arrived at the use of reason . . . harms no one, deceives no one; it is free from covetousness, knows nothing of its own will, judges no one, calumniates no one, covets nothing. It is not anxious for the present nor solicitous for the future and relies only on the judgment of others."[36] While Aelred seems to imply that infants are naturally virtuous, he essentially says they lack the vices or failings commonly found in adults, especially those living in the world (though one could also say that Aelred values infants' simplicity, a positive virtue).[37] When commenting on Christ's remark about the necessity of becoming like a little child, if one wishes to enter the kingdom of heaven (Matt. 18:3–5), St. Jerome (d. 420) had similarly spoken of little children as not being guilty of the negative behaviors commonly displayed in flawed adults: "Just as that little one, whose example I give you, does not persevere in anger, does not remember when it is injured, does not desire a beautiful woman it sees, does not think one thing while saying another, so also you, unless you shall have such innocence and purity of soul, shall not enter into the kingdoms of the heavens."[38] Jerome's list was repeated by a number of monastic authors.[39] Though Aelred does not reiterate its particulars, he can be said to convey the same basic idea. Yet even as both authors call attention to children's lack of malice, their harmlessness, and overall passivity, they do so in slightly different ways. Aelred's ideal seems to be that Cistercian monks (who, significantly, as already noted, did not begin their life in the monastery as oblates, which was a standard practice in the earlier Benedictine tradition) should be as malleable and submissive as young children.[40] Guerric of Igny, another twelfth-century Cistercian, likewise valorizes childhood in reflecting on Christ's having taken on the form of a child: "Unto us . . . a little Child is born, and emptying out his majesty God had taken on himself not merely the earthly body of mortal men but the weakness and insignificance of children. O blessed childhood, whose weakness and foolishness is stronger and wiser than any man. . . . O sweet and sacred childhood, which brought back man's true innocence, by which men of every age can return to blessed childhood and be conformed to you, not in physical weakness but in humility of heart and holiness of life."[41] In his treatise *De Jesu puero duodenni*, Aelred likewise engages in a type of idealization of childhood,[42] though he is specifically concerned with how it was exemplified by Christ, the epitome of spiritual as well as physical perfection.

Thus far we have seen how Aelred spends a relatively small amount of time discussing the concrete aspects of Jesus' childhood, specifically, how Aelred often seems eager to transition to the topic of a monk's spiritual development, as ideally running parallel to the Christ Child's human development. There is another way in which Aelred takes ample time to focus on the nonhistorical aspects of the Temple episode: in the middle section of his treatise, he offers an extended allegorical discussion of the Jews, who, like Jesus' parents on this very stressful occasion, have great difficulty finding him. Though Aelred's extensive criticism of the Jews (specifically, the Holy Family's traveling companions) for failing to appreciate Christ in their midst seems digressive, not to mention bitterly harsh, it nevertheless shares the very broad theme of conversion and enrichment through Christ's spiritual gifts that is central to Aelred's overall moral interpretation of the Temple episode. To be more precise: in this middle section, Aelred speaks of the presumed, eventual conversion of the Jews at the end of the world and of God's bestowal of graces upon the Gentiles, near to Christ, in the meantime. Rather surprisingly (considering that the figures of Mary and Ecclesia were often conflated and opposed to that of Synagoga),[43] Aelred recasts Jesus' parents as the Jews who are separated from Christ and ineffectively searching for the Messiah among their own people. In his imaginative reworking of the biblical episode, Aelred goes further by transforming the Jewish teachers in the Temple, with whom Jesus is eventually found conversing, into the Gentiles, and the Temple into the Church, into which Jesus' parents enter only after a period of time. Regarding Jesus as the Lord who will ultimately unite the Jews and Gentiles, Aelred speaks of the twelve-year-old Christ as an embodiment of both the Old and New Laws: the Ten Commandments and the dual mandate to love God and neighbor. As the *verbum abbreuiatum sed consummans* ("the Word that is abbreviated but sums up"; cf. Rom. 9:28; Isa. 10:23), Jesus brings the Law of Moses to perfection.[44] Like other medieval Christian scholars, Aelred is confident that the Jews will ultimately come over to Christ.

Since this treatise focuses heavily on the young Jesus' separation from his parents and kindred, rather than his reunion with them, it is not surprising that the middle section of this work centers on discord among people. Aelred thus seems to seize upon (or perhaps be carried away by) the dramatic potential of the episode, going so far as to position himself as a sort of spokesperson for the Christ Child vis-à-vis the Jews, to whom he speaks reprovingly. He bluntly informs them that Christ has "cast away his heritage," and proclaims that Christ's "beautiful face . . . is hidden only from those of your own house." Finding fault with the Jews for failing to recognize Christ, Aelred derogatorily contrasts them with the ox and the ass at the manger, who laudably recognized their master (Isa. 1:3).[45] Aelred depicts himself as not having success as a mediator with regard to either party; it is especially difficult for him to appease Jesus, whom he describes as *crudelissimus* ("utterly cruel") toward his own people.[46] In this scenario, the Christ Child, whose immovability is made worse by the essentially unalterable biblical past, seems unwilling to make the initial gesture of reconciliation. Alluding to Matthew 12:46, Aelred says that even though the boy Jesus "certainly" (*certe*) was told that his mother and brethren were looking for him, he still did not go out of the Temple to meet them.[47] Instead, he waits inside until, after three days, his relatives finally come in, which for Aelred signifies the Jews' eventual conversion to Christianity, in the third age of the world.

Although the abbot may zealously wish the Jews to be reconciled with Christ and for them to enjoy spiritual prosperity, he portrays the young Jesus as coldly stern toward his family members and associates who are looking for him. He also portrays the Jews as hostile, specifically by claiming that they cast an evil eye on those to whom (presumably the adult) Christ showed mercy. To be more precise, Aelred imagines Jesus criticizing the Jews more generally for their ill-will: "you raged at my gifts, you were envious at my compassion, and since your evil eye (*nequam oculus*; cf. Matt. 20:15) grudged the penitent, blinded by envy (*livor*), it was unable to see the author of its own salvation."[48] As noted in subsequent chapters, Thomas Aquinas and Birgitta of Sweden similarly called attention to Jewish envy when they imagined how Jesus might have been received by the Jewish community around him.[49] Going further than Aelred, these later authors imagine ill feelings being directed at the boy Jesus himself. As I explain in the following chapter, the apocryphal infancy legends circulating in the later Middle Ages undoubtedly create a cultural rift between Jesus and the Jewish community into which he was born. Although Aelred, in the middle section of his treatise, may be alluding to the actual tension he imagines to have existed between Jesus and the Jews of his day, the abbot, taking a broad view of things, envisions the future healing of the current division between Christians and Jews.

I have already emphasized how Aelred treats the incident in the Temple as a historical event only to a certain extent, given that he also approaches the episode metaphorically as well as allegorically. Aelred's novel yet rather spare speculations about the Boy's activities in Jerusalem are worth considering more closely, especially since they have significant points in common with other medieval sources dealing with Christ's childhood. After briefly wondering about the practical aspects of Jesus' staying behind in Jerusalem, Aelred conjectures that, on the first day, the Boy went up to heaven to consult his Father about "the ordering of the redemptive work he had undertaken (*suscepta dispensatio*)."[50] Such a novel speculation (not apparently inspired by any legend in circulation) implies that the child Jesus already knew of the mission for which he was sent, an idea that finds expression, in different ways, in other medieval sources.[51] Careful not to impute any ignorance to Christ as he engages in this divine and heavenly conference, Aelred adds that Jesus consulted his Father, "not in order to learn what he already knew from all eternity," but "to defer" to him, to "offer him his obedience, [and to] show his humility."[52] Far from imagining the young Jesus wandering around Jerusalem, Aelred claims that on the second day of the Child's brief retreat from his parents, Christ informed the angels of God's plan to make good the loss of their numbers due to the rebellion of the bad angels. Only then, on the third day, did he "gradually" give the Jewish scholars some insight into "the promise contained in Scripture," that is, the Father's plan for the redemption.[53] Aelred interprets the Child's answering of questions, as well as his listening to and questioning of the teachers, as a sign of his humility—of his choosing to act "as a boy who learns."[54]

Yet, at the same time, the boy Jesus instructs the doctors in a subtle way, seeking to shed some light on divine matters without causing alarm or offense.

Despite his tactfulness vis-à-vis the learned doctors, Aelred's Christ Child could still be considered an exceptional boy and also a *puer-senex* (a boy endowed with the maturity of an adult). The abbot emphasizes how the fellow pilgrims to Jerusalem were drawn to the Boy, attracted as they were to the "signs of heavenly powers shining forth" from him, as well as the Christ Child's revelation, in some way, of "the mystery of the wisdom that saves."[55] Aelred also calls attention to the Boy's serious demeanor and weighty speech, by which "the boys of his own age are kept from mischief."[56] Despite such details, which clearly distinguish Jesus from ordinary boys, in this treatise he is in no way portrayed as preternaturally odd or obnoxious, as he is in the apocrypha (and as some children are in medieval saints' vitae).[57] Toward the end of the first (that is, historical) section of the treatise, Aelred directly, though briefly, touches upon the issue of what Luke meant when he said that Jesus "advanced in wisdom" (2:52). Although he offers two views, without explicitly endorsing one and discounting the other, he seems to believe that Jesus did not actually advance in wisdom, since he states that "what can be said of God in his nature could be said of Christ, even when he was in his Mother's womb."[58] Yet Aelred acknowledges the alternative view, which relies upon the argument that if Christ lacked the fullness of beatitude during his life, then he probably also lacked wisdom in his youth.[59] In any case, Aelred does not spend much time on this vexed question, stating that he is concerned with devotion rather than theology.[60]

Aelred's devotional agenda explains why he emphasizes Mary's intense feelings on the occasion of her loss, search for, and recovery of Jesus, and why he only briefly touches upon the question of what she thought of her son's behavior and identity, which, again, has more to do with theological issues. When, toward the beginning of the treatise, he questions both the Christ Child and the Virgin, specifically wondering why Jesus did not have compassion on his mother, and expressing his bemusement as to why Mary looked for him if she knew that he was God, Aelred seems to be finding fault with both parties. In any case, he is clearly expressing his inability to comprehend their actions and motives, as well as his astonishment that such a mix-up could have happened in the first place. Around a century later, an English Franciscan poet, Walter of Wimborne, similarly pondered the crisis caused by Christ's lingering in the Temple, going so far as to act as Mary's lawyer in an imaginative

court case, in which the twelve-year-old Jesus is accused of impiety because
he caused his mother such emotional suffering.[61] Although Aelred does not
exaggerate the misunderstanding between Mother and Child to such proportions, he does depict Mary as a very solicitous and dutiful mother, saying that
she was "on fire with such anxiety" over the loss of her son. He also adds tender human touches, for example, by suggesting that Mary suspected that Jesus
had gone off with other boys and was worried that he suffered injury from
one of them.[62] As already noted, Aelred conveys Mary's sense of relief when
she finally found her son (which echoes the exclamation of the bride in the
Song of Songs: "I have found him"). He is careful, though, to point out that
her negative feelings were caused more by being deprived of the delights caused
by her son's presence, than by overwhelming anxiety over his safety (which is
later emphasized in the *Meditationes vitae Christi*).[63] After all, he bluntly states,
Mary knew that he was God.[64] Along similar lines, Aelred remarks, in response to Luke's comment that his parents did not understand Jesus' words
when they found him (Lk. 2:50), that Mary "could not be ignorant of any purpose of her son."[65] This implies that she somehow knew of her son's redemptive mission, though the abbot here says too little to indicate what he actually
thought about Mary's understanding of the young Jesus.[66] As we shall see,
late medieval writers sometimes portrayed Mary as being aware of her son's
future sacrifice through her knowledge of prophecies, or learning about it
early on and sometimes being reluctant to accept it as God's will.

    While Aelred touches upon (what we might call) some Mariological and
Christological issues and certainly adds some tender, human notes to the episode of the three-day separation, his main purpose in the *De Jesu puero duodenni* is ostensibly to foster the soul's union with Christ, which is here
symbolized by Mary's finding of Jesus on the third day of her troubling
search.[67] In the course of promoting such spiritual development, the Cistercian abbot has undeniably expanded the basic story about Christ's staying
behind in the Temple to great proportions. He achieves this not so much by
adding mundane details that seem to derive from his own imagination (such
as the idea the Jesus begged for food, which he mentions only briefly)[68] but
by applying passages from different parts of the Bible (especially the Song of
Songs) to an anecdote about Jesus' childhood. His overall goal is to treat of
the soul's progress toward greater intimacy with and also resemblance to
Christ. Indeed, in some way the treatise can be said to be not so much about
the Christ Child after all, but rather about the soul of its intended monastic
reader.

While the other medieval texts I will explore in this book similarly add color to their depiction of the Christ Child by drawing on passages from different parts of the Bible, none of them seem to interweave biblical verses quite so intricately as does Aelred in the *De Jesu puero duodenni*. Although Aelred inserts some realistic details, much of what he adds to the Temple episode does not apparently derive from his exercise of poetic license or from oral or apocryphal traditions but from the Bible in some way (including the novel idea about Jesus' conference with his Father, which builds upon Christ's assertion that he had to be "about [his] father's business" [Lk. 2:49]).

In the *De Jesu puero duodenni*, Aelred has not relied on any apocryphal infancy texts, as he does, admittedly in only one instance, in the *De institutione inclusarum* (discussed below), yet in both cases he evinces a fairly open-minded attitude toward material that is not strictly rooted in Scripture, in which, as we have seen, he is wonderfully immersed. He briefly addresses this issue in the *De Jesu puero duodenni*, when, in the course of speculating about who might have cared for the Child in his parents' absence, he remarks, "It is attractive (*libet*) to form opinions or conjectures or surmises on all these matters, but it is wrong to make any rash assertions."[69] The apocryphal infancy legends explored in the following chapter have, as I have already noted, a quasi-dogmatic bent in their presentation of Christ's childhood, in the sense that their narrators do not pause to offer alternatives or state that things might have happened differently. In an essay in which she concentrates on medieval French redactions of Christ's apocryphal childhood, and contrasts them with the Franciscan *Meditationes vitae Christi* (which I discuss in the latter part of this chapter), Evelyn Birge Vitz draws an astute parallel between these two genres of texts (namely, apocryphal and meditative). It is helpful to consider her observation here since the *Meditationes* and the two aforementioned treatises by Aelred all encourage reflection on and visualization of the life of Christ, which, while guided, still leaves readers a good deal of freedom and, most importantly, invites them to see the biblical scenes and characters with their own inner eyes: "when one reads the Gospels, or any part of the Bible, as soon as one wishes to go beyond the schematic narrative and the theological formulations and tries to reconstruct in the mind's eye a scene—tries to see Jesus in action—one automatically produces apocryphal, non-canonical details. Meditation is, thus, by its very nature, what I would term 'apocryphogenic.'"[70] While it is true that meditational texts and apocryphal narratives, broadly speaking, engage the reader's imagination by going beyond the bare narrative of the biblical text, it is important to reiterate that the authorial

narrators of the apocrypha do not invite their readers to speculate about Jesus'
boyhood or in any way suggest that he himself may enlighten them about his
life or about other issues or concerns. As I have already stated, such narrators
pretend to offer historical accounts and do not foster much creative visualization of the child Jesus himself or of homely details about his childhood (such
as what his sleeping conditions were like),[71] beyond the reader's envisioning
of the scenes that form the backdrop of certain incidents—the remarkable
episodes deemed worthy of recollection. Yet, as the observation by Vitz suggests, the authors of these genres all participate in and foster an imaginative
freedom that allows them and their readers, to varying degrees, to explore the
life of Christ in concrete though hypothetical ways.

The visual orientation of Aelred's *De Jesu puero duodenni* and his *De institutione inclusarum* (discussed in the following section) is clearly central to the
abbot's experiential approach to monastic spirituality. Speaking of Jesus as the
bridegroom desired by the soul, both texts emphasize the Boy's extraordinary
beauty and encourage the reader to imagine his physical appearance and, even
more so, to yearn to see him. At the very beginning of the *De Jesu puero duodenni*, Ivo is reminded of how he is accustomed to gaze at the Boy's "most
beautiful face."[72] Later, Aelred surmises that on the trip up to Jerusalem "the
grace of heaven shone (*refulsisse*) from that most beautiful face (*speciossimus
vultus*) with such charm as to make everyone look at it."[73] In describing Jesus
as beautiful, Aelred and other medieval writers undoubtedly took their cue
from Psalm 44:3, which speaks of one who is "beautiful above the sons of men."
William of St. Thierry, for example, cites this verse in Bernard of Clairvaux's
vita, when he recounts the pious boy's vision of the Christ Child that occurred
before Mass one Christmas Eve: "It was as if Bernard saw re-enacted the birth
of the infant Word, more beautiful than all the sons of men. . . . And this
made young Bernard's heart overflow with a love and longing unheard of in
a mere boy."[74] Like Bernard, Aelred regards Jesus' beauty as having a powerful
influence on the beholder. His beauty is not simply skin-deep, but divinely
radiant and deeply affecting. As we shall see, the Christ Child's face is similarly
described as powerfully radiant in the *De institutione inclusarum*.

By encouraging his reader to look at Christ's face without, it should be
noted, actually providing a detailed description of it, Aelred increases his reader's desire for the beatific vision, which was thought to transcend human experience (cf. 1 Cor. 13:12). At the end of his treatise on Jesus' childhood, Aelred
claims that when the soul has reached its twelfth year, so to speak, it will be
able to gaze on the bridegroom, who is more comely than the sons of men

(Ps. 44:3); in return the Lord will look back through the lattices (Sg. 2:9). Such language reinforces the Christian reader's conviction that, although Jesus is hidden, he desires to make contact with and even be united with the human soul.[75] Aelred concludes his treatise by encouraging Ivo to extend the gaze of his mind's eye "into heaven's secret places" (*oculus mentis in ipsa caeli secreta radium porrexit*).[76] Like an eagle,[77] the monk is to look up at the radiant sun, seeking to be more profoundly imbued with Christ's mysteries as he continues to make spiritual progress. Rather than offer hidden knowledge about Christ's childhood, along the lines of the purveyors of apocryphal lore, Aelred urges his reader to gain an experiential sort of knowledge of Christ through personal prayer and to proceed from there to a more contemplative level of spirituality. Although he modestly refrains from claiming that the book stems from the inner workings of his own interior life, his biographer Walter Daniel asserted that Aelred's *De Jesu puero duodenni* came "out of the library of his heart."[78] Thus, in this treatise Aelred presumably shared his own experience in approaching divine mysteries. In short, in addressing the desire of his addressee Ivo for deeper knowledge about the Christ Child, Aelred does not disseminate secrets he gleaned from reading esoteric books, such as those containing apocryphal childhood narratives, which had such an allure for medieval audiences. Instead, Aelred offers imaginative and rhetorical prompts that will propel his reader along the course toward a greater intimacy with Christ through prayer and meditation.

## The Christ Child in Aelred's *De institutione inclusarum*

In the 1160s, Aelred wrote the *De institutione inclusarum*, at the request of his sister, a recluse, in order to provide her, and other women drawn to the anchoritic way of life, with appropriate guidance and inspiration.[79] Significantly, only a relatively small proportion of this epistolary treatise deals with the Christ Child: a passage on Jesus' infancy that occurs within the section of the text that focuses retrospectively on the life of Christ. The majority of Aelred's letter is aimed at explaining why one should be a recluse and, more importantly, how to be a good one. Aelred's underlying premise, with which he assumes his reader agrees, is that a female recluse, as a bride of Christ, exists in a state of expectation; having died to the world, she preserves her virginity in this life for her bridegroom, with whom she will finally be united in heaven. At the beginning of the treatise, Aelred tells his sister that one of the main reasons that people in the past have chosen the solitary life is so that they might "enjoy greater freedom in expressing . . . ardent longing for Christ's embrace."[80] Like other women, she has prudently enclosed herself in a cell, having little contact with other human beings. Yet she has not simply assumed a defensive posture; her goal of union with Christ is lofty. At different points in the treatise, Aelred invites the recluse to embrace Christ in her imagination and thus experience a foretaste of heavenly bliss.

Besides seeking to inspire and encourage his reader, Aelred recommends ways for her to avoid spiritual dangers. To fortify herself against the devil's attack, the recluse should "never cease to ponder for whose bridal chamber she is being embellished, for whose embraces she is being prepared." The sensuality of such imagery is presumably not at odds with the communal nature of heaven, for Aelred also tells the recluse to envision Mary leading the dance of the virginal brides of Christ.[81] Approaching the issue of spiritual safeguarding more concretely, Aelred advises the recluse on how she should decorate her cell so as to avoid vanity; by sticking to the bare essentials, she will conform her lifestyle to that of her heavenly spouse, "who became poor although he was rich and chose for himself a poor mother, a poor family, a poor little house also and the squalor (vilitas) of the manger."[82] The recluse ought to recall Christ's sacrifice as well as his childhood. By having a crucifix on the altar, specifically a representation of Jesus with outstretched arms, she will undoubtedly be reminded of his love for her.[83] On the whole, Aelred emphasizes the idea that Christ is the recluse's spouse, even as he employs the image of Jesus as mother, specifically by prompting the recluse to imagine a maternal Christ nursing her with his naked breasts.[84]

It is in Part Three of the epistolary treatise that Aelred focuses on the life of Christ in a brief and basically linear fashion. Aelred does not simply summarize the course of Jesus' life but serves as a virtual tour guide, imaginatively leading the reader from one place to another in the Holy Land—locations once graced by Christ's presence. Imaginatively entering into Jesus' life, the recluse is to carry out the actions that Aelred recommends as a sort of stage director, at times telling her to pause, and at other times rushing her on to the next site, in order to commemorate another event. Marsha Dutton, seeking to distinguish between the two Aelredian works under discussion, says that the treatise addressed to Ivo urges imitation of Christ, whereas that addressed to his sister fosters a participatory experience of Christ, through the reader's envisioning of herself as a companion of Jesus and also of Mary.[85] In my view, though these texts may be said to have different emphases, in reality they overlap a good deal. For example, the reader of the *De Jesu puero duo-denni* is, like the reader of the *De institutione inclusarum*, encouraged to imagine what it would have been like to experience the presence of the Christ Child, as well as his absence. Admittedly, however, the treatise for Ivo centers on a metaphorical finding of the boy Jesus in the Temple as the ultimate goal of one's spiritual journey, which in its various stages imitates Christ's physical development. The focus of the *De institutione inclusarum*, in contrast, is on the literal details of Jesus' childhood and the latter part of his life; Aelred's sister is instructed to enter into the drama of Christ's earthly life and have an imaginatively tactile experience of him, rather than ponder how her life metaphorically parallels that of Christ. The point of such meditations, Aelred states, is to increase the recluse's love of God by providing a foretaste of Jesus' sweetness through imagined intimacy with his historical person.[86]

Although Aelred does not write extensively about the early life of Jesus in Part Three of the *De institutione inclusarum*, the relevant contents of this section are worth considering here, mainly because of their connection to details found in later medieval devotional works, some of which are discussed below. Assuming that the recluse habitually engages in the reading of Scripture, Aelred recommends that she ponder the writings of the prophets, along with Mary, who was similarly engaged in her room before the arrival of the archangel Gabriel. This view of the Virgin as reading at the moment of the Annunciation differs from what we find in the influential *Gospel of Pseudo-Matthew*, where Mary is said to have been engaged in textile work.[87] Preferring a more contemplative Mary or at least one who uses books to enrich her prayer life, Aelred tells the recluse to imagine what "great sweetness" and fire of love Mary must have experienced upon becoming pregnant with the Lord; she is to focus on "the Virgin, whom she has resolved to imitate, and her son, to whom she is wed."[88] Aelred tells his reader to follow Mary to her cousin Elizabeth's home and focus her gaze on the wombs of the two pregnant women, "in which the salvation of the whole world takes its origin." He reminds the recluse that even as a fetus, Jesus was her spouse, telling her to "embrace your Bridegroom" in Mary's womb and Jesus' "friend" in the womb of Elizabeth.[89] As we have already seen, medieval theologians commonly spoke of the Christ Child as a spouse. In addition, medieval Christians often envisioned Jesus as a *homunculus* while in the womb (that is, as a perfectly formed, yet diminutive human).[90] Building upon Luke 1:41, which notes that John the Baptist leapt in the womb of his mother when she was greeted by the pregnant Mary, Aelred further endows the fetal John with personality by making him seem on friendly terms with his cousin. Making no mention of Joseph, Aelred tells the recluse to be present with Mary at the Nativity—to observe her child with joy. Urged to become even further engaged in this domestic event, so to speak, the reader is to "embrace him in that sweet crib, let love overcome your reluctance, affection drive out fear. Put your lips on those most sacred feet, kiss them again and again"[91]—a piece of advice recycled in later devotional texts. Aelred clearly views imaginary contact with Christ's feet as a way to gain access to him and to experience a foretaste of future intimacy with the divine bridegroom. Later on, along similar lines, he tells the reader to visualize Mary Magdalene kissing Jesus' feet.[92] The fear he automatically assumes his reader will feel when she is told to kiss the Infant's feet may stem from her presumed sense of awe as well as her reserve, an inclination Aelred considers inappropriate in Christ's bride. Even the otherwise bold housewife-turned-holy-woman Margery Kempe, who flourished in the early fifteenth century, felt some reserve toward Christ (though mostly because of her sense of inferiority stemming from her status as a wife). Hence when she swaddles him in a vision, she does so very gently.[93] Yet the Lord mystically assured Margery on another occasion, saying: "thu mayst boldly, whan thu art in thi bed, take me to the [i.e., embrace me] as for this weddyd husband . . . and as thy swete sone."[94] While not all medieval Christians intermingled erotic and maternal imagery so readily, the spousal connotation of the Christ Child, clearly present in Aelred's anchoritic text, was in fact quite common, as already noted.

After Aelred tells his reader to meditate on the visit of the shepherds and that of the Magi, he instructs her to accompany the Christ Child to Egypt. He then recounts the story about how the Holy Family was held up by robbers as they fled there. It is important to note that Aelred is apparently the first writer in the West to relate this apocryphal legend, which is ultimately based on a tale included in the early medieval *Arabic Infancy Gospel*.[95] A chapter from this apocryphal text tells how the Holy Family encountered two adult thieves on the Flight into Egypt, one of whom prevented the other from harming the Holy Family. Out of gratitude, the infant Jesus promised his mother that he would reward the good thief's kindness, prophesying that the two men would be crucified with him, but that the one on his right, the good thief, would enter with him into Paradise. Mary vocalizes her prayer that God protect her son from such a fate, but we are not told whether the infant Jesus responds.[96] This basic story was transmitted to the Greek-speaking world (and thence to Western Europe) through an interpolation made in the apocryphal *Gospel of Nicodemus*.[97] Background information about the good thief is provided right after the Greek writer mentions the exchange of words between the two thieves crucified beside Christ, as recorded in Scripture (Lk. 23:39–43).[98] The apocryphal Greek text gives these thieves names: the bad one on the left is called "Gestas," while the good one on the right is named "Dismas."[99] The name Dismas and the tale of his early encounter with the Holy Family became well known in the West by the later Middle Ages.[100] This figure can be seen as one of many late medieval elaborations on the Passion story and, more specifically, as a part of the widespread devotional trend of the Proleptic Passion, which I explore in more detail below.

Whereas Mary plays a key role in both the Arabic and Greek redactions of this legend, in Aelred's version the emphasis is on the interaction between the good thief and Jesus as they hung on the cross in close proximity. Struck by the beauty of the Lord hanging beside him, and far from being scandalized by Jesus' execution as a criminal, the thief in Aelred's account, who insists on Jesus' innocence, reminds Christ of the good deed he himself had previously done for him, several years ago. It is worth quoting this passage from the *De institutione inclusarum* in full since, besides positing a close connection between Jesus' infancy and Passion, it includes a number of important details, some of which resonate with sources discussed below. In addition, this is the only apocryphal infancy legend that Aelred relates here or elsewhere, so he must have had a good reason for its inclusion. Although the recluse is initially urged to accompany the Child on the Flight into Egypt, in this case, she is not at all told to intervene in the scene. Instead, she is meant to behold the miracle of a quasi death-bed conversion, which reveals Jesus' lavish mercy:

Accept as true the legend that [Jesus] was captured by robbers on the way and owed his escape to a young man (*adolescentulus*) who is supposed to have been the son of the robber chief. After seizing his booty he looked at the Child in his Mother's bosom and was so impressed by the majesty that radiated from his beautiful face as to be convinced that he was something more than man. Inflamed with love he embraced him and said: "O most blessed of children, if ever the occasion arises to take pity on me, then remember me and do not forget the present moment." This is said to be the thief who was crucified at Christ's right hand and rebuked the other thief when he blasphemed. "What," he said, "have you no fear of God, when you are undergoing the same sentence? And we justly enough; we receive no more than the due reward of our deeds; but this man has done nothing amiss." Then, turning to the Lord and seeing in him that majesty which had distinguished him as a child, he remembered his agreement and said: "Remember me when you come into your kingdom." So, in order to kindle love I consider it worthwhile to accept this legend as true, without making any rash assertions as to its authority.[101]

In this story, emphasis is given to the striking appearance of Jesus when he was both an infant and an adult—in both cases, the majesty of his divinity shines through the humble human circumstances of Jesus' childhood and his death as a criminal. Recall that in the *De Jesu puero duodenni*, the Christ Child's face, along similar lines, was said to be *speciossimus* (most beautiful), a description which echoes Psalm 44:3. Significantly, in both treatises, light is said to gleam from Jesus' face.[102]

Aware of its lack of certitude, Aelred still recounts this pious anecdote (in a sketchy fashion, as if he expects his reader to be already familiar with the tale), and then tells the recluse why he did so: it is useful in instilling love. He gives his reader freedom to believe it or not, though at the outset of his narration, he urges her to accept it as true: "Believe that what is said is true. . . . Therefore I judge it not at all useless for the enkindling of love to hold this opinion, with all boldness of affirming it far away."[103] In the *De Jesu puero duodenni*, as I noted above, Aelred makes a comparable statement.[104] As we shall see in the following chapter, clerics similarly justified (or at least tolerated) the transmission of apocryphal material because of its perceived devotional utility, without worrying whether such legends were actually true. Along similar lines, medieval hagiographers customarily composed biographical narratives about holy people on the basis of what they considered appropriate behavior for those who came to be recognized as saints, rather than from what they knew to be the facts, or in the absence of biographical materials. In addition, they often knowingly used sources that were not completely reliable. For example, the thirteenth-century Dominican Jacobus de Voragine, who was essentially a compiler, repeatedly tells what we (and probably his learned readers) would consider farfetched tales and occasionally alerts his readers to the apocryphal nature of his accounts, saying that he himself regards them as doubtful. He explicitly leaves it up to his readers to judge for themselves whether such stories are worth retelling.[105]

Aelred similarly tells his anchoritic reader that the tale about the robber's son is a pious "opinion."[106] He undoubtedly sees much value in the apocryphal legend about the Holy Family's encounter with a good thief. For him, it is pious fiction worthy of attention, unlike, for example, the fictional romances about King Arthur that lay people and even monks were attracted to and took so seriously—worthless material as far as Aelred was concerned, especially when it became an inordinate drain on Christians' emotions.[107]

We might wonder how Aelred became acquainted with the story about the good thief, which originated in the East. As I mention in the following chapter, a few legends about the Holy Family deriving from Eastern sources were, in the later Middle Ages, incorporated into apocryphal infancy narratives that circulated in Latin and the vernacular languages. Such tales were also added to the repertoire of Christian iconography.[108] Yet given that the story about the good thief was generally not incorporated into the apocryphal infancy narratives circulating in Latin in the West, it is probably the case that the legend about the Holy Family's encounter with thieves was originally transmitted orally. This was perhaps a result of Europeans' greater contact with eastern Mediterranean cultures, due to their more frequent travel to and interest in that region. Oral transmission seems to account, at least in part, for the appearance in Europe of another tale about the Holy Family, namely their visit to the garden of Matariya near Cairo, which resulted, according to legend, in precious balm growing in that special location for centuries to come, on account of Mary's washing of the baby Jesus and his clothes in that spot (fig. 18, upper register).[109]

## The Christ Child in the Piety of St. Francis and St. Clare of Assisi

While it was by means of his writings that Aelred of Rievaulx, as far as we know, encouraged both monks and recluses to meditate on the early life of Jesus and to imitate his development by making spiritual progress, Francis of Assisi's deep devotion to the child Jesus manifested itself very strongly through performance both on special occasions and day-to-day; without doubt, his dramatic words and deeds left a lasting impression upon his fellow Franciscans and also the laity. The most dramatic manifestation of Francis's piety toward the child Jesus occurred on Christmas Eve in 1223 (three years before his death), when he arranged for a public manger to be set up in Greccio, a small town between Assisi and Rome. Those who have heard of the incident but are unfamiliar with the early accounts of Francis's life may assume that, at Greccio, he simply participated in a Nativity play or paraliturgical activity of some sort.

Yet he actually made arrangements for a Christmas Eve Mass, which he creatively embellished with audiovisual aides and enhanced by his preaching as a deacon. In this section, I will examine the Greccio episode in detail, after discussing the biographical sources for Francis and his disciple Clare that underscore their love for the Christ Child and their efforts to imitate him, especially his embrace of poverty. The corpus of Francis's writings is quite small, and Clare's even smaller, but they themselves speak of the Christ Child in a few passages, as do the hagiographical writings centered on these saints. Significantly, both Francis and Clare focused on Luke's account of the Nativity, apparently disregarding the apocryphal legends about Jesus' birth. As I explain below, at Greccio, Francis capitalized on the apocryphal detail about the ox and the ass, which seem part and parcel of his love of animals and of all creation more generally. The non-canonicity of these animals' presence at Christ's manger was probably not worrisome to Francis and his Christian contemporaries, considering that, at that time, these animals were widely assumed to have been present at the baby Jesus' manger, which was literally a feeding box. On the whole, Francis, Clare, and their followers seem to have done very little, if anything, with the traditional apocryphal infancy legends. Instead, the two saints called attention to Jesus and Mary's embrace of poverty at the Nativity despite their status as royalty—an embrace of poverty that is implied by the Gospel account but assumes central place in the Franciscan vision of Christ's life and their attempts to imitate it exactly.

As we have seen, the Cistercians also meditated on the poverty of the infant Jesus and strove to imitate it by the simplicity of their monastic lifestyle, but they seem to have reflected more generally upon the poverty of the divine Word's self-emptying (cf. Phil. 2:7), that is, his descent from his heavenly throne, assumption of human flesh, and living as a real human being, among other humans. In other words, the Cistercians did not apparently become fixated on specific circumstances surrounding Jesus' birth, such as the feeding bin in which he was placed and the meager strips of fabric with which he was swaddled—biblical details that captured the imagination of the Franciscans.[110] In my view, the difference between early Franciscan and Cistercian approaches to the Nativity can be readily perceived by looking at two short and arguably representative passages that involve a visualization of the Mother and Child. In his *De Jesu puero duodenni*, Aelred encourages his reader to see "with the eyes of an enlightened mind" the Christ Child "lying in a manger, crying in his mother's arms, hanging at her breasts"—an embodiment of God's goodness, he says.[111] The image of a lactating Virgin and Child that Francis supposedly offered his followers is much more concrete and emotionally intense. According to Thomas of Celano, the Franciscan who authored two of the earliest vitae of the saint, Francis "used to observe the Nativity of the Child Jesus with an immense eagerness above all other solemnities, affirming it was the Feast of Feasts, when God was made a little child (*parvulus*) and hung on human breasts." Here, God's amazing condescension in becoming a child is highlighted by his literal dependency on *human* (that is, his mother's nourishing) breasts. Thomas immediately goes on to note that Francis "would lick the images of the baby's limbs with a hungry meditation, and the melting compassion of his heart toward the child [Jesus] also made him stammer sweet words as babies do. This name [Jesus] was to him like honey."[112] Francis manifests his love for the Christ Child physically, by licking an effigy of Jesus and, further, by becoming like an infant, through his slippage into baby talk.[113] So, while both Aelred and Francis imagine the infant Jesus nursing at Mary's breast, Francis touches and even tastes the Christ Child with his inner senses, which are activated by external objects. Granted, the Franciscan text I have just quoted is a biographical one, whereas the Cistercian text that I have cited is not. Still, I think it is fair to say that Francis, in comparison to Aelred, was more concrete in the way he imagined the Christ Child and much more demonstrative in his piety toward the infant Jesus.

The aforesaid passage about Francis, which comes from Thomas of Celano's *Vita secunda* (1245–47), contains the claim that Francis's favorite feast was Christmas; it is this aspect of the saint's piety that I will consider first. By affirming that the Nativity of the child Jesus "was the Feast of Feasts," Francis (as he is presented by Thomas) gives the impression that he considers Christmas more important than Easter, the feast of Christ's Resurrection, traditionally regarded as the climax of the liturgical year. In a sermon aimed at preparing Christians for the upcoming fast of Lent, Pope Leo the Great (d. 461) enunciates the common idea that Christmas is subordinate to Easter when he says: "we well know that the Paschal Mystery is the chief [of festivals], and the calendar of the whole year disposes us to enter into it properly and worthily."[114] Francis, I suspect, would have agreed with this idea; nonetheless, he sees the two feasts as inextricably linked and chooses to place rhetorical emphasis on the feast that commemorates the beginning of Christ's life. In *The Assisi Compilation* (1244–60), an early Franciscan collection of stories about the saint, we are given Francis's reason for holding Christmas in such high esteem: "although the Lord may have accomplished our salvation in his other solemnities, nevertheless, once he was born to us . . . it was certain that we would be saved."[115] In this passage, Francis cites part of Isaiah 9:6 ("For a child [*parvulus*] is born to us, and a son is given to us"). For Francis, this verse, which became the Introit for the Third Mass of Christmas, encapsulates the idea that the Son of God was born in order to be offered to God as a sacrifice that would redeem humankind. Francis seems to have been quite enthusiastic about this surprising and paradoxical mystery at the root of Christianity. Hence the verse occurs in the Office for the Passion that Francis himself composed, specifically, as the antiphon for the Vespers that were to be used from the Nativity to Epiphany: "This is the day the Lord has made / let us rejoice and be glad in it (Ps. 117:24). / For the Most Holy Child has been given to us (Isa. 9:6) / and has been born for us on the way [i.e., to Bethlehem] / and placed in a manger / because he did not have a place in the inn."[116] These verses express joy on account of the Father's gift of the Son, who already begins to suffer at his Nativity, because of the lowly conditions in which Mary gave birth to her child. For Francis, then, the feast of Christmas commemorates the beginning of grace and points forward to Passiontide and, beyond it, to Easter; thus, the two main feasts of the liturgical year celebrate one and the same divine plan for the redemption. This explains why, at Christmas, Francis is not simply optimistic and merry, but confident of salvation and filled with profound joy. According to Thomas of Celano, the saint told his friars that they should eat meat if Christmas occurred on a Friday; he wanted "even the walls to eat meat on that day" or "at least be rubbed with grease!" He also desired that the poor be fed by the rich, and that oxen and asses be given extra hay. In addition, he wished to beseech the Emperor to issue a decree that wheat and grain be thrown on the roads for "our sisters the larks."[117]

Yet joy was not the only emotion Francis experienced at Christmas. In the same chapter from the *Vita secunda*, Thomas goes on to recount how Francis was filled with compassion when he considered the circumstances of the Nativity: "He could not recall without tears the great want surrounding the little, poor Virgin (*paupercula Virgo*) on that day. One day when he was sitting down to dinner a brother mentioned the poverty of the Virgin, and reflected on the want of Christ her Son. No sooner had he heard this than he got up from the table, groaning with sobs of pain, and bathed in tears ate the rest of his bread on the naked ground. He used to say this must be a royal virtue, since it shone so remarkably in a King and Queen."[118] As is clear from such courtly language, Francis regards the *paupercula* Mary and her infant son as the ultimate royalty.[119] The influential Franciscan theologian and Minister General Bonaventure (d. 1274) likewise emphasized the poverty that

Christ embraced: "Christ was poor at his birth, poor during the course of his life, and poor at his death. In order to make poverty lovable to the world, he chose a most poor Mother." For Francis, Christ's wilful embrace of poverty required a radical response. Thus, in the anecdote mentioned above, he thinks it inappropriate for one who is Mary and Jesus' subject (namely himself) to enjoy greater comfort than they, and so sits on the ground, a position associated with humility.[120] As we shall see, Francis similarly speaks of the Christ Child as "the poor King" when he preached as a deacon at Greccio. Francis's fondness for courtly imagery, reflected in the passage above, is also seen in his comparison of the friars to minstrels and to the knights of the Round Table.[121] As the greatest of knights, like Lancelot, Francis seems to live flamboyantly in a quasi-Arthurian world, ruled by Christ and Mary.[122]

Another anecdote about Francis sitting on the floor at Christmas is worth considering since it likewise suggests that the saint associated the Nativity with poverty and (to a lesser extent) humility. One Christmas the friars in Greccio were expecting a visit from a Minister of the Franciscan Order, and so set the table elegantly, presumably to show him honor. Francis, who was staying with these friars at that time, knocked at the door and asked for alms, disguised as a beggar, but he was immediately recognized by his fellow friars. After coming in and taking a dish of food, Francis sat on the floor, rather than at the table on the dais with the other brothers. Sighing, Francis explained his disappointment: "When I saw the table finely and elaborately prepared, I considered that this was not a table of poor religious, who go door-to-door [i.e., begging] each day. For more than other religious, we should follow the example of poverty and humility in all things."[123] This anecdote provides a glimpse into Francis's response to Christ's birth on the feast of Christmas itself, but his thoughts (to the extent that hagiography gives us access to them) seem to have been filled with the Nativity, and his actions shaped by his reflection on it, all the time.

As is well known, Francis's biographers interpret his reception of the stigmata at La Verna in 1224, two years before his death, as the culmination of his perpetual efforts to imitate the crucified Savior during his life. Yet, if we read the sources carefully, it becomes clear that the saint strove to imitate Christ in the manger, as well as Jesus on the cross. Francis's life as a friar began when he stripped himself publicly before the bishop of Assisi. Returning his fine clothing to his father, a wealthy cloth merchant, Francis informed him that his primary allegiance would henceforth be to his Father in heaven.[124] In a rendering of this famous episode by the modern Italian printer Rolando

Dominici (fig. 5), Francis is portrayed covered from the waist down with the bishop's mantle, the way he is depicted in the fresco dedicated to this event in the Upper Church of San Francesco in Assisi. Dominici seems to suggest a source of inspiration for Francis at this crucial moment, by his placement of the half-swaddled baby Jesus lying practically on the ground in front of Francis.[125] The implication that the young convert Francis was, as it were, swaddled like the poor naked Christ Child may seem novel, but it is actually rooted in the written sources. Recall that in Aelred's *De Jesu puero duodenni* infancy signified spiritual conversion. Bonaventure echoes this idea in his spiritual treatise *De quinque festivitatibus pueri Jesu*, a short devotional text that, like Aelred's treatise on the twelve-year-old Jesus, makes an extended analogy between the earliest events of Christ's life, on the one hand, and the soul's conversion and spiritual growth, on the other.[126] A comparison between Francis at the beginning of his conversion and the infant Jesus is appropriate because, in his youth, the future saint experienced a spiritual rebirth, in which he embraced a sort of newness. Like a newborn, who has no clothing or other possessions, Francis divested himself of all material goods, even his underwear, when he severed his ties with his father and rejected his worldly ways.[127] Thomas of Celano comments on the advantage Francis gained by taking off his clothes: "Now he wrestles naked with the naked"—a reference to the traditional idea of spiritual combat, as well as an allusion to the ancient practice of *pankration* (which involved wrestling in the nude).[128] Thomas adds that now "only the wall of the flesh would separate [Francis] from the vision of God," implying that clothing and other earthly goods are a hindrance to one who intensely seeks union with the divine.

Throughout his life as a friar, Francis—who, again, could have dressed in fine clothes in life, because of his social standing, but decisively opted not to, just as the Word himself chose poverty—insisted on having only one rough tunic, which he often shared or gave away when he saw a person in need.[129] At his death, he ordered that he be laid naked on the "naked ground." A connection between the saint's nakedness at the beginning and end of his religious life is explicitly made by Bonaventure, whose vita of Francis became the official version for the Franciscan Order in 1266: "In all things he wished without hesitation to be conformed to Christ crucified who hung on the cross poor, suffering, and naked. Naked he lingered before the bishop at the beginning of his conversion; and, for this reason, at the end of his life, he wanted to leave this world naked."[130] In praising Francis's nakedness, Bonaventure may have in mind the famous remark of Job (1:21; cf. Ecclesiastes 5:14) about his

Figure 5. The converted St. Francis stripped of clothes standing next to the baby Jesus lying on the ground. Print by Rolando Dominici (twenty-first century). By permission of the artist.

exiting from his mother's womb naked and leaving the world in that state as well. Yet, by saying that Francis was naked "at the beginning" (of his life as a religious), Bonaventure may also have in mind the nearly naked Christ Child. The popular Franciscan-authored devotional text *Meditationes vitae Christi* (about which I will say more below) draws attention to Christ's lack of clothing at his birth and at his death when it describes Mary wrapping the baby Jesus in her veil and later "girding him with her head covering," when he was stripped completely naked at the Passion.[131]

Bonaventure himself conflates Christ's infancy with his Passion in a few places of his writings. For instance, in his *De perfectione vitae ad sorores*, he remarks that "from the first day of his life to his last, from the instant of birth to the instant of death, pain and sorrow were his companions. So he himself has said through the prophet: 'I am afflicted and in agony from my youth' (Ps. 87:16); and elsewhere: 'I have been scourged all the day' (Ps. 72:14), meaning all his life."[132] In his *Vitis mystica*, Bonaventure reiterates the idea that Jesus' entire life was filled with suffering, when he explains that "the term 'passion'" does not apply "to the one day only on which he died, but to the whole extent of his life."[133] He again cites Psalm 87:16 in support of this interpretation.[134] In a later chapter, Bonaventure reflects on the idea that "the crucifixion of Jesus actually began at his birth," explaining that it was not an accident that he was "born in a strange place, in mid-winter, in the depth of the night, outside the inn, of a Mother poor and humble. Although at this time there was no shedding of his blood, it did come about after only seven days had passed," that is, at the Circumcision.[135] Along similar lines, St. Anthony of Padua, in a sermon for the feast of the Circumcision, observed, "Christ's whole life was in blood . . . Christ was blood-red at the beginning and at the end of his life."[136] In light of such passages, which presumably distill the spirituality of the order's founder, I think it is fair to say that Francis of Assisi was thought to have imitated Christ in the sufferings he endured, not just at his Passion, but throughout his life—including its earliest moments. Indeed, all of Christ's life entailed suffering that stemmed from poverty.

The centrality of Christ's poverty to the Franciscan way of life is evident from the *Regula non bullata*, the Rule that Francis composed for his friars and that Pope Innocent III orally approved in 1209. When Francis says that the friars ought to "strive to follow the humility and poverty of our Lord Jesus Christ," having nothing but food and clothing, he likely has in mind the Christ Child as well as the adult Jesus, who lived as an itinerant preacher content with bare necessities. Francis continues by telling the brothers not to be ashamed to beg, since Jesus himself was not ashamed to do so. "He was poor and a stranger and lived on alms—he, the Blessed Virgin, and his disciples."[137] A more nuanced presentation of Jesus as a mendicant (literally, "one who begs") is found in the Franciscan *Meditationes vitae Christi*, in the chapter on the Holy Family's return from Egypt. Here, the boy Jesus seems to accept alms with unease: when his neighbors offered him money for traveling expenses for the family's return from Egypt, "the boy was embarrassed . . . but out of his love of poverty, he opened his hand, shamefacedly accepted the money and expressed thanks."[138] The implication is that by going against his natural disinclination to accept handouts, the Christ Child reveals his love of poverty as well as his nobility.[139] In the depiction of this incident in the well-known illustrated manuscript containing an Italian version of the *Meditationes* (Paris, Bibliothèque nationale de France, ital. 115, fol. 45r; fig. 6), a small-looking Christ Child (who, according to the text, would be about nine years old) appears a bit overwhelmed by the situation, as he opens his hand to receive money from an old man standing behind him.[140] Aelred of Rievaulx had earlier suggested that the young Jesus had begged for necessities, specifically during his three-day sojourn in Jerusalem, yet he did not elaborate on that detail.[141] Just as Francis and his followers can be said to have acted like the child Jesus by begging, so, by wearing "poor clothes" patched "with sackcloth and other pieces" (namely, "a tunic with a hood"),[142] they arguably patterned themselves after the new-born Christ Child, who was humbly wrapped with swaddling clothes (Lk. 2:7).

While Francis himself, in the surviving texts written by him, does not explicitly speak about the strips of fabric Mary used to swaddle her infant, his disciple Clare of Assisi did. In the monastic Rule she wrote for her sisters, Clare emphasizes that the infant Jesus was scantily covered, a detail she weaves into her instructions concerning the nuns' clothing: "Out of love of the most holy and beloved Child wrapped in poor swaddling clothes (*pauperculis panniculis involutus*) and placed in a manger and of his most holy mother, I admonish, beg, and encourage my sisters to wear poor garments."[143] Similarly, in her Fourth Letter to Agnes of Prague (a Bohemian princess who had become a Poor Clare nun around twenty years earlier), Clare urges her to contemplate Christ, her heavenly spouse: "Look, I say, at the border of this mirror, that is, the poverty of him who was placed in a manger and wrapped in swaddling clothes (*in panniculis involutus*). O marvelous humility! O astonishing poverty! The King of angels, the Lord of heaven and earth, is laid in a manger!"[144] Clare's use of the diminutive form of the word *panni* ("strips of fabric"), which appears in Luke 2:7, is suggestive of rags, or at least of paltry pieces of cloth—

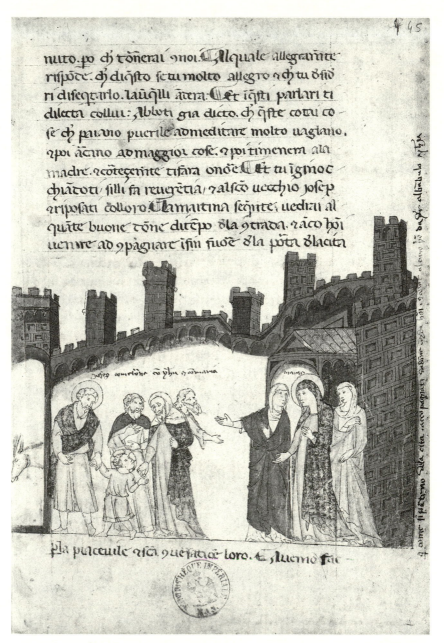

nuito.po ch tônerai mei. Alquale allegrariñte
rispôde. ch dichsto se tu molto allegro ach tu ôsiô
ri disegtarlo. Lauqlli adera: Et ichsti parlari ti
dileta colluí: Abloti gia ducto. ch chste cotu co
se ch paruio puerile admeditare molto uagliano.
zpoi acuino admaggioi cose. zpoi timenera ala
madre. zcotegeriñte tisara onôe Et tu igmoc
chiatoti silli fa reuerétia. zalsco uecchio josep
aripofati colloro Tamartina seguite. uediti al
quate buone tône ditepo ôla grada. zaco hoi
uenire ad cpagniare isin suoe ôla pôta ôlacitia

Josep camertône cô ghu z marina

mariîa

pla piîceuile zisei guefatiae loro. E, lucino fa

Figure 6. The Christ Child accepting alms, in an illustrated manuscript of the *Meditationes vitae Christi*. Paris, BnF, ital. 115, fol. 45r (fourteenth century). By permission of the Bibliothèque nationale de France.

pitiful strips of fabric that barely, and not at all worthily, cover the royal Babe.[145] Like Francis, Clare calls attention to the Infant's royalty, which makes the humble conditions of the Nativity seem even more astonishing. Moreover, such a characterization emphasizes the nobility of Agnes's heavenly spouse, a fitting match for a princess. Just as Francis was extremely ascetic as regards his use of clothing, occasionally appearing naked in public and instructing other friars to do so, as a form of penance,[146] so Clare, a woman of the nobility, "was content with only one tunic of *lazzo* (a rough fabric) and one mantle," as a witness testified in Clare's Process of Canonization.[147] Modestly wearing her rough-hewn garment, in deference to social norms, Clare nevertheless boldly envisioned herself fighting naked against the devil.[148] Although Francis himself does not employ the image of *pankration*, as Clare rather remarkably does, they both seem to have thought of Christ's poverty as fundamentally consisting of a lack of clothing.

That Francis's fellow friars thought of him as a mirror image of the Christ Child is indicated by the comparisons they made between Francis and the baby Jesus. Franciscan sources recount how Lady Jacoba, an ardent admirer of Francis, was mystically summoned to the saint as he approached death. She brought fabric for his burial shroud, wax and incense for his funeral, as well as the ingredients needed for making the confection (marzipan) that Francis was extremely fond of. Although Lady Jacoba was a solo bringer of provisions for the one she so admired, the sources compare her to the Three Kings who offered gifts to the child Jesus. In his request for sweets (and his lack of fear of death), Francis seems childlike, yet he resembles the Christ Child most properly in his embrace of poverty. As the *Assisi Compilation* states: the Lord "inspired the Kings to travel with gifts to honor the child, his beloved Son, in the days of his birth and his poverty. So too he willed to inspire this noble lady in a faraway region to travel with gifts to honor and venerate" the body of Francis, "who loved the poverty of his beloved Son with so much fervor and love in life and in death."[149]

Francis's admirers extended the comparison of the saint to the Christ Child even further in the following century, when they claimed that Francis was born in a stable, in proximity to an ox and an ass. According to legend, when his mother Lady Pica came to term but had not yet entered into labor, she was told by a mysterious stranger, who knocked at the door, that she should leave her chamber and go into the stable where she would be able to give birth. Today, in Assisi, one can still read the following inscription over the door of the chapel S. Francesco il Piccolo: "This oratory was the stable of the ox and the ass in which St. Francis, the mirror of the world, was born."[150] Although the legend seems to have emerged only in the second half of the fourteenth century and the house of Pietro Bernardone, Francis's father, was apparently located elsewhere in the town of Assisi, the tale about Francis's birth remains valuable since it reveals how Francis's life was believed to mirror Christ's at its very beginning, not simply later on, most visibly when he received the stigmata. The Renaissance artist Benozzo Gozzoli (d. 1452) transmits this legend in his cycle on the life of St. Francis that adorns the sanctuary walls of the church of S. Francesco in Montefalco (fig. 7).[151] Significantly, a handmaiden who has just given the newborn Francis his first bath holds him up naked so that the other women, and also animals in attendance, may see this remarkably Christ-like child. Francis's birth, like that of other infants destined to become saints, was accompanied by a mysterious occurrence that presaged his future career: following his conversion in his youth, Francis earnestly imitated Christ's

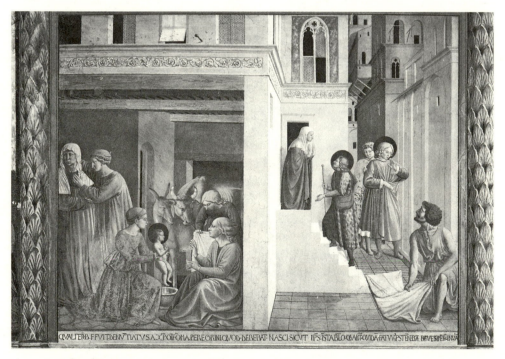

Figure 7. The legendary birth of Francis of Assisi in a stable. Fresco by Benozzo Gozzoli, Church of S. Francesco, Montefalco (fifteenth century). By permission of Scala/Art Resource, NY.

Figure 8. St. Francis of Assisi held by Christ; the Christ Child held by Mary. Stained glass lancets, Upper Church of the Basilica of San Francesco, Assisi (late thirteenth century). By permission of G. Ruf, www.assisi.de.

lowliness (including his nakedness) and strove to spread love of the baby Jesus.[152] Francis is similarly likened to the Christ Child in a pair of late thirteenth-century stained glass lancets in the Upper Church of San Francesco in Assisi; in parallel fashion, the windows represent a standing figure holding a smaller, child(like) figure (fig. 8). On the left, Christ with a crossed nimbus embraces an adult yet miniature version of Francis of Assisi bearing the stigmata, who, as it were floating before Christ, holds a book and a cross. On the right, the Virgin holds the Christ Child frontally, almost as if he were seated on her lap, while his hands are basically in the same position as those of Francis. The suggestion is that Francis is the perfect image of Christ by virtue of sharing in his sufferings at the Passion and also by imitating the Christ Child. Furthermore, the image encourages the viewer to regard Francis as maternally cared for by Jesus and also as a brother to the Christ Child.[153] From such examples we can see how, from the perspective of Francis's followers, he and Christ were mirror images of each other.

The merging of the figures of Francis and the Christ Child is also manifested in another way: in the attribution to the child Jesus of Franciscan features. We have already encountered an example of this in the portrayal of the Boy as a recipient of alms found in the *Meditationes vitae Christi*. The depiction of Jesus as a Franciscan can also be seen in an early fourteenth-century painting of the Madonna and Child, ascribed to the Primo Maestro di Santa Chiara, now in the Museo Diocesano in Spoleto. Here the Christ Child is dressed as a Franciscan, with brown wool habit, triple-knotted cord, and bare feet.[154] The anonymous author of the late thirteenth-century *Meditatio pauperis in solitudine* emphasizes Christ's Franciscanism even more explicitly, stating that Christ "was the first and true Lesser Brother (*frater minor*) according to the perfection of the . . . virtues [viz., poverty, love and humility] which shone out in him in a most perfect way."[155]


## The Christ Child—Alive Again—at Greccio


Having made the case that Francis and Clare sought to imitate the Christ Child, particularly the Infant's embrace of poverty, I will now consider the famous episode at Greccio on Christmas Eve in 1223. On this occasion, Francis celebrated the feast of the Nativity with an outdoor Mass, using props and the setting of nature to help his audience visualize the first Christmas, when the Son of God came forth from Mary's womb to live among humans—a descent of the divine to earth that was later repeated by Christ's embodiment in the Eucharist. The saint's motives for orchestrating a celebration of Christmas that was certainly more dramatic than usual were, in my view, primarily devotional: he wished to draw his audience's attention to the virtues of the Christ Child, which he himself had cultivated for many years, to awaken the participants' piety toward the baby Jesus, and to help them realize that the Child was perpetually in their midst and accessible to them, in the consecrated Eucharistic host.

Franciscan belief in the comforting and indeed unfailingly protective presence of the child Jesus hidden within the Eucharist is dramatically illustrated by a story told about how St. Clare once pleaded with the Lord, before the Eucharistic host, that he defend the nuns from the Saracens who were on the verge of invading her convent of San Damiano. In the most detailed account of this incident that survives, a chapter from the *Legend of Saint Clare*, it is the Christ Child who answers her prayers: a voice, "as if of a little child," resounded in her ears: "I will *always* defend you." So even when the child Jesus was not audible or visible to his devotees, he continually watched over them through his abiding presence in the Eucharist.[156] Fourteenth-century frescoes depicting this incident, in the oratory of the convent of San Damiano, depict Clare and her nuns kneeling before the Christ Child, who stands in the niche where a tabernacle or pyx used to be kept. The nuns' reliance upon the power of the Christ Child, who blesses the sisters with his right hand, is vividly commemorated in this scene (fig. 9).[157]

Belief in the Christ Child's presence in the Eucharist and a commemoration of the deprivations attending his Nativity, rather than his mighty power, stressed in the aforesaid tale about Clare and her convent, is central to the early accounts of the Christmas celebration at Greccio. In what follows, I will focus on Francis's devotional motives, seeking to deduce from details found in the legendary accounts of the episode what he most admired about the Christ Child. In this section, I will cite the description of the event at Greccio that Thomas of Celano provides at the end of Book One of his *Vita prima*, since this is the earliest source we have, yet I will also refer to Bonaventure's later account, which includes a few details not found in the earlier version. At Greccio, Francis emphasizes the poverty and suffering of the Christ Child, seeing the Nativity and the Passion as part of a single continuum, which is accessible to Christians, in various times and places, in a special way through the Eucharist.

Thomas begins his chapter on the incident at Greccio by saying that Francis continuously strove to trace Christ's footsteps and meditated on his words

Figure 9. *Above*, St. Clare of Assisi and the nuns of San Damiano, in need of protection against the invading Saracens, praying before the Christ Child in a Eucharistic niche. *Opposite*, detail of the Christ Child blessing his devotees. Fresco, Oratory, San Damiano Convent, Assisi (fourteenth century). By permission of Stefan Diller.

and deeds so assiduously "that he scarcely wanted to think of anything else." He adds that Francis was totally focused on the humility of the Incarnation and the charity of the Passion, a remark that implies that the saint concentrated on both the beginning and endpoints of Jesus' life. As we have seen, Francis rejoiced at Christmas because he saw the Nativity as the first step of a divinely planned course of events that would, of necessity, lead to redemption. In a short exhortatory text he authored, Francis says that it was the Father's will that the Son, "whom he gave to us and who was born for us (Isa. 9:6), should offer himself through his own blood as a sacrifice and oblation on the altar of the cross (*ara crucis*)."[158] Francis's association of the Nativity

with the Passion and with the Eucharist is reflected in this passage and also (though more subtly) in Thomas's account of Christmas at Greccio.

Thomas's statement that Francis's greatest desire was "to retrace [Jesus'] footsteps completely" speaks to the saint's eagerness to experience the life of Christ vicariously rather than as a disinterested observer, and to be perfectly conformed to it. Yet Thomas's remark also raises the question of whether Francis sought to walk in Christ's footsteps literally by making a pilgrimage to the Holy Land. Francis took great pains to visit the Sultan Malik al-Kamil in Egypt a few years prior to the incident at Greccio, probably wishing to achieve more than one end by his trip: his own martyrdom, the conversion of Muslims, and the securing of peace in the Holy Land, which was then under the sultan's authority.[159] While none of the early sources say that Francis went to Jerusalem, some later historians suggested and even claimed that he did.[160] This position is no longer considered tenable, but it is worthwhile speculating here about Francis's attitude toward pilgrimage, especially to the Holy Land, given that, in the episode under consideration, Greccio is made to resemble Bethlehem. Chiara Frugoni raises the possibility that the saint erected the manger scene at Greccio as a devotional alternative to pilgrimage to Bethlehem, which had been closely linked with the crusade movement. This is certainly one way of interpreting Thomas of Celano's remark that "out of Greccio was made a new Bethlehem."[161]

Perhaps Francis wished to convey the message that making a pilgrimage to the manger of Bethlehem was easier than it seemed, since Christmas was reenacted—or rather mystically recurred—on the altar at every Mass. Frugoni cites a passage from an anonymous treatise from the late twelfth century, in which a monk who wishes to go to Bethlehem is told that every altar, in every church, is the manger of the Christ Child: "You have no need to travel since you could find all these things at home. Christ, who was once born in Bethlehem according to the flesh, and was found in a manger, is now found everywhere, on all the altars of Holy Church . . . Therefore you do not need to go across the sea to seek in one place that which is found everywhere. Your altar a short way off is your Bethlehem."[162] The idea that the altar is the manger and also the cross is expressed in numerous homilies and commentaries on Scripture from the patristic and medieval periods.[163] But if a medieval Christian, grasping such mystical conflations, still insisted on making contact with a relic of the Nativity, he or she could travel less distantly by going to Rome, to the Basilica of Santa Maria Maggiore, where purported relics of the manger from Bethlehem had been venerated for centuries. There, in a special chapel, midnight Mass of Christmas Eve was celebrated at an altar that stood over "five small boards of Levantine sycamore venerated as the crib of Christ."[164] While Francis, at the Christmas celebration at Greccio, may have consciously imitated the nocturns and the Midnight Mass of the Roman liturgy as they were prayed in Santa Maria Maggiore ("supra praesepe"),[165] I very much doubt that it was his intention to draw pilgrims away from either Rome or Bethlehem.

In all likelihood, Francis simply wanted to reinvigorate people's devotion to the Christ Child as the loving Redeemer who incredibly humbled himself at the Incarnation and to reiterate the traditional belief that Jesus is incarnated on the altar at Mass. The transformation of the bread and wine into Christ's body and blood (an age-old doctrine officially promulgated as "transubstantiation" a few years earlier, at the Fourth Lateran Council of 1215) paralleled Jesus' assumption of flesh within Mary. In one of his "Admonitions," Francis explains that when Christians view the host, they are unable to see Jesus in his humanity, just as the people around Christ were unable to see his divinity during his lifetime. Francis elaborates on this analogy: "Behold, each day he humbles himself as when he came from the royal throne (Wis. 18:15) into the Virgin's womb; each day he himself comes to us, appearing humbly; each day he comes down from the bosom of the Father upon the altar in the hands of the priest. As he revealed himself to the holy apostles in true flesh, so he reveals himself to us now in sacred bread. . . . And in this way the Lord is *always* with his faithful, as he himself says: 'Behold I am with you until the end of the age'" (Matt. 28:20).[166] In this passage, Francis calls attention to the divine humility fundamental to the Incarnation and also to the Eucharist; in both cases, God puts aside his royal magnificence and invites humans to exercise faith in his presence, which cannot be truly, that is, fully, seen. By conflating the baby Jesus with the Eucharistic host, Francis underscores the continual presence of the Lord, which is also a perpetual manifestation of his humility.

To return to what can only be speculations regarding Francis's attitudes toward the role of specific geographic places within Christians' spirituality: might his undeniable belief in Jesus' Eucharistic omnipresence, in time and place, have led him to regard pilgrimage to Bethlehem and the other holy sites as unnecessary and otiose? While this is possible, I think that Francis would have encouraged European Christians to go to the Holy Land if they had the means to do so, given his intense focus on the historical life of Christ as transmitted by the canonical gospels.

Both Thomas and Bonaventure are fairly specific when it comes to enumerating the physical objects that Francis requested be prepared for the upcoming celebration at Greccio. It is important to note the objects that are named and those that are not, rather than assume that the mise-en-scène devised by Francis was identical to the large, if not life-size, manger scenes that in modern times have been displayed at Christmastime.[167] Thomas of Celano relates that Francis summoned a friend of his, a virtuous layman named John (the knight Giovanni Velita), and gave him instructions about what he should prepare. He also shared with him his reasoning for bringing about such a celebration: "For I wish to enact the memory of that babe who was born in Bethlehem: to see with my own bodily eyes the discomfort of his infant needs (*infantilium necessitatum eius incommoda*), how he lay in a manger (*praesepe*), and how with an ox and an ass standing by, he rested on hay."[168] This instruction regarding props, so to speak, is fairly simple yet its language is precise and thus in need of careful examination.

First, though, we might consider an objection regarding the whole scenario: given that Francis (according to Thomas of Celano) continuously meditated on the Gospel, it seems superfluous for the saint to have insisted upon seeing the Nativity with his bodily eyes. However, given that religious art (and presumably also the liturgy and religious drama) had a powerful effect upon him, Francis's desire to use props and appropriate scenery should not surprise us. When praying before the crucifix in the church of San Damiano, in the early stage of his conversion, Francis heard Christ tell him to rebuild his church: there, at the cross, a wonder occurred, for "with the lips of the painting (*labiis picturae deductis*), the image of Christ crucified spoke to him."[169] Considering that he was profoundly influenced by religious art, I think it is fair to assume that Francis would have agreed with the thirteenth-century Dominican John Balbi of Genoa, who says that there are "three reasons for the institution of images in churches. First, for the instruction of the uneducated, who seem to be taught by them as if by books. Second, so that the mystery of the Incarnation and the examples of the saints may be the more in our memory while they are daily represented to our eyes. Third, to excite the feeling of devotion, which is more efficaciously aroused by things seen than by things heard."[170] Balbi's first point reiterates the ancient view of Gregory the Great, which was repeated, more recently, by Peter Comestor, who said that pictures in churches serve, as it were, as books for the laity.[171] Drama, as a "quick" (that is, living) book, was thought to have an even stronger impact on the imagination than a picture or a series of pictures.[172]

Scholars have often suggested that Francis's Christmas celebration at Greccio was a popularization of the Christmas plays that had been performed in monasteries and cathedrals for at least two centuries. These plays imitated the dramatizations performed at Easter, which, as is well known, originally developed from an elaboration of the "Quem quaeretis" trope—the chanted question "Whom do you seek?" supposedly posed by an angel to the women who came to Jesus' tomb on Easter Sunday morning.[173] In medieval Christmas plays, midwives ask a similar question of the shepherds or the Magi.[174] Such plays often involved a manger (*praesepe*) and an image of the Mother and Child, or just the Child, placed in or near it.[175] According to the fourteenth-century liturgical ordinary for the *Officium Pastorum* performed at the cathedral at Rouen, "a manger is to be prepared behind the altar and an image of St. Mary placed in it." When the shepherds tell the midwives that they are in search of "the Savior Christ," the women, "opening a curtain, show them the Child, saying: 'The infant is here.'"[176] Although Francis may have been influenced by such plays performed in a number of monastic settings, he probably borrowed the idea of having Mass said over a manger more directly from the Christmas liturgy as it was executed at Santa Maria Maggiore. Francis certainly employed props at Greccio, but his manger scene—as far as we know—did not involve performers with scripted actions and speeches. As Erwin Rosenthal stated a number years ago: "The *mise-en-scène* at Greccio . . . cannot be called a liturgical play . . . but it does have in common with the 'sacre rappresentazioni' the intention of materializing the legend, of transposing it into living image. But," he emphasizes, "there was no dialogue, there were no players in Greccio."[177]

Let us pursue the question of Francis's liturgical props further. According to Thomas of Celano, the saint asked for a manger (*praesepe*); he did not explicitly request that an image of the Christ Child (or of the Madonna and Child) be brought to the Christmas celebration. I think there are two possibilities here. First: that Francis was concerned that the participants in the Mass at Greccio recognize the Christ Child on the altar, in the Eucharistic host, and so did not actually use an effigy—a hypothesis to which I will return shortly. The second, and more likely, possibility is that when Francis asked for a *praesepe* he meant that an effigy of the Christ Child should be brought with a manger. But this Latin word is admittedly problematic. As Rudolph Berliner pointed out, the Latin words *praesepe* or *praesepium* literally "mean 'a stable' or 'a manger.' In this special case [of the Nativity], the words can mean the whole cave as well as only that concavity which was the actual resting place of the Child."[178] Although it is possible that Francis wanted a whole stable-like cave prepared when he requested a *praesepe*[179] (the mountain in Greccio on which the event occurred is indeed rocky and cavernous),[180] I suspect that by using the latter word he simply meant a "manger," probably with an effigy in it. In his account of what actually happened that Christmas at Greccio (which, significantly, he describes in the present tense, as if the event were happening anew), Thomas noted that "over the manger (*supra praesepe*) the solemnities of the Mass are celebrated."[181] "Praesepe" here obviously means "feeding bin," above (or perhaps near) which was placed a portable altar of some sort, since the Mass took place outdoors.[182] Thomas describes the setting as a forest (*silva*), which would have been able to accommodate a large number of people, who might have gathered around an outdoor grotto. As we shall see, this rustic setting is important because it enabled people, animals, and even the natural surroundings to participate in the joyful re-presentation of the Savior's birth.

The early artistic representations of the Mass of Greccio, which vary in detail, do not provide a definitive answer to the question of the actual furniture and accessory props used on this occasion (or the precise setting), nor do they help much in determining if some kind of Christ-Child statue was used. In the scene that depicts the Greccio episode in the Bardi Dossal (ca. 1245), in the Basilica of Santa Croce in Florence, we see a priest at an altar and, in front of it, a swaddled infant Jesus lying upon a rocky mound.[183] In the fresco (s. XIV/XV) depicting the Greccio episode in the Chiesa di San Francesco in Pistoia, we see a box-like manger placed next to an altar, both of which are underneath a simple wooden structure surrounded by a leafy setting.[184] In a number of images, the Mass occurs within a church, as in the "Miracle of the Crib at Greccio" fresco in the Upper Church of San Francesco in Assisi, which probably depicts the annual commemoration of the Greccio Mass in the Lower Church, rather than the historical event itself (fig. 10).[185] My concern, though, is not so much with the setting of the event, but rather with the question of whether Francis used an effigy of the Christ Child in that liturgical celebration. All of the surviving depictions of Greccio show a swaddled baby, either lying in the manger or being embraced by Francis hovering over it.

After calling attention to the saint's preaching about the Christ Child's poverty, both Thomas and Bonaventure speak of the sudden appearance of "a little child lying lifeless in the manger," whom Francis "approach[ed] and waken[ed] . . . from a deep sleep." Bonaventure adds that the child was "beautiful" and that Francis "embraced" it.[186] While both authors certainly imply

Figure 10. The Celebration of the Nativity at Greccio, with an appearance of the baby Jesus to St. Francis. Fresco, Upper Church of the Basilica of San Francesco, Assisi (ca. 1288–1297). By permission of Scala/Art Resource, NY.

that the child was Jesus, they speak about the boy in vague terms. This can be considered analogous to the way in which the Christ Child is spoken about in other hagiographical texts that recount how he unexpectedly appeared to someone, often to a holy person as a reward or to provide some consolation. For example, in the Life of St. Dorothy (appended to the *Legenda aurea*), right before the virgin is beheaded, a mysterious child appears to her, "dressed in purple, barefooted, with curly hair, with stars on his garment, bearing in his hand . . . a little basket, with three roses and as many apples."[187] The beauty of the Child who mysteriously appears to a holy person usually reveals who he is (both to the saint and to the reader), and it is in this sense that we should understand Bonaventure's remark that John of Greccio saw a "puerulus quidam valde formosus" (literally, "a certain very beautiful little boy").[188] Both Thomas and Bonaventure indicate that only one of the bystanders saw the lovely child who suddenly appeared (Thomas omits the beholder's name). The other participants' lack of awareness of the miracle may symbolize their spiritual tepidity, but it may also be a way for the authors to indicate the special holiness of the beholder John—his being granted a special, mystical privilege to share in Francis's intimacy with the baby Jesus. Thomas explicitly offers a symbolic interpretation of this apparition: the boy's sleeping represents the lamentable fact that "in the hearts of many," the Child had "been given over to oblivion." Francis woke him as he lay dormant in the participants' hearts, and impressed him upon their memory.[189] Bonaventure concurs, adding that "the truth [that the miracle] expresses proves its validity."[190] Thus, both hagiographers credit Francis with reinvigorating people's devotion to the Christ Child at Greccio. Whether he actually did this for European Christians in general is debatable, but given the tremendous influence wielded by the friars in the later Middle Ages, as well as Francis's undeniable and very dramatic devotion to the Nativity, it seems fair to surmise that the increasing attention given to the Christ Child at that time was owing, to a large extent, to the charisma and impact of St. Francis of Assisi.

While John of Greccio supposedly beheld a living child in the manger, the other bystanders probably saw a mere effigy. Perhaps Francis approached it spontaneously and embraced it, hoping that Jesus would respond to him through it, as he did through the crucifix at San Damiano (which, at least with its lips, came to life).[191] Effigies of the Christ Child from fourteenth- and fifteenth-century Italy have survived to the present day, the most famous of which is the Santo Bambino of Ara Coeli in Rome, supposedly carved by a Franciscan friar using wood from the Holy Land.[192] Even though extant statues of the Christ Child, as far as I am aware, do not date as far back as the early thirteenth century, Francis probably made use of one such effigy at Greccio, perhaps one that had already been employed in a Christmas play or in a private devotional context. A passage from the *Vita secunda* already cited demonstrates that Francis himself was fond of such devotional statuettes. After telling the reader about the saint's love of Christmas, Thomas of Celano notes that "he would lick the images of the baby's limbs."[193] Along similar lines, in the *Book of Margery Kempe*, while the English holy woman was in Italy she came across a woman, traveling with two Franciscans, who carried an effigy of Jesus in a chest. When this woman with the prized possession arrived in different cities, she would give other women the opportunity to lavish their affection on the statuette, which they did by putting clothes on it as if it were a real baby, kissing it "as thei it had ben [as if it were] God hymselfe."[194] Along similar lines, the *Revelations* of Margaret Ebner (d. 1351), a Dominican nun of the Monastery of Maria Medingen, recount how she received "a lovely statue from Vienna—Jesus in the crib." One night, Margaret was called to come to the statue in the choir. "Then great delight in the childhood of our Lord came over me," she recalls, "and I took the statue of the Child and pressed it against my naked heart as strongly as I could. At that I felt the movement of His mouth on my naked heart." Another sister later tells her of the dream she had of giving Margaret her statue: "it was a living child . . . and [you] wanted to suckle it."[195] The dynamics among Margaret, the statue, and the other nun can be seen as analogous to the triangular relationship that pertains among Francis, the mysterious boy in the manger, and the observer John. While Margaret clearly relates to the Child as a mother, Francis wakes him up and then simply hugs him. Francis's follower Anthony of Padua similarly embraced the child Jesus, according to the man who, when he happened to peer into the friar's chamber, saw him doing so.[196] Perhaps at the celebration at Greccio, Francis embraced the infant Jesus to comfort him in a maternal way, considering Francis's well-known compassion for the discomforts attending Jesus' birth.[197] Caroline Walker Bynum's remark that Francis "is described as cradling all creation—from a rabbit to the baby Jesus—in his arms as a mother" strikes me as somewhat of an exaggeration,[198] but it is nonetheless true that Francis's personality may be regarded, in some ways, as maternal.

In the Upper Church of San Francesco, the inscription underneath the fresco that depicts Francis's encounter with the baby Jesus at Greccio provides evidence that an effigy was part of the manger scene that Francis had arranged. All the inscriptions accompanying the Life of St. Francis cycle in the Upper

Church are based upon Bonaventure's *Legenda major*, the text that became the official biography of Francis in 1266, around a generation prior to the execution of the cycle.[199] Although only some of the letters of the inscription for the Christmas fresco are still legible, the text has been reconstructed and reads, in translation, as follows: "How Blessed Francis, in memory of the birth of Christ, had a crib (*praesepium*) prepared, hay brought, an ox and ass led in, and preached concerning the birth of the poor king, and likewise, as the holy man was in prayer, a certain knight saw the child Jesus in the place of the one that the saint had brought."[200] These words are closely based on Bonaventure's text, which repeats Thomas's earlier description of the props almost verbatim. What is new here, though, is the statement that the Christ Child appeared in place of the boy whom the saint had brought; this implies that a statue was included in the manger scene and that it came to life or was, in some way, temporarily replaced by a living Christ Child. Regardless of whether Francis himself brought an effigy of the infant Jesus to the Christmas Eve Mass or told John to do so (when he instructed him to bring a *praesepe*), there seems to have been a statue of an infant placed in the manger at Greccio. Having a replica of the newborn Jesus before their "bodily eyes" would undoubtedly have helped the participants imagine the Nativity and, in addition, recognize the Child's Eucharistic presence on the altar.

According to Thomas, Francis wanted to see "the discomfort[s] (*incommoda*) of [Jesus'] infant needs"—he admittedly does not actually say that Francis wanted to have an effigy of the Christ Child present at the celebration. By proceeding to list the manger, the beasts, and the hay (*foenum*), Thomas implies that all of these things made the Nativity an unpleasant, if not a painful, experience for the baby Jesus. Francis's frequent practice of refusing "straw mattresses and blankets" and instead, sleeping naked on the "naked ground," sometimes making use of "a stone or a piece of wood as his pillow,"[201] may very well have been an attempt, on his part, to imitate the infant Jesus, who had nowhere (suitable) to lay his head (Lk. 9:58). Emphasizing the Christ Child's uncomfortable place of repose along similar lines, the author of the *Meditationes vitae Christi* encourages the reader to imagine Mary "plac[ing] Jesus] in the manger" and positioning "his head on a small stone with perhaps just a little straw (*feno*) in between."[202] In setting up the manger at Greccio, Francis might have thought that the hay provided a little, though not sufficient, padding for the baby Jesus; perhaps he also regarded the hay as scratchy and irritating to the Infant's bare skin. Such a view is expressed in a fourteenth-century German Sister-Book, which recounts how a nun had a vision of "the Christ

Child lying before the altar on stiff hay, which pricked his tender body so that it had red furrows."[203] The ox and ass were likewise regarded as indications of the Christ Child's early suffering. The author of the *Meditationes vitae Christi* (likely taking a cue from *Pseudo-Matthew*)[204] claims that the beasts "knelt, positioned their mouths over the manger and through their nostrils breathed down on him, almost as if they had reason to believe that a child so scantily covered would need warmth in a time of such intense cold."[205] By creating such wintry weather as the setting for the Nativity, the author of the *Meditationes* suggests that the Babe's paltry swaddling clothes must not have done much to alleviate his discomfort. The harshness of the conditions in which Christ was born is stressed to an even greater extent by the fourteenth-century Franciscan Bartholomew of Pisa, who, like Francis, emphasizes that the baby Jesus, the Lord of the whole world, chose not to luxuriate in the lap of luxury or bask in magnificence but to suffer in the freezing cold.

> Who, I ask, could keep from weeping . . . to see with the eyes of the mind the child Jesus, most noble, most beautiful and the very little king of all and the Lord crying out at his birth, wracked with cold, nakedness, and the unsuitableness of the place, and want of all things. For who is Jesus? Is he not the prince of peace, leader and lawgiver, king of kings . . . and emperor of heaven and earth? . . . Why therefore does the stony heart not have compassion on that little Jesus? . . . But since it was a time of great coldness, with what clothes was he covered up? Not, I say, those of great price but cheap and modest ones; he who clothes the whole world with variegated decoration is wrapped up with base clothes.[206]

To return to Francis's representation of the infant Jesus' discomforts: what do the earliest sources claim that Francis did and said at the celebration of Christmas held at Greccio, apart from hugging the baby Jesus? As Chiara Frugoni has remarked, we unfortunately lack a transcript of the sermon that Francis preached at this Mass, yet we can speculate about what he said, based on Thomas of Celano's comments in this chapter. After noting that the props Francis had requested were duly brought in, Thomas remarks (probably echoing the saint's expression of pleasure at a job well done): "There simplicity is given a place of honor, poverty is exalted, humility is commended, and out of Greccio is made a new Bethlehem."[207] While the first part of this statement speaks of God's condescension at the Nativity and the virtues modeled by the infant Christ, the latter part references both the dramatic commemoration of the Nativity as a historical event, and its mystical recurrence in the Mass. Thomas uses another rhetorical paradox when he claims that Francis, in his role of deacon, preached about "the birth of the poor king in the poor city of Bethlehem." Thomas here is likely summarizing at least part of the saint's sermon; the phrase "poor king," in particular, sounds like something Francis would say, judging from other statements attributed to him in early hagiographical writings. Recall how (according to the *Vita secunda*) Francis once sat on the bare floor and was "bathed in tears" when he heard about the "royal virtue" of the Christ Child and his mother—their embrace of poverty.[208] At Greccio, Francis may very well have stressed this virtue out of the three that Thomas mentions (simplicity, poverty, and humility). Elsewhere, Thomas tells us why Francis liked Greccio so much: its inhabitants were "rich in poverty."[209] So poverty was clearly uppermost in Francis's mind on Christmas Eve in Greccio.

Although Thomas does not explicitly say that Francis cried on that occasion, he calls attention to the saint's intense emotionality when he says that he stood "before the manger, filled with heartfelt sighs." He was no doubt thinking about the Babe's poverty, and likely reflected on his pitiful swaddling clothes, as well as his makeshift crib.[210] In his account of this episode, Bonaventure, in comparison to Thomas of Celano, places greater emphasis upon Francis's emotional response, specifically by saying that he was "bathed in tears," a phrase which echoes the aforementioned passage from the *Vita secunda*.[211] Along similar lines, in his *Liber miraculorum*, the Cluniac abbot Peter the Venerable (d. 1156), noted that "it is the custom of the same monastery [that is, Cluny] to celebrate the birthday of the Savior with a certain singular affection, more devotedly than other feast-days, and to solemnize it earnestly with the spirits of the angels, by means of the melodies of songs, lengthy readings, the burning of many sorts of candles, and—what is far more remarkable—with special devotion and much shedding of tears."[212] Although Francis was by no means the inventor of the Christmas Eve celebration, of the manger as a paraliturgical object,[213] or of compassion for the sufferings of the lowly Christ Child,[214] he breathed new life into the feast of the Nativity by emphasizing realistic details surrounding Christ's birth, particularly the manger. He was also one of the first medieval Christians to manifest publicly and intentionally a tender sensibility for the Infant's bodily sufferings and to encourage others to experience feelings of compassion as well as joyful gratitude for the Incarnation. Thus, in my view, it is fair to say that "compassion for the suffering Savior"—in both his infancy and at his Passion—"was given an archetypal expression in Francis and through him was channeled into Western devotion, art, and culture as a whole."[215]

During his sermon, Francis manifests his "sweet affection" for the Child by his inability to utter the word "Bethlehem" without bleating like a sheep. Thomas says that he tasted the words "Jesus" and "babe of Bethlehem," savoring their sweetness.[216] Such gustatory imagery expresses the intensity of the saint's loving meditation on Christ's infancy, his experience of its immediacy, and his desire for union with the tender lamblike babe of Bethlehem, not to mention his devotion to the name of Jesus.[217] Anna Vorchtlin, a nun at Engelthal, expressed this sentiment, but with more gusto, when she told the baby Jesus, whom she saw in a vision, "If I had you, I would eat you up, I love you so much!"[218] Perhaps Francis's indulgence in mystical sweetness compensated for the sorrow he experienced on this occasion when he recollected the sufferings that attended Christ's birth.

Besides expressing his love for the infant Jesus and speaking of the incommodious conditions of his Nativity, Francis, by both his words and actions, likely reminded his audience of the presence of the Christ Child in the consecrated host. Indeed, by licking his lips, the saint may be manifesting his spiritual appetite for this heavenly food.[219] In one of his "Admonitions" (which I have already mentioned), Francis emphasizes the importance of Christians seeing God in the Eucharist with their spiritual eyes. Just as, at Greccio, the bystanders (with the exception of John and Francis) were unable to see Jesus in the manger, so they, like the other participants at Mass, were unable to see Christ, in his human form, on the altar. Might Francis, during his sermon, have pointed to the manger under (or next to) the altar, telling his listeners that they would soon see, in the hands of the priest, the same child who was wrapped in swaddling clothes and placed in the manger in Bethlehem hundreds of years ago? Perhaps he expressed, in simple terms, the metaphor that the early Cistercian Guerric of Igny (and others) had enunciated: that the sacramental species of bread and wine covered the divinity, as the swaddling bands enveloped the Christ Child.[220]

While the image of the lamb that Francis dramatically introduces into his sermon by bleating reveals, in a charming manner, his love of animals (lambs were definitely his favorite),[221] he probably intended it as an imaginative cue that would prompt his audience to think of the Lamb of God who was sacrificed at the Passion (cf. Isa. 53:7), and still offered up by the priest at the altar at every Mass. The fresco depicting the Mass at Greccio in the Upper Church in Assisi may in fact represent the very moment in the liturgy when, at the beginning of the canon of the Mass, the choir chants the "Agnus Dei." Like a snapshot, the scene captures a small number of friars singing, with opened mouths, as the priest bends over the host at the altar. Perhaps, though, the scene represents Francis seizing the baby Jesus at the very moment when the priest consecrates the host, which shortly thereafter would be elevated for adoration and viewing, with the priest saying: "Ecce Agnus Dei." This could possibly explain why no one in the fresco (and all but one person in the written sources) seems to notice Francis's encounter with the baby Jesus: while Francis holds the Lamb of God in his infant form, the other participants are about to behold Christ hidden under the Eucharistic species.[222] At the end of the chapter, Thomas reintroduces the image of the lamb when he notes that a permanent altar was built over the manger and a church around it, "so that where animals once ate the fodder of hay (*foeni pabulum*), there humans . . . would eat the flesh of the immaculate and spotless lamb, our Lord Jesus Christ, who 'gave himself for us.'" Thomas here cites Paul's letter to Titus (2:14), where he speaks of Christ's giving of himself "for us, that he might redeem us from all iniquity," but he also echoes Isaiah 9:6 ("A child is born to us, and a son is given to us"), which, for Francis, as we have seen, powerfully encapsulates God's loving plan for the redemption of the human race.

Now that we have considered how some of Francis's earliest followers viewed his devotion to the Christ Child, it is worth reflecting on how this devotion of the saint tends to be viewed more generally and popularly. In an essay on the Old English poem *Christ III*, the Anglo-Saxonist scholar Thomas D. Hill contrasts the "dark" Anglo-Saxon view of the Nativity with the modern-day festive attitude toward Christmas, which he traces back to St. Francis of Assisi.[223] Contextualizing the Old English poem within early medieval culture, as well as viewing it within the development of Christian piety over the centuries, Hill connects the Anglo-Saxon poet's presentation of the infant Christ as "covered in a pauper's clothes" and "laid . . . in the darkness . . . on a hard stone" with contemporary iconography of the newborn Christ placed on an altar-like manger, as seen, for example, in the tenth-century Benedictional of Æthelwold (London, British Library, MS Add. 49598, fol. 15v). Significantly, the image in question lies opposite a blessing for Christmas taken from a homily of Gregory the Great, an early and influential source for the conflation of the Christ Child and the Eucharist, and the manger and the altar.[224] Although Hill in this article seems predominantly to have in mind the jovial side of Francis's personality as well as his typical association with affective piety, Francis's view of the Nativity was in fact rooted in the same patristic-based imagery that is reflected in the illuminated Anglo-Saxon liturgical book and in *Christ III*. Hill contrasts the "square, block-like" altar mentioned in the poem and similarly depicted in the Benedictional with Francis's "crib filled with straw" ("comfortable enough").[225] Yet the Italian saint's display of compassion for the "discomforts" of the Nativity and the connection he almost certainly made in his sermon between the Infant in the manger and the Child soon to be present on the altar demonstrates that Francis's Christmas was not merely an occasion for sentimentality and merry-making. Francis was just as aware of the biblical theme of "the sacrifice of the well-beloved son" (a phrase used by Hill) as was his predecessors—a mystery culminating in Christ's Passion and death and his perpetuation of his sacrifice in the Eucharist.[226] Yet rather than glumly view the sacrificial offering of Jesus as "dark," Francis expresses heartfelt compassion for Jesus' suffering and, at the same time, delights in the lovableness of the "son given to us," looking forward optimistically to the fullness of redemption, which was effected by both the birth and death of Christ and culminated in the Resurrection.

Francis's overall approach to the Nativity, which is simultaneously rustic and mystical, should be kept in mind when trying to understand the attention he gives to the ox and the ass at Greccio and his wish, expressed on another occasion, that these beasts be given double fodder on Christmas.[227] Scripture does not mention the presence of these animals at the manger, but the apocryphal *Gospel of Pseudo-Matthew* does, going so far as to describe how they bent their knees and adored the Infant who had been placed in their feeding bin,[228] after the Holy Family had moved from the cave to the stable on the third day after Jesus' birth. The anonymous author of that apocryphal text was by no means the first Christian to link Luke's mention of the manger with Isaiah's statement (Isa. 1:3) that "The ox knoweth his owner, and the ass his master's crib (*praesepe domini sui*)."[229] Early exegetes had already interpreted this passage as a prophecy of Christ's Nativity, typically seeing the ox as the Jews, chained to the law, and the ass as the Gentiles (pagans), who bore the burden of idolatry.[230] Artistic representations of the Nativity rendered the passage from Isaiah literally,[231] which had the effect of lodging the presence of these two animals at Christ's manger even further in the popular imagination. René Grousset claims that the ox and the ass gradually lost their symbolic meaning,[232] but it is not self-evident that literal and metaphorical views of the beasts could not coexist in the mind of the same person (or within the culture at large), at the same time. For Francis, the beasts around the baby Jesus were probably both reverent, rustic animals, as well as symbols of humans who were meant to feast

on the bread that had come down from heaven at Christmas and is present at
every Mass.

I wish to close this section by responding to two insightful scholarly treatments of the Greccio episode, which I have already mentioned in passing. Chiara Frugoni, who offers an ecumenical reading of the scene at Greccio, bases
the crux of her argument on Francis's inclusion of the ox and the ass, which, for
her, represent the peaceful coming together of Christians and non-Christians
(particularly Muslims).[233] Frugoni notes that the Greccio incident took place
shortly after the approval of the modified Rule of St. Francis (the *Regula bullata*), which eliminated Francis's earlier instructions for dealing with the Saracens. In chapter 16 of the earlier Rule, Francis had suggested two approaches:
one more ecumenical (the friars could live peacefully among the Saracens
and other unbelievers, subject to their authority), and the other more directly
missionary (they could preach the Gospel openly).[234] Lamenting that these
options (particularly the first) were removed from the later Rule, Frugoni
claims that Francis erected the Christmas manger to encourage his fellow
Christians to heed the message of peace delivered by the angels to the shepherds at Christ's birth (Lk. 2:14, a biblical passage which Francis, judging
from his own writings and from his devotional performativity described
in the early legends, does not seem to have emphasized at Christmastime).[235]
The Christmas Mass at Greccio, from this perspective, was a protest against
the Church-sponsored warfare of the Crusades, which were proving to be a
failure by that time.[236] Though Frugoni's historical and ideological contextu-
alization of the Greccio episode is illuminating, her insistence upon the
connection between this event and Francis's concern about inter-faith relations
seems reductionistic. Moreover, while Francis's bleating at Greccio would have
made his audience think of a lamb, we actually do not know if he explicitly
referred to the ox and the ass (let alone the message of the angels to the shepherds) in his sermon—and it is on the symbolism of these latter animals that
Frugoni's argument is based.

Lisa Kiser, for her part, considers Francis's emphasis upon the ox and the
ass in light of his well-known love of nature.[237] She argues that the novelty of
the Greccio incident was that Francis had real, live animals brought to the
(para)liturgical performance centered around the manger. The wording of
Francis's instructions, which John of Greccio faithfully carried out, supports
this view: "the manger is prepared, the hay is carried in, and the ox and the
ass are led (*adducuntur*) to the spot." Although Kiser emphasizes Francis's inclusion of real animals at Greccio, she does not focus on the ox and the ass

qua animals, but rather as representatives of the working classes who habitu-ally employed them to help carry out their work. In my view, while there is certainly basis for associating Francis with ecumenism, environmentalism, and contemporary efforts to promote social justice, it would be misleading to ig-nore or seriously downplay the saint's devotional aims in orchestrating the Mass under the stars at Greccio. His main goals were, in all probability, to inculcate a more tender devotion to the child Jesus and to remind his fellow friars and the laity of Jesus' swaddled presence, so to speak, in the conse-crated host.

Michael Robson captures a key element of the Greccio incident, which is easy for us to lose sight of, due to our familiarity with the story: Francis "wished to share with others his own sense of wonder. He was impelled to communi-cate to them the riches he had unearthed in the Gospel."[238] The newness of Greccio, in the most important sense, consisted in the participants' experi-ence of wonder, which Francis, like a child, seems to have possessed in great abundance and been able to share with others. As a cleric with an intuitive pastoral sensibility, Francis devised a plan for spreading his own enthusiasm for the Nativity, recognizing the impact that a multimedia presentation of a touching Gospel story would have upon ordinary people. Thomas of Celano conveys a sense of the excitement experienced by the participants when he says that they were delighted by the brightness of candles and torches that lit up the night, and "ecstatic at this new mystery of new joy."[239] The event at Greccio entailed not only an eye-catching spectacle, but also loud sounds: the singing of God's praises, which, mixed with animals' utterances, reverberated against the boulders, so that all of nature seemed to rejoice in the Nativity, just as it sorrowed at the Passion.[240] In the previous century, Aelred of Rievaulx had expressed disapproval of elaborate singing at Mass.[241] He lamented that a practice that was "instituted to awaken the weak to the attachment of devo-tion" had the effect of causing people to lose a sense of the sacred—to fail "to honor that mystical crib . . . where Christ is mystically wrapped in swaddling clothes, where his most sacred blood is poured out in the chalice."[242] Francis of Assisi, in contrast, seized the opportunity to embellish the liturgy with sights and sounds (and even smells), which would catch people's attention and make an annual feast seem like a "new mystery"—without apparently worrying that the engagement of the senses would detract from the Real Presence. In the broadest sense, the "novelty" of the event at Greccio, which both Thomas of Celano and Bonaventure underscore, was the combination of the tangible and the everyday, with the mystical and the sacred. In my reading of the episode,

Francis emphasized both the actual conditions of Christ's Nativity, as it occurred hundreds of years ago, and the repeated sacramental embodiment of Christ upon the altar of every church.


## The Meek and Ordinary, Though Peculiar Christ Child of the *Meditationes vitae Christi*

Francis of Assisi was so intensely focused on the Nativity and Passion of Christ—the central events of the Gospel—and the Lord's enduring presence in the Eucharist that he might not have speculated much, if at all, on what Jesus did during the so-called "hidden years" of his childhood and adolescence. But, hypothetically speaking, if Francis had wondered about Christ's "hidden years," he would probably have reflected on the hardships that that phase of his life entailed and the virtues, such as humility, that Christ manifested at that time. Before moving on to consider, in the next chapter, the apocryphal portrayal of Jesus as a boy who displays his wisdom and power so dramatically that he calls much attention to himself, I will close this chapter by discussing the main features of the treatment of Jesus' early life in the *Meditationes vitae Christi*, a Franciscan text I have already mentioned.[243] The anonymous author of this popular devotional text owes much to Francis of Assisi and probably also to Aelred of Rievaulx, as regards the virtues of Christ he emphasizes, and the types of responses he hopes to elicit, when recounting the infancy and childhood of Christ. Although the *Meditationes vitae Christi* was not the only extensive treatment of Jesus' youth in the later Middle Ages, it was very influential from the time of its appearance (probably in the early fourteenth century, possibly at its beginning) until the end of the medieval period and even into the Early Modern era.[244]

That this widespread devotional text has, in the past, been misattributed to Bonaventure, a prolific Franciscan writer canonized in 1482, is not surprising considering the latter's fame and the features that Bonaventure's *Lignum vitae* shares with the *Meditationes vitae Christi*. In his short treatise *Lignum vitae*, Bonaventure touches upon Christ's early life only briefly, unlike the author of the *Meditationes vitae Christi*, who is almost novelistic in the imaginary scenarios and extra-biblical details about Christ's infancy and childhood he conjures up. Still, both authors repeatedly invite their readers to insert themselves into the life of Christ as it unfolds within their imaginations, thereby giving them the opportunity to engage in what Ewert Cousins has called the "mysticism of the historical event," which Francis clearly exemplified at Greccio.[245] That Bonaventure employs this mode of commemoration in the *Lignum vitae* is evident from the way he closes his brief account of the Nativity, with an instruction to enter into the event: "Now, then, my soul, embrace that divine manger; press your lips upon and kiss the boy's feet." Echoing what he says elsewhere, Bonaventure goes on to assert that Jesus began to suffer for humanity at the beginning of his life, "not delaying to pour out for you the price of his blood," which he did at the Circumcision.[246] A little further on, the reader is urged to join the Magi in "venerat[ing] Christ the King," and then to imitate the old man Simeon at the Purification: "Let love overcome your bashfulness; let affection dispel your fear. Receive the Infant in your arms and say with the bride: 'I took hold of him and would not let him go' (Sg. 3:4). Dance with the old man."[247] The reader is further told to accompany the Holy Family on the Flight into Egypt, "when the evil Herod sought to kill the tiny King." Immediately afterward, the reader is instructed to search with Mary for her twelve-year-old son, who supposedly had never left his parents before. Linking these crisis situations through his narrative, Bonaventure tells his reader to imagine himself accompanying the young mother fleeing with her little son and later seeking him when he was twelve and then, when he is found in the Temple, questioning him about his apparently callous actions.[248]

While some of these passages seem to be closely modeled on Part Three of Aelred's *De institutione inclusarum*, which is concerned with the biblical past, Bonaventure—not surprisingly, considering his intense focus on biblical details—omits the apocryphal tale about the encounter between the Holy Family and the good thief, which appeared in the earlier, Cistercian text.[249] In addition, although Bonaventure cites a verse from the Song of Songs (3:4) in his account of Jesus' early life (when describing how Simeon held Mary's babe and did not want "to let him go"),[250] his meditative text is not suffused with the erotic language of yearning for union with the child Jesus that is so prominent in Aelred's *De institutione inclusarum* as well as his *De Jesu puero duodenni*. Another important distinction worth noting is that, whereas Bonaventure elsewhere, namely in his *De quinque festivitatibus pueri Jesu*, tells his reader to express her affection for the Christ Child and tend to him in a spiritual way (by "wrapp[ing] him up in the chaste folds of desires," for example), in the *Lignum vitae*, he simply recommends embracing Jesus physically, as if his reader were truly in the Child's presence.[251] So the *Lignum vitae* is quite biblical and fairly straightforward in the imaginative and affective responses it seeks to elicit to the conventional events of Jesus' infancy and childhood (that is, the incidents recounted in Scripture).

Like the *De institutione inclusarum* and the *Lignum vitae*, the *Meditationes vitae Christi* repeatedly urges its reader, originally a Poor Clare nun, to enter imaginatively into Jesus' life. In addition, it frequently scripts the feeling of compassion as the appropriate response to the hardships and sufferings experienced by Jesus and Mary. A striking example of this occurs in the chapter on the Circumcision, which is the first time the reader is told to weep.[252] The author claims that Mary herself circumcised her son, using a stone knife, and says that the Infant cried because of the sharp pain he felt in his "real flesh subject to pain (*ueram carnem et passibilem*)."[253] The reader ought to "suffer together with him" and even to cry with him. She is also to share in the psychological pain of his mother, who was "terribly upset at the pain and tears of her son."[254] The psychological suffering of both Mother and Child is increased by each of them witnessing the other suffer, which likewise happens at the crucifixion,[255] but on this occasion they pacify and comfort each other as the pain presumably subsides. As did Bonaventure in the *Lignum vitae*, the author of the *Meditationes vitae Christi* emphasizes that Jesus "began to suffer for us" at that time (that is, at the Circumcision).[256] Jesus' suffering and self-abasement are in fact highlighted throughout the text, even before this incident. For example, the author earlier remarks that Jesus humbly cloistered himself in Mary's womb, "just like everyone else." The reader is urged to "feel compassion for him [in the womb] that he reached so great a depth of humility." In addition, she is informed that Jesus "was in ongoing affliction" from the moment of his conception until his death, and that his continual mental anguish, especially at the thought of the loss of souls (to the devil), was even greater than his physical suffering.[257] When describing the Holy Family's return from Egypt, the author claims that it was even more difficult than the journey there (which, as other texts emphasize, was an unexpected, anxiety-ridden flight from murderous pursuers), since the seven-year-old Jesus was too big to be carried the whole way and too small to walk very far. The author then references Psalm 87:16 as a prophecy of Jesus' childhood (as did Bonaventure earlier): "O noble and delicate child, king of heaven and earth, how hard you have labored for us, and how early you have taken on those labors!"[258] By eliciting the emotion of compassion for both the adult and child Jesus, the *Meditationes vitae Christi* certainly did much to promote affective piety for its Poor Clare readers and other late medieval Christians.

The Poor Clare reader is encouraged to experience delight as well as sorrow when meditating on the childhood of Christ, and to relate to the Boy on a simple level, as if she were a gentle child in his presence. At Greccio, Francis of Assisi may very well have interacted in such an intimate way with the Christ Child who, as I have already recounted, seems to have miraculously appeared during the Christmas Eve Mass celebrated there. In his *Vita secunda*, Thomas of Celano says that Greccio was the place where the saint "recalled the birth of the Child of Bethlehem, becoming a child with the Child (*factus cum Puero puer*)"—an intriguing comment upon which the author unfortunately does not expand.[259] Citing this latter passage, Leah Marcus remarks that Francis was "far from scorning puerility." Speaking of medieval Franciscans more generally, she claims that they "sought to infuse Christianity with a childishly playful spirit"; their "mingled gaiety and reverence" was "quite consciously childlike in its spontaneity and lack of decorum."[260] While Francis may be considered childlike on account of his simplicity, playfulness, and sense of wonder, he may also be thought to have become "a child with the Child" in a deeper sense, perhaps experiencing, as if vicariously, some of the divine child's lowliness and abasement. Although we cannot pin down his meaning, it is fair to say that Thomas of Celano's phrase "factus cum Puero puer" is echoed by the author of the *Meditationes vitae Christi* in the chapter on the Flight into Egypt, which instructs the reader to "become a little girl with the little child."[261]

The chapter from the *Meditationes vitae Christi* dealing with the Flight to Egypt is worth examining more closely, since the author proposes much fruit for meditation regarding the seven years that the Holy Family spent in exile. To instill compassion in the reader, the author tells her what the family did to earn their living during that time. Implying that Joseph, an old man, brought home only a modest income as a carpenter, the author says that Mary plied the distaff and needle—a scene depicted in an illustrated *Meditationes vitae Christi* in Latin (Oxford, Corpus Christi College, MS 410, fol. 24v, bottom register; fig. 11) and also in an illustrated Italian version (Paris, Bibliothèque nationale de France, ital. 115, fols. 41r and 43r).[262] When he was old enough to do so, the child Jesus acted as his mother's agent in her home-based sewing business, returning the items she finished and sometimes suffering rude treatment from her clients. Immediately after being told how the Holy Family supported themselves, the reader is prompted to consider what Mary did whenever she became aware that her growing boy was hungry (whether this was between meals or more continuously is unclear): as a solicitous and loving mother, Mary must have deprived herself of food in order to feed her son. Having given the reader a few glimpses into the Holy Family's humble and close-knit domestic life, the author invites her to delve more deeply into Jesus' boyhood, telling her to make use of the material he has given her, as she sees fit:

> Enlarge on it . . . and be a little girl with the child Jesus, and disdain neither such humble activities nor meditating on what seems childish. For they are thought to produce devotion, enkindle love, induce compassion, bestow purity and simplicity, add to the strength of your humility and poverty; preserve intimacy, and produce unanimity (*conformitatem facere*), as well as raise your hope. . . . Do you see how many good results derive from [such meditation]? As I said, become like a little girl with the little child (*sis . . . cum paruulo paruula*) and grow with him as he grows.[263]

As Robert Worth Frank, Jr., points out, this enumeration of the good effects that will result from such a meditative exercise is a "large order, and an important statement."[264] While modern readers tend to respond to the *Meditationes* condescendingly, claiming that it fostered only a sentimental type of piety,[265] the anonymous author here claims that the activity he proposes will have a profound spiritual effect. Not merely a game of make-believe aimed at triggering a fleeting emotional response, meditation on Jesus' boyhood will enable the devout reader to become like the Child himself. She will not only grow in the virtues that the young Jesus manifests, she will also achieve a greater oneness, or familiarity, with Christ through the process of imaginatively concentrating on him and his experiences.[266]

Frank cites a passage from the following chapter of the *Meditationes vitae Christi* (which deals with the Holy Family's return from Egypt) to illustrate the text's effectiveness at "increasing love and preserving familiarity."[267] The reader, who, in her imagination, has already visited the Holy Family in Egypt, is told to go back there before they leave and then accompany them on their journey.

> When perchance you have found him outside with the children, he will catch sight of you and run up to you immediately; for he is so friendly and easy to talk with and caring (*curialis*, lit., "courteous"). Kneel and kiss his feet, and sweeping him into your arms with a

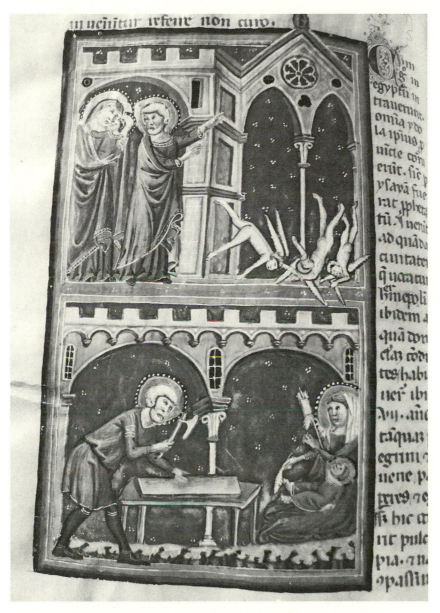

Figure 11. The fall of the idols in Egypt (upper register); Joseph and Mary at work (lower register), in an illustrated manuscript of the *Meditationes vitae Christi*. Oxford, Corpus Christi College, MS 410, fol. 24v (fourteenth century). By permission of the President and the Fellows of Corpus Christi College, Oxford.

hug, find a bit of sweet respite with him. Then he will say to you,
"We've been given permission to return to our own land, and
tomorrow we must leave. You've come at a good time, because
you will be going back with us." Answer him at once that you are
overjoyed at this; and that you hope to follow him wherever he goes
(Rev. 14:4). In conversations like these you can take your delight
with him.[268]

The charm of the child Jesus, who is here brimming with friendliness, is quite
inviting. Students of medieval literature might usefully contrast the imaginary interaction between the Poor Clare reader and the Christ Child in this
scene with the strained relationship between the jeweler-narrator and his deceased daughter in the Middle English poem *Pearl*. Though she had died at
age two, the deceased girl around whom the poem centers appears to her father
in a vision as a young maiden. Her demeanor is certainly more mature than
what we would expect of one who, just a short while ago, was a little girl: she
maintains her reserve and seems lacking in compassion, as she explains her
new, exalted status as a bride of Christ. Toward the end of his dream vision,
the narrator, after being coldly admonished by his daughter for his excessive
grief and inability to understand basic Christian teachings, is nevertheless
granted the privilege of seeing her in the heavenly Jerusalem, her new home,
as she participates in a procession with the other spotless maidens who have
become brides of Christ. Viewing her from an insurmountable distance, the
bereft father is clearly cut off from the bliss and perfection of her world, even
though he painfully yearns to be part of it.[269] In contrast, the gap between
the Poor Clare reader and the child Jesus, in the passage cited above, is quickly
closed up, since the Child, as soon as he sees her, leaves his playmates, runs
up to her, and then converses with her. He is happy that she is there and invites her to join his family. Though he is still a child, Jesus' welcoming attitude here can be said to illustrate a statement he made to his disciples when
he was an adult: "Suffer the little children, and forbid them not to come to
me" (Matt. 19:14). In this and in other chapters from the *Meditationes vitae
Christi* dealing with the Christ Child, the reader is certainly welcomed into
Jesus' presence; she is encouraged to follow the Holy Family in her imagination, as they go from place to place, serving the boy Jesus and his parents in
a concrete way.[270]

Like the two treatises by Aelred considered above, the *Meditationes vitae
Christi* does not attempt to provide definitive answers about Christ's life, but

instead offers meditational materials that will help the reader engage in prayer-ful interaction with the Lord and other holy personages. In his prologue to the work, the author praises St. Cecilia for "ruminating on [Gospel] episodes with sweet and gentle relish (*dulci ac suaui gustu ruminans*)."[271] Cecilia, in other words, engaged in *lectio divina*, the monastic practice of spiritual reading that was commonly likened to "chewing the cud."[272] The reader of the *Meditationes vitae Christi* is given devotional stories and images that she is likewise to assimi-late and transform to her own liking within her soul. Since the author's main goals are affective and moral, rather than historical (as regards the specific de-tails of Jesus' biography), he remains open-minded to his own and his reader's reconstruction of Christ's life. So, although the *Meditationes vitae Christi* can be said to resemble a gospel harmony, a text that synthesizes information from the canonical gospels to form a continuous narrative, the author of the Fran-ciscan text is more concerned about the possibilities of meditative expansive-ness than about producing a historically accurate, restrained yet detailed, linear account of Jesus' life.[273] He thus alludes in his prologue to Augustine's well-known argument for an expansive mode of exegesis, which encourages mul-tiple interpretations of a biblical passage, all of which are valid so long as they not contradict the law of charity.[274] Admittedly, despite the Franciscan au-thor's statements about the open-ended nature of his project, he often prefers one way of filling in the gaps left by the scriptural account of Christ's life to another, insofar as one particular approach seems more conducive to incul-cating piety and good morality, especially as regards Franciscan values. A memorable example of this is his response to the gastronomical question that he himself raises: what kind of food did Jesus want the angels to bring him after his forty-day fast in the desert? As a son devoted to his mother, Jesus must have wanted some of her cooking more than anything else.[275] While the apocryphal narratives considered in the next chapter do not speculate about such matters, they do, however, follow a similar sort of logic in their recon-struction of Jesus' hidden years: assuming that Jesus had certain traits (because Scripture seems to indicate as much or it just seems proper for him to be such-and-such a way), one can fill in details about his truly human, yet also very exceptional, life.

The Franciscan text's general open-endedness can be seen in the author's use of multiple and different kinds of sources for the chapters dealing with Christ's early years. To be more precise: in the early part of his work, he fre-quently quotes passages from Bernard of Clairvaux's sermons in order to re-inforce the importance of particular virtues[276]; he occasionally borrows details from Peter Comestor's *Historia scholastica*;[277] he once refers to the revelations of a St. Elizabeth, to convey the intensity of the young Mary's desire to please God;[278] and he cites what he claims is an unnamed friar's vision of the Nativity.[279] These sources add credibility and value to the meditations he proposes, but the author mainly uses them eclectically to create a framework for meditation and to provide some valuable details that will help fill out the space created by his narrative. He does not suggest that these sources are completely accurate, in a historical sense, nor does he limit himself or his reader to what they have to say.

The author also makes use of the apocryphal *Gospel of Pseudo-Matthew*, which he (wrongly) refers to as a writing of Jerome, in order to tell how Mary divided the hours of the day when living in the Temple during her girlhood.[280] The author arguably also incorporated a few apocrypha-related details (without explicitly designating them as such) in order to reinforce his depiction of the Christ Child's piety. He mentions, for example, that the boy Jesus must have drawn water from a well for his mother—a scenario that appears in the apocrypha.[281] Not only is the number of these details very small, but their traditional and legendary quality means that they were practically canonical; this is especially the case with the widespread belief that the idols fell down when the Christ Child entered into Egypt with his parents.[282] Significantly, with the exception of the incident just mentioned, that is, the fall of the idols, which is depicted in one of the few surviving illustrated copies of the *Meditationes* (Oxford, Corpus Christi College, MS 410, fol. 24v, top register; fig. 11), apocryphal legends concerning Jesus' purportedly numerous childhood miracles are not incorporated into the narrative, not even the benign miracles, such as the Child's commanding of a tree to bend down so that his mother might be refreshed by its fruits.[283] In an aside, the anonymous Franciscan author actually reveals his disapproval of the apocrypha, probably as a body of legendary lore that others took so seriously, or at least found so appealing, when he says, when treating the Flight into Egypt: "because so little that is authentic can be found, I am not going to bother to relate the events that happened to them in the desert and along the way."[284] This remark clearly implies that he is aware of the apocryphal infancy stories (a number of which are set on the Flight to Egypt), yet has consciously chosen to disregard them in the composition of his narrative.

That the Franciscan author's primary concern is to produce an affective response is evident from his treatment of the biblical episode in which the boy Jesus stays behind in the Temple. The majority of this chapter (which, significantly, is short, compared to Aelred's handling of it in the *De Jesu puero duo-*

*denni*) describes the anguish that Jesus' parents experienced upon realizing that he was lost and when they were searching for him with much difficulty. Echoing Aelred's musings on the Child's physical well-being during those few days, the Franciscan author briefly suggests that Jesus found food and lodgings at a hospice. In addition, he notes the Boy's humility in listening to "the learned doctors, serene of countenance, wise and reverent . . . as if igno-rant." The author also points out Jesus' humility in returning home with his parents, even though the Boy had stated his intention to focus on his Father's business.[285] Probably not incidentally, in this retelling of the Temple episode, the teachers' response of amazement at the Boy's speech (Lk. 2:47) is not at all mentioned. It was presumably this particular aspect of the story that seemed to justify the apocryphal authors' presentation of Jesus as a wonder-child, a depiction out of sync with the Franciscans' focus on their own self-abnegation and that of Jesus, their model of ideal human behavior.

Significantly, the idiosyncratic chapter from the *Meditationes vitae Christi* on what Jesus did from age twelve to thirty is much longer than the chapter on the episode about the Finding in the Temple.[286] The Bible's silence on what Christ did for so many years is here remedied by a Franciscan reconstruction of the young Jesus as a good-for-nothing, who purposely sought the scorn of those around him by doing nothing remarkable. The young Jesus is said to have withdrawn from the public, engaged in prayer, and carried out domestic chores. He is not portrayed as playing with other boys or even as going to school—the main activities ascribed to the Christ Child in the apocrypha, which are also things we would typically expect to hear about children. The author presents biblical support for this view of Jesus' unimpressive youth: the comments of Jesus' contemporaries, when he later began his public ministry, that he was merely the son of a carpenter (Matt. 13:55); John the Baptist's role as his precursor, which would have been unnecessary if Jesus had already begun preaching and distinguishing himself in other ways; and the fact that the Evangelists wrote nothing about this period of Christ's life. The adult Jesus' description of himself as "meek and humble of heart" (Matt. 11:29) also makes this depiction seem plausible, as does the way in which Jesus spoke of himself as the brother of his fellow human beings (John 20:17, Matt. 25:40)—biblical passages that are explicitly cited in this chapter. In addition, the anonymous author clearly has in mind Luke's comment, at the end of his account of the Holy Family's visit to the Temple, that the twelve-year-old Jesus went home with his parents and "was subject to them" (Lk. 2:51), which he cites at the outset of the chapter dedicated to Jesus' hidden years.[287]

The emphasis of the *Meditationes vitae Christi* upon the self-abnegation of the young Jesus is clearly an attempt to fashion his persona according to the model of Francis of Assisi. The saint's desire to be perceived as a fool is strikingly illustrated by a detail Thomas of Celano includes in his *Vita prima*.[288] Francis was clearly a talented preacher, for "even without preparation . . . [he] used to say the most amazing things to everyone." Although he was apparently able to do so, Francis did not always preach impromptu. Even the absence of Francis's anticipated preaching had a powerful effect, as Thomas attests: "Sometimes [Francis] prepared for his talk with some meditation, but once the people gathered he could not remember what he had meditated about and had to say. Without any embarrassment he would confess to the people that he had thought of many things before, but now could not remember a thing . . . [H]e would give a blessing and send the people away with this act alone as a very good sermon."[289] In a similar way, the young Jesus of the *Meditationes vitae Christi* paradoxically did amazing things by doing (or saying) nothing worth recording in Scripture, apart, of course, for the incident in the Temple, which the anonymous Franciscan author relates (in chapter 14) mainly to instill compassion for Mary in the reader. In this following chapter (15), the author switches gears, as it were, by claiming that, although Jesus had originally shown considerable promise after his return with his family from the Temple (cf. Lk 2:52), thereafter he did nothing commendable until the beginning of his public ministry. This led his neighbors to conclude: "He is an idiot, a no-good [person], foolish, and stupid."[290] Emphasizing the scorn that was directed at the young Jesus, the author adds: "He had no formal schooling, and among the people he was generally thought of as oafish and unbalanced (*grandis et captivus*)." Significantly, although this Franciscan Jesus seems incredibly passive, he nevertheless retains a faint trace of the vigor traditionally associated with Christ (especially in the earlier Middle Ages), when the anonymous author comments that the young Jesus wielded the paradoxical "sword of humility" in order "to bring low the haughty enemy."[291] But even this detail, because of its emphasis upon Christ's self-emptying (that is, the Son's putting aside of his glory in becoming human, and a poor and powerless one at that), can be seen as characteristically Franciscan.

Jaime Vidal effectively summarizes, and also offers a rationale for, the *Meditationes vitae Christi*'s treatment of Jesus' inconspicuous youth when he says: "The hidden life at Nazareth has hidden from his people the wonders which the Infancy Narrative has shown to us, and thus made possible the Messianic secret and the possibility of rejection."[292] The overarching theme of the chapter in which the Franciscan author ponders what Jesus did from age twelve to twenty-nine is that Christ is a *Deus absconditus* (Isa. 45:15), a passage that is explicitly quoted in this chapter.[293] As we shall see in subsequent chapters of this book, many medieval Christians believed that Jesus kept a low profile during his childhood and believed that this was not accidental but that he chose to do so for good reasons.

Jesus was thought to have concealed the greatness of his identity not only from his human contemporaries, but also, and most importantly, from the devil. Back in the chapter on the Circumcision, the author of the *Meditationes vitae Christi* remarks that one of the reasons that Jesus cried on that occasion was to hide himself from the devil—so his crying was a stratagem, not just a response to pain.[294] Similarly, in the chapter on Mary's life with Joseph after the Annunciation, we are told that one of the reasons why Mary had a husband was "so that the birth of the Son of God . . . be kept hidden from the devil"—an idea backed by a long exegetical tradition.[295] In other words, by giving the appearance of being conceived and born in the normal manner, the Christ Child successfully escaped the attention of the devil, which allowed him to mature gradually and later face his adversary at the appropriate time and, in a way, to catch him off guard. While the Franciscan author provides this theological rationale for Jesus' hiddenness, he seems more concerned about Jesus' personality, specifically, more interested in the Boy's lowliness—the abjection that revealed his profound humility—than in his apparent normalcy, both of which could be construed as a clever stratagem. The possibility of confusion about the Christ Child's full identity is likewise suggested in the chapter in the *Meditationes vitae Christi* on the Epiphany, where the Magi are commended for believing that "this tiny child" was "king of the Church and true God," despite the "worthless straits" (*vilia*) in which they found him.[296]

Although the text emphasizes the meekness of the boy Jesus, it does not shy away from indicating his uniqueness, particularly his uncanny understanding of what was going on around him. As did other medieval religious writers, the author claims that Jesus was "perfect" from the moment of his conception, both intellectually and, in a way, physically, in terms of the formation of his various body parts, which were already present from the very beginning, though in minuscule form. As a *homunculus*, Jesus simply grew in size within Mary's womb, instead of gradually acquiring a more complex body as did other unborn children.[297] From this principle, the author logically infers that the Christ Child possessed full understanding; and although Jesus did not at first speak, he is described as communicating his wishes to those around him by means of gestures. In fact, he is said to have done this on more than one occasion: when soothing his mother at his Circumcision, when averting his glance from the gold given by the Magi, and when nodding to his mother to convey his wish to be handed to Simeon.[298] The infant Jesus' uncanny sense of self-awareness and self-determination is likewise reflected in the author's characterization of him as a giant rejoicing to run the race as he exited his mother's womb (Ps. 18:6)—an image suggesting the Savior's eagerness to fulfill his mission, which was employed by other medieval authors.[299] In short, it seems as if the Franciscan author perceived no problematic contradiction between portraying the Christ Child as an ordinary boy and, at the same time, as a mature person, from his earliest years, one who was aware of what was going on around him and also intent upon his mission of redemption. Francis of Assisi had earlier summed up the Christ Child's duality when he spoke of him as the "poor King," but the author of the *Meditationes vitae Christi* goes further by portraying the Child at times as a *puer-senex* (a boy endowed with adultlike characteristics, which in the case of Jesus stem from his divinity, not simply a special infusion of divine grace). As suggested in the previous chapter, the portrayal of the child Jesus as mature and intelligently attuned to his surroundings indicates that the more traditional, hieratic view of the Christ Child continued to hold sway, even as Christians, in the later Middle Ages, became increasingly interested in Jesus' experience of human boyhood and in the poverty and humble circumstances of his family.

As we shall see in the following chapter, the tellers of apocryphal tales likewise strove to represent the Christ Child's duality, by calling attention to his childishness and love of play, on the one hand, and his preternatural wisdom and miracle-working abilities, on the other hand. While the Franciscan author of the *Meditationes vitae Christi* and the promoters of apocryphal lore may seem diametrically opposed to each other, in that the latter emphasizes the Boy's activity and feistiness and the former, his passivity, humility, and sweetness,[300] all of these tale-tellers seem to have engaged in a sort of intellectual and imaginative juggling act in attempting to reconstruct the childhood of a Boy who was paradoxically both human and divine. In addition, they all creatively, though differently, seized the opportunity to capitalize on Scripture's silence regarding Jesus' hidden years, rather than simply allowing their fellow Christians to ignore or make what they would of this void, without providing any hints or suggestions. In other words, a host of medieval authors (and artists) provided various suggestive ideas and images that were intended to help bring Jesus' childhood back to life and they succeeded in doing so in both complementary and contradictory ways.

# CHAPTER 3

# Aquinas and the Apocryphal Christ Child in the Later Middle Ages

As we have seen from our discussion of select Cistercian and Franciscan materials in the previous chapter, new attention was given to the events of Christ's childhood and an even greater concern shown for their spiritual applicability in the twelfth and thirteenth centuries. Rooted in the traditional practice of *lectio divina* and the celebration of the liturgical feasts connected with the Christ Child, this development was bolstered by the increasing emphasis placed upon Christ's humanity in the high and later Middle Ages. Other factors were at play as well. One of these may have been Western Europe's economic expansion, which, as David Herlihy suggested, helps account for the greater attention given to children and thus to the Christ Child in the later Middle Ages.[1] Another likely source of influence was Western Europe's increasing scientific approach to childhood, which may have resulted in a more positive reception of the apocryphal legends' depiction of the Christ Child acting as a normal boy, in many ways.[2] Whereas thinkers in the Augustinian tradition tended to regard children pessimistically as the victims of original sin whose hope of moral improvement lay in the discipline afforded by adults, medieval scholars who read about children in medical and natural philosophical texts would have probably been more willing to tolerate children's typical behavior.[3] In a cultural milieu in which adults were more attentive than before to the children around them, and, in addition, more intrigued by the very nature of childhood, European Christians probably wondered more about the early stages of Jesus' life than they had previously, and were more disposed to imagine the Christ Child resembling the children they actually knew.

As discussed in the previous chapter, both the Cistercians and Franciscans provided insight into Christ's childhood experiences and fostered imitation of the Child's pious ways. Yet because of their reluctance to stray too far from the Bible's scanty account of Jesus' childhood, members of these two religious orders may have actually increased medieval Christians' curiosity about his hidden years rather than satisfied their inquisitiveness about it. In the high Middle Ages, apocryphal narratives about Christ's early years—narratives that had been around for roughly a millennium—experienced a revival in Western Europe. This entailed the incorporation of new stories into centuries-old Latin texts and the transmission of both old and new tales in the vernacular languages.

In this chapter, I focus on Thomas Aquinas's view of the apocryphal narratives about Christ's childhood, arguing that, when he speaks about them, he evinces an awareness of trends within popular culture (such as stories about incubi and child murder) and that he had probably read later medieval redactions of these legends. As we shall see, Aquinas argues that these legends cannot be true, because if the Christ Child had worked miracles, it would have been harmful to Christians' faith, leading them to doubt the humanity (specifically the physical reality) of the boy Jesus and to regard him as a magician or some kind of supernatural being with demonic affiliations. Aquinas also considers it inappropriate for stories to portray Jesus as exercising his extraordinary power and displaying his unearthly wisdom before his adulthood, believing that this is not at all likely: if Christ would have done so, then he would have left a bad example for future generations of children and youths, who would have felt justified in disregarding social expectations for those their own age. Aquinas seems to think that such stories could do harm to Christians of the present day, especially considering the anti-somatic ideologies that had gained a foothold in parts of Europe. Further on in this chapter I suggest that those who propagated apocryphal legends about Jesus' infancy and boyhood in the later Middle Ages offered what they thought would be useful and appealing to their fellow Christians, while, in many cases, keeping in mind the objections to these legends posed by Aquinas and other highly learned clerics.

Since my interests in this chapter are pan-European—the reception of apocryphal stories about the Christ Child in Western Europe in the later Middle Ages—I will refer to apocryphal texts written in Latin that were produced and circulated in both England and on the Continent, as well as to select vernacular redactions. By the later Middle Ages, apocryphal legends about the Christ Child had been translated into numerous languages, including Middle English, French, Italian, German, Welsh, and Irish.[4] The legends were also transmitted in various art forms.[5] A careful study of these numerous textual and visual traditions and their interrelationships would indeed be valuable,[6] but it lies outside the scope of the present chapter. Of these vernacular narratives, I usually cite examples from the Middle English poems on Christ's childhood, in accordance with the special attention this book gives to late medieval English culture, and also because these texts will be linguistically accessible to many of my readers.[7] The diverse late medieval redactions of the apocryphal Christ-Child legends discussed in this chapter and William Caxton's printing of the *Infantia salvatoris* (ca. 1477), a Latin text recounting many of the childhood miracles, which is summarized in the Appendix, demonstrate that the apocryphal legends about Jesus' childhood piqued Christians' interest until the very end of the Middle Ages. Although their readership remained (I would venture to say predominantly) within the domain of the clergy, who were usually fluent in Latin, the audience of these legends expanded beyond it to include the laity. The latter would have learned about Jesus' hidden years, as transmitted through the apocrypha, by reading (or hearing) vernacular narratives based on centuries-old apocryphal texts as well as newer legendary material and also by seeing art objects inspired by apocryphal texts and traditions.[8]

After introducing the apocrypha, I will first provide an overview of Thomas Aquinas's objections to the legends about Jesus' childhood, stressing areas of overlap between his remarks and facets of contemporary folklore (such as the belief in fairies and in ritual murder). I will then offer explanations for the appeal of these legends in the later Middle Ages, within what seems to be a firmly rooted, largely orthodox, Christian culture. The hold that the apocryphal legends had on people's imaginations may seem surprising when we consider their depiction of Jesus as a troublesome child and contemporary canon law's stigmatization of "apocryphal" texts as books that Christians ought to avoid. Yet even though apocryphal legends about Christ's childhood were in many ways questionable, churchmen appear to have voiced objections against them only occasionally and apparently often promoted them. These legends may thus be called "popular," not because they were reiterated and represented as often as, say, the widespread stories of the posthumous miracles worked by the Virgin Mary, but because they were consumed and propagated by the clergy and laity alike.[9] In the context of this generally positive reception of the apocryphal infancy legends, Aquinas's arguments against them stand out and appear strikingly harsh.

I focus on the thirteenth-century Dominican theologian Thomas Aquinas (d. 1274) because, as the most well-known and accomplished scholar of the age of scholasticism, he represents the uppermost echelons of the medieval intellectual world. His comments about the apocryphal infancy legends give us insight into a particular end of the spectrum of medieval views about them. Surprisingly, scholars have almost completely ignored Aquinas's attitude toward the "alternative" version of Christ's childhood offered by the apocrypha, even though his Christology has received recent critical attention.[10] Considering his aristocratic background, we might assume that Aquinas was far removed from what ordinary people imagined, thought, and did. Yet Aquinas's elite status apparently did not prevent him from being respectful of people with little or no education, whose simple faith and honest deeds were meritorious; nor did it hinder him from acknowledging that, in Christianity, salvation is offered to all.[11] Regardless of the virtues that people not highly educated might have or be able to acquire, Aquinas probably thought they needed to be protected from religious material that might appeal to them but be doctrinally harmful. With respect to the legends considered here, it is worth noting that, while Aquinas goes so far as to call the apocryphal miracles worked by the boy Jesus "mendacious and fictitious," he never recommends the censorship or destruction of books that transmit apocryphal tales—a maneuver that would, in fact, exceed his work as a professional theologian.[12] While Aquinas's negativity toward the apocrypha is unmistakable, there were other churchmen whose response to the apocryphal childhood of Christ was even more extreme. An anonymous French Celestine monk considered the *Livre des enfances Jhesucrist* blasphemous on account of its depiction of Jesus as a naughty boy ("comme malvaiz garçon"); with impassioned speech, he expresses his eagerness to destroy every last copy of that book.[13] Refraining from the expression of anger toward such material, if he indeed felt any, Aquinas probably realized that intellectuals like himself were unlikely to be able to counteract completely the popular culture that welcomed such stories as both entertaining and devotional narratives. Although it is difficult if not impossible to determine Aquinas's views about how these legends ought to be dealt with practically, and doubtful that he had even formulated such a policy, I think we can fruitfully speculate about his familiarity with certain aspects of popular culture that intersect with the apocryphal legends, particularly the folk belief in beings who only appear to have bodies and in highly unusual children who have some kind of supernatural parentage or affiliation. On the whole, my analysis of late medieval apocryphal narratives about Jesus' childhood and their cultural contexts demonstrates that, in the later Middle Ages, the legends had a strong hold on the imagination of both the clergy and the laity alike. Furthermore, the controversy surrounding these legends, even if only a few learned people debated about them, might have encouraged late medieval writers and artists to approach Jesus' hidden years in innovative ways. Even if writers and artists responded to the apocrypha negatively by rejecting them on the whole or in part, they still might have appropriated certain details, or simply have devised alternate approaches to dealing with important issues that the apocrypha raised and caused audiences to ponder.

## Reasons for the Emergence and Continuing Popularity of the Apocrypha

Apocryphal stories about Jesus' birth and childhood originated in the Early Christian era (around the second century), primarily as a way of supplementing the official accounts about Jesus' early life that were offered by the Church in the canonical gospels. The renowned French art historian Émile Mâle succinctly characterized the impulse that led to the composition of these stories when he said, "Le peuple trouvait les Évangiles trop brefs et ne pouvait se résigner à leur silence." In other words, people experienced curiosity about Christ and his contemporaries and sought to satisfy it by looking for possibilities beyond the canonical gospels. This way of viewing things suggests that the apocrypha came into being and developed because Christians viewed the New Testament not as erroneous but rather as insufficient, in the sense of not fully answering the questions one might have after considering its contents. Mâle suggests that the Bible itself was thought to justify noncanonical expansions upon its incomplete treatment of the life of Christ: "Il [le peuple] prenait à la lettre la parole de saint Jean [21:25]." In other words, Mâle finds a prooftext in the end of John's Gospel (21:25), where the Evangelist remarks, as if to acknowledge the limitations of his own account: "But there are also many things which Jesus did, the which, if they should be written every one, I suppose that even the world itself could not contain the books that should be written."[14] John's comment implies that very many of Christ's deeds went unrecorded by the Evangelists, but were fondly remembered and transmitted orally. If this is really how people preserved the memory of Jesus, then apocryphal stories about him can be seen as not just a response to perceived gaps in the canonical gospels, but also as a setting down in writing of preexisting traditions that, for one reason or another, were not included by the inspired writers of the Bible.

John's remark about the inability of books to preserve a full account of Christ's deeds privileges human beings as repositories of historical information. To late antique and medieval Christians, this view might have suggested that Mary had thorough knowledge of her son's infancy and childhood, which the Evangelists recorded only partially. According to Luke (2:19, 51), when Mary witnessed the homage paid to the baby Jesus by the shepherds and, later, heard her twelve-year-old son's explanation of why he stayed behind in the Temple, she kept these experiences in her heart and pondered them. Might her memories, or those of other people who knew Jesus, have been transmitted to others besides the four Evangelists (or in noncanonical texts sometimes attributed to them, like the *Gospel of Pseudo-Matthew*)? Anonymous authors of apocryphal texts might have had such biblical verses in mind when relating miracles that the boy Jesus performed at home for his parents or within a semiprivate setting. The so-called *Vita rhythmica*, a long Latin poem on the lives of Mary and Jesus thought to have been composed by an anonymous thirteenth-century German monk,[15] who makes extensive use of the apocrypha and stridently justifies doing so, relates a story from Mary's kitchen. Once, when Joseph unexpectedly brought home guests for dinner, Mary had only a piece of bread to offer them—surely not enough to feed such a gathering. Seeing his parents' predicament, the boy Jesus multiplied the bread and set it on the table for the guests, who admired the bread's tastiness, "without knowing what Jesus had done, except his mother alone."[16] This episode is depicted in an illustrated version of the poem, found in what appears to be a fifteenth-century German or Flemish manuscript (London, British Library, Add. 29434, fol. 57r; fig. 12) The poet relates another household miracle performed by Jesus: when the herbs he had gathered for his mother's cooking turned out to be bitter, he instantaneously made them sweet and flavorful for her (Add. 29434, fol. 60v).[17] These two miracle stories were not widespread, but one that was frequently included in late medieval apocryphal narratives is, like them, notably domestic in nature. On one occasion, when Jesus went to a well to draw water for his mother, his water jar broke in the jostling of the other children also headed there. Jesus nevertheless fulfilled his task, by bringing back water in the lap of his tunic. A late thirteenth-century Italian manuscript containing an illustrated version of the apocryphal *Gospel of Pseudo-Matthew* emphasizes the miraculous nature of this deed by depicting a large, pitcher-shaped mass of water supported by a flap of Jesus' garment (Paris, Bibliothèque nationale de France, MS lat. 2688, fol. 45r; fig. 13).[18] These three miracles can be seen as domestic or semiprivate incidents from Christ's childhood that

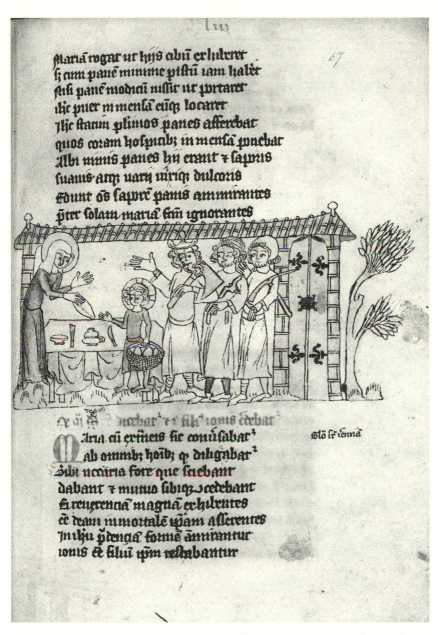

maria rogat ut hijs cibũ exhiberet
ꝗ cũ panẽ minime ꝑistũ iam haber̄
siũ panẽ modicũ misit ut ꝓrtaret
ihc puer ĩ mensã eiuꝗ locaret
Ihc statim plurimos panes afferebat
quos coram hospitib; in mensã ponebat
Albi minus panes hŭ erant ⁊ sapōris
suauis atꝗ uarij miriꝗ dulcoris
edunt õs sapōrē panis ammirantes
ꝑter solam mariã sũ ignorantes

ſr ou ſeꝗ... ducbat ⁊ ſili'ionis cēdbat
Maria cũ ertincis sic conũsabat
ab omnib; hoĩb; q̉ diligabat
Sibi uccaria fore que sciebant
dabant ⁊ mutuo sibiꝗ ꝛcedebant
ſi reuerẽciam magnã exhibentes
eē deam immortalẽ ipm asſerentes
Jnthu ꝑtenꝗ formē amirantur
ionis eē silui ip̃m restabantur

Glō ſr ienñ

Figure 12. The Christ Child's multiplication of bread at home, in an illustrated *Vita rhythmica* manuscript. London, British Library, Add. 29434, fol. 57r (fifteenth century?) By permission of the British Library Board.

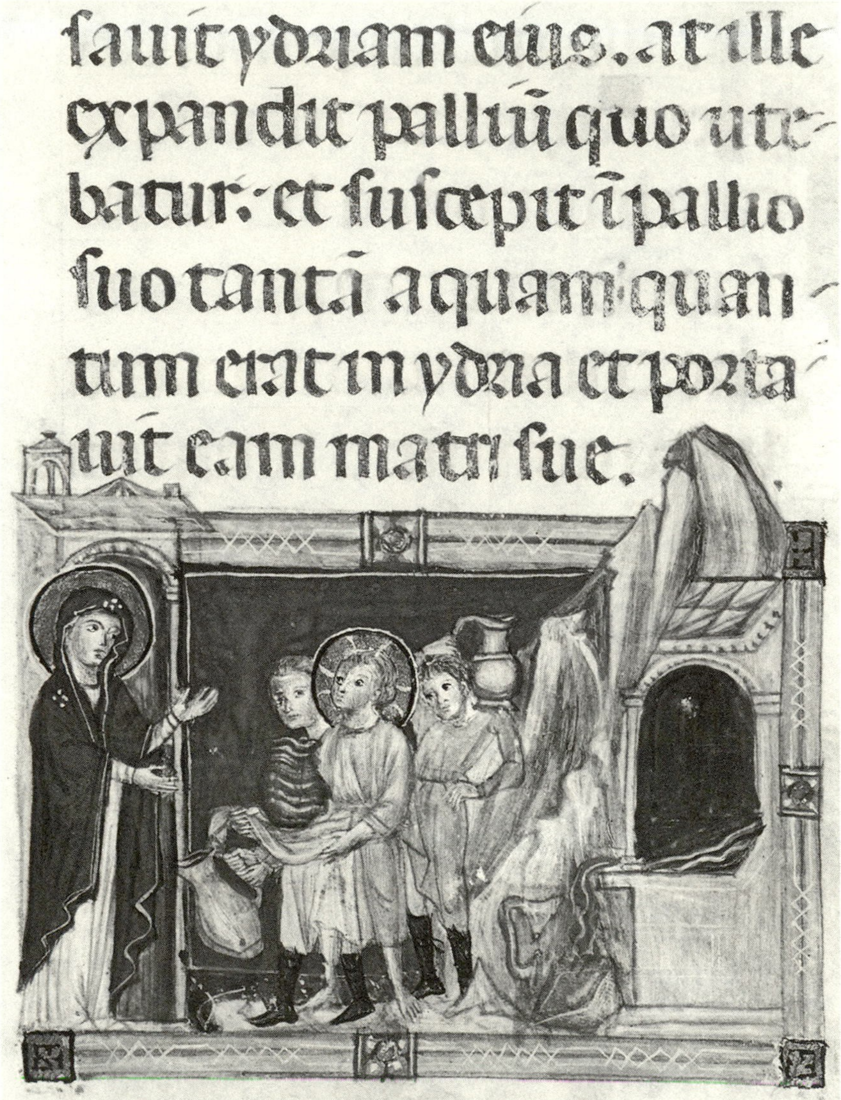

savit ydriam eius. at ille
expandit pallii quo ute
batur. et suscepit i pallio
suo tanti aquam quan
tum erat in ydria et porta
uit eam matri sue.

Figure 13. The Christ Child bearing a globe of water in his garment, in an illustrated
*Pseudo-Matthew* manuscript. Paris, BnF, lat. 2688, fol. 45r (thirteenth century). By
permission of the Bibliothèque nationale de France.

would have remained unknown to posterity had not Mary (or someone else) told others about them.

Conceiving of the apocryphal childhood narratives as records of incidents that occurred within the boy Jesus' family and community, and so rather privately, biblical scholar Raymond E. Brown posits a close connection between such tales and the Lucan account about the twelve-year-old Christ staying behind in the Temple: "in its content and tone it is a canonical example of those stories of the 'hidden life' of Jesus (that is, his life with his family at Nazareth before the ministry) which appear in the apocryphal gospels of subsequent centuries."[19] It would make sense that Mary, as a participant in the highly unusual and undoubtedly memorable event in the Temple, would have been the one to tell Luke, and possibly others, about it, though other witnesses could have done so, given that the occurrence was not completely private (as was, for example, the incident involving the herbs). As we shall see in Chapter 4, the fourteenth-century holy woman Birgitta of Sweden turned to Mary as a most valuable source of knowledge about Jesus' childhood; her approach may be considered broadly analogous to that taken by those who composed the apocryphal infancy narratives, since both Birgitta and the apocryphal writers provide more details about Christ's early life than do the canonical gospels and also claim that people who interacted with Jesus during his lifetime were their sources. On the whole, medieval Christians probably felt they had good reasons to pay attention to apocryphal legends about Jesus' childhood, despite the fact that these texts were clearly differentiated by churchmen from the canonical gospels of the Bible and considered inferior to them in terms of authority, which, ipso facto, cast at least some doubt upon their content.

## An Overview of Apocryphal Infancy Texts in the West

The apocryphal text that one must consider in any wide-ranging study of the Christ Child in the medieval West is the *Gospel of Pseudo-Matthew*, which in its fullest form was a compilation of two earlier apocryphal texts: the *Protoevangelium Jacobi* and the *Infancy Gospel of Thomas*. The *Protoevangelium Jacobi*, probably written in Greek in the second century, recounts a number of events that led up to Jesus' birth and a few that followed upon it.[20] The text derives its title from the narrator's announcement at the end of the text that his name is James; the audience may have considered him a stepbrother of Jesus (cf. Mk. 6:3), a hypothetical son of Joseph from his first marriage, though the author does not explicitly identify himself as such.[21] Although this apocryphal text is in actuality anonymous, it is somewhat logical that medieval readers could imagine its having been written by a son of Joseph who, as a member of his father's household (comprised of children from his supposed first marriage, as well as his second wife, Mary, and her son), would have witnessed some of the events narrated in the text.[22] Mary, of course, was not the only witness to what the Christ Child did; the other (hypothetical) members of Jesus' household and his neighbors were also witnesses of his deeds.

In the apocryphal *Protoevangelium Jacobi*, we are given a fairly lengthy prehistory to Christ's birth. We learn about the original childlessness of Anne and Joachim, Anne's being told by an angel (as was Joachim) that she would conceive a child, the offering of this child Mary, who was destined for renown, in the Temple at age three, her pious life there, her marriage to Joseph, her virginal conception of Jesus, and the Lord's miraculous birth. The text concludes with Herod's order that all of the infants two years old and younger be killed (cf. Matt. 2:16). Notable details from this text that made their way into medieval legend and iconography include, besides the incidents just mentioned, the reunion of Mary's parents at a gate after Joachim returns from the wilderness, where he fled on account of his shame at being childless (ch. 4).[23] We also hear about how the toddler Mary ascended the Temple steps without looking back (ch. 7), how Joseph was initially reluctant to marry the twelve-year-old girl since he was an old man with children from a previous marriage (ch. 9), and how Mary was assigned the enviable task of spinning the purple and scarlet threads for the veil of the Temple, an activity in which she was engaged at the Annunciation (chs. 10–11).[24] The *Protoevangelium* also recounts the attestation to Mary's virginity by two midwives, immediately after the birth of Jesus in a cave (chs. 19–20).[25]

Two rather odd details appearing near the end of the *Protoevangelium* (ch. 22) are also worth noting. The first ties in to the related themes of deception, disguise, and hiddenness that appear in some medieval texts (ideas briefly mentioned in the previous chapter, where I noted how Jesus was thought to have prudently concealed his divinity during his youth).[26] Upon learning that Herod ordered the slaughter of infants, Mary attempts to hide the baby Jesus by wrapping "him in strips of cloth, and put[ting] him in a feeding trough used by cattle," a ruse that works.[27] Mary's cousin Elizabeth, in order to save her own infant son, flees with him into the hill country and is engulfed by a mountain that hides them from little John the Baptist's would-be slayers.[28]

Somewhere in the process of this text's translation into Latin and its incorporation into *Pseudo-Matthew* these interesting details dropped out of the narrative.

The other apocryphal text that served as a source for the *Gospel of Pseudo-Matthew*—though only for certain manuscript families of this text, those which date from the high to late Middle Ages—is the *Infancy Gospel of Thomas*. Like the *Protoevangelium*, the *Infancy Gospel of Thomas* seems to have been composed in Greek in the second century. At the start, it is important to clarify its title: the reference to Thomas in the modern title has led some to associate it erroneously with the Gnostic *Gospel of Thomas*, a collection of sayings of Jesus in the Nag Hammadi corpus.[29] A connection between heretical sects and material found in the *Infancy Gospel of Thomas* is, however, suggested by a passage from Irenaeus of Lyons's second-century treatise *Adversus haereses*. Irenaeus mentions that the Marcionites, who were known to be Docetists as well as Gnostics, had a text in which Jesus discusses the alphabet with a schoolmaster.[30] This clear allusion by Irenaeus to an episode from the *Infancy Gospel of Thomas* (ch. 6) does not necessarily mean that the latter text originally emanated from heretical circles, even though the Gnostics, who believed in salvation through esoteric knowledge, would likely have found the image of a boy Jesus speaking about the mysterious meaning of the letters of the alphabet appealing.[31] Yet, given that this apocryphal tale apparently circulated among the Marcionites, it is possible that other apocryphal stories about the Christ Child were transmitted in some fashion (if not first created) by a heretical group or groups.[32] In any case, the passage in Irenaeus's treatise helps scholars date the *Infancy Gospel of Thomas*, since it indicates that at least some of its contents were already in circulation by the end of the second century.

The *Infancy Gospel of Thomas*'s original title was probably "The Boyhood Deeds of the Lord Jesus Christ," or something similar—a fitting designation, considering that the text focuses entirely on Christ's boyhood, without attempting to provide an exhaustive biography of the first part of Jesus' life. The narrative begins in medias res with a scene in which the five-year-old Jesus plays with other children at a riverside. It concludes with a slightly different version of the story recounted in Luke (2:41–52) about how the twelve-year-old Jesus traveled to Jerusalem with his parents to celebrate Passover and stayed behind in the Temple after their departure. In both texts (the canonical and the apocryphal), Jesus' parents eventually find him sitting among the teachers, who are amazed by the Boy's questions and comments on the law. After Mary asks her son for an explanation of his behavior and Jesus

responds rather cryptically and almost defensively,[33] the Boy returns home
with his parents. It is not difficult to imagine how Luke's account of the Christ
Child astounding the Jews could have prompted the author of the *Infancy
Gospel of Thomas* to tell stories about how Jesus repeatedly attracted the attention of his elders during his boyhood, most noticeably by performing miracles.[34] In both the Temple episode and in the other stories, Jesus is a wonder
boy. As already noted, this incident from the Gospel of Luke is the only canonical detail provided about Jesus' early life, apart from the sequence about
the Nativity and its immediate aftermath.

The apocryphal *Gospel of Pseudo-Matthew* is thought to have been originally composed sometime between the middle of the sixth and the end of the
eighth century (probably in the early seventh century) by an anonymous monk
who used a Latin translation of the *Protoevangelium* and probably an anonymous account about the Flight into Egypt.[35] A prologue, consisting of a set of
spurious letters between two bishops (named Chromatius and Heliodorus) and
St. Jerome, was later attached to *Pseudo-Matthew*. In these fictive epistles, the
bishops ask the renowned scholar to translate an account of Mary's origin
and Christ's infancy, which Matthew the Apostle supposedly wrote in Hebrew. They present an urgent need for a faithful translation of this account,
which they hope would serve as an antidote to a heretical text on this same
topic that they claim is in circulation. Jerome agrees to carry out the translation, though, in actuality, the real Jerome (d. 420) was repulsed by apocryphal infancy narratives, at least the apocryphal account of the Nativity
(which includes the detail of the two Jewish midwives arriving on the scene
after Jesus' birth) and the claim that Joseph had children from a previous
marriage.[36] It is due to this preface about the text's origins that modern scholars designate this early medieval apocryphal text as the *Gospel of Pseudo-
Matthew* (and that medieval scholars sometimes associated it with St. Jerome).
In the medieval period, the text was usually referred to as the *Infantia salvatoris* or by some similar title.[37] This is in fact how William Caxton entitled the
apocryphal text he printed around 1477.

Whereas the *Protoevangelium* concludes with the attempts of Mary and
Elizabeth to protect their baby boys, the early versions of *Pseudo-Matthew* end
with a brief account of the Holy Family's Flight into Egypt to avoid Herod's
murderous wrath. On this journey, the infant Jesus does wondrous deeds, such
as taming some dragons and wild beasts and causing a tree to bend down so
that his mother, who is fatigued from the journey, may be refreshed by its
fruit.[38] In addition to working these miracles, Jesus shortens his family's jour-

ney to Egypt at the weary and elderly Joseph's prompting.[39] Later on, when Jesus and Mary enter a temple in the city of Sotinen, located in Egypt, the idols immediately fall to the ground, a wonder that causes the governor Affrodosius to acknowledge the mother and child as divine (see fig. 11, upper register).[40]

Manuscript families of *Pseudo-Matthew* from the later Middle Ages continue the narrative beyond the Flight into Egypt by recounting what Jesus did as he was growing up; the section that contains these stories has been called the "Pars altera," since it was an addendum to, rather than an intrinsic part of, the original text.[41] Jesus' deeds often disturb the peace of village life and are usually miraculous in nature or at least unconventional. While the bulk of the material comes from the *Infancy Gospel of Thomas*, stories emanating from and/or transmitted by oral tradition and non-Western sources were also added to *Pseudo-Matthew* in the high and later Middle Ages. These include a tale about how Jesus changed his playmates into pigs when the boys' parents, who were concerned about their children's well-being, hid them in an oven, in order to protect them from Jesus, who was often implicated in, if not the sole cause of, the injuries and even deaths of his playmates. This story ultimately derives from the early medieval *Arabic Infancy Gospel*,[42] which recounts how Jesus, on one occasion, transformed his playmates into goats, rather than pigs.[43] Another story derived from the *Arabic Infancy Gospel* that was incorporated into the expanded *Pseudo-Matthew* (that is, the *Infantia salvatoris*) tells how the Christ Child dyed a number of clothes various colors despite placing them in the same dyeing vat.[44] While the tales about the pigs and the dyeing of cloths appear infrequently in Latin manuscripts, they are common in Middle English and medieval French redactions of the *Infantia salvatoris*.[45] Another story that was sometimes added to late medieval apocryphal narratives recounts how, on the Flight into Egypt, Mary or Joseph tells a sower to say to their pursuers that a family with a child passed by his field when he was sowing his grain.[46] This statement is in fact true, but essentially equivocal. When Herod's men come upon the sower and see the grain ready for harvesting around him (as a result of its having miraculously grown, that is, without the normal passage of time), they are given a misleading message. Because they misinterpret it, assuming that the family the sower is speaking of must not be the one they are looking for, they fail to realize that they were indeed hot on the trail of Jesus and his parents. This episode seems to have originated in oral folklore rather than in old and influential apocryphal texts.[47]

Many of these apocryphal stories underscore the reality of Christ's boyhood even while they demonstrate his exceptionality vis-à-vis his playmates.

The fact that Jesus is a normal boy becomes clear when we consider his motives, not just the amazing quality of his deeds. The reason Jesus is annoyed that his playmates have been hidden in an oven, for example, is that he wants to interact with children his own age. Along similar lines, he curtails his activity of dyeing cloth in the conventional way, according to the instructions he has been given, miraculously achieving the stipulated outcome instead, because he wants to play outside with other children at the same time that he is supposed to be carrying out the task assigned to him. In these tales, Jesus employs his divine power to achieve his desired end or to express his chagrin at being thwarted in it, yet in both cases he is behaving in a boyish manner. As I have stated above and argued elsewhere,[48] increasing interest in the nature of childhood from the high Middle Ages onward likely resulted in a more positive reception of the type of Jesus we find in the *Infancy Gospel of Thomas* and in related material.

## Aquinas's Disapproval of the Portrayal of Jesus in the Apocryphal Infancy Legends

Thomas Aquinas explicitly mentions the *Infantia salvatoris* in only a few places; when he does so, he usually refers to key Christological principles that were earlier expressed in patristic sources. As we shall see, Aquinas opposes the legends about Jesus' childhood, not only because they contradict Scripture, but also because their portrayal of the Christ Child would, in his estimation, likely result in a denial of Jesus' physicality and lead to inappropriate behavior in youths, though, interestingly, he does not hone in on the portrayal of Jesus as a bad boy. In his discussion of the apocryphal Christ Child, Aquinas gestures at what we might generally characterize as folkloric ideas—notions of incubi, changelings, and magicians, and anti-Judaic rumors of the Jews as murderers of children. In doing so, Aquinas probably wished to endow the legends with sinister associations and thus further discredit them in the view of his fellow friars and other clerics, who he likely hoped would discourage the laity from taking an interest in them.

In examining Aquinas's response to the apocryphal Christ Child I will focus on a few passages from the *Tertia pars* of the *Summa theologiae*, specifically from the section of that work that has been called a "Life of Christ." Dating from the end of his life (ca. 1272–73, when Aquinas was writing in Naples), this section is not a narrative account of the major incidents in Jesus' life; rather, Aquinas follows its chronological sequence with the "intention . . . to write about the 'mysteries' of the life of Christ."[49] This section on "what the Incarnate Son of God did and suffered in the human nature united to him," as Aquinas himself puts it,[50] is divided into four subsections: Christ's *ingressus* into this world, his *processus* (or life) within it, his *exitus* from this world, and, lastly, his *exaltatio* (or life in glory after this life)—a structure, Torrell observes, that "establishes the exemplary value of the mysteries of the life of Jesus."[51] In a question found within the first part of this section (encompassing Questions 27–59), Aquinas asks "Whether Christ's birth should have been made known to all" (q. 36, a. 1).[52] He responds negatively, citing in his *sed contra* two verses from Isaiah (45:15, 53:3) in which God is said to be hidden (*absconditus*) and the "look" of the Suffering Servant "hidden and despised" (*quasi absconditus vultus eius et despectus*). Such a characterization implies that Christ would not have wanted himself to be announced as the Incarnate Word at his birth or even later on. In his response, Aquinas cites St. Paul's comments about "the princes of this world" (whom medieval exegetes commonly interpreted as the Jewish leaders contemporaneous with Christ): "If they had known it, they would never have crucified the Lord of glory" (1 Cor. 2:8). Aquinas's argument here is that if Christ's birth had been manifested to all, then he would not have been crucified and thus would not have saved humankind. As we shall see, the question of the Jews' understanding of Jesus is central to the medieval reception of the apocryphal legends concerning his childhood.

In the body of the article, Aquinas mentions another problem that would have arisen if Christ's birth had been made manifest: others would not have had the opportunity to exercise belief in him (presumably as a Redeemer who was both human and divine), since it would have been obvious to all that he was no ordinary child. "If," Aquinas says, "when Christ was born, his birth had been known to all by evident signs, the very nature of faith would have been destroyed, since it is 'the evidence of things that appear not'" (Heb. 11:1). Aquinas goes on to cite St. Augustine in support of his point that if Christ had appeared out of the ordinary at his birth, then he would have likely prevented people from acknowledging "the reality of his human nature" (*veritas humanitatis*). In his letter to Volusian, Augustine puts forth a rhetorical question, which Aquinas quotes as follows: "If he had not passed through the different stages of babyhood to youth, had neither eaten nor slept, would he not have strengthened an erroneous opinion, and made it impossible for us to believe that he had become true man? And while he is doing all things wondrously, would he not have taken away that which he accomplished in his mercy?"[53]

Aquinas's argument in this part of the article is that if Christ had not looked and acted like a normal human being all the time, then those around him would have doubted that he was truly human.

It is worth recalling that the tremendously influential Doctor of the Church, Augustine (d. 430), whom Aquinas cites in this particular question (q. 36, a. 1) and of course elsewhere, was writing at a time when Christological heresies were a threat to the doctrine that the Early Church was engaged in developing and defending. Augustine himself had been a Manichaean, that is, one who regarded matter as evil and thus could not accept the idea that the Word had truly become flesh. In the passage above, Augustine mentions the basic bodily functions of eating and sleeping, which are clearly more noticeable than the gradual development that a human being undergoes during infancy and childhood. His point is that Christ, in his physicality, followed the law of nature for human beings so that people would conclude correctly that he was truly human. While the high Middle Ages might not have been as doctrinally tumultuous as were the first centuries of Christianity, we should keep in mind that heresies were still in circulation at that time and that Aquinas's order was founded to combat them, particularly Catharism, an anti-somatic ideology like Manichaeism. It is thus appropriate that Aquinas cites a former Manichaean when discussing Christ's infancy and childhood: ensuring the *veritas* of Christ's humanity was a central concern to Aquinas as well as to his influential predecessor.

Elsewhere, Augustine balks at the idea that Christ was psychologically like other infants. He denies that "this ignorance [i.e., of babies] was present in that infant in whom the Word was made flesh . . . nor do I think that there was in the little Christ that weakness of mind that we observe in little ones." Here Augustine insists on the Infant's exceptionality, but, as he does in the passage above, he claims that Jesus developed physically in a normal manner: "because there was in Christ the likeness of sinful flesh [Rom. 8:3], he chose to undergo changes in age, beginning from infancy, so that it seemed his flesh could come to death by growing old."[54] While the phrase "likeness of human flesh" (Rom. 8:3; cf. Phil. 2:7) may, through a strained interpretation, suggest that Christ's humanity was a mere appearance and thus in a way deceptive, Augustine's statement that Christ "chose to undergo" the phases of the human life cycle implies that he actually experienced them, rather than simply giving people the false impression that he was doing so.[55] As we shall see, Augustine was not the only Christian thinker who envisioned the God-man in his early life as both normal and exceptional; for Augustine, Jesus was normal physically but not psychologically.

To return to Aquinas: in a later article of the *Summa theologiae* (ST, 3, q. 36, a. 4) concerned with Christ's manifestation of himself to others at the Nativity,[56] Aquinas reiterates the basic principles that undergird his answer to the previous question: Christ chose to appear as an ordinary infant and child, so as (1) to safeguard humans' faith in his humanity and (2) not to obstruct the divine plan for his crucifixion (which was intended to occur in his adulthood). In the *sed contra* Aquinas quotes the fifth-century pope Leo the Great, who claims (in a homily on the Epiphany) that the Magi found the baby Jesus "in no way different from the generality of human infants."[57] In the body, he explains that Christ "presented a likeness of human weakness" (by implication a spectacle true to reality) so that those who saw him might think that he was truly human. At the same time, Aquinas notes that the Magi benefitted from certain extraordinary signs, for "by means of God's creatures," Christ "showed the power" of his godhead. Aquinas is probably referring to the star that led the Magi to the infant Jesus (Matt. 2:2). The angels that appeared to the shepherds likewise announced the birth of Christ in an extraordinary fashion. It is also possible that Aquinas here has in mind nonbiblical material, for Jesus' birth was widely thought to have been marked by wonders that occurred at that time. A number of these traditional "signs" are mentioned in the chapter on the Nativity in the thirteenth-century Dominican-authored *Legenda aurea*. Among these is the famous legend about the Basilica of Santa Maria in Ara Coeli: on the day of the Nativity, "a virgin holding a child in her lap," enveloped by the sun, appeared to the Sibyl, who then informed the emperor that the child she had seen was greater than he and thus ought to be worshipped by him. The room where the vision occurred became a church dedicated to St. Mary. Jacobus mentions another wonder that occurred around the time of the Nativity: the star that appeared to the Magi "had the shape of a most beautiful boy over whose head a cross shone brilliantly," and who actually told them to go to Judea, where they would find the newborn babe.[58]

Whereas Aquinas in the earlier article (q. 36, a. 1) briefly alluded to Jesus' transition from infancy to youth by citing Augustine, in this article (q. 36, a. 4) he seems to widen the scope of his inquiry more noticeably to encompass both the birth and childhood of Christ. As before, Aquinas is unwilling to attribute unusual behavior to the Christ Child. In the second objection he considers whether it was useless for Christ, who had "the treasure of wisdom and grace [perfectly] from the beginning of his conception," to hide these gifts in his early life (given that Ecclesiasticus 20:32 says that there is no profit in hidden wisdom). Aquinas responds by saying that "there is no need for a wise man to make himself known at all times, but at a suitable time," adding that Christ actually manifested his wisdom by at first hiding it. As we shall see, the principle that certain types of behavior are appropriate at certain stages of the life cycle is fundamental to Aquinas's discussion of the early period of Christ's life. In objection 3, Aquinas introduces the possibility of the Child having been a wonder-worker, a topic not unrelated to his consideration of the appropriate time for Jesus to manifest his wisdom. In this objection, Aquinas explicitly refers to the *Liber de infantia salvatoris*: in that book "we read . . . that in his infancy (*pueritia*) Christ worked many miracles." Although the word *infantia* appears in the title of the book, which Aquinas cites by name, he indicates that its contents deal with Christ's *pueritia*. While we tend to think of "infancy" as referring to the very first stage of life (that of babies), in the six-age scheme of the life cycle that was popular in the Middle Ages and propounded by Isidore of Seville, among others, *infantia* is said to last seven years. The first age is followed by *pueritia*, which lasts the same amount of time.[59] Significantly, the expanded *Infantia salvatoris* deals with both the Christ Child's infancy and his childhood, as these ages were defined by Isidore, for example.

Aquinas replies to the objection that the Christ Child worked miracles, first of all by discounting the text known as the *Infantia salvatoris* as an authority that can be employed in a theological argument. He is clearly referring to a book with a specific, well-known Latin title, rather than to a tradition that was merely oral, even though apocryphal legends about the child Jesus circulated in both manners. The fact that Aquinas refers to the *Infantia salvatoris* by its title, without specifying its contents precisely, reveals an assumption on his part that his readers have at least a basic acquaintance with this text. Aquinas himself probably read it, for informational rather than devotional purposes. By calling the *Infantia salvatoris* "apocryphal," Aquinas implies that it is unreliable and therefore lacks authority. He does not, however, state that it is completely worthless and should never be read by Christians. Aquinas also assumes that his clerical readers are familiar with the so-called Gelasian Decree, an early sixth-century document that gives the names of the canonical books of the New Testament, followed by a long list of apocryphal texts.[60] This latter portion of the list is introduced by an emphatic statement of the Church's rejection of such books, which serves as an implicit warning against reading and placing trust in them as reliable sources of information:

"The catholic and apostolic Roman church in no way receives the remaining works, which have been written or preached by heretics or schismatics; we have thought that a few of these, which have come to mind and are to be avoided by Catholics, should be listed below."[61] At the end of the list, the anonymous author proclaims that "these works and those things similar to them [which a number of heretics or schismatics have taught or written] are not only repudiated but also rejected (*eliminata*) by the entire Roman and apostolic church, and are permanently condemned (*damnata*) by the indissoluble bond of anathema, along with their authors and their followers."[62] Included in the list of books are three that ostensibly contain apocryphal infancy material: the *Evangelium nomine Iacobi minoris* (item 8), the *Liber de infantia salvatoris* (item 15), and the *Liber de nativitate salvatoris et de Maria vel obstetrice* (item 16). While the first item of the three just mentioned seems to refer to the *Protoevangelium*, it is not obvious which texts the other two titles designate.[63] It would make sense that one of them refers to *Pseudo-Matthew*, but the date of the latter text's composition probably postdates the document. Although modern scholars disagree on the identification of items 15 and 16, a book with the title *Infantia salvatoris* is undeniably included in the Gelasian Decree, and this text presumably has close affiliations with *Pseudo-Matthew*, if it is not in fact an early form of it.

In the *Summa theologiae*, q. 36, a. 4, Aquinas indicates that the *Infantia salvatoris* is concerned with "many miracles" that were performed during Christ's *pueritia*. Although he may be thinking of the wonders that occurred not that long after Jesus' birth (relatively speaking), such as, on the Flight into Egypt, the bending down of a palm tree at the Infant's command, the phrase "many miracles" in the objection under consideration (q. 36, ad 4), together with the remarks in his reply to it, suggest that Aquinas has in mind a depiction of the boy Jesus as a wonder-worker who frequently called attention to himself over a significant period of time. The expanded version of *Pseudo-Matthew*, as well as the *Infancy Gospel of Thomas* in Latin, are possibilities, since both of these texts were in circulation in Aquinas's day and recount the Boy's miracles.[64] Aquinas may very well have read a text similar to that printed by William Caxton around 1477, who may have obtained his text directly from what he found in a manuscript, perhaps one that had been copied for centuries, or from another printed text, which may perhaps have derived from a text found in a manuscript.[65] Caxton's *Infantia salvatoris* begins with a compressed account of Christ's Nativity (chs. 1–7) and then devotes seven chapters to the miracles that occurred on the Flight into Egypt, followed by twenty chapters on the

wonders that Jesus did during his childhood. Given that most of the text deals
with the latter, it can be considered closer to the *Infancy Gospel of Thomas* in
Latin than to *Pseudo-Matthew*, a text that typically begins further back with
the childlessness of Mary's parents and often lacks the childhood miracles.[66]
In any case, Caxton's text certainly focuses on the remarkable events of
Christ's childhood.

Aquinas and his learned contemporaries would have been familiar with
the Gelasian Decree on account of Gratian's reiteration of it in his *Decretum*,
the standard collection of canon law that dates to the middle of the twelfth
century. To better understand what Aquinas and others mean when they call
the *Infantia salvatoris* "apocryphal," we must look closely at the actual words
of the *Decretum* and their interpretation by medieval scholars, as indicated by
the *Glossa ordinaria* to the *Decretum*, which was initially composed around
1215–18 and revised around 1245. The Greek-derived word "apocryphal" attracted the attention of some Latin scholars, who explained it etymologically,
as in this gloss: "Apocryphal means hidden and secret, as the word comes from
*apo* meaning 'of' and *crysis* meaning 'concealed.' Therefore, a book is called
apocryphal, that is, concealed and secret, when its author is unknown. It is
not received by the Church but, one might say, rejected, in that it may be read,
not in church, but elsewhere privately (*non in Ecclesia, sed remote et secrete ab
Ecclesia est legendus*). This follows Hug. [Huguccio]. So it is called apocryphal
in Greek and *secreta*, that is 'concealed places' in Latin."[67] Centuries earlier
Isidore of Seville had offered the word "secret" as a synonym for the word
"apocryphal." He explains why apocryphal texts are regarded as dubious: "their
origin is hidden and not evident to the Church Fathers, from whom the authority of the true scriptures has come down to us." Some of these texts, he
notes, are attributed to apostles but in reality are composed by heretics. They
are thus rightly "set apart by canonical authority under the name apocrypha."[68]
Rather than cite Isidore, however, the gloss in the *Glossa ordinaria* quoted
above cites a more recent authority: the twelfth-century canonist Huguccio,
who was undoubtedly indebted to his predecessor. Huguccio states that a book
that is called " 'apocryphal'—that is "hidden" and "secret," on account of the
uncertainty surrounding its authorship—such a book "is not received by the
Church but rejected, as if not to be read in church, but secretly and remotely
from church."[69] There are two aspects of Huguccio's comment that ought to
be emphasized: first, that while apocryphal books have a certain stigma attached to them, they are not automatically regarded as totally false and worth-

less;[70] and second, that canon law allows Christians to read such books privately. The thirteenth-century Dominican Giovanni Balbi offered a similar etymology for "apocryphus" in his *Catholicon*, where he makes the additional remark that apocryphal texts contain "multa vera" but also "plura falsa." This stance, which seems more negative than agnostic toward apocryphal texts, can also be seen in the Wycliffite Bible, which, relying on the *Catholicon*, divides apocryphal books into two categories: those "þe treuþe þerof is open," and others, for which "men doutiþ þe treuþe þerof," an example of which is "þe book of þe ȝong childhed of þe Sauyour."[71] This gives us clear proof that the *Liber de infantia salvatoris* was circulating in late medieval England and that it was regarded with suspicion, at least by scholars of canon law and theology.

While Huguccio may seem to offer a novel, permissive interpretation of the Gelasian Decree, it is extremely unlikely that he was trying to introduce a new approach or policy. The fourth-century Council of Laodicea had long ago decreed that "it is not proper that books not canonized be read in church," a statement that leaves open the possibility that they could be read by Christians elsewhere.[72] Along similar lines, the Gelasian Decree does not dictate against the reading of apocryphal books in a space that is not within a church. In short, by describing the *Infantia salvatoris* as "apocryphal," Aquinas implies that its status is dubious and that it should not be employed within a theological argument; in other words, his use of the adjective "apocryphal" for the *Infantia salvatoris* does not in itself imply that he considers the book to be filled with errors and worthy of destruction.

That Aquinas does not think highly of this book's contents, however, is clear from the remaining remarks he makes about it in ST 3, q. 36, a. 4, ad 3. Aquinas quotes John Chrysostom (d. 407), a Greek Father of the Church whose writings had been translated into Latin fairly recently.[73] Backed by the authority of Chrysostom, Aquinas emphasizes two points: that the *Infantia salvatoris* contradicts Scripture and that its contents are highly implausible as a historical account of Christ's childhood. In Chrysostom's homily 21 on the Gospel of John (which Aquinas cites here), he begins his criticism of the apocryphal legends about the childhood of Christ by pointing out their most obvious problem: their contradiction of what the Evangelist says at the end of his account of Jesus' transformation of water into wine at a wedding feast at Cana: "This beginning of miracles did Jesus in Cana in Galilee" (John 2:11). Rather than stop there, Chrysostom continues by assuming, for the sake of argument, that the boy Jesus worked miracles. Aquinas quotes him as follows:

> If he had worked miracles at an early age (*secundum primam aeta-tem*), there would have been no need for anyone else to manifest him to the Israelites; whereas John the Baptist says (John 1:31): "That he may be made manifest in Israel; therefore am I come baptizing with water." Moreover, it was fitting that he should not begin to work miracles at an early age. For people [i.e., the Israelites] would have thought the Incarnation to be unreal (lit., "a phantasm": *Existimas-sent enim phantasma esse incarnationem*), and, out of sheer spite (*livore liquefacti*), would have crucified him before the proper time.[74]

The underlying reasoning in this passage is that of *reductio ad absurdum*: absurdity arises from the apocryphal legends' contradiction of the scriptural presentation of John the Baptist as Jesus' herald, even apart from their ostensible clash with John 2:11. First, if the Christ Child had been a wonder-worker, then there would have been no need for John the Baptist to indicate that Jesus was the *Agnus Dei* (John 1:29). When Chrysostom mentions the Baptist's role in manifesting Christ to the Israelites, he implies that Christ's supreme special-ness was hidden during his early life. In other words, the adult Jesus was in need of a herald because he had spent his childhood and adolescence in obscurity.[75] In the same homily, Chrysostom explains why a wonder-working Christ Child would have caused such a stir: if Jesus' renown spread so quickly when he worked miracles for a relatively brief time as an adult, then his fame would have spread even more quickly had he worked miracles as a child: "The things which happened would have seemed to be more amazing, since they were done by a boy, and the time [during which he worked miracles] would also have been double, or triple, or more."[76]

Aquinas, still citing Chrysostom, argues that the boy Jesus' working of miracles would not only have been unseemly—a case of exhibitionism—but would also have disrupted the divine plan for the redemption of humanity, particularly the role that the Jews were to play in it. Instead of seeking to crucify Jesus when he was an adult, the Jews, had they been exposed to a wonder-working Christ Child, "would have crucified him (*cruci eum tradidis-sent*, literally, "delivered him to the cross") before the proper time," since they would have been *livore liquefacti* (literally, "enervated by malice") at the sight of his marvelous deeds.[77] The text is not entirely clear whether the Jews, in this hypothetical scenario, would have handed Jesus over to the authorities or would themselves have nailed him to the cross, though the former interpre-tation seems to correspond more closely to the phrasing of the Latin text.

Note, too, that the word *livor* used here is probably better translated with the broader meaning of "malice" than with the narrower meaning of "envy,"[78] though both words are, in fact, applicable to the Jews as they are presented in late medieval apocryphal legends and in other anti-Judaic sources.[79] For example, the extensive Middle English biblical paraphrase *Cursor Mundi* (c. 1300), which interpolates into its narrative the apocryphal account of Jesus' childhood (as transmitted by the expanded *Pseudo-Matthew*), provides a physiological description of the "envy" felt by one of Jesus' teachers: "At ihesu was he ful tene [very angry] / For he spak so skilfuly / To him had he greet enuy / Þourȝe swellyng of his herte."[80] This derogatory characterization of Jesus' elder may stem in part from the increasing emphasis that biblical commentaries placed, from the high Middle Ages onward, on the Jews' ill will toward Jesus and his followers, and on the Jews' alleged agency in the crucifixion.[81]

Aquinas's supposition that the Jews would have been unable to restrain themselves if a miracle-working Christ Child had been in their midst (which results in another *reductio ad absurdum*, since it leads to the idea of Christ's premature death) reveals his low estimation of the Jews of Jesus' day, at least the Jewish leaders. While Aquinas is obviously reiterating the views of Chrysostom, an eastern bishop known for his anti-Semitism,[82] it is not impossible that the thirteenth-century scholastic had in mind the slanderous rumors of his time that Jews murdered children, usually for ritualistic purposes.[83] Christian children found dead were sometimes presumed to be murdered by Jews, vicariously in place of Christ, whom the Jews could no longer harm in his historical body. In his lengthy account of the death and finding of the body of William of Norwich, generally considered the first medieval victim of ritual murder, the Benedictine monk Thomas of Monmouth makes a clear link between the Jews' supposed murder of the boy William during Easter Week of 1144 and the Passion of Christ: "The boy, like an innocent lamb, was led to slaughter. . . . Having shaved his head, they stabbed it with countless thorn-points. . . . While these enemies of the Christian name were rioting in the spirit of malignity around the boy, some of those present adjudged him to be fixed to a cross in mockery of the Lord's passion, as they would say, 'Even as we condemned the Christ to a shameful death, so let us condemn the Christian' . . . After these many and great tortures they inflicted a frightful wound in his left side, reaching to his inmost heart."[84] A victim of the Jews' cruelty, William is undoubtedly presented here as an *alter Christus*.

Along similar lines, about three centuries later, Geoffrey Chaucer's Prioress draws powerful parallels between the child Jesus and the "little clergeon" (a seven-year-old schoolboy), who was cruelly killed because his singing in praise of the Virgin angered the Jews in the vicinity. At the end of her tale, the Prioress explicitly refers to a more recent case of ritual murder (1255), that of "yonge Hugh of Lyncoln, slayn also / With [by] cursed Jewes."[85] Collapsing the present and the past even further, and erasing an age difference of about five years (the amount by which her child victim is younger than the one found in Chaucer's sources), the Prioress casts the little clergeon as a martyr like one of the Holy Innocents, who themselves were killed in place of Christ.[86] The Prioress links the Jews with Herod, both of whom were thought to have been disturbed by the news of the birth of the "king of the Jews" (Matt. 2:2–3).[87] In the poem recounting the apocryphal childhood of Jesus found in the London Thornton manuscript, the Holy Family's pursuers are, significantly, Jews rather than (gentile) Romans, as one might expect.[88] Thus, all these children could be seen as innocent victims of Jewish malice: the infant Jesus, the multitudinous murdered babies age two and under, and the boy martyrs of later centuries.[89] The child Jesus hidden in the Eucharist—occasionally thought to be stabbed, placed in boiling water, or otherwise harmed by Jews—could also be included in this group of innocent children subjected to violent cruelty.[90] Christian writers and artists presumably produced much pathos and undoubtedly also feelings of hostility in their audiences by employing the trope of an innocent child cruelly murdered or tortured by Jews.

By mentioning the possibility of child murder, Aquinas seems to endow the *Infantia salvatoris* with unpleasant connotations; his hypothesis suggests that, if the apocryphal text's contents were true, than Christ would have met with bitter antagonism from his tender years, even if he had not been killed early on. Although it is extremely doubtful that Aquinas himself believed in rumors of ritual murder, considering, among other things, that certain aspects of the legend blatantly contradicted Judaism and that the accusation was illogical in other ways as well, not to mention bigoted,[91] the fact that Aquinas, in his arguments against the *Infantia salvatoris* conjures up images of envious and violent Jewish neighbors of Christ implies that he thought such an idea would have resonated with his readers and Christians more broadly. Aquinas elsewhere emphasizes the fittingness of Christ's dying as an adult, a point that reinforces his remarks elsewhere about the inappropriateness of Jesus being killed as a child. He apparently holds that the sacrifice of an adult is of much greater value than that of a child, since, in his view as well as that of many of his contemporaries, a person enjoys a greater fullness of humanity in (the prime years of ) adulthood (or "juventus") than in childhood.[92] The idea of the crucifixion of the Christ Child is thus both unbiblical and inappropriate.

In reference to Aquinas's hypothesis regarding a premature death for Christ, it is worth noting that he explicitly associates the Christ Child with the Passion in a different text: his *Commentary on the Epistle to the Hebrews*. In chapter 10 of the New Testament text, where the author compares the multiple sacrifices of animals of old with the sacrifice of Christ himself, there occurs a citation of Psalm 39:7–8, which Christian exegetes regarded as a prophetic statement of Christ: "Sacrifice and oblation thou wouldst not: but a body thou hast fitted to me: Holocausts for sin did not please thee. Then I said (*tunc dixi*): Behold I come (*ecce venio*): in the head of the book it is written of me: that I should do thy will, O God." In commenting on this passage, Aquinas, referring to the Gloss to the Vulgate Bible, provides a meticulous explanation as if in the voice of Christ: " 'Then' [*tunc*], namely, when Thou had fitted a body for Me in the conception, 'said I: Behold I come' [*Ecce venio*], that is, I propose to come to the Passion. I Jn. 5:6: *This is He that came by water and blood, Jesus Christ.* Or better, this refers to His coming into the world thus: 'Then,' namely, when the holocausts did not please Thee, 'said I: Behold I come' through the Incarnation. Jn. 16:28: *I came forth from the Father, and am come into the world* to offer Myself for the Passion."[93] The crucial idea here is that Christ became incarnate to offer himself as a sacrifice at the Passion. Aquinas here implies that Jesus himself was aware of his end when he came to earth and that as an infant he was already thinking of his death, yet such an idea was not (what we might at first consider) a morbid peculiarity of Aquinas. The Dominican theologian and exegete was, in fact, one of many Christians in the later Middle Ages who associated the Christ Child with death in some way.

To return to Aquinas's reply to the objection mentioned above (q. 36, a. 4, obj. 3) that Jesus worked miracles as a child: besides speculating that the boy Jesus would have been murdered, he argues that another major problem would have arisen if the Christ Child had worked wonders. Jesus would have caused those around him not only to desire his death but also to conclude that his humanity was a mere illusion. In putting forth this hypothesis, Aquinas does not make explicit his train of thought, but he may be imagining that the attention of Jesus' contemporaries would have been so riveted on the manifestations of the Boy's divine power that they would have failed to take note of the gradual human development that he was undergoing, or even suspected that he was a god or a demon who deceptively assumed the appearance of a human being and/or worked wonders through demonic powers. Centuries earlier, Gregory the Great had made it clear that miracles could be worked by evil agents as well as by saints; the principle that miracles are ambiguous, that is, not irrefutable proofs of sanctity, could very well have been considered applicable here.[94]

Although the Latin translation of Chrysostom's homily on the Gospel of John that Aquinas quotes is very close to the original Greek, there is a slight divergence between the two texts when it comes to the idea that the Christ Child would have been associated with an illusion. Aquinas's "Existimassent enim phantasma esse incarnationem" clearly harks back to Augustine's concern, mentioned earlier, that the *veritas humanitatis* of Christ would have been endangered if he, as a boy, had not followed the ordinary course of the human life cycle (by developing gradually) and engaged in the everyday human activities of eating and sleeping.[95] While Chrysostom, who was Augustine's contemporary, might have had this idea in mind, his phrasing is slightly vague: "He [Jesus] did not begin his miracles at once from his earliest years, since people would have thought the phenomenon an illusion [μορφωσέων]."[96] In the same homily, we find a similar statement a few lines later: if the boy Jesus had been a wonder-worker and been "hurried . . . to the cross," due to the Jews' malice, then "the actual details of the Redemption would not have been believed [καὶ αὐτὰ τὰ τῆς οἰκονομίας ἠπιστήθη πράγματα]."[97] While "the phenomenon," in the first passage, may refer to God's embodiment in a child, it seems more directly to signify the Christ Child's hypothetical miracle working. The implication seems to be that the people around the boy Jesus would have thought that he was performing feats of magic. This idea might have occurred to Chrysostom because, according to Scripture, a similar accusation was leveled against the adult Christ: he was thought by some of his contemporaries to have worked miracles by the power of Beelzebub (Matt. 12:24; Mk. 3:22; Lk. 11:15). Chrysostom makes explicit the connection between the latter view of Jesus as a sort of magician and his hypothesis regarding the likely misinterpretation of a wonder-working Christ Child: "If, when he had reached manhood, many actually did have this suspicion, they would have had it much the more if he had worked wonders when still only a lad."[98] To the contrary, Chrysostom asserts that the only wonderful thing that the boy Jesus did was to astound the Jewish masters in the Temple at the age of twelve.[99] In contrast to the anonymous author of the *Infancy Gospel of Thomas*, who seems to have used the Lucan episode as a basis for reconstructing the bulk of Christ's wonder-filled childhood, Chrysostom and others who shared his train of thought regard the scriptural incident as completely atypical.

Whereas Aquinas uses the noun *phantasma* in ST 3, q. 36, a. 4, ad 3 to speak of the likely response of the Holy Family's neighbors to a wonder-working Christ Child (*Existimassent enim phantasma esse incarnationem*), he uses the adjective *phantasticus*, though in a semantically similar way, in q. 39, a. 3, in which he asks whether Christ was baptized at a fitting time.[100] In one of the objections Aquinas considers (obj. 2), it is taken as a given that Christ was baptized before teaching or working miracles. The claim is then made that "it would have been more profitable to the world if he had taught for a longer time, beginning at the age of twenty, or even before," which implies that, hypothetically, Christ should have been baptized a lot earlier than age thirty. Such an idea about the benefit of Christ teaching for a longer time echoes the objection Aquinas raised earlier (q. 36, a. 4, obj. 2) that it would have been ineffectual for Christ to hide his wisdom during his early life. His response here (q. 39, a. 3, ad. 2) reemphasizes that certain activities should be done at their proper time, and that human beings benefit from Christ's self-restraint (a principle that presumably applies to Christ's contemporaries as well as to his followers who lived at later times):

> The profit which accrues to men from Christ is chiefly through
> faith and humility: to both of which he conduced by beginning to
> teach not in his boyhood or youth (*in pueritia vel adolescentia*), but
> at the *perfect age* (*in perfecta aetate*). To faith, because in this manner
> his human nature is shown to be real (*ostenditur in eo vera humanitas*),
> by its making bodily progress with the advance of time; and lest
> this progress should be deemed imaginary (*phantasticus*), he did
> not wish to show his wisdom and power before his body had
> reached the *perfect age* (*ante perfectam aetatem corporis*): to humility,
> lest anyone should presume to govern or teach others before
> attaining to *perfect age*.[101]

Although Aquinas does not explicitly mention the *Infantia salvatoris* in this passage, it is extremely likely that he was thinking of this text here, given that he knew about it and that it focuses on Christ's unabashed display of wisdom and power during his childhood. In the passage quoted above, Aquinas gives us a better sense of the confusion that, he thinks, would have been created if Jesus had allowed himself to appear singular: those who saw Christ as he was growing up would have denied the evidence of their senses, which indicated that he was developing like other children, and concluded erroneously that what they saw was a mere illusion, that is, that the young Jesus was not a real human being. After all, not only would Christ's miracle working have caused others to have a false view of him as not truly human, but it would also have set a bad example (of precociousness) for youths, for centuries to come. Wishing to imitate Jesus' extraordinary behavior, youths might have presumptuously attempted to do and say things that were improper for someone their age. Elsewhere Aquinas concedes that, through the influx of grace (that is, the strength conferred by the Holy Spirit), there might be a large disjunction between a person's bodily and spiritual age, as in the case of the child martyrs.[102] In support he cites Wisdom 4:8: "For venerable old age is not that of long time. . . . And a spotless life is old age." Yet despite Aquinas's belief in the possibility of Christians transcending their age, namely, by being more mature in spirit than they are in their bodies, he clearly dislikes the view of Jesus' not having acted in conformity with his bodily age.

Whereas Aquinas takes it as a given that the Christ Child was humble and discreet (cf. Matt. 11:29),[103] the authors of the apocryphal legends about his childhood usually do not depict him in that way. In these texts, Jesus repeatedly acts like a know-it-all child when placed under the tutelage of his teachers, for example. Rather than behave in a docile way toward these figures of authority, Jesus humiliates them, by proving that their wisdom is superficial and their sense of self-esteem inflated. In the Middle English redactions of these legends, the Christ Child attempts to instruct his Jewish teachers about the Trinity, whereas in the school scenes found in the *Infancy Gospel of Thomas* and in the expanded *Pseudo-Matthew* (which is based upon it) the Child simply shames his masters by displaying his esoteric knowledge, rather than forcefully attempting to proselytize them. In "A Disputison bitwene child Jhesu & Maistres of þe lawe of Jewus," a Middle English debate poem that clearly traces back to the *Infancy Gospel of Thomas*, we are informed at the outset of Jesus' goal in interacting with his learned elders: "gentyl Ihesu . . . þe ffalse ffei fonded to felle. / ffor wo ne wrake ne wolde he wonde / Of Trinite trewe to Iewes tell" (gentle Jesus sought to bring down the false faith; neither for difficulty nor pain would he hold back to tell the Jews of the true Trinity).[104] One of the teachers objects to the Child's having seated himself on the elevated chair, the customary position of authority and center of attention within a scholastic setting: "Þou sittest stalled in vre stage" (you sit installed upon our raised platform).[105] A lesson about the Trinity, delivered by a young boy speaking from such a place of honor and authority—all before the beginning of Christ's public ministry, as conventionally understood—would surely have attracted people's attention.[106] Significantly, late medieval depictions of the Finding of the Child Jesus in the Temple (as in a Latin gospel harmony made around 1400, Milan, Ambrosiana Library, SP II 64 [*olim* L. 58 Sup], fol. 18v; fig. 14) tend to elevate the Child to the position of a teacher, by having him sit upon a master's *cathedra*. Here, as elsewhere, the boy Jesus is shown to gesture like a scholastic disputant, with his hand raised in an authoritative way as he speaks to the learned Jewish scholars seated beneath him at a long table on which books are strewn in a disorderly fashion.[107] Perhaps to counteract contemporary portrayals of Jesus' interaction with the doctors as antagonistic, the fourteenth-century Carthusian Ludoph of Saxony diffuses the potential emotional contentiousness of this biblical scene from Luke by advising his reader to visualize the Christ Child "with a peaceful, intelligent, and reverent face . . . how he questioned and heard them, as if ignorant, which he did out of humility and also so that they would not be ashamed on account of his wonderful responses."[108]

Ludolph, Aquinas, and other clerics clearly hold that it was more fitting for the God-man—when he was a baby, a boy, and an adolescent—to have behaved as (properly socialized) human beings ordinarily do at those particular stages of life than to have made himself appear singular, as were many of the child saints who lived and were venerated in the centuries after Christ. Even in the case of the one scriptural passage (Lk. 2:46–49) that arguably portrays Jesus as a *puer-senex*, that is, as a preternaturally mature child (a trope mentioned in Chapter 2), biblical commentators tended to downplay the Boy's precociousness, which the apocryphal authors, in contrast, greatly exaggerated. Bede, for example, asserts that "the fact that at twelve years old [Jesus] sat in the Temple in the midst of the teachers, listening to them and asking them questions, is an indication of his human humility, and moreover it is also an extraordinary example of humility for us to learn."[109] Jerome, however, suggests that the boy Jesus engaged in teaching in a discreet manner: when "the Savior had completed twelve years, and questioned the elders in the Temple about points of the law, he taught while he wisely questioned."[110] According to this interpretation, Jesus cleverly exercised pedagogical agency without violating decorum.

Aquinas implicitly rejects the idea of Jesus as a *puer-senex*, especially one whose personality is so intense that he is unable to live beyond boyhood. Children with very strong and sometimes jarring personalities are often found

Figure 14. The Christ Child disputing with the doctors in the Temple. Milan, Biblioteca Ambrosiana, SP II 64, fol. 18v (c. 1400). By permission of the Veneranda Biblioteca Ambrosiana, Milano/De Agostini Picture Library.

in medieval saints' vitae, which tend to portray children and even infants behaving in preternaturally mature ways. One of the most striking examples is baby Rumwold, who demanded baptism, preached a sermon, and then died, all within three days of his birth.[111] Although Jesus might have similarly preached in his infancy, if he wanted to, many medieval Christians shied away from such an idea. As Augustine's aforementioned comments about the infant Jesus suggest, some religious writers seem to have imagined Jesus ambiguously as both an ordinary boy and an extraordinary child. On the one hand, his transcendence of the human life cycle (particularly the embarrassing aspects of child development) might have seemed appropriate on account of his divinity. On the other hand, his humanity necessitated his adherence to natural law and also to social custom. Tension between these two positions—transcendence versus conformity—can be detected in the twelfth-century abbess and physician Hildegard of Bingen. In a medical treatise, Hildegard claims that Jesus did not cry or babble as normal children do when they begin to talk, but spoke fluently at once, yet in a childlike way (*pueriliter*), probably so as not to call attention to himself.[112] In contrast, a number of Franciscan authors took delight in attributing baby talk to Jesus, apparently not at all worried about the possibility that this presumed behavior might detract from the God-man's dignity (which seems to have been of less interest to the Franciscans than was God's amazing condescension).[113] Christian Gnilka gets at the heart of the Christological issue dealt with by Hildegard, Augustine, and many other Christian thinkers when he states that "the childhood of the Redeemer was not allowed to be too far elevated into the realm of the miraculous, since the natural childhood and, more generally, the natural stages in Christ's life guaranteed his true humanity."[114] The main explanation, then, for the difference between the portrayals of children who became saints and the Christ Child is that while Jesus had to demonstrate his humanity, this was not the case with saintly children. Hagiographers mention the uncanniness of such children, which is made possible by grace, as proof that certain holy people were chosen by God from the very beginning of their life.[115] No such proof was needed for Christ—in fact, because of his special mission and his lurking enemy (the devil), he had to keep a low profile during his domestic life at Nazareth.

It is worth considering more closely the phrase "perfect age" that Aquinas uses when speaking about the age of Christ at his baptism (ST, 3, q. 39, a. 3). In medieval thought, the highpoint of Christ's life, inaugurated by his baptism, seems to have spanned about three years (from thirty to thirty-three). With the model of Christ's life in mind, theologians who speculated on the age of humans after their resurrection generally agreed that a person would be as old as Christ was when he died, which was regarded as "the perfect age."[116] The culmination of Christ's life during the few years of his public ministry also seems to have been designated as such. In the question he raises about the timing of Christ's baptism, Aquinas explicitly refers to age thirty as the "perfect age" (cf. Eph. 4:13),[117] a number based on Luke's comment (3:23) that Jesus was approximately that age at his baptism. In the body of his argument, Aquinas points out the symbolic value of this number: three represents the Trinity, ten the Decalogue. While the age at which Christ was baptized as an adult would not have set a standard for medieval Christians in the later Middle Ages concerning the age at which they themselves were baptized (considering that infant baptism was then the norm), the age at which Jesus began to teach and assume authority had practical bearing on the lives of males who aspired to a career within the Church. Medieval canon law stipulated that males were not to be admitted to the priesthood or episcopate until the age of thirty, "because the Lord himself," in the words of the influential twelfth-century theologian Peter Lombard, "was thirty when he was baptized, and so he began to teach."[118]

In the body of q. 39, a. 3, Aquinas explains the relationship between Jesus' baptism and his activities of preaching and teaching: "Christ was baptized as though for the reason that He was about . . . to begin to teach and preach: for which purpose perfect age is required." David and Ezekiel from the Old Testament are cited as examples of men who likewise undertook their mission at age thirty (2 Kgs. 5:4; Ezek. 1:1). Yet what are we to make of Daniel, in whom divine wisdom was already manifested in his boyhood (Dan. 13:45)? In his reply to the third objection, Aquinas argues that although it was acceptable for Daniel to have behaved as a *puer-senex*, it was not fitting for Christ to have begun teaching before the perfect age since he had to serve as an example for ordinary children. As to the few odd children mentioned in Scripture, it was "by special dispensation" that some holy boys were commissioned "to exercise the functions of governing or teaching." In other words, Aquinas insists that the Christ Child did not follow the pattern of the *puer-senex* to which so many saints who were venerated in the Middle Ages adhered. He reiterates the view of Gregory the Great, who likewise considered the examples of precocious boys in the Bible, seeing Ezekiel, in particular, as a prefigurement of Christ and a model for clerics: the fact that Ezekiel received the spirit of prophecy at age thirty indicates "that the faculty of preaching—because it necessitates the exercise of reason—is not granted except in the perfect age. . . . In order that men should not dare to preach while their age is weak, he who, in his divinity, always teaches the angels in heaven deigned in his twelfth year to ask questions of men on earth."[119] Elsewhere, Gregory explains that youths ought to bide their time before preaching rather than attempt to do so too soon. Perhaps recalling the unfortunate fate of the mythical Icarus, he asserts that youths "should be admonished to bear in mind that when fledglings attempt to fly upwards before their wings are fully developed, they fall down from where they tried to soar."[120] The clear implication is that children and youths ought to respect the slow developmental processes of nature.

The same general idea that there is a proper time within the life cycle for certain activities undergirds Aquinas's handling of the question of whether Christ (literally) began to work miracles at the wedding feast at Cana when he miraculously changed water into wine (ST, 3, q. 43, a. 3). As before, Aquinas is more concerned with the fittingness of Christ's having done certain deeds at a certain time than with establishing a historical fact. In the body of his argument Aquinas sets forth the relationship between Jesus' miracle-working and teaching activities: the former was ordered to the latter and was meant to confirm it. Such a subordination of wonder to teaching and evangelizing, coming from a member of the Order of Preachers, is not surprising, considering that the Dominicans valued education highly. Having already established the fittingness of Christ's baptism at age thirty (that is, before he began to teach), Aquinas easily dismisses the view that Christ began to work miracles before his thirties. In the body, Aquinas explains that, in the life of Christ, miracles served to confirm his teaching and manifest his divinity. He immediately proceeds to a reiteration of Chrysostom's view, found in homily 21, that "it was fitting that he should not begin to work wonders from his early years (*in prima aetate*): for men would have deemed the Incarnation to be imaginary (*phantasma*, literally, a "phantasm") and would have crucified him before the opportune time."[121] The implication is that Christ's childhood was not the proper time for him to manifest his divinity; this could only have been harmful to other people. It behooved him to wait until he reached the "perfect age." As Aquinas did previously, here, in his reply to objection two, he speculates that doubts would have arisen concerning Christ's Incarnation if he had worked miracles as a boy, even though he could have hypothetically done so: Jesus chose not to do this, so "as not to prejudice our belief in the reality of his flesh (*ut fidei de veritate carnis eius praeiudicium non fieret*)."[122]

The phrase "veritas carnis eius" can be seen as a variation on Augustine's *veritas humanitatis*. As Caroline Walker Bynum has demonstrated, particularly with regard to feminine spirituality in the later Middle Ages, Christ's physicality was equated with his humanity.[123] To be human, Christ had to be a child in a truly physical way. Miracle working during his boyhood would have been prejudicial to belief in Jesus' physical reality.

In the same question from the *Summa theologiae* about the miracle worked at Cana (q. 43, a. 3), Chrysostom is cited again, in the reply to the first objection, in which Aquinas explicitly mentions the *Infantia salvatoris*'s depiction of the boy Jesus as a miracle-worker. Although the passage from Chrysostom that Aquinas quoted in the body of this question and in q. 36, a. 4, ad 3 comes from homily 21, here Aquinas quotes a statement that Chrysostom makes in homily 17. In this homily, the Greek theologian explicitly says, as he only implies in the other homily, that "those miracles which some ascribe to Christ's childhood are false, and merely the products of the imagination of those who bring them to our attention [ψευδῆ καὶ πλάσματά τινων ἐπεισαγόντων ἐστίν]."[124] Since the miracles, as purely imaginary events, never happened, the legends about them are simply fiction. Aquinas enunciates this idea when he remarks, following Chrysostom, that the fact that John the Baptist had to manifest Christ to the Israelites means that "the wonders (*signa*) which some pretend (*quidam dicunt*) to have been worked by Christ in his childhood (*pueritia*) are untrue and fictitious (*mendacia et fictiones sunt*, lit., "are lies and fictions")."[125] Aquinas had not earlier explicitly pronounced on the truth value of the *Infantia salvatoris*'s contents, as he does here.[126]

Aquinas had earlier spoken disapprovingly of the *Infantia salvatoris*, namely in his *Commentary on the Gospel of John*,[127] when he turned his attention to the Evangelist's remark that Jesus worked his first miracle at the wedding feast at Cana. It is worth looking carefully at the succinct argument he offers, since it provides a useful summary of what Aquinas says in the *Summa*: the "falsity" (*falsitas*) of the apocryphal text is evident from its patent contradiction of Scripture. To discount the *Infantia salvatoris* further, Aquinas claims that the childhood miracles would have been injurious to people's belief in Christ's humanity: "he did not work miracles [during his childhood] in order that the mystery of his circumcision and Incarnation not be thought a figment of the imagination (*phantasma*), if he had not conducted himself in that age like other children."[128] Aquinas seems to assume that it would have been extremely difficult, if not impossible, for a miracle-working Christ Child to have been thought of as human. Late medieval English redactions of the apocrypha seem to challenge this assumption: in these accounts, the Christ Child's immaturity, often revealed by the types of miracles he works, confuses the Jewish leaders. After discounting the possibility that Jesus is the Messiah, they wonder whether he is the son of a devil or just a remarkably gifted yet very troublesome boy.[129] Regarding the appropriateness of the Christ Child acting like a wonderworker and the issue of how a portrayal of him might compare to that of saintly children, it is worth noting that, of all the pious children included in the *Legenda aurea*, only one of them is said to have worked a miracle in his boyhood: the young Benedict, who miraculously fixes a jar that his nurse had accidentally broken.[130] The *Legenda aurea* often mentions infants who pronounce wonderful words of wisdom and sometimes children who are strangely ascetic, yet it rarely portrays a child working a miracle that involves a change in something or someone contrary to nature. Besides the incident in which the young Benedict miraculously reunited the shards of a vessel, the *Legenda aurea* mentions only a few miracles brought about by the Christ Child (for the most part, those pertaining to the Flight into Egypt).[131]

In addition to calling attention to the importance of Christ's having conducted himself as an ordinary, respectful child, Aquinas's comments on Jesus' putative childhood miracles in the *Commentary on John* underscore the theological significance of the Circumcision. Aquinas was not the only one to remark that the shedding of Christ's blood for the first time at the Circumcision was proof that he had a real human body. According to his fellow Dominican Jacobus de Voragine, one of the reasons for Christ's circumcision was "to show that he had assumed a real human body, because he knew that there would be those who would say his body was not real but a phantasm (*dicerent ipsum non corpus uerum, sed fantasticum assumpsisse*)." That Jacobus regards the shedding of the baby Jesus' blood in a polemical light is clear from his comment: "to refute their [i.e., heretics'] errors, he chose to be circumcised and to shed blood, because no phantasm (*corpus fantasticum*) can bleed."[132] This rather curious statement is based upon the intrinsic vulnerability of the human body. Jacobus's remark not only enunciates a truism about human beings, namely, that they bleed; it also highlights a Christological problem of his own day: the heresy of the Cathars, who denied Christ's physicality.

Aquinas used the adjective "phantasticus" in his earlier *Compendium theologiae*,[133] when offering an interpretation of Luke's comment (2:52) that "Jesus advanced in wisdom, and age, and grace with God and men," a verse that is known to have "tantalized theologians over the ages."[134] Aquinas explains that Christ increased in "experimental knowledge" (that is, knowledge of sensible things gained through experience), but not in wisdom per se: "[Christ] was able to grow only in his experiential knowledge, as Lk. 2:52 says. . . . (But one can also understand this in another way, to affirm Christ's progress in wisdom because wisdom increased in others, namely, those whom his wisdom was progressively instructing, not because he himself is wiser.) And this was done designedly, to show that he was like other human beings, lest the mystery of the Incarnation would seem a fiction (*phantasticum*, lit., "phantastical") were he to have shown perfect wisdom in boyhood."[135] Aquinas's use of the adjective "phantasticus" in this context, as well as in the section of the *Tertia pars* and in his *Commentary on John* discussed above, demonstrates his persistent concern about people denying Christ's physicality. Bede had earlier put forth the idea that Christ only appeared to grow in wisdom, likewise noting how this progress indicated "his true humanity (*naturam uerae humanitatis*)," but without drawing specific attention to the tangibility of Jesus' body.[136]

The ambiguous depiction of the boy Jesus (as both meek and assertive, listening and speaking, wise yet growing in wisdom) in Luke 2:41–52 and the exegesis it spawned left medieval artists and writers without a definitive answer as to whether it was appropriate to portray the boy Jesus receiving instruction, and without clues as to how such an educational scene could be rendered. To the Dominican Antoninus, archbishop of Florence in the fifteenth century, the common theological view that Christ knew all things from the first moment of his conception implied that artistic representations of the Christ Child learning how to read and write like other children were inappropriate.[137] In his own *Summa theologica*, Antoninus expresses disapproval of artists who "paint the infant Jesus with a hornbook,"[138] thus contradicting the supposed fact that "he learned nothing from a human being."[139] In the apocryphal legends, Jesus is placed under the tutelage of a teacher on more than one occasion yet he is never said to have gained book knowledge from such encounters. The legends could thus be considered theologically orthodox, even though the way in which they dramatize acceptable Christological viewpoints may be jarring. The ability of late medieval educated Christians to draw fine distinctions between that which seems orthodox and that which seems questionable in terms of conventional Christology can be seen in an illustrated Latin gospel harmony dated around 1400, which incorporates material from the *Infantia salvatoris*. Here, Jesus, who is depicted as being taken to school by Joseph, holds a hornbook, but he is not actually shown to use it pedagogically.[140] He carries it, one might say, to fulfill his role as a "schoolboy with his satchel / . . . creeping like snail / Unwillingly to school."[141]

In a fifteenth-century Italian painting by the Master of Borsigliana, Jesus as a toddler sits upon his mother's lap; he looks down upon a hornbook, while his mother watches him.[142] Is Mary trying to teach Jesus how to read? And if so, is Jesus simply going along with this lesson but not really getting anything out of it? Or is the little Jesus perhaps just amusing himself with an object typically handled by a child? The supposition of Aquinas and other religious writers that the Christ Child progressively manifested to others the wisdom that he already had is intriguing; it suggests that Christ was pretending to be ignorant and was thus somewhat deceptive or at least secretive about his full identity.

## "Phantasms" in Medieval Culture

What might Aquinas have had in mind when he uses the words "phantasm" (*phantasma*), "fantasy" (*phantasia*) and "fantastic" or "phantastical" (*phantasticus*) when speaking of the child Jesus? In the aforesaid passage on the Circumcision from the *Legenda aurea*, which emphasizes the reality of Christ's body and blood, Jacobus de Voragine seems to be referring to a ghost when he expresses his worry about Jesus being misperceived as a "phantasm." In using similar language, Aquinas may also be thinking of a being that seems to have a body but does not actually have one.

While Aquinas, in a number of the passages cited above (some of which reiterate Chrysostom), uses the related words "fantastic" (or "phantastical"), "phantasm," or "fantasy" to refer to different but related phenomena, the notion of the human body as a "phantasm" or mere apparition is one of the most basic senses of this word. Let us briefly consider an episode from the canonical gospels (specifically, from the Vulgate version): two of the Evangelists use the word "phantasm" when speaking of the disciples' response to the sight of Jesus approaching them by walking upon the sea. According to Mark (6:49), they "thought it was an apparition (*putaverunt fantasma esse*), and they cried out." Matthew (14:26) adds that they "cried out for fear."[143] The phrasing of Mark in particular seems to be echoed in Aquinas's expression of the hypothetical response he imagines might arise in those who perceived a wonder-working Christ Child. Most bluntly, they might very well have thought that the boy Jesus was a ghost. While this supposition is not expressed in the remarkable chapter in Caxton's *Infantia salvatoris* that briefly mentions that the boy Jesus walked on water, as does the Holkham Bible, which actually depicts Jesus doing so (fig. 18, bottom register),[144] it is certainly significant that both of these late medieval sources include this odd detail (unusual even for the apocryphal narratives circulating in the West) alongside other accounts of the Christ Child's miracles.

But the situation is more complicated when it concerns what we might call "fantastic(al) children." Aquinas, in my view, was probably referring to popular Christian folklore about supernatural beings, as well as the theological subscience of demonology—areas of knowledge and belief that overlap—when he speculates that the Christ Child might have been perceived as a phantom. My suggestion will seem more plausible if we look more closely at the roughly contemporary meanings of the medieval Latin words he employs.

Broadly speaking, *phantasia*, *phantasma*, and *phantasticus* were often used to speak of visual and moral deception wrought by demons. The gossipy clerk Walter Map (d. 1209–10), who includes many stories about supernatural beings in his *De nugis curialium*, explains that the word *fantasma* "is derived from *fantasia*" and signifies "a passing apparition, for the appearances which occasionally devils make to some by their own power (first receiving leave of God), pass by with or without doing harm." In contrast, instances of *fantasia* "endure and [sometimes] propagate themselves in good succession," as is demonstrated by Map's story about a dead woman, who was snatched from a (fairy) dance by her late husband and then produced offspring with him.[145] Elsewhere, Map tells about Gerbert of Burgundy, whose fairy lover lavished much wealth upon him. When he first saw her in a forest, he "was quietly withdrawing with intent to flee, fearing a phantom (*fantasma*) or delusion,"[146] yet he ends up having a physical relationship with her that lasts for many years. Although in the first passage Map distinguishes between *fantasia* and *fantasma*, these words, when not employed in a technical, epistemological way, tended to be used by medieval writers interchangeably to refer to apparitions and phantoms or, more abstractly, to illusions and deception.[147] Placing the Anglo-Saxon hermit Guthlac in the tradition of the desert father Anthony of Egypt, a saint famously subjected to demonic apparitions, his biographer Felix comments on the place to which Guthlac retreated: Croyland, "where no one beforehand dared to inhabit on account of the terrible apparitions (*fantasiae*) of the demons who dwelt there."[148] The Franciscan author of the fourteenth-century preacher's handbook *Fasciculus morum* says that the "elves" (he switches from Latin to the vernacular here), which some "superstitious wretches" claim to see, are "nothing but phantoms (*fantasmata*) shown them by a mischievous spirit." Unlike Map, who seems to encourage his audience to believe in fairies and similar otherworldly beings, the anonymous friar says that "when the devil has subdued someone's soul into believing these things, he transforms himself, now into an angel, now into a man or a woman, now into other creatures. . . . By all of these he deludes in many ways the wretch whom he has captivated through his credulity."[149] The Annals of Dunstable similarly speak of demonic deception in a note for the year 1289, which mentions a "certain child who did not eat for half a year," which, it was later realized, existed "through the deception (*per fantasma*) of the demonic incubi."[150]

The strange behavior of this child who does not eat recalls the quirky creatures known as changelings: infant-like beings believed to be substituted by demons or fairies for real human babies.[151] What is possibly the first reference in the West to this kind of supernatural creature is the strange little visitor mentioned in the *Chronicon anglicum* of Ralph of Coggeshall (1228): "in the reign of King Richard, a certain fantastic spirit (*fantasticus spiritus*) appeared many times and for much time, speaking with the family members of the aforesaid knight, having imitated in sound the voice of a one-year-old infant; and it called itself Malekin."[152] Other early references to changelings are found in the writings of the theologian and Bishop of Paris William of Auvergne (d. 1249); the cleric Jacques de Vitry (d. 1240); and the Dominican preacher Étienne de Bourbon (d. 1262).[153] So, discussions about changelings, beings that merely looked like human children, were definitely taking place around the time when Aquinas commented on the apocryphal Christ Child. While changelings were unsettling, they were also something that Christians could joke about in the later Middle Ages. In the "Second Shepherds' Play," the most famous of the late medieval Towneley Plays, a sheep which is stolen from some shepherds is disguised as a newborn human baby. When one of the shepherds visiting the thief's home realizes that this baby has horns, the wily wife of the thief quickly accounts for its demonic looks by claiming with alarm that her infant must have been stolen by an elf and a changeling put in its place.[154]

While I do not think that Aquinas was going so far as to suggest that Christ's contemporaries would have thought that he was a changeling if he had worked miracles when he was still a child, I suspect he was aware of people's general tendency—in centuries past and in his own time—to associate children who behaved differently or looked unusual with demonic forces. Medieval writers do not seem to explain where changelings come from, but they have a good deal to say about the offspring of incubi and the human women they attack. Matthew Paris recounts that in the year 1249, "a certain creature, generated, as they say, by a nightmare demon," in the county of Hereford, "had all its teeth in less than half a year and rose to the height of a youth of about seventeen years. After its mother gave birth, she was overcome with exhaustion, at once withered away, and wretchedly died."[155]

By far the most renowned case of a child engendered by an incubus is Merlin. This well-known child figure can be seen as an analogue of the preternatural Christ Child of the apocrypha, one that, given the pervasiveness of Arthurian lore, both the learned and the unlearned might have recalled when hearing about Jesus' wonderful childhood.[156] The *Historia regum Britanniae* of Geoffrey of Monmouth (d. 1155) is the first text to claim that Merlin was the son of a demon. When the British ruler Vortigern consults his magicians about how to prevent the tower that he is trying to build from being swallowed up by the earth, they tell him to search for "a young man who had no father," who is to be killed and whose blood is to be sprinkled on the mortar and stones, which will ensure a strong foundation for the desired stucture. Vortigern's messengers soon stumble upon some youths engaged in play, who begin to fight with each other. One of them taunts the other, named Merlin, for not having a father. Thinking they have found a fatherless lad, the messengers send Merlin and his mother, a nun of noble lineage, to Vortigern. When the woman is questioned about Merlin's father, she reveals that "someone resembling a handsome young man (*quidam in specie pulcherrimi iuuenis*) used to appear to me very often, holding me tight in his arms and kissing me." He visited her many times and "often made love to me in the form of a man (*in specie hominis*), leaving me with a child in my womb." While the mysterious male visitor, from the way Merlin's mother describes him, seems as if he were tangible, he is technically "in specie hominis," which may imply that he was a demonic phantom or incubus who merely looked like a man. Amazed at this story, Vortigern asks a learned man named Maugantius if this sort of thing is possible. The sage, citing the authority of a certain Apuleius, replies that demons called incubi, which live between the moon and the earth, can "take on human form at will and sleep with women."[157]

In this last remark Geoffrey is probably referring to St. Augustine of Hippo, rather than Apuleius, since the famous and influential Church Father mentions incubi in the *De civitate Dei*, when discussing the possibility of angels having carnal relations with human beings. The topic arises from his reflection upon Genesis 6:2–4, which speaks of the "sons of God" mating with the "daughters of men."[158] According to Augustine, Scripture reliably teaches that angels appeared to humans in bodies and could be both seen and touched by them. He buttresses this view by referring to popular opinion: "Besides this, it is widely reported that Silvani and Pans, commonly called *incubi*, have often behaved improperly towards women, lusting after them and achieving intercourse with them. These reports are confirmed by many people . . . whose reliability there is no occasion to doubt. Then there is the story that certain demons, whom the Gauls called Dusii, constantly and successfully attempted this indecency. This is asserted by so many witnesses of such a character that it would seem an impertinence to deny it."[159]Augustine refrains from discussing how "some spirits with bodies of air" can mate with women, yet his comment suggests that he thinks that this is actually possible.

A couple of centuries later, Isidore of Seville (d. 633) echoes Augustine when speaking of the gods of the heathens in his famous encyclopedia. Right before he gives the etymology of the word "incubi," Isidore mentions similar beings (i.e., ghosts and witches), and then continues: " 'Hairy ones' (*Pilosus*, i.e., a satyr) are called *Panitae* in Greek, and 'incubuses' (*incubus*) in Latin, or Inui, from copulating (*inire*) indiscriminately with animals. Hence also *incubi* are so called from 'lying upon' . . . that is violating, for often they are shameless with women."[160] As is to be expected of a taxonomist, Isidore distinguishes among these various beings; medieval churchmen, though, tended to group them together somewhat indiscriminately, since they regarded all of these beings as the progeny of the devil. In the same work cited above, Augustine expresses concern over the malignant influence of demons that "have persuaded the greater part of" humans to accept them "as gods, by means of impressive but deceptive miracles (*mirabilibus et fallacibus signis*)." He emphasizes that they ought not be worshipped in any way.[161] When Aquinas, centuries later, suggests that a wonder-working Christ Child would have been perceived as a *phantasma*, he could have had in mind a number of forms that demons were alleged to assume in their attempts at deceiving human beings. His worry seems to be that Jesus would have been (and could still be) regarded as demonically deceptive, in the sense of only appearing to have the body of a human child, and also by working illusory magic tricks.

Whereas Augustine, when speaking of incubi, does not attempt to explain how demons, having airy bodies, can impregnate women, Aquinas and other theologians of the high and later medieval period, under the supposition that demons were, in themselves, pure spirits, offered a more concrete and rather mechanistic explanation of demonic insemination.[162] A common theory was that a demon, taking the form of a woman (that is, as a succubus), receives sperm from a human male, which is subsequently inserted into a human woman by a demon incubus. Taking a different, more abstract approach to uncanny experiences on one's bed, a number of medieval physicians and psychologists offered a physiological explanation for a person's feeling oppressed when sleeping. In the tradition of Macrobius, they spoke of an incubus as a nightmare (*phantasma*) occurring right before wakefulness, rather than as a demon rapist.[163] Despite this alternative view, the belief in incubi as demonic beings was widespread among both the learned and the uneducated in the later Middle Ages. As George L. Kittredge put it, "by the year 1100—to take a safe date—the Incubus Dogma was solidly established as an article of *learned* faith throughout Western Europe."[164] If Kittredge is right to draw our attention to the beginning of the twelfth century, then Geoffrey of Monmouth (whose *Historia* was completed in 1138 and later revised around 1147) was simply tapping into popular belief and making it famous by associating demonic insemination with Merlin, a central character in the Matter of Britain.

The story about Merlin, the preternaturally wise child engendered by an incubus, was further developed by Robert of Boron in his French prose *Merlin* (ca. 1200); he built upon Geoffrey of Monmouth's earlier, rather sparse account. In Geoffrey's narrative, after Merlin's mother explains how she became pregnant, the boy saves himself from destruction (recall that the blood of a fatherless boy was to be sprinkled on the mortar and stones) by informing Vortigern of the mysterious cause that prevents the tower's construction: two dragons sleeping within stones underneath a pool. When this strange phenomenon is shown to be true, "all the bystanders . . . were filled with wonder at his [the boy's] wisdom."[165] By displaying his esoteric knowledge, Geoffrey's young Merlin can be considered a sort of *puer-senex*. Robert of Boron has Merlin demonstrate his preternatural knowledge on more than one occasion, with emphasis placed on the infant's ability to speak and exculpate his mother from the charge of adultery in a legal trial. Shunned by her female attendants and awaiting a trial that may very well lead to her death, Merlin's mother laments her situation, but Merlin comforts her: "Mother, have no fear, for you will not die on my account." The woman is so surprised to hear her infant talk that she allows him to drop to the ground. Fortunately not seriously harmed by the fall, Merlin then boldly disagrees with the other women, who say that it would be better if he had never been born. They conclude: "This is no child but a demon!"[166] At the trial, Merlin clears his mother by revealing that the judge's mother became pregnant with him as a result of having relations with a priest, rather than with her husband. Merlin's mother, for her part, swears that she never "knew or saw the father" or "willingly gave myself in such a way as to be with child."[167] When questioned whether conception in that way is possible, the women say, "No, we have never heard tell of it, with the exception of the mother of Jesus Christ," a comment, we should note, which reveals that Robert of Boron definitely had the Christ Child in mind when writing about little Merlin.[168] Corroborating his mother's testimony, Merlin reveals that he is "the son of a devil who deceived my mother," and that his father "was one of a kind of demon . . . who inhabit the air."[169] Robert enhances the supernatural qualities of Merlin by setting him in the tradition of the Antichrist, whose birth, it was thought, would mirror Christ's from the Virgin Mary.[170] The boy reveals that his demonic father "bequeathed to me the power and intelligence to know everything that has been said and done," and also "knowledge of things to come."[171]

While both Merlin and the apocryphal Christ Child are preternaturally wise, they share other personality traits as well. The way that Merlin quickly becomes furious with his interlocutors reminds one of the interaction between the apocryphal boy Jesus and the Jewish elders, whom he quickly loses patience with and insults.[172] In addition, both boys laugh in circumstances that seem inappropriate and both seem disrespectful toward their elders.[173] An important difference between the two boys, though, is that while baby Merlin (who was very hairy and mature-looking) stood out as physically abnormal,[174] this is apparently not the case with the Christ Child, whose physical appearance (apart form his divine radiance) is almost never mentioned in the apocryphal narratives. In other texts, Jesus' beauty is an indication that he is no ordinary mortal.

Without doubt, the most fundamental parallel between the boys Merlin and Jesus is that they both have an unusual parentage. Although Robert of Boron might not have had any exposure to the Qur'an,[175] his description of how baby Merlin was supernaturally conceived and how he rescued his mother from the charge of adultery curiously resembles the holy book's treatment of the conception and birth of Jesus. The Islamic version of Jesus' origins was transmitted to the West at times by texts that described the geography of the East and also the people who lived there. The travel and ethnographic book attributed to Sir John Mandeville is a well-known example.[176] In Mandeville's account of Islamic beliefs we find a comment about how the Virgin Mary, before she had conceived Jesus, was on her guard because she had heard of the devious sorcerer who threatened virgins. Such a figure, while not rooted in the Qur'an itself, is analogous, albeit distantly, to the incubus father of Merlin: "Takina, that be [by] his enchauntementes cowde make him in lykness of an angel and wente often tymes and lay with maydenes. And therfore Marie [i.e., at the Annunciation] dredde lest it hadde ben Takina . . . and therfore sche coniured the angel that he scholde telle hire yif it were he or non."[177] While

Mandeville is fairly accurate (and impartial) in his summary of Islam, which occupies a chapter of his text, the evil pseudo-angel Takina, whom he mentions in this passage, derives from a misinterpretation of an Arabic word in the Qur'an transmitted to the West by the thirteenth-century Dominican William of Tripoli. In his account of the Muslim version of the Annunciation, William seems to have in mind a human rapist, who, by assuming the extraordinary beauty of an angel, resembles an incubus: "Takina," he says, "was a certain enchanter who suddenly approached virgins and, brilliant and beautiful as an angel, overcame them."[178] The fact that there were seductive and attractive male figures analogous to Takina in western European literary culture may help explain why this figure was of interest to Mandeville as well as other well-read Europeans; it also appealed to the writers of romance and other genres of fiction. To take an example: the "brilliant and beautiful" appearance that Takina assumes parallels the stunning beauty of the fairy-knight in the French lai *Tydorel,* who approaches a queen reclining in an orchard and sexually overwhelms her.[179] The child who results from this union is likewise extremely handsome yet unable to close his eyes in sleep—uncanny characteristics that inspire wonder in those who see him.[180]

In his chapter on so-called Saracen beliefs, which seeks to stress Islam's similarities with Christianity, Mandeville proceeds to recount what happened when Mary gave birth to Jesus under a palm tree. His summary seems fairly faithful to the Qur'anic text, and it is also reminiscent of the tales about baby Merlin mentioned above: "sche had gret schame that sche hadde a child, and she grette [wept] and seyde that sche wolde that sche hadde ben ded. And anon the child spak to hire and comforted hire and seyde, 'Moder, ne dysmaye the nought, for God hath hidd in the His preuytees [mysteries] for the saluacoun of the world.' And in othere many places seyth here [their] Alkaron [Qu'ran] that Ihesu Crist spak als sone as He was born."[181] The apocryphal *Arabic Infancy Gospel* similarly reports that the infant Jesus spoke to Mary when he was lying in his cradle, a detail that also arguably appears in the Qur'an.[182] Although the apocryphal *Arabic Infancy Gospel* has been dated to the eighth or ninth century, it may derive from a Syriac archetype of the fifth or sixth century.[183] In addition to ostensibly teaching that Jesus spoke in his infancy, the Qur'an recounts how those who doubted Mary's chastity were informed by the baby Jesus of his mission as a prophet; this can be seen as analogous to how baby Merlin explains his origins at the trial, thus freeing his mother from blame.[184]

While one can sense the logic behind the medieval association of Jesus with Merlin, the son of an incubus and a human mother, it is not so clear why the Christ Child, in one of the plays from the late medieval Chester Cycle, is called a "changeling,"[185] technically a pseudo-infant brought to humans by a supernatural being. In the play about the Magi, a paranoid Herod expresses his anger at the infant Jesus who, he is convinced, aims to be king of the Jews: "Alas, what presumption should move that pevish page or any elvish godlinge to take from me my crown?" Determined to cut down his opponent, Herod angrily swears by the false god he calls Muhammad that "that boye for all his greate outrage [presumption] shall die by my hand, that elfe and vile congion [changeling]."[186] In a similar way, in the York Cycle, the high priest Annas denounces Jesus as a "conjeon" who does daring deeds on the Sabbath.[187] The adult Christ is likewise called a "changeling" in John Capgrave's fifteenth-century Life of St. Catherine of Alexandria: the pagan emperor advises the convert Porphyry to "Leue þat crysten company, for sake þat elue / Ihesu of naȝareth."[188] In these cases, "elf" likely means "miscreant," a term of reproach like "conjon." But the literal sense of the term was probably also in the author's mind. Thus, when evil characters in the biblical plays call Jesus an "elf" or "conjon" to malign his character, they probably allude, at least obliquely, to Christ's undeniably unusual parentage.[189]

Another disparaging characterization of Jesus that medieval Christian writers occasionally mention is that of a magician. Earlier I noted that John Chrysostom briefly refers to the charge of magic when he said that Jesus "did not begin his miracles . . . from his earliest years, since people would have thought the phenomenon an illusion."[190] Aquinas, I suggest, has this potential misinterpretation of Jesus in mind when, in his *Commentary on the Gospel of John*, he asserts, echoing Chrysostom, that "the reason that he did not perform miracles in his childhood" was "so that human beings should not think those miracles were imaginary (*phantastica*)."[191] An episode from Bede's Life of Cuthbert helps illuminate what medieval writers may mean when speaking of a "fantastic" or "phantastical" miracle. The saint's preaching in a village was once disrupted by a sort of firework display instigated by the devil: "that most evil foe, producing a phantom fire (*fantasticus ignis*), set light to a house nearby, so that firebrands seemed to be flying all through the village." People tried to extinguish the "false flames" with "real water," but to no avail.[192] It is unclear whether this fire was a mere optical illusion, since we are not told whether the devil, after being routed, left behind real destruction. In other cases, calling a wonder "fantastic" seems to signify the underhanded means by which it was produced. The Anglo-Saxon scholar Aldhelm (d. 709) speaks of the false miracle show worked by Simon Magus (famous for his flying over

Rome) as *magicum fantasma*.[193] Much later, the fourteenth-century scholar Thomas Bradwardine refers to the wonders worked by the magicians of the Egyptian Pharaoh (Exod. 7:11, 22) as *miracula fantastica*—a synonym for magic tricks.[194] Viewing the above-cited statements by Aquinas in light of such passages helps us better appreciate his concern that the Christ Child would have been thought to be a magician if he had worked miracles. Earlier I briefly mentioned Gregory the Great's comment that while saints certainly work miracles, not all miracles are worked by saints; some, in fact, are worked by demons. That a miracle-worker's way of life is holy assures the observer that a bad agent is not at work. Recognizing the confusion that miracles can create, Jacobus de Voragine says of those worked by St. Germain: "there were so many that, had they not been preceded by his merits, they would have seemed figments of the imagination (*miracula . . . phantastica putarentur*)."[195] Here, "phantastical" miracles clearly have a negative connotation.

The view of Jesus as a magician can be found in Early Christian and also medieval polemical writings that consider the nature of his miracles. Calling the wonders worked by one's opponents magic tricks was a typical strategy of defamation (seen, for example, in a number of saints' vitae). In defense of a wonder-worker's integrity, some Christian writers insisted upon distinguishing between "miracles" and "magic tricks." In his *Dialogue with Trypho*, Justin Martyr expresses outrage that people "dared to call [Christ] a magician who misled the people." He says that Jesus should be seen, instead, as the miracle worker prophesied by Isaiah 35:5–6, who gives sight to the blind, and performs other healings. In contrast to the idle and malicious tricks of magicians, Jesus' miracles were ordered to good ends: besides healing, they instilled hope in the future resurrection.[196] Origen, in his *Treatise against Celsus*, similarly calls attention to the motives of wonder-workers: whereas magicians wish to produce an amazing show, Jesus sought to bring about moral reformation.[197] In response to the accusation that Jesus "from the temples of the Egyptians . . . stole the name of powerful angels and esoteric learning," by which he worked his magic, Arnobius of Sicca points out that Christ made no use of paraphernalia or rituals: he worked miracles "only through the power of his [own] name" and granted "only what was helpful, wholesome, and full of aids for us."[198] The high-medieval anti-Christian *Nizzahon Vetus* similarly claims that Jesus learned the art of magic in Egypt, traditionally regarded as a haunt of demons.[199] If this polemical author has the Holy Family's Flight into Egypt specifically in mind, this implies that Jesus became a magician when he was still a child. In contrast, the *Toledot Yeshu*, a slanderous medieval Jewish Life of Jesus (which existed in various versions), portrays Jesus as a rabble-rouser who deviously acquired magical powers when, in his adulthood, he broke into the Temple and stole the Ineffable Name (the Tetragrammaton), which was hidden and guarded there. He craftily inserted the scroll on which it was written into his flesh and afterward used the name to work miracles, such as the vivification of clay birds.[200]

It is worth paying closer attention to the *Nizzahon Vetus*, since it considers the possibility of the Christ Child's having been a wonder-worker, while, at the same time, interpreting the adult Jesus' miracles in a very negative light. The anonymous Jewish author asks his imaginary Christian interlocutor the following question about Jesus: "Why did he wait until he was an adult and intellectually mature before performing his wonders? He should have performed wonders while *in utero* and in his infancy . . . then everyone would have believed in him. . . . In fact, you should know that he was a sorcerer and that all his wonders were performed through sorcery; consequently, he was condemned to death legally and properly, just as we were commanded by our Lord God [cf. Ex. 22:18: "Wizards thou shalt not suffer to live"]."[201] In sum, the author contends that if Jesus had divine power in and of himself, then he should have wielded it from the very beginning of his life. Aquinas, as we have seen, responded indirectly to this idea by arguing that it was more fitting that Jesus wait until adulthood before performing miracles, since it was incumbent upon him to set a good example for other human beings and crucial that he not behave in a way that would lead others to deny his humanity. Another important point worth noting is that in the aforesaid passage Jesus' ability to work wonders is attributed not to his own power but to the art of sorcery, which he had to learn and for the use of which he was justly condemned. Elsewhere, the *Nizzahon Vetus* again calls attention to the embarrassing gap of time between Jesus' birth and his working of miracles as an adult: "the fact that we saw nothing in him during his youth to distinguish him from other infants leads us to disbelieve those wonders performed in his adulthood and to conclude that he performed them through magic." Whereas the monks and friars discussed in Chapter 2 admired Christ's childhood obscurity and uneventfulness, here, in contrast, the unremarkability of his youth is despised and considered proof of his being merely human.

The accusation that Jesus was a magician can be found in a number of sources from late medieval England, such as the York Cycle.[202] The above-cited comment from the *Nizzahon Vetus* that the Jews were obliged to put sorcerers to death helps illuminate the York trial scenes, where the charge of magic is presented as a Jewish justification for the execution of the adult Jesus. In his fourteenth-century visionary poem *Piers Plowman*, William Langland similarly weaves the motif of Jesus the magician into his narrative, especially when treating the trial of Christ.[203] Although the Anglo-Norman text of the Holkham Bible (London, British Library, Add. 47682) does not say that Jesus was thought by those around him to be a magician, he is depicted as performing what may be considered magic tricks (such as the Circe-like transformation of children into pigs), a portrayal which led W. O. Hassall to opine, in commenting on the manuscript's depiction of the Christ Child's miracles (fols. 14v–16r): they "provide reasons why the Jewish parents might come to regard Christ as an undesirable little magician."[204]

Along similar lines, in the Middle English redactions of the apocryphal *Infantia salvatoris*, there are a number of instances in which Jews, who are astounded and/or angered by the amazing deeds and words of the boy Jesus, call him a magician. For example, in the poem about the apocryphal childhood found in the London Thornton manuscript, when Jesus informs the Jewish scholars that he will save souls from hell with his blood, "thay loughe hym to hethynge [laughed at him scornfully], / And sayde, with wichecrafte þat he wroghte."[205] In the *Cursor Mundi*, when Jesus' teacher Zacchaeus has been confounded by his wise pupil, he exclaims that he has never seen such a one and does not know what he is:

> Ouþer a tregettour he most be
> Or ellis god himself is he
> Or ellis sum aungel wiþ him dwelleþ
> To teche þe wordis þat he telleþ
> Wheþen he coom what he shal be
> Not woot I by my lewte[206]

> [He must be either a magician or else he is God himself, or else some angel dwells within him to teach him the words that he says; whence he comes from, what he shall become, by my faith, I do not know!]

The Middle English verses here, as well as of the entire apocryphal childhood section, closely follow *Pseudo-Matthew*. In the Latin text, we find an explicit disavowal of the Boy's being human and then three possibilities corresponding to those listed above: Jesus' teacher says that the Boy's works, speech, and intentions "seem to have nothing in common with human beings. Therefore I do not know whether he is a (1) magician (*magus*), (2) a god, or (3) in fact an angel of god speaks in him."[207] In the analogous passage in the Greek source text, Zacchaeus only gives two possibilities: "What great thing he is—god or angel—I do not know."[208] The third option—a magician—may have been added sometime in the high Middle Ages when material from the *Infancy Gospel of Thomas* was incorporated into *Pseudo-Matthew* (and also when the West was apparently becoming more familiar with material from the *Arabic Infancy Gospel*, where the Child is already called a "sorcerer").[209] The speculation that Jesus may be a magician, which *Pseudo-Matthew* mentions first in the list of possibilities as to who Jesus is, makes the Jewish teacher seem even more incredulous. By suggesting that the Christ Child is an angel, the teacher implies that Jesus only looks like a human being—an idea that aligns with Aquinas's concern that Jesus would be considered a phantom. Perhaps Zacchaeus's exclamation in the Greek text that the boy Jesus "can even tame fire!" prompted a medieval author to think of a magician, given that burning was a punishment for witchcraft in the later Middle Ages.[210] The teacher says that the Child can make a mockery of other torments besides fire, and so suggests that he be crucified.[211] The *Cursor Mundi* repeats this when it has Jesus' teacher say: "Worþi he were on gibet honge (he deserves to be hung on a gibbet)."[212] This is by no means the only threat of capital punishment that we find in Middle English versions of the *Infantia salvatoris*. Such menacing statements recall Aquinas's hypothesis that the Jews would have wished to put a wonder-working Christ Child to death.

In other late medieval texts derived from *Pseudo-Matthew* and the *Infancy Gospel of Thomas*, Jesus is accused of being a magician because he has power over life and death. In a Latin redaction of the *Infancy Gospel of Thomas*, during the Holy Family's stay in Egypt, Jesus causes a desiccated fish to come back to life. When the widow in whose house he and his parents were staying sees this, she concludes that her guests are "magicians" (*magi*) and evicts them.[213] One of the most striking depictions of Jewish dislike of Jesus as a magician occurs in the *Vita rhythmica*, when a "certain Jew," upon seeing Jesus and the other boys making little fish ponds with connecting channels on the Sabbath, angrily treads upon the Christ Child's pond. Cursed by Jesus in retribution, he immediately falls down dead. When the parents of Jesus' victim hear about this, they demand of Joseph: "Take away (*tolle*) your son, take away the destroyer, take away the evildoer and enchanter (*maleficium et incantorem*). He has committed very many homicides against us, and he permits neither us nor our children to live. He ought to be dead. Let him be taken from our midst. It is expedient that he should die for the sake of all. That magician (*magus*) has perpetrated the greatest outrages."[214] The opening words of this passage— "tolle" repeated thrice—recall the exclamation "tolle, tolle, crucifige!" (John 19:15) uttered by the crowds before Pilate, while the statement about the expediency of one dying for all obviously repeats the same remark made by Caiaphas regarding the adult Jesus (John 11:50).

Late medieval vernacular and Latin texts not only relay the accusation of magic against Jesus but also call attention to the manner in which he supposedly worked his magic. A story that appears to have been added to the apocryphal childhood narratives sometime in the later Middle Ages recounts how a Jewish father was envious of the affection that his son had for Jesus and so locked up his own child in a tower to prevent the two boys from interacting with each other further. In William Caxton's retelling of this story, the father menacingly tells his son Joseph that "the boy Jesus with all his incantation will not help you nor free you from your prison." The child responds by professing his belief that Jesus, who is so powerful, "will not permit me to perish."[215] He is indeed correct, for the Christ Child soon arrives and wonderfully extracts the boy by pulling at his finger through a little hole, through which his entire body exits the prison. Jesus in this situation seems to work a magic trick, not by means of verbal enchantment (or magical song), as the father had suspected, but through a sort of sleight of hand. The same episode is depicted on one of the fourteenth-century Tring Tiles now in the British Museum (TT 3A-3B; fig. 15), and included in all the extant Middle English childhood of Jesus poems. In London, BL, Harley 3954, for example, the father similarly tells his son: "Jesu . . . / Out of presoun xal þe not bryng / Be no maner of sharment / Þat he kan of rede & synge (Jesus shall not bring you out of prison on account of any manner of charm that he knows how to read or sing)."[216] Contrary to what the father says, in the apocryphal narratives the Christ Child is never shown to use enchantment or any kind of implement in working miracles; he simply utters imperatives (that is, curses or commands) that have powerful effects on people, or he just makes his will come to pass, contrary to nature, as when he pulls upon and thus lengthens a beam of wood that had been cut too short.[217] In other cases, people instantly die as a result of touching the Christ Child, like the schoolmaster who strikes him or the child who willfully runs into him.[218] Such incidents recall the healing of the hemorrhaging woman that occurred when she merely touched the hem of the adult

Figure 15. The boy Jesus rescues his friend locked in a tower. Tring Tile, TT 3A-3B, London, British Museum (fourteenth century). By permission of the British Museum.

Jesus' garment (Matt. 9:20) and the death of Oza, who audaciously touched the Ark of the Covenant (1 Chron. 13:9–10). While depictions of Jesus holding what appears to be a magic wand survive from the Early Christian period,[219] those arguing in defense of Christianity at that time pointed out that Christ was not dependent upon the means that magicians typically employ to work miracles. In short, the late medieval redactors of the *Infantia salvatoris* might very well have been aware of the age-old charge that Jesus was a magician, since it appeared in the high and later Middle Ages in various forms, sometimes specifically in polemical contexts. Rather than completely ignoring it, as an offensive blasphemy, they embellished their narratives by giving voice to it, thereby increasing the tension between Jesus and his fictional adversaries, whose disbelief is underscored by their cynical view of Jesus' power.

Why did medieval Christian writers willingly reiterate the ancient charge that Jesus was nothing but a magician? As an analogous case, we might consider the 1593 note of Richard Baines, an Elizabethan spy, directed against Christopher Marlowe, which attributes a number of outrageous beliefs to him. Among other things, Baines claims that Marlowe "affirmeth that Moyses was but a Jugler [a magician]" and "That it was an easy matter for Moyses being brought vp in all the artes of the Egyptians to abuse the Jewes being a rude & grosse [ignorant and dull] people."[220] By putting blasphemous claims in the mouth of his opponent (claims which, incidentally, echo those about Jesus learning magic in Egypt), Baines effectively demonizes him, while at the same time making himself seem more righteous and truthful. Late medieval Christian propagators of the apocrypha, when fashioning their Jewish characters, seem to have adopted a similar strategy.

To return to Aquinas's comments about phantoms: whereas in some passages that allude to or mention the apocryphal childhood of Jesus the Dominican theologian raises the possibility of Christ's flesh being regarded as an illusion, elsewhere he says that the childhood miracles would themselves have been perceived as such. In both cases—whether people would have thought that Jesus' miracles were magic tricks or that he had merely assumed the appearance of a human with a child's body—the Christ Child would have been associated with demonic forces, or at least with the unethical practice of deception, in the estimation of his contemporaries as Aquinas imagines them.

Although I have stressed at length the possibility that Aquinas has folkloric ideas in mind when he expresses concern that the child Jesus would have been perceived as a phantasm or as a magician doing "fantastic" (or "phantastical") things, emphasis should also be placed on the Dominican's doctrinal approach to the notion that Jesus was a mere phantom. In his *Commentary on the Gospel of John*, Aquinas makes an apparently simple remark about the verse "Verbum caro factum est" (John 1:14), yet one that is quite relevant here. Aquinas explains that John made this statement in order "to show the truth of the Incarnation in contradiction to [the views of] the Manichaeans, who said that the Word had not assumed a true body (*veram carnem*), but only an imaginary one (*carnem . . . phantasticam*)."[221] Paul Gondreau has called this statement "perhaps Thomas' strongest anti-docetic words,"[222] and while this may be an accurate way of characterizing Aquinas's thought and its expression here, to avoid anachronism we should note that, strictly speaking, Aquinas does not use the word "docetism" to refer to the late antique heresy that held that Christ lacked a genuine human body. He instead refers specifically to the Manichaeans.[223] Aquinas makes a similar remark in his *Compendium theologiae*, in which he speaks of the principle underlying Manichaean Christology. Viewing all of creation as the work of the devil, Mani (the founder of this heresy) "held that Christ had only imaginary, not real, flesh (*non habuisse veram carnem, sed phantasticam tantum*). And he asserted that all things belonging to human nature related in the Gospel about Christ [presumably referring to sleeping and eating or other basic activities] were done in appearance (*in phantasia*), not in fact."[224]

Aquinas's desire to understand the doctrine of the Manichaeans was no doubt motivated by the Dominican Order's original (and continued) efforts to stamp out heretics, particularly the Cathars, who were dualists like the

Manichaeans; that is, he was not simply interested in church history as a sort of intellectual hobby. When, in commenting on John 2:11, Aquinas argues that the reason why Christ did "not perform miracles in his childhood" was "so that human beings should not think those miracles were imaginary (*phantastica*)," he speaks in a general way of those who might form an erroneous opinion of Christ.[225] This suggests that he has his own contemporaries in mind, not just the historical neighbors of the boy Jesus. Aquinas's preoccupation with defeating the heretical Cathars, apparently a pressing menace that was of great concern to him, is highlighted in a well-known anecdote about his abstracted behavior during a dinner he had with Louis XI, where Aquinas's companion and secretary Reginald of Piperno was also in attendance: "Suddenly he struck the table, crying, 'That settles the Manichees (*Modo conclusum est contra heresim Manichei*)!' and called out . . . 'Reginald, get up and write!' "[226] Aquinas was not the only high-medieval cleric concerned about anti-somatic heretics. An anonymous early thirteenth-century account about a dualist group in northern Italy demonstrates that the view of Christ as an angel appearing in the flesh was not simply a far-fetched fantasy in Aquinas's imagination: the theologian's contemporaries actually entertained this idea, or at least were believed to do so by orthodox clerics.[227] As I suggest below, it is possible that among the people who propagated the *Infantia salvatoris*, those who were more educated were aware of Aquinas's worry that such legends, still in circulation, would incline their contemporary audiences to disregard the reality of Jesus' human body. They may have subtly counteracted, or at least drawn attention away from, this objection by making the fictional Jews who deal with the Christ Child seem ogre-like and inhumane, and the Christ Child himself seem clever and sprightly yet in need of discipline.

## The Favorable Reception of the Apocryphal Infancy Legends in the Later Middle Ages

Before shifting to a broader discussion of the medieval reception of the apocryphal infancy legends, it will be helpful to summarize Aquinas's views of such stories and his concern about their possibly deleterious influence. The bluntness of Aquinas's statement that the legends about the Child's miracles are "lies and fictions"—a comment derived from Chrysostom, but nevertheless made by the Dominican as well—is, as we shall see, unusual among the rather infrequent remarks made by medieval churchmen about the apocryphal infancy legends.[228] Aquinas's overall position is that Jesus could have worked miracles as a boy, but chose not to do so, a view that seems consistent with John the Evangelist's designation of the changing of water into wine at Cana as Jesus' first miracle (2:11). Aquinas insists that Jesus set a good example of proper behavior for children and youths of all times. And he does not seem to be worried that a lack of wonder-working in the boy Jesus implies that he was weak. What seems to trouble Aquinas instead is that by working miracles the Christ Child would have given his contemporaries the impression that he was a mere phantom or a magician, and, probably, that Jesus' fictional persona might still incline people to this erroneous view.

The issue of Christ's power is clearly central to the legends about his childhood miracles. As Pamela Sheingorn has suggested, the Aristotelian distinction between the potential and actual use of a faculty may shed light on medieval Christians' perspective on the divine child's behavior as presented in the apocrypha.[229] Just as someone who possesses the "habit" of geometry, for example, may not wish or be able (for practical reasons) to go through, at a given point in time, the various proofs of that *scientia* (that is, to actualize or use the knowledge that he or she possesses as a habit), so one could say that Jesus had divine power and wisdom when he was a boy, but chose not to act upon them and thus reveal his full capabilities. The anonymous author of the *Vita rhythmica*, in contrast, seems to assume that Christ would not have allowed his powers to lie dormant during the many hidden years of his life. Defending his use of apocryphal sources, this pious author exclaims: "It is unbelievable that he had lived so many years and performed no miracles or wondrous works. For—alas!—it is not found in authentic writings how he lived for twenty-nine years and what he did. Neither is it found fully in apocryphal writings. For John the Evangelist writes, Jesus worked many more miracles than these! They are not, however, declared in writing in this book; instead, a few are told in order that there may be belief in Jesus."[230] In this highly emotional protestation, the anonymous author (probably a German monk) tries to defend his narration of the miracles worked by the Christ Child by alluding to John's comment about books not being able to provide a complete record of Jesus' deeds (21:25), all the while ignoring John's remark about Christ's first miracle being performed at the wedding feast at Cana (John 2:11). The author goes on to provide a reason why Jesus' childhood miracles were not included in the canonical gospels: the young Christ did not work them in the presence of the faithful and had not yet called his disciples, who were the ones who committed his deeds to writing.

Along similar lines, some medieval writers seem to have tried to qualify John's statement that the miracle at Cana was Jesus' absolutely first miracle. To give an example: the fifteenth-century Augustinian friar John Capgrave apparently thinks the canonical gospels' lack of mention of Christ's miracles before the wedding feast at Cana leaves open the question of whether he had worked any wonders earlier. Capgrave draws his own conclusion, apparently relying on the principle that Jesus already possessed divine power: "In all þese ʒeres tyl Crist was xxx ʒere of age, þe gospell makith no gret declaracion of his dedis, but withoute ony doute he lyued a parfit lyf and ded many miracles, þou þei be not wrytin in bokis (although they are not recorded in books)."[231] The anonymous author of a fifteenth-century French Life of Christ goes further, asserting that an acknowledgement of Christ's omnipotence is an act of devotion; it is thus appropriate to recount a few of the apocryphal childhood miracles, which he proceeds to do.[232]

In his justification for using apocryphal sources among other, more reputable works, which he makes in the prologue to his massive encyclopedia, the *Speculum maius,* the thirteenth-century Dominican scholar Vincent of Beauvais likewise exhibits a tolerant attitude toward the pious belief that Christ could have worked miracles that are not spoken of in Scripture. Vincent distinguishes between apocryphal books, saying that some are more reliable than others, though both types are worthy of attention: while some are of unknown authorship, but "contain pure truth," such as the *Gospel of Nicodemus,* others are of unknown authorship and dubious, such as the *Liber de infantia salvatoris.*[233] Although Vincent remarks that the sort of people who are liable to put credence in apocryphal texts are those "who believe that God could have done all those things," he does not condescendingly regard such believers as naïve.[234] Adopting a hands-off attitude toward medieval readers of apocryphal texts, he says "it is permissible . . . to read and even believe [apocryphal works] which are not contrary to the catholic faith, although they do not have the certitude of truth."[235] As a writer he remains neutral, transmitting much apocryphal material in his massive compendium without claiming that the content is either true or false.[236]

In the section of his encyclopedia where he provides a brief overview of the life of Christ and its historical context, Vincent omits the stories about Christ's miracles derived from the *Infancy Gospel of Thomas,* yet he does recount episodes from the Flight into Egypt section of *Pseudo-Matthew* and from its earlier chapters based upon the *Protoevangelium.* A limited transmission of apocryphal infancy material can also be seen in the compendia of his fellow Dominicans Jacobus de Voragine (d. 1298), Bartholomew of Trent

(d. ca. 1251), and Martin of Poland (d. 1278).[237] Considering this trend, it is not insignificant that the Holkham Bible, which contains a few scenes based upon the apocryphal childhood legends (14r–16r), opens with a depiction of "an unidentified Dominican friar standing at the shoulder of the artist (fol. 1r)."[238] Franciscan friars likewise transmitted legends concerning the Flight into Egypt, a good example being the anonymous author of the fourteenth-century preacher's handbook *Fasciculus morum*.[239] With the exception of Aquinas (who was essentially a theologian, not an author of chronicles or *pastoralia*), medieval friars seem to have promoted apocryphal stories about the Christ Child quite frequently, at least those about events that occurred before the Holy Family returned from Egypt. This is noteworthy, considering that Peter Comestor's *Historia scholastica*, a standard source for historiography and biblical lore in the later Middle Ages, recounted neither the miracles that occurred on the Flight into Egypt nor those that Christ worked during his childhood in Nazareth. Like the later, fourteenth-century author of the *Meditationes vitae Christi*, however, Comestor does mention that the boy Jesus used to draw water from a well. This detail, which would presumably have encouraged children to do their chores, seems related to the apocryphal tale about how Jesus fetched water for his mother, using his garment in place of his water jar; it also seems to reflect knowledge of an actual pilgrimage site in Nazareth.[240] Friars were by no means the only clerics who transmitted apocryphal legends about the boy Jesus in the later Middle Ages,[241] but they seem to have been on the forefront of those who propagated such lore, so much so that by doing so, they attracted the criticism of the anti-ecclesiastical Oxford scholar John Wyclif. Echoing Aquinas's comment that the *Infantia salvatoris* is false, Wyclif accused the friars of directing "their attention to pleasing their audience with apocryphal poems, fables, and lies," thus implying that they thereby adulterate the message of the Bible.[242]

Wyclif was apparently uncomfortable with the mixing of business and pleasure, specifically the efforts of some clerics to make religious material entertaining. This tactic can be seen in an anonymous French Life of Christ composed around the end of the fourteenth century, in which the author justifies his retelling of apocryphal legends in part by saying that they are "ung passetemps (a pastime)."[243] The attempt to make religious literature pleasurable, so that it could compete with secular literature, seems to have been fairly common in the later Middle Ages; in other words, it was not simply a didactically expedient approach adopted by the friars. An awareness of the ready appeal of secular tales can be seen, for example, in the *Cursor Mundi*; in the prologue to his long biblical paraphrase that incorporates many legends, the author states: "Men ȝernen iestes for to here [desire to hear poems about heroic deeds] / And romaunce rede in dyuerse manere." He then lists a number of romance heroes, implying that, although the characters of his work are biblical, they can also be viewed as heroes. These lines, together with his promise to his readers that later on "shul ȝee here many a dede / Þat ihesu dide in his childehede," suggest that the Christ Child's deeds, taken from the apocrypha, may also be viewed as heroic.[244] Along similar lines, Maureen Boulton has argued that the apocryphal infancy narratives in French were intended as alternatives to the widely popular Arthurian literature of the time or the earlier but still appealing *chansons de gestes*; such synergy seems to have existed among the genres of English literature as well.[245]

An awareness of the enticement of vernacular romances seems to explain why Robert Thornton, a member of the Yorkshire gentry, begins the poem about Christ's apocryphal childhood that he copied into one of his codices (London, BL, Add. 31042) with an incipit that calls the piece a "romance."[246] While this Middle English word, derived from French, had a variety of meanings, one of which was simply "narrative,"[247] the poem has a number of features that suggest that its redactor modeled it along the lines of a romance in the sense of a medieval adventure story. The Thornton poem about the childhood of Jesus can be considered a romance since (1) it is cast as an oral recitation in vernacular verse, (2) it is structured episodically like so many romances, (3) it focuses on the Christ Child's daring deeds (such as the rescuing of his friend from a tower), and (4) it features a special lady (the Virgin Mary) dear to the main character (her son).[248] Presumably conceiving of this poem as fundamentally devotional, John Thompson considers it odd that Thornton placed it directly after the "romance" about the "blood-thirsty" Richard Coeur de Lion.[249] Yet the poem about Christ's childhood, like other romances, contains a fair amount of violence and a good deal of conflict between simplified camps of good and evil: Jesus, his family, and his devotees (many of whom are children) on one side, and most of the Jewish adults and a number of bad boys on the other. Thompson acknowledges that the author of the poem on the childhood of Jesus was aware of its potential entertainment value, remarking that he "attempt[ed] to use the ephemeral delights of a lively narrative style for the didactic purpose of celebrating the virtues of obedience and mercy,"[250] qualities in Jesus, we should note, which are overshadowed by his playful and willful behavior as well as his irritability.

Nevertheless, Jesus' submission to his mother's wishes and his general readiness to help or heal people (who, problematically, often suffer as a result of challenging him or even by following his lead) are noticeable features that mark the apocryphal childhood narratives as being devotional in character. While Jesus' harming of others strikes many a modern reader as bizarre and offensive—as completely at odds with the way Jesus is presented in the canonical gospels—it is worthwhile approaching this depiction, as well as the text's pronounced anti-Judaic character, from the vantage point of an ordinary (that is, not highly educated) medieval Christian.[251] As I have argued elsewhere, the apocryphal Christ Child is similar to the saints who, in medieval culture, were known for being vengeful, or at least seemed to be so. Ambrose, bishop of Milan, is said to have predicted that a woman who tried to harm him would experience God's judgment; she in fact died the next day.[252] Regarding biblical passages that seem to express vengeful curses on the part of humans, Lester Little explains that "under the guise of a request for vengeance upon enemies," such statements iterate "in truth a prophecy of the punishment of the ungodly." In other words, "biblical imprecations were to be understood as predictions," with rare exceptions.[253] Medieval hagiographical writings, though, do present plenty of cases of saints inflicting punishment, whether out of a spirit of vengeance or from some other emotion is often unclear. The chapter in the *Legenda aurea* on St. Pancras, a boy martyr, mentions how a man who swore falsely over the saint's tomb could not remove his hands.[254] And of course, there is the famous observation of Gerald of Wales that the saints of Ireland "are more vindictive (*animi vindicis esse videntur*) than the saints of any other region."[255] Jesus has even more of a prerogative than the saints to see that offenders are punished, since he is God, for whom vengeance, technically speaking, was thought to be reserved (Rom. 12:19). Modern readers or viewers of the apocryphal Christ Child who find his harmful actions disturbing should consider that the ethical rules of behavior that are binding upon human beings, in these narratives, generally do not apply to him.[256] Jesus himself teaches his playmates on a number of occasions that he is exceptional and so cannot truly be imitated, as when he is described as leaping from hill to hill.[257] He encourages other boys to do so, but only to underscore their inferiority, by allowing them to experience physical pain, if not directly causing them to do so.

While the legends often present an inimitable Christ Child, those who transmitted them no doubt intended their audience to emulate the Child's respectfulness and submission to his mother. In these stories, Mary is portrayed as a powerful intercessor (Joseph having practically no governing influence over Jesus); when the Holy Family's neighbors are in trouble, they often turn to her, confident that Jesus will do whatever she asks. While Mary herself never works miracles, it is often due to her prompting (as at the wedding feast at Cana [John 2:3]) that the Christ Child works his wonders. The legends thus resemble, to an extent, the Marian miracles that were wildly popular in the later Middle Ages.[258] In short, the apocryphal tales about the Christ Child were ostensibly regarded by medieval audiences as devotional material, even though the Christ-figure they present may not be what a modern audience would expect or like to see.

As a sort of romance hero, then, the apocryphal Christ Child differs greatly from the passive and effeminate Man of Sorrows of the later Middle Ages, with whom holy women, in particular, readily identified.[259] David Aers has insightfully remarked that the image of the crucified Savior who lovingly expends his body for humanity (as a female would for her child and other loved ones) was not the only way that Christ was conceptualized in the later Middle Ages, even though such an image had great appeal. The apocryphal materials considered in this chapter confirm Aers's observation, which he makes in reference to the antiestablishment Jesus (found in Wycliffite and other texts), who is notably active in his ministry. Rather than simply apply Aers's remark to the material considered here, I would go further and suggest that the apocryphal Christ Child may have actually appealed to audiences as, in many ways, a counterbalance to the passivity of Jesus promoted by mainstream devotional culture.[260] The Man of Sorrows was admittedly a compelling image, so much so that it gave rise to the so-called Child of Sorrows (*Schmerzenskind*), the image of the Christ Child with wounds and/or the *arma Christi* (the instruments of torture used at the Passion).[261] In my view, the apocryphal Christ Child is an image that complements yet at the same time differs dramatically from this latter image: in both cases, the Child is associated with the infliction of violence, which he either escapes or passively succumbs to. The apocryphal narratives take things in a bold new direction, by making the Christ Child seem assertive, in the numerous instances in which he himself metes out suffering, though often indirectly.

As Elina Gertsman and Theresa Kenney have amply demonstrated, the figure of the Child of Sorrows was widespread in the later Middle Ages and served multiple functions.[262] These include the attempts of artists and writers to inculcate feelings of pathos for the holy babe and outrage at those who would inflict harm on a vulnerable child. Such images also emphasized the theological viewpoint that Christ took flesh to suffer and redeem humankind, a mission that commenced at once, with the Incarnation of the Son of God within Mary's womb. In various ways, the life of Christ in the later Middle Ages was imaginatively reconfigured to convey the idea that Jesus was overshadowed by the cross from the beginning of his life—an idea we have already encountered in the writings of Bonaventure and other authors.[263] According to Kenney, medieval Christians acculturated to the liturgy of the Mass, which entailed a mystical intersection of this world with divine eternity, would have readily understood Christ's transcendence of time, an idea that helps explain artistic and literary conflations of his infancy and Passion. In her essay that provides a wide-ranging overview of the medieval image of the Child of Sorrows, Gertsman begins with a late-fifteenth-century miniature that depicts the infant Jesus seated on a pillow, holding a crucifix (The Hague, Koninklijke Bibliotheek, 75 G 70, fol. 88r).[264] While he is not actually depicted as suffering—by flinching at pain being inflicted upon him, for example—the infant Jesus seems to be meditating sedately on his future Passion, as the adult Christ frequently does in late medieval images of the Man of Sorrows.[265] The baby Jesus is also pictured with one of the *arma Christi* (that is, the instruments of torture) in a miniature from the Hours of Catherine of Cleves, in which he is shown to embrace the cross as he flies down to earth, specifically to an open, hilly landscape, rather than (according to iconographic convention) to Mary, prayerfully engaged in reading or textile work at the moment of the Annunciation (New York, The Pierpont Morgan Library, MS M.945, fol. 85r; fig. 16). Yet here, as in similar scenes of the Annunciation, Jesus is absorbed in the task at hand (the Incarnation, which, paradoxically, makes possible the death of the God-man and thus salvation) rather than in pensive reflection.[266] In other, later images (such as a seventeenth-century engraving by Hieronymus Wierix, now in the Bibliothèque nationale de France, Département des Estampes et de la Photographie; fig. 17), the boy Jesus is depicted carrying the cross, as he slowly and pensively winds his way to Calvary, an image that literalizes Psalm 87:16, a verse that was frequently applied to the Christ Child, as it is here: "I am poor, and in labours from my youth."[267] Such imagery recalls late medieval depictions of Isaac as a boy carrying fagots to the site of his would-be sacrificial death; tropological texts such as the *Biblia pauperum* in fact linked the Man of Sorrows carrying the cross with the image of a young Isaac bearing the wood needed for his sacrifice.[268]

The Christ Child of the apocryphal legends differs greatly from images of the boy Jesus like these, which are redolent of the Man of Sorrows, by virtue of his being extraordinarily active and social, as is fitting for a healthy, growing boy. The images of pathos I have just mentioned, however, resemble the boy Jesus in the apocrypha (especially in the Middle English redactions) insofar as he is occasionally subject to violence and is frequently threatened

Figure 16. The baby Jesus flies down to earth. New York, The Pierpont Morgan Library, MS M.945 (Hours of Catherine of Cleves), fol. 85r (Utrecht, the Netherlands, c. 1440). By permission of The Pierpont Morgan Library, NY.

In laboribus a iuuentute mea.

Hieronymus Wierx excud. Cum Gratia et Priuilegio. Buschere.

Figure 17. The boy Jesus carrying the cross and other instruments of torture. Engraving by Hieronymus Wierix, Paris, BnF, Département des Estampes et de la Photographie (seventeenth century). By permission of the Bibliothèque nationale de France.

with capital punishment by the Jews around him. Besides hanging him (by crucifixion?), they consider stoning, burning, and cutting him up into pieces (a torture similar to the piercing of the Eucharist with knives in rumored host desecrations), yet the authorities never take things that far.[269] As a sort of trickster, Jesus always manages to elude his opponents' grasp. He is never physically wounded (despite being occasionally struck), or deeply affected by persecution, as he sometimes appears to be in images of the Child of Sorrows. Taking a broader perspective on all this iconography, it may be helpful to think of the trope of the Proleptic Passion (which, by associating the Nativity with the Passion in any number of ways, is more general than the "Child of Sorrows" motif) as encompassing both kinds of images: the Child of Sorrows and also the Boy of the apocrypha, who often angers and otherwise upsets those around him, who, in turn, scheme about how they should deal with this troublesome child.

The late medieval redactors of the *Infantia salvatoris* incorporate foreshadowing into their narratives by highlighting certain details, usually pertaining to the hostility faced by the Christ Child, which recalls the conflict that Jesus experienced as an adult. In the poem about the apocryphal childhood of Jesus in the London Thornton manuscript, for example, one of the elders is named Sir Caiaphas ("Kayface"),[270] although a Jew with this specific name does not appear in the Latin or Greek source texts. The Middle English character named Caiaphas opposed to the Christ Child is presumably the same high priest in the Gospel who interrogated the adult Christ (Matt. 26:57). Caiaphas and a handful of other Jewish adults are not the only characters portrayed as "kene" (fiercely cruel) in their stance toward Jesus.[271] So are some of the Jewish children, who are likewise envious of the Christ Child and seek to do him harm. Just as the name "Caiaphas" has been introduced to remind the reader of the unjust opposition Jesus encountered as an adult, which led to his Passion, so the boy who ruins Jesus' little dams is given the name "Judas," the implication being that the apostate apostle was wicked and also bent on harming Jesus from the very beginning of his life (cf. Matt. 26:24).[272] After destroying the pools and dams that Jesus constructed by a riverside one Sabbath, Judas is cursed by the divine child and immediately dies. As a result, the Jews threaten to kill the Christ Child and drive his parents out of town. Fortunately, Mary intervenes, gently beseeching her son to restore the boy to life. Jesus complies, yet also informs his mother that "This traytour es fulle of felonye, / Vn-to the Jewes he salle me selle / Ymanges my faamene for to dye (he will sell me to the Jews so that I will die among my enemies)."[273] Jesus later resurrects another child, for whose death he was unjustly blamed, since the real responsibility lay with other boys who pushed him down from a loft (see fig. 18, upper register). Betrayed by his playmates in this incident, Jesus takes the opportunity to tell his mother about the key roles these children will play in his future death:

> Þe childire þat are here
> Salle stande by-forne me one thaire fete,
> Agaynes me false witnesse for to bere,
> By-fore the Jewes thare thay salle sitte,
> And gyffe me boffettes, þat salle me dere,
> And nakyne me and one me spitte,
> And some with thornnes salle croune my hede
> And helpe at hange me one the Rode,
> And ȝour face sall be with blode by-wefede.[274]

> [The children that are here shall stand before me on their feet, to bear false witness against me, before where the Jews shall sit, and give me buffets that shall injure me, and strip and spit upon me; and some shall crown my head with thorns and help to hang me on the cross; and your face shall be covered with blood.]

Christ speaks of his future Passion as inevitable, but Mary naively and rather presumptuously thinks that he can prevent it by simply causing the boys not to live so long.[275] Although this striking interchange between the Christ Child and his mother seems quite novel, a passage from the Gospel of John is worth considering as being somewhat analogous since it depicts a young Jesus speaking to Mary about his future. When Mary suggested to her son that he solve the problem of wine running out at the wedding feast at Cana, he responded, "my hour is not yet come" (2:4). This rather mysterious remark—which Jesus himself seems to disregard, by going ahead to work the desired miracle anyway—indicates that Jesus knew about his future and (like Aquinas in the arguments considered above) had a sense of proper timing, specifically, that his public working of miracles was to begin at a certain period of time in his adulthood. For St. Augustine, Jesus' remark served as a springboard to clarify, contrary to heretics, that although Jesus knew of his future death, he was not subject to fate, a distinction that seems to address a more popular view of Jesus' life and death, rather than perhaps a more speculative concern regarding the necessity of the crucifixion as the divinely chosen means of the redemption. Augustine's

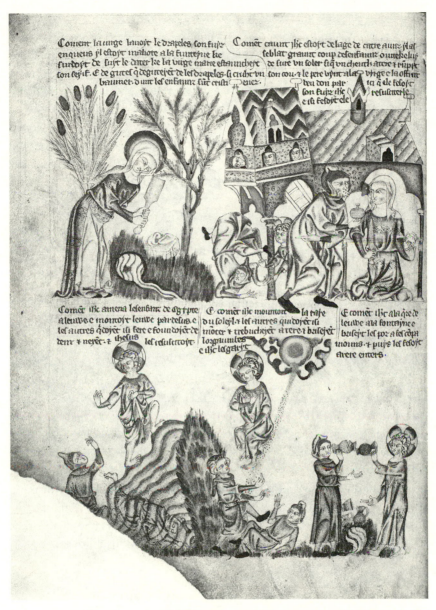

Figure 18. Mary doing laundry at Matariya, the Christ Child healing a boy who fell from a solar, and a man speaking to Mary (upper register); the boy Jesus walking on water, sitting on a sunbeam, and mending a broken pot (or pots), as the boys around him suffer misfortune (lower register). London, British Library, Add. 47682 (Holkham Bible Picture Book), fol. 15v (fourteenth century). By permission of the British Library Board.

rejection of the view that Jesus was subject to the unavoidable force of fate is worth keeping in mind when considering how later medieval authors and artists employed the trope of the Proleptic Passion, which, within some of the scenarios they sketch out, does create an ominous and even fatalistic feeling.[276]

Foreshadowing of the Passion also occurs at the beginning of the poem from the London Thornton manuscript, when the Holy Family encounters a good thief on the Flight into Egypt (an incident that is not usually included in the apocryphal Latin texts, as mentioned in Chapter 2). When the thief's son Dismas enables the Holy Family to continue on their journey unharmed, the infant Jesus, grateful for the boy's kindly deed, tells his mother that the latter will enter into bliss with him, after being crucified at his side (cf. Lk. 23: 39–43).[277] Such passages attribute a certain mature stoicism to Jesus: he knows about his future Passion, but is apparently untroubled by it—a depiction that likewise appears in the revelations of St. Birgitta of Sweden.[278]

On the whole, by incorporating the Proleptic Passion into their accounts of Christ's apocryphal childhood, the Middle English poets added theological depth and a sense of eeriness to the multiple episodes that feature hostility directed at the Christ Child, thereby increasing the poems' appeal for later medieval Christian audiences, who seem to have been drawn to the figure of a divine child bursting with potential, yet also bound to experience opposition. Is it a coincidence that the late medieval redactions of the legends almost seem to dramatize Aquinas's speculation that the Child's working of miracles would have led to his premature crucifixion? I think it not unlikely that Aquinas's views somehow reached the awareness of the (often clerical) composers and propagators of English poems dealing with Jesus' childhood and other biblically related matters.[279] Conversely, considering the wide influence wielded by popular culture, I think it is fair to say that Aquinas's hypothetical thinking about the Jews who were the Christ Child's neighbors was, to some extent, conditioned by, or at least responsive to, contemporary texts and images that characterize the Jews as maliciously hostile to Jesus and his followers.

## The Apocryphal Legends' Anti-Judaism and Playful Handling of God's Paradoxicality

The late medieval redactors of the *Infantia salvatoris* were clearly influenced by their environment and attuned to the anti-Judaic aspects of contemporary culture in their incorporation of the anti-Semitic episode about the Christ

Child's transformation of Jewish children into pigs, as well as other details of a similar nature.[280] The boys' parents seem to have two motives in trying to keep their children away from Jesus: first; they are intent upon preserving their children's physical welfare; and second, they are envious of this exceptional lad (his "giftedness" and charisma) and fearful that their children will convert to his sect.[281] The Jewish parents are thus portrayed ambiguously as being caring in a cruel and egotistic sort of way, a paradox that may be based upon Christian knowledge of the Jewish practice of *Kiddush ha-shem*, that is, Jewish parents' sacrificial killing of their children out of piety.[282] The popular tale about the Jew of Bourges similarly focuses on a Jewish father who is maliciously cruel. Discovering that his son received the Eucharistic host at Mass, along with a group of Christian boys, the father puts him in an oven, apparently to kill him, but the Virgin Mary enters into the scene and protects the child.[283] In a similar way, the Jews in the Middle English poems about Jesus' apocryphal childhood are not only eager to dispose of him, but willing to see their own children be miserable or die in order to terminate their children's attachment to Jesus. In the long Middle English redaction of the *Infantia salvatoris* found in Minneapolis, University of Minnesota, MS Z822 N81 (*olim* Phillipps MS 8122), the Jewish parents go so far as to remark that the only way that they can separate their children from Jesus is by killing them; while these parents might simply be exaggerating to make a point, the author probably intends for this to be taken literally or at least wishes to create ambiguity in the mind of his audience regarding the Jewish parents' motives.[284]

As I have suggested above, the Jews' hostility toward the Christ Child in the Middle English poems entails a transposition of the Passion narrative onto Jesus' childhood. This would have seemed logical in an imaginative way, not only on account of the principle that Jesus was born to die, but also because of the ancient biographical trope that emphasized the consistency of one's character over the course of a lifetime: following this logic, if Jesus was the victim of Jewish envy in his adulthood (cf. Mk. 15:10), then he must also have been so during his childhood. It made sense for those accustomed to this trope to imagine the boy Jesus as a miniature version of his adult self, in terms of his personality and also what happened to him and what he did later on (like weightlessly walking on water [Mk. 6:49]). Christian hagiographers commonly applied, as if retroactively, pious characteristics (especially a grave demeanor and ascetic behavior) onto the early stages of life of a person considered holy as an adult, in order to reconstruct saints' infancies and childhoods (about which often little or nothing was known). This also served to show how people who became saints were different from their peers early on. A famous case concerns St. Anthony the Abbot, who, as a boy, disdained the ordinary pleasures of childhood: he "dwelt at home in innocence" and "often went to church with his parents, and avoided both infantile games and boyish thoughtlessness."[285] As a boy, Benedict, who was to become the founder of Western monasticism, bore "the heart of an old man"—a serious demeanor that can be seen as foreshadowing his career as a monk intent on spiritual perfection. Like the apocryphal Christ Child, who miraculously reunited the shards of a shattered pitcher (fig. 18, bottom register),[286] the young Benedict, out of compassion, miraculously fixed a winnowing dish that his nurse had borrowed and accidentally broken. The local people thought the deed "so wonderful that they hung up the dish outside the porch of the church" so as to "acknowledge . . . how great was the boy's perfection right from the start."[287] The trope of biographical consistency can also be seen in secular texts from the medieval and classical periods. For example, Plutarch (d. 120), when recounting the childhood of the famous Athenian politician Themistocles, notes that "in times of relaxation and leisure, when absolved from his lessons, he would not play nor indulge in ease, as the rest of the boys did, but would be found composing and rehearsing to himself mock speeches," which "would be in accusation or defence of some boy or other."[288] The trope can involve bad as well as admirable features. Middle English legends about Judas, like the poem about Christ's childhood found in the London Thornton manuscript, portray him as already wicked in his boyhood. The *South English Legendary* relates that "Iudas bigan sone / To do luþere & qued oueral as his riʒte was to done / Children þat he come to he wolde smyte & bete / & breke ʒare heued & do ʒam harm (Judas soon began to do wickedness and evil everywhere, in accordance with his nature; children that he encountered he would strike and beat and break their heads and do them harm)."[289] Medieval legends about John the Baptist similarly employed the trope that emphasizes consistency of character, claiming that he was a hermit from the time of his childhood, a view that is actually supported by a verse in Scripture (Lk. 1:80): "the child [John] grew . . . and was in the deserts until the day of his manifestation to Israel."[290]

Such instances of children who give clear indications early on about the exceptional people they will surely become imply that, from a literary perspective, it made sense for the apocryphal authors to portray Jesus as a boy who is persecuted (by those disturbed by his unconventional behavior), and also, to a certain extent, to represent him as a *puer-senex*. Jesus' preternatural maturity is prominently displayed in the episodes in which he astounds his teachers by his extraordinary wisdom. It can also be seen in the episodes in which he takes control in crisis situations, as when the Holy Family encounters dragons on the Flight into Egypt. Whereas the other children in the entourage are terrified by the many dragons that issued forth from a cave, Jesus, "who was not yet two," went forth from his mother's bosom and "stood before them [the dragons] on his feet." After he easily tames the ferocious creatures, he tells his parents, who are extremely worried about him: "Do not think I am a little baby, for I always was and am a perfect (or "fully formed") man."[291] Those who propagated the apocrypha were apparently not at all or hardly concerned, as was Aquinas, about the Christ Child setting an example of proper, age-appropriate behavior for ordinary children.

While the apocryphal Christ Child has some features of what we would expect of an adult or old man (and also of the Lord God himself), he also behaves like a typical child. By highlighting various aspects of his personality, those who recounted the legends arguably sought to attest to Jesus' humanity as well as his divinity. I have already given the reader a sense of Jesus' boyishness, but a lot more could be said about the legends' characterization of him as a real human child, a topic I have dealt with elsewhere.[292] Here I will only make some general observations. The Christ Child enjoys playing games with his friends, as well as playing tricks on people. He quickly loses his temper, but easily forgives others or at least forgets about the recent conflicts he had with them. He is often disrespectful toward his elders and sometimes even toward his foster-father. In these ways, the child Jesus seems more to mirror normal children than to set an example for them of virtuous behavior, notable exceptions being his obedience to his mother, Mary, and the mercy he shows to those in need, as when he multiplies grain to feed the poor.[293]

At the same time that Jesus acts like a typical child, he is also shown to belong to a completely different category. Gillian Clark's remark about the late antique versions of the apocryphal legends applies, I think, to the later medieval redactions as well: "The stories of Jesus' own childhood which circulated in the apocryphal 'infancy gospels' were concerned with the power of this exceptional child and certainly not intended as models for other children."[294] This is to say that those who told such stories did not seek, primarily, to promote *imitatio Christi*, a devotional practice that was widespread in the later Middle Ages. This entailed not just an effort to emulate the suffering Christ who endured the Passion but, as we saw in the previous chapter, an admiration of and an attempt to imitate the Christ Child's presupposed virtues and gradual development, which symbolized the Christian path to perfection. To a certain degree, the late medieval redactions of the apocrypha may be seen as reacting against the increasing emphasis that was placed on the imitation of Christ in his suffering humanity and victimization.[295] On a number of occasions, the Christ Child dramatically teaches the other boys that he is different from them, specifically in terms of the power he wields; they should thus not misconstrue him as their equal. Yet, at the same time, Jesus is indeed one of the boys, since he enjoys being in their company and often does things that, one would expect, would only appeal to a child. Consider the episode in which Jesus leaps from hill to hill, like a superboy with bionic springs. All the other boys want to do this too—it looks like so much fun—but when they try to do so, they fall and break their limbs.

The legends' focus on children and childhood behavior has led some readers to wonder whether they were written for children.[296] While these stories could definitely have appealed to late antique and medieval children,[297] I do not think that the apocryphal childhood narratives were mainly written to entertain or teach children. I view the medieval redactions primarily as devotional texts that gave Christian readers who were inclined to imagine Jesus' past the opportunity to admire the Christ Child's power, and incidentally to gloat over the mean-spirited Jewish characters, who are never able to harm him seriously or truly understand the idiosyncratic divine child they are dealing with.

It is also likely that the late medieval redactors of the legends believed that, by highlighting the Boy's childlike nature, they were fortifying belief in Christ's humanity. As I have argued elsewhere, in the later Middle Ages, intellectuals as well as writers of middling education seem to have realized that children behaved in a peculiar way because their bodies were undergoing continuous development that paralleled their gradual psychological maturation. Children's behavior, in other words, was thought to stem from their condition as imperfect (literally, "not fully completed") human beings.[298] If Christ truly had a child's body and thus the type of physiological "complexion" common to children (warm and moist), then it would logically follow that he acted like a normal child. Motivated by physical restlessness as well as a spirit of adventure, he would have sat on, or slid down, a sunbeam, for example, with the same boyish gaiety as a lad climbing a tree or whizzing down a slide. Significantly, the incident involving a sunbeam is not recounted in the Greek *Infancy Gospel of Thomas*, but it appears in some Latin versions of the *Infantia salvatoris* as well as in some vernacular redactions.[299] In a scene from the Holkham Bible mentioned above (London, British Library, Add. 47682, fol. 15v; fig. 18, bottom register), the Christ Child's playmates have fallen from a mote-filled sunbeam, which Jesus either sits upon or gently slides down (rather like Milton's angel Uriel, who glides "through the even / On a sunbeam, swift as a shooting star").[300] In the Anglo-Norman poem about the apocryphal childhood of Jesus found in Oxford, Bodleian Library, Selden Supra 38, an early fourteenth-century manuscript that includes many miniatures illustrating the apocryphal narrative, Jesus is shown straddling a slightly more horizontal, solid-looking sunbeam (fol. 24r). One might assume that a being who is in some way suspended upon a ray of light without falling down lacks a real human body. Yet, if medieval readers/viewers reflected upon the types of activity likely to appeal to a child on account of its physiology, then, ironically, they might regard Jesus' stunt as proof that he had a child's body. The depiction of Jesus sitting on a sunbeam thus argues, paradoxically, against Docetism (or, more properly, Manichaeism): the view that Jesus was a mere phantom. By emphasizing the Child's boyish behavior, and thus indirectly his physicality, the late medieval redactions of the *Infantia salvatoris* can be seen as cleverly counteracting Aquinas's argument that a wonder-working Christ Child would have caused people to think that he was a mere phantom or magician. The legends, in other words, play with the idea that the almighty and all-wise Lord was once, paradoxically, embodied in a real human child who had not yet achieved total perfection, in the sense of completion.

In this discussion of the boyishness of the apocryphal Jesus, it is useful to consider the *Vita rhythmica*'s attribution of laughter to the Christ Child, a detail that István Bejczy finds highly significant. Bejczy's interpretation is similar to my hypothesis that the redactors of the apocryphal childhood narratives were aware of scholastic objections against them.[301] As I did above, Bejczy links the poet's application of the word *phantasma* to Aquinas's use of that word when speaking about the childhood of Christ in the *Summa theologiae* and also in his *Commentary on John*. The particular passage from the Latin poem that Bejczy sees as addressing Aquinas's concerns about the apocryphal childhood reads as follows: "After the boy Jesus had completed ten years, he was never accustomed afterward to laugh at anything, or to do or laugh at anything childish, and he never uttered a word without weight. Yet whatever the child spoke previously did not seem to be useless, although the little infant maintained a childish manner, so that his mystery (*sacramentum*) might, in such wise, be hidden from demons, and that it might not be recognized by them and that he not be called a phantom (*fantasma*) by the impious."[302] These remarks occur after three short sections that inform the reader of when Jesus began to walk (at the age of one year and one month), speak (at one and a half), and abstain from the breast (at two).[303] In all three cases, the anonymous author avoids attributing to Jesus the incompetent and thus embarrassing behavior of a baby. He then turns the reader's attention to another milestone: Jesus' putting aside of childishness (*modus puerilis*) at age ten—this, despite the fact that the poet makes Jesus seem somewhat like a *puer-senex* even before he reached that age.[304] The anonymous author then proceeds to recount a number of miracles that the boy Jesus worked, yet he does not say how old he was in each incident, thus preventing the reader from determining exactly which of these miracles occurred before age ten and which afterward.[305] Be that as it may, it is clear that the author, like Aquinas later on, associates the childhood miracles with the worry that Jesus might been considered a *fantasma*. The implicit argument is that since Christ manifested both childishness (though not too much) and divine power (but not excessively) during his boyhood, he did not lead others to doubt his humanity but rather provided indications of his dual nature. In this way, by occupying a sort of Aristotelian mean, the boy Jesus of the *Vita rhythmica* can have his cake and eat it too—work miracles without indirectly leading people into heresy.

Bejczy rightfully calls specific attention to the poet's attribution of laughter to the boy Jesus, a point the author makes despite the absence of a depiction of the Child as laughing in the chapters recounting his miracles.[306] Nevertheless, the idea that Jesus at one time laughed is important, because it underscores his humanity and, more particularly, his boyhood. Although laughter was generally regarded in the Christian (especially monastic) tradition as undignified—Christ, after all, in the canonical gospels is never said to have laughed—in the high Middle Ages, with the growing commitment to Aristotelianism in the schools and universities, laughter came to be viewed as an attribute essential to human beings.[307] We thus find medieval scholars making the crucial distinction between Christ's ability to laugh and his never having actually done so. More generally, laughter, perhaps the type we associate with giddiness, was seen as a special characteristic of children.[308] In Middle English and late medieval Latin accounts of the apocryphal childhood,[309] Jesus is said to laugh (or smile) on a few occasions, as when he causes the clay birds he has fashioned to come to life: clapping his hands, he "louȝh so þat it dude him guod (laughed so that it did him good)."[310] While Jesus here may be imagined as laughing naturalistically and also impishly, in response to his foster-father's question as to why he worked on the Sabbath, specifically by fashioning clay birds, at other times his laughter seems a mixed expression of jubilant triumph over his opponents and also of childlike mirth.[311] Without saying much about why the boy Jesus laughs, Bejczy argues that by being said to have once or formerly done so—that is, to have acted childishly—Jesus proves his humanity, which enabled the author to dispel the worry of scholars like Aquinas that a wonder-working Christ Child would have been perceived as a phantom.[312]

While I agree with Bejczy that the anonymous poet seems to have in mind the objection against the childhood miracle stories that Aquinas (later) enunciated, I disagree with his interpretation of the relationship between the two hypothetical outcomes of the Christ Child's miracles. Aquinas does not actually say that the Jews would have wanted to crucify the Child because they mistook him for an apparition, which is how Bejczy interprets Aquinas's remarks.[313] After all, how can one crucify a phantom? While Early Christian (and later) Docetists may have envisioned the crucifixion along these lines, mainstream piety in the West, in the later Middle Ages, emphasized the bodily nature of Christ's sufferings at the Passion. Aquinas simply says that the Jews would have wanted to kill the Christ Child out of malice, perhaps implying that they envied his amazing abilities, stupendous knowledge, and ability to attract a large contingency of followers.

## Who Do People Say I Am?

Aquinas's speculations about a wonder-working Christ Child, unfortunately very succinct and not entirely clear, raise the question of what the Jews would have thought of such a boy, and it is on this issue that I would like to conclude this chapter. My reason for reflecting more carefully on the Jewish characters in such narratives is that they bring to the forefront the question of how the boy Jesus would have been perceived and treated if he had behaved in an extraordinary manner. The Middle English redactors of Jesus' apocryphal childhood seem to imply that the Jewish leaders, while entertaining the idea that Jesus was some kind of supernatural being, mostly concluded that he was merely a human—though very troublesome—child. His disruptive and unruly behavior—what one would expect of a normal boy—indicated as much. In other words, the Christ Child's rambunctiousness and apparent willfulness prevented the Jews from realizing his *sacramentum*—the mystery that he was also God. A comment made by one of Jesus' teachers, astounded by his wisdom, encapsulates this idea. Referring to David's prophecy of a child that was to be born of a maiden (Isa. 7:14), the teacher says to Jesus: "If it ne ware thi werkes wild, / I monde wene that thou it ware" (If your deeds were not wild, I would have thought that you were it [i.e., the Messiah]).[314] Recall that in ST 3, q. 36, a. 1 Aquinas had quoted Paul's remark (1 Cor. 2:8) that the princes of this world (interpreted as Jews) would never have crucified Christ if they had known who he was, in order to argue that Christ's birth should not have been made known to all. This implies that if they had seen clear, unmistakable signs of his divinity, they would never have brought about his death. A different line of thinking appears in q. 36, a. 4, in which Aquinas argues that Christ did not work miracles during his boyhood, because if he had, then the Jews, being very irritated by him, would have crucified him at that time. This may possibly imply that they would have knowingly crucified one they inferred to be God, though such a hypothesis would seem to contradict Paul's claim about the ignorance of those who put Jesus to death. Another possibility is that the Jewish elders justifiably wanted to get rid of a wizard causing havoc in their community. The ability to work miracles, after all, could be explained in more than one way.[315] Perhaps Aquinas means that the Jews would have killed the Christ Child as if he were some kind of pesky supernatural being in their midst, which at times is how the Jews seem to regard him in the Middle English redactions of the apocryphal infancy legends. While it is not entirely clear what Aquinas has in mind, it is fair to say that he believes that Christ kept a low profile during his childhood in order to ensure the fulfillment of the divine plan for the crucifixion, which was meant to occur as the culmination of the adult Christ's public ministry.

In commenting on the aforesaid verse from Paul (1 Cor. 2:8: "if they had known it they would never have crucified the Lord of glory"), exegetes tended to distinguish between different groups of Jews and different types of knowledge. The Jewish elders were often said to know who Jesus was only to a certain degree: they knew that he was the promised one, but not that he was God. The common people, on the other hand, were said to be generally ignorant of who Jesus was; they thus went along with their leaders, turning against Jesus at their leaders' prompting. The first group was therefore thought to be more culpable than the latter. Suggestions were made as to why the Jewish leaders' understanding of Jesus could only reach so far; a common explanation was that they were simply hard-hearted and mean-spirited, and thus blind to the fullness of truth.[316]

The Middle English narratives about Jesus' childhood similarly divide his Jewish neighbors into two (or three) camps: many of the children seem drawn to Jesus, while the elders are regularly offended by him. Ordinary adults, for their part, seem to have a mixed reaction to him. Not surprisingly, those whose children have been injured or whose friends or family members have died as a result of interacting with the Christ Child are strongly opposed to him, while those for whom he works miracles (for instance, by causing a miraculous harvest)[317] are impressed by him and grateful for his benevolence. Out of all these groups, the children who simply enjoy being with Jesus, are impressed by his powers, and have no intention of harming him (or have been forced to acknowledge his superiority) are presented, at least in the Middle English poems, as most attuned to Jesus' true identity and eager to show him honor. In the *Vita rhythmica*, the boys who spend time with him go so far as to crown Jesus as their king (see fig. 1).[318] Indeed, a common theme running through these apocryphal legends is that children—who, for the most part, are portrayed naturalistically, as carefree and unregulated by social or religious customs—manifest an openness to faith in Jesus, almost as if they were proto-Christians. This depiction parallels a detail in medieval Palm Sunday processions: the children's special role in greeting Christ as he entered Jerusalem.[319] It also seems to allude to statements in the canonical gospels that speak of Christ's love of children and admiration of their virtues.[320] In the Middle English legends, the mean-spirited elders, who, on account of their book knowledge might be considered well positioned to spot the Messiah, are ironically unaware of him in their midst. Thus, the childhood narratives seem to raise the question of the Jews' knowledge of Jesus, and indicate that the group with the least learning and authority was the most adept at recognizing Christ's true nature. At one point, Jesus' boyhood friend Joseph, after seeing yet another miracle worked by his divine playmate, declares: "Me thynke, of wittes we bene to slawe; / Ilke daye thi miracle thus we see / And wele us aughte the for to knawe. / Thou arte kynge of alle pouste (It seems to me we are [mentally] too slow; each day we see your miracles, so it behooves us to know who you are; you are the omnipotent king)."[321]

The issues of Jesus' identity and the Jews' suppositions concerning it are highlighted at the end of the longest extant Middle English poem on the apocryphal childhood of Jesus—that in Minneapolis, University of Minnesota, MS Z822 N81. After claiming that his "apocrysome" (apocryphal) source text was written by an apostle,[322] the anonymous redactor/narrator states what was by then quite obvious: that Jesus was once a real human child. For him, this implies that Christ, like St. Paul (1 Cor. 13:11), must have done some "child dedes" (deeds that one would expect of a child), for this was incumbent on him by "kynde of man" (human nature).[323] The narrator then blames the Jews for failing to recognize Jesus' divinity, after the Child had worked so many miracles in their midst.[324] He goes so far as to say that they deserve eternal punishment for their lack of awareness, seemingly forgetting his own portrayal of Jesus as an unruly child, which, if accurate, would surely have made it very difficult for the Jews to see past the irritating aspects of Jesus' humanity. Quick to find fault with the Jews of Jesus' day, the narrator recalls their having witnessed the Boy's "maystryse" (lordship or power, shown by his miracles), yet having quickly shifted his attention to the task of blame, the poet here does not reemphasize Jesus' "child dedes," which can be thought to have counterbalanced his miracles, which in turn pointed to his divinity. According to the author of the *Vita rhythmica*, Jesus' behavior as a normal child hid the *sacramentum* of his identity. As the comments of both of these late medieval authorial narrators reveal, the issue of the Christ Child's duality is central to the apocryphal legends: while his miracles display his divinity, his boyishness can be seen as cleverly obscuring it. The mere fact that storytellers and audiences were willing to entertain this contradictory depiction of the divine child suggests a certain playfulness on their part in reflecting upon the unique literary possibilities afforded them by the Incarnation, particularly as it was played out in the scripturally unscripted years of Jesus' boyhood.

A number of medieval writers, such as the author of the *Meditationes vitae Christi*, emphasize the hiddenness of divinity in the Christ Child. Along similar lines, when Aquinas explains why it was appropriate for Mary to have a husband, he says that it was so "that the manner of his birth might be hidden from the devil" (ST, 3, q. 29, a. 1, c.).[325] Those who saw the Holy Family together, including the devil, must have thought that Jesus was an ordinary child, naturally engendered by a human father. While Aquinas accepts the notion that Christ outwitted the devil through the arguably deceptive appearance of having had a normal father[326] who impregnated his wife, he seems unwilling to entertain the idea that Christ cleverly hid his identity during his childhood by acting like a normal child—a child who delights in play and who has not yet learned (or simply chooses not) to harness his divine power, which often gets exercised quite irresponsibly. In short, unlike the authors and propagators of the apocryphal childhood narratives, Aquinas was not willing to play, as it were, with the paradoxicality of a divine child. Very well might he have shared the sentiment of stern Wycliffite Christians who disliked the biblical dramas on account of their perceived lack of reverence. Like them, he may have imagined the Lord saying in response to those who told such apocryphal tales: "Pley not with me but pley with thy pere."[327] In other words,

Aquinas would have considered it irreverent to imagine Christ as a sort of trickster figure.

In conclusion, although Aquinas persuasively argues against putting credence in the *Infantia salvatoris*, there were a number of appealing aspects to the apocryphal legends about Christ's childhood that resulted both in their being tolerated (and even propagated) by a number of medieval churchmen and also favorably received by the laity. Those who willingly read or heard these stories, or enjoyed seeing them depicted, were likely the type of people who were attuned to secular literature, accustomed to folklore, and desirous of knowing more about the lives of Jesus and Mary and the people with whom they interacted. Lastly, Christians in the later Middle Ages were probably also often forgetful of, or not greatly concerned about, the differences between the canonical and apocryphal gospels.

# CHAPTER 4

# A Maternal View of Christ's Childhood
# in the Writings of Birgitta of Sweden

The Virgin Mary plays a central role in the *Revelationes*, a massive compendium of the mystical experiences of the fourteenth-century laywoman Birgitta of Sweden (ca. 1303–73). Named a patroness of Europe by Pope John Paul II in 1999, Birgitta was canonized (in 1391) less than twenty years after her death. She spent the first part of her adulthood married to a Swedish nobleman, the lawman Ulf Gudmarsson, bearing him eight children. A few years after her husband's death, she moved to Rome in 1349, where, for the most part, she spent her widowhood devoted to a life of piety.[1] Although her late vocation involved founding the monastic Order of the Most Holy Savior, she lived the latter part of her life not in a cloister but in the midst of the world, going on pilgrimage, communicating with important political and ecclesiastical figures, and transcribing heavenly messages with the aid of her confessors.[2] Birgitta sometimes dictated the revelations she had received and sometimes wrote them in her mother tongue; in a collaborative effort, her confessors either transcribed these revelations or translated them into Latin, while Birgitta acted as a sort of supervisor.[3] As an older woman living in Rome, Birgitta undertook the study of Latin so that she could ensure the accuracy of these translations. Learning another language in one's adulthood is rarely an easy task, so she must have been strongly motivated in undertaking that endeavor.[4] Regarding herself as the humble yet empowered mouthpiece of Mary, Jesus, and God the Father, she apparently wished to maintain authorship over her text.[5] A chapter from Birgitta's *Revelationes* suggests that Mary herself was concerned about the faithful transmission of the *Revelationes*: the Virgin grants Birgitta permission to visit saints' shrines, but admonishes her not to put aside the study of Latin grammar.[6] Numerous chapters of this massive compendium recount conversations between Mary and Birgitta or monologues in which Mary shares her personal experiences and perspectives on the life of Christ. While God the Father and Christ often speak to Birgitta, her collection of mystical texts is by no means dominated by their utterances, unlike, for example, *Il Dialogo* of Catherine of Siena, a Dominican tertiary who lived a generation after Birgitta and shared many of her spiritual and political concerns. The group of texts that I will explore in this chapter demonstrates that Birgitta's *Revelationes*, to a large extent, transmit a private female discourse, in which Mary reveals intimate details about the Holy Family to another woman in whom she trusts.

This chapter will focus in particular on passages from Birgitta's writings that shed light on experiences from both Mary's life and Christ's, as the Virgin recounts them and also as Birgitta is mystically enabled to envision them. In the *Sermo angelicus*, a Latin liturgical text written in praise of the Virgin and supposedly dictated to Birgitta by an angel, Mary is presented as God's favorite, a woman endowed with divine wisdom and prophetic abilities. In the first lesson (or reading) for Friday, it is revealed that "[e]ven before [Mary] knew she was to be his mother, she understood from the prophecies in the bible that God willed to become man and that he would suffer painful torment in his incarnate flesh."[7] In this text, as well as in the *Revelationes*, Mary possesses foreknowledge of the Incarnation and also of Christ's future sufferings, which she typically reflects upon as she clothes his body. Like Mary, Birgitta was a mother who cared for children and continued to clothe others in her widowhood. Her canonization dossier records that "when she was at home and not engaged in prayer . . . the same lady Birgitta sewed and repaired with her own hands the garments of her servants, her *famiglia*, and of other poor people (as well as her own clothing) with the goal of rendering herself more abject."[8] It is not surprising, therefore, that Birgitta emphasizes Jesus' clothing in the meditations that she offers to her readers on his destiny to suffer and his mother's corresponding sorrow. As Caroline Walker Bynum has pointed out in her discussion of the characteristic features of female piety, holy women, even when they left secular life for the cloister, did not leave behind the female roles assigned to them by medieval society: "The somatic quality of [females'] visual experience was thus, in part, a continuation of women's social responsibility. Not only did female mystics kiss, bathe and suckle babies in visions and grieve with Mary as she received her son's dead body for burial; they actually acted out maternal and nuptial roles in the liturgy, decorating life-sized statues of the Christchild for the Christmas crèche or dressing in bridal garb when going to receive their bridegroom in the eucharist."[9]

My examination of Birgittine texts confirms this generalization for a fourteenth-century female saint who had lived as an aristocratic wife with children. In medieval society, it was a married woman's duty to produce or obtain the clothes to be worn by the members of her family and to tend to their upkeep. Even when women were not financially pressured to sew garments to clothe their family or to increase their income, women engaged in textile work in order to create a positive image of themselves as diligently using their skills and lovingly caring for others. They even continued with this work when cloth production became a male-dominated industry in the later Middle Ages.[10] Thus, by focusing on the Virgin's clothing of her son—as a baby, as a child, and also as a dead man—Birgitta calls attention to Mary's caretaking and maternal love of Christ.

While the imagery that Birgitta uses has a particularly feminine resonance on account of its association with the conventional duties of a wife and mother, it would also have had a popular appeal to both male and female readers, clerical and lay, by virtue of its emphasis upon concrete objects. In the later Middle Ages, Jesus' swaddling bands, tunic, and shroud were all venerated as relics in Western Europe. Although very few medieval Christians traveled around as much as Birgitta did or visited so many shrines, they would have been able to visualize the relics she mentions in her writings. By centering a number of her revelations on such objects, Birgitta provides a devotional aid for her readers, giving them cues to pause and focus on the concrete realities of the Incarnation as a means of apprehending theological truths. Prominent among these concepts is Mary's role as cooperator in the redemption or, in other words, as Co-Redemptrix: the tears the Virgin is said to have shed when clothing her son signify the crucial role she herself played in the redemption of the human race.[11]

By sharing in Christ's sufferings at the foot of the cross, Mary offered a joint sacrifice to God the Father along with her son. Birgitta does not simply imply that Mary was a Co-Redemptrix or argue for it abstractly; rather, she transmits Mary's experience of it in the here and now. At one point, the Virgin explains with vivid details the intimate psychological connection between her and her son that resulted in her virtual co-crucifixion with him:

He was for me like my own heart. This is why, when I gave birth to him, I felt as though half my heart was being born and going out of me. When he was suffering, it felt like my own heart was suffering. When something is half outside and half inside and the part outside gets hurt, the part inside feels a similar pain. . . . As that which is closest to the heart hurts the worst, so his pain was worse for me than for the others. As he gazed down at me from the cross and I gazed at him, my tears gushed from my eyes like blood from veins. . . . I can therefore boldly say that his pain was my pain and his heart my heart. Just as Adam and Eve sold the world for a single apple, you might say that my Son and I bought the world back with a single heart (*quasi cum uno corde*).[12] (cf. Acts 4:32)

This remarkable statement about Mary's sharing in Christ's suffering on the cross surpasses in detail and intensity the apostle Paul's remark that "we are God's coadjutors" (1 Cor. 3:9), a passage sometimes cited in modern discussions of Mary's role as Co-Redemptrix, which to date is not officially defined dogma.[13] Although the saints along with Paul (Col. 1:24) could share in Christ's sufferings, Mary's physical as well as psychological connection with Jesus was unique: "As that which is closest to the heart hurts the worst, so his pain was worse for me than for the others." Jesus and Mary, in other words, have a single heart.

In Birgitta's writings, Mary's heart symbolizes her union with Christ on many levels: the physical, the intentional, the experiential, and the emotional. Within medieval culture, the heart was generally considered the center of many vital human faculties.[14] Physicians viewed it as the focal point of blood, the source of biological life, and an organ keenly sensitive to pain. For theologians, it was the seat of the will and affections. For writers of romances and love poetry, it was the originator and sustainer of amorous feelings. Yet filial love also emanated from the heart, as did other emotions, such as anger, as Aristotle famously observed.[15] In an essay in which she argues that the heart in the late Middle Ages and Renaissance continued to be thought of as "the moral centre of the human being," Catrien Santing emphasizes the huge role played by Christianity, especially Roman Catholicism: "Christianity propagated the virtually invincible concept of the human being as one of flesh, whose heart (*kardia*) was the rational, emotional and volitional center—the hidden core of the self."[16] Although European scholars beginning in the twelfth-century increasingly spoke of the head as the seat of the soul, specifically, the place where memories were formed and saved, and also where the rational process was conducted, many people, including those who were learned, still regarded the heart as the center of one's inner person, which encompassed the recollections of one's experiences. Birgitta of Sweden was clearly one of those who emphasized the heart, which is not surprising considering her role as a mystic. For, as Esther Cohen concedes in an essay in which she traces the high-medieval emergence of the idea of the soul residing in the head (as opposed to the heart), "The heart was . . . central to mystical practices."[17] The heart's tremendous symbolic value within Western culture can be seen in an unusual (and almost marginal) scene in the Holkham Bible (London, BL, Add. 47682, fol. 17r, bottom right register): Mary is shown conversing with her young son, standing beside her, as both of them hold heart-like apples in their hands. This scene is intended to illustrate "How the Virgin and child played with an apple," yet it also conveys their deep sensitivity to one another.[18] In the passage from Birgitta's *Revelationes* cited above, mother and son have one heart, which they offer as a sacrifice to atone for the sin that Adam and Eve committed through an apple. This intimate connection between the Virgin and her son is reflected in the belief that the blood that Jesus shed on the cross was derived from the blood he received from Mary in her womb.[19] The tears she shed on Calvary and, indeed, at other points of her life in anticipation of the Passion, are analogous, if not equivalent, to the blood that Christ shed on the cross, as the passage from Birgitta cited above indicates.[20]

Claire L. Sahlin, Kari E. Børresen, and others have seen Birgitta's promotion of Mary as Co-Redemptrix as a key maneuver in her feminist agenda to correct the male-centered theology of her day.[21] Yet male authors also exalted the Virgin's role in the redemption. The twelfth-century Benedictine monk Arnold of Bonneval emphasizes the pouring forth of Mary's heart at the foot of the cross, though admittedly not to the same extent that Birgitta does. In his treatise *De laudibus beatae Virginis Mariae*, Arnold states: "At that moment [i.e., when Jesus gave up his spirit], Christ and Mary had but one single will, and both were equally offering a single holocaust to God: she with the blood of her heart; he with the blood of his body."[22]

Another clarification is in order at the outset of this chapter. Scholars have previously called attention to Birgitta's presentation of Mary as the *Mater dolorosa*,[23] but the Virgin in Birgitta's writings is not simply filled with sorrows when she stands beneath the cross; rather, she is portrayed as a clairvoyant and tender-hearted woman saddened by the thought of her son's future Passion throughout her life. Birgitta's emphasis on Mary's sadness was in fact part of a larger trend. The more recent Roman Catholic devotion to the "Seven Sorrows" of the Virgin Mary can be traced back to the later Middle Ages when Christians meditated empathetically on the human experiences of Jesus and his mother.[24] The number and list of sorrowful incidents that Mary endured was in flux at that time, but the first few were derived from the infancy and childhood of Christ. These key moments typically included the loss of the twelve-year-old Jesus during his family's trip to Jerusalem to celebrate the Jewish feast—an incident that caused Mary much anxiety, as explored for example in Aelred's *De Jesu puero duodenni*.[25] Medieval Christians generally saw a continuum of suffering in the life of Christ that began in his infancy (and even within the womb of Mary) and extended until his Passion.[26] As one late medieval author noted: "The whole life of Christ can be called a passion or passions because he not only suffered in the end, but in the beginning of his life and in the middle and in the end."[27] While such a blunt statement of the so-called Proleptic Passion is unusual, the trope can be seen in numerous medieval texts and images, where it is often employed with more subtlety. The Proleptic Passion is undoubtedly a major theme in Birgitta's writings, as noted by Gertrud Schiller many years ago and by Richard Kieckhefer more recently.[28] This feature of her works, however, has never previously been explored in detail, partly because studies of the actual contents of her writings are scarce.

This chapter investigates the connections Birgitta draws between Christ's childhood and his death upon the cross, as well as his burial, in numerous passages within her literary corpus. I am particularly interested in how Birgitta uses images of cloth to reinforce the notion that Christ's suffering and death were preordained. As I explain below, the attention Birgitta calls to Christ's clothing is related to her admiration of St. Francis of Assisi and her interest in recent controversial developments within the Franciscan Order. Though her devotion to the Christ Child and her preoccupation with his future sufferings probably owe much to Franciscan influence, Birgitta's emphasis upon the clothes that Jesus wore seems to stem more broadly from her exposure to a range of devotional materials and from her own gendered experiences and approaches to Christian spirituality.[29] In the discussion that follows I analyze passages from Birgitta's writings that pertain to events in the life of Christ, beginning with his infancy, moving on to his childhood, and lastly touching upon his Passion. While I will proceed mainly according to this chronology, teasing out, as it were, a sort of Life of Christ from this massive visionary collection,[30] a strictly sequential narrative will not emerge from my discussion, since a single chapter of Birgitta's work often makes reference to both past and future events in Jesus' life. The flexible temporality of Birgitta's treatment of Christ's life, which may unsettle the reader's experience of sequential time, can be said to gesture at a more godlike view of Jesus' years on earth.

Besides exploring the theme of the Proleptic Passion in Birgitta's writings, specifically as this motif is conveyed through the imagery of clothing, this chapter will argue that the Swedish saint was aware of apocryphal infancy legends about the birth and childhood of Christ, even though she never explicitly mentions them. While Birgitta apparently wishes to deny the validity of some of the apocrypha's details, she incorporates others into her visionary and locutionary texts. Most strikingly, in Book Six of the *Revelationes*, Birgitta gives us glimpses into the hidden life of Jesus by providing Mary's perspective on his childhood, a topic, as we have seen, about which the Bible is almost completely silent and on which the apocrypha honed in, with great detail. As a mystic in communion with heavenly beings, Birgitta is privy to knowledge about the Holy Family that ordinary medieval Christians lacked; thus, like the anonymous authors of apocryphal narratives, she has much more to say about the lives of Christ and Mary than is found in the canonical gospels. The revelations considered here, unlike the apocryphal infancy legends studied in the previous chapter, contain no ostensibly objectionable material, except perhaps for their implication that Mary was sometimes emotionally disturbed, to an excessive degree, by the thought of the suffering that God had planned for her son.[31] Medieval clerics probably valued Birgitta's depiction of the Virgin for its capacity to inspire compassion in her audience, without worrying about the theological correctness of Mary's acute emotionality. Women were considered more emotional than men anyway, so it would probably not have seemed inappropriate or inaccurate for a female mystic to focus on Mary's profound sorrows.

## Birgitta's Visionary Account of the Nativity in *Revelationes* 7.21

Birgitta's most famous revelation is recounted in Book 7, ch. 21, where she describes the birth of Jesus as she herself witnessed it in her mind's eye. The beginning of the chapter notes the location of her vision: the purported site of the manger in Bethlehem, which she visited during a divinely mandated pilgrimage to the Holy Land near the end of her life (1371–73). In this vision, Birgitta presents herself as a spectator, in contrast to other chapters dealing with the life of Christ, in which she is only told about what occurred and is given details verbally, rather than seeing events relived before her very eyes.[32] As already mentioned, late medieval devotional writers frequently encouraged their readers to enter into biblical scenes through the practice of meditation, but Birgitta maintains a respectful distance, without becoming a participant

Figure 19. Birgitta of Sweden's vision of the Nativity. Painting by Niccolò di Tommaso, Vatican City, Pinacoteca (fourteenth century). By permission of Scala/Art Resource, NY.

in sacred events. Indeed, in illustrations of this scene, which were widespread in the later Middle Ages, Birgitta is often portrayed off to the side, viewing the Nativity as a reverent spectator, rather like the viewer of a painting (as can be seen in Niccolò di Tommaso's "Birgitta of Sweden's Vision of the Nativity," Rome, Pinacoteca Apostolica Vaticana, fourteenth century; fig. 19). Birgitta had previously asked the Virgin Mary to see the manner in which Jesus was born, and her request was finally granted shortly before her death.[33] A similar curiosity may be said to have impelled her in Book 6 to pry into Jesus' childhood in the course of talking with Mary, as I explain below.

When Mary and Joseph arrive at the cave where Jesus is very soon to be born, Joseph departs, while Mary takes off her shoes, veil, and mantle.[34] Birgitta calls attention to the transparent garment that Mary keeps on, the "finely woven tunic (*subtilis tunica*) through which from without I could clearly discern her virginal flesh."[35] Mary's transparent clothing in *Revelationes* 7.21 recalls a metaphor male writers traditionally used in speaking of the fragility of women's virginity: it was like a precious balsam enclosed within a glass vessel.[36] The diaphanous chemise Mary wears is indeed glass-like; it reveals yet protects her virginity.

Birgitta's comment about Mary's see-through tunic clearly indicates her wonder at Mary's virginity, which was not at all compromised by her maternity. Yet this detail may also suggest Birgitta's knowledge of the *sancta camisia*, the relic of the Virgin's undergarment or tunic venerated at Chartres Cathedral in the Middle Ages. According to a twelfth-century miracle collection, Mary gave birth to Jesus wearing the chemise that was later treasured at Chartres.[37] Although Birgitta may have been influenced by this particular Marian relic, in her account of the Nativity she actually emphasizes Mary's clothing of her son Jesus more than what the Virgin is wearing. After divesting herself of some of her garments, Mary "then drew out two small cloths of linen and two of wool, very clean and finely woven (*subtiles*), which she carried with her to wrap the infant that was to be born, and two other small linens to cover and bind his head; and she laid these cloths beside her that she might use them in due time."[38] Mary is clearly a mother who has planned ahead for this momentous occasion. Not only that—she arranges what she will shortly need for her baby in a state of complete composure, with no hint of imminent uterine contractions. The neatness of the clothes Mary lays out may be a reflection of Birgitta's own concern for proper childcare and her appreciation of domestic order, but it also symbolizes the purity of Christ's body and that of the Virgin from which he is born. In Niccolò di Tommaso's painting of Birgitta's vision, as in other similar depictions, the pieces of cloth that Mary has brought for swaddling her newborn son are placed in a prominent spot (fig. 19).[39] The fact that they are not yet being used may be due to the artist's desire to call attention to the babe's brilliant nudity, a feature illustrating Birgitta's remark that "such great and ineffable light and splendor" emanated from the baby Jesus "that the sun could not be compared to it."[40] Significantly, this detail parallels the emphasis upon Jesus' luminosity in the apocryphal infancy legends.[41]

In an earlier book of the *Revelationes* (2.47), Christ uses the homely image of a mother and child to speak of how the Mosaic Law was precursor to the New Dispensation: "As a pregnant mother prepares her infant's clothing, so too God prepared the Law, which was just the clothing and shadow and sign of things to come."[42] On the literal level, Birgitta is referring to a medieval mother's practice of making clothes to cover her child's nakedness—a necessity that may be easily overlooked by modern-day readers who have ready access to a multitude of products for babies. Medieval medical literature provided a scientific rationale for a newborn's need for clothing: the contrast in temperatures the baby experienced when it left its mother's womb. Babies, whether newborn or otherwise, were routinely swaddled to ensure that their bodies would be sufficiently warm (undoubtedly a special concern in the northern countries), as well as straightened out and prevented from becoming desiccated.[43] Mary thus acts as a sensible mother in bringing swaddling bands with her as she travels to Bethlehem and approaches the time of childbirth. Indeed, the strips of fabric she prepared were crucial considering the rough-hewn, naturalistic setting of Christ's birth in Birgitta's vision of the Nativity. Following the tradition of Early Christian writers and the apocrypha, Birgitta locates the Nativity in a cave.[44]

A central feature of Birgitta's chapter on the Nativity is Mary's giving birth to Jesus without suffering any labor pains or injuries to her bodily integrity. While the doctrine of Mary's perpetual virginity (*pre, per,* and *post partum*) was commonly accepted in the Middle Ages,[45] the question as to whether Mary was always free from original sin was debated by medieval theologians—a question relevant to a conceptualization of the physical aspects of Mary's bringing forth at the Nativity, since women were thought to give birth in pain as a punishment for Eve's sin (Gen. 3:16). The Dominicans, following Thomas Aquinas, generally held that Mary was sanctified in her mother's womb, while the Franciscans, following Duns Scotus, preferred to regard the Virgin as sinless at all times and in every respect.[46] Clerics' views were not always so diametrically opposed, as some people held that Mary was sanctified at the very first instant of her conception, a theory implying that she was virtually always free of any kind of sin. Birgitta's belief in Mary's "Immaculate Conception," as it came to be called, is reflected in her vision of the Nativity recorded in *Revelationes* 7.21 and in other passages. In the *Sermo angelicus*, in the prayers for the first lesson on Wednesday, Birgitta praises Mary's conception within the womb of her mother Anne—the natural fruit of marital relations between her parents, who, along with other spouses, are to be commended for being "so God-fearing in all their actions that they love one another purely as God commands and only for the sake of procreating children."[47] "Surely and without doubt," Birgitta attests, "God loved the matter from which Mary was to be formed when she was conceived and assembled in Anne's womb more than every other human body ever engendered or ever to be engendered in all the world."[48] The issue of Mary's conception is also treated in *Revelationes* 6.49, where Mary reveals that her parents came together in the natural manner and that both she and her son were completely sinless. Here Mary testifies that she "was conceived without original sin and not in a state of sin."[49] Although her lineage can be traced back through a multitude of mothers to the first mother of all, the completely sinless Mary is no ordinary daughter of Eve. Building upon a long exegetical tradition, Birgitta regards Mary and Eve as diametrical opposites.[50] In contrast to Eve who suffered the punitive pangs of childbirth, Mary was thought to have been exempt from pain in giving birth to Jesus.[51] Despite this privilege, she experienced the pain of childbirth metaphorically when she beheld her son on the cross and reflected upon this horrific event.[52] Through her compassion, Mary closely assisted Christ in the work of redemption.

In Birgitta's vision of the Nativity (7.21), Jesus comes forth from his mother's body miraculously in the twinkling of an eye (*ictu oculi*), as she kneels and prays to God.[53] Birgitta's account attests to the miraculous nature of Jesus' birth without specifically describing how the baby exited from his mother's womb, which is perhaps what Birgitta particularly wished to know when she previously questioned the Virgin about the Nativity. Birgitta's version of Jesus' birth may be contrasted with that presented in the *Meditationes vitae Christi*, the popular devotional text discussed toward the end of Chapter 2.[54] In this text, the Virgin is described as leaning against a pillar as she is about to give birth to her son. Although Mary's use of a prop may suggest that parturition was physically difficult for her, the anonymous author is quick to add that Jesus left "his mother's womb without any breach or lesion, was one moment inside the womb and the next outside the womb on the hay at his mother's feet." While these two scenes thus agree in Christ's virtually instantaneous birth, the author of the *Meditationes* has Mary wash Jesus with her milk and wrap him in her veil, whereas in Birgitta's vision he is clean and is soon enveloped with the neat and spotless swaddling bands that his mother specially selected and carefully laid out for him. [55]

By calling attention to the cleanliness of the baby Jesus, Birgitta distinguishes him from other newborns, who were thought to be defiled by the fluids and membranes of their mothers' womb and birth canal.[56] "At once," she recalls, "I saw that glorious infant lying on the earth, naked and glowing in the greatness of neatness (*nudum nitidissimum*). His flesh was most clean of all filth and uncleanness."[57] Not even is the placenta, no longer a part of Mary's body or connected to that of Jesus, allowed to be messy or tossed aside.

Instead, it was "lying wrapped very neatly beside him." Similarly, no fluid or blood issues from the umbilical cord when it is delicately snipped by Mary's fingers.[58] Medieval religious art, building upon a long tradition ultimately tracing back to the apocryphal *Protoevangelium Jacobi*, which recounts the arrival of two midwives after Jesus' birth, often portrayed the Christ Child being bathed by one or two women, as Mary lay upon a bed.[59] Birgitta will have none of this: when the Christ Child is born he has no need of a bath,[60] and Mary, regaining her pre-pregnancy shape at once, tends to him herself. Like Jerome, who, centuries earlier, sought to defend Mary's perpetual virginity in his treatise against Helvidius, Birgitta has Jesus' mother take care of her baby all by herself (before Joseph soon arrives), implying that she had no need of female attendants. As Jerome put it bluntly: Mary "herself was both mother and midwife."[61]

Before she describes the Virgin wrapping the Christ Child with the pieces of cloth that she has carefully assembled beforehand, Birgitta notes that the babe, whom his mother hailed as "my Lord and my God" (cf. John 20:28), experienced the discomfort and needs of a normal child: "then the boy, crying and, as it were, trembling from the cold and the hardness of the pavement [or floor] where he lay, rolled a little and extended his limbs, seeking to find refreshment and his Mother's favor."[62] By depicting the Christ Child lying on the ground and presumably feeling some pain as a result of its hardness, Birgitta calls attention to his humanity and also, obliquely, to his future sufferings upon the cross. As did theologians before her, Birgitta claims that Jesus appeared and behaved as a regular human infant.[63] Mary responds to her baby's needs like a caring mother, picking him up and drawing him to her breast, where she warms him with her cheek. She experiences "great joy" as she does so, but also "tender maternal compassion" (*tenera compassione materna*)—sorrow, that is, at seeing her newborn's discomfort.[64] Mary literally suffers with her baby boy. The suggestion here is that even at this peaceful moment, Christ's future sufferings are on the distant horizon. Nevertheless, in this visionary chapter from Birgitta's writings, in contrast to what we find in other passages, Mary does not vocalize her emotions or thoughts, so we are not informed as to whether she was thinking of Christ's future hardships and death at this time.

Nor does Birgitta in her chapter on the Nativity comment on the utter poverty surrounding Christ's birth, as does, for example, the anonymous author of the thirteenth-century *Wooing of Our Lord*. In this text, the anchoritic reader is led to reflect upon the poverty of Jesus' birth, in words that might have been spoken by a Franciscan as well as other lovers of poverty: "you found no house-room in all the town of Bethlehem where your delicate child's limbs might rest, except in a wall-less house in the middle of the street, [where] you were poorly wrapped in rags and tatters, and coldly lodged in a beast's manger."[65] John Gower, the late fourteenth-century contemporary of Geoffrey Chaucer, similarly emphasizes the poverty into which Jesus was born, by remarking that the Christ Child was nestled, as it were, between two beasts, without a curtain to separate the newborn from them, an appurtenance one would except in a courtly "chambre."[66] Below I discuss debates that occurred in the fourteenth century about Christ's poverty and the connections Birgitta makes in other passages between his Nativity and the Passion. Here it is important to note that *Revelationes* 7.21 does not emphasize the Christ Child's poverty or imply a sense of doom, though it does call attention to the discomforts and basic human needs Jesus experienced as an infant and his dependency upon his mother, who is definitely shown to have a practical bent and a finesse in combining simplicity with elegance.

Birgitta describes Mary swaddling Jesus in a typical medieval manner. Although it may be difficult for a modern reader to visualize exactly what Mary is doing, she is clearly putting much care into her task: "And at once she began to wrap him carefully, first in the linen cloths and then in the woolen [ones], binding his little body, legs, and arms with a ribbon that had been sewn into four parts of the outer woolen cloth. And afterward she wrapped and tied on the boy's head those small linen cloths that she had prepared for this purpose."[67] Considering the emphasis placed on Birgitta's use of swaddling cloths and bands, it is interesting to note that medieval artists typically portrayed babies who suffered death and were laid to rest as being swaddled, just like their counterparts fortunate to survive into the later stages of infancy.[68] Sensing an intimation of death in the above-cited Birgittine passage, Albert Ryle Kezel comments that Mary's binding of the Christ Child echoes a detail mentioned in the Passion according to John (20:7), namely, that the cloth that had been tied around Jesus' head was found apart from the other burial clothes within the empty tomb.[69] A more obvious parallel is that the wrappings in both cases are made of linen. While medieval clerical readers steeped in the Bible would undoubtedly have been attuned to such resonances, it is impossible to know the extent to which Birgitta's readers would have perceived them here. As noted below, Birgitta makes a more explicit parallel between Christ's swaddling clothes and his burial shroud when recounting her vision of his sufferings and death in *Revelationes* 7.15. In comparison to other passages in Birgitta's

writings, her vision of the Nativity seems rather two-dimensional, tempo-
rally speaking, in the sense that its allusions to the Passion are minimal. Her
famous and influential chapter on the Nativity closes with a tender scene:
Mary and Joseph, overcome with joy, worshipping the newborn child.[70] Interestingly, here as elsewhere, Birgitta presents a positive image of Joseph; he is
certainly not a cranky old man or a morose Jew irritated by his wife's having
a baby without his involvement, which is how he is often depicted in other
late medieval sources.

   As noted earlier, Birgitta mentions Joseph at the beginning of chapter 21:
after he and Mary arrive at the cave, he ties their ox and ass to a manger and
then brings in a candle, which he affixes to a wall. He then departs "in order not
to be personally present at the birth."[71] In both the *Protoevangelium Jacobi* and
the *Gospel of Pseudo-Matthew*, Joseph brings Mary to a cave that (in *Pseudo-
Matthew*) is initially enveloped in darkness but illuminated by the presence
of Mary, who enters into it with Jesus in utero.[72] Joseph's tending to a candle
in Birgitta's text may suggest her knowledge of the apocryphal infancy tradition, because it implies that, in her vision of the Nativity, there was originally
a dark cave that Joseph sought to make more habitable. Whereas in apocryphal infancy texts Joseph departs in order to look for a midwife (who turns
out to be superfluous), in Birgitta's chapter he appears confident that Mary
can manage on her own and so leaves out of a sense of propriety. In the apocryphal texts, Joseph encounters a bright light when he returns and enters the
cave after Jesus' birth.[73] Birgitta similarly emphasizes the light from the newborn Jesus: "such great and ineffable light and splendor [went out from him]
that the sun could not be compared to it."[74] These details concerning bright
light are no doubt ultimately owing to the identification of the Son of God
with light in the Gospel of John (1:5–9; cf. 9:5), and are also related to the
centuries-old metaphor that likened Jesus' harmless entrance into and exit
from Mary to light passing through glass,[75] but the fact that such details appear
in both the apocrypha and in Birgitta's text suggests that the former influenced
the latter. While Birgitta may have borrowed the motif of a supernaturally
bright light from the apocrypha, she emphasizes the newborn's corporeality,
which undermines the suggestion of some (more obscure) apocryphal texts that
the baby Jesus was merely a dazzling spectacle of light.[76]

   Furthermore, Birgitta seems to reject the derogatory depiction of Joseph
as a suspicious husband, ineffectual father, and cranky old man, which is found
in the apocrypha and a range of late medieval sources.[77] Although Birgitta
agrees with the apocrypha in describing Joseph as a *senex* ("an old man"), at

the beginning of the chapter on the Nativity she uses the adjective *honestissimus* ("most honorable") to characterize him, and at the end describes how he weeps for joy upon reentering the cave and seeing the baby Jesus.[78] Birgitta adds another touching detail (which reinforces her positive depiction of Joseph but actually contradicts Lk. 2:7): Joseph assists Mary in placing the baby Jesus in the manger. So here Joseph actually holds his foster-son, and presumably gazes on him with eyes of wonder, such as Bernard of Clairvaux had earlier ascribed to him when speaking of how privileged Joseph was to hold his foster-son Jesus and to take care of him.[79] Also complimentary to Joseph is Birgitta's mention at the end of the chapter that both parents adored the baby Jesus on bended knee (a detail already noted). As discussed below, Birgitta similarly presents Joseph in a positive light in *Revelationes* 6.58–59, where she explicitly counters the demeaning images of him circulating in her day. With regard to *Revelationes* 7.21, it is likely that the omission (the midwives' postpartum arrival) and addition of small details (such as Joseph's crying) were intentional, and served Birgitta's aim of creating a pious and more reverent alternative to the apocryphal infancy tradition, even though these legends (as argued in the previous chapter) were apparently not considered offensive by most medieval Christians.[80]

## Swaddling the Infant Jesus in *Revelationes* 1.10 and the Friday Lesson of *Sermo Angelicus*

A synopsis of the key episodes of Mary's life can be found in *Revelationes* 1.10, where she provides her perspective on both the Annunciation and the Passion. Mary recounts these events in detail, but only briefly touches upon the Nativity and childhood of Christ. After emphasizing the joy she experienced and her absence of pain when giving birth to Jesus,[81] Mary goes on to recall the mixed feelings that came over her as she admired her son's beauty and gazed at the different members of his body:

> When I looked upon him and contemplated his beauty, knowing myself to be unworthy of such a son, joy seeped through my soul like drops of dew. When I contemplated the places where, as I had learned through the prophets, his hands and feet would be nailed at the crucifixion (Ps. 21:17), my eyes filled with tears and my heart was torn by sadness. My Son looked at my crying eyes then and

became deathly saddened. When I contemplated his divine power, I was consoled again, realizing that this was the way he wanted it and so it was the right way, and I conformed all my will to his. So my joy was *always* mixed with sorrow.[82] (emphasis mine)

This passage appears immediately after Mary's comments on giving birth to Jesus, so it may refer to her gazing upon her newborn babe. Yet Mary may also be speaking of a repeated experience, especially since she reminisces in a general way about the admixture of joy and sorrow that she "always" felt.

In this passage the Mary of Birgitta's text emphasizes the Christ Child's beauty (*pulchritudo eius*), as she does in other places, notably at the beginning of *Revelationes* 6.1, where Mary recalls how Jews, despite their ignorance of his divinity, used to come to see the infant Jesus in order to be consoled by his beauty (a challenge to the notion that there was "no beauty in him," found in Isaiah 53:2).[83] Mary does not explain how Jesus' appearance had such a soothing effect, though other texts speak to the power of his beauty. The *Book of the Blessed Angela of Foligno*, for instance, which relates the visions of a thirteenth-century Franciscan tertiary, provides a striking account of the effect of the infant Jesus' glance: when the babe whom Angela was graced to hold in her arms opened up his eyes and looked at her, she felt completely overwhelmed with love, almost as if she were struck by fire.[84] In the chapter from the *Revelationes* (6.1) just mentioned, Birgitta further emphasizes the Christ Child's physical perfection by having Mary attest that "his body . . . was so pure (*mundus*) that no lice or maggots ever touched him, for these creatures showed reverence to their creator (*vermis reuerenciam factori suo exhibebat*). Not even tangles or dirtiness were ever found in his hair."[85] This passage not only speaks to the Christ Child's pristine condition but also his lordship over creatures, a point that the apocryphal legends make repeatedly, as, for instance, when the *Vita rhythmica* recounts how beasts on the Flight into Egypt paid homage to the baby Jesus.[86]

In calling attention to Christ's beauty and bodily perfection, which she does in a few passages,[87] Birgitta undoubtedly has in mind Psalm 44:3 about the beloved's beauty exceeding that of "the sons of men"—a notion frequently applied to Christ in medieval religious texts. In the vita of St. Edmund of Abingdon, for example, the boy Edmund is struck by the attractiveness of his heavenly visitor, before he realizes who he is—none other than the Christ Child.[88]

In *Revelationes* 1.10, the vulnerability of the Christ Child's beautiful body and the looming threat of the Passion are underscored by the abrupt turn

Mary makes in her imaginative recollection: the scene of peaceful domesticity she describes quickly shifts to one of violence, as Mary visualizes the piercing of her son's hands and feet.[89] Here, as in other passages, Mary is presented
as a prophetess, or at least a biblical exegete finely attuned to prophetic utterances concerning Christ in the Old Testament. Mary's reference, in the passage cited above, to the rending of her heart ("my heart was torn by sadness")
may be an allusion to Simeon's prophecy that her heart would be pierced (Lk.
2:35), a key scriptural source of Mary's awareness of her son's future Passion.
The Christ Child's nonverbal response to his mother's sorrow (he "became
deathly saddened") foreshadows Jesus' sadness in the Garden of Gethsemane,
where his soul was "sorrowful even until death" (Matt. 26:37–38). Like the
adult Christ, whose pain was thought to be intensified when he viewed Mary
from the cross,[90] the Christ Child is filled with sadness at the sight of his
mother's emotional distress. To be sure, Christ's sensitivity to his mother's feelings demonstrates his premature intelligence and foreknowledge of his future
sufferings. Here, as elsewhere in Birgitta's writings, we see that Christ's childhood was hardly a time of continuous carefree delight for Mary and Jesus, as
might be concluded from the jocund faces of the Virgin and Child that we
tend to associate with roughly contemporary Gothic statuary.

By having Mary reflect upon and willingly accept God's will in *Revelationes* 1.10, Birgitta raises her above the level of typical female emotionality, as
it was constructed in numerous late medieval images and texts.[91] The chapter
on the Circumcision in the pseudo-Bonaventuran *Meditationes vitae Christi*,
for example, tells how Mary wept on account of her infant son's physical pain,
which he manifested by his tears. The baby Jesus, in turn, attempted to make
his mother stop crying, by gesturing to her with tenderness, to which Mary responded: "'Son, if you want me to stop crying, then you stop too. I cannot stop
crying while you are crying.' And then out of compassion for his mother, her
son eased off into little sobs."[92] Both authors, in these particular passages, show
Mary managing to moderate her sadness, yet Birgitta speaks of the Virgin's
emotional restraint on more than one occasion, here and elsewhere. One can
almost say that resignation seems Mary's way of life.

As already noted, in the *Sermo angelicus*, in the second lesson (or reading) for Friday, the day devoted to the commemoration of the Passion in the
weekly liturgical cycle, Birgitta emphasizes that Mary was gifted with prophetic insight. The lesson for this day begins by arguing analogously that if
the Hebrew prophets had foreknown the Incarnation and the Passion, then
how much more must the Virgin, "whom God had predestined before time

began to be his mother," have been aware of these future events. Inspired by the Holy Spirit, Mary is said to have understood the prophecies more than did the men who served as their mouthpieces, and thus "the reason that God chose to be clothed in human flesh in her womb (*humana carne in eius vtero dignabatur vestiri*) was not concealed from her."[93] After arguing for the perfection of Mary's prophetic knowledge, the lesson for Friday describes her musings on the Passion as she takes care of the Christ Child's body. Mary's introspection in this chapter is similar to her sense of foreboding found in *Revelationes* 1.10, except that here, her meditation on the future Passion is much more elaborate, involving details that do not refer to Old Testament prophecies per se. The passage seems to move from an instance of clothing the newborn Christ to the numerous times when Mary clothed her son during his infancy. The accumulation of descriptive details in this passage effectively conveys Mary's absorption in affective meditation:

> When the Virgin first began to touch him with her hands (*primo suis manibus tractare cepit*) after his birth, we can truly believe that she began at once to think of how he was going to fulfill the biblical prophecies. When she wrapped him in swaddling clothes, her heart considered how his body was going to be wounded all over with sharp scourges to make it appear like that of a leper (Isa. 53:4). When she bound her little Son's hands and feet with swaddling bands (*in fascia*), she called to mind how harshly they would be pierced by iron nails on the cross (Ps. 21:17). When she contemplated her Son's face, more beautiful than that of any of the sons of men (Ps. 44:3), she thought how irreverently the lips of impious men would stain it with their spit. The Mother often turned over in her mind the blows that would be struck against her Son's cheeks and the insults and reproaches that would fill his ears. Now she considered how the stream of his own blood would block his sight, then again how sour wine mixed with gall would be poured into his mouth. Then she would bring to mind how his arms would be tied with ropes, how his muscles and veins and all his joints would be pitilessly stretched out on the cross, how his vital organs would contract at the moment of death and how his entire body, inside and out, would undergo harsh and anguishing torment on the cross. The Virgin knew that when he breathed his last on the cross, a sharp lance would pierce his side and penetrate his heart.[94]

While Mary's vision of Christ's future sufferings is rooted in a tactile experience, she reads the Christ Child's body with her eyes, intellectually,[95] as if it were a Passion text recounting his sufferings and death.[96] In a number of ways the vision presented in this lesson parallels depictions of the Passion in the art and literature of the later Middle Ages. The likening of Christ to a leper, for example, while ultimately derived from Isaiah 53:4, was taken to an extreme in images that portrayed Jesus' body being completely covered with wounds.[97] The phrase "lips of wicked men" recalls the grotesque features of Christ's persecutors in late medieval art, who were often caricatured as unattractive-looking Jews.[98]

Also worth noting is that Birgitta, in the Friday lesson from the *Sermo angelicus*, shifts the reader's attention from Christ's sufferings to Mary's by relating how Mary's prophetic sensibilities dispelled her sense of joy: "Hence, of all mothers she was the happiest, when she saw God's Son born of her body. . . . Yet she was also the most sorrowful of mothers, because of her foreknowledge of his most painful sufferings."[99] Birgitta, undoubtedly recalling her own natural experience of excruciating labor pains, uses the image of a woman giving birth in order to explain the coexistence of opposing emotions within Mary's heart: "greatest happiness" (*maximam leticiam*) and "heaviest sorrow" (*grauissima mesticia*). Yet instead of comparing the Virgin—as we might expect—to a woman who, upon seeing her newborn child, suddenly forgets (or at least no longer pays attention to) the pain she just experienced, Birgitta says that Mary was like a woman who endured the pains of childbirth throughout her entire life and was grieved by the thought of her own sufferings.[100] Since the biological pains of childbirth are in actuality short-lived (relatively speaking) perhaps Birgitta here has in mind the psychological pains that mothers experience on account of their children (she herself was apparently always very concerned and anxious about the behavior and fates of her own children).[101] For Birgitta, as for Mary, spiritual motherhood was a never-ending, stressful occupation.

As mentioned above, the passage from the *Sermo angelicus* we have been considering occurs as the second lesson for Friday in the Birgittine Breviary, a book which organizes passages from the *Sermo angelicus* for the nuns' recitation at matins on the different days of the week. As the lesson draws to a close, Birgitta refers to the prophecy of Simeon that a sword would pierce the Virgin's soul (Lk. 2:35). In her appropriation of this passage here, Birgitta underscores the depths of Mary's emotional sufferings by pointing out, philosophically, that the soul is more sensitive to pain than the body.[102] Birgitta observes that the "sword of sorrow came ever nearer to the Virgin's heart as the time of her Son's [P]assion approached."[103] In its ever more menacing aspect, the sword of sorrows, as Birgitta presents it, resembles the sword hanging by an ever more tenuous horse's hair that forestalled Damocles' (vicarious) enjoyment of a tyrant's life replete with luxuries.[104] Mary's present joys are similarly dispelled by future sorrows, which continue to approach day by day. Immediately following the description of the sword of sorrow is the assurance that Jesus, having compassion for his mother's sufferings, as a good son should, consoled her, presumably throughout his lifetime. The implication seems to be that otherwise Mary would not have been able to survive until his death.[105] Similarly, the reader is encouraged to console the sorrowful Virgin as Christ himself repeatedly did.[106] This is followed by a prayer that is both in praise of Mary—who willingly endured the sword that pierced her heart—and in supplication for her help, lest the sword of spiritual death slay the sisters' souls.[107] Thus, the text not only encourages emotional involvement in the lives of Mary and Jesus, but directs the readers' attention to a consideration of the dangers threatening their own spiritual condition.

## Birgitta's Influence on Margery Kempe's Meditations on Christ's Nativity

The middle-class housewife-turned-holy woman Margery Kempe, who flourished at the beginning of the fifteenth century, was familiar with Birgitta's *Revelationes*, which a young priest seems to have read to her along with other religious texts.[108] Margery's efforts to pattern herself after Birgitta,[109] whom she admired and identified with as a non-virginal bride of Christ, indicate that, at the very least, she was familiar with the saint's vita. Retracing Birgitta's footsteps, Margery made pilgrimages to the Holy Land, Rome, and Santiago de Compostela. In Rome, Margery spoke with Birgitta's former maid and visited the chamber in which the saint had lived.[110] Back in England she visited her country's sole Birgittine foundation, Syon Abbey, to obtain the indulgence granted to pilgrim visitors; while she was there, she might have learned more about the Birgittine Order's foundress and her writings, or derivative texts, such as *The Myroure of oure Ladye*.[111] The latter includes the aforementioned Friday lesson of the *Sermo angelicus* that "tellyth of the sorowes that oure lady suffered after the byrth of her sonne, vnto the tyme of his passyon."[112]

In the early part of her autobiographical book, Margery recounts how, when Jesus instructed her to meditate on his mother, she had a vision of the childhood of Mary and the birth of Christ. Whereas Birgitta, in her famous vision of the Nativity (*Revelationes* 7.21), remains a reverent spectator, Margery, betraying a pronounced bourgeois focus on hands-on practicality and busyness, and undoubtedly influenced by the *Meditationes vitae Christi* (as well as Birgitta's writings),[113] imagines herself striving to provide for the Holy Family's necessities as they travel to Bethlehem:

> And than went the creatur forth with owyr Lady to Bedlem and purchasyd hir herborwe every nyght. . . . Sche beggyd owyr Lady fayr whyte clothys and kerchys for to swathyn in hir sone whan he wer born; and whan Jhesu was born, sche ordeyned beddyng for owyr Lady to lyg in wyth hir blyssyd sone. And sythen sche beggyd mete for owyr Lady and hir blyssyd chyld. Aftyrward sche swathyd hym wyth byttyr teerys of compassyon, havyng mend of the scharp deth that he schuld suffyr for the lofe of synful men, seyng to hym: "Lord, I schal fare fayre [behave well] wyth yow; I shal not byndyn yow soor. I pray yow beth not dysplesyd wyth me."[114]

Like the Virgin in Birgitta's vision of the Nativity, Margery is concerned that clean ("fayr white") pieces of cloth be set aside for swaddling the newborn Jesus. By inserting herself into the Nativity story as a rather intrusive attendant who prepares Mary's bedding after she has given birth, Margery builds upon the older iconographic tradition of Byzantine origin, which portrayed Mary lying next to the newborn babe, cared for by female attendants.[115] Imitating the legendary women who bathed the infant Jesus, Margery tends to the newborn, covering and also washing him with her "byttyr teerys." By clothing the infant and seeking food for him, Margery makes unnecessary Joseph's purported efforts to prepare porridge for the newborn child and also swaddling bands from his cut-up stockings (which is not surprising considering her tendency to take control within her own marriage).[116] Perhaps Margery's swaddling of the baby Jesus with her tears, rather than with actual strips of cloth—that is, with her affections rather than with physical objects—was owing to the influence of Bonaventure's *De quinque festivitatibus pueri Jesu*, a short treatise in which the Franciscan theologian and spiritual advisor encourages those who have given birth to Christ in their souls to care for the Child, as did Mary, despite his physical absence.[117] Yet unlike this and other spiritual works that encouraged devout Christians to tend to the infant Jesus who inhabited their souls, Margery, as seen through the adventures recounted in her book, insists upon seeking him out in the world.[118]

Another notable feature of Margery's vision of the Nativity is her fear that she will unintentionally cause the infant pain by swaddling him too tightly, as well as her thoughts of the Passion as she binds him: "havyng mend of the scharp deth that he schuld suffyr for the lofe of synful men," she said to him, "Lord, I schal fare fayre wyth yow; I shal not byndyn yow soor." In this scene, Margery does not simply focus on what is before her, but mentally looks forward to what is to come. Without doubt, her interaction and monologue with the infant Jesus in this vision is a direct borrowing from Birgitta of Sweden: specifically, the Virgin's premonition of the Christ Child's future death, as she herself swaddles him, which is found in both *The Myroure of oure Ladye* and the *Revelationes*.[119] However, in contrast to Mary in Birgitta's texts, Margery actually speaks to the babe, assuring him, like a comforting (though rather overanxious) nanny, that she has no intention of harming him.

## Uncovering the Hidden Life of Jesus in *Revelationes*, Book 6

Whereas the Virgin says elsewhere that the joys she experienced at the Nativity of Christ and during his childhood were tempered by the sorrow occasioned by her awareness of his future death, in *Revelationes* 6.57 she enumerates six sources, or *loci*, of her *dolores*. The first of these is her thoughts of Jesus' Passion when she was swaddling him, while the rest concern her indirect experience of the Passion as it was occurring and the difficulties she and Jesus' disciples faced on earth after his death.[120] At the beginning of the next chapter (6.58), Mary comments on the Holy Family's Flight into Egypt to escape Herod's soldiers, who sought to kill her and her loved ones, an addendum to the list of sorrows she provided earlier. Significantly, medieval representations of the Flight into Egypt often portray the Holy Family traveling at a steady pace (and sometimes resting) in a rural setting, which may draw a viewer's attention away from the mortal danger that threatened the infant Jesus and his family. Here, in contrast, Mary emphasizes the sorrow (and presumably fear) she experienced on that occasion, explaining that her emotions were more powerful than the knowledge she had of the prophecies concerning her son.[121]

In the rest of the chapter (58), Mary goes beyond the biblically recorded events of Jesus' life and provides an insider's view of his childhood: his life within the Holy Family and in the Jewish community in which he lived in the early stages of his life. Apart from a chapter on the youth of Christ in the *Meditationes vitae Christi*, in which the Franciscan author speculates on what Jesus did and did not do from age twelve to thirty, no other medieval text that I am aware of (excepting the apocryphal narratives) makes such a serious attempt at delving deeply into the hidden life of Jesus, by recovering some specific details and by sketching out some basic patterns.[122]

As we saw in Chapter 2, Bernard of Clairvaux speaks of the life of Cistercian monks as "hidden"—an idea that reappeared in Early Modern Carmelite texts that often draw attention to Jesus' childhood. The nun or monk hidden within the cloister was thought to be imitating Christ, who spent the majority of his life in obscurity. "Note well," says a seventeenth-century Carmelite spiritual writer, "that the monasteries of this order are houses of the Virgin. If you, therefore, are called to imitate Jesus Christ, contemplate the type of life he spent in the house of his mother. It was a humble life, a secluded life, an unknown life, a hidden life."[123] It seems fair to say that many monks and nuns were drawn to the mystery of Jesus' hidden years—his obscurity—because they themselves had chosen reclusion. But interest in the misty and unrecorded happenings of Jesus' youth was apparently not restricted to those who were cloistered; laypeople, whose lives were in many ways repetitive and mundane, could also have related to the Holy Family's interactions within their home at Nazareth. Moreover, a female layperson might approach this topic differently than would a male layperson, who might, for example, take a greater interest in the experiences of St. Joseph. It is thus significant that in *Revelationes* 6.58 Joseph has only a shadowy presence; while he is definitely not portrayed in a derogatory way, he is indistinct nevertheless. In shedding light on the family life of Jesus in this chapter, Mary seems concerned about conveying to Birgitta a sense of her intimacy with her son and of the joys and sorrows she herself experienced during his childhood—in other words, her perspective—rather than with recounting specific memorable events or presenting Jesus as a role model of humble obscurity (though the Virgin does speak to the, in many ways, ordinariness of her son's life). Narrated in the first person, *Revelationes* 6.58 offers the reader a glimpse into Mary's tender heart, where she stored the memories of her son's childhood, the period of his life hidden from most of his early followers and certainly from those of later centuries.

As noted above, within the Western tradition the heart is often considered the seat of affectivity and so (at least popularly) a receptacle of emotion-tinged memories. The Gospel of Luke speaks twice of Mary's heart as a treasure-house of memories: the Evangelist calls attention to Mary's storage of events when she witnesses the shepherds' visitation of her newborn son (2:19), as well as when she and Joseph, upon finding the child Jesus in the Temple, hear him say that he must be about his Father's business (2:51).[124] *Revelationes* 6.58 similarly demonstrates that the words and deeds of the boy Jesus made a deep impression upon his mother and were treasured in her heart. Other women later imitated Mary's pensive interiority, such as the handicapped Dominican tertiary Margherita da Città di Castello (d. 1320), in whom the notion of the heart as a storage-house was literalized. After her death, three stones engraved with images of the Holy Family were removed from Margherita's heart.[125]

By providing Mary's emotionally colored perspective on Christ's childhood, Birgitta presents Mary as a prototypical female who responds to day-to-day happenings from the heart and registers events and impressions there as well. In contrast, Joseph is portrayed here and elsewhere in Birgitta's *Revelationes* as a faithful father and spouse, but his perspective on Christ's childhood is not given, except only indirectly and minimally. It is Mary who speaks to Birgitta, another woman who has also been a mother, as to a confidante. Although it might seem inappropriate to use the term "gossip" to describe Mary's discussion with Birgitta, the word (in its more archaic sense) is relevant in this case since it originally referred to speech among neighbors or relatives, especially females.[126] Applying the word "gossip" to Mary's speech in *Revelationes* 6.58 is thus appropriate, even though their conversation is not—to borrow another Middle English term—mere "jangling" (or idle talk). What Mary is talking about is important: the hidden life of Jesus within the Holy Family, which the male authors of the canonical gospels apparently had no access to or simply chose to ignore.

The "secrets" that Mary reveals in this chapter are, to be sure, not "gossipy" in nature, yet they have a distinctly feminine character by virtue of their conveying Mary's emotional responses to events in her son's early life. These events from Jesus' childhood and adolescence are also "secret" in the sense that they are not contained within the canonical gospels, but are the sorts of details we would expect to find in apocryphal literature—texts concerned with hidden matters whose authorship is essentially unknown. Thus, by focusing on Jesus' hidden life, Mary's disclosure in *Revelationes* 6.58 may be seen as an alternative to the apocryphal legends of Christ's childhood that circulated in the later Middle Ages. Whereas the authorship of these latter texts was enveloped in uncertainty, this chapter of Birgitta's *Revelationes* purports to transcribe the words of the Virgin herself, who closely observed her son throughout his life, especially during his childhood. In the *Legenda aurea*, Jacobus de Voragine explains that Luke, along similar lines, derived his knowledge about the Nativity of Christ from Mary.[127] How else would he have known what transpired on that first Christmas Eve when no one else but the members of the Holy Family were present? Birgitta likewise goes to the source of the Gospel when listening to Mary tell her what happened during Christ's hidden years. Birgitta then disseminates Mary's account, thus imitating the Evangelists.

An examination of particular details in *Revelationes* 6.58 suggests even more strongly that, in writing it, Birgitta may have been influenced by the apocrypha. Even if Birgitta disapproved of apocryphal legends about the Christ Child, nevertheless, she has in common with those anonymous storytellers who composed and transmitted legends about the boy Jesus a marked curiosity about his hidden life. This curiosity probably underlies the many questions recorded by Birgitta earlier, in Book 5, purportedly asked by a monk about the obscurity and ordinariness of Jesus' childhood.[128]

Having briefly commented on the Slaughter of the Innocents in the beginning of *Revelationes* 6.58, Mary says to Birgitta, "Now you might ask what my Son did during all that time before he was to suffer."[129] While it is possible that Mary is taking the discussion in a new, though related direction on her own initiative, it is likely that she is responding to Birgitta's noticeable inquisitiveness about Jesus' childhood. Mary's answer to Birgitta's question—whether hypothetical or actual—is at first a refusal to pry into such hidden matters. The response of the Virgin agrees with the views of orthodox churchmen: Mary explains that the only thing that Scripture says about Christ's childhood is that "he was subject to his parents" (Lk. 2:51). As Jesus' constant companion, not only at the Finding of the Temple, but throughout his early life, Mary is surely in a position to fill in a large number of the lacunae left by Scripture.

Mary provides her rationale for avoiding the question put to her, and then makes the additional, rather generic comment that Jesus "behaved like other young children until he grew up."[130] As noted in Chapter 3, apocryphal legends about Christ's childhood circulating in the later Middle Ages tended to emphasize the childishness of Jesus, how he acted like a normal boy and sometimes did things that bordered on naughtiness, or were definitely mischievous. This is probably not what Mary is referring to, however. Back in Book 5, in response to an anonymous monk's questions about the Incarnation (and other matters, which Birgitta faithfully transmits), God makes the point on more than one occasion that Christ willingly subjected himself to time and the ordinary course of nature in choosing to undergo normal human development. For example, the question arises as to why Jesus remained so long within the Virgin's womb and did not come forth at once; the response given is that God chose to obey the laws of nature that he himself established, partly to forestall the conclusion that his humanity was "fantastical and untrue (*humanitatis mee assumpcio fantastica fuisset et non vera*)."[131] Birgitta even asks about Jesus' increase in size, entertaining the hypothesis that he should have been big all at once (an idea that William Langland, along similar lines, hints at, in his description of the Christ Child as "big" and "bold," even when he was still in the womb).[132] The explanation that God provides is that it behooved Christ to take on a body like that of Adam and his children whom he came to redeem, and that his body had to be that in which he "could labor from morn to evening and from year to year, even to the end of death."[133] Mary may be making a similar point when she says (in *Revelationes* 6.58) that Jesus "behaved like other young children." In other words, he did not exempt himself from the laws of nature that govern human childhood and thereby cause people to wonder about what kind of being he was. And he presumably behaved in the same obedient and respectful way as do other good children.

That Birgitta, in *Revelationes* 6.58, may have in mind the apocrypha's depiction of the Christ Child as a wonder-worker is suggested by the fact that Mary goes on to address the issue of whether *mirabilia* distinguished Jesus' childhood:[134] "Miraculous happenings (*mirabilia*) were indeed not lacking during his youth—[1] creatures that served their creator, [2] idols that became mute and many that collapsed on his coming into Egypt, [3] astrologers (*magi*) who foretold my Son to be a sign of things to come, [4] the mysterious appearance of angels (*misteria* [or *ministeria*] *angelorum apparuerunt*), [5] the absence of any unclean dirt (*immundicia*) on him or any knots (*perplexitas*) in his hair."[135] In his note on this passage, the editor of the Latin text, Birger Bergh, cites the apocryphal *Gospel of Pseudo-Matthew* (chapters 22–23), which recounts how, when the Holy Family arrived in Egypt and Mary and the Christ Child entered into the temple at Sotinen, the idols toppled over. Bergh's reference, while helpful, does not go very far toward explicating this list of wonders. *Pseudo-Matthew* could be cited as a source or analogue for the first item in the list as well; chapter 20 of this apocryphal text recounts (as already noted) how the wild beasts that the Holy Family encountered on the Flight into Egypt became tame at the Child's command and showed them the way on their journey. Mary's mention of creatures serving their Creator may refer more particularly to the ox and the ass's recognition of their master, the divine child, when he was placed in their food trough—a detail diffused widely through visual culture, which is mentioned in chapter 14 of *Pseudo-Matthew*. This first wonder enumerated by Mary also echoes a remark she made at the beginning of Book 6: that the worm showed reverence toward its Creator. The third wonder listed in *Revelationes* 6.58 probably refers to the question the Magi posed in the canonical Gospel of Matthew (2:2) about where they might find the "king of the Jews." The fourth wonder, concerning the angels' "misteria" or "ministeria" (the alternative reading) may signify the angels' announcement to the shepherds of the birth of Christ in Luke (2:8–15).[136] It may also refer to the angels who hovered around the boy Jesus, which Mary mentions later in this same chapter.[137] The fifth item in this list is one that we have encountered before, at the very beginning of Book 6, except that there the impeccable cleanliness of the Christ Child's body and the perfect neatness of his hair were not explicitly said to constitute a wonderful occurrence.[138]

Mary concludes her list of *mirabilia* by noting that it is actually not necessary for Birgitta to know these things since Scripture gives sufficient proof of Christ's humanity and divinity.[139] The fact that Mary refers to Scripture's treatment of Christ's childhood suggests that Birgitta is conscious of the importunity of her own curiosity; it may also imply an ambiguity on her part about legendary traditions concerning the childhood of Jesus. Somewhat in contradiction to what she just said, Mary goes on to provide glimpses into the boyhood of Jesus, mentioning things that one might expect a pious Jewish boy to do: Jesus was continually engaged in prayer, he celebrated the religious feasts with his family, he did honest labor with his hands. Mary also notes the powerful impression that Jesus made upon others: his appearance and his speech were so wonderful and pleasing that those who were troubled came to be consoled by the mere sight of him. This detail reiterates Mary's assertion in the first chapter of Book 6 that many Jews flocked to the Christ Child to gaze upon his beauty.[140] Echoing Luke 2:52 ("Jesus advanced in wisdom and age and grace with God and men"), Mary remarks (though in passing and not with a clear reference to the Finding in the Temple episode) that her son "grew in age and the wisdom that he had in full from the start." Through these utterances of Mary, Birgitta touches upon the vexed question as to how Christ the Incarnate Wisdom could grow in wisdom, but without offering much of an explanation. Elaborating on the comment she made elsewhere that divine solace compensated for her sorrows, Mary explains that Jesus often spoke privately to her and Joseph in words that were both consoling and indicative of his divinity (*verba deitatis*). In this particular passage, she does not explicitly mention her premonitions of the Christ Child's future sufferings and death, but rather seems to have in mind the challenges of day-to-day life: "When we found ourselves in circumstances of poverty, fear[s] or difficulties, he made no gold or silver for us but encouraged us to be patient."[141] While "fears" may allude to Mary's terror at Herod's order to slaughter all the infants as well as to her dread of Christ's future Passion, it more likely refers to the stressful situations and challenges that the Holy Family encountered in providing for their needs and seeking to live peacefully among their neighbors, who in the apocrypha, as we have seen, are often portrayed as menacing. Recall, too, the description in the *Meditationes vitae Christi* of how Mary had to sew and spin to support her family, and how the child Jesus assisted her, and in that role often had to interact with difficult clients.[142] Birgitta's Mary similarly emphasizes the Holy Family's poverty when she implies that her son did not miraculously endow his family with money though he could have done so, and when she remarks, "we had only what we needed for our upkeep and nothing superfluous."[143]

Further, Mary calls attention to the teaching that Jesus did in his youth: "Besides this he had familiar conversations at home with visiting friends regarding the law and its meanings and symbols. He had open discussions (*Disputabat eciam in aperto*) with experts so that they were amazed and said, 'Joseph's boy (*filius Ioseph*) instructs the teachers—some great spirit is speaking through him.'"[144] This latter statement echoes the pedagogical episodes in the apocrypha and also alludes to the fourth chapter in Luke, which recounts that, after the adult Jesus was tempted in the desert for forty days, he returned to Nazareth and went to the synagogue, where he read the prophet Isaiah, specifically the passage that tells of the coming of a healer and liberator (Isa. 61:1). When Jesus informed his audience that that prophecy was fulfilled that very day, they "wondered at the words of grace that proceeded from his mouth, and said: 'Is not this the son of Joseph?'" (Lk. 4:22) Although the age of Jesus in this incident is not specified, Scripture suggests that he had already turned thirty, since the fasting and temptation in the desert, which preceded the episode in the synagogue, happened after Christ's baptism, which was thought to have occurred in his thirtieth year (cf. Lk. 3:21–23, 4:1–2, 16–30).[145] Mary's description of the boy Jesus teaching in *Revelationes* 6.58 seems creatively to combine different elements from Luke, both the anecdote about the adult Jesus in the synagogue and the tale of Jesus' earlier display of wisdom. I refer, of course, to Luke's account of how Mary and Joseph found the twelve-year-old Jesus in the Temple, "sitting in the midst of the doctors, hearing

them, and asking them questions. And all that heard him were astonished at
his wisdom and his answers" (Lk. 2:46–47). A little further on in *Revelationes* 6.58, Mary calls attention to her spouse's paternal authority by noting that
Jesus was always obedient to Joseph, immediately carrying out his orders.[146]
The placement of this detail after Mary's description (in *Revelationes* 6.58) of
Jesus teaching suggests that Jesus was still a boy when he openly instructed
the teachers, since Joseph was generally believed to have died before the wedding feast of Cana, which occurred after Christ's baptism and before the
commencement of his public ministry.[147] By linking the scene in the synagogue with that in the Temple, Mary's remarks imply that Jesus disputed with
the Jewish teachers while he was still a child, which he also is depicted as
doing in the apocryphal infancy narratives. Taking the Temple scene in the
second chapter of Luke as their cue, the apocryphal legends, as we have seen,
repeatedly focus on the interaction between Jesus and his teachers, who are
alternately astounded, infuriated, and humbled by the Boy's amazing wisdom and frequently offensive candor.[148]

Before recounting how the child Jesus attracted attention to himself by
his words, Mary mentions, as if in passing, that Jesus "marvelously" protected
the Holy Family from "envious people" (*mirabiliter seruati fuimus a inuidiis*).[149]
Considering that his parents were poor and thus lacking in desirable material
goods, this envy was probably directed at Jesus on account of his talents, good
looks, or other remarkable qualities. Perhaps the Christ Child's amazing wisdom, manifested in theological discussions with elders, was a particular cause
of this envy. Mary here, unfortunately, does not elaborate, but her suggestion
of an ominous threat issuing from "invidii," while subtle, is nevertheless significant. In an earlier passage, the sense of sight is explicitly connected with
Jesus' enemies,[150] which, considering that *invidia* is at root associated with
vision,[151] may be a reference to the "invidii" spoken of here. Recall that at the
beginning of Book 6, it is specifically Jews who are said to have gazed, as if
with fascination, upon the Christ Child. So the envious and hostile people
mentioned in this chapter are probably meant to be understood as Jesus' Jewish neighbors. As we have seen in Chapter 3, Jewish envy is a central feature
of late medieval adaptations of *Pseudo-Matthew*—envy being construed in
the specialized sense of jealousy or unhappiness at another person's good for-
tune, as well as in the broader sense of ill will. The trope of the Jews as envious
was also briefly noted in Chapter 2, where it was a matter of the Jews, according to Aelred, directing envy at those who experienced the adult Christ's
mercy.[152]

Thus, according to Mary's account in *Revelationes* 6.58, tension was clearly in the air when Jesus was growing up, even though the Virgin portrays her son as a pious and cooperative child. Just as Mary ponders her son's future death elsewhere in Birgitta's writings, so in chapter 58, which provides a partial and tantalizing disclosure of Jesus' childhood, she worries about the suffering (*passio*) that he will experience—whether in the near or distant future, or both, is not clear. Having noted how the young Jesus instructed his elders, Mary recounts how he consoled her by informing her of his intention to fulfill the will of his Father:

> Once when he saw me feeling sad (*mestissima*) because I was thinking about his passion (*cogitanti mihi de passione*), he said to me: "Do you not believe, Mother, that I am in the Father and the Father in me? (cf. John 14:11) Were you defiled by my entrance or [did you feel] pain (*tribulata es*) at my emergence? Why do you feel sad? The Father's will is that I should suffer and die, and my will belongs to the Father. What I have from the Father cannot suffer, but the flesh, which I have received from you, will suffer in order that the flesh of others might be redeemed and their spirits saved."[153]

In this scene, the Christ Child seeks to console his mother by reminding her of his divinity, and thus the incapacity of his divine nature to suffer.[154] The attention Jesus calls to the intactness of Mary's virginity (which was not injured by his entry into or exit from her) may allude to Luke's account of the angel Gabriel's announcement concerning Mary's miraculous maternity, which initially caused her to be emotionally unsettled. According to Luke (1:29), when the angel told her she was blessed among women, she "was troubled (*turbata est*) at his saying, and thought within herself (*cogitabat*) what manner of salutation this should be." To allay her worries, Gabriel tells Mary not to fear and explains that the conception of Jesus within her will occur through the overshadowing of the Holy Ghost (Lk. 1:30–35). Mary's concern about her son's well-being, expressed in the passage from Birgitta quoted above, not only echoes details from the account of the Annunciation in Luke, but also seems to resonate with scenes from the apocryphal infancy narratives, in which Mary is concerned about the safety of her Child because he repeatedly incurs the envy and wrath of the Jewish elders. Yet whereas the apocryphal childhood legends also highlight Joseph's worries about his gifted foster child (which are sometimes quite severe), here it is only Mary who is emotionally troubled on account of her son.[155]

The dialogue between Mary and the young Jesus concerning his future death—the most striking aspect of *Revelationes* 6.58—is quite similar to what we encounter in some Middle English lyrics. In one such poem, considered a lullaby, found in a late fourteenth-century manuscript, the narrator relays a conversation between Mary and the Christ Child. Jesus informs his mother about his future destiny, which will necessarily entail hardship:

> "Quan the thretti yer ben spent,
> I mot beginne to fille
> Werfore I am hidre sent
> Thoru my Fadres will."

> ["When the thirty years have been completed, I must begin to
> fulfill the reason why I have been sent here through my Father's
> will."]

Mary, whom the author presumably imagines as a Jew expecting a powerful Messiah, responds by introducing the idea of Christ's future kingship. But Jesus chides her worldliness:

> "Do wey, moder," seid that suete,
> "Therfor kam I nouth,
> But for to ben pore and bales bete
> That man was inne brouth."[156]

> ["Put away that thought, mother," said that sweet child. "That is
> not the reason I came here, but to be poor and to remedy the evils
> into which man was brought."]

As we have seen in Chapter 3, Middle English versions of *Pseudo-Matthew* sometimes contain passages in which Jesus warns his mother of the physical suffering that the Jews will inflict upon him in the future. In all three cases— in the lyric, the apocryphal legends, and *Revelationes* 6.58—Jesus and Mary discuss the future Passion, the mere thought of which deeply unsettles the Virgin.[157] Whereas other passages within Birgitta's writings feature the solitary meditations of Mary on her son's future Passion (usually as she clothes him and gazes upon his body), chapter 58 features a Christ Child who responds to his mother's sorrows with words of consolation; whether he does so precociously as an infant who can speak or as a more mature child is not entirely clear.

An analogous scenario can be seen in a miniature in the fifteenth-century Hours of Catherine of Cleves (New York, The Pierpont Morgan Library, MS M.917, p. 149; ca. 1440; fig. 20). At home, the infant Jesus rolls about in his baby walker while his parents are busy with their tasks: cloth-making and carpentry. A banderole issuing from the mouth of the child, who faces his mother, reads, in Latin: "I am your consolation (*consolacium tuum*)," words of comfort that are clearly intended for Mary.[158] Jesus may simply be offering his presence as a compensation for his mother's hard work. Although there are no indications here that she is thinking of her son's future Passion, Joseph in the background seems to be making a cross.[159] Regardless of whether the Boy is cognizant of his future Passion, he is definitely sensitive to the present hardship of his mother, at the very least, her daily labor and diligent tending to practical matters. *Revelationes* 6.58 intensifies matters, for here the Christ Child is aware of his mother's sorrow and also of the grand scheme of the redemption that necessitates it. The overall tone of this passage is one of subdued sadness. Jesus is calmly aware of his future sufferings, while his mother seems resigned to them. Although she may seem passive and weak in accepting the inevitability of the Passion, there is also a suggestion of her inner fortitude, which she exercises when interacting with her son and in later telling Birgitta about it (which may involve a reliving of former pain).[160]

Similarities between the mother-and-son dialogues found in the apocrypha and in *Revelationes* 6.58 provide further evidence that Birgitta had encountered the apocryphal legends about Jesus' childhood circulating in her day. An unusual detail found near the end of this chapter likewise suggests that Birgitta was influenced by these legends in her treatment of the hidden life of Christ. After noting that Jesus was an obedient son, always doing what Joseph told him to do, Mary remarks that "he hid his divine power so well that it could not be perceived except by me and sometimes by Joseph. Many a time we saw a wondrous light shining around him and heard angelic voices singing above him."[161] Mary's statement that Jesus "hid his divine power" may imply that Christ's childhood was not in fact marked by public miracles,[162] such as those that are repeatedly recounted in the apocryphal childhood legends. Yet Mary goes on to say that "the unclean spirits who could not be cast out by the exorcists skilled in our law departed at the sight of my Son's appearance."[163] It is unclear whether these exorcisms were done publicly or occurred

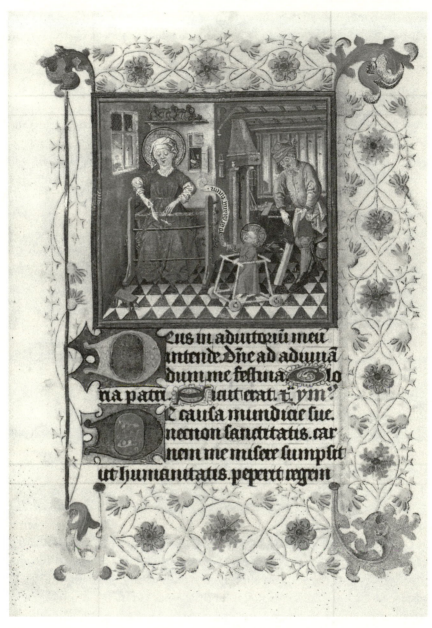

Figure 20. The domestic activities of the Holy Family. New York, The Pierpont Morgan Library, MS M.917 (Hours of Catherine of Cleves), p. 149 (Utrecht, the Netherlands, ca. 1440). By permission of The Pierpont Morgan Library, New York.

incidentally and without many witnesses, a situation more in keeping with the notion of Jesus maintaining a low profile (which Birgitta and others, such as the Franciscans, seemed to prefer). Even if the Christ Child had not publicized his divinity, it was manifested to his parents by the aureole that enveloped him. After all, who can hide a halo? Along similar lines, some versions of *Pseudo-Matthew* report that a bright light ("the splendor of God") illuminated the Christ Child whenever he slept.[164] The mention of this miraculous light may simply be an appropriation of a hagiographical motif commonly used to cast a supernatural aura around an infant or child destined for greatness, as well as an instance of the attention that was commonly given to God's radiance.[165] Aelred, for example, in both the *De Jesu puero duodenni* and the *De institutione inclusarum*, speaks of the light that gleamed from the Christ Child.[166] Nevertheless, Birgitta's attribution of an aura of light to the child Jesus may be directly owing to *Pseudo-Matthew*, especially given the other points of contact between Birgitta's revelations and the apocryphal infancy tradition—though we obviously cannot know for sure.

In the following chapter (59), Mary goes back in time to speak about the miraculous conception of Jesus within her womb and the possible scandal this might have entailed in the minds of her spouse and their Jewish neighbors. Throughout this chapter Mary emphasizes Joseph's holiness: his sense of unworthiness of being in his wife's presence, his desire to serve her, and the various virtues he manifested during their life together. Mary's praise of Joseph, which complements the slightly earlier scholastic arguments that valorized their marriage,[167] seems aimed at counteracting the derogatory characterization of him as a sort of cuckolded husband, often found in late medieval biblical plays. The latter derive, in large part, from the apocrypha and, more obliquely, from secular culture (such as the fabliaux). Mary pointedly denies that Joseph ever said anything harsh to her, an implicit rebuttal of other sources that have him accuse her of infidelity upon finding her pregnant, his harshness crudely revealing his lack of awareness of God's plan for the redemption.[168] Birgitta's ostensible challenge to apocryphal infancy material at the end of this chapter thus lends weight to my contention that the Swedish saint was knowledgeable of the apocryphal infancy legends and trying to undermine as well as provide an alternative to them in *Revelationes* 6.58.

To summarize the foregoing discussion: in her treatment of the childhood of Christ in *Revelationes* 6.58, Birgitta does not, in fact, portray him working miracles (except perhaps exorcisms), yet she records Mary as saying that his youth was not lacking in *mirabilia* ("wonderful things"), that is, out-of-the-ordinary phenomena that attracted people's attention, and even elicited their sense of wonder. In addition, Mary tells how Jesus gave subtle indications of his divinity and revealed to her his awareness of his future Passion. By shedding some light on the hidden years of Christ's childhood in this chapter, Birgitta compensates for the silence of Scripture on this topic and offers an alternative to the apocrypha.

Birgitta was not the only late medieval Christian who turned to Mary as a source of information about Christ's childhood. The anonymous (Carthusian) author of the fifteenth-century Middle English meditational text known as the *Speculum devotorum*, which at times paraphrases *Revelationes* 6.58, may have the apocrypha in mind when he argues for the reliability of Birgitta's account of Christ's childhood. Right before he relates what Jesus did from age twelve until his baptism, the author states that his text is "aftyr þe Reuela-cyon of Seyint Brygytte, as oure Lady, þat knewe best nexte God alone, tolde here."[169] The suggestion here is that Mary, as Jesus' (almost) constant companion during his childhood, stored many memories in her heart and is thus the ultimate authority on Jesus' hidden years. A similar train of reasoning is found in a thirteenth-century Latin poem on the lives of Jesus and Mary I have mentioned before, the *Vita rhythmica*, which makes extensive use of the apocrypha. The poem's anonymous author claims that Jesus worked miracles during his adolescence, which were "hidden" because they were not performed in the presence of the disciples, who were chosen later on. The implication is that the author somehow, through the mediation of other sources, learned about these incidents from eyewitnesses, the most authoritative of which is Mary, who stored all things in her heart.[170]

At the end of *Revelationes* 6.58, which focuses exclusively on Jesus' boyhood, Mary enjoins her "daughter" Birgitta to keep these memories continually in mind and to thank God for having been chosen as the channel through which he wishes to reveal Jesus' infancy.[171] Birgitta thus continues Mary's role as guardian of the secrets of Christ's childhood, yet duly propagates this knowledge, rather than keeping it to herself. By spreading knowledge of the Christ Child's virtues, unusual deeds, and interactions with those around him, Birgitta undoubtedly sought to increase her readers' admiration of the child Jesus and appreciation of Mary's privileged perspective, as the one who participated in his life most intimately.

The Virgin reveals additional hidden knowledge about Christ's childhood near the end of Book 6, in a chapter (112) that concerns the relic of the holy foreskin. Mary informs Birgitta that the relic of Christ's foreskin is currently in Rome (without specifying its precise location), and explains how it managed to survive to the present day. As to the immediate fate of the holy prepuce, Mary says that she preserved it when it was cut off at the time of Jesus' circumcision and later entrusted it to St. John, along with the blood collected from Christ's wounds when he was removed from the cross.[172] Mary's mention of the relic of Christ's blood would have prompted medieval readers to think of Joseph of Arimathea, who, in medieval legend, was believed to have collected Christ's blood in the vessel used by the Lord at the Last Supper. Yet whereas the so-called grail, a contact relic, was thought to have passed from Joseph to his descendants (who then, purportedly, made their way to England),[173] the holy prepuce, a piece of Christ's body, was entrusted to John and his successors, later hidden "in a perfectly clean spot underground" during a time of persecution, and eventually discovered through the help of an angel.[174] The *Arabic Infancy Gospel* contains a similar detail about the prepuce, recounting how an old Hebrew woman, present at the Circumcision, took the foreskin and placed it in a jar of ointment; it was subsequently sold to Mary (Magdalene) the sinner, who used the substance to anoint Jesus' feet.[175] The Virgin Mary does not say how the relic of her son's foreskin was preserved and ended up in Rome, but she does express her displeasure at the Romans' unintentional neglect of it, by lamenting, "O Rome, O Rome, if you only knew, you would surely rejoice, and if you only knew how to weep, you would weep ceaselessly, for you have a treasure that is most dear to me and you do not treat it with reverence." Mary calls the prepuce her "thesaurum . . . carissimum" (dearest treasure) and indicates why: Jesus' flesh was derived from her own sinless flesh.[176]

Birgitta is one of a number of female saints from the later Middle Ages who venerated the holy foreskin, though Catherine of Siena and Agnes of Blannbekin, who are better known for this devotion, did not focus on it primarily as a relic, as did the Swedish saint.[177] For Catherine it was a symbol of God's union with humanity, presumably because it showed that the Son became man in all things but sin (Heb. 4:15). It conveyed this doctrine in a more meaningful way than, say, his baby teeth, because it signified his maleness.[178] While the prepuce relic appears to have had erotic associations for some women, there were also males who treasured it.[179] That Birgitta mentions this holy remnant of the Lord's flesh is not surprising, especially given her emphasis on Mary's care for her son's body, but the chapter on Jesus' foreskin in Book 6 is also tied to Birgitta's belief in the centrality of Rome—to the past, present, and future vitality of the Church. Though she worked tirelessly to bring the Avignon popes back to their proper seat, Rome, she boldly criticized the city's decadence, no doubt believing in the principle that the corruption of the best is the worst. Mary's emotionally charged criticism of Rome in the *Revelationes* is thus in keeping with Birgitta's esteem for and disappointment in this great city. Passing over the theoretical difficulties involved in the existence of such a relic on earth,[180] Birgitta focuses (in *Revelationes* 6.112) on Mary's veneration of this piece of flesh to showcase her tender love for her son and care for his physical welfare.

## Franciscan Influences on Birgitta's Treatment of the Childhood of Christ

Whereas in *Revelationes* 6.112 Mary expresses displeasure about people's neglect of a precious remnant of her son's body, in *Revelationes* 3.25 she laments more generally that the Christ Child has been forgotten and is neglected in modern times. Indeed, she seems almost angry about humankind's indifference toward the amazing humility demonstrated by God in assuming the form of a child. While Mary's emotional sensitivity is featured throughout the *Revelationes*, here, presumably to tone down the acuteness of Mary's affectivity, we are explicitly told that her sinlessness prevents her from experiencing the negative emotion of anger.[181] This statement is understandable given medieval scholars' assumption that humans almost always sin when they are angry (though righteous anger was regarded as commendable).[182] Rather than being seen as simply venting her emotions, Mary may be viewed as taking positive action against people's indifference toward the Christ Child: to be specific, she provides a unique insight into Jesus' hidden life, speaks at length about the admirable deeds and qualities of her son, and encourages Birgitta to make them known. As we have seen in Chapter 2, Francis of Assisi likewise strove to make the Christ Child more intimately known and tenderly loved by the people of his day, especially by setting up a public manger scene one Christmas at Greccio. According to Thomas of Celano, Francis drew fresh attention to the child Jesus, who, "in the hearts of many . . . has been given over to oblivion."[183] In *Revelationes* 3.25 Mary similarly uses the verbs *obliviscor* and *neglego* to speak of humans' forgetfulness of her son. While this close verbal parallel may be a coincidence, both Francis and Birgitta undoubtedly attempted to remind their contemporaries that the Christ Child was deserving of greater devotion. Another parallel that may be drawn between the two saints is their attentiveness to the sufferings of the infant Jesus. As I have already shown, in her vision of the Nativity (7.21), Birgitta subtly notes the discomfort experienced by the newborn babe. In a similar way, Francis told his friend John of Greccio, who prepared the manger scene at his request, that he wished "to see as much as possible with my bodily eyes the discomfort[s] of his infant needs."[184]

Without a doubt, the chapter that most clearly reveals the influence of Franciscan thought on Birgitta's own way of thinking (about Mary and Jesus' interaction and about poverty) is *Revelationes* 7.8. Whereas a handful of passages from Birgitta's works speak of Mary's swaddling of the infant Jesus, in this chapter the Swedish saint focuses on the clothing that Jesus wore as a lad and into his adulthood. In the middle of the chapter, Mary directs Birgitta's attention to the seamless tunic, "which [she] made with [her] own hands," and "over which the crucifiers cast lots" at the time of Christ's Passion (John 19:24; Ps. 21:19).[185] While Mary does not specify the exact manner in which she made Jesus' tunic, she says she did so "with her own hands." This might imply knitting, a technique which would cause a garment to be both seamless and elastic—characteristics that Mary attributes to her son's tunic. Her emphasis upon the tunic as her handiwork suggests her loving care for her son and possibly the humble circumstances of the Holy Family,[186] though in the Middle Ages aristocratic and royal ladies also seem to have engaged in textile work.[187] According to Ruth Mazo Karras, such activity symbolized the virtues of a married woman, but single women also engaged in such work as a suitable way to occupy themselves.[188]

Mary did not make Jesus' seamless tunic when he was an adult, as we might assume, but rather while he was still a child. Birgitta does not explicitly make this point, but she implies that this is the case when she records Mary saying that she used to clothe her son with that garment, by implication during his childhood. As Jesus' closest companion for many years, Mary asserts,

> I . . . bear witness to the fact that the same Jesus Christ, my son, had one personal possession and that he alone possessed it. This was that tunic that I made with my own hands (*propriis meis manibus feci*). And the prophet witnesses to this fact, saying in the person of my Son: "Over *my* garment, they cast lots." [Ps. 21:19; John 19:24] Behold and be attentive to the fact that he did not say "*our* garment" but "*my* garment." Know too that, as often as I

dressed him in that tunic for the use of his most holy body, my
eyes then filled at once with tears and my whole heart was wrung
with trouble and grief and was afflicted with intense bitterness. For
I well knew the manner in which that tunic would in [the] future
be separated from my Son, namely, at the time of his [P]assion
when, naked and innocent, he would be crucified by the Jews. And
this tunic was that garment over which his crucifiers cast lots. No
one had that same tunic while he lived, but only he alone.[189]

This passage resembles those (considered above) that describe Mary's visualization of her son's future wounds while she wrapped him in baby clothes and
was filled with sadness as she did so. Yet here Jesus is no longer an infant being swaddled, but a young boy who is dressed in a tunic. This locution may
have prompted Birgitta to visualize the tunics worn at the time of Christ, yet
she probably also had in mind the clothing worn by little boys in her own
day, which consisted of gowns.[190] Birgitta and her contemporaries, therefore,
might have regarded the tunic of the adult Jesus as simply a larger version of
that which he wore as a boy. A rare depiction of Mary apparently clothing the
boy Jesus with the tunic is found in a fourteenth-century Venetian manuscript
containing a prose version of the *Vita rhythmica* (Oxford, Bodleian Library,
Canon. Misc. 476, fol. 51v, ca. 1340; fig. 21). This Life of Mary, which makes
ample use of the apocrypha and other legends, explicitly states that Jesus' tunic
increased in size as he grew up.[191]

Whereas the swaddling clothes that Mary mentions in other passages
symbolize the burial garments that would envelop him within the sepulcher,
in *Revelationes* 7.8 Christ's tunic makes Mary think of the nudity that he will
suffer at the crucifixion when his clothing will be abruptly torn from him.[192]
As in the passages that focus on Jesus' swaddling clothes, Mary's premonition
of the Passion in *Revelationes* 7.8 derives from her knowledge of the prophets.
She cites Psalm 21:19, which was thought to prophesy the role that Christ's
seamless garment would play in his Passion: "upon my vesture they cast lots."
John the Evangelist in fact reiterates this verse in his account of the Passion
when he mentions the distribution of the crucified Christ's clothing. Mary goes
on to explain that the tunic that she made for Jesus when he was a child is the
same one he wore at the crucifixion: "this tunic was that garment over which his
crucifiers cast lots. No one had that same tunic while he lived, but only he alone."
By saying that Jesus "had" (*habuit*) the garment, Mary implies that he possessed

Figure 21. The Virgin Mary clothing Jesus with the seamless tunic. Oxford, Bodleian Library, Canon. Misc. 476, fol. 51v (ca. 1340). By permission of the Bodleian Library.

it; and by adding that "he alone" (*ipse solus*) did so, she suggests that it was his personal belonging rather than an item held in common.

Mary as she is presented by Birgitta has a definite purpose in mind in stating that the garment worn by the adult Jesus was the same as that worn by the Christ Child. Although we might at first assume that the Virgin wishes to stress her son's poverty, the way in which Jesus lived like a medieval monk or a friar with regard to frugality in clothing, this is not the point she wishes to make. Nor does Mary wish to call attention to the magical quality of the garment that graced Jesus' body—its ability to increase in size as Christ's body grew during his childhood and adolescence. This amazing feature of the seam-less garment is in fact implied by Mary's words, but she makes no effort to call attention to it. Nor is it Mary's central aim to point out the ontological stability of Christ's identity—that he was the same person in his childhood as he was in his adulthood, as is symbolized by the sameness of his garment. Nor even is it Mary's main purpose to convey that the Christ Child was destined to suffer the Passion from the very beginning of his life, the idea of the Proleptic Passion that, as we have seen, was expressed in a number of late medieval texts and images. No—Mary's agenda, and I think it would be fair here to characterize her motive and remarks as such, is much simpler: it is to demonstrate that Jesus actually owned something during his earthly life. This fact enables her to undercut the position of extremist Franciscans, known as the Spirituals, who held that Jesus never owned anything and be-lieved that they, too, should own nothing.

Mary's argumentative stance in *Revelationes* 7.8 is aimed at supporting the orthodoxy of John XXII, one of the Avignon popes, who died in 1334 at age ninety when Birgitta was about thirty and still living in Sweden. Although Birgitta was not intensely active in politics during John's reign, she was inter-ested in his papacy in the later part of her life, if not earlier. Mary reveals her partiality for this pope (and thereby Birgitta's) by framing her remarks about the Christ Child's seamless garment between statements that assert the ortho-doxy of John XXII and that defend the authority of popes in general. It is important to note that chapter 8 is a continuation of the questioning of the Virgin begun in the previous chapter, in which Birgitta makes known to Mary the concerns of a certain Franciscan friar whom she had encountered in Rome, known as Peter of Trastevere.[193] After expressing her sense of unworthiness to serve as Mary's mouthpiece, Birgitta conveys the Virgin's response to the ques-tion posed to her by the friar. He, in turn, is encouraged to persevere in his vocation, and instructed, in particular, that "he is not to have an overabun-dance of clothing but only necessary things, according to the Rule of Saint Francis, so that pride and cupidity may not ensue." As an incentive to the prac-tice of poverty in dress, Mary assures Birgitta that "the less costly and valu-able his clothes have been, the more lavish shall be his reward." The friar is further advised: "let him humbly obey all of his superior's instructions that are not contrary to God and that the friar's own ability permits him to per-form."[194] Mary's advice concerning dress might be interpreted by a Francis-can extremist as implying that he is to cover himself with a mere rag, with only a scrap of fabric, but Mary's emphasis upon obedience seems to forestall such an ascetically strict interpretation: she says that the friar is to follow the Rule and the instructions of his superior. Obedience, in other words, takes precedence over absolute poverty. At the same time, the friar is to exercise careful discernment: a superior's instructions that are clearly contrary to God's will are, by implication, to be disregarded.

It is helpful here to turn briefly to the original documents that established the Franciscan lifestyle, as a sort of addendum to Francis's own modus vivendi. While in the following I may seem to be meandering from my main topic—the medieval Christ Child—this broad and excursive consideration of thirteenth- and fourteenth-century context is valuable because it shows how far the varying images of, and motifs concerning the Christ Child could extend their influence. The Earlier Rule of St. Francis begins with the author Francis promising obedience to the pope and his successors; Francis's followers, in turn, are enjoined to obey him and those who will later oversee the friars. After the preface, a brief summary of the Rule is offered in chapter 1: the brothers are "to live in obedience, in chastity, and without anything of their own, and to follow the teaching and footprints of our Lord Jesus Christ, Who says: 'If you wish to be perfect, go sell everything you have and give it to the poor, and you will have treasure in heaven; and come, follow me.' (Matt. 19:21)"[195] The Rule goes on to cite additional biblical statements of Christ that invite his followers to a complete and radical commitment to him and the spreading of the Gospel. These evangelical counsels to poverty, chastity, and obedience, found at the beginning of the Rule of Francis, are of course derived from earlier monastic tradition. Emphasis here is given to poverty, since the first thing mentioned after the exhortation to follow in the footsteps of Christ is his injunction to give away one's worldly goods. This is what we would expect of Francis, who took Lady Poverty as his bride and can be said to have lived this ideal perfectly. Trying to imitate him exactly, however, became problematic when the number of his followers grew and the order started to become institutionalized—incorporated into the structures of contemporary society; in other words, it became increasingly difficult for the friars to live as mere vagabonds. The early history of the Franciscan Order is thus marked by struggles among different groups within it over how the evangelical injunction to poverty should be practiced if the friars are to imitate Christ and their beloved founder, and, at the same time, function effectively within society. The early solution to the need for money, which the Rule had forbidden the friars to have or even touch, was the appointment of a trustee who would receive and hold money on behalf of the friars, thus providing them the use of money and goods without their technically owning anything.[196]

Chapter 2 of the Earlier Rule explains how poverty is to be manifested in the friars' dress. That clothing should be given so much attention is not surprising considering that the young Francis, the son of a wealthy cloth merchant, dramatized his conversion to a radically religious way of life by publicly divesting himself of his clothing and returning it to his father in the presence of the local bishop and townspeople.[197] In a similar way, the Rule stipulates that those who wish to become brothers are to sell everything they have and give the proceeds to the poor, rather than to the friars to create or enrich an endowment. They are to be allotted "the clothes of probation for a year, that is, two tunics without a hood, a cord, trousers, and a small cape reaching to the cord." Once the brothers promise obedience, they are to "have one tunic with a hood and, if it is necessary, another without a hood and a cord and trousers." While they are permitted the use of more than one tunic, the phrase "without anything of their own" (in Chapter 1) suggests that no tunic is actually owned by an individual friar. The Rule goes on to indicate that the friars are to get as much use as possible out of their tunics: "Let all the brothers wear poor clothes and, with the blessing of God, they can patch them with sackcloth and other pieces."[198] The tunics worn by Francis that are today displayed in the Basilica of San Francesco in Assisi and at the Sanctuary of La Verna have clearly been patched up as the Rule instructs. Birgitta's daughter Katarina evinced a similar minimalist attitude toward clothing; in one of Birgitta's revelations, the Virgin Mary praises Katarina for preferring an "old and repaired tunic" to a new one.[199]

This background information about Franciscan ideals of poverty, specifically as regards clothing, will help us better understand Mary's description of Christ's clothing in *Revelationes* 7.8. As we shall see, some important differences emerge in what seems to have been the outlooks of Birgitta and some early extremist friars. Although both Jesus and the friars wear a tunic, Mary claims that her son wore the same seamless tunic throughout his entire life. In other words, he had only one tunic, while the Franciscans were permitted the use of two. Whereas the friars were expected to patch their garments to extend their durability, Mary, in Birgitta's revelation, says nothing about Jesus doing so. She alludes to the legend that Christ's seamless garment increased in size with its wearer, which explains how Jesus could wear the same tunic over the course of so many years. The friars' tunics, in contrast, wore out or were given away to the poor, and so eventually had to be replaced. No mention is made in *Revelationes* 7.8 of the monetary value of Jesus' tunic, but the fact that it was the seamless garment mentioned by John (19:24), for which the soldiers eagerly cast lots, may imply that it was of considerable value. Passages from the Rule of St. Francis and other Franciscan texts dealing with the clothing to be worn by the friars, particularly the material of which it was to be constructed, suggest that their garments would have been of relatively little market value.[200]

By far the greatest difference between the clothing worn by Christ and that to be worn by the Franciscan friars concerns the ownership of it. Mary clearly states that her son owned (at least) one thing, referring to Psalm 21:19 (as a prophetic utterance of Christ) to reinforce this point: " 'Over my garment, they cast lots.' Behold and be attentive to the fact that he did not say 'our garment' but 'my garment.' " The emphasis here is on the possessive adjective *meam* (modifying *vestem*), which is explicitly contrasted with *nostram*, also a possessive adjective; the latter refers to the collective "we," whereas the former is governed by the singular "I." As Kezel has noted, Birgitta probably has in mind the monastic custom of referring to commonly owned objects with the plural "noster."[201] Mary's point is that Jesus did not share his garment with his disciples or consider it common property; he regarded it as his own. Ironically, his having only one tunic is not used here specifically to support the strict poverty advocated in the Franciscan Rule, but to argue against the extremist position that Jesus owned absolutely nothing.

What Francis intended to convey in the Rule and what it seemed to say were, of course, matters of dispute among the Franciscans in the thirteenth and fourteenth centuries. A friar who favored a strict interpretation of the Rule might in fact have seen an inconsistency between Mary's claim that Jesus "had one thing which was his own (*vnum proprium habebat*)" and the injunction to the friars, found in chapter 1, to live "without anything of their own (*sine proprio*)." The *Anonymous of Perugia*, a thirteenth-century text that idealizes the first friars, states that "Whatever they had, a book or a tunic, was used in common and no one called anything his own (*nullus suum aliquid esse dicebat*), just as it was done in the primitive church of the Apostles" (cf. Acts 4:32).[202] The language here is clearly at odds with that used in *Revelationes* 7.8. According to Mary, Jesus did not share his tunic or consider it common property.

A contemporary and a virulent opponent of John XXII, the Franciscan philosopher William of Ockham (d. 1347), dealt at length with the question of Christ's poverty in his *Opus nonaginta dierum*, a treatise that provides a fine-tuned series of counter-objections to John XXII's views. In chapter 94, Ockham argues against the position that Christ had universal lordship of all things from the moment of his conception, initially citing scriptural passages quoted by his opponents that seem to indicate that Christ in fact "had clothes."[203] Like the Virgin in *Revelationes* 7.8, Ockham's opponents support their position by pointing out that, in the Scriptures, possessives are used of the material goods employed by both Christ and the apostles. Ockham responds by making a distinction: these words, he says, "sometimes . . . imply lordship and ownership, sometimes use of fact (*usus facti*), sometimes licit power of using, sometimes custom of using, sometimes custody; and they can be taken in almost countless other ways. It can therefore be conceded that Christ had various things in respect of use, and in respect of a licit power of using and in respect of a custom of using, or in respect of some kind of stewardship or management, although he did not have lordship or ownership." Ockham continues in this chapter by addressing the issue of Christ's clothing more specifically, taking the position that Christ used articles of clothing, without offering a definitive statement as to who really owned them. To show that possessive adjectives do not always imply ownership, Ockham gives an example from Scripture: Luke says that Mary and Joseph returned to "their city, Nazareth" (2:39), but this of course does not mean that they owned it. He interprets the statement that Christ "put aside his garments" when he washed the disciples' feet (John 13:4) as meaning that "those clothes were Christ's in respect of his custom of using them." Similarly, the adjective "my" in the phrase "they parted my garments" (John 19:24) simply means that the clothes "were Christ's in respect of his custom of wearing them."[204]

William of Ockham was only one of a group of Spiritual Franciscans and others who opposed John XXII in the Franciscan poverty controversy. The pope sought to end the long-standing debate about this issue among the Franciscans by issuing the bull *Cum inter nonnullos* on November 12, 1323, in which he asserted that it was heretical to hold that Christ and his disciples had owned nothing, either individually or in common.[205] In offering a definitive answer to this question, John seemed, to many, to contradict his predecessor Nicholas III, who in his decretal *Exiit qui seminat* (1279), gave his approbation to the Spiritual Franciscans who claimed that they were following Christ by completely renouncing all possessions.[206] About a decade before John's *Cum inter nonnullos*, Clement V took a middle-of-the road position in *Exivi de Paradiso* (1312), in which he declared that poverty of clothing and the Rule's prohibition against granaries and cellars were to be observed, but that these matters were to be subject to the discretion of superiors. John went further in *Quorumdam exigit* (1317) by putting all of the emphasis upon obedience: "to admit the Pope's power of dispensation over the rule was to abandon the [Spirituals'] view . . . that the Franciscan rule, written under divine inspiration, was like the Gospel and not subject to alteration by any human hand." The persistent protest of four friars against this bull ultimately resulted in their being burned as heretics in Marseilles in 1318. John's authoritarian stance against the Spirituals succeeded in polarizing them and encouraging the Joachimite impulses within the movement.[207]

Birgitta refers again to John XXII in *Revelationes* 3.18, though not by name. After Mary predicts harsh punishment for "those friars who have scorned the rule of Dominic," Birgitta dares to ask her a question: "Given that the pope relaxed the austerity of the rule for them, should they be censured for eating meat or anything else set before them?" As Bridget Morris notes, Birgitta has in mind the dispensation that John XXII granted in 1326 to the Dominicans in Scandinavia, which allowed them to eat meat when they were away from their houses. Mary responds by explaining that John "reasonably" made that concession to them, "not that they might appear lazy and lax," but to enable them to preach more effectively: "For this reason, we excuse the pope for permitting it."[208] As in *Revelationes* 7.8, Mary's defense of John XXII can perhaps be interpreted as Birgitta's way of resolving her own doubts and serious concerns about him, in particular, her questioning of his tendency to dilute the primitive rigor of the mendicant lifestyle.[209]

The political and religious contexts I have just summarized underlie the revelations prompted by Peter of Trastevere in *Revelationes* 7.7–8. Like other chapters in Birgitta's writings, chapter 8 reveals hidden information about Jesus' childhood, at the same time that it speaks to contemporary concerns. The friar apparently wondered about John's eternal fate,[210] but Mary defends the pope on the issue of Christ's poverty, by saying that his decretals dealing with this matter are without error.[211] On the whole, Mary's revelation concerning the Christ Child's seamless garment is a supporting argument in defense of John XXII, particularly his denial of Christ's complete and utter poverty.

Although Birgitta has sometimes been called a Franciscan Tertiary and been claimed by the members of the order as one of their own, she probably never officially became a Franciscan. Henrik Roelvink maintains that Birgitta became more involved with the Franciscans after she left Sweden, as evidenced, for example, by the friendship that developed between her and the Poor Clares

in the convent at San Lorenzo in Panisperna in Rome, so her connections with
the Franciscans were obviously close.[212] The most notable instance in the *Revelationes* of Birgitta's devotion to St. Francis is the chapter that describes her
visit to Assisi after being told by the saint "to eat and drink" with him in his
"chamber," when visiting the church of San Francesco a Ripa in Rome on the
saint's feast day (October 4) in 1351.[213] As Kezel points out, it does not seem
coincidental that this event is related toward the beginning of Book 7, the book
in which Birgitta recounts her visions of the Nativity and the Passion, which
occurred during her pilgrimage to the Holy Land, the sacred sites of which
were by that time in Franciscan custody.[214] Book 7 is also the place where Birgitta deals with the Franciscan poverty controversy. Birgitta's admiration of
Francis can be seen in other passages from the books of the *Revelationes* as
well. On more than one occasion, Birgitta praises the great founders of religious orders, especially Francis and Benedict.[215] She obviously believed that
consecrated religious should strictly follow the Rules of the orders to which
they belong, and, on occasion, she gives the impression of sympathy with the
Spirituals.[216] Yet, at the same time, in the passage about the life-long seamless
tunic cited above, Birgitta, through Mary, essentially argues for the correctness of John XXII's stance toward Christ's poverty.

In the Rule for the monastic order she established, the *Regula Salvatoris*
(thought to have been dictated by Christ himself), Birgitta, like the founders
of religious orders who preceded her, stresses the importance of poverty, a further indication of her affinity for Franciscan values. Chapter 2 of her Rule
explicitly forbids private property: "It is therefore not permitted to anyone to
own anything, not even the least little thing, nor possess or handle money"
(literally, touch it with their hands, "attrectare manibus"), a restriction that
echoes the Rule of St. Francis.[217] Chapter 4 of the *Regula* specifies the religious garb the nuns are to have: "two chemises (*camisie*) of white wool, one
for daily use, the other to be used when this is being washed; a tunic (*tunica*)
of gray wool; and a cowl." The sisters are also to have "a cloak, of gray wool."[218]
Though it is possible that Birgitta permitted the nuns to have the use of a spare
tunic to be worn while the tunic stipulated in the Rule was being washed (as
is the case with their *camisie*), she literally says that they are to have one tunic.
The regulations regarding clothing in the *Regula Salvatoris* interpreted literally thus echo Mary's comment in *Revelationes* 7.21 that Jesus had only one
tunic. And regardless of how Birgitta wished her nuns to deal with the basic
necessity of laundry,[219] she undoubtedly considered frugality in clothing a serious matter—a sentiment in line with Franciscan spirituality. Further on in

the Birgittine Rule (in chapter 18), a protocol is given for punishing a nun found having private property. As Ingvar Fogelqvist points out, such a sin is considered grave, as in other Rules, but here it is made more so because it is the only fault whose correction is explicitly stipulated.[220] Judging from other points she made concerning material goods, it is fair to say that, on the whole, Birgitta sought to ensure the collective poverty of the monastic community in addition to the individual poverty of each of its members.[221] Thus, while the Birgittine nuns' cloistered and contemplative lifestyle was in line with the old monastic tradition, the spirit of poverty in which they lived was clearly indebted to the Franciscan movement.

My overview of the Franciscan poverty controversy and of Birgitta's attitude toward poverty indicates that Mary's remarks about the seamless tunic in *Revelationes* 7.8 (her making it and her clothing Jesus with it), while similar to her reflections on the Christ Child in other chapters of Birgitta's writings, do not simply serve to elicit compassion in Birgitta's readers and to underscore the closeness of Jesus and Mary. Rather than pertaining simply to private, domestic matters, this locution addresses contemporary concerns about authority within the fourteenth-century Church, especially that of the papacy. Birgitta's employment of a poignant devotional motif centered on the Christ Child within a weighty ecclesiastical debate is a novel approach, yet the idea of Mary's weaving the seamless garment while Jesus was still a boy did not originate with the Swedish saint, as I shall show in what follows. Although in the preceding section it may have seemed that we were digressing widely from a discussion of devotion centered on the Christ Child, Christians at all levels of the Church were keenly interested in the humanity of Christ, which encompassed the seemingly insignificant details of his childhood, such as what he wore at that time. The above case study has shown how in later medieval society the cult of the child Jesus influenced and became interwoven within a wide range of issues and situations that people were willing to pray and argue about, as well as fight (and even die) for.

## Birgitta and the Legend of the Holy Tunic

As we have seen in the previous section, in *Revelationes* 7.8 Mary confides to Birgitta that she made Jesus' seamless tunic with her own hands, and that she herself clothed him with it when he was a boy. Legends about the holy tunic treasured in Argenteuil, which can be traced back to at least the middle of

the twelfth century, speak, as does Birgitta, of Mary's making the seamless
tunic. The cult of the holy robe venerated in Trier also encompassed this
idea, though Birgitta does not seem to have been influenced by this particular
relic, at least not directly. Below I briefly discuss early attestations of the legend that Mary made the seamless tunic during Christ's boyhood, as well as
the medieval metaphor that Mary made the tunic, so to speak, of Christ's
flesh, but I will first mention a few artistic representations of Mary working
on her son's garment.[222] A striking and well-known illustration of Mary knitting the seamless tunic appears in Master Bertram's early fifteenth-century
Buxtehude Altarpiece (Hamburg, Hamburger Kunsthalle; fig. 22), which
shows the Christ Child rather contentedly occupying himself with a book
while his mother peacefully knits his tunic.[223] Any serenity a viewer may vicariously experience from this peaceful domestic scene is, however, quickly
disrupted by the presence of visual omens of Jesus' future Passion. As shown
in the previous section, Birgitta likewise associates the seamless tunic with
both Jesus' childhood and his crucifixion on Calvary. Yet an important difference distinguishes the painting from Birgitta's treatment of the seamless
garment (and her handling of Jesus' clothing and the Proleptic Passion more
broadly). In the image, the boy Jesus, who looks behind him at the *arma
Christi* borne by the angels standing beside him,[224] seems to be musing on his
future fate, especially considering that he has temporarily put aside his reading, perhaps a book containing the psalms, many of which (e.g., Psalm 21)
were thought to speak of the Man of Sorrows (a figure rooted in Isaiah 53:3).[225]
Even the toy top lying beside Jesus points to the Passion, since medieval Christians associated the whip used to spin a top with the whips wielded against
Christ at his scourging long ago.[226] In the altarpiece, Mary (unlike her son
who sees beyond the here and now), seems oblivious to Jesus' future sufferings, absorbed as she is in knitting his tunic, although, according to some
medieval meditations on the Passion, that, too, would directly cause Jesus
pain on Calvary when the garment, which had adhered to his skin on account
of his dried blood, would be rudely torn from his body.[227]

   A situation analogous to that found in the Buxtehude Altarpiece is presented by an engraving of the Holy Family within a domestic setting by the
Silesian Master, Veit Stoss.[228] In this late fifteenth-century depiction of Mary
preparing the seamless garment Jesus occupies himself not with a book, as in
the other work, but with fabric strewn before Mary's feet, while she knits his
tunic. Although there is no clear indication that the Child, who looks up at
his mother rather than at weapon-bearing angels, is thinking about his

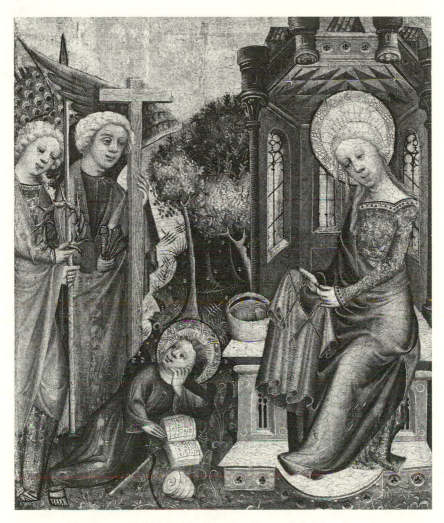

Figure 22. The Christ Child beholds the *arma Christi* while Mary knits his garment. Master Bertram, Buxtehude Altarpiece, Hamburg, Hamburger Kunsthalle (ca. 1400–1410). By permission of Art Resource, NY.

future suffering, the cross-shape of both Mary's garment frame as well as Joseph's carpentry tool undoubtedly recall, or rather foreshadow, the Passion. Taking things further than both these artists, Birgitta, who explores Mary's interiority in her visionary literature, in several passages presents the Virgin as dwelling on and emotionally responding to her son's future Passion, and even at times communicating with him about it. That such a conversation transpired between mother and son is suggested by the fresco "Madonna del Ricamo" by Vitale da Bologna (Bologna, Pinacoteca Nazionale, 1330–40; fig. 23), which depicts Mary apparently talking to the boy Jesus seated next to her, as she sews his garment, with her sharp needle held aloft. By viewing the life and death of Jesus from Mary's perspective and communicating the Blessed Mother's thoughts and feelings through her own writings, Birgitta effectively conveys the poignancy of the swordlike needle that menaced the Virgin and her son as she tended to the clothing and covering of Jesus' body at different points of his life. Indeed, throughout her work, Birgitta is quite emphatic that the Virgin was the *Mater dolorosa* even when Christ was still a child, and that the simple things of her day-to-day life held great meaning for her.

Mary's confiding to Birgitta (in *Revelationes* 7.8) that she made the seamless garment with her own hands during Jesus' childhood may have been influenced by a number of texts or images about the Child's tunic that date sometime before the middle of the fourteenth century. Yet we can reasonably conclude that Birgitta learned about the origins of Jesus' tunic (or at least was prompted to reflect upon them) as a result of visiting the Abbey of Saint-Denis or being in its environs. From roughly the middle of the twelfth century, the monks at the Priory of St. Mary at Argenteuil, a nearby sisterhouse of the renowned abbey of St. Denis, claimed to have Christ's seamless tunic, which they believed Charlemagne had brought back from Constantinople around four centuries earlier. Prelates, dignitaries, and other Christians gathered there to pay homage to this relic and to receive plentiful indulgences in return, according to a legendary account about the finding (or *inventio*) of the relic (extant in Oxford, The Queen's College, MS 348) and a charter of 1156 issued by the Archbishop of Rouen Hugh of Amiens. Significantly, both of these documents speak of the textile relic as the "cappa pueri domini Jesu."[229] A number of chronicles from the late twelfth, thirteenth, and fourteenth centuries make note of the discovery of the seamless tunic at Argenteuil, with different authors including different details, such as the explicit claim that Jesus' tunic increased in size as he grew up.[230]

To explain how the Swedish saint would have almost certainly been influenced by legends surrounding Argenteuil's prized possession, Jesus' lifelong seamless tunic, we need to return to an earlier stage of St. Birgitta's life, a little before she started her career as a pious widow and several decades before she crowned her lifestyle as a devout laywoman with a trip to the Holy Land in the early 1370s. There are a number of indications that

Figure 23. The Madonna talks with her son as she sews. Tempera and oil on panel, detached painted mural, Vitale da Bologna, "Madonna del Ricamo," Bologna, Pinacoteca Nazionale (1330–1340). By permission of Mondadori Portfolio/Electa/ Art Resource, NY.

Birgitta went on a pilgrimage with her husband Ulf to Santiago de Compostela in the early 1340s.[231] The precise route they took there and back cannot be determined since there is no record of their point of entry on the
Continent, and there were a number of possible routes they could have taken
down through Germany and France and westward across northern Spain.
While the Swedish couple and their entourage had a number of routes to
choose from for their return, it is very likely that Birgitta traveled through
Paris and stopped off at the Abbey of Saint-Denis, and also at the priory at
Argenteuil, on her way back from Compostela.[232] Medieval depictions of
Birgitta often show her with a pilgrim's staff, scrip, and hat, on which at
times can be seen one or more badges indicating the pilgrimage sites she
visited.[233] While we cannot know which badges she managed to acquire, it
is not impossible that she had some from Argenteuil and Saint-Denis. The
survival of pilgrim badges from the once-thriving monasteries located at
these holy sites attest that both places were pilgrimage centers in the later
Middle Ages.

My suggestion that Birgitta visited the Abbey of Saint-Denis and possibly also Argenteuil is not simply based on the fact that the former was a
famous place and that, in addition, Birgitta was accustomed to visiting shrines.
A few passages from Birgitta's *Revelationes* and canonization dossier reveal
that she had a special devotion to St. Denis. Indeed, she is said to have had
several visions of him, one of which occurred on the way back from Santiago
de Compostela.[234] The revelation in question (chapter 92 of the *Extravagantes*)
specifies the location of this particular revelation: Arras, a medieval town
about 160 kilometers northeast of Paris. Significantly, there was a pilgrimage
route that connected these two cities.[235] Birgitta seems to have proceeded
along that course on her return trip, as far as we can know of it. To be more
precise: chapter 92 recounts how her husband, Ulf, had fallen ill in Arras, and
Birgitta feared that he would be unable to make it back to Sweden alive. In
such a difficult situation, it was certainly fitting that Birgitta would turn for
spiritual aid to the patron of the monastic community at Saint-Denis, and
indeed of all of France, considering that she would have just traveled through
that country. St. Denis appeared to Birgitta and told her that she had been
entrusted to his protection; as a sign of this, he promised that her husband
would not die at that time.[236] Upon their return to Sweden the couple agreed
to discontinue marital relations and enter into monastic life.[237] Ulf, however, soon died at the Cistercian monastery of Alvastra in 1344 (or 1346).
Shortly afterward, Christ transmitted to Birgitta the *Regula Salvatoris*, the

rule of life for the new monastic order she was divinely commissioned to establish.

## Birgitta and the Image of Clothing

While Birgitta was not the first person to claim that Mary made the seamless garment for her son, she was unique among those who propagated this legend, since only she records the Virgin speaking about her handiwork in the first person. In *Revelationes* 7.8, Mary's reflections and insights span a wide expanse of time: speaking to Birgitta in the present and addressing recent developments within the Church, Mary's memory harks back to the time when Jesus was still a boy. She prompts Birgitta to imagine how she used to clothe the Christ Child, and then encourages her to move forward in time to the Passion, and see as she saw—both as a prophet and eyewitness—the horrific sufferings endured by her son. As is the case with the passages that describe how Mary meditated upon Jesus' future death as she swaddled his little body, the initial theme of nurturing introduced in *Revelationes* 7.8, which tells of the Virgin clothing the boy Jesus with his tunic, quickly turns into one of ignominy and violence. Mary tells Birgitta she "well knew the manner in which that tunic would in future be separated from [her] Son, namely, at the time of his [P]assion, when, naked and innocent, he would be crucified by the Jews." The fact that the seamless tunic belonged to and was worn by Jesus practically his entire life makes its forceful separation from him seem all the more like a violation of his dignity. The Crucifixion Play from the Towneley Cycle similarly focuses on Mary's reaction to her son's sufferings as she beheld them at the foot of the cross. In the play, however, Mary is not pained at her son's divestiture, as she is in *Revelationes* 7.8, but by the injuries he suffers in his body, which she speaks of metaphorically as the clothing that she has sewn for him: "His robe is all to-ryffen, / That of me was hym gyffen, / And shapen with my sydys" (his robe, which was formed in my womb and given to him by me, is completely torn).[238] The dramatist's reference to Mary's "sides" (that is, loins or womb) would have prompted the audience to imagine the fabrication of the Christ Child's body within his mother's.

Birgitta's conceptualization of Mary knitting the Christ Child's garment may possibly include the idea that this was begun in the womb, but she focuses almost exclusively on the literal tunic worn by her son throughout his life. A rare example of Birgitta's use of the trope of Mary's womb as a holy place where Christ dons the garment of his flesh occurs in *Revelationes* 3.29. "It was indeed in my temple," Mary remarks, "that he dressed himself spiritually in the priestly garb in which he offered a sacrifice for the world."[239] This remark is a striking attestation to the belief that Christ was a priest throughout his life and from the very first moment of his existence, an idea I touched upon early on, in Chapter 1. In a couple of other passages, Birgitta speaks of a pregnant mother preparing clothing for her child, but in these cases she seems to have in mind the physical clothing that the child will wear once it has left the womb, rather than the child's body itself.[240] In talking about women's work, therefore, Birgitta tends to be literal-minded. This may be related to the fact that she continued to sew and mend clothing even after she left Sweden. In one vision, Mary tells her to repair her daughter Katarina's old tunic.[241] That this directive is in keeping with Birgitta's habits is indicated by her canonization dossier, which notes that she used to sew and repair the clothing of her retinue and of the poor, as well as her own garments.[242] Imitating their foundress, the Birgittine sisters engaged in sewing and other handiwork, ultimately in imitation of the Virgin Mary.[243] For Birgitta, manual labor, mysticism, and authorship went hand in hand. In one revelation, the virgin martyr St. Agnes once consoled Birgitta for having been criticized by a man who questioned the spirit from which she spoke and opined that it "would be better for you to spin and sew after the fashion of women and not to discuss scripture."[244] Yet Birgitta did both. In the words of Bynum discussing holy women more generally, Birgitta did not abandon "women's social responsibility" even when she dedicated herself to an especially devout life. In fact, Birgitta actually uses the language of sewing to talk about the act of composition. Though she was not original in speaking thus, given that the trope that likens literary texts to textiles has a long history, the fact that she does so is no doubt owing, at least in part, to her own experiences, as a wife, mother, and caretaker of others.[245] In the prologue to the *Sermo angelicus*, the angel who dictated the text tells her that she is to put the finishing touches on the "dress" (*tunica*) of the Virgin; in other words, she is to edit or, like a seamstress, "alter" the text she has divinely received for the use of human readers.[246]

In a number of other places Birgitta uses the metaphor of clothing to speak of the virtues that should "adorn" the soul, and which should guide it in its actions. I have already referred to the passage in *Revelationes* 1.47, in which one set of clothes is used to signify the Old Law and another set, the New. "When the clothing of the Old Law was ready to be put aside," God says, "I put on the new clothing, that is, the New Law, and gave it to everyone who wanted to have me and my clothing." Here the image of clothing alludes to Paul's injunction to "put on the new man" (*induite novum hominem*, Eph. 4:24; cf. Rom. 13:14 and Col. 3:10), as well as to his likening of baptism to an investiture ceremony, in which Christ is "put on" (Gal. 3:27). Though this passage speaks of a pregnant woman preparing clothing for her child, the reader is prevented from thinking that clothing signifies an infant's body by God's matter-of-fact statement: "As a boy grows up, his old clothes get exchanged for new ones."[247] The mother, in other words, is preparing clothes externally, and these will be replaced by larger garments in due time.

While Birgitta employs metaphors that refer to garments to convey more abstract ideas, when she speaks of a woman clothing a child, she normally means this in a literal sense. Her imagination seems to have been captivated by the idea of the Virgin's having woven the seamless tunic, a concrete embodiment of her maternity with which Birgitta could readily relate. She was probably also familiar with the apocryphal legend that Mary busied herself with textile work as a young woman, an idea commonly expressed in works of art, especially those influenced, in some way, by the Byzantine tradition.[248] Considering her emphasis on the mental, emotional, and physical energy Mary expended on her child, it is fair to say that, on the whole, the Virgin served for Birgitta as a female role model—more as a pattern for thinking, feeling, and action than as a cue for abstract theological reflection and argumentation detached from lived experience. Lastly, it is worth reflecting that Birgitta's focus on relics of a textile nature likely stems from her own experience of being a wife and mother as well as a feminine leader attuned to ordinary people's needs.

## Birgitta's Visionary Account of the Passion

Before closing this chapter, it is important to treat Birgitta's vision of the Passion, which she received in Jerusalem in 1372 and recollects in *Revelationes* 7.15—a text that is retrospective rather than forward-looking, as are many of her chapters dealing with the Christ Child. In this vision, Birgitta emphasizes the co-Passion that Mary endured by mentioning more than once the sword of sorrow that pierced her heart, that is, the intense pain she felt on account of her son's sufferings, about which Simeon prophesied at the Presentation.[249] Birgitta describes Mary fainting at the foot of the cross, thereby suggesting, as did other medieval writers, that Mary's labor pains were experienced not at the Nativity, but at a later time, and in a psychological, rather than physical, sense.[250] The most striking way in which Birgitta causes her readers to recall the Nativity is by her description of how Mary laid (*reclinavit*) the lifeless body of Jesus on her knee—a literary version of the late medieval image of the pietà. Along similar lines, a Middle English lyric dating to the fifteenth century presents the Virgin as the most sorrowful mother of all, since she tends to a dead child. Addressing the audience directly, Mary in the lyric solicits compassion for her plight by contrasting herself as she mourns the death of her son, whose corpse she tenderly holds, to mothers who dandle their sprightly little children upon their knees:

> Off alle women þat euer were borne
> That berys childur, abyde and se
> How my son liggus me beforne
> Vpon my kne, takyn fro tre.
> Your childur 3e dawnse vpon your kne
> With la3yng, kyssyng and mery chere;
> Be-holde my childe, be-holde now me,
> ffor now liggus ded my dere son, dere.[251]

> [(O You) of all women who have ever lived or borne children, abide
> and see how my son lies before me, upon my knee, taken from the
> tree. You dandle your children upon your knee, with laughing,
> kissing, and merry expression. Behold my child, behold now me,
> for now my dear son, dear, lies dead.]

The accusatory speech of the *Mater dolorosa* in this lyric, as in other similar devotional sources, stems from the medieval tradition of reflecting on one's sinfulness in light of Jesus' "Reproaches" in the Good Friday liturgy, a series of first-person statements in which Christ accuses his people of indifference toward his sufferings, despite the abundance of divine favors they have received.[252] In a similar manner, Mary addresses the females who read or hear the lyric, reproaching them for joyfully interacting with their children rather than meditating on her misfortune of being a mother with a dead child lying across her knees. Jesus, in other words, is still Mary's vulnerable and precious child, even in his adulthood; their maternal-filial relationship never ends.

It is not surprising, then, that in a number of pietàs from the later Middle Ages, Jesus is in fact made to seem childlike by a diminution of his size, as can be seen, for example, in a miniature from the fifteenth-century Rohan Hours (Paris, Bibliothèque Nationale de France, MS lat. 9471), on folio 41r.[253] The passages examined in this chapter demonstrate that a similar conflation of the adult and infant Jesus regularly occurs in Birgitta's works. As Mary tended to her son's bodily needs in his infancy, so she does at his death (treated in *Revelationes* 7.15): receiving her son's body after the deposition, "she laid him (*reclinauit*) on her knee . . . . And then, with her linen cloth, his most mournful Mother wiped his whole body and its wounds . . . . She wrapped (*inuoluit*) him in a clean cloth of fine linen."[254] Kezel points out that this action imitates Mary's swaddling of the Christ Child, though in reverse order. Whereas in Luke (2:7) and in Birgitta's vision of the Nativity (7.21) Mary first wraps Jesus' body in swaddling clothes and then places him in a manger, here she lays him across her lap and then wraps his body in burial shrouds. The same verbs (*inuoluit* and *reclinauit*) are used in both passages.[255] Although Birgitta provides insight into Mary's emotions when she tended to her son's body during his childhood and stood beneath the cross, we are not told that Mary cast her thoughts back to the early stages of her son's life when she enshrouded his body, though she might very well have done so, considering the parallelism of her earlier and later actions toward Christ, as they are described by Birgitta. Like Luke when he describes Mary tending to the newborn Christ, Birgitta, with an apparent concern for practicality, recounts Mary's actions after the deposition. Mary brings clean linen cloth to both the Nativity and the Passion with the express purpose of wrapping up her son's body. For medieval adults living in a culture with a high infant mortality rate, the association of infancy with death, found in this passage and in other sources, would probably not have seemed as morbid as it does to us.[256]

The famous Franciscan preacher Bernardino of Siena (d. 1444) likewise connects Mary's care of Jesus' body at both the beginning and end of his life. In a sermon on the Passion, Bernardino states that the sword of sorrow pierced Mary's heart when she witnessed her son's death. He then goes on to describe Jesus "reclining" at his mother's breast (or lap), thereby making him seem childlike. Mary, he says, "is obliged to wrap (*involvere*) the body of her dead son in the linen cloths that someone else has provided her: the same son, whom, as a newborn infant, she wrapped in cheap swaddling clothes; and to add to her grief, she is obliged to place in a stranger's tomb—a thing unnatural for a mother—the same son whom she laid (*reclinavit*) in a poor manger when he was a crying child."[257] Whereas Birgitta, by birth a noblewoman, insists upon Jesus having his own swaddling bands and burial cloths (of good quality), just as he had his own tunic, Bernardino emphasizes, as is to be expected of an Observant Franciscan who embraced extreme poverty, that Jesus was wrapped with shabby cloths that belonged to another person and was placed in somebody else's tomb (cf. John 19:41).[258] The poverty of Christ's death matches that of his birth. In contrast to Bernardino and other writers who emphasized that Jesus was placed in a beasts' manger, Birgitta does not underscore the Babe's lack of personal belongings. He has clean clothes and two very loving parents: what more could he need? This difference, together with Birgitta's advocacy of poverty elsewhere, suggests her ambiguity toward poverty, a central Christian virtue. Christiania Whitehead has, in fact, made a similar point with reference to an image that appears in *Revelationes* 2.26: a house filled with textiles, which Birgitta is to prepare in accordance with the wishes of her heavenly spouse. Whitehead claims the Swedish mystic must have had in mind one of her prior functions as a chatelaine, "overseeing the management of her husband's rural estate." Christ's instructions regarding bountiful textiles imply that material wealth is a good thing. Yet, as Whitehead points out, the same chapter contains a meditation on the Passion by St. Lawrence that underscores the waywardness of wearing fine clothes.[259]

Bernardino was not unique in seeing a connection between the infancy and death of Jesus with regard to the objects in or upon which his body was placed, especially the manger and tomb,[260] where he was bodily contained at his birth and at his death, respectively. Medieval exegetes commonly spoke of the "leaps of Christ," which he made down from heaven to the Virgin's womb, to the manger, then to the cross and sepulcher, and finally back up to heaven in the Resurrection.[261] Such imagery configures Jesus as an active subject, indeed as an athlete running a race; in contrast, the metaphors that involve clothing found in Birgitta's writings place emphasis upon Mary's ministrations upon Jesus' passive body and her premonitions of his future suffering.

In sum, Birgitta's linkage of the theme of the Proleptic Passion with images of textiles may very well have stemmed from her own experiences as a mother and caretaker of others, particularly the efforts she made to ensure that her children and her followers were properly clothed. In her visionary writings, Birgitta conveys the Virgin's femininity by drawing attention to Mary's interiority—her thoughts, emotions, and intuition—often as they focus on the material aspects of childcare. In short, through her mystical charism, Birgitta provides insights into the private lives of Jesus and his mother, telling her readers what transpired during the hidden years of Christ's childhood, within the community in which Jesus lived, at home, and also what went on within the hidden recesses of Mary's heart. Identifying with the Virgin as a prophetess infused with divine insight, Birgitta may very well have sought to bolster her own authority as a visionary, who, through "gossip," was gifted with the secret knowledge of Jesus' childhood. Birgitta undoubtedly believed that the experiential knowledge she was privileged to transmit to others surpassed the hearsay of the apocrypha, whose unreliable male authors could not hold a candle to the *auctoritas* of the Virgin Mary.

# CHAPTER 5

# Conclusion

## The Yearning of the Quest

A, a, a! (Jer. 1:6)

In this book we have heard many medieval voices attempting to compensate for the canonical gospels' silence regarding the early years of Jesus' life. In seeking to add sound and color to Christ's infancy and childhood, a number of creative approaches were taken, including the exegetical, visionary, and performative. Many of these reveal an awareness of apocryphal infancy legends even when they implicitly reject them.

The revelations of Birgitta of Sweden concerning the Christ Child and his family and those around them focus on the painful separation between Mary and her son at the Passion and also earlier on in Jesus' life, when the Virgin prophetically envisions the sufferings that both she and her son will endure, a looking ahead that is often triggered by her interaction with some form of clothing. Birgitta presents this painful separation between mother and son as necessary for the redemption, and thus crucial in the grand scheme of things. Christians' forgetfulness of Jesus' childhood in modern times likewise saddens the Virgin, who knows the price her son has paid to redeem mankind. In a number of revelations, Birgitta stresses the Boy's beauty, perspicacity, and love for his mother, rather than the physical hardships, poverty, and antagonism that the young Jesus endured, though she also mentions these features of his childhood as experiences shared by mother and child. In one locution, Birgitta hones in on Jesus' seamless tunic, woven by Mary in his boyhood, a practical yet sentimental object that psychologically knit mother and child together, as did the pieces of cloth with which Mary covered Jesus' body in his infancy and after his death. While Birgitta admired St. Francis of Assisi and his followers, she chose not to imitate their tendency to emphasize the Boy's self-abasement and complete detachment from material things. Birgitta also denies the veracity of certain details about Jesus' childhood popularized by the apocrypha: for example, that Mary availed herself of the assistance of midwives at his birth, that Joseph was an ill-natured spouse lacking in understanding and patience, or that Jesus' wild behavior caused his parents a lot of grief. She does, however, echo the apocrypha in her description of Jesus as glowing with brightness, both at his birth and later on, and her mention of other marvels associated with Christ's childhood.

Although the apocryphal legends could be faulted for focusing on the tensions between the gifted Christ Child and those around him and, more generally, for introducing and elaborating on a number of characters in Jesus' early life, without having solid biblical support for this, they were nevertheless quite appealing, as the various surviving late medieval redactions and artistic renditions attest. The popularity of these legends can largely be explained by their creation of a vigorous Christ Child and their successful filling in of the void of Jesus' otherwise obscure years with numerous action-packed adventures. As discussed above, Thomas Aquinas and other learned clerics regarded the apocryphal infancy narratives about Jesus' childhood with suspicion because of their obscure origins. They also objected to their contents, noting their blatant contradiction of Scripture, especially John the Evangelist's claim that Jesus worked his first miracle at the wedding feast of Cana. Clerics also perceived the legends' disagreement with the widespread, biblically supported supposition that Jesus was a meek and gentle child who waited for the proper time to preach and work wonders, thus setting a good example for ordinary children for years to come. Moreover, theologians and church leaders were sensitive to the possible heretical implications of such apocryphal legends, namely the view that Jesus was not physically human like other children and that his miracles were basically magic tricks. Yet other medieval Christians seemed to have regarded the presumed imperfections of the Christ Child, which caused him to get into numerous predicaments early on, as proof of his humanness, and to have taken delight in envisaging the young Jesus as not very prudently displaying his divine superpowers and preternatural knowledge to those around him, thereby inspiring a host of reactions, including amazement, gratitude, envy, and frustration. As suggested above, the entertainment value derived from such tales and their work in helping to fashion

Christian identity (as at odds with Judaism) seemed to override the concern expressed by Aquinas that if the boy Jesus would have called much attention to himself, especially by working miracles early on, then the divine plan for Christ's crucifixion as an adult would have been thwarted.

Without doubt, the Franciscans greatly emphasized the young Christ's obscurity and lowliness, which for them was most noticeably seen in his embrace of poverty, hard work, and endurance of the disdain of those around him. Rather than encouraging Christians to yearn for a Savior who was beyond their imaginative and psychological grasp, Francis of Assisi offered the mystical in the ordinary—the Eucharistic Christ Child in the manger of every altar, which professed religious, the laity, and even animals were invited to approach. Furthermore, by his very life Francis demonstrated how the Savior was to be imitated in his wholehearted embrace of poverty and suffering; Francis also modeled the feeling of compassion for all of the hardships that Christ and his parents had endured. Reflection upon the concrete aspects and events of Jesus' human life, such as his pitiful lack of clothes at the Nativity, inspired the Franciscans to reciprocate—to the extent that they could—the love that drove the deity to the heights of generosity and to rejoice in the redemption being virtually accomplished with Christ's birth. Whereas Aquinas had rejected the apocrypha without offering a compelling imaginative substitute, and without really acknowledging the plausible viewpoint that "just as everything else about [Christ] was extraordinary, so his boyhood was extraordinary as well,"[1] Francis gracefully sidestepped the apocryphal childhood legends by, instead, dramatically focusing on God's incredible condescension in the Incarnation and in the Eucharist. Reflecting upon these two mendicants' approaches to the Christ Child, it is fair to say that that of Aquinas was negative and thus unappealing, whereas Francis's was joyful and inviting.

While the Cistercians likewise encouraged imitation of the Christ Child, they placed more emphasis than did the Franciscans on the metaphorical dimension of the God-man's childhood development and also on the elusiveness of God, who hides himself, so to speak, in the temple of his heavenly existence. Aelred did not accidentally center the meditational treatise he addressed to Ivo on the biblical episode about the twelve-year-old Jesus' lingering in the Temple; monks who desired union with God could undoubtedly relate to Jesus' parents search for their mysteriously disappearing and hard-to-find son. Aelred saw this domestic mishap of separation and eventual reunion as paralleling the Cistercians' arduous quest for perfection and mystical union with the transcendent deity—the divine lover who was yearned for and who, reciprocally, looked out through the lattices, so to speak, out of love for human beings. While Aelred in his treatise on the twelve-year-old Jesus does suggest some concrete ways of envisioning the Christ Child, by emphasizing the latter's beauty and charm, for example, his overall approach is geared toward the monastic specialist.

Nevertheless, the variety of Christ-Child images circulating in the later medieval period arguably offered something for everyone. The apocryphal Christ Child's popular appeal seems to have stemmed, to a large measure, from the liveliness and dynamic situations of his hypothetically reconstructed day-to-day life. These tales' playful coupling of the strength and self-confidence of the divinity with the inherent imperfection of childhood led to the creation of a whimsical and touchy Christ Child who often acted unpredictably and self-defensively instead of suffering passively the abuse and disregard of those around him. This was a Lord to be reverenced and one who often caused surprise, rather than an innocent Savior to be pitied—the typical response elicited from the multiple manifestations of the so-called Child of Sorrows. Though the apocryphal Christ Child was human, he was clearly *sui generis* and thus a figure of great interest.

The lack of a fleshed-out portrayal of the Christ Child in the canonical gospels meant that medieval Christians could entertain a variety of complementary and even contradictory images of him, since the question of what the boy Jesus was really like and what he did and experienced all those years long ago was ultimately left unsettled. Christians sought greater knowledge of the Christ Child in many ways, such as through personal prayer, participation in the liturgy, and the undertaking of pilgrimages to the sites where Jesus was born, had lived, and was put to death. Pastors, visionaries, poets, storytellers, and artists similarly brought contemporary Christians into imaginative and spiritual contact with Christ by encouraging them to reflect on the probable, though unavoidably hidden, events of Jesus' boyhood. The ultimate inscrutability of it all seems to have been a source of great creativity and also of anxiety, as we saw earlier in the case of Margery Kempe, who in her search for Jesus on earth was never fully satisfied.

One could easily forget in all this fervor propelled by curiosity as well as a desire for deeper spirituality and intimacy with the God-man that the quest for Jesus was actually a mutual pursuit. Bernardino of Siena explicitly makes this point in a sermon aimed at conveying the love of God for the human soul. Using as a springboard Jesus' parable about the shepherd who turns aside from his ninety-nine sheep to go in search of the one that is lost (Lk. 15:4–6),

Bernardino details how the love-crazed Jesus (*amorosissimus Iesus*) became in-carnate, undertook a difficult pilgrimage and toilsome way of life, and, lastly, suffered the Passion in order to find and regain the lost sheep, that is, the human soul that had wandered astray.[2] The baby Jesus himself expressed the ardor of God's love for the human soul when he cried as children are wont to do:

> He hardly came forth from the Virgin's womb and calls the
> beloved soul in the manner of infants: "A, a, a!" [Jer. 1:6] That is,
> "My soul (*anima mea*), my soul, my soul, I seek you, I undertake
> this pilgrimage in order to find you! I was tortured with coldness
> in the middle of the night and encompassed by enriching poverty
> for your sake, I have undertaken a laborious life for you!" On the
> eighth day the child is circumcised for you and . . . now begins to
> pour forth his sacred blood for you. Consider, my soul, how the
> little Jesus cries out on account of the pain of his wound and
> sweetly seeks you, when wailing he says, "A, a, a!"[3]

Jesus, who was the *Verbum Abbreviatum* ("Abbreviated Word") in more ways than one, can hardly express his love for human souls. Whereas Adam and Eve's children cried out "Ah" and "E" to express their sorrow as well as their neediness,[4] Mary's child gave utterance to a different kind of pain. Just as his short cry "A, a, a!" was laden with deep meaning but not easily explicated in human terms, so to posterity Jesus leaves the wondrous mysteries of his early life largely enveloped in silence. This indeed seems fitting considering the es-sential paradoxicality and incomprehensibility of God's becoming a child. Yet, as we have seen, in the later Middle Ages, European Christians seem often not to have been content with such silence or the briefness of a few cries. They sought to break through the silence, to find answers in the here and now, or at least a temporarily satisfying hypothesis.

A different approach can be seen in the modern proponent of spiritual childhood, known as "Saint Thérèse of the Child Jesus," a nineteenth-century Carmelite nun, who had a deep devotion to the child Jesus and to the entire Holy Family. In one of her musings as she approached death (which she suf-fered at the age of twenty-four due to sickness), Thérèse reflected on what life must have been like in the Lord's home at Nazareth. She imagines the young Jesus wanting to fast but being told by his mother that he was not quite ready for it physically. She also fancies that many local women would have wanted the little Jesus to play with their children. Quite confident in her understanding of the faith, Thérèse puts forth her own view of what life must have been like for the Holy Family in general: "une vie toute ordinaire." She continues, explaining why she rejects the opposite possibility: "It wasn't everything that they have told us or imagined. For example, that the Child Jesus, after having formed some birds out of clay, breathed upon them and gave them life. Ah! No! little Jesus didn't perform useless miracles like that, even to please his mother. Why weren't they transported into Egypt by a miracle which would have been necessary and so easy for God. In the twinkling of an eye, they could have been brought there. No, everything in their life was done just as in our own." Thérèse goes on to express pity for all the sufferings the Holy Family must have endured. As she herself patiently awaits death, she expresses childlike confidence in soon finding out, in heaven, all about Jesus' hidden years: "How charming it will be in heaven to know everything that took place in the Holy Family!"[5] In contrast to the secure and serene attitude manifested by Thérèse, many medieval Christians seem to have been impatient to know more about what Christ's childhood was like and also undecided as to what they should think; they thus entertained a variety of hypotheses about Jesus' early life. Without doubt, many medieval Christians remained open-minded to the possibility that Jesus performed miracles and displayed his knowledge early on, for whatever reason he had, whether didactically, practically, uselessly, or simply because he was truly a child—who knows? In short, the viability of the apocryphal legends about Jesus' childhood—their not being easily brushed aside as definite untruths—and their attempt to answer the difficult question of what a God embodied as a child might have been like seem to have fostered in the later medieval period a multiplicity of literary and artistic reconstructions of the way that God had spent the many years of his youth.

# APPENDIX

## Summary of William Caxton's *Infantia salvatoris* (c. 1477)

1. Mary and Joseph journey to Bethlehem for the census. On the way Mary has a vision of two peoples: weeping Jews and rejoicing Gentiles. When Mary enters a cave to give birth, it radiates with splendor.

2. Joseph brings two midwives to the cave in which Mary had already given birth. The hands of one of the midwives become lame because she doubted that a virgin gave birth, but she is healed when she touches the fringes of the newborn's swaddling bands.

3. Prompted by angels and seeing a huge star shine above the cave, shepherds hasten to the Savior.

4. The Holy Family moves to a stable on the third day, where an ox and an ass adore the baby Jesus placed in the manger.

5. The Child is brought to the Temple on the eighth day to be circumcised. The old man Simeon receives the baby Jesus in his hands and kisses his feet.

6. Magi bring gifts and adore the Child and bypass Herod on their return.

7. Herod orders that all the children two years old and under be killed. The Holy Family flee to Egypt at an angel's prompting.

8. When the Holy Family stop to rest on their journey, Jesus is adored by dragons that issue from a cave.

9. Lions, leopards, and wolves adore the Child and show the Holy Family the way in the desert.

10. The Holy Family encounter the thief Barabbas and his son Dismas, but are left unharmed. Jesus tells his mother that Dismas will suffer death with him and then enter into paradise.

11. Jesus orders a palm tree to bend down so that his mother and those with her might be refreshed by its fruits. He also orders water to gush forth from the tree's roots.

12. The next day, Jesus orders the tree to stand up and commands an angel to take one of its branches to paradise.

13. Jesus miraculously shortens the journey at Joseph's request.

14. When Mary, with the Child on her bosom, enters the temple in the city of Sotinen, the idols fall down. The leader Affrodosius and his people adore the Child.

15. When Jesus returns to Galilee at age five, he plays with some children along the Jordan River on the Sabbath and creates seven pools with connecting rivulets. When a bad boy ruins his handiwork, Jesus curses him and causes him to die. The boy's parents complain

to Joseph, who consults with Mary, who, in turn, asks her son why he harmed the boy. Jesus kicks the boy and, so as not to upset his mother, commands him to rise up.

16. On a Sabbath, Jesus makes twelve sparrows out of mud and commands them to fly forth. Some people wonder at him, while others blame him.

17. A boy who was the son of a priest destroys Jesus' riverside pools and channels with a rod. The boy immediately dries up and dies.

18. A boy intentionally rushes against Jesus, but is cursed by him and dies. The people level charges against Jesus, but he grabs the boy by the ear and brings him back to life.

19. Joseph and Mary hand Jesus over to the teacher Levi. After being struck by his teacher with a switch, the Child discourses on the mysterious meaning of the letters of the alphabet. Ashamed at being overcome by a child, Levi opines that his pupil ought to be killed. The Holy Family withdraw to Nazareth.

20. On a Sabbath, Jesus plays with some children in a loft. One of them, named Zeno, is pushed down by another boy and dies. Jesus jumps down from the loft and commands Zeno to come back to life to vouch that he is not to blame for his death.

21. The Holy Family travel to Jericho. Jesus, now six, goes to draw water from a well for his mother, but another child dashes against him and breaks his jar. So Jesus brings back water in his cloak instead.

22. The following day, at the same well, Jesus hangs his water pitcher on a sunbeam and tells the other children to do the same, but their jars break. Having pity on the crying boys, Jesus miraculously fixes their pitchers.

23. With a handful of grain, Jesus causes a field of wheat to grow overnight. Through Joseph, he hires reapers to harvest it. After paying them with grain, he gives the remainder to the less fortunate. The next day Jesus takes some ears of grain from a field, cooks them, and then eats them. Henceforth that field yields much grain.

24. Jesus finds a dry fish by the seaside, puts it in a basin, and orders it to swim, which it does. Thinking the boy is a magician, the widow in whose house the Holy Family were staying evicts them. Jesus often walks on water and preaches to sailors on their ships. He satisfies a thousand people with a loaf of bread.

25. At age eight Jesus goes forth from Jericho and visits a lioness and her cubs, which adore him. Jesus reproaches the people for not recognizing their Lord. Jesus crosses the Jordan, which divides into two parts for him and his train of lions. He sends the lions away and then returns to his mother.

26. Joseph, who was a carpenter, receives an order for a bed. He instructs a servant to cut two pieces of wood, but one turns out to be too short. Jesus perceives his father's worry and tells him to pull the end of one of the beams, while he pulls the other. Once the wood is the right size, Jesus tells Joseph to finish his job.

27. Once again Jesus is handed over to a teacher, who gets angry with him and strikes him on the cheek. Jesus curses his teacher, who immediately falls down and dies. The other boys rejoice that their teacher is dead.

28. The Holy Family come to Bethlehem, where Joseph's son James goes into a garden to gather herbs. A snake comes out and bites his hand. Jesus grabs the snake's tail and throws it to the ground, whereupon it dies. Then he heals the boy by blowing on his wound.

29. Jesus goes out with some boys to two lofty hills. Challenging them to imitate him, he jumps from one hill to the next and scampers back to the first, but when the other boys

try to scale the distance by leaping, they break their limbs. Jesus heals the children who got hurt. They adore him and tell their parents what happened.

30. When Jesus is twelve, a boy who lived in his village accidentally chops off his toes when cutting wood. Jesus has compassion on him and heals his foot.

31. Some parents hide their children from Jesus by putting them in an oven and placing a guard there to watch and feed them. Jesus comes along and asks the guard what is in the oven. When he replies "Pigs," Jesus says, "So let them be pigs." The guard and the parents lament the children's transformation into pigs and beseech Mary for help. Granting his mother's prayer, Jesus changes the pigs back into children.

32. A rich man imprisons his son Joseph so that he can longer play with Jesus. Soon Jesus comes along and pulls his friend out through a hole into which Jesus told the boy to insert his finger.

33. At her son's request, Mary arranges for Jesus to learn the art of dyeing. Before the dyer goes out to lunch, he tells Jesus to dye pieces of cloth different colors, but Jesus lights a fire under a cauldron and goes out to play. Seeing his apprentice out playing, the master heads home. Yet Jesus rushes back and throws all the clothes into one cauldron. The master, seeing this, laments his loss and throws a firebrand at Jesus but misses him. The brand hits the ground and then germinates and blossoms. From the same vat Jesus pulls out pieces of cloth that are now of different colors. The master asks Jesus for forgiveness, which he grants.

34. Everybody in Judea and Samaria offers Jesus a gift, but he gives what he has received to the poor. He grows daily in age and grace with God and human beings. Whenever Jesus sleeps or does anything else, a light shines around him.

35. The anonymous author wishes that those who read this treatise fare well. He says he found his account in the books of the Jews and encourages readers to believe his story.

(Caxton adds that the Virgin lived for sixty-three years.)

CHAPTER I. INTRODUCTION: RECOVERING CHRIST-CHILD IMAGES

1. Kempe, *The Book of Margery Kempe*, bk. 1, ch. 35, pp. 190–91. See further Dzon, "Margery Kempe's Ravishment."

2. On the origins of the feast of Christmas, see Gianotto, "L'origine de la fête de Noël au IVᵉ siècle." On the emergence of compassion for Jesus and Mary, and on affective piety more generally, see Fulton, *From Judgment to Passion*; and McNamer, *Affective Meditation*. On the new religious sensibility, see Southern, *The Making of the Middle Ages*, ch. 5, and Mâle, *Religious Art in France: The Late Middle Ages*, chs. 3 and 4.

3. See, e.g., Marsha L. Dutton, "The Face and the Feet of God."

4. Constable, *Three Studies in Medieval Religious and Social Thought*, part II.

5. Grundmann, *Religious Movements in the Middle Ages*, chs. 1 and 2.

6. Chenu, "Theology and the New Awareness of History," esp. p. 168. Hanning, *The Individual in Twelfth-Century Romance*. On the rise of individualism in the high Middle Ages, see Colin Morris, *The Discovery of the Individual*.

7. Isidore of Seville, *Etymologiae*, 2:11.2.1–2; idem, *The* Etymologies *of Isidore of Seville* (hereafter referred to as *Etymologies*), p. 241. On the term "child," see further Boswell, *The Kindness of Strangers*, pp. 26–35. Goodich, *From Birth to Old Age*, p. 59 et passim. See also Schultz, *The Knowledge of Childhood*, pp. 21–22 et passim. Orme, *Medieval Children*, pp. 6–7.

8. The so-called *Protoevangelium of James* closes with an epilogue, in which the author identifies himself as "James . . . who wrote this account at the time when an uproar arose in Jerusalem at the death of Herod." As Hock notes, this James "is presumably the elder stepbrother of Jesus (see Mark 6:3), hence an eyewitness of the very events he narrated, at least since the time Mary had been taken by Joseph from the temple"; *The Infancy Gospels*, p. 77. The *Infancy Gospel of Thomas*, for its part, opens with a certain "Thomas the Israelite" saying he wishes to make known what Jesus "did after his birth in my region." As Hock notes (p. 105), a version of this Greek text (referred to as C) attributes this account to James, an attempt to link this apocryphal text with the *Protoevangelium*. Some manuscripts of *Pseudo-Matthew* open with the author identifying himself as "Iacobus filius Ioseph fabri," who has written what he has seen "oculis meis"; Gijsel, *Pseudo-Matthaei Evangelium*, pp. 275–77. In other manuscripts, the text begins with a claim that the account that follows was written by Matthew the Evangelist; pp. 280–81. A Latin version of the *Infancy Gospel of Thomas* closes with a certain "Thomas Israelita" stating he has written what he has seen and remembered ("scripsi quae vidi et recordatus sum"); Tischendorf, *Evangelia Apocrypha*, p. 179. Some redactions of apocryphal infancy gospels say nothing explicit about their authorship.

9. Schneemelcher, "General Introduction," pp. 38–40. See further Chapter 3.

10. I generally use the terms "apocryphal infancy legends" and "apocrypha" synonymously and in a broad sense to refer to stories that tell of events that led up to Jesus' birth, the Nativity itself, or the incidents that occurred during his childhood. To be clear: in this study, by "apocrypha" I mean folklore related to the New Testament, not the Deuterocanonical books of the Old Testament. For a useful collection of apocryphal infancy episodes organized topically, see J. K. Elliott, *A Synopsis*.

11. The sacrifice of Isaac, e.g., was interpreted as a foreshadowing of Christ's crucifixion, a parallel noted in the *Biblia pauperum* and related texts; Chapter 3, n. 268.

12. On this apocryphal story, see Dzon, "Jesus and the Birds."

13. An allusion to the story appears in Ovid's *Metamorphoses*, bk. 9, p. 107, line 67. On the trope of foreshadowing a child's future greatness in saints' vitae, see Dzon, "Saintly and Other Children."

14. Noye, "Enfance de Jésus," p. 658. St. Augustine frequently pairs and contrasts the Son of God with the human son of Mary; for example: "The Ruler of the stars nurses at a mother's breasts, He who feeds the angels! He who speaks in the bosom of His Father, is silent in the bosom of His mother"; *Sermons for Christmas*, p. 132. Sermo 196, PL 38:1020.

15. Quoting here Nature's discourse on the pregnant Mary's knowledge of the divine infant in her womb, in Jean de Meun's continuation of the *Romance of the Rose*; Guillaume de Lorris and Jean de Meun, *The Romance of the Rose*, p. 295; Guillaume de Lorris and Jean de Meun, *Le Roman de la Rose*, vol. 3, lines 19099–102.

16. Isidore of Seville, *Etymologiae*, 11.2.8. *Etymologies*, p. 241. Repeated by Huguccio of Pisa, *Derivationes*, p. 450.

17. On medieval discussions of wonder, see Bynum, "Wonder." See further Auerbach's discussion of the *humilis* motif in Early Christian writings, which contrasts the sublimity of God with the lowliness of the Incarnation; *Literary Language and Its Public*, pp. 40–45 et passim.

18. Damian, Sermo 61, pp. 359–60.

19. Bernard of Clairvaux, "On the Eve of the Lord's Birth, Sermon Three," *Sermons for Advent and the Christmas Season*, pp. 65–66. *Sermones I*, pp. 216–17.

20. *Sermons for Advent and the Christmas Season*, p. 68. *Sermones I*, p. 218.

21. "On the Lord's Birthday, Sermon Three," *Sermons for Advent and the Christmas Season*, pp. 113–14. *Sermones I*, pp. 257–58. Later in the same sermon Bernard remarks that the baby Jesus cried but not "for the same reason others do. In others the senses prevail, in Christ unwavering affection. Other babies whimper from suffering (*ex passione*), Christ from co-suffering (*ex compassione*)"; *Sermons*, p. 116; *Sermones I*, p. 260. Bernard here evinces a neutral, even sympathetic view of infants' crying, in contrast to Augustine, who, centuries earlier, considered it proof of their selfishness; *Confessionum libri XIII*, bk. 1, chs. 6 and 7, pp. 4 and 6. Medical writers offered physiological reasons for infants' crying, seeing it, e.g., as an expression of the pain they feel in teething; MacLehose, "The Holy Tooth," pp. 214–15. On babies' crying, see also Chapter 4, n. 63, and the Conclusion, n. 4.

22. *Sermons for Advent and the Christmas Season*, p. 115. *Sermones I*, p. 259. The weakness of the infant Christ was, in fact, a point of contention in Jewish-Christian polemical debates. See, e.g., Berger, *The Jewish-Christian Debate*, pp. 350–54.

23. On infants' softness, see, e.g., Philip L. Reynolds, "Infants of Eden"; and MacLehose, *"A Tender Age,"* pp. 19–21. The remedy for human babies' formlessness was swaddling and, more generally, nurses' careful handling of their bodies. See Bartholomaeus Anglicus, *De rerum pro-*

*prietatibus*, bk. 6, ch. 4, p. 238; Trevisa, *On the Properties of Things*, p. 299; and Shahar, *Childhood in the Middle Ages*, p. 87. On medieval interest in the Christ Child's physicality, see further Dzon, "Boys Will Be Boys."

24. "The history of the Christ Child has strangely received little attention," MacLehose, *"A Tender Age,"* p. 160. For the main scholarship on the topic available up until that time, MacLehose cites two German studies dealing primarily with mystical visions of the Christ Child in Eucharistic or other settings (Browe, *Die eucharistischen Wunder des Mittelalters*, pp. 100–111; Rode, *Studien zu den mittelalterlichen Kind-Jesu-Visionen*, and also Marcus, "The Christ Child as Sacrifice." For a recent volume of conference proceedings focusing mainly on Christmas, which touches on various aspects of the medieval cult of the Christ Child, see Boyer and Dorival, *La Nativité et le temps de Noël*. Another recent book in French includes a chapter on the Christ Child in the Middle Ages as background for later manifestations of the cult; La Rocca, *L'Enfant Jésus*, ch. 1. Very helpful on medieval visions of the child Jesus, especially those associated with the Eucharist, is a section of Poignet's thesis "Recherches sur les récits de visions du Christ en Occident," pp. 70–99. See also Barnay, *Le Ciel sur la terre*. Horton's *The Child Jesus*, an older book-length study on the Christ Child geared toward a popular audience, provides a useful overview of medieval treatments of the Child and his family. Acres's recent book *Renaissance Invention* concentrates on allusions to the Passion in depictions of the Nativity and of the Christ Child more generally. Stephen J. Davis's *Christ Child*, which approaches the *Infancy Gospel of Thomas* through cultural memory studies, focuses mainly on the stories' connections to Greco-Roman culture and their implication for interfaith relations. Boulton's *Sacred Fictions* deals with the lives of Christ and Mary in medieval French literature; such texts often rely on older apocryphal sources.

25. Jacques de Vitry recounts the vision of a Cistercian monk, who saw the Virgin offering the Christ Child to crusaders as a reward for their receiving the cross with a contrite heart; *The Exempla*, pp. 55–56. In the early thirteenth-century *Life of Abbot John of Cantimpré* by Thomas of Cantimpré we learn of the knight William of Floss, who, having been influenced by heretics, denied the Real Presence of Christ in the Eucharist. But when he saw the Christ Child appear in the host, "he recanted his heresy and took the crusaders' vow"; Simons, *Cities of Ladies*, p. 18, citing Thomas of Cantimpré, "Une oeuvre inédite de Thomas de Cantimpré," pp. 260 and 264; "The Life of Abbot John," here bk. 1, ch. 10, p. 66. On the use of tales about Eucharistic apparitions of the Christ Child to fortify faith by vividly underscoring the sacrament's corporeality, see Justice, "Eucharistic Miracles and Eucharistic Doubt."

26. See Chapter 4, which deals in part with the clothing of the Christ Child. Space does not permit me to explore here the range of relics and holy places that medieval people associated with Christ's childhood. For studies along these lines, see MacLehose, "Relics of the Christ Child"; MacLehose, "The Holy Tooth"; Dzon, "Out of Egypt"; and Durand, "Byzantium and Beyond."

27. The essay is reproduced with slight modifications in Dzon and Kenney, *The Christ Child in Medieval Culture*, pp. 3–28. Its new title is "The Christ Child as Sacrifice: A Medieval Tradition and the English Cycle Plays." For a recent treatment of the story of the child Jesus appearing in the host, see Burns, "Child Sacrifice."

28. Bynum, *Holy Feast and Holy Fast*, pp. 131, 250. Also cited in Bynum, "Women Mystics and Eucharistic Devotion," pp. 129–30. The quotation is attributed to Anna Vorchtlin; Christina Ebner, *Der Nonne von Engelthal Büchlein*, p. 36.

29. See, e.g., Hale's discussion of the theme of "the birth of the Son in the soul" in the sermons of Eckhart and Tauler, who present "an immovable and silent Mary" (p. 94), in

contrast to the solicitous, nurturing, and maternal Mary found in the Sister-Books; Hale, "The 'Silent' Virgin."

30. Dinzelbacher, "The Beginnings of Mysticism Experienced in Twelfth-Century England," p. 130, n. 63: "Eucharistic apparitions of this kind recently have been claimed as typical of female piety of the middle ages and have been interpreted in a feminist sense, but there are, too, many and earlier examples of men having had the very same experiences." Although Dinzelbacher's claim that the experiences of male and female mystics were "the very same" now seems untenable, his general point is well taken. His comment follows upon an example he gives from the Life of Waltheof, a twelfth-century abbot of the Cistercian house at Melrose, "one of the innumerable visionaries who had the privilege of seeing the host transformed into the figure of the divine child," and who "benefit[ted] from a very close and loving bodily contact with Jesus." For Dinzelbacher's translation of this passage, see p. 121. The encounter occurs at Christmas Mass, at the consecration, when Waltheof found a beautiful little infant in his hands, beaming with brightness; Jocelin of Furness, *Vita Waldevi*, ch. 1, p. 255. Dinzelbacher also mentions (p. 122) the twelfth-century hermit Godric of Finchale's visions of the Christ Child.

31. Steinberg's concern with Christ's sexuality (*The Sexuality of Christ*) led him to focus on the Circumcision and Western Europeans' concern for Christ's penis, and, in my view, to overlook the wider contexts of medieval Christ-Child images. For a recent study of Christ's Circumcision that focuses on Jewish-Christian interrelations, see Jacobs, *Christ Circumcised*.

32. Kempe, *The Book of Margery Kempe*, bk. 1, ch. 83, p. 360.

33. This is not to underplay recent studies related to the medieval Christ Child, such as the book on St. Anne by Nixon (*Mary's Mother*), Sheingorn's numerous publications on St. Joseph (e.g., "'Illustrius patriarcha Joseph'" and "Joseph the Carpenter's Failure at Familial Discipline"), and works by literary scholars interested in the Christ Child primarily as a backdrop for understanding the figure of the child in literature (as in Lee Patterson's "'What Man Artow?'").

34. In addition to the studies by McNamer and Fulton cited in n. 2, see the work of Bynum (e.g., *Holy Feast and Holy Fast*); Bestul, *Texts of the Passion*; Ross, *The Grief of God*; and Bale, *Feeling Persecuted*. These studies mention the child Jesus sporadically or hardly at all.

35. On this devotional motif and related images popular in the later Middle Ages, see Hourihane, "Defining Terms."

36. See, e.g., Bale, *Feeling Persecuted*; Rubin, *Gentile Tales*; idem, "The Passion of Mary"; Despres, "Cultic Anti-Judaism"; and idem, "Mary of the Eucharist."

37. Rubin, *Mother of God*. Fulton, *From Judgment to Passion*. See also Ellington, *From Sacred Body to Angelic Soul*; and Williams Boyarin, *Miracles of the Virgin*.

38. *Vita b. Hermanni Josephi*, p. 685. See further Muir, "Bride or Bridegroom?" as well as her *Saintly Brides and Bridegrooms*. On males' love for Mary, see, e.g., Katherine Allen Smith, "Bodies of Unsurpassed Beauty."

39. Ward, *Catalogue of Romances*, vol. 2, p. 697; London, British Library, Add. 32248, fol. 4v.

40. Interest in the child Jesus as an individual did not result in disregard for the family and community in which he lived; these, in fact, received more attention as the cult of the Christ Child grew, as witnessed by the late medieval cult of the Holy Kinship. See Sheingorn, "Appropriating the Holy Kinship"; Brandenbarg, "St. Anne and Her Family," and idem, "Saint Anne: A Holy Grandmother." On the cult of the Holy Family, see Hahn, "Joseph Will Perfect"; and Erlemann, *Die Heilige Familie*. Bynum helpfully explains that medieval people's in-

dividualism was not inimical to their sense of community; "Did the Twelfth Century Discover the Individual?"

41. Jacobus de Voragine (quoting an anonymous text on the Assumption) observes: "Surely she served him and ministered to him in every way, carrying him in her womb and bringing him forth to the world, feeding and warming him, putting him to rest in the manger, hiding him on the flight to Egypt, following him from childhood to the cross, never being far from where he was"; GL, vol. 2, p. 96; LA, ch. 115, vol. 2, p. 809.

42. GL, vol. 2, p. 155; LA, ch. 127, vol. 2, p. 909. While it is not impossible that the woman used a chisel, the story seems to presuppose that the effigy of Jesus is detachable; for an example, see Borenius, *A Catalogue of the Pictures*, plate 59. See also Gerald of Wales, *Gemma ecclesiastica*, dist. 1, ch. 33, pp. 105–6. For a brief overview of the tale of the Image Held Hostage, which is considered one of the numerous Marian Miracles, see Glover, "Illustrations of the Miracles of the Virgin," pp. 175–84; figs. 124–29. Glover cites an analogue from the exempla collection of Jacques de Vitry (d. 1240) that underscores the intimacy between—indeed, the inseparability of—Mother and Child. To make explicit the moral of the story about the ransomed Christ Child, Jacques paraphrases the age-old dictum that honor (or dishonor) given to the Mother redounds to her son; *The Exempla*, no. 276, pp. 115–16.

43. Dzon and Kenney, "Introduction: The Infancy of Scholarship," p. xxii, n. 2. See also Laneyrie-Dagen, "'Lorsque l'enfant paraît.'"

44. I would agree with Elisabeth Dutton ("Review," pp. 1172–73), regarding the differences medieval people perceived between the boy Jesus and other children, that the exception proves the rule—an idea that is applicable to saints' vitae that touch upon their protagonists' early years and often contrast the budding saint with his or her coevals. At the same time, I think matters concerning Jesus are not so clear-cut, since the Boy's transcendence paradoxically allows him to act like an ordinary child without shame or serious censure. Thus, Dutton's claim that Jesus is "always an exceptional child" strikes me as an oversimplification. On the child Jesus as boyish, see my essays "Wanton Boys" and "Boys Will Be Boys."

45. Cawley, *Ida the Eager of Louvain*, bk. 1, ch. 15, p. 30. *Vita venerabilis Idae*, p. 168. Commenting on this scene Roisin states, "Unique en son genre, cette anecdote semble ravaler les sentiments du Seigneur au niveau des passions humaines"; *L'Hagiographie cistercienne*, p. 173.

46. Cawley, *Ida the Eager of Louvain*, bk. 2, ch. 11, p. 56. *Vita venerabilis Idae*, p. 177. Cf. Shahar, *Childhood in the Middle Ages*, p. 96.

47. Herlihy, "The Family and Religious Ideologies in Medieval Europe," p. 171. Shahar also mentions the episode, *Childhood in the Middle Ages*, p. 96.

48. Oosterwijk, "Swaddled or Shrouded?" and idem, "'I cam but now.'" On the high infant mortality rate in the later Middle Ages, see Youngs, *The Life Cycle*, p. 24 et passim. On the association of infants and death, through the conflation of the Christ Child with the Eucharist, see Gertsman, *The Dance of Death*, pp. 149–59. See further Part I of Dzon and Kenney, *The Christ Child in Medieval Culture*.

49. McDevitt, "'The Ink of Our Mortality.'" Clanchy, "Did Mothers Teach Their Children to Read?" Cf. the description of Mary teaching the boy Jesus about his destiny in Gerson's *Josephina*, pp. 45–46; and a brief reference to Joseph's instruction of his foster son in Gerson, *Considérations*, p. 66. On Gerson's view of Jesus' parents, see further McGuire, "When Jesus Did the Dishes"; idem, *Jean Gerson*, pp. 235–39; and idem, "Becoming a Father and a Husband," pp. 52–57.

50. Herlihy, "Medieval Children," p. 219.

51. Ibid., pp. 238–41. In another essay, in which he makes the same point, Herlihy refers more broadly to the mendicants; "The Making of the Medieval Family," p. 150. Unfortunately, Herlihy does not elaborate on the contributions of non-Franciscan mendicants, except for mentioning the apparition of Christ "as a schoolboy of surpassing charm" to the Dominican Heinrich Suso. See *The Life of the Servant*, in Suso, *The Exemplar*, ch. 11, p. 82. The Child's beauty is also emphasized in ch. 10, p. 80. Idem, *Heinrich Seuse*, pp. 30 and 32. On the Dominicans see below, n. 129.

52. See, e.g., Hanawalt, *Growing Up in Medieval London*, ch. 4; and idem, *The Ties that Bound*, ch. 11. On the mysterious nature of children, see further Berthon, "Le Sourire aux anges."

53. Herlihy says the cult "of childhood itself" was "ill concealed behind" the "cult of the Holy Child"; "The Making of the Medieval Family," p. 150. Elsewhere he states: "The cult of the child Jesus enjoys great popularity, at least from the twelfth century. Did it not conceal beneath it a cult of childhood?"; "The Family and Religious Ideologies," p. 170. Cf. *Medieval Households*, p. 125.

54. See the remark on children's readiness to forgive found in the chapter on Christmas in Jacobus de Voragine, *Legenda aurea*, LA, ch. 6, vol. 1, p. 73. GL, vol. 1, p. 42.

55. "Medieval Children," p. 238.

56. Ariès, *Centuries of Childhood*, p. 36. Idem, *L'Enfant et la vie familiale*, p. 27.

57. *Centuries of Childhood*, pp. 33–37, and 128. *L'Enfant et la vie familiale*, pp. 23–27, and 134. In contrast to Ariès, Hanawalt reemphasized the continuities between medieval and modern childhood; Hanawalt, "Medievalists and the Study of Childhood."

58. From his study of mainly pre-thirteenth-century visions of the Christ Child, Poignet concludes, along similar lines, that, "Avant le XIIIᵉ siècle, il est . . . fort rare qu'un récit décrive une vision de l'Enfant en et pour lui-même"; "Recherches sur les récits de visions du Christ," p. 93.

59. Marcus, *Childhood and Cultural Despair*, pp. 18 and 20. For the *laude* (dubiously) ascribed to Jacopone da Todi that Marcus cites, see Miles, *Christmas in Ritual and Tradition*, p. 39. In the famous Greccio episode that Marcus mentions, as recounted in the *Vita prima* by Thomas of Celano, Francis is not explicitly said to have used diminutives when speaking of the Christ Child; Francis instead calls him "pauper Rex" and "puer de Bethlehem"; FF, p. 361. Thomas of Celano, "The Life of Saint Francis," p. 256. See further the discussion of Christmas at Greccio in Chapter 2.

60. For a *lauda* in praise of the Virgin, in which the speaker becomes speechless when imagining Mary's maternal care of the Christ Child, see Jacopone da Todi, *The Lauds*, no. 2, pp. 70–71. In his first canticle on the Nativity (no. 64), Jacopone celebrates God's new accessibility through the Incarnation, pp. 194–95. In his second canticle on the Nativity (n. 65), Jacopone focuses on the madness of divine love that drove God to become a child, pp. 196–203. The anthology *Quelques poésies de Fra Jacopone da Todi* includes the Latin hymn "Stabat Mater Speciosa" (pp. 386–88), which highlights Mary's joy at the Nativity but also calls attention to Jesus' suffering—at that time and in the future. This alternately tender and lachrymose hymn echoes the famous hymn on Mary's compassion "Stabat Mater Dolorosa," as, e.g., when the Christian prays: "Cause me to rejoice truly, to adhere to little Jesus while I am in exile," p. 387. See further Ozanam, *The Franciscan Poets in Italy*, pp. 240–41, 297–304.

61. An example occurs in the "Philomena" by John Pecham, a thirteenth-century Franciscan who was also Archbishop of Canterbury. In this Latin poem, which covers the stages of Christ's life sequentially following the liturgical hours, the narrator expresses his desire to in-

teract with the Christ Child, commenting: "I believe that this loving infant would not be adverse to that, but would perhaps smile (*arrideret*) in the manner of a little one." Pecham, "Philomena," ed. Blume and Dreves, p. 605, stanza 31. For another translation (here not very literal), see *Philomena*, trans. Dobell, p. 15.

62. See, e.g., Anselm's third prayer to Mary, where the speaker exclaims: "With what affection should we love / this brother and this mother, / with what familiarity should we commit ourselves to them, / with what security may we flee to them!" He goes on to wonder at so "great a Lord, our eldest brother (*maior frater*)"; *The Prayers and Meditations of Saint Anselm*, p. 123, lines 270–73; p. 124, line 288. "Oratio 7," *Opera Omnia*, vol. 3, pp. 23–24. For further references to Jesus as our "brother," see Duffy, "Mater Dolorosa, Mater Misericordiae," pp. 220–22.

63. In Caxton's *Infantia salvatoris*, some of Jesus' playmates whose limbs become broken and even Mary and Joseph address Jesus as "Lord"; chs. 13, 15, 20, 23, and 29, pp. 8–9, 12, 17–18. For an example of a child who addresses Jesus as "Lord" from a Middle English text, see the poem on Jesus' childhood in London, BL, MS Harley 3954, which retells apocryphal tales. Here, one of Jesus' playmates "Josep" proclaims, in front of his friends, that "Jhesu is lord of gret poste [power], / Wel aut we hys myth to knowe / For þe meraclys þat we se / Fro day to day"; Horstmann, "Kindheit Jesu," in *Sammlung altenglischer Legenden*, p. 106, lines 370–33. The boy is confident that Jesus can miraculously fix his broken pitcher, if the "Lord" wishes to do so. In the same scene found in the poem recounting the apocryphal childhood in the London Thornton manuscript (BL, Add. 31042), this same friend of Jesus professes: "Thou arte kynge of alle pouste (you are the omnipotent king)." If Jesus would but blow on his pitcher, he says, it would be made whole. Horstmann, "Nachträge zu den Legenden," p. 332, lines 356–59. In this poem, after Jesus heals the boys whose limbs break when they try to imitate him (viz., his sitting on a sunbeam), "Þay hoppede and sange & made gude chere," while one of them states (the cold, hard truth): "We aughte to lufe hym, if we ware wysse," that is, on account of Jesus' superior power, apparently not because of his personal charm or gentleness, for example; p. 334, lines 516, 520.

64. For an edition of the original thirteenth-century Latin text, see Vögtlin, *Vita beate virginis Marie et Salvatoris rhythmica* (hereafter referred to as *Vita rhythmica*), p. 91, lines 2564–67. The tale derives from the *Arabic Infancy Gospel*; Walker, "The Arabic Gospel of the Infancy," ch. 41, p. 413. The anecdote in the *Vita rhythmica* recalls the adult Christ's entry into Jerusalem as performed in the York Cycle (Play 25), which involved a procession of children singing, "With braunches, floures, v[r]ysoune [prayer]"; Beadle, *The York Plays*, p. 203, line 262. As Chambers notes, children commonly greeted Christ in Palm Sunday processions (cf. Matt. 21:15–16); *The Mediaeval Stage*, vol. 2, pp. 4–5.

65. For a recent study that seeks to gender the practice of affective meditation as feminine, see McNamer, *Affective Meditation*. On Bynum's claim that Mary of Oignies anticipated Francis of Assisi's piety toward the Christ Child, see below, n. 122.

66. In *English Spirituality*, Mursell similarly uses the motif of a quest for the title of ch. 4: "The Quest for the Suffering Jesus: Late Medieval Spirituality (1300–1500)."

67. By "devotional literature" I have in mind works that aim to produce a certain religious disposition or affective response as well as to convey a religious teaching, and that often share characteristics with medieval literary texts. The term is admittedly (but necessarily) imprecise, as Bartlett and Bestul (as well as others) have noted; *Cultures of Piety*, p. 2. Bestul, though, provides a fairly specific yet encompassing definition elsewhere: "Devotional and Mystical Literature," p. 694. On devotional images, see Belting, *Likeness and Presence*, pp. 362, 409–19; and Van Os, *The Art of Devotion*.

68. For a study of the reception and adaptations of the apocryphal infancy gospels in the patristic and medieval periods, with an emphasis on the earlier centuries, see Stephen J. Davis, *Christ Child*. On Jesus' life in medieval French literature, see Boulton, *Sacred Fictions*. For a study of Middle English texts on the birth of Jesus and the very first part of Christ's life, see Bates, "Christ's Birth and Infancy in Middle English." Bates helpfully explores medieval English drama, which I say relatively little about here, mainly because the dramatists generally ignore the apocryphal childhood of Jesus. Two exceptions are Mary's desire for fruit on the Flight into Egypt (Gijsel, *Pseudo-Matthaei Evangelium*, ch. 20, pp. 58–61), which gets moved from the Flight to the journey to Bethlehem in the drama, and is later transformed into the so-called "Cherry Tree Carol"; and Mary's anxiety about the Jews' dislike of her gifted son, in the N-Town play "Christ and the Doctors." See Spector, *The N-Town Play*, p. 153, lines 32–43; p. 205, lines 221–24. See further Carr, "The Middle English Nativity Cherry Tree."

69. These topics are discussed in Chapters 2 and 3, respectively. See also my essay on Langland's portrayal of the Christ Child as knightly, " 'Bold in His Barnhoed.' "

70. Children were traditionally thought to be imperfect human beings since they were undergoing the process of development toward becoming a complete ("perfect") person, an idea expressed, e.g., by Thomas Aquinas in his commentary on 1 Cor. 13:11–12; *Super epistolas s. Pauli lectura*, p. 387. See further, Traina, "A Person in the Making"; Philip L. Reynolds, "Infants of Eden"; idem, "Thomas Aquinas and the Paradigms of Childhood"; and Sheingorn, "Reshapings of the Childhood Miracles," p. 263, p. 290, n. 28. For earlier attitudes toward children, see Bakke, *When Children Became People*; and Horn and Martens, *"Let the Little Children Come to Me."*

71. Vidal, "The Infancy Narrative in Pseudo-Bonaventure's *Meditationes vitae Christi*," pp. 355–56, n. 68.

72. Forsyth, *The Throne of Wisdom*.

73. This latter representation was admittedly uncommon in the medieval West, unlike the hieratic Christ Child seated regally on Mary's lap (*Sedes Sapientiae*). In an apsidal painting (c. 1337) above the altar of prothesis in the church of St. Nicholas in the monastery of Ljuboten, Serbia, Christ Emmanuel, blessing with his hand, is featured above a striking depiction of the infant Jesus lying on the paten. See Garidis, "Approche 'réaliste' dans la représentation du Mélismos," fig. 3. On the latter image, see also Vloberg, *L'Eucharistie*, vol. 1, pp. 51–53. On Christ Emmanuel, see further Hennessy, *Images of Children in Byzantium*, passim; and Linardou, "Depicting the Salvation," p. 141, nn. 38–40.

74. Pseudo-Bonaventure, *Meditations on the Life of Christ* (hereafter referred to as *Meditations*), ch. 9, p. 35. Idem, *Meditaciones vite Christi* (hereafter referred to as *Meditaciones*), ch. 9, p. 42. The author goes on to tell how the Infant, through a gesture, indicated his disdain for the gold.

75. Burrow, *Gestures and Looks in Medieval Narratives*, p. 53.

76. Aelred of Rievaulx, *De spiritali amicitia*, bk. 2, par. 24, p. 307. Idem, *Spiritual Friendship*, p. 76.

77. The eldest king likewise kisses the Child's feet in an illustrated fourteenth-century Italian *Meditationes vitae Christi* manuscript (Notre Dame, Snite Museum of Art, University of Notre Dame, 85.25, fol. 20r; c. 1350), and in the spectacular *Adoration of the Magi* by Gentile da Fabriano (1423, Florence, Uffizi Gallery); Pérez-Higuera, *La Nativité dans l'art médiéval*, pp. 164–65. On the Italian manuscript, see Phillips, "The *Meditations on the Life of Christ*." On the significance of Jesus' feet, see Cannon, "Kissing the Virgin's Foot," and Marsha L. Dutton, "The Face and the Feet of God."

78. Burrow, *The Ages of Man*, p. 136. The *Opus imperfectum*, a fifth-century text that circulated in the later Middle Ages, approaches the paradoxicality of the Epiphany with arguably greater subtlety when it states: the Magi "did not honor his youthfulness, which could not understand anything, but rather they honored his divinity, which knew everything." Kellerman, *Incomplete Commentary on Matthew*, p. 38. PG 56:642.

79. Ratzinger, *Jesus of Nazareth: The Infancy Narratives*, p. 52. For a much earlier statement see the "Definition of Faith" in the Council of Chalcedon: Tanner, *Decrees of the Ecumenical Councils*, pp. 77–82. In Chapter 3, I suggest that some medieval Christians, though generally orthodox in belief, perceived a parallel between Christ and other humans who had some kind of supernatural origin.

80. On apocryphal infancy scenes in Books of Hours, see Kathryn A. Smith, "Canonizing the Apocryphal," vol. 1, pp. 227–80; and her *Art, Identity and Devotion in Fourteenth-Century England*, passim. The early twelfth-century wooden ceiling panels in St. Martin Church in Zillis, Switzerland, depict scenes from the life of Christ as recounted in the New Testament, though some of the episodes (such as Jesus vivifying clay birds) derive from the apocrypha. See Garcia, "Les diverses dimensions d'apocryphité"; Murbach, *The Painted Romanesque Ceiling of St. Martin*, specifically, plates G-II and H-II, and p. 44; and Stephen J. Davis, *Christ Child*, Appendix C. Another series on the life of Christ that includes apocryphal material is the early fifteenth-century German altarpiece from the Cologne School, now in the Gemäldegalerie in Berlin; see Eisler, *Masterworks in Berlin*, pp. 44–45. The depiction of the child Jesus as a miracle worker is also found in two frescoes (s. XV/XVI) in a small parish church in Momo, Italy; here, under the watchful gaze of his mother, the Christ Child benignly restores a child to life and heals a blind adult; Temporelli, *Oratorio della Santissima Trinità*. Even more striking, because of their complete focus on the apocryphal childhood, and certainly more well known, are the early fourteenth-century Tring Tiles, executed in the delicate sgraffito technique. See Strickland, "Gazing into Bernhard Blumenkranz's *Mirror of Christian Art*"; Casey, "Conversion as Depicted on the Fourteenth-Century Tring Tiles"; Eames, *Catalogue of Medieval Lead-glazed Earthenware Tiles*, vol. 1, pp. 56–61, and 70–71, pl. 2; vol. 2, drawings 15–30; and James, "Rare Mediaeval Tiles and Their Story." The tiles are closely related to the miniatures accompanying the Anglo-Norman poem on the apocryphal childhood found in Oxford, Bodleian Library, MS Selden Supra 38; see Boulton, *Les Enfances de Jesu Crist*; idem, "The 'Evangile de l'Enfance,'" and her recent essay, "Telling the Story of the Christ Child." For a translation of the Anglo-Norman text, see Boulton, "The Childhood of Jesus Christ," pp. 97–123. Depictions of the Christ Child working miracles are also included in fourteenth-century encyclopedias, specifically: Le Palmer, *Omne Bonum*, vol. 1, p. 123, fig. 101; and Blangez, *Ci nous dit*; vol. 1, chs. 35–42, pp. 56–60, and vol. 2, pp. 267–69; Heck, *Le Ci nous dit*, pp. 93–95, and 278. A broad overview of artistic renderings of the apocrypha is provided in Cartlidge and Elliott, *Art and the Christian Apocrypha*. On the folkloric aspect of such images, see Kauffmann, "Art and Popular Culture"; and Kathryn A. Smith, "Accident, Play, and Invention." For a survey of the figure of the Christ Child in medieval art, which includes some apocryphal scenes, see Pérez-Higuera, *La Nativité dans l'art médiéval*, esp. pp. 247–57. See also Zuffetti, *Il bambino Gesù*.

81. Such as the thirteenth-century nun Mechthild of Hackeborn, who mentions the Christ Child when speaking of liturgical feasts dealing with key events from the early life of Christ. See Mechthild of Hackeborn, *Liber specialis gratiae*, vol. 2 of *Revelationes Gertrudianae ac Mechthildianae*, pp. 15–17, 29–30, and 38. Idem, *The Booke of Gostlye Grace of Mechtild of Hackeborn*, pp. 94–95, 98–99, 119–20, and 138. On "the intersection between divine time and human

time" in the liturgy, see Larrington, "The Candlemas Vision and Marie d'Oignies's Role in Its Dissemination," esp. p. 196.

82. See Dzon, "'Bold in His Barnhoed.'"

83. The *Protoevangelium* tells how the young Mary was assigned the special task of spinning the purple and scarlet threads for the veil of the Temple, and was engaged in this task when Gabriel brought news of her unique calling; Hock, *The Infancy Gospels*, pp. 51 and 53. Cf. Gijsel, *Pseudo-Matthaei Evangelium*, ch. 9, pp. 376–79.

84. On this legend, see, besides Chapter 4, Dzon, "Birgitta of Sweden and Christ's Clothing."

85. On this question, see Part III of Dzon and Kenney, *The Christ Child in Medieval Culture.*

86. GL, vol. 1, p. 42. LA, ch. 6, vol. 1, p. 73. The story is also recounted by Étienne de Bourbon, who adds that the prostitute used to be a nun and that she adjured the Christ Child "per benignitatem infantie sue quod misereretur eius"; Étienne de Bourbon, *Tractatus de diversis materiis praedicabilibus*, p. 73.

87. A common view seems to have been that the post-Resurrection Christ was polymorphous, in the sense that he could appear to humans as a child or as an adult, and in specific guises, such as a pilgrim on the way to Emmaus (Lk. 24:13–31); see Garcia, "L'enfant viellard"; Scavone, "Joseph of Arimathea, the Holy Grail, and the Edessa Icon," p. 5, and pp. 18–19, nn. 10–11; and Jensen, *Face to Face*, pp. 139–42. On Jesus as a pilgrim, see Bériou, "Parler de Dieu en images." Karl Rahner's remark that visions of Jesus as a child must not be real visions since Jesus no longer exists as a child runs contrary to the possibilities entertained by at least some medieval believers; Rahner, *Visions and Prophecies*, p. 41. Thomas Aquinas briefly considers the validity of visions of the Christ Child in the host, stating: "Nor does it matter that sometimes Christ's entire body is not seen there, but part of His flesh, or else that it is not seen in youthful guise, but in the semblance of a child, because it lies within the power of a glorified body for it to be seen . . . under its own semblance or in a strange guise (*in effigie . . . aliena*)"; Thomas Aquinas, *Summa theologiae*, 3, q. 76, a. 8, c. (Ottawa edition, cols. 2957b–58a); idem, *St. Thomas Aquinas: Summa Theologica* (hereafter referred to as *Summa Theologica*), vol. 5, pp. 2455–56. Thomas of Cantimpré, a thirteenth-century clerical author of exempla, hagiography, and natural history, recounts how, once when he was in a church at Douai, when he was looking at a Eucharistic host, he suddenly saw the Savior's "face in the measure of the fullness of the age of Christ" (Eph. 4:13), while others saw the host transformed into Christ on the cross, coming in judgment, or as a child; Thomas of Cantimpré, *Bonum universale de apibus*, bk. 2, ch. 40, pp. 399–401. This anecdote illustrates a point Aquinas makes in the body of the aforesaid article: that sometimes different beholders see different forms in the sacrament. "Nor is there any deception there, as occurs in the feats of magicians (*in magorum praestigiis*), because such species is divinely formed in the eye," while at other times an apparition "comes about not merely by a change wrought in the beholders, but by an appearance which really exists outwardly." In both cases, the miraculous apparition occurs "to show . . . that Christ's body and blood are truly in this sacrament"; ST, 3, q. 76, a. 8, c. (2957b–58a), *Summa Theologica*, vol. 5, pp. 2455–56. On the association of Jesus with magic and deception (which Aquinas, in the first question, links with Jesus' appearance on the road to Emmaus, 2957b; p. 1455), see further Chapter 3. See also Dyan Elliott, "True Presence/False Christ."

88. Bernard of Clairvaux, *Cistercians and Cluniacs*, p. 36; idem, *Apologia*, p. 83. Cf. Bernard's remark that a little one (*parvulus*) can be easily placated; "In Epiphania, Sermo I," in idem, *Sermones I*, p. 295. Idem, *Sermons for Advent and the Christmas Season*, p. 157.

89. Henry of Lancaster, *Le Livre de Seyntz Medicines*, pp. 36–37. Henry also says that since Jesus' life is eternal, his childhood always lasts, and that we need not fear to speak to a child. Idem, *Henry of Grosmont*, pp. 107–8. See further Batt, "Henry, Duke of Lancaster's *Book of Holy Medicines*."

90. Trevisa, *On the Properties of Things*, vol. 1, p. 300. Bartholomaeus Anglicus, *De rerum proprietatibus*, bk. 6, ch. 5, p. 239. Centuries earlier Leo the Great recommended imitating children's lack of vengefulness: "To inflict and to pay back injury belongs to the wisdom of this world, but 'to repay evil for evil to no one' (Rom. 12:17) represents the childhood of Christian self-possession." Leo the Great, *St. Leo the Great: Sermons*, p. 161. Idem, *Tractatus septem et nonaginta, Tractatus 37* ("Item alius de Epiphania"), vol. 1, p. 203.

91. Bernard of Clairvaux, in a sermon on the Epiphany, remarks that "Christ appears first of all as a child with his virgin mother, teaching us that before all else we have to seek simplicity and modesty. Simplicity is natural to children"; Bernard of Clairvaux, *Sermons for Advent and the Christmas Season*, p. 175. Idem, *Sermones I*, p. 309. Children's simplicity also appealed to St. Hugh of Lincoln, a twelfth-century Carthusian monk and bishop. His biographer Adam of Eynsham notes that since he "set great store by sincerity and simplicity (*simplicitatis et munditie*, lit., 'cleanliness'), the saint had an unusual affection for children because of their complete naturalness (lit., 'the holy man cherished not only the sincerity of childhood but also its age')"; Adam of Eynsham, *Magna vita Sancti Hugonis*, vol. 1, p. 129.

92. On children's status as *(in)capax doli*, see Edwards, "Canonistic Determinations," pp. 70–71; and Dzon, "Wanton Boys," pp. 92–93.

93. Trevisa, *On the Properties*, p. 300. Bartholomaeus Anglicus, *De rerum proprietatibus*, bk. 6, ch. 5, p. 239. On children's love of apples, see further Chapter 4, n. 18.

94. For a discussion of premodern manifestations of "spiritual childhood," often associated in modern times with St. Thérèse of Lisieux, see Barnay, "De l'Enfant-Jésus à l'enfance spirituelle"; and Berrouard, Sainte-Marie, and Bernard, "Enfance spirituelle."

95. For an early sixteenth-century statement of the need for adults to imitate the Christ Child and to become children again, see Erasmus's "Homily on the Child Jesus" (*Concio de puero Jesu*), a sermon he wrote for the Feast of the Boy Bishop at St. Paul's. For a thirteenth-century expression of this sentiment, see Walter of Wimborne's description of schoolboys and his yearning to become a child again (*repuerascere*): *The Poems of Walter of Wimborne*, p. 64, stanza 161, lines 1–4.

96. Peter the Florentine, *Vita Margaritae Faventinae*, ch. 2, p. 849. Idem, "Concerning the Blessed Margarita of Faenza," p. 155 (translation slightly altered). The preceding chapter relates how once Margaret was privileged to hold the baby Jesus but did not wish to give him back to his mother.

97. Vito of Cortona, *Vita Æmilianae seu Humilianae, viduae Florentiae*, ch. 2, p. 390. Idem, "The Life of Umiliana de' Cerchi of Florence," p. 109. See further Magginis, "Images, Devotion, and the Beata Umiliana." On clerics' suspicion of visions of the Christ Child, see further Kieckhefer, "*Ihesus ist unser!*" pp. 191–92.

98. See further Dzon, "Boys Will Be Boys."

99. Raby, *A History of Christian-Latin Poetry*, pp. 443–49.

100. Jerome foretells a sorry end for the powerful people of this world and those who cultivate secular literature and philosophy, but envisions a positive outcome for the simple, who will be able to say: "Behold my crucified Lord, behold my judge. This is He who was once an infant wrapped in swaddling clothes and crying in a manger. This is He whose parents were a workingman and a working-woman (*operarii et quaestuariae filius*)"; Epistle 14, in *St. Jerome:*

*Letters and Select Works*, p. 18; Jerome, *Epistulae: Pars I*, p. 61. Along similar lines, the Breviary readings for Advent, as well as sermons for that season, associate the first and last "comings" of Christ; see Vaughn, "The Three Advents," pp. 497–502. See further Binski, "The Faces of Christ."

101. Herbert, *Catalogue of Romances*, vol. 3, no. 213, pp. 647–73, here p. 647. London, BL, Add. 27336, fols. 48v–49r. This story shows that Franciscans did not always envision the Christ Child sentimentally as one who was mild and genial.

102. Caesarius of Heisterbach, *Dialogus miraculorum*, vol. 4, bk. 9, ch. 57, p. 1872. Cf. Ps. 26:9.

103. For a recent study and edition of this narrative, see Deitch, "*Ypotis*: A Middle English Dialogue." See further Suchier, ed., *L'Enfant Sage*. A similar case of a child instructing a wise man is the anecdote about the mysterious boy playing by the seashore who basically tells St. Augustine that he will never comprehend the Trinity; see Marrou, "Saint Augustine et l'ange," esp. p. 145, n. 45, where he cites, as the first known textual example, a passage from a homily by Caesarius of Heisterbach, which reappears in his *Libri VIII miraculorum*. Of relevance is Caesarius's remark that he thinks the boy might have been an angel or, more likely, "ipsum 'speciosum forma pre filiis hominum' (Ps. 44:3), Christus Ihesum, qui multis modis in se credentibus apparuere dignatus est"; Caesarius of Heisterbach, *Die Wundergeschichten des Caesarius von Heisterbach*, vol. 3, bk. 2, ch. 1, p. 76. Marrou notes that the depiction of Augustine with the mysterious boy spread in the fifteenth century, and that artists endowed the boy with a crossed nimbus, thereby indicating that he was Jesus. The story is also recounted in the *Golden Legend*; Jacobus de Voragine, *Legenda aurea*; LA, ch. 120, vol. 2, p. 864. For a depiction of the episode among the frescoes on the life of St. Augustine in the Church of Sant'Agostino, San Gimignano, see Ahl, *Benozzo Gozzoli*, no. 78. See also Laneyrie-Dagen, " 'Lorsque l'enfant paraît,' " p. 56, fig. 47.

104. See his vita attributed to Bertrand of Pontigny, *Vita s. Edmundi Cantuariensis archiepiscopi et confessoris*, cols. 1778–79.

105. "If you do not suckle me, then I will draw away from you and you will take no delight in me," Ebner, *Margaret Ebner*, p. 132. On Margaret Ebner's devotion to the Christ Child, see further Hale, "Rocking the Cradle."

106. Kieckhefer, "*Ihesus ist unser!*" p. 174.

107. Jesus can be said to play with Margaret both as a child and as a flirtatious lover. Rublack describes the Christ Child in his relations with German nuns as "an utterly paradoxical but real lover: omnipresent, nurturing, and equal, a child even, and yet also absent, demanding, and almighty"; Rublack, "Female Spirituality and the Infant Jesus in Late Medieval Dominican Convents," p. 36. See further Lagorio, "Variations on the Theme of God's Motherhood."

108. Berengario di Donadio, *Life of Saint Clare of Montefalco*, p. 15. Idem, "La vita di Santa Chiara," p. 589. On Mary's mantle as a protective enclosure, see Perdrizet, *La Vierge de miséricorde*.

109. Cf. medieval treatments of Jesus' post-Resurrection appearance to Mary Magdalene, where he often appears as a gardener. See Baert, "The Gaze in the Garden," pp. 212, 220–21. On Jesus in the guise of a pilgrim, and in other forms, see above, n. 87.

110. Vito of Cortona, *Vita Æmilianae*, ch. 5, p. 397. Idem, "Umiliana de' Cerchi of Florence," p. 129. Cf. an episode from the vita of the thirteenth-century Dominican tertiary Benvenuta of Cividale: when a mysterious boy appears to her, she begins to teach him the "Ave Maria," only to find out very quickly that he himself is the "fruit of Mary's womb" mentioned in the prayer; *Vita b. Benevenutae de Bojanis*, ch. 6, p. 163. The same basic tale is found in Caesarius of Heisterbach's *Dialogus miraculorum*, vol. 4, bk. 8, ch. 8, pp. 1524–29.

111. *Vita II b. Osannae Mantuanae*, tractatus 1, ch. 1, p. 606.

112. Cf. Caxton, *W. Caxtons Infantia salvatoris*, ch. 33, pp. 20–21: when a fiery dart thrown at Jesus hits the ground, it blossoms.

113. GL, vol. 2, pp. 10–14; LA, ch. 96, vol. 2, pp. 663–69. Van Hout discusses the tale with reference to an early sixteenth-century depiction of the encounter, in which Jesus is actually seated on a globe, which Christopher carries on his shoulders; Van Hout, "*The Legend of St Christopher*," fig. 2. This unusual Atlas-like portrayal literalizes the Child's explanation (in the *Legenda aurea*) that Christopher had the world as well as the Creator of the world on his shoulders. The earliest narratives about Christopher were *passiones* that focused on his martyrdom. See further Farmer, *The Oxford Dictionary of Saints*, pp. 105–6. As Jansen notes, the feast days of Christopher and other dubiously legendary saints "were summarily expunged from the Roman calendar" in 1969, thanks to the "exacting scholarship" of the Bollandists; Jansen, *The Making of the Magdalen*, p. 335.

114. For an interesting analogue, see Oscar Wilde's tale "The Selfish Giant," in *The Complete Shorter Fiction*, pp. 110–14.

115. Strikingly, the boy Jesus in the anecdote about retribution from Ida of Louvain's vita mentioned in this chapter is described as wearing a "seamless tunic reaching down to the ankles"; *Vita venerabilis Idae Lovaniensis*, p. 168.

116. In a passage from the *Antiquities* of Josephus, the high priest is said to wear what appears to be a seamless tunic; Josephus, *Flavius Josephus*, bk. 3, sections 159–61, pp. 274–75. See further Pemberton, "The Seamless Garment," p. 53, n. 14. A fifteenth-century painting in the Louvre portrays the Christ Child standing beside an altar and next to his mother, who is clearly wearing liturgical vestments; see Cardile, "Mary as Priest"; and Purtle, "Le Sacerdoce de la Vierge."

117. Cattin, *Musica e Liturgia a San Marco*, vol. 1, p. 367, plate 93; manuscript described on pp. 253–57.

118. Kenney and I made this suggestion in "Introduction: The Infancy of Scholarship," pp. xx–xxi, where we discuss "the baby on the stone" in Anglo-Saxon sources and in later materials, in light of Hill's view that a new image of the Christ Child came about as a result of the Franciscans. On the issue of continuity or lack thereof in Christian piety, see also Shoemaker, "Mary at the Cross, East and West"; and Rubin, "From 'Theotokos' to 'Mater Dolorosa.'"

119. On Jerome's account of Paula's piety in Letter 108 (Jerome, *Epistulae LXXI-CXX: Pars II*, pp. 306–51; idem, *St. Jerome: Letters and Select Works*, pp. 195–212), see Cain, "Jerome's *Epitaphium Paulae*."

120. Bernard of Clairvaux, *In Praise of the New Knighthood*, ch. 11, p. 65. Idem, *Liber ad milites de laude novae militiae*, p. 229.

121. This outlook is reflected by Mandeville, *The Book of John Mandeville*, p. 4, and n. 6. Idem, *Le Livre*, pp. 89–90.

122. Jacques de Vitry, the author of Mary's vita, explicitly refers to Jerome's account of how St. Paula, "cum veniret Bethleem, vidit eum ut parvulum iacentem in presepio." (This is not surprising given that Jacques mentions Jerome and Paula in the chapter on Bethlehem in his *Historia orientalis*, ch. 59, p. 240.) In the vita, Jacques goes on to say that Mary saw Jesus as an infant on certain feasts. On the feast of Christmas he appeared to her "quasi puer ubera matris Virginis lactans vel in cunabilis vagiens"; idem, *Vita Marie de Oegnies*, bk. 2, ch. 8, pp. 139–40; idem, "The Life of Mary of Oignies by James of Vitry," p. 110–11. Bynum asserts that "it was a Low Country woman, Mary of Oignies, not Francis of Assisi, who invented the Christmas crèche," but the corresponding note does not provide a clear source in support of

her claim; Bynum, "The Mysticism and Asceticism of Medieval Women," p. 56. Along similar lines, in her *Holy Feast and Holy Fast* (p. 115), Bynum describes Mary (who died thirteen years before Francis) as a "precursor in many of the devotional practices of Francis of Assisi." In a standard study on the Beguines, McDonnell remarks that "the twelfth century witnessed the growth of devotion to the humanity of Christ—the child in the crèche"; McDonnell, *The Beguines and Beghards in Medieval Culture*, p. 150. A brief note (50) cites Van Rooijen (*Theodorus van Celles*, pp. 146–48) to the effect that the vita of Mary of Oignies "offers the earliest example of this particular motif." In the aforesaid passage, Van Rooijen points out that Mary's concern for the poor of Liège was influenced by Jesus' lying in a manger on account of his poverty. Mary's love of poverty is indeed stressed in Jacques de Vitry, *Vita Marie de Oegnies*, bk. 2, ch. 2, pp. 96–97: "Attendens enim frequenter et recolens Christi paupertatem, cui nato non fuit locus diversorio, qui non habuit ubi caput reclinaret." Idem, "The Life of Mary of Oignies," p. 81. Greven had earlier compared Mary and Francis, but, for chronological reasons, denied that Mary was influenced by the Franciscans; Greven, *Die Anfänge der Beginen*, pp. 100–101. Although Jacques de Vitry mentions Mary's mystical interactions with the Christ Child, specifically her vision of him at Christmas lying in a manger (*in praesepio*), and also her embrace of poverty, inspired by the poor babe of Bethlehem, he does not say anything about Mary using a crèche as a devotional object. Nor is she said to have popularized the manger at Christmastime within a public setting, as Francis of Assisi did. Given the parallel Jacques sees between the two holy women Mary of Oignies and Paula (mentioned above in this note), the friend of Jerome, it seems as if he wants his reader to think of Mary as, in some way, having seen, rather than handled, a manger. While it is not impossible that Mary had some kind of physical crèche (crib/cradle), the surviving examples from Northern European convents postdate her. See, among others, Bynum, "The Female Body," pp. 198–99; idem, *Christian Materiality*, pp. 62–63, fig. 11; LeZotte, "Cradling Power"; and Keller, *Die Wiege des Christuskindes*, pp. 195–209. In short, although Mary of Oignies imitated Christ's poverty and contemplated the crèche, she is not said to have used an actual object, as a sort of replica of the Christ Child's resting place, in doing so. As discussed in Chapter 2, Francis of Assisi's first hagiographer devotes a chapter to "the manger (*praesepium*) he made in celebration of the Lord's birthday," on Christmas in 1223. Thus, in my view, Mary of Oignies cannot, in a strict sense, be said to be Francis's precursor in the devotion to the crèche, as an actual object used to foster devotion to Christ's infancy.

123. Raymond of Capua, *Legenda beate Agnetis de Monte Policiano*, ch. 10, p. 24. Agnes had earlier acquired a relic of the Christ Child, a small cross that he wore on a string around his neck. She pulled it from him when she resisted Mary's effort to take back her child, during a vision, after the Virgin had graciously allowed Agnes to hold her son for a short while (Sg. 3:4); ch. 8, p. 20. On late medieval images of Jesus wearing a (typically coral) necklace, see Alexandre-Bidon, "La Parure prophylactique de l'enfance." A similar case of an object handled during a visionary experience being brought back to ordinary life appears in the chapter on the Purification in the *Legenda aurea*; LA, ch. 37, vol. 1, p. 250; GL, vol. 1, p. 150.

124. Adomnán, "The Holy Places," p. 185. Idem, *De locis sanctis*, bk. 2, ch. 3, p. 207. This anecdote entails a connection between a material object and a presupposition about Jesus' childcare that does not actually have a basis in the apocrypha. For a pilgrimage account that clearly links an apocryphal text with objects from Christ's childhood (the book [*tomus*] in which he wrote and the bench [*trabis*] on which he sat with other children), see Piacenza Pilgrim, "Travels from Piacenza," pp. 131–32. Idem, *Antonini Placentini Itinerarium*, pp. 130–31.

125. "It must be remembered," remarks Ure, "that the First Crusade, as preached by Pope Urban II and by Peter the Hermit, was presented as a campaign to reopen the pilgrim routes

to Palestine and to protect the peaceful pilgrims on their innocent and vulnerable journey"; *Pilgrimages: The Great Adventure*, p. 166. On medieval pilgrimage, see, among others, Chareyron, *Pilgrims to Jerusalem in the Middle Ages*; and Whalen, *Pilgrimage in the Middle Ages*.

126. The "First Bath" of the newborn Jesus, an event lacking textual (both canonical and apocryphal) basis, is commonly represented in Byzantine art and occasionally appears in Western art. See Juhel, "Le Bain de l'Enfant Jésus"; Arad, "The Bathing of the Infant Jesus in the Jordan River"; and Sonne de Torrens, "*De fontibus salvatoris*." See also Dzon, "Out of Egypt," passim.

127. See further Saward, *Perfect Fools*, chs. 5 and 6, esp. pp. 62–68, 80–89.

128. On late medieval and Renaissance Franciscan authors who imagined the intimate interaction between Joseph and his little son Jesus, see Armon, "Servus, Pater, Dominus."

129. The Dominicans, generally more intellectual than the down-to-earth and arguably sentimental Franciscans, also cultivated devotion to the child Jesus, though scholarly discussions of the medieval cult of the Christ Child rarely give them due credit. On the importance of Christmas for Dominicans, see Scarciglia, *Il Natale nella mistica domenicana*. On Dominicans' piety toward the human Christ, see, e.g., Gaston, "Affective Devotion and the Early Dominicans," and Cannon, "Dominic *alter Christus*?" In the introduction to *The Christ Child in Medieval Culture*, Kenney and I mention the case of the fourteenth-century Dominican Heinrich Suso, who took delight in a "cheerful little tune about the baby Jesus" (supposedly the carol *In dulci jubilo*) sung to him by a heavenly minstrel; Suso, *The Exemplar*, part 1, ch. 5, pp. 73–74. Idem, *Heinrich Seuse*, pp. 21–22. Instances of devotion to the Christ Child manifested by other Dominicans prove that Suso was not a mere idiosyncrasy among the members of his order. In his *Vitae fratrum*, the thirteenth-century Dominican Gerard of Frachet recounts a vision of a friar on the Feast of Thomas Becket. Having fallen asleep in church, where he lay prostrate before the altar, the brother beheld the two-year-old Jesus come down from there. "As he saw the lovely feet with which he [Jesus] condescended to touch the earth where we mortals live, for joy and devotion he exclaimed like the Apostle Thomas, 'You are my Lord Jesus! you are my Lord Jesus!' [cf. John 20:28] He kept repeating the same thing with tears, as he held his right foot in his hands and lovingly kissed it over and over"; Gerard of Frachet, *Vitae fratrum ordinis praedicatorum*, appendix, no. 12, p. 319. Translation by Joseph Kenny: http://www.dhspriory.org/kenny/VF4.htm#4.24. There are many other Dominicans who played a role in the cult of the Christ Child, by personally focusing their devotion on him, by spreading knowledge of and affection toward him, and also by trying to counteract what they regarded as erroneous views of him. The present study mentions a number of these Dominicans: Bartholomew of Trent, Vincent of Beauvais, Thomas of Cantimpré, Thomas Aquinas, Martin of Poland, Jacobus de Voragine, Agnes of Montepulciano, Margaret Ebner, Catherine of Siena, Raymond of Capua, Giovanni Dominici, Antoninus of Florence, as well as the English Dominican thought to have commissioned (or in some way been involved with) the Holkham Bible.

CHAPTER 2. THE CHRIST CHILD IN TWO TREATISES OF AELRED
OF RIEVAULX AND IN EARLY FRANCISCAN SOURCES

1. Bernard of Clairvaux, *Bernard of Clairvaux on the Song of Songs, II*, sermon 43, pp. 220–24. Idem, *Sermones super Cantica Canticorum 36–86*, pp. 41–44.

2. The theme of the deprivations surrounding Jesus' Nativity is also featured in Bernard's sermons for the liturgical season of Christmas. See, e.g., his third sermon for the Nativity,

Bernard of Clairvaux, *Sermons for Advent and the Christmas Season*, pp. 114–15. Idem, *Sermones I*, pp. 258–59.

3. Elsewhere, in his *Homilies in Praise of the Blessed Virgin Mary*, Bernard notes how privileged Joseph was to interact with the Christ Child: "To him it was given not only to see and to hear what many kings and prophets had longed to see and did not see, to hear and did not hear, but even to carry him, to take him by the hand, to hug and kiss him, to feed him and to keep him safe"; p. 29. Idem, *In laudibus virginis matris*, homily 2, p. 34.

4. Astell, *The Song of Songs in the Middle Ages*, pp. 48–49.

5. Jacques de Vitry, "The Life of Mary of Oignies," p. 110 (translation modified). Idem, *Vita Marie de Oegnies*, bk. 2, ch. 8, p. 139.

6. A chronology of Aelred's life is provided by McGuire, *Brother and Lover*, pp. xvi–xviii. On the treatise, see the introductions to Aelred of Rievaulx, *Quand Jésus eut douze ans*, and idem, *Aelred of Rievaulx: Treatises & Pastoral Prayer*. For another twelfth-century meditational treatise that focuses on the Christ Child (though only in part), and draws together many biblical passages, see Leclercq and Müller, "Les méditations d'un moine au XIIᵉ siècle," pp. 9–14.

7. Aelred of Rievaulx, *Jesus at the Age of Twelve* (hereafter referred to as *Age of Twelve*), sect. 32, p. 39. Idem, *De Iesu puero duodenni* (hereafter referred to as *De Iesu puero*), p. 278. The plural form of "meditatio" suggests the multifacetedness of the points of reflection Aelred provides. The phrase "meditationis . . . semina" appears earlier in the treatise; *Age of Twelve*, sect. 1, p. 3. *De Iesu puero*, p. 249. For a brief overview of "meditatio," see Bestul, "*Meditatio/ Meditation.*"

8. Dzon, "Cecily Neville and the Apocryphal *Infantia Salvatoris*." On the manuscripts containing Latin versions of the *Infancy Gospel of Thomas*, see Burke, *De infantia Iesu euangelium Thomae graece*, pp. 144–60. See further Voicu, "La tradition latine des *Paidika*," and idem, "Notes sur l'histoire du texte de L'*Histoire de l'Enfance de Jésus*."

9. Gilbank briefly compares these works in "The Childhood of Christ and the Infancy of the Soul," p. 176. See also Despres, "Adolescence and Interiority."

10. *Age of Twelve*, sect. 1, p. 3. *De Iesu puero*, p. 249.

11. *Age of Twelve*, sect. 1, p. 4. *De Iesu puero*, p. 250.

12. I use the traditional phrase "hidden years" broadly to speak of the period of Jesus' early life, about which Scripture says very little.

13. *Age of Twelve*, sect. 24, pp. 31–32. *De Iesu puero*, p. 271.

14. Newhauser, "The Sin of Curiosity and the Cistercians." Cf. Aquinas, ST, 2.2, q. 167, a.1; idem, *Summa theologiae*, vol. 3, cols. 2245a–46b; idem, *Summa Theologica*, vol. 4, pp. 1868–69. In a Wycliffite sermon, Christians who wish to know more than is contained in the canonical gospels are accused of curiosity: "hold we us payed on þe mesure þat God hath ʒyuen vs and dreme we noht aboute newe poyntis þat þe gospel leuyth, for þis is synne of curiouste þat harmeth more þan profiʒteth," Hudson, *English Wycliffite Sermons*, p. 241.

15. Seeing little value in the apocrypha, Hervieux remarks that these legends, though "showing sometimes a touch of devotion," evince "at others an excess of curiosity which passes from the grotesque to the trivial"; Hervieux, *The New Testament Apocrypha*, p. 95. See further Chapter 3.

16. *Age of Twelve*, sect. 1, p. 5. *De Iesu puero*, p. 250.

17. *Age of Twelve*, p. 4, n. 6.

18. On the view, though, that Jesus is still a boy in heaven, see Chapter 1, n. 89.

19. "Item amant se mutuo." In support he cites Ecclus. 13:19: "Omne animal diligit simile sibi." Commenting on Lk. 18:17, Hugh notes, "Pueri hos amant, cum quibus ludere consueverunt"; Hugh of Saint-Cher, *In evangelium*, vol. 6, fols. 189v and 240v.

20. "Work and seclusion (*latebrae*) and labor and voluntary poverty"; Bernard of Clairvaux, *On the Conduct and Office of Bishops*, p. 81. Idem, *De moribus et officio episcoporum* (letter 42), sect. 37, p. 130. On the monastic life as "hidden," see further "La vie cachée," ch. 9 in Leclercq, *Chances de la spiritualité occidentale*, pp. 179–296.

21. On the Cistercians' response to oblation see further McGuire, "Children and Youth in Monastic Life."

22. Aelred of Rievaulx, *The Mirror of Charity*, bk. 1, ch. 34, p. 149 (translation slightly altered). Idem, *De speculo caritatis*, p. 58. The abbot's lament for Simon has been cited in support of his homosexuality, since, among other things, he talks about Simon's beauty; see McGuire, *Friendship and Community*, pp. 308–14.

23. *Age of Twelve*, sect. 5, p. 9. *De Iesu puero*, p. 253.

24. *Age of Twelve*, sect. 24, p. 32. *De Iesu puero*, p. 271.

25. McGuire goes on to say that this "fantasy . . . was perfectly legitimate in view of the fact that his flesh was pure and holy"; McGuire, *Brother and Lover*, p. 35.

26. McGuire remarks: "Despite Boswell's attempt to make the twelfth century look relatively tolerant toward gay sexuality, Aelred belongs to a monastic tradition that can be traced back to at least the Early Middle Ages, where homosexual behavior was judged more seriously than heterosexual"; McGuire, "Sexual Awareness and Identity in Aelred of Rievaulx," p. 199. See further Boswell, *Christianity, Social Tolerance, and Homosexuality*, pp. 221–26; and Marsha L. Dutton, "The Invented Sexual History of Aelred of Rievaulx."

27. Bynum, "Jesus as Mother and Abbot as Mother."

28. *Age of Twelve*, sect. 22, p. 30. *De Iesu puero*, p. 270.

29. On the four senses of scriptural interpretation practiced by patristic and medieval exegetes, see De Lubac, *Medieval Exegesis*, vol. 1.1: *The Four Senses of Scripture*.

30. On the etymology of "Bethlehem" and the idea of the Eucharist/Christ Child as food in the manger, see below, n. 163.

31. *Age of Twelve*, sect. 4, p. 7. *De Iesu puero*, p. 252. Augustine had earlier spoken of the Christ Child as food placed in the manger: "He lies in the manger as the Food of the faithful beasts of burden"; Augustine of Hippo, *Sermons for Christmas*, p. 104. Idem, *Sermo* 190, PL 38:1008.

32. *Age of Twelve*, sect. 4, p. 8. *De Iesu puero*, pp. 251–52.

33. Origen, *Origen: Homilies on Luke*, homily 20, p. 87. Idem, *Die Homilien zu Lukas*, pp. 123–24. Origen uses this distinction to explain how Christ truly progressed in (bodily) age (Lk. 2:52).

34. *Age of Twelve*, sect. 11, pp. 15–16. *De Iesu puero*, pp. 11–12.

35. *Age of Twelve*, sect. 19, pp. 25–26, 38. *De Iesu puero*, pp. 265–66, 277.

36. *Age of Twelve*, sect. 19, p. 26. *De Iesu puero*, p. 266.

37. On children's simplicity, see Chapter 1, n. 91.

38. Jerome, *Commentariorum in Matheum libri IV*, p. 157.

39. Authors who repeat Jerome include Bede, Columban, Isidore, and Smaragdus; see Boynton and Cochelin, "The Sociomusical Role of Child Oblates," p. 7.

40. On the treatment of children within Cluniac monasteries, see Cochelin, "Besides the Book."

41. Guerric of Igny, *Liturgical Sermons*, vol. 1, Sermon 6:2 (The First Sermon for Christmas), p. 38. Idem, *Guerric of Igny: Sermons*, vol. 1, pp. 166–68.

42. On the idealization of children in the eleventh and twelfth centuries, see Riché, "L'enfant dans la société chrétienne aux XIᵉ–XIIᵉ siècles," esp. pp. 285–88. See further Saward, *Perfect Fools*, ch. 5; Barnay, "De l'Enfant-Jésus à l'enfance spirituelle"; and Bakke, *When Children Became People*, pp. 58–63.

43. On this iconography, see Rowe, *The Jew, the Cathedral, and the Medieval City*.

44. *Age of Twelve*, sect. 13, p. 17. *De Iesu puero*, p. 260.

45. *Age of Twelve*, sects. 14 and 17, pp. 18–19, 22. *De Iesu puero*, pp. 260–61, 263.

46. *Age of Twelve*, sect. 17, p. 22. *De Iesu puero*, p. 264.

47. *Age of Twelve*, sect. 15, p. 19. *De Iesu puero*, p. 262.

48. *De Iesu puero*, sect. 18, p. 265 (my translation).

49. The Gospel of Mark notes that the high priests "delivered him up out of envy (*per invidiam*)" (15:10). The portrayal of the Jews as envious has a long history in the Christian tradition. See Cohen, "The Jews as the Killers of Christ."

50. *Age of Twelve*, sect. 7, p. 10. *De Iesu puero*, p. 255.

51. Although Aelred suggests that the boy Jesus was aware of his future Passion, he does not draw an explicit parallel between the three-day death of Christ and the three-day loss of the Christ Child—as Ambrose did, for example: Ambrose, *Expositio evangelii secundum Lucam*, bk. 2, sect. 63, p. 58.

52. *Age of Twelve*, sect. 7, p. 10. *De Iesu puero*, p. 255.

53. *Age of Twelve*, sect. 8, p. 11. *De Iesu puero*, p. 255.

54. *Age of Twelve*, sect. 2, p. 6. *De Iesu puero*, p. 251.

55. *Age of Twelve*, sect. 5, p. 9. *De Iesu puero*, p. 253.

56. *Age of Twelve*, sect. 5, p. 9. *De Iesu puero*, p. 253. The text literally says the boys were deterred by Jesus' seriousness but does not specify from what, though, in the case of children, the opposite of "gravitas" (applied to the Christ Child here) is usually "levitas," "lasciviae," or a similar word or phrase. For example, Nalgod says of the young Maïeul, who became a Cluniac abbot, "You would see in the innocent child the wanton levity of boyhood condemned by the austerity of censorious gravity"; *Vita sancti Majoli abbati Cluniacensis in Gallia*, p. 659.

57. Such as the legend about St. Quiricus, a three-year-old martyr who scratched the face of the pagan governor holding him and then professed that he was a Christian; LA, ch. 78, vol. 1, pp. 532–33; GL, vol. 1, p. 324. On the *puer-senex* trope in hagiography, see further Dzon, "Saintly and Other Children."

58. *Age of Twelve*, sect. 10, p. 13. *De Iesu puero*, p. 258.

59. Along similar lines, Aquinas paradoxically characterized Christ, during his human life, as both a "wayfarer" and a "comprehensor"; Aquinas, *Summa Theologica*, ST, 3, q. 15, a. 10, corpus, p. 2016. Idem, *Summa theologiae*, vol. 4, col. 2526a.

60. *Age of Twelve*, sect. 11, pp. 13–14. *De Iesu puero*, p. 258. A similar distinction between devotion and theology is later made by Bonaventure in his *Itinerarium mentis in deum*, trans. Hayes, pp. 38–39. At the end of his work (pp. 136–39), Bonaventure emphasizes that the reader's goal should be to pass over into divine mysteries.

61. Dzon, "Conflicting Notions of *Pietas*."

62. *Age of Twelve*, sect. 2, p. 5. *De Iesu puero*, p. 250. This is indeed what happens in Gerson's *Josephina*, p. 45. See also McGuire, "When Jesus Did the Dishes," pp. 145–46. In the ballads of "The Bitter Withy" and "The Holy Well," Jesus' playmates taunt him on account of his lowly parentage. See Gerould, "The Ballad of *The Bitter Withy*"; and Graves, "'The Holy Well.'"

63. In the *Meditationes vitae Christi*, Mary goes so far as to wonder whether she was a negligent parent. Pseudo-Bonaventure, *Meditations on the Life of Christ*, ch. 14, p. 54. Idem, *Meditaciones*, pp. 61–62.

64. *Age of Twelve*, sect. 8, p. 12. *De Iesu puero*, p. 256.

65. *Age of Twelve*, sect. 9, p. 12. *De Iesu puero*, p. 257.

66. On patristic and medieval responses to this verse, see Laurentin, *Jésus au temple*.

67. Though Aelred implies that both of Jesus' parents were upset over his disappearance, Joseph is hardly mentioned, which is not surprising considering that devotion to Joseph was barely emerging in the twelfth century. On Aelred's treatment of Joseph, see Sheingorn, "Joseph the Carpenter's Failure at Familial Discipline." See also Hahn, "'Joseph Will Perfect.'" On Joseph more generally, see Dzon, "Joseph and the Amazing Christ-Child"; Armon, "Servus, Pater, Dominus"; Lavaure, *L'Image de Joseph au Moyen Âge*; and Payan, *Joseph: Une image de paternité*.

68. *Age of Twelve*, sect. 6, p. 10. *De Iesu puero*, p. 254.

69. *Age of Twelve*, sect. 6, p. 10. *De Iesu puero*, p. 254.

70. Vitz, "The Apocryphal and the Biblical," p. 144. On connections among such texts, see also Lamy, "Les apocryphes dans les premiers chapitres des deux célèbres 'Vies du Christ.'"

71. Cf. Pseudo-Bonaventure, *Meditations*, ch. 15: "their home was . . . rather small. You might even think of it as three beds in some kind of little room," p. 61. *Meditaciones*, p. 71.

72. *Age of Twelve*, sect 1., p. 4. *De Iesu puero*, p. 250. Late medieval interest in the appearance of the twelve-year-old Jesus is implied by the claim that an "imago Christi in etate xii annorum" was kept within the Sancta Sanctorum chapel at the Lateran in Rome; Hulbert, "Some Medieval Advertisements of Rome," p. 406. Along similar lines, Gerald of Wales recounts how, after the Ascension, Mary asked Luke to paint a portrait of her son, describing for him the contours of her son's body. When the image was finally finished (with miraculous assistance, according to some sources), Mary asserted, "Hic est Filius meus," a statement which may perhaps have been taken to refer to the young Jesus. Gerald of Wales, *Speculum ecclesiae*, bk. 4, ch. 6, p. 278. The twelfth-century *Descriptio Lateranensis Ecclesiae* simply speaks of an "imago Salvatoris mirabiliter depicta"; John the Deacon, *Descriptio Lateranensis Ecclesiae*, p. 357. On the legend that Mary collaborated with St. Luke, see also Chapter 4, n. 127.

73. *Age of Twelve*, sect. 5, p. 9. *De Iesu puero*, p. 253. A few lines earlier, he says that his traveling companions were blessed "to contemplate certain signs of heavenly powers shining forth (*radiare*)," sect. 5, p. 9. *De Iesu puero*, p. 253. The sun-like brilliance of Jesus' face recalls the biblical description of Christ's face as snow-white at the Transfiguration (Matt. 17:2). Along similar lines, in *Pseudo-Matthew*, when the girl Mary was growing up in the temple, "her face shone as snow so that one hardly could look at her countenance"; Gijsel, *Pseudo-Matthaei Evangelium*, ch. 6 (the reading in P), pp. 330–33. A similar passages occurs in McNamara et al., *Apocrypha Hiberniae. I: Evangelia Infantiae*, vol. 2, ch. 16, p. 947. On radiant faces, see further Twycross, "'As the Sun with His Beams When He Is Most Bright'"; and Dzon, "Out of Egypt," pp. 166–69. On light emanating from the boy Jesus' head, see Tischendorf, *Evangelia Apocrypha*, p. 111; and Birgitta of Sweden, *Revelaciones: Book VI*, 6.58.13, p. 202; *The Revelations of St. Birgitta of Sweden*, vol. 3, p. 121 (discussed in Chapter 4).

74. William of St. Thierry, Arnold of Bonneval, and Geoffrey of Auxerre, *St. Bernard of Clairvaux: The Story of His Life*, ch. 2, p. 17. Idem, *Vita prima s. Bernardi*, PL 185:229. This incident was popularized by the *Golden Legend*; LA, ch. 116, vol. 2, p. 812; GL, vol. 2, pp. 98–99. Birgitta of Sweden likewise emphasizes Christ's attractive appearance in a few passages; see Chapter 4 of this volume.

75. *Age of Twelve*, sect. 20, p. 27. *De Iesu puero*, p. 267.

76. *Age of Twelve*, sect. 29, p. 36. *De Iesu puero*, p. 276.

77. In bestiaries (Barber, *Bestiary*, p. 119), the eagle is said to have the peculiar ability to look into the sun, a belief transmitted by Isidore of Seville in *The* Etymologies *of Isidore of Seville*, p. 264. Idem, *Etymologiae*, vol. 2, 12.7.11.

78. Daniel, *The Life of Ailred of Rievaulx by Walter Daniel*, ch. 32, pp. 40–41.

79. On the treatise, see the introduction in Aelred of Rievaulx, *Aelred of Rievaulx: Treatises & Pastoral Prayer*, and idem, *La Vie de recluse*.

80. Aelred of Rievaulx, *Rule of Life*, sect. 2, p. 45. Idem, *De institutione inclusarum* (hereafter *De institutione*), p. 637. For a well-known description of a female recluse embracing the Christ Child (who comes to free his "sorely tested spouse" from the urges of lust), see the vita of Christina of Markyate; L'Hermite-Leclercq and Legras, *Vie de Christina de Markyate*, vol. 2, pp. 142–45; Talbot, *The Life of Christina of Markyate*, p. 48. This vision is thought to have an erotic aspect, since when Christina "held him at one moment to her virginal breast, [she] at another felt him in her innermost being."

81. *Rule of Life*, sect. 14, pp. 63–64. *De institutione*, p. 651.

82. *Rule of Life*, sect. 24, p. 71. *De institutione*, pp. 656–57.

83. This image became widespread in the later Middle Ages. It is reflected in Kempe, *The Book of Margery Kempe*, e.g., bk. 1, ch. 4, p. 66. For an early example, see Pseudo-Anselm, "Tenth Meditation: Of the Passion of Christ," pp. 133–34. PL 158:761–62. See further Lipton, " 'The Sweet Lean of His Head.' "

84. Marsha L. Dutton, "Christ Our Mother"; Bynum, "Jesus as Mother and Abbot as Mother."

85. In my view, Dutton makes the contrast too stark by saying that, in the *De institutione inclusarum*, the recluse's "place in Paradise is earned not by imitating him [as in the *De Jesu puero duodenni*] but by ministering to him." Marsha L. Dutton, "Christ Our Mother," p. 28.

86. *Rule of Life*, sect. 29, p. 79. *De institutione*, p. 662.

87. Gijsel, *Pseudo-Matthaei Evangelium*, ch. 9: the angel appears to her "dum operatur purpuram digitis suis." Three days earlier, he met her at a well, as she was drawing water; pp. 376–77.

88. *De institutione*, sect. 29, p. 663 (my translation). Marsha L. Dutton emphasizes how Aelred casts his reader as a mother of Christ ("Christ Our Mother"), yet he seems to call even more attention to the recluse's spousal relationship with Jesus.

89. *Rule of Life*, sect. 29, p. 81. *De institutione*, p. 663. O'Connell claims that Aelred "breaks through a narrowly imaginative perspective [of the Visitation] and suggests the future development of each child's mission"; O'Connell, "Aelred of Rievaulx and the 'Lignum Vitae' of Bonaventure," p. 60.

90. See, e.g., Pseudo-Bonaventure, *Meditations*, pp. 15–16; idem, *Meditaciones*, ch. 4, p. 22; and Bartholomaeus Anglicus, *De rerum proprietatibus*, bk. 6, ch. 4 (*De infantulo*), p. 237; Trevisa, *On the Properties of Things*, vol. 1, p. 298. In the preceding chapter (*De creacione infantis*), Bartholomaeus talks about the gradual formation of a child's body in the womb (pp. 233–34; Trevisa, pp. 298–300). See further Saward, *Redeemer in the Womb*, pp. 13–20.

91. *Rule of Life*, sect. 29, p. 81. *De institutione*, pp. 663–64. A similar injunction occurs in the *Meditationes*; Pseudo-Bonaventure, *Meditaciones*, ch. 7, p. 35; *Meditations*, p. 28.

92. *Rule of Life*, sect. 31, pp. 86, 92. *De institutione*, pp. 667, 672–73. Marsha L. Dutton, "The Face and the Feet of God."

93. On Margery's vision of tending to the baby Jesus, see further Chapter 4, n. 114.

94. Kempe, *The Book of Margery Kempe*, bk. 1, ch. 36, p. 196.

95. For a brief account of this text, see Dzon, "Out of Egypt," pp. 150, 152, n. 6.

96. Walker, "The Arabic Gospel of the Infancy of the Saviour," ch. 23, p. 402.

97. Specifically the Byzantine recension "B."

98. See Gounelle, "Une Légende apocryphe relatant la rencontre du Bon Larron et de la Sainte Famille."

99. In the Latin *Gospel of Nicodemus*, the two thieves have these same names; Kim, *The Gospel of Nicodemus*, pp. 24–25. Gounelle and Izydorczyk, *L'Évangile de Nicodème*, p. 153, n. 83. The interpolation in the Greek text is a flashback that tells how the robber Dismas meets the Holy Family as they are fleeing to Egypt and brings them home with him.

100. For a detailed study of the Holy Family's encounter with a good thief, see Dzon, "Out of Egypt." On the good thief in late medieval culture, see Klapisch-Zuber, *Le voleur de paradis*.

101. *Rule of Life*, sect. pp. 81–82. *De institutione*, p. 664. This story is repeated almost verbatim by the fourteenth-century Carthusian Ludolph of Saxony, who wrongly cites Anselm as his source; Ludolph of Saxony, *Vita Christi*, vol. 1, prima pars, ch. 13, p. 66.

102. *Age of Twelve*, sect. 5, p. 9. *De Iesu puero*, p. 253. The youth's conversion in the *De institutione inclusarum* as a result of looking upon Jesus parallels the power of a woman's appearance in secular texts. Along similar lines, Jacobus de Voragine emphasizes the impact of the Virgin's beauty: LA, ch. 37, vol. 1, p. 247. GL, vol. 1, p. 149. See also Dzon, "Out of Egypt," p. 168, n. 46.

103. *De institutione*, sect. p. 664 (here my own literal translation).

104. *Age of Twelve*, sect. 6, p. 10. *De Iesu puero*, p. 254.

105. LA, ch. 45, vol. 1, p. 280; ch. 51, vol. 1, p. 352; ch. 63, vol. 1, p. 456; Izydorczyk noted these passages in "The *Evangelium Nicodemi* in the Latin Middle Ages," p. 81. See also Maggioni, "La Littérature apocryphe"; and De Gaiffier, "L' 'Historia Apocrypha' dans la Légende dorée."

106. Dumont (Aelred of Rievaulx, *La Vie de recluse*, p. 122, n. 3) observes that Aelred makes a similar remark with regard to Mary's bodily Assumption; Aelred of Rievaulx, Sermo 20, *Opera Omnia: Sermones I-XLVI*, p. 163. See further Dumont, "St. Aelred and the Assumption," p. 206. Cf. *Age of Twelve*, sect. 6, p. 10 (idem, *De Iesu puero*, p. 254), where Aelred asks Jesus who took care of him for three days and then remarks that conjectures on this point are permissible.

107. I borrow the expression "pious fiction" from Boulton, "Transmission or Transformation," p. 14; idem, *Sacred Fictions*, p. 4. For Aelred's dismissive comments on Arthurian legends, which he calls "fabulae" and "mendacia," see Aelred of Rievaulx, *De speculo caritatis*, bk. 2, ch. 17, pp. 90–91. Idem, *The Mirror of Charity*, pp. 198–99. Aelred objects to monastic novices being so emotionally involved in fiction and so apathetic toward Christ's sufferings.

108. Smith has suggested that the *Arabic Infancy Gospel* may have been translated into Latin in the high Middle Ages, but we know of no such translations. Kathryn A. Smith, "Canonizing the Apocryphal," pp. 255–56.

109. The legend is illustrated in the fourteenth-century Anglo-Norman Holkham Bible on folio 15v; see Brown, *The Holkham Bible*, p. 51. It is also related in Mandeville, *The Book of John Mandeville*, ch. 7, p. 31; idem, *Le Livre*, p. 153. See further James, "An English Bible-Picture Book," p. 15; and Dzon, "Out of Egypt," pp. 210–19.

110. This is not to say that the Christ Child's poverty was not a central concern for Bernard of Clairvaux (see above, n. 2). According to Foulon, Bernard differs from the Church Fathers by emphasizing the mercy that God showed by assuming the human condition and also by choosing poverty; Foulon, "La Nativité dans la prédication de saint Bernard." See also Wareing, "The Teaching of St. Ailred of Rievaulx on Poverty." Wareing cites a passage from *The Mirror of Charity*, in which Aelred tells his reader that if he has "preferred the poverty of Jesus to all the world's wealth" and "traded regal platters for the fare of coarse bread and the cheapest vegetables," then he has commendably passed from this world; Aelred of Rievaulx, *The Mirror of Charity*, bk. 2, ch. 15, p. 189. Idem, *De speculo caritatis*, p. 83. Along similar lines, the thirteenth-century Cistercian Stephen of Sawley emphasized the Christ Child's poverty by describing the Babe in the manger as "ragged" (*puerum Iesum pannosum*); Stephen of Sawley, "Les méditations d'Étienne de Salley," p. 345.

111. *Age of Twelve*, sect. 25, p. 33. *De Iesu puero*, p. 272.

112. Thomas of Celano, "The Remembrance of the Desire of a Soul," bk. 2, ch. 151, in *The Founder*, FAED, p. 374. For the Latin texts of early Franciscan sources, I cite *Fontes Franciscani*, ed. Menestò and Brufani, here *Vita secunda*, FF, pp. 616–17. (I have altered the translation, since *lambebat* means "he licked" rather than "kissed." I also provide a different translation for *famelica cogitatione*, since "thinking of hunger" misses the mark.) The Franciscan John Pecham likewise imagined the delight derived from licking ("lambere") the Christ Child's hands and feet; Pecham, "Philomena," ed. Blume and Dreves, p. 604, stanza 29. Idem, *Philomena: A Poem*, trans. Dobell, pp. 12–13. Along similar lines, in his poem *Marie Carmina* the Franciscan Walter of Wimborne expresses a yearning to lick Mary's womb, which he likens to a wine-cask; *The Poems of Walter of Wimborne*, p. 212, stanza 152, lines 1–2.

113. Armon discusses Franciscan authors who describe how Joseph felt incredible sweetness in hearing his son speak baby talk. She traces this trend back to Thomas of Celano's account of the Christmas celebration at Greccio. Armon, "Servus, Pater, Dominus," pp. 219–20, 270.

114. Leo the Great, *St. Leo the Great: Sermons*, sermon 47, p. 201. Idem, *Tractatus septem et nonaginta*, vol. 2, p. 274.

115. *Assisi Compilation*, sect. 14, in *The Founder*, p. 130. *Compilatio Assisiensis*, FF, p. 1494.

116. Francis of Assisi, "Office of the Passion," in *The Saint*, FAED, p. 156. *Officium passionis Domini*, FF, p. 162.

117. Thomas of Celano, *Vita secunda*, bk. 2, ch. 151, in *The Founder*, FAED, p. 374. FF, pp. 616–17.

118. *Vita secunda*, bk. 2, ch. 151, FAED, pp. 374–75. FF, p. 617.

119. Bonaventure, *Defense of the Mendicants*, ch. 7, p. 182. Idem, *Apologia pauperum*, vol. 8, p. 274.

120. Cf. Isidore of Seville: "Humble (*humilis*), as if inclined to the ground (*humus*)"; *Etymologies*, p. 220. *Etymologiae*, vol. 1, 10.H.115.

121. *Assisi Compilation*, sects. 83 and 103, in *The Founder*, FAED, pp. 186 and 208. *Compilatio Assisiensis*, FF, pp. 1598, 1643. Francis resembles a troubadour in *Vita prima*, bk. 1, ch. 7: "Once when he was singing praises to the Lord in French, in a certain forest, thieves suddenly attacked him"; Thomas of Celano, "The Life of Saint Francis," in *The Saint*, FAED, p. 194. *Vita prima*, FF, p. 291.

122. Thomas of Celano calls attention to Francis's desire for knighthood at the beginning of the *Vita prima*, when he tells of the young man's desire to gain military recognition at Apulia

and his dream of a house filled with knightly equipment; "The Life of Saint Francis," in *The Saint*, bk. 1, ch. 2, FAED, p. 186. FF, pp. 280–81.

123. *Assisi Compilation*, sect. 74, *The Founder*, FAED, p. 175. FF, p. 1579. Thomas of Celano (in *Vita secunda*, bk. 2, ch. 31) says the feast was Easter, probably because of the resonance of this story with the Emmaus episode. Yet considering the tale's emphasis on the poverty of both Mary and Christ, it seems more likely that the incident occurred at Christmas; *The Founder*, FAED, p. 287. FF, pp. 498–99.

124. Thomas of Celano, *Vita prima*, bk. 1, ch. 6, *The Saint*, FAED, p. 193. Idem, *Vita secunda*, bk. 1, ch. 7, *The Founder*, FAED, p. 251. FF, pp. 290, 454.

125. The figure of the baby is apparently based on the bambino in Filippo Lippi's "Adoration of the Child," 1455, Florence, Uffizi; see Beretta, *San Francesco e la leggenda del presepio*, p. 105.

126. Bonaventure begins with the spiritual conception of Jesus, whereas Aelred parallels the start of the soul's progress with Jesus' birth.

127. Thomas of Celano notes: "He did not even keep his trousers (*femoralia*, i.e., "breeches") on, and he was completely stripped bare before everyone"; *Vita prima*, bk. 1, ch. 6, in *The Saint*, FAED, p. 193. FF, p. 290.

128. Cf. Gregory the Great, *Gregory the Great: Forty Gospel Homilies*, homily 32, p. 258. Idem, *Homiliae in Evangelia*, p. 278.

129. According to the Divine Office of St. Francis (c. 1228–32), attributed to Julian of Speyer, "No use he had for staff, or shoes, / Or scrip. A rope around his waist, / No spare tunic would he wear (*duplicibus dimissis*)"; sect. 14, *The Saint*, FAED, p. 335. FF, p. 1112. Francis's detachment from clothing is also noted in Thomas of Celano, *Vita prima*, bk. 1, ch. 28: "Though he was content with a ragged and rough tunic, he often wished to divide it with some poor person," in *The Saint*, FAED, p. 247. FF, p. 351. (Cf. Sulpicius Severus, *Vie de Saint Martin*, vol. 1, ch. 3.1, pp. 256–59.) Numerous passages indicate that Francis wanted minimal clothing or none at all.

130. Bonaventure, *The Major Legend*, ch. 14, in *The Founder*, FAED, pp. 642–43. FF, p. 902. See further Châtillon, "*Nudum Christum Nudus Sequere.*"

131. Pseudo-Bonaventure, *Meditations*, chs. 7 and 78, pp. 25 and 252. *Meditaciones*, pp. 31 and 271. Cf. Pseudo-Anselm, *Dialogus beatae Mariae et Anselmi de passione Domini*, ch. 10; PL 159:282.

132. Bonaventure, *De perfectione vitae ad sorores*, 6.8, p. 122. Idem, *On the Perfection of Life Addressed to the Sisters*, p. 244.

133. Bonaventure, *The Mystical Vine*, p. 163. Idem, *Vitis mystica*, 5.2, p. 169. The idea that suffering permeated all of Christ's life is powerfully expressed in a sermon mistakenly attributed to Henry Chambron, a fourteenth-century Oxford Franciscan: "the whole of Christ's life can be called a passion or passions so that not only did he suffer in the end, but in the beginning of his life, in the middle, and in the end"; London, British Library, MS Harley 331, fol. 81r. For an edition and translation (based on Oxford, Balliol College, MS 149, fols. 1r–15v), see Johnson, *The Grammar of Good Friday*, pp. 250–51. See also Wenzel, *Preachers, Poets, and the Early English Lyric*, p. 164. The belief that Christ suffered throughout his entire life is also expressed by Thomas à Kempis in his early fifteenth-century treatise *De imitatione Christi*: "Not even our Lord Jesus Christ spent one hour without the anguish of the Passion as long as he lived. . . . Christ's entire life was a cross and a martyrdom" (bk. 2, ch. 12). Later, Christ is given to say: "From the hour of my birth until my death on the cross I was never without sorrow," bk. 3,

ch. 17. À Kempis, *Imitation of Christ*, pp. 49, 75; Idem, *De imitatione Christi*, pp. 124, 180. See further Esther Cohen, *The Modulated Scream*, pp. 221–25; and Mossman, *Marquard von Lindau*, passim.

134. For the Psalm's connection with the image of the boy Jesus carrying the wood of the cross, see Chapter 3, n. 268.

135. Bonaventure, *The Mystical Vine*, p. 192. Idem, *Vitis mystica*, 18.1, p. 183. In this passage Bonaventure connects Isaiah's "Puer natus est nobis . . . cuius imperium (or "principatus") super humerum eius" (Isa. 9:6) with Christ's carrying of the cross, an interpretation derived from Jerome; Jerome, *Commentariorum in Esaiam libri I–XI*, p. 126.

136. Anthony of Padua, *Sermons for Sundays and Festivals*, IV, p. 69. Idem, *Sermones Festivi*, p. 62. On the Circumcision as the first of Christ's bloodlettings, see Swanson, "Passion and Practice," p. 17, n 53.

137. Francis of Assisi, "Earlier Rule" (*Regula non bullata*), ch. 9, in *The Saint*, FAED, p. 70. Idem, FF, pp. 193–94.

138. Pseudo-Bonaventure, *Meditations*, ch. 13, p. 50. *Meditaciones*, p. 57. A rich man, "feeling sorry about their poverty, called the boy over and offered some money for his expenses. The boy was embarrassed to take it, but out of his love of poverty, he opened his hand, shamefacedly (*uerecunde*) accepted the money and expressed his thanks." Accepting alms is obviously not the same thing as begging. Much stronger claims that the boy Jesus engaged in begging can be found in the late fourteenth-century *De conformitate vitae beati Francisci ad vitam domini Iesu nostri redemptoris* by Bartholomew of Pisa (Erickson, "Bartholomew of Pisa: Francis Exalted," p. 260), and in the thirteenth-century *Cronica* of Salimbene de Adam, p. 63.

139. Vidal explains that, although "*verecundia* was seen as a temptation against humility which must be overcome, it was a temptation for which . . . the Friars seem to have had a certain sympathy: it was a sign of a *gentil cor* and its presence distinguished the man who begged for spiritual reasons from the callous professional beggar"; Vidal, "The Infancy Narrative in Pseudo-Bonaventure's *Meditationes vitae Christi*," p. 334, n. 16.

140. The images from this manuscript are reproduced in Pseudo-Bonaventure, *Meditations on the Life of Christ: An Illustrated Manuscript*. For a study, see Flora, *The Devout Belief of the Imagination*.

141. Aelred of Rievaulx, *Age of Twelve*, sect. 6, p. 10. *De Iesu puero*, p. 254.

142. Francis of Assisi, "Earlier Rule," ch. 2, *The Saint*, p. 65. *Regula non bullata*, FF, p. 173. On the connection between Christ's clothing and that of the friars, see further Chapter 4.

143. Clare of Assisi, *The Form of Life of Saint Claire*, ch. 2, p. 112. Idem, *Regula*, FF, p. 2295.

144. "Fourth Letter to Agnes," sects. 19–20, Armstrong, *The Lady*, p. 56. FF, pp. 2282–83.

145. William Durandus, when speaking of the interior of churches, conveys the same idea, but by using the adjective *vilis*: "those churches which on the Nativity suspend curtains of poor texture . . . typify that Christ did then 'take on himself the form of a servant' [Phil. 2:7], and was clothed with miserable rags (*uilibus pannis*)"; Durandus, *The Symbolism of Churches and Church Ornaments*, sect. 40, p. 61. Idem, *Rationale divinorum officiorum*, bk. 1, ch. 3, sect. 40, p. 48. Along similar lines, Pecham emphasizes that the Christ Child was poorly clad and then remarks how such reflections on the lowliness of Christ's infancy move one to desire poverty, specifically "vestis vilitatem"; Pecham, *Philomena*, ed. Blume and Dreves, p. 605, stanza 33; idem, *Philomena: A Poem by John Peckham*, trans. Dobell, pp. 12–15. On the poor quality of Christ's swaddling clothes, see Chapter 4, n. 257.

146. Thomas of Celano, *Vita prima*, bk. 1, ch. 28, p. 248. FF, pp. 351–52.

147. *The Acts of the Process of Canonization*, second witness, no. 4, Armstrong, *The Lady*, p. 151. *Il Processo*, FF, p. 2463.

148. In her "First Letter to Agnes," Clare explains that "one clothed cannot fight another naked, because she who has something to be caught hold of is more easily thrown to the ground." Clare commends Agnes for casting aside her "garments, that is your earthly riches"; sect. 27–29, in Armstrong, *The Lady*, p. 46. FF, p. 2266. Mueller notes that Gregory the Great's statement about wrestling naked (see above, n. 128), Clare's ultimate source, "was used in Matins, 12th lesson for the Common of a Martyr," *Clare's Letters*, p. 49. Cf. Heffernan, *The Passion of Perpetua and Felicity*, sect. X.7, pp. 112, 262–63.

149. *Assisi Compilation*, sect. 8, *The Founder*, FAED, pp. 122–23. FF, pp. 1478–80. Cf. *A Mirror of Perfection* (sect. 11), *The Prophet*, FAED, p. 222. FF, p. 1761.

150. Cited (with a word missing) in Jørgensen, *St. Francis of Assisi*, pp. 18–20. Fortini, *Francis of Assisi*, pp. 85–86, note a. In some sources, a stranger knocks at the door and, like Simeon at the Presentation (Lk. 2:25–35), embraces the child and prophesies concerning his holiness. For a defense of the chapel as the place of Francis's birth, see Abate, *La casa dove nacque S. Francesco d'Assisi*. Abate dates the inscription to 1316; plates 3–4, fig. 1.

151. Ahl, *Benozzo Gozzoli*, p. 56, and figs. 55a and 60.

152. Along similar lines, legend has it that when Dominic's godmother lifted him from the baptismal font, she saw a "brilliant star" on his forehead, which illuminated "the whole world"—a presage of the Dominicans' widespread preaching activities. LA, ch. 109, vol. 2, p. 719; GL, vol. 2, p. 45. See further Loomis, *White Magic*, pp. 15–26.

153. Poulenc argues that, in addition to expressing the Franciscan belief that Francis was a perfect image of Christ, this stained glass window conveys the idea of Jesus as mother, which became increasing popular in the High Middle Ages; see Bynum, "Jesus as Mother." Poulenc refers to a passage from the Franciscan-authored *Stimulus amoris* (by James of Milan), in which the narrator is meditatively present with Christ and Mary at both the cross and the manger, where he partakes of a sweet and health-giving drink mixed from blood and milk. Poulenc, "Saint François dans le 'vitrail des anges.'" See further Cook, *Images of St Francis*, no. 20, pp. 43–44.

154. On the symbolism of the cord, see Derbes, *Picturing the Passion in Late Medieval Italy*, p. 220, n. 84; p. 235, n. 75, et passim.

155. Murray, *A Meditation in Solitude of One Who Is Poor*, part I, ch. 8, p. 58. Delorme, *Meditatio pauperis*, p. 94.

156. *The Legend of Saint Clare*, part 3, ch. 14, pp. 300–301 (emphasis mine). FF, ch. 21, pp. 2428–29. In the *Process of Canonization*, a child is not explicitly mentioned in the recounting of this incident, though a nun, Francesca, testified that Clare was answered by "a voice of wonderful sweetness." Sister Francesca (ninth witness) also explains that since Clare was ill at that time, she had asked to be brought to the entrance of the refectory, where she prostrated herself before "a small box where there was the Blessed Sacrament." This same nun also claimed to have seen "a very small and beautiful young boy" next to Clare when the saint received communion shortly before her death. *The Acts of the Process of Canonization*, pp. 174–75, 177. *Il Processo di Canonizzazione*, FF, pp. 2486, 2489.

157. On the iconography of this episode, see Debby, *The Cult of St Clare of Assisi*, pp. 28–29 et passim. Frugoni discusses the invasion of the Saracens as well as Clare's devotion to the Eucharistic Christ Child; Frugoni, *Una solitudine abitata*, pp. 164–83.

158. Francis of Assisi, *Later Admonition*, no. 11, *The Saint*, FAED, p. 46. Idem, *Epistola ad fideles*, FF, p. 80.

159. Thomas of Celano implies that Francis was mainly motivated by a desire for martyrdom; Thomas of Celano, *Vita prima*, bk. 1, ch. 20; *The Saint*, FAED, pp. 229–31. FF, pp. 328–32.

160. Tolan, *Saint Francis and the Sultan*, ch. 13. Sabatier, *Vie de S. François d'Assise*, pp. 313–14.

161. Thomas of Celano, *Vita prima*, bk. 1, ch. 30, in *The Saint*, FAED, p. 255. FF, p. 360.

162. *Tractatus de poenitentia et tentationibus religiosorum*, ch. 26; PL 213:891. Frugoni, "Sui vari significati del Natale di Greccio," p. 42, n. 15. Cf. Horace's aphorism: "caelum, non animum, mutant, qui trans mare currunt"; Horace, *Horace*, bk. 1, epistle 11, line 27, p. 325. For objections against pilgrimage, see further Constable, "Opposition to Pilgrimage in the Middle Ages"; Whalen, *Pilgrimage in the Middle Ages*, passim; Webb, *Pilgrims and Pilgrimage*, ch. 12; and Dyas, *Pilgrimage in Medieval English Literature*, ch. 8.

163. Germanus, the Patriarch of Constantinople, expressed this idea in the eighth century: "Altare . . . dicitur praesepe et sepulchrum Domini," PG 98:390. Important references to the motif in the Latin Church Fathers include (1) Augustine, Sermons 189–90, *Sermons for Christmas and Epiphany*, pp. 100 and 104; PL 38:1006–8; (2) Gregory the Great, Homily 8, *Gregory the Great: Forty Gospel Homilies*, p. 51; idem, *Homiliae in Evangelia*, pp. 54–55; and (3) Bede, *Bede the Venerable: Homilies on the Gospels: Book One*, homily 1.6, pp. 56 and 58–59; idem, *Homiliarum evangelii libri II*, pp. 40–42. The frequently repeated etymology of Bethlehem as "House of Bread" appears, early on, in Jerome, *Epistulae: Pars II, Epistula 108*, sect. 10, p. 316; idem, *St. Jerome: Letters and Select Works*, p. 199. Art historians who treat of this trope include Nilgen, "The Epiphany and the Eucharist"; Lane, "'Ecce Panis Angelorum'"; idem, *The Altar and the Altarpiece*; as well as Gertsman, "Signs of Death." For studies by literary scholars, see Marcus, "The Christ Child as Sacrifice"; and Kenney, "The Manger as Calvary and Altar."

164. McNamara, "Crib, Christmas," p. 364. See further Keller, *Die Wiege des Christuskindes*, fig. 2. The *Descriptio Lateranensis Ecclesiae* mentions both a cradle and a crib/manger at Santa Maria Maggiore: "Cunabulum Domini ibi est, in quo puer iacuit. De praesepio Domini sunt ibi reliquiae"; John the Deacon, *Descriptio Lateranensis Ecclesiae*, p. 359.

165. De La Roncière, "La Nativité dans la dévotion de saint François d'Assise."

166. Francis of Assisi, "The Admonitions," ch. 1.17–19, in *The Saint*, FAED, p. 129 (emphasis mine). Idem, "Admonitiones," FF, p. 26. Cf. the Christ Child's words to Clare; cited above, n. 156.

167. Cockerell notes that Nativity scenes with "individual, freely movable figures . . . developed in Italy from the mid-sixteenth century." However, "from the end of the 13th century, Italian records describe fixed, life-sized reconstructions of the Nativity in devotional rooms set aside for them." Cockerell, "Nativity Group," p. 680. Arnolfo di Cambio's sculpture of the Nativity (consisting of eight figures) for the Sistine Chapel of S. Maria Maggiore dates to 1289; Beretta, *San Francesco e la leggenda del presepio*, pp. 94–95. See further Janet Robson, "Assisi, Rome and *The Miracle of the Crib at Greccio*."

168. Thomas of Celano, *Vita prima*, bk. 1, ch. 30; *The Saint*, FAED, p. 255. FF, p. 360.

169. Thomas of Celano, *Vita secunda*, bk. 1, ch. 6, no. 10; *The Founder*, FAED, p. 249. FF, p. 452.

170. Balbi, *Catholicon*, entry for "imago," n.p.

171. On the reception of Gregory the Great's comments about art, see, e.g., Kessler, "Gregory the Great and Image Theory." For Peter Comestor's reiteration of this aphorism in his *Historia scholastica*, see PL 198:1540.

172. Davidson, *A Tretise of Miraclis Pleyinge*, p. 98. Aronson-Lehavi, "*A Treatise of Miraclis Playing*," p. 132.

173. Bevington, *Medieval Drama*, p. 25.

174. According to the apocrypha, these women came to assist Mary in giving birth, yet arrived belatedly and were not needed, because the miraculous birth of Christ had already occurred. In late medieval artworks, handmaidens, apparently taking the place of the unpalatable midwives, assist Mary with childcare. They often tend to the Infant by bathing him while Mary rests. For the appearance of the midwives in the apocrypha (the *Protoevangelium* and *Pseudo-Matthew*), see Hock, *The Infancy Gospels*, pp. 66–69; and Elliott, *The Apocryphal New Testament*, pp. 93–94. For the Latin, see Gijsel, *Pseudo-Matthaei evangelium*, 417–27. See further Toubert, "La Vierge et les sages-femmes"; and Juhel, "Le Bain de l'Enfant Jésus."

175. Forsyth, *The Throne of Wisdom*, pp. 49–59.

176. Karl Young, *The Drama of the Medieval Church*, vol. 2, pp. 14–15. See also pp. 9 and 51. The stage directions seem to refer to a painted panel portraying the Virgin and Child.

177. Rosenthal, "The Crib of Greccio and Franciscan Realism," pp. 58–59.

178. Berliner, "The Origins of the Crèche," p. 253. Berliner here refers to the ancient view that the Nativity took place in a cave. The idea is transmitted by the apocryphal infancy gospels (*Protoevangelium*, chs. 18–19, in Hock, *The Infancy Gospels*, pp. 64–67; Gijsel, *Pseudo-Matthaei Evangelium*, ch. 13, pp. 414–19), though it did not originate with such texts. Ancient witnesses to the tradition include: Justin Martyr, *St. Justin Martyr: Dialogue with Trypho*, ch. 78.5–6, pp. 121–22; and Origen, *Origen: Contra Celsum*, pp. 47–48. While Nativity scenes from the East tended to portray a cave, those in the West usually featured a stable; Comet, "L'iconographie de la Nativité à l'époque médiévale," pp. 204–5.

179. St. Jerome uses the word *praesepe* in the broader sense when he calls himself "a lover of the inn at Bethlehem and of the Lord's stable (*praesepe*) in which the virgin travailed with and gave birth to an infant God"; Epistle 77.2, in Jerome, *St. Jerome: Letters and Select Works*, p. 158. Idem, *Epistulae: Pars II*, p. 38. Cf. Epistle 46.11: "With what expressions and what language can we set before you the cave (*spelunca*) of the Saviour? The stall (*praesepe*) where he cried as a babe can be best honored by silence. . . . Where are the spacious porticoes? . . . Behold, in this poor crevice (*foramen*) of the earth the Creator of the heavens was born." Jerome, *Letters and Select Works*, p. 64. Idem, *Epistulae: Pars I*, p. 341.

180. Tozzi, "L'iconografia della natività nei luoghi del primo Presepe."

181. Thomas of Celano, *Vita prima*, bk. 1, ch. 30, *The Saint*, FAED, p. 256. FF, p. 361.

182. Frugoni notes that the Franciscans had earlier been granted the privilege of using portable altars; Frugoni, "Sui vari significati del Natale di Greccio," p. 73. The term "portable altar" refers to a small rectangular box with an inset slab of stone; this would have to be placed somewhere, such as on a table set up for Mass in a non-permanent location.

183. Cook, *Images of St Francis of Assisi*, pp. 98–102. Beretta, *San Francesco e la leggenda del presepio*, pp. 76–77.

184. Cook, *Images of St Francis of Assisi*, p. 99. Beretta, *San Francesco e la leggenda del presepio*, pp. 71–72. See further Lunghi, "Il presepe di Greccio."

185. Mulvaney, "The Beholder as Witness."

186. Bonaventure, *The Major Legend*, ch. 10, in *The Founder*, FAED, p. 610. *Legenda major*, FF, pp. 869.

187. Jacobus de Voragine, *Legenda aurea vulgo Historia lombardica dicta*, ch. 210, p. 911. For a depiction of the Christ Child standing next to St. Dorothy, see Dzon, "Wanton Boys," p. 97, fig. 2. The anonymous quality that medieval authors attribute to the Christ Child in visions may, in part, be a way for them to underscore the ordinariness assumed by the Word in becoming a human being; in some cases it suggests the Child's desire to test others by appearing,

as it were, incognito, as in the case of the vita of Edmund of Abingdon; Bertrand of Pontigny, *Vita S. Edmundi Cantuariensis archiepiscopi et confessoris*, ch. 6, cols. 1778–79.

188. Bonaventure, *Legenda major*, ch. 10, *The Founder*, FAED, p. 610. FF, p. 869. Thomas says "puerulus unus," p. 361. FF, p. 361. Bonaventure's description of the boy is similar to how a nun once saw "a very small and beautiful young boy" appear to Clare when she received communion at Mass (referred to above, in n. 156); *The Acts of the Process of Canonization*, ninth witness, no. 10, p. 177. FF, p. 2489.

189. Thomas of Celano, *Vita prima*, bk. 1, ch. 30, *The Saint*, FAED, p. 256. FF, pp. 361–62.

190. Bonaventure, *Legenda major*, ch. 10, in *The Founder*, FAED, p. 610. FF, p. 869.

191. Vincent of Beauvais tells a story about a little boy offering a piece of bread to an image of the Christ Child (*ymago cunctipotentis parvuli*), which comes to life, embraces the boy, and predicts that he will "eat pap" with him in heaven within three days; the boy indeed dies in three days' time. This story implies that the Christ Child associates with other children in heaven; see Vincent of Beauvais, *Speculum historiale*, bk. 8, ch. 99, p. 258. On images that come to life, see further Freedberg, *The Power of Images*, ch. 11.

192. Van Hulst, "La storia della devozione a Gesù Bambino"; and Schlegel, "The Christ Child as Devotional Image in Medieval Italian Sculpture." See also LeZotte, "Cradling Power"; and Klapisch-Zuber, "Holy Dolls"; Van Os et al., *The Art of Devotion*, pp. 99–103; and Van Os, "The Madonna and the Mystery Play." As Jung recently remarked, "a catalogue of medieval Baby Jesus dolls remains a desideratum"; Jung, "The Tactile and the Visionary," p. 236, n. 129.

193. Thomas of Celano, *Vita secunda*, bk. 2, ch. 151, p. 374. FF, p. 617.

194. Kempe, *The Book of Margery Kempe*, bk. 1, ch. 30, pp. 176–77. That the effigy is "sett . . . in worshepful wyfys lappys" (p. 177) suggests that it might have been thought to be talismanic as regards fertility. On this episode, see further Dzon, "Margery Kempe's Ravishment."

195. Ebner, *Margaret Ebner*, p. 134. See further, Hale, "*Imitatio Mariae*"; idem, "Rocking the Cradle"; and Rublack, "Female Spirituality."

196. Attributed to Arnaldo de Serranno, *Liber miraculorum*, ch. 3, p. 220. Herlihy notes that "this legend . . . appears more than a century after Anthony's death [1231], but gains wide popularity in the late Middle Ages. This story is first recounted in the *Liber Miraculorum*, which was written about 1370"; Herlihy, "Medieval Children," p. 240, n. 73. The lack of artistic representations of this legend in the later Middle Ages suggests that it may not have been as popular then as Herlihy suggests; see Canova, "Contributo alla iconografia antoniana," and Mâle, *L'Art religieux du XVII^e siècle*, pp. 171–72. *The Deeds of Blessed Francis and His Companions* recounts that the Virgin once permitted the friar Conrad of Offida to embrace and kiss the Christ Child; Ugolino Boniscambi of Montegiorgio, *The Deeds of Blessed Francis*, p. 528. *Actus B. Francisci et sociorum eius*, FF, p. 2182. For an account of a Cistercian lay brother, Arnulf of Villers, embracing the Christ Child, see Goswin of Bossut, "The Life of Arnulf," p. 158; idem, *Vita b. Arnulfi*, p. 567. Both Conrad and Arnulf derive much sweetness from their brief encounter with the Christ Child.

197. The Virgin likewise embraces and comforts her son in Birgitta of Sweden's vision of the Nativity; see Chapter 4.

198. Bynum, "Women's Stories, Women's Symbols," p. 35. A number of late medieval texts that describe Joseph hugging the young Jesus suggest that embracing one's child was not considered a strictly maternal gesture; Armon, "Servus, Pater, Dominus," pp. 371–72 et passim.

199. *The Founder*, FAED, p. 503. Mulvaney, "The Beholder as Witness," pp. 169–70.

200. Smart, *The Assisi Problem and the Art of Giotto*, p. 276.

201. Thomas of Celano, "The Life of Saint Francis," *The Saint*, ch. 19, FAED, p. 227. FF, p. 326.

202. Pseudo-Bonaventure, *Meditations*, ch. 8, p. 30. *Meditaciones*, p. 37.

203. Christina Ebner, *Der Nonne von Engelthal Büchlein von der Genaden Überlast*, p. 36. Cited by Kieckhefer, "*Ihesus ist unser!*" pp. 179–80.

204. Gijsel, *Pseudo-Matthaei Evangelium*, ch. 14, p. 431.

205. Pseudo-Bonaventure, *Meditations*, ch. 7, p. 25. *Meditaciones*, p. 31.

206. Bartholomew of Pisa, *De vita et laudibus B. Mariae Virginis*, pp. 443–44.

207. *The Saint*, bk. 1, ch. 30, FAED, p. 255. FF, p. 360.

208. "Perfusus lacriminis," in Thomas of Celano, *Vita secunda*, bk. 2, ch. 151, p. 375. FF, p. 617. On crying in the Middle Ages, see among others Nagy, "Religious Weeping."

209. Thomas of Celano, *Vita secunda*, bk. 2, ch. 7, in *The Founder*, FAED, p. 269. FF, p. 474.

210. Thomas of Celano, *Vita prima*, bk. 1, ch. 30, in *The Saint*, FAED, p. 255. FF, p. 361.

211. "Respersus lacrimis," Bonaventure, *Legenda major*, FF, p. 868. Idem, *The Major Legend*, ch. 10, *The Founder*, FAED, p. 610. For the passage from the *Vita secunda*, see above, nn. 118 and 208.

212. Peter the Venerable, *De miraculis libri duo*, bk. 1, ch. 15, p. 50. The chapter goes on to recount how a certain monk (thought to be St. Hugh of Cluny) had a vision of the Christ Child rejoicing at Christmas and triumphing over the ancient enemy. Such sentiments resonate with Francis of Assisi's joyful confidence of the redemption on the feast of Christmas.

213. Although Mary of Oignies meditated upon the baby Jesus' manger, we do not know if she used a baby Jesus statue or a replica of the manger as devotional objects. See Chapter 1, n. 122.

214. On the emergence of compassion in the religious sensibility of the West, see, among others, McNamer, *Affective Meditation*; and Fulton, *From Judgment to Passion*.

215. Cousins, "Francis of Assisi," p. 175.

216. Carruthers emphasizes the rhetorical aspect of this concept ("Sweetness"), while Posset ("*Christi Dulcedo*") stresses its emotional and spiritual valences.

217. Lutton, "The Name of Jesus."

218. Cited by Bynum, "Women Mystics and Eucharistic Devotion," p. 348, n. 36. Herlihy and Klapisch-Zuber note that "la sensibilité italienne était ouverte au charme spécifique de l'enfance et cette attitude s'est révélée durable. Au début du 15e siècle, Giovanni Dominici condamne les mères florentines qui passent leur temps à embrasser et dorloter leurs enfants, les 'léchant' et chatouillant sans se lasser"; Herlihy and Klapisch-Zuber, *Les Toscans et leurs familles*, p. 569. Dominici, *Regola del governo di cura familiare*, p. 151.

219. Thomas of Celano, *The Life of Saint Francis*, bk. 1, ch. 30, *The Saint*, FAED, p. 256. FF, p. 361. Cf. Marcus, who notes how Francis of Assisi delighted in "tasting" of the baby Jesus when he thought of him on Christmas Eve; Marcus, "The Christ Child as Sacrifice," pp. 8–9.

220. Guerric of Igny, *Liturgical Sermons: Book I*, Fifth Sermon for Christmas (10.5), p. 66. Idem, *Guerric d'Igny: Sermons*, vol. 1, p. 234. Cf. Aelred of Rievaulx, Sermon 3.39–40, *The Liturgical Sermons*, p. 105. Idem, *Opera omnia: Sermones I-XLVI*, p. 36. John Chrysostom expressed a similar idea centuries earlier; see Kenney, "The Manger as Calvary," p. 47.

221. "But among all the different kinds of creatures, he loved lambs (*agniculi*) with a special fondness and spontaneous affection"; Thomas of Celano, *Vita prima*, bk. 1, ch. 28, *The Saint*, FAED, p. 248. FF, p. 352.

222. A pillar supporting the ciborium prevents the viewer from seeing the priest's hands fully, yet he is clearly concentrating on what he is doing. Mulvaney claims that the layman behind the altar with his head bent down is "staring directly downward into the face of the baby," but the direction of his gaze is debatable. Mulvaney, "The Beholder as Witness," pp. 184–85.

223. Hill, "The Baby on the Stone." For a facing-page translation, see Clayton, *Old English Poems of Christ and His Saints*, here pp. 70–71.

224. "The bread of angels . . . the food of the faithful animals in the crib of the church" (see above, n. 163); Prescott, *The Benedictional of St. Æthelwold*, p. 12. Schiller suggested that "the tall structure of the manger" (seen in this image and in others) alluded to the "altar . . . built over the grotto of the Nativity in the church at Bethlehem" as well as to "the connection between the Incarnation of God and his expiatory death." The structure "may also serve to emphasize generally the dignity of the divine Child"; *Iconography of Christian Art*, vol. 1, pp. 63 and 70.

225. Hill, "The Baby on the Stone," pp. 72–73.

226. Ibid., p. 77.

227. See above, n. 117.

228. Cf. the famous account of how a mule reverently bent down before the Eucharist at the prompting of St. Anthony of Padua; Arnaldo de Serranno, *Liber miraculorum*, pp. 168–71.

229. Gijsel notes that Habakkuk 3:2 was paired with Isaiah 1:3. The former passage ("In the midst of the years thou shalt make it known" ["in medio annorum notum facies"]; Weber, *Biblia sacra*) was mistranslated in the Septuagint (and Vetus Itala), which in turn gave rise to a faulty translation in the Vulgate: "In medio duorum animalium innotesceris," Gijsel, *Pseudo-Matthaei Evangelium*, p. 430.

230. On Aelred's interpretation of the ox and the ass in the *De Iesu puero*, see above, n. 31.

231. The earliest of these depictions (from the fourth century) predate *Pseudo-Matthew*.

232. Grousset, "Le boeuf et l'âne," p. 342.

233. Frugoni downplays the patristic and medieval idea that individuals from these groups of people are able to come together—indeed, eat at the same Eucharistic table—once they have all acknowledged the Lord, meaning converted to Christianity.

234. Francis of Assisi, *Regula non bullata*, ch. 16, in *The Saint*, FAED, p. 74. FF, p. 199.

235. The verse "peace to men of good will" (Lk. 2:14) is not mentioned or alluded to by either Thomas of Celano or Bonaventure in their accounts of the Greccio incident. In her biography of Francis, in the chapter "Greccio and Damietta," Frugoni remedies this omission by noting that Francis mentioned Luke 2:14 in his prayer for Christmas vespers, which she glosses as follows: "Christ has come to bring peace, that peace which men cannot find in the holy places where he was born, the peace which Francis had gone to proclaim." She continues: "the crib at Greccio does away with the need to travel to the Holy Land or to defend it. . . . Bethlehem is everywhere, even at Greccio, because above all it must be in people's hearts." Frugoni, *Francis of Assisi*, p. 115.

236. Francis was in Egypt in 1219 during the Fifth Crusade, but the Mass at Greccio took place in 1223 after it had already ended (in 1221).

237. Mathews maintains that the welcoming of the animal kingdom into the religious sphere is central to Christianity, providing evidence for it in the Early Christian period; Mathews, "The Chariot and the Donkey," p. 48.

238. Michael Robson, *St. Francis of Assisi*, p. 227.

239. Thomas of Celano, *Vita prima*, bk. 1, ch. 30, in *The Saint*, FAED, p. 255. FF, p. 361.

240. Robson, *St. Francis of Assisi*, p. 227. The creation-wide celebration of Christmas at Greccio that Francis orchestrated may be said to parallel Francis's slightly later "Canticle of the Creatures"; Francis of Assisi, "The Canticle of the Creatures," *The Saint*, FAED, pp. 113–14. Idem, "Canticum fratris solis," FF, pp. 39–41. Cf. Swanton, "Dream of the Rood," p. 97, line 55.

241. Holsinger says that Aelred is "almost certainly referring to polyphony"; Holsinger, *Music, Body, and Desire in Medieval Culture*, p. 160.

242. Aelred of Rievaulx, *Mirror of Charity*, bk. 2, ch. 23, no. 68, p. 211. Idem, *De speculo caritatis*, p. 98.

243. McNamer has recently argued that the original form of this text was a short version in Italian authored by a woman (the sole copy of which survives in a fifteenth-century manuscript: Oxford, Bodleian Library, MS Canon. Ital. 174), and suggests 1305–1315 as the date of the text's composition; McNamer, "The Author of the Italian *Meditations on the Life of Christ*." In "The Origins of the *Meditationes vitae Christi*," she argued for this text's precedence over the other vernacular and Latin versions and recapped her earlier argument that the long Latin text was composed later than had previously been assumed. Falvay and Tóth have recently questioned McNamer's dating of the long Latin text, pushing the date back, as previous scholars had thought, to the early 1300s; see Falvay and Tóth, "New Light on the *Meditationes Vitae Christi*," as well as Falvay's "St. Elizabeth of Hungary in Italian Vernacular Literature." Since my purpose here is to provide an overview of the treatment of the Christ Child in the long Latin version of the *Meditationes vitae Christi*, so that it may serve as a comparison for the portrayal of the Christ Child in other late medieval texts that touch upon Jesus' childhood, I shall put aside the difficult question of the dating of the *Meditationes vitae Christi*. For a recent study of the illustrated Italian version in Paris, BnF, MS ital. 115, see Flora, *The Devout Belief of the Imagination*, and for a translation, Pseudo-Bonaventure, *Meditations*. For a useful overview of contemporary scholarship on the *Meditationes* and related texts, see Maxwell, "Mapping the Meditations." See also Johnson and Westphall, *The Pseudo-Bonaventuran Lives of Christ*, and Kelly and Perry, *Devotional Culture*, as well as ch. 4 of Karnes, *Imagination, Meditation, and Cognition*.

244. Thomas More referred to the *Meditationes vitae Christi* as one of three "englishe bookes as moste may norysshe and encrease deuocyon"; More, "The Confutation of Tyndale's Answer," in *The Complete Works of St. Thomas More*, vol. 8, part 1, p. 37.

245. "In this type of consciousness, one recalls a significant event in the past, enters into its drama and draws from it spiritual energy, eventually moving beyond the event towards union with God"; Cousins, "Francis of Assisi: Christian Mysticism at the Crossroads," p. 166.

246. Bonaventure, "The Tree of Life," Fructus 1, sect. 4, and Fructus 2, sect. 5, in *Bonaventure*, p. 129. Idem, *Lignum vitae*, p. 72.

247. "The Tree of Life," Fructus 2, sect. 7, p. 131. *Lignum vitae*, p. 72.

248. "The Tree of Life," Fructus 2, sect. 8, p. 132. *Lignum vitae*, pp. 72–73.

249. O'Connell, "Aelred of Rievaulx and the 'Lignum Vitae,'" pp. 55–56, 62–63.

250. "The Tree of Life," Fructus 2, sect. 7, p. 131. *Lignum vitae*, p. 72.

251. Bonaventure, *De quinque festivitatibus*, 2.3, pp. 91–92. Idem, *Bringing Forth Christ*, p. 8. This shift from a more mystical relationship with the Christ Child to one that is more concrete can be seen in the vita of Agnes of Montepulciano (d. 1317). Mary is said to have given her the Child to hold, but the nun was not willing to return him to his mother—likely a literalization of Sg. 3:4. See Raymond of Capua, *Legenda beate Agnetis de Monte Policiano*, Prima Pars, ch. 10, p. 24. For similar encounters, see Greenspan, "Matre Donante."

252. Flora, "Women Wielding Knives."

253. On the Circumcision as proof of Jesus' real physicality, see Chapter 3, n. 132.

254. Pseudo-Bonaventure, *Meditations*, ch. 8, pp. 30–31. *Meditaciones*, pp. 37–38.

255. See *Meditations*, ch. 78, p. 254. *Meditaciones*, pp. 272–73. This mutual increase of suffering is also featured in the *Revelationes* of St. Birgitta; see Chapter 4.

256. *Meditations*, ch. 8, p. 30. *Meditaciones*, p. 37. Bonaventure, "The Tree of Life," 2.5, p. 129. Idem, *Lignum vitae*, p. 72: "sanguinis sui pretium non pro te non tardans effudere."

257. *Meditations*, ch. 6, pp. 22–23. *Meditaciones*, pp. 29–30. Possibly because he is concerned with drawing an analogy between the nun's reclusion and that of the fetal Jesus, the author does not explicitly say that Jesus' stay within the womb was unpleasant, as does St. Jerome, e.g., *Epistula ad Eustochium* (Letter 22), sect. 39, *St. Jerome: Letters and Select Works*, p. 40; idem, *Epistulae: Pars I*, p. 206. Cf. Millett, *Ancrene Wisse: Guide for Anchoresses*, part 6, p. 142. Idem, *Ancrene Wisse: A Corrected Edition*, vol. 1, p. 142.

258. *Meditations*, ch. 13, p. 51. *Meditaciones*, p. 58. For analogous comments by Bonaventure, see above, nn. 132–33, 135.

259. Thomas of Celano, *Vita secunda*, bk. 2, ch. 7, in *The Founder*, FAED, p. 269. FF, p. 474.

260. Marcus, *Childhood and Cultural Despair*, pp. 16–17.

261. *Meditations*, ch. 12, p. 45. *Meditaciones*, pp. 52–53.

262. Reproduced in Pseudo-Bonaventure, *Meditations on the Life of Christ: An Illustrated Manuscript*, pp. 73 and 75, figs. 62 and 63; and in Flora, *The Devout Belief of the Imagination*, pp. 128–29, figs. 34 and 35.

263. *Meditations*, ch. 12, p. 45. *Meditaciones*, pp. 52–53.

264. Frank, "*Meditationes Vitae Christi:* The Logistics of Access to Divinity," p. 43.

265. Steinberg calls the *Meditationes vitae Christi* "a work of naïve sentimental piety . . . aimed at the common reader"; Steinberg, *The Sexuality of Christ*, p. 57. More recently, Watson has remarked that Nicholas Love's translation of the text into Middle English, which followed in the wake of the Arundel Constitutions, seems "designed to divert lay readers from doctrinal inquiry and to remind them of their childlike dependence on clerics who think for them"; Watson, "Censorship and Cultural Change," p. 853. Aers, for his part, dislikes Love's text because it "domesticate[s] the prophet and mobile layman" Christ, thus negating "the powerful prophetic figure" found in *Piers Plowman*; Aers, *Sanctifying Signs*, pp. 169, 175.

266. Karnes, "Nicholas Love and Medieval Meditations on Christ," pp. 392–93. See also Hundersmarck, "Reforming Life."

267. Frank, "*Meditationes Vitae Christi:* The Logistics of Access to Divinity," p. 43.

268. *Meditations*, ch. 13, pp. 49–50. *Meditaciones*, pp. 56–57.

269. Gordon, *Pearl*, pp. 40–41, lines 1093–152. The narrator is dismayed when he realizes that "my little quene" (line 1147) is beyond his reach. Spearing, who compares the narrator to "a fond father . . . watching his daughter acting in a school play," considers "the contrast between the tender and unpretentious intimacy of his feelings and the unreachable grandeur of her new position . . . painfully moving"; Spearing, *Medieval Dream-Poetry*, p. 125.

270. She thus resembles the woman who is sometimes represented as Mary's assistant in Nativity scenes and as the Holy Family's traveling companion in depictions of the Flight into Egypt; see Booton, "Variation on a Limbourg Theme"; Del Popolo, "Anastasia levatrice di Maria"; James, "Legends of St. Anne and St. Anastasia"; Hassall, *The Holkham Bible*, p. 88; and Van Os, *The Art of Devotion*, pp. 139–40.

271. *Meditations*, p. 1. *Meditaciones*, p. 7.

272. Carruthers, *The Book of Memory*, pp. 206–7.

273. On "medieval lives of Christ" as a genre related to the gospel harmony, see Salter, *Nicholas Love's "Myrrour of the Blessed Lyf of Jesu Christ,"* ch. 4, esp. pp. 57–61. An early instance of a sequential account of Christ's life is Tatian's *Diatessaron*. For a translation, see Tatian, *The Diatessaron of Tatian*. Sargent (Nicholas Love, *The Mirror*, p. 2) mentions the gospel harmony of Clement of Llanthony's *Unum ex quattuor* and (part of) Comestor's *Historia scholastica* as twelfth-century biblical texts loosely analogous to the *Meditationes vitae Christi*.

274. *Meditations*, p. 4. *Meditaciones*, p. 10. Augustine of Hippo, *On Christian Teaching*, bk. 3.15, p. 80.

275. *Meditations*, ch. 17, p. 77. *Meditaciones*, p. 90.

276. An example from Bernard's writings is the passage from the latter's "Third Christmas Sermon" (quoted above, n. 2), in which he asserts that the Christ Child chose poverty, an idea obviously close to the heart of the Franciscans; Bernard of Clairvaux, *Sermons for Advent and the Christmas Season*, pp. 114–15. *Sermones I*, pp. 258–59. *Meditations*, ch. 7, p. 27. *Meditaciones*, p. 34.

277. For instance, the author explains that on their way to Bethlehem, Mary and Joseph "were forced to turn off at a kind of roadside shelter, where people would slip in during a rainstorm"; *Meditations*, ch. 7, p. 24. *Meditaciones*, p. 31. The Nativity takes place in this shelter, closed in by Joseph. Mary and Joseph bring the ox and ass with them, rather than finding these animals in a stable (or cave). Cf. Comestor, *Historia scholastica*, ch. 5; PL 198:1540.

278. *Meditations*, ch. 3, pp. 9–11. *Meditaciones*, pp. 15–16. Cf. McNamer, *The Two Middle English Translations of the Revelations of St Elizabeth of Hungary*, pp. 62–67, 77–79.

279. *Meditations*, ch. 7, p. 31 (the editor, Stallings-Taney, does not identify a specific source here). *Meditations*, p. 24. A much fuller and more well-known vision of the Nativity was that of St. Birgitta, but this postdates the *Meditationes*; see Chapter 4.

280. *Meditations*, ch. 3, p. 11. *Meditaciones*, pp. 17–18. Gijsel, *Pseudo-Matthaei Evangelium*, ch. 6, pp. 332–41. The apocryphal detail that Mary engaged in weaving in the Temple supports the *Meditationes vitae Christi*'s depiction of Mary as a textile worker in the chapter (12) on the Holy Family's life in Egypt. Much earlier, Jerome had spoken of Jesus as a son of "a working-man and a working-woman"; Epistle, 14, quoted in Chapter 1, n. 100. A summary of Mary's rule of life likewise appears in the GL, vol. 2, p. 153. LA, ch. 127, vol. 2, p. 905.

281. *Meditations*, ch. 13, p. 52. *Meditaciones*, p. 59. The immediate source is Comestor, *Historia scholastica*, ch. 23; PL 198:1550, additio. This detail is related to a pilgrimage site (see, e.g., Pseudo-Odoric, *De terra sancta*, ch. 1, p. 146) as well as a tale in *Pseudo-Matthew*; Tischendorf, *Evangelia apocrypha*, ch. 33, p. 103. See further Chapter 3, n. 240, and Dzon, "Out of Egypt," pp. 216–17, n. 170.

282. *Meditations*, ch. 12, p. 44. *Meditaciones*, p. 51. Gijsel, *Pseudo-Matthaei Evangelium*, ch. 23, pp. 474–75.

283. For the story about the tree, see Gijsel, *Pseudo-Matthaei Evangelium*, ch. 21, pp. 461–63. The fourteenth-century artist who illustrated Oxford, Corpus Christi College, MS 410, was clearly familiar with apocryphal infancy tales: he not only depicts the fall of the idols as the Holy Family enter Egypt (fol. 24v; upper register; fig. 11), but also Mary's pulling on the branches of a palm tree (fol. 28r), presumably to gather some fruit, on the Holy Family's return from Egypt (the apocryphal legends tell of a fruit-laden tree miraculously bending down to Mary on the way there). Although the former apocryphal incident is (briefly) mentioned in the text of the *Meditationes*, the latter is not. On the representation of both incidents, see Mâle, *Religious Art in France: The Thirteenth Century*, pp. 220–22. On the illustrations in MS 410, see further Bartal, "Repetition, Opposition, and Invention."

284. *Meditations*, ch. 12, p. 44. *Meditaciones*, p. 51. Cf. the remark of the twelfth-century French poet Herman de Valenciennes in his biblical paraphrase: "Des miracles qu'il fist ne vos ai pas conté / Molt en ot fait ançois quel païs fust entrés" (I have not told you of the miracles which he did; he had performed very many of them before he entered into the country [of Egypt]); Herman of Valenciennes, *La Bible von Herman de Valenciennes*, p. 98, lines 3731a–b. On this French work see Boulton, *Sacred Fictions*, pp. 83–109 et passim. On legends about the Flight, see further Valensi, *La Fuite en Égypte*.

285. *Meditations*, ch. 14, pp. 53–55. *Meditaciones*, pp. 60–64.

286. Burrow ("God and the Fullness of Time," p. 301) similarly notes the extreme nature of this presentation, which he uses as a backdrop to discuss William Langland's handling of Jesus' youth; see also Dzon, "'Bold in His Barnhoed.'" Both of these late medieval authors emphasize the obscurity of Jesus' youth.

287. The illustrator of the Holkham Bible represents this verse by showing the boy Jesus engaged in household chores: he fetches water, prepares a fire, and sets the table for his parents; Brown, *The Holkham Bible*, fol. 18r. Jean Gerson, in his long poem *Josephina*, similarly describes Jesus doing his chores; see McGuire, "When Jesus Did the Dishes," pp. 131–52, and 188–93.

288. This perception of Francis is reflected in the story mentioned above (in n. 121), about how Francis encountered some thieves in a forest and told them he was "the herald of a great King!" They pushed him into a ditch, saying: "Lie there, you stupid herald of God!" Thomas of Celano, *The Life of Saint Francis*, bk. 1, ch. 7, *The Saint*, FAED, p. 194. *Vita prima*, FF, p. 294. On this theme, see further Saward, *Perfect Fools*, esp. pp. 80–89.

289. Thomas of Celano, *Vita prima*, bk. 1, ch. 27, p. 245. FF, p. 348. Cf. Francis's remark in the *Regula non bullata*, ch. 17: "Let all the brothers . . . preach by their deeds"; FAED, *The Saint*, p. 75. FF, p. 200.

290. *Meditations*, ch. 15, p. 57. *Meditaciones*, p. 65.

291. *Meditations*, p. 58. *Meditaciones*, p. 67. On the warrior connotations of Christ, see, e.g., Duncan, "'Quid Hinieldus cum Christo?'"

292. Vidal, "The Infancy Narrative," p. 328.

293. *Meditations*, ch. 15, p. 61. *Meditaciones*, p. 71.

294. *Meditations*, ch. 8, p. 31. *Meditaciones*, p. 38.

295. *Meditations*, ch. 6, p. 21. *Meditaciones*, p. 28. Stallings-Taney cites Peter Comestor as the source (*Historia scholastica*, ch. 3: "ut diabolo occultaretur Dei partus"; PL 198:1539), but the idea was common among theologians. Cf. Thomas of Hales, *The Lyf of Oure Lady*, p. 45. See further Schapiro, "'Muscipula Diaboli,' The Symbolism of The Mérode Altarpiece," esp. note 25. See further Chapter 3, n. 325.

296. *Meditations*, ch. 9, pp. 34, 36. *Meditaciones*, pp. 41, 43.

297. See above, n. 90.

298. The anonymous author similarly endows baby John the Baptist with non-normal or adultlike characteristics, by claiming that Jesus' cousin, "quasi intelligens," refused to turn his face away from the Virgin as she handed him back to his mother; *Meditations*, ch. 5, p. 19. *Meditaciones*, p. 26. John here, as in other late medieval texts, is said to have gone out to the desert to live penitentially as a hermit when he was still a boy; *Meditations*, ch. 13, p. 51. *Meditaciones*, p. 59. See further Lavin, "Giovannino Battista: A Study" and idem, "Giovannino Battista: A Supplement." On childhoods that foreshadow a well-known person's adulthood, see further Chapter 3.

299. On the applicability of this verse to Christ in *Piers Plowman*, see Dzon, "'Bold in His Barnhoed.'"

300. Vitz also noted the differences between the Franciscan and apocryphal Christ Child; Vitz, "The Apocryphal and the Biblical," pp. 142–43.

## CHAPTER 3. AQUINAS AND THE APOCRYPHAL CHRIST CHILD IN THE LATER MIDDLE AGES

1. Herlihy, "Medieval Children." Herlihy later made the same point in *Medieval House-holds*, where he remarked: "as civilization grew more complex, more critically based on learned skill, medieval society had to invest heavily in the training of the young. And where treasure is, so also is the heart" (p. 125). Another factor he mentions is "the ravages of the times," which caused people to pay "more attention to children" and "show a greater willingness to invest in their welfare" (p. 130).

2. Dzon, "Boys Will Be Boys."

3. MacLehose, "Health and Science."

4. On the apocryphal infancy material in the vernacular languages, see Reinsch, *Die Pseudo-Evangelien von Jesu und Maria's Kindheit*. See further the vernacular versions mentioned by Hall, "The Miracle of the Lengthened Beam," pp. 119–22. For late medieval French versions of the apocryphal childhood legends (Old French and Anglo-Norman), see the editions by Boulton: *The Old French Évangile de l'enfance* and *Les enfaunces de Jesu Crist*. Boulton provides a translation of the latter in *Piety and Persection*, pp. 97–123. For the legends in Occitan, see Giannini and Gasperoni, *Vangeli occitani dell'infanzia di Gesù*. See also Boulton, "Telling the Story of the Christ Child."

5. See Chapter 1, n. 80.

6. For an ambitious attempt to trace the evolution of apocryphal narratives about the childhood of Jesus over the centuries and across linguistic registers, see Gero, "The Infancy Gospel of Thomas." On the elasticity of apocryphal materials across different time periods and cultures, see Reed, "The Afterlives of New Testament Apocrypha."

7. The number of extant Middle English texts on the apocryphal childhood of Jesus is relatively small; they are all in verse. Three of these poems are closely related and are found in the following manuscripts: London, British Library, MS Add. 31042 (London Thornton Manuscript; s. XV^med); London, BL, MS Harley 2399 (s. XV); London, BL, MS Harley 3954 (s. XIV or s. XV^in). Of these manuscripts, the first is the most well known, since it is an important repository of Middle English romances and religious literature; see Couch, "Apocryphal Romance." Horstmann edited all three texts: the first in "Nachträge zu den Legenden," the second and third (as "Kindheit Jesu") in *Sammlung altenglischer Legenden*, pp. 101–10, 111–23. Horstmann also edited a longer poem on the apocryphal childhood found in Oxford, Bodleian Library, MS Laud Misc. 108 (s. XIII/XIV), a manuscript containing the *South English Legendary*, an early Middle English collection of saints' lives; Horstmann, "Kindheit Jesu," in *Altenglische Legenden*, pp. 1–61; see Couch, "Misbehaving God"; and Kline, "The Audience and Function of the Apocryphal *Infancy of Jesus Christ*." By far the longest Middle English poem on the apocryphal childhood is that found in Minneapolis, University of Minnesota, MS Z822 N81 (s. XV^med); Parker, *Middle English Stanzaic Versions of the Life of Saint Anne*, pp. 1–89 (henceforth referred to as *The Life of Saint Anne*). On this text, see Dzon, "Wanton Boys." Also

relevant is the *Cursor Mundi*, a long Middle English biblical paraphrase from the early fourteenth century, which has a section on the apocryphal childhood of Jesus; see Fowler, *The Southern Version of* Cursor Mundi, pp. 91–116, lines 11928–12712. Couch compares the sequence of episodes in this text to that in the London Thornton manuscript; Couch, "Apocryphal Romance," pp. 233–34. A related text, an elaboration of Luke 2:41–52 that parallels the contentious school scenes of the apocrypha, appears in the Vernon Manuscript (Oxford, Bodleian Library, MS Eng. Poet.a.1), a well-known compilation of Middle English devotional writings from the end of the fourteenth century; see "A Disputison bitwene child Jhesu & Maistres of þe lawe of Jewus," no. 45 in Furnivall, *The Minor Poems of the Vernon MS.: Part II*, pp. 479–84. See further my forthcoming edition, *Middle English Poems on the Apocryphal Childhood of Jesus*, which will also contain a translation of Caxton's *Infantia salvatoris* (ca. 1477), an incunable surviving in a single copy now in The Pierpont Morgan Library; *Early Printed Books*, no. 30, n.p.

8. On a fifteenth-century dowager duchess's reading of the *Infantia salvatoris*, along with other devotional works, see Dzon, "Cecily Neville and the Apocryphal *Infantia Salvatoris*."

9. By "popular," most properly I mean "shared" among different sectors within society; see Boyle, "Popular Piety in the Middle Ages." See also Smoller, " 'Popular' Religious Culture(s)."

10. Hassall briefly though helpfully noted, when commenting on the apocryphal childhood miracles found in the Holkham Bible (London, BL, Add. 47682), that "according to St. Thomas Aquinas, Christ's life would have been a normal human life between his Birth and his Ministry, but Aquinas had less honour in his own generation than now"; Hassall, *The Holkham Bible*, p. 96. Noting Aquinas's general silence on the "vie cachée," Torrell remarks: "À notre connaissance, seuls de rares travaux ont été consacrés à ce suject"; Torrell, *Le Christ en ses mystères*, p. 210. For some recent studies on Aquinas's Christology see, e.g., Gondreau, *The Passions of Christ's Soul*; and Madigan, *The Passions of Christ in High-Medieval Thought*. Both books deal with issues pertinent to the medieval Christ Child (e.g., Christ's emotionality and growth in wisdom).

11. Lacroix and Landry, "Quelques thèmes de la religion populaire chez le théologien Thomas d'Aquin." On medieval scholastics' views of the religiosity of "simple" people, see Biller, "Intellectuals and the Masses."

12. "Mendacia et fictiones," ST, 3, q. 43, a. 3, ad 1. For the Latin, I cite the Ottawa *Summa theologiae*, vol. 4: *Tertia Pars*, here col. 2695a; and for an English translation, *Summa Theologica*, trans. Fathers of the English Dominican Province, vol. 4, p. 2245.

13. The author acknowledges that there are many truthful things in the book, but believes that its sweetness insidiously covers up the poison it contains. As far as he is concerned the book "est plein de blasphemes, de fables et de moqueries, et est plus digne d'estre brulez que d'estre recité"; Lieberman, "Saint Joseph, Jean Gerson et Pierre d'Ailly dans un manuscrit de 1464," pp. 50–51. Jean Gerson, chancellor of the University of Paris in the fifteenth century, also condemned the book *De l'enfance du Sauveur*, objecting to its portrayal of Joseph as an old widower when he married the Virgin, and its "autres erreurs et folies." He also claims the book offers poison enveloped in honey (apparently the many "veritable et proffitable" things contained therein), likening it to the *Romance of the Rose* as well as the Qur'an; see Gerson, "Considérations sur Saint Joseph," pp. 76–77. On Gerson's efforts to promote the veneration of Joseph, see, McGuire, "Becoming a Father and a Husband"; idem, *Jean Gerson*, pp. 235–39; idem, "When Jesus Did the Dishes"; Sheingorn, "Illustris patriarcha Joseph"; as well as Armon, "Servus, Pater, Dominus," pp. 256–69. For Mandeville's observations on the overlap of the Qur'an and the New Testament, see below, n. 181.

14. Mâle, *L'Art religieux du XIII^e siècle en France*, p. 207. In translation, this passage loses some of its impact: "The people found the Gospel stories too brief and remained curious about what was not related there." Idem, *Religious Art in France: The Thirteenth Century*, p. 211. On the memory of Jesus' youth in Late Antiquity, see further Stephen J. Davis, *Christ Child*.

15. Vögtlin, *Vita rhythmica*, p. 3. See also Hoffman, "Vita Beatae Virginis Mariae et Salvatoris Rhythmica"; and Mimouni, "Les *Vies de la Vierge*," pp. 246–47.

16. Vögtlin, *Vita rhythmica*, p. 90, line 2555.

17. Ibid., pp. 94–95, lines 2664–83.

18. This episode derives from the *Infancy Gospel of Thomas*, ch. 11; see Hock, *The Infancy Gospels*, pp. 127–28. For a discussion of the illustrated *Pseudo-Matthew* in Paris, BnF, lat. 2688, see Sheingorn, "Reshapings."

19. Brown continues: " 'Hidden life' stories show that he was God's Son even as a boy by having him work miracles just as he did in his ministry, and by having him speak in the high Christological language of the ministry. . . . [It] is no accident that, at the end of his sequence of 'hidden life' stories about Jesus, the author of the *Infancy Gospel of Thomas* presented an adaptation of Luke 2:41–52. He had recognized kindred material." Brown, *The Birth of the Messiah*, pp. 480–81.

20. For an edition and translation, see Hock, *The Infancy Gospels*, pp. 32–77. See also J. K. Elliott, *The Apocryphal New Testament*, pp. 48–67; and Ehrman and Pleše, *The Apocryphal Gospels*, pp. 31–71. For several essays on the apocryphal infancy gospels, see Clivaz et al., *Infancy Gospels*. See also Gregory and Tuckett, *The Oxford Handbook of Early Christian Apocrypha*.

21. Hock, *The Infancy Gospels*, ch. 25, p. 77, and note to 25:1; and pp. 8–9. See also J. K. Elliott, *The Apocryphal New Testament*, p. 49. When the priests pressure Joseph into taking Mary as a wife, he initially objects, "I already have sons." Hock, *The Infancy Gospels*, ch. 9, p. 49. See below, n. 36, and also Chapter 1, n. 8.

22. *Pseudo-Matthew* (ch. 31) recounts how James, a son of Joseph, went into a garden to pick some vegetables and was bitten by a snake; the boy Jesus followed him and miraculously healed him; Tischendorf, *Evangelia apocrypha*, p. 110. In the source text (the *Infancy Gospel of Thomas*), James goes out to gather wood when this incident occurs; although he is said to be Joseph's son, his relationship to Jesus is not explicitly stated; Hock, *The Infancy Gospels*, ch. 16, p. 137.

23. On this episode, see Chapter 4, n. 47.

24. As mentioned in Chapter 1 (n. 83) the depiction of the Virgin as a textile worker played a role in the development of the legend that Mary made Jesus' seamless tunic.

25. The text also tells how the Jewish high priest tested the chastity of Joseph and Mary, when she was unexpectedly found pregnant, by having them drink some special water as part of a truth-revealing ritual (ch. 16), but this scene was rarely portrayed in art (for an example, see Horton, *The Child Jesus*, p. 68, fig. 35, which reproduces a scene from Oxford, Bodleian Library, Canon. Ital. 280, fol. 40r). Giotto's Life of Joachim and Life of Mary cycles in the Scrovegni chapel in Padua are probably the most famous example of late medieval artwork ultimately based upon the *Protoevangelium*. On the birth and early life of Mary in art, see Lafontaine-Dosogne, *Iconographie de l'enfance de la Vierge*.

26. See the discussion of the *Meditationes vitae Christi* in the last section of Chapter 2.

27. Hock, *The Infancy Gospels*, ch. 22, p. 73. Hock notes that this incident, which seems to contradict Matthew's account of the Flight into Egypt (2:13–15), is omitted in some manuscripts. This detail is analogous to Gil's deceptive hiding of a stolen sheep in the famous

"Second Shepherds' Play." After disguising the sheep as a baby and placing it in a cradle, she threatens to eat it when the shepherds, who have come looking for their stolen sheep, get suspicious; "Second Shepherds' Play," p. 148; lines 773–76. See also below, n. 154.

28. Hock, *The Infancy Gospels*, ch. 22, p. 73.

29. Burke explains that the two texts are not related, as scholars had previously thought; see Burke, *De infantia Iesu*, pp. 45, 88, 94–95, 113, et passim. Quasten, among others, believed that the *Infancy Gospel of Thomas* was "probably an expurgated and abbreviated edition of the original [*Gospel of Thomas*]"; Quasten, *Patrology*, p. 123. For a discussion and translation of the Gnostic *Gospel of Thomas*, see J. K. Elliott, *The Apocryphal New Testament*, pp. 123–47.

30. Cullmann, "Infancy Gospels," p. 442. For the passage in *Adversus haereses* (bk. 1, ch. 20.1), see Irenaeus of Lyons, *Contre les hérésies*, p. 288. Idem, *Irenaeus against Heresies*, p. 79.

31. Hock says that "both in its original form as an apophthegm and in its later expanded form this story is easily understood as merely showing Jesus' superiority over his teachers"; Hock, *The Infancy Gospels*, p. 99. For a selection of gnostic legends concerning the Christ Child, see Cullmann, "Infancy Gospels," pp. 453–55.

32. Some scholars have proposed that the apocryphal text that Irenaeus was referring to was later expurgated, and that the *Infancy Gospel of Thomas*, as we know it, is a distant relative of a gnostic text. See Burke, *De infantia Iesu*, pp. 3–5, 45–46, 269–75, et passim.

33. "Why are you looking for me? . . . Don't you know that I have to be in my father's house?" Hock, *The Infancy Gospels*, ch. 19, p. 143. This account is basically the same as Luke 2:42–51.

34. Brown seems to suggest that Luke was influenced by the apocrypha (see above, n. 19). See further Burke, *De infantia Iesu*, pp. 182–88, 197–200.

35. Beyers, "Introduction générale," p. 13. See also Beyers, "The Transmission of Marian Apocrypha," pp. 128–30, 133, 137.

36. Jerome famously denounced the "deliramenta apocryphorum" in a treatise written in defense of Mary's virginity; see Jerome, *Liber adversus Helvidium*, PL 23:203. Idem, "On the Perpetual Virginity of the Blessed Virgin Mary," p. 39. Jerome also used this derogatory phrase in his *Commentary on Matthew*, where he says that Jesus' *fratres* (Matt. 12:47) were his cousins, not his step-siblings; see Jerome, *Commentariorum in Matheum libri IV*, pp. 100–101. For the passage involving the midwives, see Hock, *The Infancy Gospels*, pp. 64–69.

37. J. K. Elliott, *The Apocryphal New Testament*, p. 85. See, in addition, Dzon, "Cecily Neville," pp. 263–64.

38. Gijsel, *Pseudo-Matthaei Evangelium*, ch. 20, pp. 458–61. J. K. Elliott, *The Apocryphal New Testament*, p. 95.

39. Gijsel, *Pseudo-Matthaei Evangelium*, ch. 22, pp. 470–71. J. K. Elliott, *The Apocryphal New Testament*, p. 96.

40. Gijsel, *Pseudo-Matthaei Evangelium*, chs. 23–24, pp. 474–81. J. K. Elliott, *The Apocryphal New Testament*, pp. 96–97. Stephen J. Davis notes that Sotinen, "otherwise unknown," is near Hermopolis; "Ancient Sources for the Coptic Tradition," in Gabra, *Be Thou There*, p. 142.

41. Tischendorf, *Evangelia apocrypha*, pp. 93–112. For an edition of the expanded *Pseudo-Matthew* in a thirteenth-century manuscript (Paris, Bibliothèque nationale de France, MS lat. 11867), see Dimier-Paupert, *Livre de l'Enfance du Sauveur*. Gijsel, clearly interested in the earlier versions of *Pseudo-Matthew*, did not include stories about Jesus' childhood years in his edition, though he did describe the manuscripts that include the extra material.

42. Burke notes that the *Arabic Infancy Gospel* "is believed to have originated in the eighth or ninth century;" Burke, *De infantia Iesu*, p. 166. J. K. Elliott, *The Apocryphal New Testament*,

p. 100. James, *The New Testament Apocrypha*, pp. 67–68. See also the connection of this text to Aelred of Rievaulx's *De institutione*, discussed in Chapter 2.

43. In the Arabic text, the boys hide themselves; Walker, "The Arabic Gospel of the Infancy," ch. 40, p. 413.

44. Idem, ch. 23, p. 409; ch. 37, p. 412.

45. Both stories are found in the apocryphal infancy text published by William Caxton, *W. Caxtons Infantia salvatoris* (hereafter referred to as *Infanta salvatoris*), chs. 31 and 33, pp. 18–21. The story of the dyer is also present in the redaction of the Latin *Infantia salvatoris* contained in Oxford, Merton College MS 13 (A. 1. 1), fol. 29v, in the section of the manuscript which dates to the late fifteenth century. An illustrated Latin gospel harmony that dates to around 1400 (Milan, Biblioteca Ambrosiana, SP II 64) also recounts this tale; Degenhart and Schmitt, *Evangelica Historia*, vol. 1, fol. 12r–v, vol. 2, pp. 192–93.

46. In one case, it is Mary who does so, in another case, it is Joseph, instructed by Jesus, and in yet another case, Jesus is simply said to throw a handful of seed on the ground, which immediately grows into wheat that is ready to be harvested; see Horstmann, "Nachträge zu den Legenden" (London Thornton MS), p. 327, lines 23–25; Boulton, "Transmission or Transformation," p. 16 (*Histoire de Marie et de Jésus* in BnF, fr. 1533); and Meiss and Beatson, *La Vie*, p. 26 (BnF, fr. 992). See also Boulton, *Sacred Fictions*, pp. 302, 322, et passim.

47. Kauffmann, "Art and Popular Culture," pp. 55, 58, fig. 7. See further Kathryn A. Smith, "Canonizing," pp. 229–30; and Breeze, "Instantaneous Harvest."

48. Dzon, "Boys Will Be Boys."

49. Torrell, *Saint Thomas Aquinas*, pp. 261–62; and idem, *Aquinas's* Summa, pp. 56–58. For an overview of this section of the *Summa theologiae*, see also Dodds, "The Teaching of Thomas Aquinas."

50. ST, 3, q. 27, prologue (Ottawa ed.: 2587a), citing the translation in Torrell, *Saint Thomas Aquinas*, p. 262.

51. Torrell, *Aquinas's* Summa, p. 58.

52. Aquinas, *Summa theologiae*, vol. 4, cols. 2645a–b. *Summa Theologica*, vol. 4, pp. 2204–5.

53. *Summa Theologica*, vol. 4, p. 2206. *Summa theologiae*, vol. 4, col. 2645b. For the text by Augustine, see "Epistula 137" in *Epistulae: Pars III*, p. 108. For a translation see idem, "Letter 137," in *Letters 100–150*, p. 217. Augustine immediately goes on to say that Christ "temper[ed] the extraordinary to the ordinary." The question of the naturalness of Christ's infancy and childhood is earlier raised in Augustine, "Letter 135," *Letters 100–150*, p. 209; idem, "Epistula 135," in *Epistulae: Pars III*, pp. 91–92.

54. Augustine of Hippo, "The Punishment and Forgiveness of Sins and the Baptism of Little Ones," p. 111. Idem, *De peccatorum meritis et remissione et de baptismo parvulorum*, bk. 2, ch. 29, pp. 118–19.

55. Steinberg suggests that Augustine here is guilty of Docetism; Steinberg, *The Sexuality of Christ*, p. 235.

56. *Summa theologiae*, cols. 2648b–49a. *Summa Theologica*, pp. 2207–8.

57. The original passage includes a few realistic observations about the nature of infants: "They saw and adored the Child, small when it came to size, dependent on others for help, unable to speak, and in no way different from the general condition of human infancy"; Leo the Great, *St. Leo the Great: Sermons*, p. 146. Idem, *Tractatus 34, Tractatus septem et nonaginta*, vol. 1, p. 183. Leo makes a similar observation about the baby Jesus in a homily on the Nativity; see below, n. 325.

58. On the wondrous occurrences that manifested the Nativity according to Jacobus de Voragine, see LA, ch. 6, vol. 1, pp. 68–72. GL, vol. 1, pp. 39–41. See further Hall, "The Portents at Christ's Birth." See also Chapter 4, n. 134. Jacobus attributes the detail about the star to (John) Chrysostom (LA, ch. 6, vol. 1, p. 69; GL, vol. 1, p. 40), but in reality it derives from the fifth-century *Opus imperfectum in Matthaeum*, a text that, in the Middle Ages, was misattributed to Chrysostom; *Incomplete Commentary on Matthew*, trans. Kellerman, vol. 1, p. 32; PG 56:638. That this text was admired by Aquinas means that he would have certainly been familiar with the detail about the star; Van Banning, "Saint Thomas Aquinas et l'*Opus imperfectum in Matthaeum*." See William of Tocco, *Ystoria sancti Thome de Aquino*, p. 172. Cornell associates the star-cum-child with other medieval images of the Christ Child with a cross, such as depictions of the Annunciation in which a baby, gliding on a cross, flies down to Mary; Cornell, *The Iconography of the Nativity of Christ*, pp. 50–56. For a more detailed description of the star-cum-child, see Schaer, *The Three Kings of Cologne*, pp. 54–55.

59. Isidore of Seville, *Etymologiae*, 2:11.2.1–2. *Etymologies*, p. 241. (See also Chapter 1, n. 7.) Elsewhere, in speaking of "age," Isidore states that the "term . . . properly is used in two ways: either as an age of a human—as infancy, youth, old age—or as an age of the world"; *Etymologiae*, 1:5.38.5. *Etymologies*, p. 130. While Isidore clearly holds that there are more than three ages of man, it nonetheless seems significant that here he singles out these three, perhaps because these terms seem most representative of man's arc-shaped course of life. On different schemata of the life cycle, see Burrow, *The Ages of Man*, and Sears, *The Ages of Man*.

60. Metzger states that it is "not a Papal work at all, but a private compilation that was drawn up in Italy . . . in the early sixth century"; Metzger, *The Canon of the New Testament*, p. 188.

61. Dobschütz, *Das Decretum Gelasianum*, p. 11. A translation of the Decree is also given, in excerpted form, in Hennecke and Schneemelcher, *New Testament Apocrypha*, pp. 38–40; and J. K. Elliott, *The Apocryphal New Testament*, pp. xxiii–xxv.

62. Dobschütz, *Das Decretum Gelasianum*, pp. 58–60. I take "eliminata" literally as "turned out of doors," or "cast over the threshold," rather than as a cognate of our English word "destroyed." See "elimino" in Lewis and Short, *A Latin Dictionary*.

63. Dobschütz, *Das Decretum Gelasianum*, p. 294. Dobschütz suggests that items 15 and 16 refer to *Pseudo-Matthew* and the *De nativitate Mariae*, an apocryphal text based upon the latter, but he mentions other possibilities as well. For an edition of the *De nativitate Mariae*, see Beyers, *Libellus de nativitate sanctae Mariae*. See also Amann, *Le Protévangile de Jacques*, p. 104; J. K. Elliott, *The Apocryphal New Testament*, p. 86; James, *The New Testament Apocrypha*, p. 288; idem, *Latin Infancy Gospels*, p. 22; as well as Beyers, "The Transmission of Marian Apocrypha," pp. 118–23.

64. Gijsel includes codicological descriptions of families Q and R, which typically contain material from the *Infancy Gospel of Thomas*. Q, the earlier family, is conjectured to have arisen in the middle of the twelfth century; R, around 1200. *Infancy Gospel of Thomas* material occasionally appears in other manuscript families, as in P³; Gijsel, *Pseudo-Matthaei evangelium*, pp. 94–97, 150–86. On the *Infancy Gospel of Thomas* in Latin, see Voicu, "La tradition latine des *Paidika*"; idem, "Notes sur l'histoire du texte de L'*Histoire de l'Enfance de Jésus*"; and idem, "Ways to Survive for the Infancy Apocrypha," pp. 411–13. For an edition of a Latin redaction of the *Infancy Gospel of Thomas* (based mainly upon a fourteenth-century manuscript, Vatican City, Biblioteca Apostolica Vaticana, Vat. lat. 4578), see Tischendorf, *Evangelia Apocrypha*, pp. 164–80. The so-called "Compilation J," which combines material from *Pseudo-Matthew* and other texts, was also at times referred to as the *Infantia salvatoris*; see Gijsel, *Pseudo-Matthaei*

*evangelium*, pp. 211–17. For editions of the latter text, see James, *Latin Infancy Gospels*; and McNamara et al., *Apocrypha Hiberniae: I. Evangelia Infantiae*, vol. 2. For a translation, see Ehrman and Pleše, *The Apocryphal Gospels*, pp. 115–55. See also Beyers, "Dans l'Atelier des compilateurs." See also Burke, *De infantia Iesu*, p. 60, and esp. pp. 149–50.

65. See further Dzon, *Middle English Poems on the Apocryphal Childhood of Jesus*.

66. The extant Middle English texts that recount Christ's apocryphal childhood, with the exception of the poem in MS Z822 N8, similarly begin rather abruptly with the Nativity and the Flight into Egypt.

67. Gratian, *Gratian: The Treatise on Laws*, p. 57. For the Latin text (with the gloss), see idem, *Decretum*, vol. 1 of *Corpus iuris canonici* (Rome, 1582), Prima pars, D. 15, c. 3, col. 74, viewable at http://digital.library.ucla.edu/canonlaw/librarian?ITEMBREAK=CJC1_0105&SIZE=1.0 &INUM=0. See also idem, *Corpus iuris canonici*, ed. Friedberg and Richter, vol. 1, col. 38.

68. Isidore of Seville, *Etymologiae*, vol. 1, 6.2.51–3. *Etymologies*, p. 138. Isidore here refers to Augustine, *De civitate Dei*, bk. 15, ch. 23; see Augustine, *De civitate Dei: Libri XI–XXII*, p. 491.

69. Huguccio, *Summa decretorum*, gloss on D.16, c.1 s.v. *constat esse remota ab autoritate canonica atque apostolica et deputata inter apocripha*; *Summa Decretorum*, pp. 242–43. Cf. Huguccio, *Derivationes*, p. 291.

70. Izydorczyk, "The *Evangelium Nicodemi* in the Latin Middle Ages," pp. 78–79.

71. Dove, *The Earliest Advocates of the English Bible*, p. 5. For the passage in the *Catholicon*, see Balbi, *Catholicon*, "apocryphus," n.p. As indicated by criticisms of the French versions of the *Infantia salvatoris* (see above, n. 13), an acknowledgement that the book contains some truths is not necessarily complimentary.

72. Martínez Díez and Rodríguez, *Concilium Laodicenum*, pp. 170–71.

73. Haskins, "The Greek Element in the Renaissance of the Twelfth Century." Bouhot, "Les traductions latines de Jean Chrysostome du V^e au XVI^e siècle."

74. Aquinas, *Summa theologiae*, 4:2649a–b. The translation of Aquinas cited above (*Summa Theologica*, 3:2208) loosely translates "livore liquefacti" as "out of sheer malice." For an English translation of Chrysostom's homily, see *Saint John Chrysostom: Commentary on Saint John the Apostle and Evangelist: Homilies 1–47* (hereafter referred to as *Homilies 1–47*), pp. 201–12, here 205–6. For the Greek text, see PG 59:127–31, here col. 130.

75. The commentary on the Bible attributed to Hugh of Saint-Cher, a thirteenth-century Dominican scholar who, like Aquinas, worked in Paris, similarly cites Chrysostom's comments on John the Baptist's recognition of Christ and links this issue with the apocryphal *Infantia salvatoris*; Hugh of Saint-Cher, *In evangelium*, fol. 287r.

76. Chrysostom, *Homilies 1–47*, p. 205. PG 59:130.

77. The translation of the passage from Aquinas cited above renders "cruci eum tradidissent" not completely literally as: "people . . . would have crucified him" (Aquinas, *Summa Theologica*, 4:2208). In the Latin, the subject of this verbal phrase is not expressed; but it is presumably the "Israelites" mentioned earlier rather than "people" more generally.

78. The Latin word *invidia* ("envy"), a synonym of *livor* in its metaphorical sense, is related to the word *invidere* ("to cast an evil eye upon"); see Chapter 4, n. 151. In late medieval Italian art, the Christ Child is frequently depicted wearing coral jewelry, which was considered a talisman against the evil eye that might be cast upon him; Callisen, "The Evil Eye in Italian Art"; Acres, *Renaissance Invention*, passim, and idem, "Porous Subject Matter," p. 262, n. 59. As we saw in Chapter 2 (n. 48), Aelred accuses the Jews of having an evil eye, but he does not say that it was directed at Christ himself. According to Trachtenberg, "the evil eye was expressly attributed to Jews during the Middle Ages"; Trachtenberg, *The Devil and the Jews*, p. 232, n. 35.

See also pp. 70–71. On the vice of envy, see further Balint, "Envy in the Intellectual Discourse of the High Middle Ages."

79. *Pseudo-Matthew* calls attention to Jewish ill will directed at Jesus through the words *odium, seditio*, and *malitia*; Tischendorf, *Evangelia Apocrypha*, ch. 26, p. 94; ch. 29, p. 97; ch. 38, p. 107. The *Vita rhythmica*, along similar lines, has a section devoted to the "invidia Judeorum contra puerum Jesum"; Vögtlin, *Vita rhythmica*, pp. 93–94, lines 2640–63.

80. Fowler, *The Southern Version of Cursor Mundi*, p. 96, lines 1280–83. A similar anti-Judaic legend is transmitted in an early Office for St. Joseph (possibly from the thirteenth century). When "malicious and envious" (*malitiosi et invidiosi*) Jews learned that Jesus was becoming renowned on account of his wonderful works, they called Joseph to them and asked him about his son's fame. When Joseph told them that Jesus was the son of God and was conceived in Mary by the Holy Ghost, they became "filled with rage and anger" and "killed the man of God with a cruel death"; ed. Bertrand, "Un office du XIIIe siècle," p. 165. See further Armon, "Servus, Pater, Dominus," pp. 245–52.

81. Cohen, "The Jews as the Killers of Christ in the Latin Tradition." See also idem, *Christ Killers*.

82. In some of his homilies, Chrysostom goes so far as to call the Jews "Christ-killers"; see, e.g., *Saint John Chrysostom: Discourses against Judaizing Christians*, discourse 6, sect. 2, p. 154. Chrysostom's harsh words toward Jews should be seen in light of his efforts to counteract Judaizers; see Wilken, *John Chrysostom and the Jews*.

83. See Hannah R. Johnson, *Blood Libel*; Wasyliw, *Martyrdom*, ch. 8; and Bale, "Fictions of Judaism," pp. 130–35. While some popes ostensibly believed the rumor of ritual murder, as Roth notes, "Not only Innocent IV, but also Gregory X (1272), Martin V (1422), Nicholas V (1447), and Paul III (1540) denounced as false all charges of Jewish ritual murder"; Roth, "Ritual Murder," p. 569.

84. Thomas of Monmouth, *The Life and Miracles of St William of Norwich*, bk. 1, ch. 5, pp. 19, 21–22. See also idem, *The Life and Passion of William of Norwich*, pp. 16–17. The side wound of Christ, caused by Longinus's spear, was traditionally, though not always, thought to be on his right side. See Gurewich, "Observations on the Iconography of the Wound."

85. "The Prioress's Tale," VII.684–85, in Chaucer, *The Riverside Chaucer*, p. 212. For Matthew Paris's description of the Jews' crucifixion of Little Hugh, see Paris, *Chronica majora (1248–1259)*, p. 517.

86. Hamilton, "Echoes of Childermas." Bonaventure speaks of the infant Jesus as mystically slain in the babies slaughtered by Herod's men; Bonaventure, *Lignum vitae*, p. 72. Idem, "The Tree of Life," Fructus 2, sect. 8, p. 132.

87. The Prioress addresses the Jews who arranged for the murder of the little clergeon as "cursed folk of Herodes al newe"; Chaucer, *Riverside Chaucer*, VII.574, p. 211.

88. Horstmann, "Nachträge," p. 327, line 25.

89. On visual parallels between the Christ Child and victims of ritual murder, see Gertsman, "Signs of Death," pp. 84–86; and Schreckenberg, *The Jews in Christian Art*, pp. 273–91. See also MacLehose, *A Tender Age*, ch. 3, esp. pp. 108–9, 143–52.

90. The Christ Child often appeared unexpectedly in place of (or with) the host, and was thought to be perpetually hidden in the host under the accidents of bread. See, among others, Marcus, "The Christ Child as Sacrifice"; Despres, "Cultic Anti-Judaism and Chaucer's Litel Clergeon"; and Rubin, *Corpus Christi*, pp. 135–39. In *Gentile Tales*, Rubin mentions transformations of the host into a child that occur within the context of stories about Jewish host desecrations. See esp. fig. 12, a detail from Jaime Serra's altarpiece (for the monastery of

Sijena, Catalonia, c. 1400) that depicts the child Jesus standing in a boiling cauldron as a Jewish man stabs a host with a dagger. The late fifteenth-century Croxton *Play of the Sacrament* centers around a similar occurrence of host desecration, which climaxes, among other wonders, with "A chyld apperyng with wondys blody"; see Davis, "The Play of the Sacrament," p. 83, line 804. For analogues, see Homan, "Two *Exempla*."

91. On Aquinas's views of the Jews, see Hood, *Aquinas and the Jews*. As Hood notes, Innocent IV, in an appendix to a previous document on the Jews, "strongly condemned the 'ritual murder' charge"; p. 31.

92. When treating Christ's Passion, Aquinas considers whether Christ suffered at a suitable time. He counters the objection that Christ should have lived longer, until old age even, by giving three reasons why Christ died as a youth (*in iuvenili aetate*), one of which is that he wished "to commend his love by giving up his life for us when he was in his most perfect state of life." Another reason is that "it was not becoming for Him to show any decay of nature nor to be subject to disease"; ST, 3, q. 46, a. 9, ad 4 (Aquinas, *Summa theologiae*, vol. 4, col. 2724a; *Summa Theologica*, vol. 4, p. 2268). Aquinas's view is comparable to that of Dante, who conceptualizes the life cycle as four-staged and arc-shaped. Dante asserts that Christ died in his thirty-fourth year (when he was almost 35), at the perfect time: "for it was not suitable for the Deity to have place in the descending segment; neither is it to be believed that He would not wish to dwell in this life of ours even to the summit of it, since He had been in the lower part even from childhood"; Alighieri, *Il Convivio*, bk. 4, ch. 23, p. 294; idem, *The Banquet*, p. 251. The high point of the life cycle (which Dante believes to be "in the perfectly natural man," best exemplified by Jesus Christ, "at the thirty-fifth year," p. 251) was clearly the best time for Christ to die and sacrifice himself to the Father. See also Burrow, *The Ages of Man*, pp. 142–43. Regarding the question of Christ's age at death, Camille has argued that the Christ in Meister Francke's early fifteenth-century panel painting of the Man of Sorrows in Leipzig is intended to look young; as an analogue (which relies upon the uncertainty of *iuventus*), he cites a Latin prayer addressed to the Man of Sorrows in a late-thirteenth-century devotional manuscript containing the *Supplicationes variae* (Florence, Biblioteca Medicea Laurenziana, Plut. 25.3): "Most sweet youth (*amantissime iuvenis*), what hast thou done that thou shouldst suffer so?" Camille, "Seductions of the Flesh," p. 252. Van Os, "The Discovery of an Early Man of Sorrows," p. 74. While Aquinas and others emphasize the value of Christ's dying "in iuvenili aetate," one senses a tendency in late medieval culture to make it seem as if Christ died at an even younger age. Comparing Christ's cleansing of sinners with the cleansing of leprosy "cum sanguine calido pueri," a belief reflected in the legend of Constantine's conversion, the Dominican Jacobus of Lausanne states, "Sic lepram peccati generis humani oportuit abstergi sanguine Christi adolescentis, figura Leuitici xiiii"; Jacobus de Lausanne, *Opus moralitatum*, fol. 172v.

93. *Ad Hebraeos*, caput 10, lectio 1, in Aquinas, *Super epistolas s. Pauli lectura*, vol. 2, p. 443. Idem, *Commentary on the Epistle to the Hebrews*, p. 206. Torrell remarks that Aquinas's commentary on Hebrews "may be the fruit of teaching during the years 1265–68 in Rome"; Torrell, *Saint Thomas Aquinas*, p. 340. The *Glossa Ordinaria*, to which Aquinas refers in his explication, sheds further light on the divine reason for Christ's coming, when (on Heb. 10) it offers the following gloss on "dixi venio": "ad me offerendum, vt faciam et compleam voluntatem tuam, quia tu es meus Deus. . . . quia ita scriptum est et prefiguratum de me in consilio deitatis que est caput mei, qui sum liber humani generis"; Froehlich and Gibson, *Biblia Latina cum Glossa Ordinaria*, vol. 4. I am grateful to Andrew Seeley for locating the aforesaid passage from Aquinas. Mâle seemed to refer to it years ago when he claimed that Thomas Aquinas had said: "au

moment de sa conception la première pensée du Christ fut pour sa croix"; Mâle, *L'art religieux du XVIIᵉ siècle: Italie, France, Espagne, Flandres*, p. 287. The source he cites is not Aquinas himself but *Discorsi del P. Gregorio Mastrilli della Compagnia di Giesu sopra la passione e morte di Christo nostro Redentore* (1607), p. 52.

94. Gregory lists the kinds of beings that can work miracles: God, angels, demons, magicians, good and also bad Christians; Gregory the Great, *Gregory the Great: Forty Gospel Homilies*, p. 230. Idem, *Homiliae*, p. 248. Cited in the LA, ch. 68, vol. 1, p. 499–500.

95. In his extensive *Vita Christi*, the Carthusian monk Ludolph of Saxony (formerly a Dominican) explicitly refers to Aquinas's comments on the miracles attributed to the boy Jesus. In discussing the obscurity of Jesus' life from his twelfth to his thirtieth year, Ludolph notes that he did not perform miracles at that time or beforehand, and explains why, paraphrasing Aquinas; Ludolph of Saxony, *Vita Christi*, part 1, ch. 16, p. 77. In this passage, Ludolph emphasizes (along the lines of Augustine) the importance of Jesus' having behaved like a normal child; at the same time, he worries that Jesus' humanity would be thought to be illusory if he worked miracles in his childhood (thus echoing Aquinas). Ludolph goes on to commend Christ as the greatest teacher of virtue, praising, in the exact words of the author of the *Meditationes vitae Christi*, the way in which Jesus rendered himself "inutilem et abjectum et insipientem"; ibid, p. 77; Pseudo-Bonaventure, *Meditaciones*, ch. 15, p. 65; *Meditations*, p. 56.

96. Chrysostom, *Homilies 1–47*, p. 206. PG 59:130.

97. Chrysostom, *Homilies 1–47*, p. 206. PG 59:130.

98. Chrysostom, *Homilies 1–47*, p. 206. PG 59:130.

99. Chrysostom, *Homilies 1–47*, pp. 205–6. PG 59:130. Cf. the contrary remark by Origen, cited in Chapter 5, n. 1.

100. *Summa theologiae*, 2268a–69b. *Summa Theologica*, pp. 2223–24.

101. *Summa theologiae*, 2669b. *Summa Theologica*, p. 2224, emphasis mine.

102. When considering the age at which a person might receive the sacrament of confirmation, which was thought to advance one spiritually to "perfect age," Aquinas answers that the sacrament should be given even to children since "the age of the body does not affect the soul. Consequently even in childhood man can attain to the perfection of spiritual age." In the body of the question, Aquinas remarks that someone may attain "perfectam aetatem" in youth or childhood. He apparently holds that there are two kinds of perfect age. ST, 3, q. 72, a. 8, ad 2; *Summa Theologica* 4:2424. *Summa theologiae* 4:2917a. Cf. Origen's distinction between physical and spiritual age; Chapter 2, n. 33. See further Dove, *The Perfect Age*, pp. 47–48.

103. Cf. Henry of Lancaster, *Le Livre de Seyntz Medicines*, pp. 31–34. Idem, *The Book of Holy Medicines*, pp. 102–5, and the accompanying notes.

104. Furnivall, *The Minor Poems of the Vernon MS.: Part II*, p. 479, lines 3–6.

105. Idem., p. 479, line 16. In a sermon on the Finding of Jesus in the Temple, the fifteenth-century Dominican Vincent Ferrer objected to such a portrayal: "Some say that Christ sat in the master's chair, and he has been painted thus; wrongly enough"; Ferrer, *A Christology*, p. 69.

106. A similar depiction of the infant Jesus as teacher can be seen in the Middle English poem "Ypotis," in which an extremely wise child, unidentified at first, instructs an emperor about the truths of the Christian faith. Questioned at the end of the catechism lesson whether he is an angel, the child reveals that he is the God-man and then ascends into heaven. See the edition by Deitch, "*Ypotis*: A Middle English Dialogue."

107. For a similar image of the Christ Child seated on a *cathedra* found at the start of a fourteenth-century canon law manuscript, see L'Engle and Gibbs, *Illuminating the Law*, fig. 35

(Cambridge, Fitzwilliam Museum, MS 183, fol. 1r). For other depictions of Jesus among the doctors, see Schreckenberg, *The Jews in Christian Art*, pp. 197–211. Burrow, *The Ages of Man*, pp. 137–38, pl. 12. The image from the Ambrosiana manuscript, by presenting an enthroned Jesus at the top of a pyramidal structure and the doctors at the bottom, with contorted bodies and messy books, arguably resembles the iconography of the Triumph of St. Thomas Aquinas; see, e.g., Geiger, "Filippino Lippi's *Triumph of Saint Thomas Aquinas.*"

108. Ludolph of Saxony, *Vita Christi*, vol. 1, part 1, ch. 15, p. 75.

109. Bede, *Homeliarum evangelii libri II*, ed. Hurst, Homily I.19, pp. 135–36. Idem, *Bede the Venerable: Homilies on the Gospels*, vol. 1, p. 189.

110. Jerome, "Epistola 53," in *Epistolae: Pars I*, p. 449. The translation here is mine, but see Jerome, *St. Jerome: Letters and Select Works*, p. 98. Cf. the brief comment by Aelred on Jesus' humble interaction with the learned doctors (cited in Chapter 2); *Age of Twelve*, sect. 2, p. 6. *De Iesu puero*, p. 25.

111. Love, *Vita S. Rumwoldi*. Rumwold's profession of the Christian faith parallels that of St. Quiricus, a three-year-old martyr from the beginning of the fourth century: "I too am a Christian!" he told his persecutor; Jacobus de Voragine, *The Golden Legend*, vol. 1, pp. 323–24. LA, ch. 78, vol. 1, pp. 533–34. Both saints are mentioned in Wasyliw, *Martyrdom*, passim. On Quiricus, see also Dzon, "Saintly and Other Children."

112. Hildegard says of the infant Jesus: "Cuius corpusculum postquam tanti roboris factum est, quod verba proferre potuit, non verba balbuciendo more aliorum infantum, verba plana et perfecta pueriliter tamen protulit"; Hildegard of Bingen, "Berliner Fragment," p. 426. While Hildegard may have been influenced by "legends about the childhood of Christ" with regard to his miraculous birth (Newman, *Sister of Wisdom*, pp. 176–77), she clearly rejects the apocryphal portrayal of the boy Jesus as a wonder-worker. At the same time, the learned abbess can be said to agree with the apocrypha's portrayal of Jesus as a very wise and (in many ways) very mature child, for she immediately goes on to claim: "Et iam ossibus et nervis ac venis corporis eius aliquantum confortatis, cum sex annorum esset, intellexit et sciebat, se filium dei esse; quod tamen miraculis signorum nondum ostendit."

113. Ubertino da Casale, *Arbor vitae crucifixae*, part 2, ch. 6, p. 124. Similar references to Joseph delighting in his son's baby talk appear in other Franciscan writings, such as Peter John Olivi's *Commentary on Matthew* and Bernardino of Siena's sermon "De sancto Joseph." See Armon, "Servus, Pater, Dominus," p. 219, n. 118; p. 270.

114. Gnilka, *Aetas Spiritalis*, p. 241.

115. See further Dzon, "Wanton Boys."

116. Dove, *The Perfect Age*, p. 58. On the bodily issues implicated in medieval Christians' belief in the Resurrection, see further Bynum, "Bodily Miracles and the Resurrection," esp. p. 92, n. 36, and idem, *The Resurrection of the Body*.

117. In support of thirty as the perfect age for men, Jerome points out, "It is written in Leviticus and in Exodus that the priests did not begin their duties until they were thirty years old"; Jerome, *Tractatus in Marci evangelium*, p. 500. Idem, "Homily 84," pp. 191–92. Cf. Augustine, *De civitate Dei: Libri XI–XXII*, bk. 22, ch. 15, 834. Idem, *Concerning the City of God*, p. 1056. Avicenna similarly saw thirty as a turning point between the age of "adolescence," that is, the period of growth (which lasts until thirty) and the prime of life (which lasts until thirty-five or forty); Avicenna, *A Treatise on the Canon of Medicine*, p. 68. See further Youngs, "Adulthood in Medieval Europe."

118. Lombard, *Sententiae in IV libris distinctae*, liber 4, dist. 25, ch. 7, pp. 415–16. Idem, *The Sentences: Book 4*, p. 156. Cf. Gratian, *Decretum*, in *Corpus iuris canonici*, vol. 1, prima pars,

dist. 78, chs. 2, and 5, p. 276. The *Clementines* (liber 1, titulus 6, ch. 3) permits advancement to the priesthood at age twenty-five; idem, *Corpus iuris canonici*, vol. 2, col. 1140. On Christ's age as the exemplar for clerical ordination, see further Metz, "L'accession des mineurs à la clérica-ture," p. 554.

119. Gregory the Great, *Homiliae in Hiezechihelem prophetam*, book 1, homily 1, p. 18.

120. Gregory the Great, *Pastoral Care*, p. 180. Idem, *Règle pastorale*, vol. 2, bk. 3, ch. 25, p. 434.

121. *Summa Theologica*, 4:2245. *Summa theologiae*, 4:2695a. Cf. Chrysostom, *Homilies 1–47*, p. 206. PG 59:130.

122. Aquinas's general way of phrasing this suggests that the danger to belief is not lim-ited to a particular historical point in time.

123. Bynum, "The Body of Christ in the Later Middle Ages," and idem, *Holy Feast and Holy Fast*.

124. Chrysostom, *Homilies 1–47*, trans. Goggin, p. 167. PG 59:110–11.

125. Aquinas, *Summa theologiae*, 3, q. 43, a. 3, ad 1 (2695a). *Summa Theologica*, vol. 4, p. 2245.

126. As noted above (n. 75), the Dominican Hugh of Saint-Cher had stated that the con-tents of the *Infantia salvatoris* constituted a "falsehood" (*mendacium*). Aquinas's mentor Al-bertus Magnus had similarly called narratives about Christ's childhood miracles "false"; like Chrysostom, Albertus makes this remark when commenting on the Gospel of John, viz., John 2:11. Albertus also distinguishes between the wonders that occurred in Jesus' early childhood, through the Father, and those he did as a man "per se"; Albertus Magnus, *In evangelium Joan-nis*, p. 100.

127. According to Torrell, this was probably written between 1270 and 1272, so a little before the "Life of Christ" section of the *Tertia pars*; *Saint Thomas Aquinas*, p. 339.

128. Aquinas, *Super evangelium s. Ioannis lectura*, p. 53.

129. A good example of this mixed response is the remark of one of Jesus' teachers (in the poem about Christ's childhood in the London Thornton manuscript): "If it ne ware this wer-kes wilde, / I monde wene that thou it ware (if your deeds were not wild, I would have thought that you were it [the Messiah])"; Horstmann, "Nachträge," p. 33, lines 466–67.

130. LA, ch. 48, vol. 1, p. 309; GL, vol. 1, p. 186. See also below, n. 287.

131. The text mentions two miracles pertaining to the Flight into Egypt, the first of which is caused by the Child more indirectly: the fall of the idols and the bending down of a tree in Egypt; LA, ch. 10, vol. 1, p. 99; GL, vol. 1, p. 10. Both of these incidents are recounted in the *Liber de infantia salvatoris*, though only in the second case does Jacobus cite the latter; Gijsel, *Pseudo-Matthaei Evangelium*, pp. 462–63 (bending down of palm tree); pp. 474–75 (fall of idols). The *Legenda aurea* mentions some other miracles worked by the Christ Child in chapters that are not centered on him: how the Christ Child caused St. Christopher's staff to blossom and how the boy Jesus vivified birds he fashioned from clay, a tale Jacobus correctly attributes to the Qur'an; LA, chs. 96 and 177, vol. 2, pp. 666, 1262; GL, vol. 2, pp. 12, 371. Apart from the miracle involving clay birds, which is recounted in the *Infancy Gospel of Thomas* and the *Arabic Infancy Gospel*, as well as elsewhere, Jesus' boyhood miracles per se are not mentioned in *Leg-enda aurea*. See further Dzon, "Jesus and the Birds."

132. LA, ch. 13, vol. 1, pp. 124–25. GL, vol. 1, p. 74. Similar remarks about heretics main-taining that Christ's body was unreal (or "phantastical") occur in LA, ch. 62, vol. 1, p. 444 (GL, vol. 1, p. 267); and LA, ch. 120, vol. 2, p. 842 (GL, vol. 2, p. 118). Jacobus's language about Christ's "true body" is echoed in the anonymous (probably fourteenth-century) Eucharistic

hymn "Ave verum," which hails the "true body of Christ born from the Virgin Mary (*verum corpus natum / Ex Maria virgine*)." Christ's blood (which flowed from his side) is also proclaimed in the hymn as "true" (*vero . . . sanguine*); hymn quoted in Bynum, *Holy Feast and Holy Fast*, p. 32. On Christ's blood at the Circumcision (as a sign of his human suffering), see further Bynum, "The Body of Christ in the Later Middle Ages," pp. 91–92. On the polemics surrounding Christ's Circumcision, primarily in Late Antiquity, see Jacobs, *Christ Circumcised*.

133. Torrell dates the first part of the *Compendium* (in which occurs the passage cited here) ca. 1265–67; Torrell, *Saint Thomas Aquinas*, p. 349.

134. Bonaventure, *Saint Bonaventure's Disputed Questions on the Knowledge of Christ*, p. 30.

135. Aquinas, *Compendium of Theology*, p. 174. Idem, *Compendium theologiae*, in *Opera omnia*, vol. 42, ch. 216, p. 171. Madigan (*The Passions of Christ*, ch. 3) claims there was a development in Aquinas's thinking on the issue of Christ's growth in knowledge, owing to his increasing acceptance of Aristotelian epistemology.

136. Bede, *Homeliarum evangelii libri II*, ed. Hurst, "Homily I.19," pp. 139–40. Idem, *Bede the Venerable: Homilies on the Gospels*, pp. 193–94. The idea that Christ appeared to grow in wisdom was earlier put forward by John Chrysostom; see Madigan, *The Passions of Christ*, p. 28.

137. In the passage by Bede just cited, e.g., we find the common idea that Jesus was "a prima conceptionis hora spiritu sapientiae plenus." See also Alexander of Hales, *Summa theologica*, vol. 2, p. 270.

138. That is, a board with letters on it that medieval children used when learning how to read; see Orme, *Medieval Children*, pp. 256–59.

139. Antoninus also regards as "contrary to the faith" depictions of the Trinity with three heads and of the Christ Child "already formed, being sent into the Virgin's womb"; Antoninus of Florence, *Summa theologica*, vol. 3, titulus 8, capitulus 4.10, col. 320. On this passage, see further Gilbert, "The Archbishop on the Painters of Florence, 1450"; and Mills, "Jesus as Monster," p. 38. On the depiction of the Christ Child flying down to earth, see fig. 16, as well as above, n. 58, and below, n. 266. See also Schapiro, "A Note on the Mérode Altarpiece." In the sixteenth century Johannes Molanus disapproved of these two aforesaid images; Molanus, *Traité des saintes images*, vol. 1, bk. 2, ch. 4, p. 134; bk. 3, ch. 13, p. 370; vol. 2, pp. 43–44, 274–75; figs. 3 and 11. On the potential of images to convey unorthodoxy, see Schmitt, "'Unorthodox' Images?"

140. Degenhart and Schmitt, *Evangelica Historia*, fols. 16r–v, vol. 2, pp. 197–98. On the apocryphal childhood section of this manuscript, see Sheingorn, "Reshapings." For more on such educational scenes, see Frojmovic, "Taking Little Jesus to School," as well as Bagley, "Jesus at School."

141. Shakespeare, *As You Like It*, ed. Hattaway, 2.7.145–47, p. 140.

142. Schreiner, "Marienverehrung, Lesekultur, Schriftlichkeit," plate 19. On images of Jesus with a book or scroll, see further McDevitt, "'The Ink of Our Mortality.'"

143. Luke omits this episode. John mentions it (6:19), and notes the disciples' fear, but does not explicitly say that they thought that the figure was a ghost. Aquinas connects this passage with Matt. 14:26, but quotes the latter verse as "aestimabant eum phantasma esse," which is very similar to the phrasing he uses when speaking of the wonder-working Christ Child; Aquinas, *Super Evangelium S. Ioannis*, p. 166. Jerome, in commenting on Matthew 14:26, links the view that Jesus was "non . . . natus ex uirgine sed uisus in fantasmate" with the heretics Marcion and Manes (Jerome, *Libri IV Commentariorum in Matheum*, p. 124), a passage that Aquinas himself quotes in his *Catena aurea in quatuor evangelia*, vol. 1, ch. 14, section 5, p. 233; Aquinas, *Catena Aurea*, vol. 1, trans. Pattison, p. 540.

144. Caxton, *Infantia salvatoris*, ch. 24, p. 14. According to the caption found in the Holkham Bible, "Jesus led the children of Egypt to the water and walked upon it, and the others followed suit and fell into it and were drowned, and Jesus resuscitated them"; Brown, *The Holkham Bible*, p. 52, fol. 15v. Intriguingly, the ballad "The Bitter Withy" provides an analogue to this tale: the boy Jesus successfully walks across a bridge of sunbeams, but when his playmates try to do so, they drown. See Gerould, "The Ballad of *The Bitter Withy*," pp. 142–43.

145. Map, *De nugis curialium*, dist. 2, chs. 12–13, pp. 159–60. Along similar lines, right before the knight featured in Chaucer's "Wife of Bath's Tale" finds the ugly old woman who gives him the answer to the perplexing question that will save his life, "he saugh upon a daunce go / Of ladyes foure and twenty, and yet mo"; Chaucer, *The Riverside Chaucer*, III.991–92, p. 118. These ladies are presumably the fairies whose absence from the England of her day, along with that of the incubi, the Wife attributes to meddlesome friars; III.857–80, p. 116. Eleanor of Aquitaine was reputed to have been a demonic phantom who, like Map's *fantasiae*, produced offspring; see Caesarius of Heisterbach, *Dialogus miraculorum*, vol. 2, bk. 3, ch. 12, p. 540. On fairies, see further Wade, *Fairies in Medieval Romance*; and Purkiss, *At the Bottom of the Garden*, ch. 2.

146. Map, *De nugis curialium*, pp. 352–53. Gerbert later repents of this liaison when he becomes pope (Silvester II).

147. Latham, *Dictionary of Medieval Latin from British Sources*, fasc. 10, pp. 2261–62. Delany notes: "As a strictly technical term . . . *phantom* denotes a mental process, or the product of a mental process, which is deceptive in that it does not accurately mirror the phenomenal world. . . . The scientific term was externalized to designate visual rather than conceptual appearances, the object perceived rather than a stage in the act of perception"; Delany, " 'Phantom' and the *House of Fame*," pp. 70–71.

148. Here citing Matthew Paris's reiteration of Felix's Life of Saint Guthlac; Paris, *Chronica majora (The Creation to A.D. 1066)*, p. 325. The key phrase in the original text is "demorantium fantasias demonum"; Felix, *Felix's Life of Saint Guthlac*, p. 88.

149. Wenzel, *Fasciculus morum*, pp. 578–81.

150. Luard, *Annales Monastici*, p. 353.

151. According to Harf-Lancer, the medieval notion of a fairy emerged sometime before the twelfth century when the *Fata* and *sylvaticae* of classical mythology fused to form a supernatural female figure, with traits of a godmother and a lover; Harf-Lancer, "Fairies."

152. Ralph of Coggeshall, *Chronicon anglicanum*, pp. 120–21. See further Briggs, *The Fairies in English Literature and Tradition*, p. 7.

153. William of Auvergne notes that *cambiones* are said to be "thin, always wailing, [and] drinking so much milk that it takes four wet-nurses to feed one"; William of Auvergne, *De universo*, vol. 1, pars 2.3, ch. 25, pp. 1072–73; Goodey and Stainton, "Intellectual Disability and the Changeling Myth," p. 227. Jacques de Vitry comments that a *chamium* (changeling) is a being that nurses at the breast ravenously but never seems to grow; Jacques de Vitry, *The Exempla or Illustrative Stories*, p. 129. Étienne de Bourbon describes a ritual involving sickly babies, performed over the burial mound of a greyhound that saved a nobleman's infant son, as an attempt of women to get the fauns (*fauni*) to return their real babies to them; see Étienne de Bourbon, *Anecdotes historiques*, pp. 325–28; Schmitt, *The Holy Greyhound*. See further Gaiffier, "Le Diable, voleur d'enfants"; and Kuuliala, "Sons of Demons?"

154. Stevens and Cawley, *The Towneley Plays*, vol. 1, Play 13, lines 867, 890, pp. 151–52. For depictions of a changeling baby with horns lying in a cradle, see Gaiffier, "Le Diable, voleur d'enfants," figs. 1, 5, 9, and 12.

155. Paris, *Chronica majora (1248–1259)*, p. 82. The destructive behavior of this infant recalls the more famous boy Robert the Devil, sent to his mother from the devil; Gaucher, *Robert le Diable*, pp. 92–93. Cf. Étienne de Bourbon, *Anecdotes historiques*, pp. 145–48. The wild child Gowther featured in a Middle English romance is clearly the offspring of a devil who has slept with Gowther's mother; the narrator explicitly compares Gowther to Merlin; Mills, *Sir Gowther*, p. 148, lines 7–10. Both children wreak havoc on their nursemaids.

156. A comparison made by Micha, "Robert de Boron's Merlin"; and Ogle, "The Discovery of the Wonder Child."

157. Geoffrey of Monmouth, *The History of the Kings of Britain*, bk. 6, sections 106–7, pp. 136–39. Looking at Geoffrey's source, Nennius, who says very little about Merlin's mother, Curley observes: "The nun's recollection of her encounter with the beautiful youth is entirely Geoffrey's creation, though it was probably suggested to him by the evocation of the Annunciation in the words of the child's mother in Nennius's *Historia Britonum* (*virum non cognovi*). . . . By altering the mother's response from 'virum non cognovi' to 'aliter uirum non agnoui,' Geoffrey completely transformed the experience of the young woman," that is, into an encounter with an incubus. Curley, "Conjuring History," p. 223. For the key phrase, see Geoffrey of Monmouth, *The History of the Kings of Britain*, p. 139.

158. Tatlock notes that Apuleius, in his *De Deo Socratis* "says merely (ch. 6, 13, 15) that the air contains demons intermediate between gods and men, who have human feelings, and some of whom are evil; he says nothing anywhere of incubi or their relations with women"; Tatlock, *The Legendary History of Britain*, p. 171. Tatlock (p. 172, n. 3) suggests Pseudo-Bede, *De elementis philosophiae* (PL 90:1131) as Geoffrey's source.

159. Augustine of Hippo, *Concerning the City of God*, bk. 15, ch. 23, p. 638. Idem, *De civitate Dei: Libri XI–XXII*, pp. 488–89.

160. Isidore of Seville, *Etymologies*, p. 190. *Etymologiae*, vol. 1, 8.11.101–3. On medieval views of ghosts, see Schmitt, *Ghosts in the Middle Ages*. See also Van der Lugt, "La personne manquée."

161. Augustine of Hippo, *Concerning the City of God*, bk. 8, ch. 22, pp. 329–30. Idem, *De civitate Dei: Libri I–X*, p. 239.

162. Dyan Elliott, *Fallen Bodies*, pp. 56–58, 150–54. See also Stephens, *Demon Lovers*, ch. 1.

163. Macrobius, *Macrobius: Commentary on the Dream of Scipio*, p. 89, bk. 1, ch 3. Idem, *Commentaire au Songe de Scipion*, bk. 1, ch. 3.7, p. 12. See further Van der Lugt, "The Incubus in Scholastic Debate"; and idem, *Le Ver, le démon et la vierge*. See also Petrina, "Incubi and Nightmares in Middle-English Literature"; and MacLehose, "Fear, Fantasy and Sleep."

164. Kittredge, *Witchcraft in Old and New England*, p. 166 (emphasis mine). Curley, however, quotes William of Newburgh (a twelfth-century historian and Augustinian canon) as saying: "Et hunc quidem Merlinum patre incubo daemone ex femina natum fabulantur"; "Conjuring History," p. 238, n. 67. So at least some people were skeptical about the story of Merlin's incubus father.

165. Geoffrey of Monmouth, *The History of the Kings of Britain*, bk. 6, section 108, pp. 140–41.

166. Robert of Boron, *Merlin and the Grail*, pp. 55–56. Idem, *Merlin*, pp. 53, 55.

167. Robert of Boron, *Merlin and the Grail*, p. 57. Idem, *Merlin*, p. 58. A little later, the reader learns of her claim that she conceived the child "while she slept, without having any pleasure of a man," which makes her seem more passive than Merlin's mother in Geoffrey of Monmouth, who admitted that a very attractive male visitor "often made love to me." Robert

of Boron, *Merlin and the Grail*, p. 58. Idem, *Merlin*, p. 61. Geoffrey of Monmouth, *The History of the Kings of Britain*, pp. 138–39.

168. "Nenil, nos n'en oïmes onques paller, fors de la mere Jhesu Crist," Robert of Boron, *Merlin*, p. 59 (missing from the English translation [p. 57]).

169. Robert of Boron, *Merlin and the Grail*, p. 60. Idem, *Merlin*, p. 68.

170. After noting that Merlin, according to Geoffrey's *Historia*, was engendered by an incubus, Gervase of Tilbury (d. ca. 1222) transmits the belief that the Antichrist will be born in that way too; *Otia Imperialia*, bk. 1, ch. 17, pp. 96–97.

171. Robert of Boron, *Merlin and the Grail*, p. 60. Idem, *Merlin*, p. 68. Along similar lines, one of Jesus' teachers, angered by the lad's esoteric knowledge and insubordination, exclaims: "I not ȝwat Deuel hine bi ȝat (I do not know what devil begot him)," Horstmann, "Kindheit Jesu," in *Altenglische Legenden*, p. 29, line 849.

172. At one point at the trial "the child [Merlin] was furious and said: 'I know my father better than you ever knew yours!' " Robert of Boron, *Merlin and the Grail*, p. 58. Idem, *Merlin*, p. 62. To take an example of the Christ Child being easily angered: when his teacher strikes him on the head, apparently out of frustration, "Jesus was wroth, wel mai man wite (Jesus was angry, as one might imagine)." The teacher drops down dead, right after Jesus informs him: "ful sone a wreke i schal be (I shall very quickly be avenged)," Horstmann, "Kindheit Jesu," in *Altenglische Legenden*, p. 49, lines 1468–79. Jesus similarly causes the boy who ruined his little pools to drop down dead. In the Old French infancy narrative, Jesus tells his mother that his emotions got the best of him: "Douce mere, mout m'en pesa / Ne me poi tenir du maldire, / Car trop en oi au cuer grant ire / Et pour ce est li felon mort (Sweet mother, it caused me much pain [that] I was not able to refrain from cursing, for I had much anger in my heart, and for this reason the cruel boy has died)"; Boulton, *The Old French Évangile de l'enfance*, p. 41, lines 610–13. For an example of Mary expressing anger, see Chapter 4, n. 181.

173. For instance, eight days before his mother's presumed execution, Merlin "saw his mother weeping and began to laugh in apparent delight"; Robert of Boron, *Merlin and the Grail*, p. 56. Idem, *Merlin*, p. 56. Jesus, for his part, laughs perversely when the children who have tried to imitate his sitting on a sunbeam fall down and break their limbs; Horstmann, "Nachträge," p. 333, lines 475–83. In another text, he "louȝh so þat it dude him guod" after he makes birds from clay on the Sabbath and causes them to fly away; Horstmann, "Kindheit Jesu," in *Altenglische Legenden*, p. 15, line 386.

174. The women in attendance at Merlin's birth notice that he has "more and far longer hair than they had ever seen on children." And when he was nine months old, "he looked at least a year or more (lit., 'II ans ou plus')." Robert of Boron, *Merlin and the Grail*, p. 55. Idem, *Merlin*, pp. 51–52.

175. Though this was theoretically possible, given that the Qur'an was translated into Latin in the mid-twelfth century by Robert of Ketton at the request of the Cluniac Abbot Peter the Venerable. See further d'Alverny, "Deux translations latines du Coran au Moyen Âge."

176. Hamelius earlier noted the parallel between baby Merlin and the infant Jesus; Mandeville, *Mandeville's Travels, Edited from MS. Cotton Titus*, ed. Hamelius, p. 82.

177. Mandeville, *Mandeville's Travels*, ed. Seymour, ch. 15, p. 97. For the passage in the French text, see Mandeville, *Le Livre des Merveilles*, ch. 15, pp. 273–74. Idem, *The Book of John Mandeville*, p. 83.

178. "*Taquius* erat quidam incantator, qui subito intrabat super virgines et supprimebat eas speciosus et pulcher ut angelus." The passage occurs in (Pseudo-)William of Tripoli's *De statu sarracenorum*, see *Kulturgeschichte der Kreuzzüge*, ch. 32, p. 592. (Recall that the incubus

in Geoffrey of Monmouth was similarly said to be "handsome"; see above, n. 157.) Seymour notes that the "legend of Takina is based ultimately on a misunderstanding, preserved by William of Tripoli, of the Arabic *taki* 'God-fearing' "; Mandeville, *Mandeville's Travels*, ed. Seymour, p. 244, n. to 97/7. See also Mandeville, *The Book of John Mandeville*, pp. 240–41. Mandeville simplifies this passage by saying that Takina used to appear "in lykness of an angel." In his sermon on the Annunciation, John Mirk similarly reports that Mary was afraid of a "man þat cowth myche of wychecrafte," who "be helpe of þe fende" could make himself "lyk an angel"; Mirk, *John Mirk's Festial*, vol. 1, p. 93. An analogous scenario is found in one of Boccaccio's tales in the *Decameron* (4.2), which tells of a charlatan friar who, putting on wings, claims to be the angel Gabriel, who has chosen to assume the friar's human form. This ruse enables the friar to engage in repeated intercourse with a married woman, who is vainly flattered by the angel's praise of her beauty; Boccaccio, *The Decameron*, 4.2, pp. 264–73. See further Friedman, "Nicholas's 'Angelus ad Virginem,' " pp. 164–65. A less risqué but still secular coloring is given to Gabriel in texts that speak of him as a "paranymphus" (bridesman) to the Virgin. In his *Sermones aurei de Maria Virgine*, Jacobus de Voragine explains why Gabriel took on this role: "A secret marriage was celebrated in Mary's chamber, in which Gabriel the bridesman (*paranymphus*) intervened lest the devout Virgin refuse"; Jacobus de Voragine, *Sermones aurei de Maria Virgine*, sermon 73, fol. 89v. Aelred earlier commented on Gabriel's role as "paranymphus": "in these nuptials the angel did not lose its dignity"—an effort, perhaps, to distinguish Gabriel from disreputable go-betweens; Aelred of Rievaulx, *Opera omnia: Sermones I–XLVI*, sermo 9, p. 74. Idem, *The Liturgical Sermons*, p. 160. Gabriel is also called a "paranymphus" in Pseudo-Bonaventure, *Meditaciones*, ch. 2, p. 20; *Meditations*, p. 14.

179. Donnelly, "The Anonymous Fairy-Knight Lays," pp. 30–33, lines 40–44, 69–70. See further Ogle, "The Orchard Scene." In *Pseudo-Matthew*, St. Anne's conception of Mary is presaged by an angel's visit to her in an orchard, where he informs her that her childlessness will soon come to end. In the *De nativitate Marie*, the angel at first tells her: "Ne timeas, Anna, neque putes fantasma esse quod uides. Ego enim sum angelus ille qui preces et elemosinas uestras obtuli in conspectu domini"; Beyers, *Libellus de nativitate sanctae Mariae*, ch. 4, p. 293. In *Pseudo-Matthew*, we get a less direct reference to the idea of a menacing angel: here Mary is fearful at the Annunciation because "ingressus est ad eam iuuenis cuius pulcritudo non potuit enarrari"; Gijsel, *Pseudo-Matthaei Evangelium*, ch. 9, pp. 377, 379. When Joseph notices that Mary is pregnant and questions her virginal female companions about it, he is told that she was visited during his absence only by an angel. Joseph responds with the suspicion that a man took on a false angelic appearance: "Quid seducitis me ut credam uobis quia angelus dei eam impraegnauit? Potest fieri ut quicumque finxerit se angelum et deceperit eam"; ibid., ch. 10, p. 385. Echoing the tradition of the lascivious angel, Bernard of Clairvaux (commenting on Lk. 1:30: "Ne timeas Maria") imagines Gabriel saying to Mary: "You need not suspect any harm, or any trap. I am not a man, but a spirit, an angel of God not of Satan;" Bernard of Clairvaux, *Homilies in Praise of the Blessed Virgin Mary*, homily 3, p. 41. Idem, *In laudibus virginis matris*; *Sermones I*, p. 42.

180. Donnelly, "The Anonymous Fairy-Knight Lays," pp. 34–37, lines 116–17, 122, 179–82. Such characteristics parallel those of the Christ Child, whose beauty is noted in many medieval texts, and who, in *Pseudo-Matthew*, is enveloped by a radiance when he sleeps; Tischendorf, *Evangelia Apocrypha*, pp. 111–12, as noted in Chapter 4, n. 164. Thus, in the "Luve Ron" of Thomas of Hales, the speaker commends "þe gode þewes of þisse childe, / he is fere & bryht on heowe (the good qualities of this young knight [Christ]; he is fair and bright in complexion)"; lines 90–91, cited by Levy, "The Annunciation," p. 124. (On Christ's beauty, see also Chapter 4,

nn. 83–84.) Although the young hero William of Palerne was not of supernatural parentage, he was so beautiful that when the emperor of Rome first saw him, he thought "þat fei3þely it were of feyre for faireness þat it welt (that truly it was of supernatural origin because of the beauty that it [the child] possessed)"; Bunt, *William of Palerne*, p. 132, line 230. See further Wade, *Fairies in Medieval Romance*, pp. 13–14 et passim.

181. Mandeville, *Mandeville's Travels*, ed. Seymour, p. 97. In the so-called Defective Version of this text, the infant Jesus' injunction ("*Ne timeas Maria*") more clearly repeats the angel Gabriel's reassuring and prophetic words as reported by Luke (1:30–33); Mandeville, *The Defective Version*, p. 57. For the passage in the French version, see Mandeville, *Le Livre des Merveilles*, ch. 15, p. 274. Idem, *The Book of John Mandeville*, p. 83. Cf. Haleem, *The Qur'an*, Suras 19.22–25, p. 192. Dawood, *The Koran*, p. 204. In this section of his text, Mandeville relies for the most part on (pseudo-)William of Tripoli's aforementioned treatise (see above, n. 178); Mandeville, *Le Livre*, p. 284, n. 1. See also Dimmock, "Mandeville on Muhammad."

182. Walker, "The Arabic Gospel of the Infancy," ch. 1, p. 405. Cf. Sura 3.46 and Sura 5.110. Dawood, *The Koran*, pp. 36, 80–81. In both passages, Haleem translates what Dawood renders as "cradle" as "infancy" instead; Haleem, *The Qur'an*, pp. 38, 78–79.

183. J. K. Elliott, *The Apocryphal New Testament*, p. 100. See also Cullmann, "Infancy Gospels," p. 456; and above, n. 42.

184. Haleem, *The Qur'an*, Sura 19.29–33, p. 192. Dawood, *The Koran*, p. 204.

185. This late medieval characterization of Christ was brought to my attention by Richard Firth Green's 2007 Opening Address "Christ the Changeling" in Toronto. He also mentions the motif in "Changing Chaucer," pp. 43–44. See now his *Elf Queens and Holy Friars*.

186. Lumiansky and Mills, *The Chester Mystery Cycle*, Play 8, lines 325–28, p. 171. In the Play of the Innocents, this word is used again of Jesus by Herod and a soldier; Play 10, lines 145 and 166, pp. 190–92; line 196, p. 192. The chapter on the Holy Innocents in the *Legenda aurea* likewise relates that Herod feared that the child Jesus "might be a changeling (*timens pueri morphoseon*)"; LA, ch. 10, vol. 1, p. 100. GL, vol. 1, p. 57. Although an explanation is not provided, Herod's fear may perhaps be related to the Child's eerie control over and even transmutation of himself into the star that directed the Magi to the Holy Family. See above, n. 58.

187. Beadle, *The York Plays*, Play 32, line 49, p. 293.

188. Capgrave, *The Life of St. Katharine of Alexandria*, bk. 5, ch. 29, p. 392, line 1629.

189. Although the MED notes that *conjon* is derived from Continental French *chanjon*, meaning a "changeling," it does not actually give the latter definition as a possible meaning. On the meaning of the word in medieval French, see Meyer, "*Chanjon*, Enfant changé en nourrice." Like Middle English "conjon," the English word "bastard" has a technical meaning ("one begotten and born out of wedlock"), but is often (simply) used as a term of reproach. See also the entries for "bastard" and "congeon" in the OED.

190. Chrysostom, *Homilies 1–47*, p. 206. PG 59:130.

191. Aquinas, *Super evangelium s. Ioannis lectura*, p. 72.

192. Bede, "Bedae Vita Sancti Cuthberti," ch. 13, pp. 198–99.

193. St. Peter "completely banished the magical practices (*magicum . . . fantasma*) of the false Simon. . . . For Simon had climbed the lofty summits of a new tower and . . . set off flying"; Aldhelm, *Carmina ecclesiastica*, 4.1, in *Aldhelm: The Poetic Works*, p. 50; idem, *Carmina ecclesiastica*, in *Aldhelmi opera*, p. 20. The story comes from the apocryphal *Acts of Peter*, in which Peter prays that Simon fall to the ground while an amazed audience watches him fly; J. K. Elliott, *The Apocryphal New Testament*, p. 422. See further Ferreiro, *Simon Magus*.

194. Bradwardine, *De causa Dei contra Pelagium et de virtute causarum*, bk. 1, ch. 1, coroll. pars 32, p. 63.

195. LA, ch. 103, vol. 2, p. 690. GL, vol. 2, p. 228. Jacobus is here citing Jean de Mailly almost verbatim; Jean de Mailly, *Abbreviatio*, ch. 106, p. 273.

196. Justin Martyr, *St. Justin Martyr: Dialogue with Trypho*, ch. 69, pp. 108–9.

197. Origen, *Origen: Contra Celsum*, p. 63.

198. Arnobius of Sicca, *The Case against the Pagans*, bk. 1.43, pp. 91–92. Lactantius similarly notes that Christ healed others "not with his hands or with any ointment but by a word of command"; Lactantius, *Lactantius: Divine Institutes*, bk. 4.4, p. 249. Kieckhefer, *Magic in the Middle Ages*, pp. 34–35. On different kinds of magic, Christian and other, see further Flint, *The Rise of Magic*.

199. Berger, *The Jewish-Christian Debate in the High Middle Ages*, pp. 63–64.

200. For a translation of the text, see Goldstein, *Jesus in the Jewish Tradition*, pp. 148–54. For a more recent study, see Osier, *L'evangile du ghetto*. This text was transmitted in Latin by the thirteenth-century Spanish Dominican Ramon Martí; see Osier, *L'evangile du ghetto*, pp. 161–65. For the reception of the text among Martí and other Latin writers, see Karras, "The Aerial Battle in the *Toledot Yeshu*." On the story about the birds derived from the *Infancy Gospel of Thomas*, see Gribetz, "Jesus and the Clay Birds," and Dzon, "Jesus and the Birds."

201. Berger, *The Jewish-Christian Debate in the High Middle Ages*, p. 204.

202. See, e.g., Beadle, *The York Plays*, Play 29, lines 58, 97, pp. 243–44; Play 36, line 278, p. 349; Play 38, line 104, p. 369. Nicholson, "The Trial of Christ the Sorcerer in the York Cycle." The *Gospel of Nicodemus*, which served as a source for the play, gives utterance to the accusation; Kim, *The Gospel of Nicodemus*, ch. 1.1, p. 14. Gounelle and Izydorczyk, *L'Évangile de Nicodéme*, p. 127.

203. Langland, *Piers Plowman: A New Annotated Edition of the C-text*, Passus 18, line 150, p. 302; Passus 20, lines 46, 72, pp. 324–25. Idem, *The Vision of Piers Plowman*, Passus 18, lines 46, 69, pp. 308–9.

204. Michelle P. Brown, *The Holkham Bible*, p. 98. These miracles include the transformation of children into pigs and the miraculous dyeing of clothes (both on fol. 16r). Cf. Caxton, *Infantia salvatoris*, chs. 31 and 33, pp. 18–21.

205. Horstmann, "Nachträge," p. 333, lines 418–19.

206. Fowler, *The Southern Version of* Cursor Mundi, p. 101, lines 12247–52.

207. Tischendorf, *Evangelia apocrypha*, ch. 31, p. 102.

208. Hock, *The Infancy Gospels of James and Thomas*, ch. 7, p. 123.

209. Walker, "The Arabic Gospel of the Infancy," ch. 36, p. 412.

210. Russell suggests that the increasing use of fire as a punishment for heresy and the related crime of sorcery, from the twelfth century onward, developed out of the ancient practice of trial by ordeal; Russell, *Witchcraft in the Middle Ages*, p. 150.

211. Tischendorf, *Evangelia apocrypha*, ch. 31, p. 101.

212. Fowler, *The Southern Version of* Cursor Mundi, p. 100, line 12218.

213. Tischendorf, *Evangelia Apocrypha*, p. 165 (variant provided in note). Cf. Caxton, *Infantia salvatoris*, ch. 24, p. 14. In the *Arabic Infancy Gospel*, the fathers of Jesus' playmates, when they see him bring clay birds to life, similarly warn their sons to beware "of keeping company with him again, for he is a wizard; flee from him, therefore, and avoid him, and do not play with him again after this"; Walker, "The Arabic Gospel of the Infancy," ch. 36, p. 412.

214. Vögtlin, *Vita rhythmica*, p. 100, lines 2846–52.

215. Caxton, *Infantia salvatoris*, ch. 32, p. 19.

216. Horstmann, "Kindheit Jesu," in *Sammlung altenglischer Legenden*, p. 108, lines 551–54. In the *Gospel of Nicodemus (B)*, Joseph of Arimathea is miraculously released from the windowless prison (into which the Jewish leaders placed him) in a much more dramatic though less magical way than the boy Joseph is rescued from his place of imprisonment. Joseph of Arimathea testifies how four angels lifted up the prison, whereupon Jesus "entered like a flash of lightning" and grabbed him "by the hand." Ehrman and Pleše, *The Apocryphal Gospels*, pp. 472–75. Cf. Kim, *The Gospel of Nicodemus*, p. 33. J. K. Elliott, *The Apocryphal New Testament*, p. 182.

217. Caxton, *Infantia salvatoris*, ch. 26, pp. 15–16. Following James ("Rare Mediaeval Tiles and Their Story"), Eames notes that an episode in which "Jesus straightens the beam of a plough" (an analogue to the lengthening of the beam miracle?) is depicted in three scenes on the Tring Tiles; Eames, *Catalogue of Medieval Lead-glazed Earthenware Tiles*, vol. 1, p. 58; vol. 2, figs. 26–28. On this miracle and its wider folkloric context, see Hall, "The Miracle of the Lengthened Beam." A related tale concerns the tree that sprang from Adam's grave, which Solomon cut down and tried to use in the construction of the Temple, but it was always too long or too short, so eventually deemed useless for that project; LA, ch. 64, vol. 1, p. 460; GL, vol. 1, pp. 277–78.

218. Caxton, *Infantia salvatoris*, chs. 18–19, pp. 10–11. Along similar lines, in the apocryphal account of Mary's passing from this world by Pseudo-Melito, the Jew who tries to overturn the Virgin's bier is instantly punished by having his hands wither and stick to the bier; J. K. Elliott, *The Apocryphal New Testament*, p. 712.

219. Mathews, "The Magician."

220. Kendall, *Christopher Marlowe and Richard Baines*, Appendix A, p. 332.

221. Aquinas, *Super evangelium s. Ioannis lectura*, p. 34.

222. Gondreau, *The Passions of Christ's Soul*, p. 142, n. 16.

223. Cf. a statement in the Marian creed found at the end of the *Psalter of the Blessed Virgin Mary*: "Let the Manichean be confounded who says: that Christ has an unreal body (*fictum . . . corpus*)"; *The Mirror of the Blessed Virgin Mary*, trans. Sr. Mary Emmanuel, p. 298. *Psalterium Beatae Mariae Virginis* (Basel, ca. 1473–75), fol. 202v. Christ's physicality was not simply an abstract issue; it influenced how people imagined his birth. The early fourteenth-century inquisitional record of Jacques Fournier, in noting the Eucharistic doubts of Aude Fauré, mentions her supposed disgust at the association of the infant Jesus with "the disgrace [*turpitudo*, filth or afterbirth] that women bring forth . . . in giving birth"; see Peters, *Heresy and Authority*, p. 262; and Anderson, "The Real Presence of Mary," pp. 754–55.

224. Aquinas, *Compendium theologiae*, ch. 207, p. 171. Idem, *Compendium of Theology*, p. 156. The phrase "in fantasia" was similarly used in a specialized, doctrinal sense by John of Cornwall in his christological treatise written for Pope Alexander III (shortly before 1179); John of Cornwall, "The *Eulogium ad Alexandrum Papam tertium* of John of Cornwall," p. 299.

225. Aquinas, *Super evangelium s. Ioannis lectura*, p. 72.

226. Recounted in Carruthers, *The Book of Memory*, p. 5. Cf. William of Tocco, *Ystoria sancti Thome*, ch. 43, pp. 173–74.

227. Dondaine, "La Hiérarchie cathare en Italie, I," p. 311; quoted by Hamilton, "The Virgin Mary in Cathar Thought," p. 42.

228. See above, nn. 12 and 126.

229. Sheingorn, "Reshapings," p. 263.

230. Vögtlin, *Vita rhythmica*, p. 118, lines 3404–13.

231. Capgrave, *Abbreuiacion of Cronicles*, p. 48.

232. "Cy apres sont recitez moult de miracles que l'enffant Jhesus peut faire en sa jeunesse, lesquelz ne sont point en l'euvangille; mais quelque personne devote contemplant la puissance de Dieu, lequel peut faire toutes choses, les mist en escript (Hereafter many miracles are recited which the infant Jesus was able to do in his youth, which are not in the Gospel, but which have been put into writing by a devout person contemplating the power of God, which can do all things)"; Meiss and Beatson, *La Vie de Nostre Benoît Sauveur*, pp. 26–27. The anonymous author of Caxton's *Infantia salvatoris* makes a similar remark in ch. 35, p. 22.

233. Vincent of Beauvais, *Préface au Speculum Maius*, p. 124. On the *Evangelium Nazareorum* as a title for the *Gospel of Nicodemus*, see Izydorczyk, "The *Evangelium Nicodemi* in the Latin Middle Ages," pp. 77–78, 91–92 (cf. above, n. 71).

234. Vincent of Beauvais, *Préface au Speculum Maius*, p. 124.

235. Ibid.

236. Ibid., pp. 124–25.

237. LA, ch. 10, vol. 1, p. 99. GL, vol. 1, p. 57. Cf. Bartholomew of Trent, *Liber epilogorum in gesta sanctorum*, ch. 17, p. 33. Martin of Poland, *Chronicon pontificum et imperatorum*, p. 408. See also Chapter 1, n. 129.

238. "Holkham Picture Bible," in Hourihane, *The Grove Encyclopedia of Medieval Art and Architecture*, vol. 3, p. 343. Folio 1r depicts a Dominican telling the artist/scribe to do a good job in executing the manuscript, since it will be shown to a "riche gent." See further Kauffmann, "Art and Popular Culture," pp. 46–47, 62–63. Brown, however, holds that "the prefatory miniature does not necessarily indicate that the book was commissioned by the Dominican friar depicted therein"; Brown, *The Holkham Bible*, pp. 4, 16. Cf. Pickering, *The Anglo-Norman Text of the* Holkham Bible, pp. xviii–xix.

239. Wenzel *Fasciculus morum*, pp. 238–41. The author acknowledges his debt to the Dominican Martin of Poland.

240. PL 198:1549. Comestor, though, does recount the fall of the idols in Egypt, an event commonly seen as a fulfillment of Isa. 19:1; PL 198:1543. Mention of the legend that Jesus used to draw water from a well for his mother occurs in an *additio* to the text; PL 198:1550, additio. Depictions of Jesus doing this chore include: Caxton, *Infantia salvatoris*, ch. 21, pp. 12–13; Brown, *The Holkham Bible*, p. 55, fol. 18r; and an early fifteenth-century German Life of Christ: Chantilly, Musée Condé, MS 35 [olim 1455], fol. 47v. See Meurgey, *Les Principaux manuscrits à peintures*, pp. 74–75, plates 48–49. This legend seems to be connected with Gabriel's Well, a pilgrimage site in Nazareth; see "The Church of St Gabriel," no. 170, in Pringle, *The Churches of the Crusader Kingdom of Jerusalem*, pp. 140–44. See also Chapter 2, n. 281.

241. Extraordinary occurrences on the Flight into Egypt are mentioned by the Exchequer official James Le Palmer in his massive fourteenth-century encyclopedia *Omne bonum*. He explicitly cites the *Libellus de infantia salvatoris* as his source. See Le Palmer, *Omne Bonum*, vol. 1, p. 150, note 95. For two apocryphal scenes pertaining to the Flight into Egypt (Jesus commanding a tree and also taming lions), see fig. 101.

242. Wyclif, *De fundatione sectarum*, p. 41. Wyclif makes a similar remark in "Exposicio textus Matthei XXIII," p. 331. See further Deanesly, *The Lollard Bible*, p. 148, n. 4. Elsewhere, Wyclif tries to draw a lot out of the sparse canonical account of Christ's childhood, claiming that Luke has Mary and Joseph marvelling at the wonders that occurred at Jesus' birth; Wyclif, *Sermones*, Sermo 5, p. 29. On the legendary signs that occurred at the Nativity, see above, n. 58. On Wycliffite attitudes toward the apocrypha, see also above, n. 71. Thomas of Hales likewise criticized "fables" when he remarked, repeating a comment of John Damascene, that

Jesus was born the customary way, "although certain people transmit the fable (*fabulantur*) that the childbearing of the Mother of God transpired through the rib itself"; Thomas of Hales, *The Lyf of Oure Lady*, p. 57; Damascene, *De fide orthodoxa*, pp. 323–34.

243. *La Vie*, pp. xv, 36. Cited by Boulton, "Transmission or Transformation," p. 14.

244. Horrall, *The Southern Version of* Cursor Mundi, p. 33, lines 1–2; p. 38, lines 165–66. Thompson notes the significance of these opening lines in "The *Cursor Mundi*, the 'Inglis tong,' and 'Romance.'" For the apocryphal childhood section in the *Cursor Mundi*, see Fowler, *The Southern Version of* Cursor Mundi, pp. 79–112, lines 11595–12576.

245. Boulton, "Transmission or Transformation," p. 14. Boulton cites as an example (in n. 8) the narrator's comment, in the prologue to the Old French *Évangile de l'Enfance*, that the romances his audience has heard about the Round Table are not truthful, whereas his narrative will be of great profit to them. See Boulton, *The Old French Évangile de l'enfance*, p. 24, lines 13–22. As we saw in Chapter 2 (n. 107), Aelred of Rievaulx sensed a competition between religious and Arthurian narratives.

246. "Here Bigynnys the Romance of the childhode of Jhesu Criste þat clerkes callys Ipokrephum"; Horstmann, "Nachträge," p. 327. See further Couch, "Apocryphal Romance." Quasten, following M. R. James, had earlier described the apocrypha as "romantic literature" (and as "romance"), but they seem to be using these words as synonyms for "folkstories" (and "folklore"), rather than referring to the narrative genre of romance (a popular type of vernacular literature in the later Middle Ages). Quasten noted that apocryphal writings "abound in accounts of alleged miracles which at times descend to absurdity"; Quasten, *Patrology*, pp. 106–7.

247. On possible meanings of the Middle English word "romance," see Mehl, *The Middle English Romances*, pp. 15 and 17.

248. See also Couch, "Apocryphal Romance." Williamson ("Enfances") suggests that the poem on the apocryphal childhood in Old French is patterned after the genre of *enfances*: "composed after the narration of the [epic] heroes' adult exploits," such texts "seek to outline the origins of their lineage. . . . The heroes' exploits mark them as destined for greatness."

249. Thompson, *Robert Thornton*, p. 48.

250. Ibid.

251. On the striking contrast between Jesus in the canonical gospels and in the apocryphal childhood narratives, see, among others, Vitz, "The Apocryphal and the Biblical," esp. pp. 141–44.

252. LA, ch. 55, vol. 1, p. 380. GL, vol. 1, p. 230. Dzon, "Boys Will Be Boys," pp. 212–13.

253. Little, *Benedictine Maledictions*, pp. 96–97. In support of the idea that holy people do not truly curse (or, by implication, seek vengeance), Lester (p. 97, n. 30) mentions a passage from Gregory the Great in which he clarifies that the woebegone Job did not curse the day he was born out of anger (Job 3:1–3), just as "when holy people pronounce a curse, they do not blurt it out with a desire for revenge but state it with righteous judgment"; Gregory the Great, *Moral Reflections on the Book of Job*, vol. 1, p. 243. Idem, *Moralia in Iob, Libri I–X*, bk. 4, ch. 1, pp. 163–66.

254. LA, ch. 71, vol. 1, p. 514. GL, vol. 1, p. 312.

255. Gerald of Wales, *The History and Topography of Ireland*, p. 91. Idem, *Topographia hibernica, et Expugnatio hibernica*, part 2, ch. 55, p. 137.

256. On the Christ Child's objectionable behavior in the *Infancy Gospel of Thomas*, see, e.g., Upson-Saia, "Holy Child or Holy Terror?" On the portrayal of the apocryphal Christ Child as vengeful, see Birenbaum, "Virtuous Vengeance," ch. 2.

257. Cf. Caxton, *Infantia salvatoris*, ch. 29, pp. 17–18.

258. For a recent study of this genre in Middle English, see Williams Boyarin, *Miracles of the Virgin*.

259. In an article in which he concentrates on Meister Francke's "Man of Sorrows" in the Leipzig Museum, Camille claims that the figure of Christ in late medieval iconography was both feminized and infantilized; Christ was not only a "sex object" but "weak, female, child-like, and helpless"; Camille, "Seductions of the Flesh," p. 259. Cf. above, n. 92.

260. Aers points to the Lollards' version of Christ as an alternative; Aers, "The Humanity of Christ."

261. For a survey of this motif with a focus on English culture, see Cooper and Denny-Brown, *The* Arma Christi *in Medieval and Early Modern Material Culture*.

262. Gertsman, "Signs of Death"; Kenney, "The Manger as Calvary and Altar." See also Marcus, "The Christ Child as Sacrifice."

263. See Chapter 2, nn. 132–33, 135.

264. Gertsman, "Signs of Death," fig. 1. Schiller, *Iconography of Christian Art*, vol. 2, pp. 195–97, figs. 669, 674–80; and Newman, "Love's Arrows," p. 267, fig. 2, provide other examples of the Christ Child bearing or surrounded by Passion-related implements. See also Greef, "*Uterus Cordis*."

265. Here I am using the term "Man of Sorrows" more generally to refer to a variety of images of Christ in his Passion. For a more precise definition, see Hourihane, "Defining Terms."

266. For a brief commentary, see As-Vijvers at al., *From the Hand of the Master*, p. 100. A descending Christ Child can also be seen in the Mérode Altarpiece (Schapiro, "'Muscipula Diaboli,'" pp. 2–4; idem, "A Note") and in other Annunciation scenes, such as that depicted in a fifteenth-century stained glass window from Norwich, as pointed out by Gibson, *Theatre of Devotion*, p. 146; and fig. 6.4.

267. This psalm appears prominently below the image. See further Mauquoy-Hendrickx, *Les estampes des Wierix, Première partie*, pp. 86–87, and pl. 62. See further Knipping, *Iconography of the Counter Reformation*, vol. 1, pp. 112–14, pl. 112; Le Brun, "La dévotion a l'Enfant Jésus au XVIIᵉ siècle"; and Hansen, "The Infant Christ with the *arma Christi*."

268. Cornell, *Biblia Pauperum*, pp. 276–77, pl. 10. See also the juxtaposition of Christ carrying the cross with a young Isaac carrying "sua ligna" in an English *Speculum humanae salvationis* (ca. 1400): New York, PML, MS M.766, fol. 43v, reproduced in Wilson and Wilson, *A Medieval Mirror*, fig. II-26, and pl. IV-I. "That child bearing wood prefigures You, O Christ," in Labriola and Smeltz, *The Bible of the Poor*, pp. 38, 123. See further Woolf, "The Effect of Typology on the English Medieval Plays of Abraham and Isaac."

269. To consider but one text: in the poem about Christ's apocryphal childhood found in Harley 2399, the Jews threaten to inflict several forms of punishment: the stoning of Jesus and also of his parents (Horstmann, "Kindheit Jesu," in *Sammlung altenglischer Legenden*, p. 114, lines 169–72), the chopping up of Jesus and the hanging of his parents (p. 114, lines 201–2), and the hanging of all three (p. 116, line 306). For an example of the Holy Family being threatened with burning (in Harley 3954), see Horstmann, "Kindheit Jesu," in *Sammlung altenglischer Legenden*, p. 107, lines 441–44. In these Middle English poems, there is also frequent talk of the desirability of "slaying" Jesus, who is occasionally hit by his angry teachers. In the poem in MS Z822 N81, e.g., Joseph at one point confides his fear to Mary that, because of Jesus' many "wykkid" deeds, "Some hasty man forþi . . . / . . . sum tym sal sla hym (some angry man therefore shall at some point slay him)," Parker, *The Life of Saint Anne*, p. 55, lines 2105–6. A few lines earlier, after Jesus stumps his teacher with a question about the meaning of the letters of the alphabet, "Þe master [who] was a dispitous man, / Ihesus fortene he smate (the teacher who

was a spiteful man struck Jesus because of anger)," p. 55, lines 2096–97. As for some analogous Eucharistic images: Rubin includes scenes in which the baby Jesus appears as the Eucharistic host is being stabbed by Jews; in Rubin, *Gentile Tales*, figs. 17 and 21. In the well-known Croxton *Play of the Sacrament*, Jews strike a stolen Eucharistic host with daggers and then, after trying to boil it, behold the Christ Child appear with bloody wounds; Davis, "The Play of the Sacrament," *Non-Cycle Plays*, p. 83, lines 804–5. (Cf. above, n. 90.) The description here parallels the angels' joyful tidings to the shepherds in *The N-Town Play*—that "Sacramentys þer xul be vij / Wonnyn þorwe þat childys wounde (there shall be seven sacraments obtained through that child's wounds)"; Spector, *The N-Town Play*, vol. 1, p. 163, Play 16, lines 5–6. An even more violent image appears in St. Colette of Corbie's vision of the baby Jesus chopped up on a platter, which the Virgin Mary attributes to humans' sins; Pierre de Vaux, *Vie de soeur Colette*, p. 91. The incident is mentioned by Bynum (*Holy Feast and Holy Fast*, p. 139), who cites the Latin version of Colette's vita: *Vita b. Coletae*, p. 558. For another example of this motif, in which Mary speaks of people's sins wounding her son, see Gertsman, "Signs of Death," pp. 76–77. In the Byzantine liturgy, which avoided the image of the sacrificial lamb, the child Jesus was imagined as pierced with a knife—an idea reflected in related art works; Garidis, "Approche 'réaliste'"; Vloberg, *L'eucharistie dans l'art*, vol. 1, pp. 51–53 (see Chapter 1, n. 73, in this volume).

270. Horstmann, "Nachträge," p. 330, line 194.

271. The narrator of the poem about the apocryphal childhood found in the Minnesota manuscript speaks of Jesus working miracles "Emang þe Iewes so kene"; Parker, *The Life of Saint Anne*, p. 89, line 3447.

272. In *Pseudo-Matthew*, he is an anonymous Jewish boy referred to as "the son of the devil" (*filius diaboli*), "the son of death" (*filius mortis*), "the son of Satan" (*filius satanae*), and "the son of iniquity" (*filius iniquitatis*); Tischendorf, *Evangelia apocrypha*, pp. 94–95. Considering that Jesus in the Gospel of John suggests that Judas "is a devil," it does not come as a complete surprise that here the malicious child acquires the name Judas. In John 6:71–72, Jesus, presumably having in mind the betrayal of Judas at the Last Supper, says that one of his apostles "is a devil." In another context (John 8:44), Jesus tells the Pharisees that "You are of your father the devil, and the desires of your father you will do," i.e., seek to kill him. Cf. Bale, *The Jew in the Medieval Book*, p. 11.

273. Horstmann, "Nachträge," p. 329, lines 190–92.

274. Ibid., pp. 334–35, lines 559–67. The bad boys that Jesus speaks of here resemble the mean-spirited boys that are sometimes included in medieval accounts of the Passion (who, in turn, are linked with the "little boys" who mocked the prophet Elisha and were cursed by him [4 Kgs. 2:23–24]); see Ziolkowski, *Evil Children*, ch. 3.

275. Horstmann, "Nachträge," p. 335, line 571.

276. Augustine of Hippo, *Homilies on the Gospel of John 1–40*, pp. 179–80. Idem, *In Iohannis evangelium*, pp. 88–89. Augustine discusses this issue again in Homily 31 (*Homilies on the Gospel of John 1–40*, pp. 507–9; idem, *In Iohannis evangelium*, pp. 295–97), where he argues that Jesus, who is master of time, willingly chose to die at a certain time, meaning that his death was not fated. In his book on St. Anselm, Southern helpfully addressed the related issue of the necessity of the Incarnation (and the Atonement), which was of great interest to high-medieval intellectuals: "The traditional Christian view was that God could have chosen other methods, but he choose [the Incarnation] because he willed it. This might suffice as an explanation for Christians; but it was clearly inadequate as an answer to the Jewish complaint that the chosen method was an unnecessary outrage to the dignity of God. . . . In seeking a proof

of the necessity of the Incarnation [in his *Cur Deus Homo*] . . . Anselm was seeking to satisfy both his own criterion of 'fittingness' and the requirements of unbelievers"; Southern, *Saint Anselm*, pp. 201–2.

277. Horstmann, "Nachträge," p. 328, lines 63–64. On legends about this biblical character, typically called Dismas, see Chapter 2.

278. On Birgitta's characterization of Jesus as rather stoic, see Chapter 4, n. 153.

279. On this point, see, e.g., Dzon, "Wanton Boys," pp. 127–29. Since, in my view, there is a good deal of overlap between learned and popular cultures that, in some way, touch upon the figure of the apocryphal Christ Child, I would disagree with Boulton that "the vernacular versions [of the stories of the childhood of Jesus ultimately derived from the apocryphal gospels] seem very far removed from learned sources"; "Telling the Story of the Christ Child," p. 123.

280. This episode is undoubtedly the most anti-Semitic tale among the apocryphal childhood legends. In the version found in MS Laud Misc. 108, the pigs are not turned back into children. The narrator explains that, henceforth, the Jews abstained from eating pork; Horstmann, "Kindheit Jesu," in *Altenglische Legenden*, p. 36, lines 1044–50. Cf. Brown, *The Holkham Bible*, p. 52, fol. 16r. See further Dzon, "Cecily Neville," pp. 249–54, fig. 1; Kathryn A. Smith, "Canonizing the Apocryphal," pp. 252, 256–61, 269–73; idem, *Art, Identity and Devotion*, pp. 275–81; Steel, *How to Make a Human*, pp. 188–89; and Pareles, "Inhuman Infants and Pork Futures."

281. The narrator of the Old French poem on the apocryphal childhood explicitly says: "les Juïs si se doutoient / Que Jesus nes convertisist / Et a sa loi ne les treïst (The Jews feared that he would convert them and draw them to his law)"; Boulton, *The Old French Évangile de l'enfance*, p. 67, lines 1454–56.

282. Minty suggests that the Christian image of the Jew who is cruel toward children was influenced by Christian knowledge of and horror at the historical cases of Jews taking the lives of their own children to forestall their forced conversion or death at the hands of Christians, at the time of the First Crusade; Minty, "*Kiddush ha-shem* in German Christian Eyes"; and idem, "Responses to Medieval Ashkenazi Martyrdom."

283. Rubin also connects these two stories; Rubin, *Gentile Tales*, pp. 7–39, esp. p. 25.

284. "Bot we our child ys lyfe refe / Ihesus company will he no3t lefe (unless we deprive our child of life, he will not depart from Jesus' company)"; Parker, *The Life of Saint Anne*, p. 64, lines 2476–77. Another possible allusion to Jewish self-martyrdom occurs in Laud Misc. 108: when the Jewish father finds out that his son has been freed from the tower in which he placed him, he is so angry that "him seolf he þou3te forto spille (he considered killing himself )"; Horstmann, "Kindheit Jesu," in *Altenglische Legenden*, p. 26, line 742.

285. In the fourth century, Evagrius of Antioch translated Anthanasius of Alexandria's vita of Anthony into Latin. I cite Burrow's translation of this passage; Burrow, *The Ages of Man*, p. 97. PL 73:127.

286. Brown, *The Holkham Bible*, p. 52, fol. 15v. To give a Middle English example: in the poem about the apocryphal childhood of Jesus found in Laud Misc. 108, after Jesus' playmates maliciously break his pitcher, he miraculously fixes it and then shows it to them ("hole and sound," line 630), hoping that everyone will put aside ill feelings; Horstmann, "Kindheit Jesu," in *Altenglische Legenden*, pp. 22–23, lines 613–38. Cf. idem, "Nachträge," p. 331, lines 340–41.

287. Gregory the Great, *Dialogues*, pp. 126, 128 and 130. Idem, *The Life of Saint Benedict*, pp. 3–4. The incident with the broken sieve is depicted in Spinello Aretino's fresco cycle on the life of St. Benedict in the Basilica of San Miniato, Florence. The episode parallels a story in the

*Glory of the Martyrs* by Gregory of Tours, which tells how a deacon accidentally broke a crystal chalice but prayed to Victor of Milan, a martyr, who "fuse[d the fragments] together again." In both cases, the miraculously restored vessel was hung up so that posterity could admire the saint's power. Gregory of Tours, *Glory of the Martyrs*, p. 68.

288. Plutarch, *Plutarch's Lives*, vol. 2, p. 5. Giannarelli mentions this anecdote in her discussion of the "concetto classico di immutabiltà del carattere," which was appropriated by Christian hagiographers; Giannarelli, "Infanzia e santità," p. 35.

289. D'Evelyn and Mills, *South English Legendary*, p. 694, lines 47–49. Medieval legend has it that Judas killed his stepbrother when he found out that he himself was a foundling; Baum, "The Mediæval Legend of Judas Iscariot," p. 494. See further Beringer, "Before the Betrayal."

290. See Lavin, "Giovannino Battista: A Study," and idem, "Giovannino Battista: A Supplement." For some medieval references to the legend, see Alexander of Ashby, *Meditaciones*, pp. 415–16; and Pseudo-Bonaventure, *Meditaciones*, ch. 13, p. 59. Cf. Jerome: "Iohannes in solitudine praeparatur"; *Epistula* 107, in *Epistulae: Pars I*, p. 293. Because of his leaping in the womb (Lk. 1:41), John the Baptist was thought to know who Jesus was even while he was still a fetus, thus assuming the role of "a prophet before he was man"; LA, ch. 81, vol. 1, p. 546; GL, vol. 1, p. 333. In late medieval artworks he is sometimes shown reverencing his Lord on bended knee; see Velu, *La Visitation dans l'art*, passim. On the young John the Baptist, see further Chapter 2, n. 298.

291. Gijsel, *Evangelium Pseudo-Matthaei*, ch. 18, pp. 448–51. Significantly, in Hrotsvitha of Gandersheim's redaction of *Pseudo-Matthew* into Latin verse, known as "Maria," she has Jesus here call himself a "parvus homuntio" (lit., a small little man); Hrotsvitha, "Maria," in *Hrotsvit: Opera Omnia*, p. 29, line 725. For some striking depictions of Jesus' encounter with dragons, see Paris, BnF, lat. 2688, fol. 6r; BL, Add. 29434, fol. 46r; and Biblioteca Ambrosiana, SP II 64, fol. 8r (Degenhart and Schmitt, *Evangelica Historia*, vol. 2, p. 187). On the idea that Jesus was fully formed even when he was in the womb, see Chapter 2, n. 90.

292. Dzon, "Boys Will Be Boys"; idem, "Wanton Boys."

293. Cf. Caxton, *Infantia salvatoris*, ch. 23, pp. 13–14.

294. Clark, "The Fathers and the Children," p. 20.

295. For an overview, see Constable, *Three Studies in Medieval Religious and Social Thought*, Part II.

296. Aasgaard, *The Childhood of Jesus*, ch. 12. Sheingorn, "Reshapings," p. 259.

297. Note, for example, how in one episode the children rejoice when Jesus causes their odious teacher to die; Caxton, *Infantia salvatoris*, ch. 27, p. 16. A similar sentiment, that of frustration with one's master, is expressed in a macaronic song that was sung by schoolboys at Christmas, in which they threaten: "we've a stick to carry, / and the usher's [i.e., schoolmaster's assistant] head with it, we shall hit and harry!"; Orme, *Fleas, Flies, and Friars*, p. 97; Wright and Halliwell, *Reliquiae Antiquae*, pp. 116–17.

298. On this basically Aristotelian view of children, see Tress, "Aristotle's Children"; and Philip L. Reynolds, "Thomas Aquinas and the Paradigms of Childhood."

299. Boulton, *Les Enfaunces*, pp. 65–67, lines 1157–232. See also idem, *The Old French Évangile de l'enfance*, pp. 68–71, lines 1491–580; Brown, *The Holkham Bible*, fol. 15v; and, for an instance of the tale in a Middle English text, Horstmann, "Nachträge," p. 333, lines 472–83. A similar incident appears in the Armenian "Infancy of Our Lord Jesus Christ" (Terian, *The*

*Armenian Gospel*, p. 68), as Boulton points out ("The Childhood of Jesus Christ [*Les Enfaunces Jesu Crist*]," in *Piety and Persecution*, p. 112), but a Latin text was probably the source, since the episode sometimes appears in expanded versions of *Pseudo-Matthew* (e.g., Florence, Biblioteca Medicea Laurenziana, Gaddi 208, fol. 64r–v, as noted in Tischendorf, *Evangelia apocrypha*, p. 106, note to ch. 37). For a discussion of the beam (both as sunbeam and beam of wood), see Kathryn A. Smith, "Accident, Play, and Invention," pp. 362–63; and Boulton, "The 'Evangile de l'Enfance,'" p. 61. In a ballad, the Christ Child avenges himself upon his friends who teased him about his lineage: Jesus walks upon a bridge made of sunbeams, but when the boys try to imitate him they drown. See Gerould, "The Ballad of *The Bitter Withy*," and King, "A Thematic Reconsideration." On the hagiographical motif of hanging objects on a sturdy sunbeam, see Loomis, *White Magic*, p. 29.

    300. The Anglo-Norman caption reads (in translation): "And how Jesus mounted a sunbeam, and the others did likewise and fell to earth and broke their legs, and Jesus healed them"; Brown, *The Holkham Bible*, p. 52. Cf. Milton, *Paradise Lost*, 4.555–56, p. 253. See further Frye, *Milton's Imagery*, pp. 174–76.

    301. Bejczy, "Jesus' Laughter and the Childhood Miracles."

    302. Vögtlin, *Vita rhythmica*, p. 89, lines 2522–32.

    303. On Jesus learning how to walk, see above, n. 112. For an example of Jesus using a baby-walker, in this case being helped by an angel, see the anonymous fifteenth-century retable of the Cathedral of Barcelona; Gudiol, *Pintura Gótica Catalana*, p. 254, fig. 61. On baby animals, unlike human infants, knowing how to walk right away, see Philip L. Reynolds, "Infants of Eden," and Dzon, "Boys Will Be Boys," pp. 186–87, n. 33.

    304. Along similar lines, the narrator of the apocryphal childhood narrative found in MS Z822 N81 implies, by paraphrasing St. Paul's remarks abouts his own childhood (1 Cor. 13:11), that Jesus eventually put aside his childish ways or, more neutrally, the behavior to be expected of a child (Parker, *The Life of Saint Anne*, p. 89, lines 3433–44). See Dzon, "Wanton Boys," pp. 126–27.

    305. The author says that the Holy Family fled into Egypt when Jesus was one (Vögtlin, *Vita rhythmica*, p. 77, lines 2140–41) and spent seven years there (p. 88, lines 2478–79). It is not clear whether all or only a portion of Jesus' miracles were worked during the Holy Family's stay in Egypt, since the author mentions the return to Judea twice.

    306. Instead of being prone to laughter, the Child "maturus erat moribus et disciplinatus"; Vögtlin, *Vita rhythmica*, p. 93, line 2633. Later, in the section that comments more generally on Jesus' childhood and teenage years, we learn that he was "nunquam levis," and that he was "hilarus" (cheerful), yet "nunquam ridens"; p. 107, lines 3102, 3109–10.

    307. Porphyry's *Isagogue*, which transmitted Aristotelian logic to the West, repeatedly gives human beings' capacity to laugh as an example of a "property" in an Aristotelian sense; Porphyry, *Isagogue*, pp. 29–30, 48, 60. On medieval attitudes toward laughter, see Le Goff, "Laughter in the Middle Ages"; and Le Brun, "Jésus-Christ n'a jamais ri?" See also Davidson, *Tretise of Miraclis Pleyinge*, pp. 31, 95, and 126; Aronson-Lehavi, "A Treatise of Miraclis Playing," pp. 129–30 et passim.

    308. Bartholomaeus remarks that children "continue clamant & garriunt & cachinant, vix silent quando dormiunt vel dormitant"; Bartholomaeus Anglicus, *De rerum proprietatibus*, bk. 6, ch. 5, pp. 239–40. Trevisa, *On the Properties of Things*, vol. 1, p. 301. Caxton offered a favorable interpretation as to why children laugh in their sleep: they hear the music of the spheres; Caxton, *The Mirror of the World*, p. 128.

309. There are also some instances of this in Greek; Hock, *The Infancy Gospels of James and Thomas*, pp. 112–13, and 122–23; Aasgaard, *The Childhood of Jesus*, p. 238 et passim.

310. Horstmann, "Kindheit Jesu," in *Altenglische Legenden,* p. 15, line 386.

311. For example, in the childhood narrative found in Harley 2399, Jesus "lawe & mayd hys play" (laughed and behaved playfully) when the children who imitated his sitting on a sunbeam fall down; Horstmann, "Kindheit Jesu," in *Sammlung altenglischer Legenden*, p. 118, line 459. A little earlier in the poem, he informs his good friend Joseph that the other boys will be sorely hurt, since they always wished to be his equal, p. 115, lines 287–88.

312. Since the *Vita rhythmica* was probably written a few decades before Aquinas's *Summa theologiae*, Bejczy speaks in a general sense of the author's effort "to circumvent scholarly criticism" of the childhood miracles; Bejczy, "Jesus' Laughter," p. 58.

313. Ibid., p. 54.

314. Horstmann, "Nachträge," p. 333, line 466. Also cited above, n. 129.

315. On medieval theories of miracles, see Goodich, *Miracles and Wonders*; and Twelftree, *The Cambridge Companion to Miracles.*

316. See Jeremy Cohen, "The Jews as the Killers," and also Hood, *Aquinas and the Jews*, ch. 4. On the image of the Jew and Synagoga as blind, see Rowe, *The Jew, the Cathedral, and the Medieval City.*

317. Parker, *The Life of Saint Anne*, pp. 68–69, lines 2614–52.

318. Vögtlin, *Vita rhythmica*, p. 91, lines 2564–67. The story about the Christ Child being crowned king by other boys is derived from the *Arabic Infancy Gospel*; Walker, "The Arabic Gospel of the Infancy," ch. 41, p. 413. See further Chapter 1, n. 64, and fig. 1.

319. Chambers, *The Mediaeval Stage*, pp. 4–5. Commenting of Luke 18:16–17, in which Jesus bids his disciples to let the little children come unto him, Bonaventure draws a sharp contrast between the chief priests, who saw the wonders that Jesus did, and the children who sang "Hosanna" to him as the Son of David; Bonaventure, *Commentary on the Gospel of Luke*, p. 1739; idem, *Commentarium in evangelium Lucae*, p. 459.

320. It should be noted, however, that Christ's injunction to "Suffer the little children to come unto me" (Mk. 10:14) did not seem to have a big impact on medieval art and literature (Schiller, *Iconography of Christian Art*, vol. 1, p. 157), an exception arguably being the Middle English poem *Pearl* (Gordon, *Pearl*, p. 26, lines 709–20), where the verse is mentioned by the deceased maiden who appears to her father in a vision. Her behavior, though, is not that of a little girl, despite the fact that she died when she was quite young. See further Kline, "Resisting the Father in *Pearl*," pp. 21–24.

321. Horstmann, "Nachträge," p. 332, lines 353–56. Also cited in Chapter 1, n. 63.

322. Parker, *The Life of Saint Anne*, p. 89, line 3428. On the authorship claimed for such apocryphal infancy texts, see Chapter 1, n. 8.

323. Parker, *The Life of Saint Anne*, p. 89, lines 3436–37.

324. Ibid., lines 3445–50. As should be clear from the bulk of this chapter, the *Infantia salvatoris* (the extended version of *Pseudo-Matthew*) and its vernacular redactions are undeniably anti-Judaic in character. In considering the earlier version of *Pseudo-Matthew* (which does not cover Jesus' childhood per se) and its source, the *Protoevangelium*, Luomanen concludes they "are free from outright anti-Judaism," though he does call attention to their attitude of "supersessionism"; Luomanen, "Judaism and Anti-Judaism in Early Christian Apocrypha," p. 339.

325. Aquinas quotes Ignatius of Antioch, via Jerome's *Commentary on Matthew* (*Commentariorum in Matheum libri IV*, bk. 1, 1.18, p. 10), who explains why Mary conceived as a betrothed

woman: "ut partus . . . celaretur diabolo, dum eum putat non de uirgine sed de uxore generatum." Cf. Ignatius of Antioch, "Epistle to the Ephesians," section 19, p. 81. On Gregory of Nyssa's influential metaphor that likens Christ's body on the cross to bait on a fishhook, which the devil foolishly "bit" into ("Address on Religious Instruction" or "Catechetical Oration," translated in *Christology of the Later Fathers*, p. 301; PG 45:66), see Marx, *The Devil's Rights*, pp. 11–12; Wee, "The Temptation of Christ"; Schapiro, "'Muscipula Diaboli'"; and Boenig, *Saint and Hero*, pp. 82–83. Boenig additionally cites popes Leo the Great and Gregory the Great. To be precise, in a homily on the Nativity (22), Leo claims that the devil "thought the birth of this boy [begotten for the salvation of the human race] to be no less subject to himself than that of anyone else who happens to be born. For the devil saw him whimper and cry. . . . He noticed in addition the usual 'growth of boyhood' (cf. Lk. 2:40, 52), and right up through manhood did not have any doubts about natural developments"; Leo the Great, *Tractatus*, vol. 1, p. 96; idem, *St. Leo the Great: Sermons*, p. 84. The key passage from Gregory the Great appears in his *Moralia in Iob*, where he states that the Redeemer's body was the bait on the hook that caught the Leviathan; Gregory the Great, *Moralia in Iob, Libri XXIII–XXXV*, bk. 33, ch. 7, pp. 1684–85. A related image is that of a mousetrap, which seems to be the device that Joseph is working on in the Mérode Triptych; see Schapiro, "'Muscipula Diaboli,'" and Acres, *Renaissance Invention*, passim.

326. On the folkloric view of God as a trickster, see Ashley, "The Guiler Beguiled."

327. Davidson, *A Tretise of Miraclis Pleyinge*, p. 94. Aronson-Lehavi, "*A Treatise of Miraclis Playing*," p. 129. On the playful aspect of these legends, see further Dzon, "Boys Will Be Boys," pp. 220–22.

## CHAPTER 4. A MATERNAL VIEW OF CHRIST'S CHILDHOOD IN THE WRITINGS OF BIRGITTA OF SWEDEN

1. For a modern scholarly biography of Birgitta, see Morris, *St Birgitta of Sweden*; and the "General Introduction" in vol. 1 of Birgitta of Sweden, *The Revelations of St. Birgitta of Sweden* (hereafter *Revelations*), See also the introduction to idem, *Birgitta of Sweden: Life and Selected Revelations* (hereafter *Selected Revelations*). For a brief account of Birgitta's children, see Morris, *St Birgitta of Sweden*, pp. 46–52. Two of Birgitta's sons died in childhood. Three of her four daughters were married at a young age, while the fourth entered a convent. In *Extravagantes* (ch. 95), Birgitta is described as having "felt sorry about leaving them [her children] to get on without her motherly affection" and as being "particularly anxious that they might in some way become bolder in sinning against God after she withdrew"; Birgitta of Sweden, *Extravagant Revelations*, in *Revelations*, vol. 4, p. 306. Idem, *Den heliga Birgittas Reuelaciones extrauagantes*, ch. 95.1, p. 218.

2. According to her vita by Prior Peter of Alvastra and Master Peter of Skänninge, Birgitta was not clothed and consecrated as a nun until right before her death; *Selected Revelations*, p. 98. Collijn, *Acta et processus*, p. 101.

3. *Selected Revelations*, pp. 59–60.

4. Another fourteenth-century female mystic who sought to acquire Latin literacy as an adult is Catherine of Siena; see Raymond of Capua, *The Life of Catherine of Siena*, pp. 96–97. Idem, *Vita s. Catharinae Senensis*, part 1, ch. 7, p. 890. See further Cooper-Rompato, *The Gift of Tongues*, pp. 62–64, 94–100.

5. For the vision in which Birgitta was called to be God's *canale* ("channel" or "conduit"), see Collijn, *Acta et processus*, pp. 80–81; *Selected Revelations*, p. 78; and Morris, *St Birgitta of Sweden*, pp. 64–67.

6. *Revelaciones: Book VI*, 105.3, p. 266. *Revelations*, vol. 3, p. 170.

7. Birgitta of Sweden, *The Angel's Discourse*, in *Revelations*, vol. 4, p. 182 (hereafter referred to as *The Angel's Discourse*). Idem, *Sancta Birgitta: Opera minora II: Sermo angelicus*, ch. 16.8, p. 120 (hereafter referred to as *Sermo angelicus*). Mary's rootedness in the prophets is similarly featured in late medieval Annunciation scenes that depict her reading the prophet Isaiah, particularly the verse "Ecce concipiet virgo" (7:14), when the archangel Gabriel appears to her. See, e.g., Aelred of Rievaulx, *De institutione*, sect. 29, pp. 662–63; Idem, "Rule of Life," p. 80. See further Laura Saetveit Miles, "The Origins and Development of the Virgin Mary's Book."

8. Collijn, *Acta et processus*, p. 312.

9. Bynum, "The Female Body and Religious Practice," p. 198.

10. Karras, "'This Skill in a Woman Is By No Means to Be Despised,'" p. 104.

11. Reynolds, *Gateway to Heaven*, chs. 3 and 6.

12. *Revelations*, vol. 1, 1.35.2–7, p. 112. *Revelaciones: Book I*, pp. 343–44.

13. For an overview of this Mariological issue, see Carol, "Our Lady's Coredemption," who notes that the term "Coredemptix" "can be traced back to at least the fourteenth century"; pp. 422–23.

14. Heather Webb, *The Medieval Heart*. Birgitta's depiction of an autobiographical and highly subjective Mary reflects the later medieval tendency to speak of the heart as a "book of experience" and to elevate the heart above the head, more generally; see Jager, *The Book of the Heart*, and Le Goff, "Head or Heart?"

15. Cf. Chaucer, "Parson's Tale": "Ire, after the Philosophre, is the fervent blood of man yquyked in his herte"; *The Canterbury Tales*, X.535, *The Riverside Chaucer*, p. 305. As Siegfried Wenzel notes, the ultimate source is Aristotle's *De anima*, 1.1.24; *The Riverside Chaucer*, p. 960.

16. Santing, "'And I Bear Your Beautiful Face Painted on My Chest,'" p. 276.

17. Cohen goes on to say that "late medieval devotional stress upon the heart affected neither medical opinions, which were divided [between Aristotelian and Galenic schools of thought], nor political ones"; Esther Cohen, "The Meaning of the Head," p. 74. Earlier, in the same essay, she asserts that "the so-called 'head or heart controversy' was not a direct controversy between parties who knew each other's work and responded to it"; p. 69. She helpfully cites Isidore of Seville's medical-based argument: "It is said that the heart of a human being is made first, because it is the seat of all life and wisdom"; pp. 64–65. Taken from Isidore of Seville, *Etymologiae*, vol. 2, 11.1.143. Idem, *Etymologies*, p. 240. On learned medieval views of human psychology, see further Harvey, *The Inward Wits*; Carruthers, *The Book of Memory*, esp. 48–49 (where she mentions the traditional association of the heart with memory); and Karnes, *Imagination, Meditation, and Cognition*.

18. According to Brown, this depiction of Mary and Jesus "signif[ies] their role in redeeming humanity from the Fall, in which the apple is also featured"; Brown, *The Holkham Bible*, p. 54. Commenting on this scene, Hassall links the "fruit of life" produced by Mary ("vite fructum," mentioned in a Nativity sequence by Adam of Saint-Victor, *Liriche sacre*, p. 12, line 13) with the "forbidden apple" offered by Eve ("vetitum pomum," mentioned in an earlier medieval Latin work); Hassall, *The Holkham Bible Picture Book*, p. 102. The anonymous fourteenth-century English Franciscan author of the *Fasciculus morum* links the heart with an apple, and both

with the Christ Child, when he says, "just as a child, however often he gets angry on account of an apple . . . is quickly pacified, so does Christ, however often he is angered by being offended, forgive the offense for a small price. For as he was offended on account of an apple, thus he forgives for the apple of a contrite heart (*pro pomo cordis contriti*)"; Wenzel, *Fasciculus morum*, pp. 452–53. Later the author likens God to "a child with whom one can strike an easy bargain; if the child has some money, one can talk him out of it for an apple" (p. 507). The thirteenth-century Franciscan Bartholomaeus Anglicus similarly noted children's love of apples (as well as pears and, indirectly, their immature love of the pleasures of the moment): "plus de amissione pomi vel pyri quam de amissione patrimonii plangunt & plorant"; Bartholomaeus Anglicus, *De rerum proprietatibus*, bk. 6, ch. 4, p. 239. Trevisa, *On the Properties of Things*, p. 301. Cf. Henry of Lancaster, *Le Livre de Seyntz Medicines*, p. 34. Idem, *The Book of Holy Medicines*, p. 105.

19. Bynum, *Wonderful Blood*, pp. 158–59.

20. On the conflation of tears and blood, see Breeze, "The Virgin's Tears of Blood."

21. Sahlin, "'His Heart Was My Heart.'" Børresen, "Religious Feminism in the Middle Ages."

22. Arnold of Bonneval, PL 189:1694; cited by Gambero, *Mary in the Middle Ages*, p. 150. On Mary's co-crucifixion with her son, see further Fulton, *From Judgment to Passion*, passim.

23. In addition to Sahlin, "'His Heart Was My Heart,'" see also Graef, *Mary*, pp. 306–9.

24. Schuler, "The Seven Sorrows of the Virgin."

25. See Chapter 2.

26. See, e.g., Bonaventure's comments about the Proleptic Passion cited in Chapter 2, nn. 132–33, and 135.

27. London, British Library, MS Harley 331, fol. 81r. Johnson, *The Grammar of Good Friday*, pp. 250–51 (also cited in Chapter 2, n. 133).

28. Schiller, *Iconography of Christian Art*, vol. 2, p. 196. Kieckhefer, *Unquiet Souls*, pp. 106–7. See also Acres, *Renaissance Invention*.

29. The present chapter does not discuss Birgitta's mystical pregnancy—her feeling of having the infant Christ within her—which obviously emphasizes her close identification with Mary. See Sahlin, "'A Marvelous and Great Exultation of the Heart.'"

30. An anonymous medieval reader of Birgitta constructed a Middle English Life of the Virgin Mary by taking extracts from the Swedish saint's writings. This derivative text survives in the fifteenth-century section of Oxford, Bodleian Library, MS Rawlinson C. 41; see Pezzini, ed., "Una 'Vita Beate Marie' tratta dalle 'Revelaciones.'"

31. Duffy remarks that "in much of the literature produced" under the influence of the cult of Mary's sorrows, "Mary is an hysterical figure, who faints, shrieks, tears her hair and pleads for death: at times she resembles the banshee more than the austerely sketched figure of the Fourth Gospel." He notes, however, that "the whole tradition of the grief-stricken mother by the cross has deep roots in Christian tradition, both in the Latin west and in Eastern Christendom." "Mater Dolorosa, Mater Misericordiae," pp. 215 and 218.

32. On the different types of sight featured in medieval religious texts, see Newman, "What Did It Mean to Say 'I Saw'?"

33. *Selected Revelations*, pp. 159–60. *Revelations*, vol. 3, pp. 205–6. *Revelaciones: Bok VII*, 7.1, p. 114. Cf. Collijn, *Acta et processus*, p. 96.

34. *Selected Revelations*, pp. 202–3. *Revelations*, vol. 3, p. 250. *Revelaciones: Bok VII*, 7.21.2–4, pp. 187–88.

35. *Selected Revelations*, p. 202 (translations taken from this text). *Revelations*, vol. 3, p. 250. *Revelaciones: Bok VII*, 7.21.1, p. 187. Mary's clothes are similarly described in a chapter from Birgitta's canonization dossier, in which we learn that Birgitta almost died in childbirth; Collijn, *Acta et processus*, p. 79.

36. Atkinson, "'Precious Balm in a Fragile Glass.'"

37. Jean le Marchant, *Miracles de Notre-Dame de Chartres*, pp. 161–66. Burns notes the ambiguity of medieval records regarding the relic of the Virgin at Chartres; "Saracen Silk and the Virgin's Chemise."

38. *Selected Revelations*, p. 203. *Revelations*, vol. 3, p. 250. *Revelaciones: Bok VII*, 7.21.5, p. 188.

39. Ali and Svanberg, *Imagines Sanctae Birgittae*, vol. 2: pl. 65a, 66, 68, 69, and 71; Cornell, *The Iconography of the Nativity of Christ*, passim; and Schiller, *Iconography of Christian Art*, vol. 1, pp. 78–81.

40. *Selected Revelations*, p. 203. *Revelations*, vol. 3, p. 251. *Revelaciones: Bok VII*, 21.8, p. 188.

41. The account of the Nativity in the so-called "J-Compilation," an unusual apocryphal infancy text in Latin (which survives in London, BL, Arundel 404, and Hereford, Hereford Cathedral Library, O.3.9) places particular stress on light; see Ehrman and Pleše, *The Apocryphal Gospels*, pp. 122–27, and also McNamara et al., *Apocrypha Hiberniae*, vol. 2, pp. 804–13. The formation of the baby Jesus from light implies a docetic viewpoint on the part of the anonymous author, as James suggested (*Latin Infancy Gospels*, pp. xxi and xxv), though the two most recent editors of the text, Ehrman and Pleše, deny this. The key passage in the Arundel MS reads: "Ipsa autem lux paulisper in se residens assimilauit se infanti et in continenti factus est infans ut solent infantes nasci"; Ehrman and Pleše, *The Apocryphal Gospels*, p. 126. The Hereford MS stresses that the baby is made from the light: "Ipsa uero lux paulisper in sese residere cepit et assimulauit se infanti. Et continenti splendore natus est infans sicut solent alii infantes nasci"; James, *Latin Infancy Gospels*, pp. 69 and 71. That Jesus' body is insubstantial is supported by an additional detail found in both manuscripts: the child's lack of weight. In Arundel, the midwife who has come to help at the birth of Jesus witnesses the supernatural event and then raises up a weightless newborn. Ehrman and Pleše, *The Apocryphal Gospels*, p. 127. Cf. James, *Latin Infancy Gospels*, p. 71. On the "J-Compilation," see further Jean-Daniel Kaestli and Martin McNamara, "Latin Infancy Gospels: The J Compilation," in McNamara et al., *Apocrypha Hiberniae*, vol. 2, pp. 621–70, and Beyers, "Dans l'Atelier des compilateurs." The theme of light is present, but not as pronounced, in the account of the Nativity found in other apocryphal texts; in the *Protoevangelium* the light recedes as the babe becomes "visible"; Hock, *The Infancy Gospels of James and Thomas*, p. 67; cf. Gijsel, *Pseudo-Matthaei Evangelium*, p. 414, n. 2, and p. 415. Flores similarly notes parallels between the apocryphal infancy gospels and Birgitta's revelations; Flores, "The Nativity Scene in the 'Lives of Mary.'"

42. *Revelations*, vol. 1, p. 132. *Revelaciones: Book I*, 1.47.1, p. 382.

43. Shahar, *Childhood in the Middle Ages*, p. 87. Trevisa, *On the Properties of Things*, vol. 1, p. 299. For the Latin, see Bartholomaeus Anglicus, *De rerum proprietatibus*, bk. 6, ch. 4, p. 238.

44. Gijsel, *Pseudo-Matthaei Evangelium*, p. 415. Hock, *The Infancy Gospels of James and Thomas*, p. 65. See Chapter 2, nn. 178–79.

45. Rubin, *Mother of God*, pp. 29–30 et passim.

46. Boss, "The Development of Mary's Immaculate Conception." See further Lamy, *L'immaculée conception*.

47. *The Angel's Discourse*, p. 173. *Sermo angelicus*, ch. 10.10, p. 103. Elsewhere Mary speaks of the moment in which she was conceived as "a golden hour," which is perhaps an allusion to

the fanciful idea that she was conceived at the Golden Gate where her parents met and kissed after a period of separation; *Revelaciones: Book VI*, 6.55.2, p. 196. *Revelations*, vol. 2, p. 116. Neither the apocryphal *Protoevangelium* nor *Pseudo-Matthew*, however, says that Mary was conceived when her parents embraced at their reunion (which only in *Pseudo-Matthew* specifically occurs at the Golden Gate), though both texts emphasize the importance and joy of her parents' meeting at a gate, as an angel had arranged; Hock, *The Infancy Gospels of James and Thomas*, p. 39; Gijsel, *Pseudo-Matthaei Evangelium*, pp. 319 and 321. The early fourteenth-century encyclopedia-like compendium *Ci nous dit* transmits the idea that Mary was conceived at the Golden Gate ("Et adonc s'entrencontrerent souz la Porte Doree, et la fut concheüe Nostre Dame"; Blangez, *Ci nous dit*, ch. 15, vol. 1, pp. 45–46), but I have not found much textual evidence in support of this view elsewhere. Regardless, Birgitta's comment about Mary's "golden" conception clearly suggests a wish, on her part, to counter apocrypha-inspired legends.

48. *The Angel's Discourse*, p. 174. *Sermo angelicus*, ch. 10.15, p. 174.

49. *Revelations*, vol. 3, p. 102. *Revelaciones: Book VI*, 6.49.2, p. 176. Mary compares the chaste and dutiful conjugal relations of her parents to a person's eating even though fasting is personally preferred.

50. For an example from the *Sermo angelicus*, see *The Angel's Discourse*, p. 169. *Sermo angelicus*, ch. 7.10–11, p. 95.

51. See, e.g., Hildegard of Bingen, *Scivias*, 3.8, pp. 336–37.

52. Neff, "The Pain of *Compassio*."

53. *Selected Revelations*, p. 203. *Revelations*, vol. 3, p. 251. *Revelaciones: Bok VII*, 7.21.8, p. 188.

54. Cornell, *The Iconography of the Nativity*, ch. 2.

55. Pseudo-Bonaventure, *Meditations*, ch. 7, pp. 24–25; *Meditaciones*, p. 31.

56. MacLehose, *"A Tender Age,"* ch. 1. The account of the Nativity in the "J-Compilation" similarly calls attention to the baby's shiny cleanness; Ehrman and Pleše, *The Apocryphal Gospels*, p. 127.

57. *Selected Revelations*, p. 203. *Revelaciones: Bok VII*, 7.21.11, p. 188. In Birgitta's *Revelationes*, the Child's brightness and cleanliness continue throughout his youth, as I note below; cf. n. 135. The Middle English poem *Cleanness* similarly emphasizes the spotlessness of the baby Jesus at his coming into the world: "Þenne watȝ her blyþe barne burnyst so clene / Þat boþe þe ox & þe asse hym hered at ones; / Þay knewe hym by his clannes for kyng of nature, / For non so clene of such a clos come neuer er þenne" ("At that moment her merry child was so cleanly pure that both the ox and the ass worshipped him immediately. They knew him for the king of nature, for none before then had ever come so clean from such an enclosure"); Gollancz, *Cleanness*, pp. 40–41, lines 1085–88. *Pseudo-Matthew*, in contrast, provides no explicit explanation as to why the ox and the ass adored the newborn Jesus. On cleanness, see further Bayless, *Sin and Filth*, and Cuffel, *Gendering Disgust*, both of whom mention the Christ Child. Bayless (pp. 150–51) cites Jerome, who, in a homily on the Nativity, remarks that Jesus "was born in dung, that is, in a stable . . . where the filth was our sins. For that reason he is born in dung, so that he may lift up those who come from dung"; Jerome, "Homilia de Nativitate Domini," p. 524. The *Opus imperfectum* likewise stresses the dirtiness of the Christ Child's surroundings when it tells of the arrival of the Magi; Kellerman, *Incomplete Commentary on Matthew*, p. 37. PG 56:642. On the moral valence of Jesus' cleanness, seen as a stark contrast to sodomy, see Jacobus de Voragine's comment that on the night of Christ's birth, all the Sodomites were destroyed, so "that no such uncleanness (*immunditia*) might be found in the nature he [Christ] had assumed"; LA, ch. 6, vol. 1, p. 72; GL, vol. 1, p. 41.

58. *Selected Revelations*, pp. 203–4. *Revelations*, vol. 3, p. 251. *Revelaciones: Bok VII*, 7.21.12 and 17, pp. 188–89. Note that Mary is not explicitly said to have wrapped up the placenta, although, according to Birgitta, she cut the umbilical cord with her fingers. Tasioulas argues for Birgitta's belief in the "naturalness" of Jesus' gestation within Mary, on the basis of the saint's mentioning of the afterbirth; Tasioulas, "'Heaven and Earth in Little Space,'" p. 30. Earlier I referred to an inquisitorial report of a French woman's disgust at the thought of Jesus being associated with the afterbirth (*turpitudo*); Chapter 3, n. 223.

59. Apocryphal sources mention two midwives but say nothing about their bathing of the newborn; Hock, *The Infancy Gospels of James and Thomas*, pp. 67 and 69; and Gijsel, *Pseudo-Matthaei Evangelium*, pp. 417–27. On the midwives, see Toubert, "La Vierge et les sages-femmes." On the late medieval image of Mary reclining after having given birth, see Gibson, *The Theater of Devotion*, pp. 62 and 64; and Schiller, *Iconography of Christian Art*, vol. 1, pp. 169–84. On the late medieval Shrine Madonna as a representation of Mary's giving birth, see Gertsman, *Worlds Within*, ch. 2.

60. Hilary of Poitiers, though, in speaking of Christ's birth, notes that the Magi adored the filth of the baby Jesus' cradle (*cunarum sordes*), perhaps implying his clothes were soiled; Hilary of Poitiers, *De trinitate*, bk. 2, ch. 27, p. 63. On the setting of the Nativity as dirty, see the comment by Jerome cited above in n. 57. By emphasizing Jesus' amazing cleanliness, Birgitta suggests that the Christ Child did not need to be bathed later on. On legends in which Mary washes her infant and/or his clothes, see Dzon, "Out of Egypt." See also below, n. 79.

61. *Selected Revelations*, pp. 203–4. *Revelations*, vol. 3, pp. 251–52. *Revelaciones: Bok VII*, 7.21.13. pp. 188–89; 7.21.21, p. 189. Jerome is emphatic that there were no midwives present to assist Mary; Jerome, *Liber adversus Helvidium*, PL 23:201; idem, "On the Perpetual Virginity of the Blessed Virgin Mary," p. 23.

62. *Selected Revelations*, p. 203. *Revelations*, vol. 3, p. 251. *Revelaciones, Bok VII*, 7.21.14–15, p. 189.

63. In his hymn "Pange, lingua," Venantius Fortunatus similarly describes the baby Jesus crying: "Set within the narrow manger, / lacking speech, the infant wails"; Fortunatus, *One Hundred Hymns*, pp. 98–99. The crying of newborns was generally regarded as a token of the misery of humankind, as noted by Augustine, *De civitate Dei: Libri XI–XXII*, bk. 21, ch. 14, p. 780; idem, *Concerning the City of God*, p. 991; and later Lotario di Segni (future Pope Innocent III) in his *De miseria condicionis humane*, part 1, chs. 5–6, pp. 102–3. On Leo the Great's emphasis upon the normalcy of Jesus' babyhood, see Chapter 3, n. 57 and n. 325. In Sermon 22, Leo explicitly says that "the devil saw [the Christ Child] whimper and cry"; Leo the Great, *St. Leo the Great: Sermons*, p. 84. Idem, *Tractatus*, vol. 1, p. 96.

64. *Selected Revelations*, p. 203. *Revelations*, vol. 3, p. 251. *Revelaciones, Bok VII*, 7.21.16, p. 189.

65. Savage and Watson, *Anchoritic Spirituality*, p. 252. Thompson, *The Wohunge of Ure Lauerd*, pp. 28–29. On the Christ Child's poverty in the Franciscan tradition, see Chapter 2. The *Meditationes vitae Christi* actually describes the animals breathing on the newborn Jesus: "the ox and the ass knelt, positioned their mouths over the manger and through their nostrils breathed down on him, almost as if they had reason to believe (*ac si racione utentes cognoscerent*) that a child so scantily covered would need warmth in time of such intense cold"; Pseudo-Bonaventure, *Meditations*, ch. 7, p. 25; *Meditaciones*, p. 31. (For a depiction of the kneeling animals in BnF, ital. 115, fol. 19ᵛ, see idem, *Meditations on the Life of Christ: An Illustrated Manuscript*, p. 34). Although Birgitta, at the beginning of her chapter on the Nativity, notes that Joseph

tied the ox and the ass they brought with them to a manger (*Selected Revelations*, p. 202. *Revelations*, vol. 3, p. 250. *Revelaciones, Bok VII*, 7.21.3, p. 187), she makes no mention of these beasts when she tells of what happened immediately following Jesus' birth.

66. Gower, *Mirour de l'Omme (The Mirror of Mankind)*, p. 368. Idem, *Mirour de l'Omme*, in *The Complete Works of John Gower*, vol. 1, pp. 311–12, lines 28054–63.

67. *Selected Revelations*, p. 204. *Revelations*, vol. 3, p. 251. *Revelaciones: Bok VII*, 7.21.18–19, p. 189. On the swaddling of babies, see further Alexandre-Bidon, *L'enfant à l'ombre des cathédrals*, pp. 94–99; and Demaitre, "The Idea of Childhood and Child Care," pp. 471–72.

68. Oosterwijk, "Swaddled or Shrouded?" See further Forsyth, "Children in Early Medieval Art," p. 38.

69. *Selected Revelations*, p. 306, n. 778.

70. *Selected Revelations*, p. 204. *Revelations*, vol. 3, p. 252. *Revelaciones: Bok VII*, 7.21.22, pp. 189–90.

71. *Selected Revelations*, p. 202. *Revelations*, vol. 3, p. 250. *Revelaciones: Bok VII*, 7.21.2–3, p. 187.

72. See Hock, *The Infancy Gospels of James and Thomas*, pp. 65 and 67. Gijsel, *Pseudo-Matthaei Evangelium*, pp. 365, 415, 417, and 419. In the "J-Compilation," cited above, when Mary enters the cave, it "welcomed the daylight and shone as if it were noon"; Ehrman and Pleše, *The Apocryphal Gospels*, p. 123.

73. Gijsel, *Pseudo-Matthaei Evangelium*, p. 415.

74. *Selected Revelations*, p. 203. *Revelations*, vol. 3, p. 251. *Revelaciones: Bok VII*, 7.21.8, p. 188.

75. The fourteenth-century English Dominican John Bromyard, for example, links the analogy to John 8:12, and suggests that it be used by a Christian in arguing with a Jew about Mary's virginity. Bromyard, *Summa praedicantium*, vol. 2.1, article 2, section 17, p. 10. See further Gros, "La *semblance* de la *verrine*." Along similar lines, the sexless creation of a pearl (by means of sunlight penetrating an oyster shell) was seen as a natural analogy for Mary's conception of Christ. The idea that Mary conceived through the ear, like a weasel, was another way to defend her physical intactness, according to Hassig (*Medieval Bestiaries*, pp. 29–30, 206–7, nn. 12–16), though Bettini has recently questioned this supposedly common medieval association in *Women and Weasels*, p. 293, n. 163.

76. See above, n. 41.

77. On the negative portrayal of Joseph as a suspicious spouse, see Chapter 3, n. 179. See further, among others, Sheingorn, "Joseph the Carpenter's Failure at Familial Discipline." On Joseph in late medieval culture, see Payan, *Joseph*, and Lavaure, *L'Image de Joseph au Moyen Âge*.

78. *Selected Revelations*, p. 204. *Revelations*, vol. 3, p. 251. *Revelaciones: Bok VII*, 7.21.20, p. 189.

79. Whereas Birgitta has Joseph help Mary care for her newborn, Thomas of Hales (following the twelfth-century scholar Zachary of Besançon [*In unum ex quatuor*, PL 186:74]) says: "Ioseph autem non audebat attingere, quem sciebat de se non esse generatum"; Thomas of Hales, *The Lyf of Oure Lady*, p. 55. For Bernard's praise of Joseph on account of his privileged intimacy with the Christ Child, see Bernard of Clairvaux, *In laudibus virginis matris*, homily 2, p. 34. Idem, *Homilies in Praise of the Blessed Virgin*, p. 29. On Bernard's visualization of the interaction between Joseph and Jesus, see further McGuire, "Becoming a Father and a Husband." A late fifteenth-century author, Bernardino of Busto, in his *Mariale*, not only imagines Joseph helping his wife swaddle the infant Jesus, but also washing his linens; cited in Armon, "Servus, Pater, Dominus," pp. 332–33.

80. See Chapter 3.

81. *Revelaciones: Book I*, 1.10.12, p. 265; *Revelations*, vol. 1, p. 67.

82. *Revelations*, vol. 1, p. 67; *Revelaciones: Book I*, 1.10.13–14, p. 266.

83. *Revelations*, vol. 3, p. 19. *Revelaciones: Book VI*, 6.1.3–4, p. 59. Along similar lines, the consolation Joseph experienced in beholding his (beautiful and precious) son is a theme found in a number of medieval writers, such as Peter John Olivi, Jean Gerson, and Bartholomew of Pisa; Armon, "Servus, Pater, Dominus," pp. 128, 222, 263–65 et passim.

84. Angela of Foligno, *Angela of Foligno*, p. 274. Idem, *Il "Liber*," instructio 19, p. 123. Mary's beauty was also said to be extremely powerful, so much so that it drove away all lust; see, e.g., Felix Fabri, *The Wanderings of Brother Felix*, pp. 512–13. Idem, *Evagatorium*, p. 407; and also Chapter 2, n. 102.

85. *Revelations*, vol. 3, p. 19. *Revelaciones: Book VI*, 6.1.5, p. 59. Cf. *Revelaciones: Book IV*, 4.70.30, p. 212. *Revelations*, vol. 2, p. 128. Along similar lines, Jacobus de Voragine notes that the Magi offered the baby Jesus myrrh "to strengthen the child's limbs and drive out hateful worms," which implies that at least the Magi assumed that the baby Jesus' medical needs were the same as other infants'; LA, ch. 14, vol. 1, p. 139; GL, vol. 1, p. 83. The remark is derived from Bernard of Clairvaux, *Sermones I*, p. 308. Idem, *Sermons for Advent and the Christmas Season*, p. 173. On humans' unavoidable contact with worms more generally, see Conlee, "A Disputacioun betwyx þe Body and Wormes," p. 58, lines 121–34.

86. Vögtlin, *Vita rhythmica*, pp. 78–79, lines 2182–89. This passage (flamboyantly illustrated in BL, Add. 29434, fol. 48r) is an elaboration of a similar passage found in Pseudo-Matthew, Gijsel, *Pseudo-Matthaei Evangelium*, ch. 19, pp. 453–57. Before the arrival of these animals, dragons come out of their cave and adore the Christ Child; Vögtlin, *Vita rhythmica*, p. 78, lines 2172–81; Gijsel, *Pseudo-Matthaei Evangelium*, pp. 451–53.

87. Birgitta praises the different parts of Christ's body in one of the *Quattuor oraciones* (*Selected Revelations*, pp. 229–30; *The Four Prayers*, in *Revelations*, vol. 4, pp. 207–9; *Opera minora III: Quattuor oraciones*, pp. 82–87). This physical description of Jesus, which focuses on different parts of his body, resembles that found in the apocryphal *Letter of Lentulus*; Dobschütz, *Christusbilder*, p. 319. Kuczynski discusses Middle English versions of this text in "An Unpublished Middle English Version of the *Epistola Lentuli*." On medieval physiological explanations of the beauty of Christ and Mary, see Resnick, "Ps.-Albert the Great on the Physiognomy of Jesus and Mary." See also Spicq, *Ce que Jésus doit à sa mère*, pp. 36–37.

88. *Vita s. Edmundi Cantuariensis archiepiscopi et confessoris*, col. 1778e. On Jesus' beauty see also Chapter 3, n. 180.

89. For a visual analogue, see an early sixteenth-century French woodcut in which Mary looks upon a seated Christ Child, gashed with many wounds; Greef, "Uterus Cordis," p. 77, fig. 23.

90. *Selected Revelations*, p. 133. *Revelations*, vol. 2, p. 303. *Revelaciones: Book V*, 5.8.15, p. 143.

91. See, e.g., Minnis, "Chaucer's Criseyde and Feminine Fear."

92. Pseudo-Bonaventure, *Meditations*, ch. 8, pp. 30–31. *Meditaciones*, p. 38. See further Flora, "Women Wielding Knives."

93. *The Angel's Discourse*, p. 183. *Sermo angelicus*, ch. 17.1–5, p. 122. On the traditional metaphor of clothing to express the enfleshment of the Word, see, for example, Brock, "Clothing Metaphor as a Means of Theological Expression"; and Evangelatou, "The Purple Thread of the Flesh." For this image in the West, see Gibson, "Swaddling Cloth and Shroud," a summary of which appears in her "The Thread of Life in the Hand of the Virgin"; and Coletti, "Devotional Iconography."

94. *The Angel's Discourse*, pp. 183–84. *Sermo angelicus*, ch. 17.6–12, pp. 122–23. The word *fascia*, which Birgitta uses early on in this passage, can mean both "swaddling bands" and "burial shroud"; Latham, *Dictionary of Medieval Latin*, vol. 4, p. 907.

95. Mary's "rehearsing" of the Passion parallels (though it is more cerebral than) the one-woman reenactment of it by the thirteenth-century holy woman Elizabeth of Spalbeek; whereas the drama of the Passion takes place in Mary's imagination and vicariously in that of Birgitta's audience, it is singularly and dramatically performed in Elizabeth's body. See Simons and Ziegler, "Phenomenal Religion in the Thirteenth Century," esp. p. 126.

96. One of the miniatures in the Rohan Hours (Paris, BnF, lat. 9471, fol. 133r) depicts the Christ Child lying within an opened book, over which Mary prays as if her son were in a cradle. For a facsimile, see Meiss and Thomas, *The Rohan Master*. On the trope that likens Jesus' body to a legal text (the "Charter of Christ"), see Steiner, *Documentary Culture*.

97. Marrow, *Passion Iconography in Northern European Art*, pp. 52–54.

98. Mellinkoff, *Outcasts*. On the trope of Jewish ugliness contrasting with Jesus' beauty, see further Bale, *Feeling Persecuted*, ch. 3, and Resnick, *Marks of Distinction*.

99. *The Angel's Discourse*, p. 184; *Sermo angelicus*, ch. 17.14, p. 123.

100. *The Angel's Discourse*, p. 184; *Sermo angelicus*, ch. 17.15–17, p. 123 (translation altered).

101. Morris, *St Birgitta*, pp. 46–52.

102. For medieval scholastic discussions of pain, see Mowbray, *Pain and Suffering in Medieval Theology*, and Esther Cohen, *The Modulated Scream*.

103. *The Angel's Discourse*, p. 184; *Sermo angelicus*, ch. 17.18–21, p. 124.

104. The anecdote appears in Boethius, *Philosophiae consolatio*, bk. 3, ch. 5, p. 44; and in Cicero, *Tusculan Disputations II & V*, 5.61–62, pp. 112–13.

105. *The Angel's Discourse*, p. 184; *Sermo angelicus*, ch. 17.21, p. 124.

106. After the text from *Sermo angelicus*, ch. 17.22, the Breviary adds "Tu autem"; Collins, *The Bridgettine Breviary of Syon Abbey*, p. 88.

107. Collins, *The Bridgettine Breviary*, p. 88.

108. Kempe, *The Book of Margery Kempe*, bk. 1, ch. 58, p. 280; cf. bk. 1, ch. 17, p. 115.

109. Margery speaks of outdoing Birgitta in ibid, bk. 1, ch. 20, p. 129.

110. Ibid., bk. 1, ch. 39, p. 202.

111. Ibid., bk. 2, ch. 10, p. 420. See Windeatt's note to line 8269 on p. 418.

112. Blunt, *The Myroure of oure Ladye*, p. 244.

113. Kempe, *The Book of Margery Kempe*, pp. 11–12, and 77, n. to line 585.

114. Ibid., bk. 1, ch. 6, pp. 77–78.

115. Gibson, *The Theater of Devotion*, ch. 3. Margery used to pray in the "gesine" (childbed) chapel in St. Margaret's Church, Lynn; Kempe, *The Book of Margery Kempe*, 1.63, pp. 297–98. The midwife Salome from apocryphal infancy legends seems to have become the figure of Anastasia, who occasionally appears in late medieval art; see M. R. James, "Legends of St. Anne and St. Anastasia," Rosalie Green, "The Missing Midwife," and Chapter 2, n. 270.

116. Hale, "Joseph as Mother." Gibson, *The Theater of Devotion*, pp. 58–59. Oosterwijk, "The Swaddling-Clothes of Christ."

117. On this text, see Chapter 2.

118. On the presence of Jesus in the soul, see Greef, "*Uterus Cordis*," and the discussion of Aelred's *De Jesu puero duodenni* in Chapter 2. On Margery's pursuit of the male Jesus along the streets of Rome, see the beginning of Chapter 1.

119. Kempe, *The Book of Margery Kempe*, p. 78, n. 589. Windeatt remarks that the juxtaposition of "the joy of Christ's Nativity with the coming anguish of his Passion was a commonplace

of devotional tradition," but does not emphasize Margery's indebtedness to Birgitta on this point.

120. *Revelations*, vol. 3, p. 119. *Revelaciones: Book VI*, 6.57.7, p. 199.

121. *Revelations*, vol. 3, p. 120. *Revelaciones: Book VI*, 6.58.1–2, p. 200.

122. See the last section of Chapter 2.

123. *Préparation à la vie religieuse*, pp. 465–66. I am grateful to Julie Tracz for this reference. See further Mâle, *L'Art religieux après le Concile de Trente*, pp. 327–29; and Chorpenning, "Icon of Family and Religious Life," who mentions that the sixteenth-century Carmelite nun and mystic St. Teresa of Ávila thought of her convents as homes of the Holy Family.

124. Luke does not say that Mary pondered Simeon's prophecy in her heart. Yet medieval people would have likely imagined Mary taking his words "to heart."

125. Lungarotti, *Le Legendae di Margherita da Città di Castello, Recensio maior*, ch. 26, p. 77; *Recensio minor*, ch. 8, pp. 99–100. Margherita is explicitly said to have meditated daily on Jesus, Mary, and Joseph; *Recensio maior*, ch. 22, p. 74; *Recensio minor*, ch. 6, p. 97. See further Park, "Impressed Images."

126. Cf. "The Wife of Bath's Prologue," *The Canterbury Tales*, III.529–38, in Chaucer, *The Riverside Chaucer*, p. 112. Phillips, *Transforming Talk*, pp. 6 and 149–50.

127. LA, ch. 152, vol. 2, p. 1069. GL, vol. 2, p. 254.

128. Morris contends that, in Book 5, Birgitta was criticizing the excessive curiosity of her first confessor Master Mathias, a renowned theologian; "The Monk-on-the-ladder."

129. *Revelations*, vol. 3, p. 120. *Revelaciones: Book VI*, 6.58.2, p. 200.

130. *Revelations*, vol. 3, p. 120. *Revelaciones: Book VI*, 6.58.3, pp. 200–201.

131. *Revelaciones: Book V*, interrogacio 10.3 and 22, pp. 124, 126–27; *Selected Revelations*, pp. 122–23. *Revelations*, vol. 2, pp. 290–91.

132. Langland, *Piers Plowman*, C-text, 18.117–39, pp. 301–2. See further Dzon, "'Bold in His Barnhoed.'"

133. *Revelaciones: Book V*, interrogacio 11.4 and 28–30, pp. 130, 132–33. *Selected Revelations*, pp. 124 and 126. *Revelations*, vol. 2, pp. 294–96. The reference to Christ's continual labors echoes the remark from Harley 331; see above, n. 27, and Chapter 2, n. 133.

134. Mary similarly speaks of the "wonders of God" (*mirabilia Dei*) surrounding the event of the Nativity in 7.22.5, lamenting the fact that people were so busy with the census that the wonders that occurred at Jesus' birth were ignored; *Revelaciones: Bok VII*, pp. 190–91. *Selected Revelations*, p. 204. *Revelations*, vol. 3, p. 252. On medieval lists of the wonders surrounding the birth of Christ, see Chapter 3, n. 58.

135. *Revelations*, vol. 3, p. 120. *Revelaciones: Book VI*, 6.58.4, p. 201. (The numbers in the translation are mine).

136. *Selected Revelations*, p. 205. *Revelations*, vol. 3, p. 253. *Revelaciones: Bok VII*, 7.23.2, p. 191. Cf. Mark 1:13, where the adult Christ is said to have been accompanied by angels in the desert, who "ministrabant illi." In the chapter on the fasting and temptations of Christ, Pseudo-Bonaventure's *Meditationes vitae Christi* describes angels delivering his mother's cooking to Jesus after his forty-day fast in the desert (*Meditaciones*, ch. 17, pp. 89–91; *Meditations*, pp. 76–78). See the depiction of this episode in BnF, ital. 115, fol. 71r–v (*Meditations: An Illustrated Manuscript*, p. 125–26). See also the busy yet charming early fifteenth-century Rheinish painting of the Nativity in which angels do chores around the recumbent Mary: one of them fluffs the Virgin's pillow, while two others help bring water for Jesus' bath and yet two others apparently prepare a receiving blanket; Panofsky, *Early Netherlandish Painting*, vol. 1, pp. 94–95, vol. 2, fig. 110.

137. Mary says that she and Joseph heard "angelic voices singing above him"; *Revelations*, vol. 3, p. 121. *Revelaciones: Book VI*, 6.58.13, p. 202. In Niccolò di Tommaso's painting of the Nativity (fig. 19), a whole host of angels surrounds the cave in which Jesus has just been born and gaze down in adoration of the divine child. Stephen of Sawley had earlier called attention to the angels surrounding the baby Jesus when he remarked that Jesus played with them ("infantem . . . angelis alludentem"); Stephen of Sawley, "Les méditations d'Étienne de Salley," p. 346.

138. Bartholomaeus Anglicus noted children's proneness to getting dirty and their dislike of being cleaned, that is, washed and combed (deloused?) by their mothers; Bartholomaeus Anglicus, *De rerum proprietatibus*, bk. 6, ch. 5, p. 240. Trevisa, *On the Properties of Things*, p. 301.

139. *Revelations*, vol. 3, p. 121. *Revelaciones: Book VI*, 6.58.5, p. 201.

140. *Revelations*, vol. 3, p. 19. *Revelaciones: Book VI*, 6.1.3–4, p. 59. See above, n. 83.

141. *Revelations*, vol. 3, p. 121. *Revelaciones: Book VI*, 6.58.5–8, p. 201.

142. *Meditations*, pp. 44–45. *Meditaciones*, ch. 12, pp. 51–52.

143. *Revelations*, vol. 3, p. 121. *Revelaciones: Book VI*, 6.58.9, p. 201.

144. *Revelations*, vol. 3, p. 121. *Revelaciones: Book VI*, 6.58.10, p. 201.

145. Cf. Tatian, *The Diatessaron of Tatian*, sections 4–5, pp. 49–51.

146. *Revelations*, vol. 3, p. 121. *Revelaciones: Book VI*, 6.58.13, p. 202. Bernard of Clairvaux earlier noted Jesus' obedience to his father, for Mary's sake; Bernard of Clairvaux, *In laudibus virginis matris, Homilia I*, p. 19. Idem, *Homilies in Praise of the Blessed Virgin*, p. 11. In his sermon "Jacob autem," Jean Gerson similarly marveled that "he who made (*fabricavit*) the dawn and the sun was subject to a carpenter (*faber*) . . . to a woman who was a weaver (*femina textrina*)"; Gerson, "Jacob Autem," in *L'Œuvre Oratoire*, vol. 5, p. 358. See further McGuire, "Becoming a Father and a Husband"; Hahn, "Joseph Will Perfect," pp. 58–59; and Filas, *Joseph and Jesus*.

147. On the Early Christian apocryphal account of Joseph's death, which has survived complete in Coptic, see "The History of Joseph the Carpenter," in J. K. Elliott, *The Apocryphal New Testament*, pp. 111–17; and Hennecke and Schneemelcher, *New Testament Apocrypha*, vol. 1, pp. 483–85. On knowledge of this text in the West, see Sheingorn, "'Illustrius patriarcha Joseph,'" p. 101, n. 35; and also Armon, "Servus, Pater, Dominus," p. 17.

148. Tension between Jesus and the masters is also heightened in the medieval English "Jesus and the Doctors" plays. In the N-Town play "Christ and the Doctors" (no. 21), Mary verbalizes her fears that people are envious of her son's giftedness: "I am aferde þat he hath fon / For his grett wytts and werkys good. / Lyke hym of wytt forsoth is non; / Euery childe with hym is wroth and wood (I am afraid because he has enemies, on account of his intelligence and good works; indeed, no one is as smart as he; every child is angry and furious with him)"; Spector, *The N-Town Play*, p. 205, lines 221–24. See further Kline, "Structure, Characterization, and the New Community."

149. *Revelations*, vol. 3, p. 121. *Revelaciones: Book VI*, 6.58.8, p. 201.

150. *Revelaciones: Book IV*, 4.70.28, p. 212. *Revelations*, vol. 2, p. 128.

151. The Latin noun "invidia" derives from the verb "invideo," literally meaning "to look askance at"; Lewis and Short, *A Latin Dictionary*, p. 995. Medieval iconography underscores the visual aspect of this vice. In illustrated manuscripts of the allegorical *Roman de la Rose*, Envy has daggers shooting from her eyes; Bloomfield, *The Seven Deadly Sins*, p. 231. In Dante's *Purgatorio*, the envious are punished by having their eyes sewn shut; Alighieri, *Purgatorio*, canto 13, lines 70–73, pp. 276–77.

152. See Chapter 2, n. 48.

153. *Revelations*, vol. 3, p. 121 (slightly modified). *Book VI*, 6.58.11–12, p. 121.

154. Statements concerning God's impassibility occur in a number of places in the *Revelationes*, but here the boy Jesus claims this peculiar quality as his own. See, e.g., *Revelaciones: Book VI*, 6.11.2–3, p. 75. *Revelations*, vol. 3, p. 32. One of the earliest as well as clearest statements of God's impassibility appears in Leo the Great's letter (28) to Flavian, Bishop of Constantinople, cited in the Council of Chalcedon, in *Decrees of the Ecumenical Councils*, vol. 1, p. 79.

155. On Joseph's inability to deal competently with the apocryphal Christ Child, see Dzon, "Joseph and the Amazing Christ-Child."

156. Greene, *The Early English Carols*, pp. 93–94. On ominous discussions between Mother and Child featured in Middle English lyrics, see Kenney, "The Manger as Calvary and Altar," pp. 50–51; Bale, *Feeling Persecuted*, pp. 40–43; and Vines, "Lullaby as Lament." On the Child's foreknowledge of the Passion more broadly, see Janson, "Omega in Alpha," and Acres, *Renaissance Invention*. For a striking image in which the infant Jesus foresees his future sacrifice, symbolized by an altar in heaven (cf. Heb. 9:24), see Ringbom, "Vision and Conversation"; and also Acres, pp. 124–25, fig. 93. On the necessity of Jesus' crucifixion, see Chapter 3, n. 276.

157. Urbach similarly notes analogues of such conversations in "'Ego sum deus et homo.'"

158. See also Plummer, *The Hours of Catherine of Cleves*, no. 92.

159. Cf. the account of the origin of the cross found in the Early Christian apocryphal *Gospel of Philip*: "Joseph the carpenter planted a garden because he needed the wood for his trade. It was he who made the Cross from the trees which he planted"; Wilson, *The Gospel of Philip*, p. 49. On traditions concerning Joseph's trade (cf. Matt. 13:55), see Cooper, *Artisans and Narrative Craft*, pp. 96, 214, n. 128.

160. Birgitta's Mary can be linked with the figure of the sacrificial mother, who, motivated by piety, passively allows her children to be injured or killed; see Newman, "'Crueel Corage.'"

161. *Revelations*, vol. 3, p. 121. *Revelaciones: Book VI*, 6.58.13, p. 202. The *Speculum devotorum*, a Middle English meditational text that borrows from the *Revelaciones*, alters this passage slightly by noting that Mary and Joseph often saw "merueylus lygth schyne abowte hym"; Patterson, *A Mirror to Devout People*, p. 58, line 57.

162. Cf. *Revelaciones: Book V*, interrogacio 12.17 and 12.22, pp. 137–38, where Christ tells how he came "in secrecy to make war with the devil." *Selected Revelations*, pp. 129–30. *Revelations*, vol. 2, p. 299.

163. *Revelations*, vol. 3, p. 121. *Revelaciones: Book VI*, 6.58.14, p. 202. The *Arabic Infancy Gospel* similarly recounts how a demoniac boy was healed when a cloth used to cover the infant Jesus was placed on his head, p. 406. Satan similarly departs from the boy Judas, "in the shape of a dog," when he strikes Jesus on the right side (where the crucified Jesus is later struck with the lance), Walker, "The Arabic Gospel of the Infancy," p. 412. The poem about Jesus' apocryphal childhood in MS Z822 N81 similarly portrays the young Jesus working exorcisms: "deluels out of þam [he] kest"; Parker, *The Life of Saint Anne*, p. 80, line 3108. It also notes that he cleansed temples of "fals gods" (thought to be demons); p. 69, lines 2661–62; p. 73, lines 28331–32. Like many apocryphal infancy narratives, this poem earlier recounts how the idols ("All þas fals godys") fell down on their faces when Mary and the infant Jesus entered the temple in Sotinen; p. 44, lines 1681–82.

164. Tischendorf, *Evangelia apocrypha*, ch. 42, p. 111.

165. Loomis, *White Magic*, p. 21. Cf. Smithers, *Havelok*, p. 20, lines 589–91.

166. Aelred of Rievaulx, *Rule of Life*, pp. 81–82; "splendor majestatis," in idem, *De institutione*, p. 664. Idem, *Age of Twelve*, pp. 8–9; idem, *De Iesu puero*, p. 253. See further Chapter 2.

167. Dyan Elliott, *Spiritual Marriage*, pp. 143–44; Hahn, " 'Joseph Will Perfect,' " pp. 61–64, and Resnick, "Marriage in Medieval Culture."

168. *Revelations*, vol. 3, p. 123. *Revelaciones: Book VI*, 6.59.12, pp. 203–4. A well-known example of Joseph speaking harshly to Mary occurs in "The Cherry Tree Carol," where he in curmudgeonly fashion tells his pregnant wife: "Let him pluck thee a cherry / that brought thee with child"; Carr, "The Middle English Nativity Cherry Tree," p. 142. Cf. Parker, *The Life of Saint Anne*, p. 20, lines 767–78, where Joseph assumes that Mary committed adultery, after having been seduced by a young man disguised as an angel. On the idea of a lascivious angel, see Chapter 3, nn. 178 and 179.

169. Patterson, *A Mirror to Devout People*, p. 57, lines 22–23.

170. Vögtlin, *Vita rhythmica*, p. 70, lines 1906–7; p. 90, line 2555; p. 107, line 3092; pp. 117–18, lines 3394–401.

171. *Revelations*, vol. 3, p. 121. *Revelaciones: Book VI*, 6.58.15, p. 202.

172. *Revelations*, vol. 3, p. 175. *Revelaciones: Book VI*, 6.112.1–2, p. 272. Although Mary discusses the major events of Christ's infancy, for which there were liturgical feasts, she does not include a visionary account of the Circumcision. The care which Mary claims to have given to the prepuce may be compared to the attention she shows to the umbilical cord and the afterbirth in Birgitta's vision of the Nativity; *Selected Revelations*, pp. 203–4. *Revelations*, vol. 3, p. 251. *Revelaciones: Bok VII*, 7.21.12 and 17, pp. 188–89. Both of these bodily remnants were thought to be kept in the Sancta Sanctorum chapel at the Lateran; John the Deacon, *Descriptio Lateranensis Ecclesiae*, p. 356.

173. The thirteenth-century bishop of Lincoln Robert Grosseteste mentions Joseph of Arimathea's collection of Jesus' blood, when he was brought down from the cross; see Grosseteste, "De sanguine Christi," pp. 138 and 140. See further Bynum, *Wonderful Blood*.

174. *Revelations*, vol. 3, p. 175. *Revelaciones: Book VI*, 6.112.3, p. 272. On the finding and relocation of relics in hagiography, see Otter, *Inventiones*, passim, and also Geary, *Furta Sacra*.

175. Walker, "The Arabic Gospel of the Infancy," ch. 5, pp. 405–6.

176. *Revelations*, vol. 3, p. 175. *Revelaciones: Book VI*, 6.112.3–4, p. 272. On medieval veneration of the relic of the foreskin in multiple locations, see Palazzo, "The Veneration of the Sacred Foreskin(s) of Baby Jesus." See further MacLehose, "Relics of the Christ Child," and Jacobs, *Christ Circumcised*, pp. ix–x, 139–41.

177. Bynum, "The Female Body and Religious Practice," pp. 185–86, n. 11; and idem, *Holy Feast and Holy Fast*, p. 377, n. 135.

178. MacLehose, "The Holy Tooth."

179. And in some cases the power embedded in it. A case in point is Charlemagne, who supposedly obtained the relic; LA, ch. 13, vol. 1, p. 129; GL, vol. 1, p. 77. See also Vigneras, "L'abbaye de Charroux et la légende du Pèlerinage du Charlemagne." See further Remensnyder (*Remembering Kings Past*, pp. 149, 172–81, 258), who notes that the relics of the cross and foreskin "represent, as it were, the alpha and omega of the Incarnation" (p. 176).

180. Vincent, *The Holy Blood*, ch. 5. See also MacLehose, "The Holy Tooth."

181. *Revelations*, vol. 1, p. 308. *Revelaciones: Book III*, 3.25.2, p. 164. One of the miracles of Gautier of Coincy features Mary speaking angrily (*iréement*) at a cleric who abandoned his total dedication to her by taking a wife; Gautier de Coincy, *Miracles de la Sainte Vierge*, p. 637.

182. *Revelations*, vol. 1, p. 308. *Revelaciones: Book III*, 3.25.2, p 164. In Chaucer's "Parson's Tale," as in other ethical works, a distinction is made between acceptable and reprovable anger; *The Canterbury Tales*, X.537–39, 542, 547, *The Riverside Chaucer*, p. 305. See also above, n. 15.

183. Thomas of Celano, "The Life of Saint Francis," bk. 1, ch. 30, in *The Saint*, FAED, p. 256. Idem, *Vita prima*, FF, p. 362: "puer Iesus in multorum cordibus oblivioni fuerit datus." Cf. Ps. 30:13. See further Chapter 2.

184. Thomas of Celano, "The Life of Saint Francis," *The Saint*, FAED, p. 255. *Vita prima*, FF, p. 360.

185. *Selected Revelations*, p. 170. *Revelations*, vol. 3, p. 217. *Revelaciones: Bok VII*, 7.8.4, p. 134.

186. Along similar lines, in a fifteenth-century lyric, Mary is said to have made the boy Jesus' rather shabby clothes. Here, after Jesus himself says that he was born "ine a powur howse wher bestys ete ther mete," he adds an unusual detail about his childhood: "I lede my yought wyth children in the strette, / Poorly a-rayed in clothes bare and thyne, / Suche as my mother for me dyde make & spyne"; Carleton Brown, *Religious Lyrics of the XVth Century*, no. 109, p. 170, lines 33–35.

187. This is reflected, for instance, in the legend that Charlemagne had his own daughters engage in textile work. See Dzon, "Birgitta of Sweden and Christ's Clothing."

188. Karras, '"This Skill in a Woman,'" p. 104.

189. *Selected Revelations*, pp. 170–71. *Revelations*, vol. 3, p. 217. *Revelaciones: Bok VII*, 7.8.4–8, pp. 134–35 (emphasis mine). On medieval exegetes' views of the Jews' role in the Passion, see Jeremy Cohen, "The Jews as the Killers of Christ."

190. Gilchrist, *Medieval Life*, pp. 79–80. On children's clothing, see further Orme, *Medieval Childhood*, pp. 73–75; and Ariès, *Centuries of Childhood*, ch. 3.

191. Vögtlin, *Vita rhythmica*, pp. 105–6, lines 3046–61.

192. On Christ's near nakedness, see *Revelaciones: Book I*, 1.10.22, p. 268, *Revelations*, vol. 1, p. 68; and *Revelaciones: Book IV*, 4.70.8, p. 209. *Revelations*, vol. 2, p. 126. On nudity, see Lindquist, *The Meanings of Nudity in Medieval Art*.

193. For the identification of this friar, see *Selected Revelations*, p. 285, n. 555; and Collijn, *Acta et processus*, p. 382.

194. *Selected Revelations*, p. 169. *Revelations*, vol. 3, p. 216. The commands to be obeyed are "que non sint contra Deum"; *Revelaciones: Bok VII*, 7.7.11–12, pp. 132–33.

195. Francis of Assisi, "The Earlier Rule," ch. 1, in *The Saint*, FAED, pp. 63–64. Idem, *Regula non bullata*, 1.1–2, in FF, pp. 185–86.

196. Lawrence, *Medieval Monasticism*, pp. 244–50.

197. On Francis's spirituality of clothing, see further Chapter 2.

198. "The Earlier Rule," ch. 2, in *The Saint*, FAED, pp. 64–65. *Regula non bullata*, 2.8 and 2.13, in FF, pp. 186–87.

199. Birgitta of Sweden, *Den heliga Birgittas Reuelaciones extrauagantes*, 69.3, pp. 191–92.

200. For an ethnographical musing on the seamless tunic, see Thomas Aquinas, *Super evangelium s. Ioannis lectura*, p. 451, citing John Chrysostom; Chrysostom, *Commentary on St. John the Apostle and Evangelist: Homilies 48–88*, homily 85, p. 431. PG 59:461. See also Ludolph of Saxony, *Vita Christi*, vol. 4, p. 104.

201. *Selected Revelations*, p. 286, n. 571.

202. *Anonymous of Perugia*, ch. 6, in *The Founder*, FAED, p. 46. FF, p. 1331.

203. Among the verses he cites are Matt. 17:2, John 13:4, John 19:24, all of which use possessive adjectives in speaking of Jesus' clothing. William of Ockham, *A Translation of William*

*of Ockham's Work of Ninety Days*, vol. 2, pp. 626–39. Idem, *Guillemi de Ockham Opera Politica*, vol. 2, pp. 705–15.

204. William of Ockham, *A Translation of William of Ockham's Work of Ninety Days*, pp. 636–38. Idem, *Guillemi de Ockham Opera Politica*, pp. 713–14.

205. John XXII, *Extravagantes Ioannis Papae XXII*, ch. 4, cols. 1229–30. For a history of the controversy, see Burr, *The Spiritual Franciscans*. See further Nold, "Pope John XXII, the Franciscan Order and Its *Rule*."

206. Douie, *The Nature and the Effect of the Heresy of the Fraticelli*, p. 155.

207. According to Malcolm Lambert, "The decision against the rule, as they saw it, helped to confirm the identification of John XXII with the mystical Antichrist who, it was prophesied, would strike against Francis and his true followers"; Lambert, *Medieval Heresy*, pp. 229–30. John XXII was also criticized for his idiosyncratic ideas about the Beatific Vision. See Mollat, *The Popes at Avignon*, pp. 21–23.

208. *Revelations*, pp. 295–96. *Revelaciones: Book III*, 3.18.16–17, p. 143.

209. On Birgitta's attitude toward John XXII and the Spirituals, see further Schiwy, *Birgitta von Schweden*, pp. 246–50; and Petrén, *Kyrka och makt*, pp. 61–62.

210. At the beginning of chapter 8, Mary says that "it is not licit for you to know whether the soul of Pope John XXII is in heaven or in hell." *Select Revelations*, p. 170. *Revelations*, vol. 3, p. 217. *Revelaciones: Bok VII*, 7.8.1–2, p. 134.

211. *Select Revelations*, p. 170. *Revelations*, vol. 3, p. 217. *Revelaciones: Bok VII*, 7.8.1–3, p. 134.

212. Roelvink, *Franciscans in Sweden*, p. 40; idem, "Var den heliga Birgitta medlem i den franciskanska tredje orden?"; and idem, "Andlig släktskap mellan Franciskus och Birgitta." Birgitta's body was kept at the Clarissan convent of San Lorenzo in Rome before it was sent to Sweden.

213. *Selected Revelations*, pp. 160–61. *Revelations*, vol. 3, pp. 207–8. *Revelaciones: Bok VII*, 7.3, pp. 116–17.

214. *Selected Revelations*, p. 282, n. 513. For an overview see Andersson, *St. Birgitta and the Holy Land*.

215. *Den heliga Birgittas Reuelaciones extrauagantes*, 45.3, p. 161. See also *Extrauagantes*, 23, p. 133; 67.2, p. 190; and 90, p. 215. *Extravagant Revelations*, in *Revelations*, vol. 4, pp. 245, 264, 285, and 304.

216. See, e.g., *Revelaciones: Bok VII*, 7.20, pp. 182–87, where she records Christ's displeasure at the failure of many Franciscans to follow the Rule of St. Francis; *Selected Revelations*, pp. 199–202. *Revelations*, vol. 3, pp. 247–50.

217. *Opera minora I: Regula Salvatoris*, ch. 2, p. 105 (henceforth cited as *Regula Salvatoris*). *The Rule of the Savior*, in *Revelations*, vol. 4, p. 126. Cf. Francis of Assisi, "The Earlier Rule," ch. 8, in *The Saint*, FAED, p. 70. FF, p. 193.

218. *Regula Salvatoris*, ch. 4, p. 106. *The Rule of the Savior*, in *Revelations*, vol. 4, p. 127.

219. *The Rule of St. Benedict* at first says that monks are to have one cowl and one tunic, but then concedes a spare of each; Benedict of Nursia, *La Règle de Saint Benoît*, 55.4 and 55.9, pp. 618 and 620.

220. *Regula Salvatoris*, ch. 18, pp. 201–2. *The Rule of the Savior*, in *Revelations*, vol. 4, p. 137. Fogelqvist, "The New Vineyard," pp. 232–33.

221. Fogelqvist, "The New Vineyard," p. 235.

222. See further Dzon, "Birgitta of Sweden and Christ's Clothing."

223. On the image, see Meinardus, "Zur 'Strickenden Madonna,'" and Acres, *Renaissance Invention*, p. 75, fig. 37; p. 123. Scholars have related this painting to other portrayals of the Virgin sewing or knitting; see van Os, "Mary as Seamstress"; Wyss, "Die Handarbeiten der Maria"; and Rutt, *A History of Hand Knitting*, pp. 44–50. Landolt-Wegener ("Darstellung der Kindheitslegenden Christi," p. 220, fig. c) reproduces an unusual image from a fifteenth-century Picture Bible (St. Gallen, Kantonsbibliothek Vadiana, VadSlg MS 343d, fol. 53r) that depicts Mary sewing the Christ Child's garment as he sits beside her naked, waiting patiently. See also Biscoglio, "'Unspun' Heroes."

224. Jászai, "Der Besuch der Engel." Schiller's *Iconography of Christian Art* provides examples with the angels bearing the *arma Christi* near the adult Christ, vol. 2, pp. 215, 217, figs. 744, 752, and 758.

225. On the reception history of Isa. 53:3, see Sawyer, "'A man of sorrows and acquainted with grief.'"

226. Tops were thus used during Lent; Orme, *Medieval Children*, pp. 184 and 186–87.

227. On this motif, see Bestul, "The Passion Meditations of Richard Rolle," p. 61, n. 35.

228. For a reproduction of this image, see Acres, *Renaissance Invention*, p. 130, fig. 101; and Hahn, "Joseph as Ambrose's 'Artisan of the Soul,'" p. 519, fig. 2.

229. The legendary account in Oxford, The Queen's College, MS 348 is by Odo of Deuil (d. 1162), who succeeded Suger as abbot of Saint-Denis. For the document by Hugh, see Hugh of Amiens, "Charta Hugonis." On these texts, see further Dzon, "Birgitta of Sweden and Christ's Clothing," pp. 135–37. While Hugh's short text speaks of the "cappa" somewhat vaguely as the "indumentum quo sese humanata induere sapientia dignata fuit" (the garment with which the incarnate Wisdom deigned to clothe himself), the text by Odo is much more clear that the garment in question was the one for which the soldiers cast lots at the crucifixion. For a detailed history of the traditions surrounding the tunic at Argenteuil, see Dor, *La tunique d'Argenteuil*. See also Brown and Waldman, "Eudes de Deuil et la première ostension de la sainte tunique."

230. In his chronicle of the Normans, Robert of Torigni (d. 1186), abbot of Mont-Saint-Michel, noted that the relic of the Savior's tunic ("cappa Salvatoris") was found by divine revelation at Argenteuil. He also claimed that Jesus' "glorious mother made it for him while he was still a boy, as a letter (or letters, an inscription?) found with it indicated (*sicut litterae cum ea repertae indicabant*)"; Robert of Torigni, *Chronique de Robert de Torigni*, p. 299. One of the earliest statements that the seamless tunic increased in size is found in the *Flores historiarum* attributed to Matthew Paris (d. 1259), a monk at St. Albans, who stated that "the seamless tunic of Christ" "grew as [Jesus] himself grew (*crevit Ipso crescente*)"; Paris, *Flores historiarum*, p. 73. The latter remark does not appear in Paris's earlier notice of the tunic's discovery in the *Chronica majora*, of which his *Flores* is an abridgement with some additional material. See Paris, *Chronica majora (1067–1216)*, p. 212. As noted above (n. 191), the *Vita rhythmica* likewise remarked that the boy Jesus' tunic increased in size as he grew up.

231. Morris, *St Birgitta*, pp. 59–60, 120.

232. Morris remarks, "they probably travelled over the Baltic to Lübeck or Straslund and then to Cologne"; *St Birgitta of Sweden*, p. 59. See further Almazán, "Saint Birgitta on the Pilgrimage Route to Santiago," pp. 17–18; Salmesvuori, "Birgitta of Sweden and Her Pilgrimage."

233. See the woodcut of St. Birgitta in the Nuremberg Chronicle: *Register des Buchs der Croniken und Geschichten*, fol. 232r. On the standard dress of pilgrims, see Sumption, *The Age of Pilgrimage*, pp. 244–50.

234. Klockars suggests that this vision happened on October 9, the feast of St. Denis, and that Birgitta visited his reliquary at Saint-Denis; Klockars, "Giorni di festa e di lavoro nella vita di santa Brigida," p. 130.

235. See the map of the pilgrimage routes in Reilly, "Santiago de Compostela," p. 734, and charts of the routes in Shaver-Crandell and Gerson, *The Pilgrim's Guide to Santiago de Compostela*, pp. 418–20.

236. *Den heliga Birgittas Reuelaciones extrauagantes*, ch. 92, pp. 216–17. *Extravagant Revelations*, in *Revelations*, vol. 4, p. 305. The text stresses the continuing relationship between Birgitta and her patron. The canonization records confirm this vision; Collijn, *Acta et processus*, pp. 482 and 618.

237. Morris, *St Birgitta*, p. 60.

238. Stevens and Cawley, *The Towneley Plays*, play 23, lines 405–7, p. 299.

239. *Revelations*, vol. 1, p. 317. *Revelaciones: Book III*, 3.29.14, p. 178. For concise expressions of this idea in earlier, Latin writings, see Sicard of Cremona, *Mitrale*, bk. 3, ch. 2 (PL 213:92); Honorius of Augustodunensis, *Gemma animae*, bk. 1, ch. 5 (PL 172:544); and Durandus, *The Symbolism of Churches*, ch. 1.38, p. 33; idem, *Rationale divinorum officiorum I–IV*, p. 23. That all three male authors use the word "sacrarium," in contrast to Birgitta's "templum," may suggest their greater focus on the literal aspect of the place where priests vest themselves for Mass.

240. I have already mentioned *Revelaciones: Book I*, 1.47.1, p. 382. (*Revelations*, vol. 1, p. 132.) See also *Revelaciones: Book IV*, 4.26.6, p. 132; and 4.38.13, p. 151. (*Revelations*, vol. 2, pp. 73 and 87.)

241. *Extravagant Revelations*, in *Revelations*, vol. 4, p. 286. *Reuelaciones extrauagantes*, 69.3, pp. 191–92.

242. Collijn, *Acta et processus*, p. 312.

243. Though also distantly in the shadow of Eve. *Regula Salvatoris*, ch. 23, p. 128. "Intextura" (weaving, embroidery) is mentioned in *Regula Salvatoris*, ch. 2, p. 105. *The Rule of the Savior*, in *Revelations*, vol. 4, pp. 126, 141. Although the Rule, in ch. 23, does not specify the type of manual labor with which the nuns are to occupy themselves, we know from other records that it involved needlework and other domestic manual labor; see Olsen, "Work and Work Ethics in the Nunnery of Syon Abbey," pp. 129–43.

244. *Revelations*, vol. 2, p. 210. *Relevaciones: Book IV*, 4.124.2, p. 332.

245. E.g., Augustine, *Confessionum libri XIII*, bk 1, ch. 14, p. 13.

246. *Sermo angelicus*, prologue, sect. 12, p. 76. *The Angel's Discourse*, p. 159.

247. *Revelations*, vol. 1, p. 132. *Revelaciones: Book I*, 1.47.1–2, p. 382. Cf. Lk. 5:36–9.

248. See, e.g., Evangelatou, "The Purple Thread of the Flesh"; and Zervou Tognazzi, *Teologia visiva*, pp. 93–95, 105.

249. According to Birgitta, when Mary beheld her son pierced with a lance, her face showed that "her soul was then being penetrated by the sharp sword of sorrow"; *Selected Revelations*, p. 190. *Revelations*, vol. 3, p. 237. *Revelaciones: Bok VII*, 7.15.31, pp. 167–68.

250. Birgitta "saw his mournful Mother lying on the earth, as if trembling and half-dead"; *Selected Revelations*, p. 189. *Revelations*, vol. 3, p. 235. *Revelaciones: Bok VII*, 7.15.13, p. 165. She attributes slightly more composure to the Virgin when she says that Mary wished to fall upon the ground; *Revelaciones: Bok VII*, 7.15.25, p. 167. *Selected Revelations*, p. 190. *Revelations*, vol. 3, p. 237.

251. Carleton Brown, *Religious Lyrics of the XVth Century*, p. 13.

252. Duffy, "Mater Dolorosa," p. 219. Sticca, *The Planctus Mariae*.

253. Dzon, "Birgitta of Sweden and Christ's Clothing," fig. 5.2. Cf. Mâle, *Religious Art in France: The Late Middle Ages*, pp. 119–20, fig. 69.

254. *Selected Revelations*, p. 190. *Revelations*, vol. 3, pp. 237–38. *Revelaciones: Bok VII*, 7.15.32, 34, p. 168. Cf. *Revelaciones: Bok VII*, 7.21.32 and 34, p. 168.

255. *Selected Revelations*, p. 299, n. 689. Serra argues that Luke himself had Jesus' infancy in mind when he described the winding of Jesus' corpse in burial garments; *Sapienza e contemplazione di Maria*, pp. 214–15. Cf. Gregory Nazianzen, "The Third Theological Oration," who remarks that Christ "was wrapped in swaddling cloths—but He took off the swathing bands of the grave by his rising again"; Nazianzen, "Select Orations of Saint Gregory Nazianzen," p. 308.

256. See, e.g., Gertsman, *The Dance of Death*, pp. 148–49, fig. 5-22, which reproduces an image of Death at a baby's cradle, in the Dance of Death at Meslay-le-Grenet (ca. 1500).

257. Bernardino of Siena, *S. Bernardini Senensis ordinis fratrum minorum opera omnia*, vol. 2, p. 268. Similar emphasis upon the baby Jesus' poverty is found in Ekbert of Schönau's *Sermo de vita et passione Jesu Christi* (Pseudo-Anselm, *Meditation* 9): "nor hadst Thou cradle to receive Thy frail and delicate frame; but Thou . . . wast laid, wrapt in rags, in the vile manger of a filthy cattle-shed"; p. 105; "Meditatio IX: De humanitate Christi," PL 158:750.

258. Kim, *The Gospel of Nicodemus*, p. 27. J. K. Elliott, *The Apocryphal New Testament*, p. 178.

259. *Revelations*, vol. 1, pp. 239–42. *Revelaciones: Book II*, 2.26, pp. 109–12. Batt, Renevey, and Whitehead, "Domesticity and Medieval Devotional Literature," pp. 232–33.

260. For artistic parallels, see Schiller, *Iconography of Christian Art*, vol. 1, pp. 169–75. See also Hill, "The Baby on the Stone."

261. The metaphor of the "leaps of Christ," which relies on Christological interpretations of Cant. 2:8 as well as Wis. 18:14–15, expresses the idea that the Son of God leapt down to earth, into the manger, then onto the cross, and lastly back up to heaven. As Twomey points out, the "allegorical topos of Christ's 'leaps' . . . was a way of highlighting the important moments of his earthly existence, skipping over (so to speak) his ministry and focusing instead on . . . the central events of the Incarnation and Redemption"; Twomey, "Christ's Leap and Mary's Clean Catch," pp. 167–68. On the related image of Jesus running the race of life (cf. Ps. 18:6), see Dzon, " 'Bold in His Barnhoed.' "

## CHAPTER 5. CONCLUSION: THE YEARNING OF THE QUEST

1. Origen, *Origen: Homilies on Luke*, homily 19, p. 81. Idem, *Die Homilien zu Lukas*, p. 115.

2. "Sermo 51: Feria Secunda post Dominicam Olivarum," in *S. Bernardini Senensis ordinis fratrum minorum opera omnia*, vol. 2, pp. 148–52. The Latin edition reads *amororissimus*, which I have corrected to *amorosissimus*. For an extensive allegorical treatment of Christ's journey to and life on earth as a pilgrimage, see Guillaume de Deguileville's fourteenth-century *Le pelerinage de Jhesucrist*. See also Amblard, *La vie de Jésus*.

3. "Sermo 51," in *S. Bernardini Senensis ordinis fratrum minorum opera omnia*, vol. 2, p. 149.

4. In his treatise *De miseria condicionis humane*, Lotario di Segni expresses the common view that a baby's cry is an expression of "sorrow or great pain." While males cry "Ah," females cry "E." Both are born of Eva, whose name thus signifies dual sorrow; Lotario di Segni, *De miseria condicionis humane*, pp. 102, 288. William of Conches explains scientifically why new-

borns feel pain: "because the child has been fed in heat and moisture, while the earth into which it comes is cold and dry, it senses the contrast and lets out a wailing cry"; William of Conches, *A Dialogue of Natural Philosophy*, p. 141. See also Chapter 1, n. 21; Chapter 4, n. 63.

5. Thérèse of Lisieux, *J'entre dans la vie: Derniers entretiens*, pp. 138–39. Idem, *St. Therese of Lisieux: Her Last Conversations*, p. 159. On Thérèse of Lisieux's "spiritual childhood," see Chapter 1, n. 94.

# WORKS CITED

## MANUSCRIPTS CITED

Cambridge, Fitzwilliam Museum, MS 183
Chantilly, Musée Condé, MS 35
Florence, Biblioteca Medicea Laurenziana, Gaddi 208
    Plut. 25.3
The Hague, Koninklijke Bibliotheek, 75 G 70
Hereford, Hereford Cathedral Library, O.3.9
London, British Library, Add. 27336
    Add. 29434
    Add. 31042 (London Thornton Manuscript)
    Add. 32248
    Add. 47682
    Arundel 404
    Harley 331
    Harley 2399
    Harley 3954
Milan, Biblioteca Ambrosiana, SP II 64
Minneapolis, University of Minnesota, MS Z822 N81
New York, The Pierpont Morgan Library, MS M.766
    MS M.917 (Hours of Catherine of Cleves)
    MS M.945 (Hours of Catherine of Cleves)
Notre Dame, University of Notre Dame, Snite Museum of Art, 85.25
Oxford, Balliol College, MS 149
Oxford, Bodleian Library, Canon. Ital. 174
    Canon. Ital. 280
    Canon. Misc. 476
    Eng. Poet.a.1 (Vernon Manuscript)
    Laud Misc. 108
    Rawlinson C. 41
    Selden Supra 38
Oxford, Corpus Christi College, MS 410
Oxford, Merton College, MS 13 (A. 1. 1)
Oxford, The Queen's College, MS 348

Paris, Bibliothèque nationale de France, fr. 992
    fr. 1533
    ital. 115
    lat. 2688
    lat. 9471 (Rohan Hours)
    lat. 11867
St. Gallen, Kantonsbibliothek Vadiana, VadSlg MS 343d
Vatican City, Biblioteca Apostolica Vaticana, MS Vat. lat. 4578
Venice, Biblioteca Nazionale Marciana, cod. lat. cl. III, 111 (*Missale Sancti Marci*)

## PRIMARY SOURCES

*The Acts of the Process of Canonization of Clare of Assisi*. In *The Lady: Clare of Assisi: Early Documents*, edited and translated by Regis J. Armstrong, 141–96. Hyde Park, N.Y.: New City Press, 2006.

Adam of Eynsham. *Magna vita Sancti Hugonis: The Life of St Hugh of Lincoln*. Edited and translated by Decima L. Douie and David Hugh Farmer. Vol. 1. Oxford: Clarendon Press, 1985.

Adam of Saint-Victor. *Liriche sacre*. Edited by Giuseppe Vecchi. Bologna: Forni Editore, 1953.

Adomnán. "The Holy Places." In *Jerusalem Pilgrims before the Crusades*, translated by John Wilkinson, 167–206. Rev. ed. Warminster: Aris & Phillips, 2002.

———. *De locis sanctis*. Edited by L. Bieler. In *Itineraria et alia geographica*, CCSL 175, 183–234. Turnhout: Brepols, 1965.

Aelred of Rievaulx. *Aelred of Rievaulx: Treatises & Pastoral Prayer*. Introduction by David Knowles. CF 2. Kalamazoo, Mich.: Cistercian Publications, 1995.

———. *De Iesu puero duodenni*. Edited by A. Hoste. In *Opera ascetica*, edited by Hoste and Talbot, 249–78.

———. *De institutione inclusarum*. Edited by C. H. Talbot. In *Opera ascetica*, edited by Hoste and Talbot, 637–82.

———. "Jesus at the Age of Twelve." Translated by Theodore Berkeley. In *Aelred of Rievaulx: Treatises & Pastoral Prayer*, introduction by David Knowles, 1–39.

———. *The Liturgical Sermons: The First Clairvaux Collection: Sermons One–Twenty Eight*. Translated by Theodore Berkeley and M. Basil Pennington. CF 58. Kalamazoo, Mich.: Cistercian Publications, 2001.

———. *The Mirror of Charity*. Translated by Elizabeth Connor. Introduction by Charles Dumont. CF 17. Kalamazoo, Mich., Cistercian Publications, 1990.

———. *Opera omnia: Opera ascetica*. Edited by A. Hoste and C. H. Talbot. CCCM 1. Turnhout: Brepols, 1971.

———. *Opera omnia: Sermones I–XLVI*. Edited by Gaetano Raciti. CCCM 2A. Turnhout: Brepols, 1989.

———. *Quand Jésus eut douze ans*. Edited by Anselme Hoste, translated by Joseph Dubois. SC 60. Paris: Cerf, 2005.

———. "Rule of Life for a Recluse." Translated by Mary Paul Macpherson. In *Aelred of Rievaulx: Treatises & Pastoral Prayer*, introduction by Knowles, 41–102.

————. *De speculo caritatis*. Edited by C. H. Talbot. In *Opera ascetica*, edited by Hoste and Talbot, 3–161.

————. *De spiritali amicitia*. Edited by A. Hoste. In *Opera ascetica*, edited by Hoste and Talbot, 287–350.

————. *Spiritual Friendship*. Edited by Marsha L. Dutton. Translated by Lawrence C. Braceland. CF 5. Collegeville, Minn.: Liturgical Press, 2010.

————. *La Vie de recluse; La Prière pastorale*. Edited and translated by Charles Dumont. SC 76. Paris: Cerf, 1961.

Albertus Magnus. *In evangelium Joannis*. Vol. 24 of *Opera omnia*. Edited by Auguste Borgnet and Émile Borgnet. Paris: L. Vivès, 1890.

Aldhelm. *Carmina ecclesiastica*. Translated by Michael Lapidge. In *Aldhelm: The Poetic Works*, translated by Michael Lapidge and James L. Rosier, with an appendix by Neil Wright, 46–58. Cambridge: D. S. Brewer, 1985.

————. *Carmina ecclesiastica*. In *Aldhelmi opera*, edited by R. Ehwald, MGH, Auctores Antiquissimi 15, 11–32. Berlin: Weidmann, 1919. Reprint, Munich, 1984.

Alexander of Ashby. *Meditaciones*. Edited by Thomas H. Bestul. In *Opera omnia. Pars 1: Opera theologica*, edited by Thomas H. Bestul and Franco Morenzoni, CCCM 188, 403–51. Turnhout: Brepols, 2004.

Alexander of Hales. *Summa theologica*. Vol. 2. Quaracchi, 1928.

Alighieri, Dante. *The Banquet of Dante Alighieri*. Translated by Elizabeth Price Sayer. London: G. Routledge & Sons, 1887.

————. *Il Convivio*. Edited by Fredi Chiappelli and Enrico Fenzi. In vol. 2 of *Opere Minori di Dante Alighieri*, 65–322. Turin: Unione Tipografico-Editrice Torinese, 1986.

————. *Purgatorio*. Translated by Jean Hollander and Robert Hollander. New York: Anchor Books, 2003.

Amblard, Paule, trans. *La vie de Jésus selon Guillaume de Digulleville, moine du XIV<sup>e</sup> siècle: ouvrage réalisé à partir du manuscrit 1130 de la Bibliothèque Sainte-Geneviève*. Paris: Le Pommier, 1999.

Ambrose. *Expositio evangelii secundum Lucam*. In *Opera, Pars IV*, edited by M. Adriaen, CCSL 14, 1–400. Turnhout: Brepols, 1957.

Angela of Foligno. *Angela of Foligno: Complete Works*. Translated by Paul Lachance. Mahwah, N.J.: Paulist Press, 1993.

————. *Il "Liber" della Beata Angela da Foligno: edizione in fac simile e trascrizione del ms. 342 Biblioteca Comunale di Assisi, con quattro studi*. Edited by Enrico Menestò. Spoleto: Fondazione Centro Italiano di Studi sull'alto Medioevo, 2009.

*Anonymous of Perugia*. In FAED, vol. 2: *The Founder*, 34–58.

*Anonymus Perusinus*. In FF, 1311–51.

Anselm of Canterbury. *Opera Omnia*. Vol. 3: *Orationes sive Meditationes necnon Epistolarum Librum Primum*. Edited by F. S. Schmitt. Edinburgh: Thomas Nelson & Sons, 1946.

————. *The Prayers and Meditations of Saint Anselm*. Translated by Sr. Benedicta Ward. Foreward by R. W. Southern. London: Penguin, 1973.

Anthony of Padua. *Sermones Festivi, Indices*. Vol. 3 of *Sermones Dominicales et Festivi*. Edited by Beniamino Costa et al. Padua: Edizioni Messaggero, 1979.

————. *Sermons for Festivals and Indexes*. Vol. 4 of *Sermons for Sundays and Festivals*. Translated by Paul Spilsbury. Padua: Edizioni Messaggero, 2010.

Antoninus of Florence. *Summa theologica*. Vol. 3. Verona, 1740. Reprint, Graz: Akademische Druck - u. Verlagsanstalt, 1959.

Aquinas, Thomas. *Catena Aurea: Commentary on the Four Gospels*. Translation by Mark Pattison. Vol. 1: St. Matthew. 1841. Reprint, London: Baronius Press, 2009.

——. *Catena aurea in quatuor evangelia*. Edited by Angelico Guarienti. Vol. 1: *Expositio in Matthaeum et Marcum*. New ed. Turin: Marietti, 1953.

——. *Commentary on the Epistle to the Hebrews*. Translated by Chrysostom Baer. Preface by Ralph McInerny. South Bend, Ind.: St. Augustine's Press, 2006.

——. *Compendium of Theology by Thomas Aquinas*. Translated by Richard J. Regan. Oxford: Oxford University Press, 2009.

——. *Compendium theologiae*. In *Opera omnia*, vol. 42, 75–205. Rome, 1979.

——. *In decem libros ethicorum Aristotelis ad Nichomachum expositio*. Edited by Raymund M. Spiazzi. Turin: Marietti, 1949.

——. *St. Thomas Aquinas: Summa Theologica*. Translated by the Fathers of the English Dominican Province. Vols. 4 and 5. New York: Benziger Bros., 1948. Reprint, Notre Dame, Ind.: Christian Classics, 1981.

——. *Summa theologiae*. Vol. 3: *Secunda secundae*, and vol. 4: *Tertia pars*. Ottawa: Commisio Piana, 1953.

——. *Super epistolas s. Pauli lectura*. Edited by R. Cai. Vol. 2. 8th, revised ed. Turin: Marietti, 1953.

——. *Super evangelium s. Ioannis lectura*. Edited by R. Cai. Vol. 2. 7th ed. Turin: Marietti, 1952.

Armstrong, Regis J., ed. and trans. *The Lady: Clare of Assisi: Early Documents*. Hyde Park, N.Y.: New City Press, 2006.

Arnobius of Sicca. *The Case against the Pagans (Adversus Nationes)*. Translated by George E. McCracken. Vol. 1. Ancient Christian Writers 7. New York: Newman Press, 1949.

Arnold of Bonneval. *Tractatus de septem verbis domini in cruce*. PL 189:1677–726.

Aronson-Lehavi, Sharon, trans. "*A Treatise of Miraclis Playing*: A Modern Version of *A Tretise of Miraclis Pleyinge*" (Appendix). In *Street Scenes: Late Medieval Acting and Performance*, 127–44. New York: Palgrave, 2011.

*Assisi Compilation*. In FAED: vol. 2: *The Founder*, 118–230.

Augustine of Hippo. *On Christian Teaching*. Translated by R. P. H. Green. Oxford: Oxford University Press, 1997.

——. *De civitate Dei: Libri I–X*. Edited by Bernard Dombart and Alphonsus Kalb. CCSL 47. Turnhout: Brepols, 1955.

——. *De civitate Dei: Libri XI–XXII*. Edited by Bernard Dombart and Alphonsus Kalb. CCSL 48. Turnhout: Brepols, 1955.

——. *Concerning the City of God against the Pagans*. Translated by Henry Bettenson. With a new introduction by G. R. Evans. London: Penguin, 2003.

——. *Confessionum libri XIII*. Edited by L. Verheijen. CCSL 27. Turnhout: Brepols, 1981.

——. "Epistula 135"; "Epistula 137." In *Epistulae: Pars III*, edited by Alois Goldbacher, CSEL 44, 89–92, 96–125. Vienna: F. Tempsky, 1904.

——. *Homilies on the Gospel of John 1–40*. Edited by Allan D. Fitzgerald. Translated by Edmund Hill. The Works of Saint Augustine III/12. Hyde Park, N.Y.: New City Press, 2009.

——. *In Iohannis evangelium tractatus CXXIV*. Edited by R. Willems. CCSL 36. Turnhout: Brepols, 1954.

———. "Letter 135"; "Letter 137." In *Letters 100–150*, edited by Boniface Ramsey, translated by Roland J. Teske, 208–9, 212–24. The Works of Saint Augustine II/2. Hyde Park, N.Y.: New City Press, 2003.

———. *De peccatorum meritis et remissione et de baptismo parvulorum ad Marcellinum libri tres*. In *Opera (Sect. VIII, Pars I)*, edited by C. F. Urba and J. Zycha, CSEL 60, 1–151. Vienna: F. Tempsky, 1913.

———. "The Punishment and Forgiveness of Sins and the Baptism of Little Ones." In *Answer to the Pelagians, I*. Translated by Roland J. Teske, 34–137. The Works of Saint Augustine I/23. Hyde Park, N.Y.: New City Press, 1997.

———. *Sermons for Christmas and Epiphany*. Translated by Thomas Comerford Lawler. Ancient Christian Writers 15. New York: Newman Press, 1952.

———. *Sermones 189–90, 196 (In Natali Domini, VI, VII, XIII)*. PL 38:1006–9, 1019–20.

Avicenna. *A Treatise on the Canon of Medicine*. Translated by O. Cameron Gruner. New York: AMS Press, 1973.

Balbi, Giovanni. *Catholicon*. Mainz, 1460. Reprint, Westmead: Gregg International, 1971.

Barber, Richard, trans. *Bestiary: Being an English Version of the Bodleian Library, Oxford M.S. Bodley 764*. Woodbridge: Boydell Press, 1992.

Bartholomaeus Anglicus. *De rerum proprietatibus*. Frankfurt, 1601. Reprint, Frankfurt am Main: Minerva, 1964.

Bartholomew of Pisa. *De vita et laudibus B. Mariae Virginis libri sex*. Venice, 1596.

Bartholomew of Trent. *Liber epilogorum in gesta sanctorum*. Edited by Emore Paoli. Florence: SISMEL, 2001.

Beadle, Richard, ed. *The York Plays: A Critical Edition of the York Corpus Christi Play as Recorded in British Library Additional MS 35290*. Vol. 1. EETS s.s. 23. Oxford: Oxford University Press, 2009.

Bede. "Bedae Vita Sancti Cuthberti." In *Two Lives of Saint Cuthbert*, edited and translated by Bertram Colgrave, 141–307. Cambridge: Cambridge University Press, 1940.

———. *Bede the Venerable: Homilies on the Gospels: Book One*. Translated by Lawrence T. Martin and David Hurst. CS 110. Kalamazoo, Mich.: Cistercian Publications, 1991.

———. *Homeliarum evangelii libri II*. In *Bedae opera: Pars III: Opera homiletica; Pars IV: Opera rhythmica*. Edited by D. Hurst. CCSL 122. Turnhout: Brepols, 1955.

Benedict of Nursia. *La Règle de Saint Benoît*. Edited by Jean Neufville. Translated by Adalbert de Vogüé. Vol. 2. SC 182. Paris: Cerf, 1972.

Berengario di Donadio. *Life of Saint Clare of Montefalco*. Edited by John E. Rotelle. Translated by Matthew J. O'Connell. Augustinian Series 9. Villanova, Pa.: Augustinian Press, 1999.

———. "Vita di Santa Chiara da Montefalco scritta da Berengario di S. Africano." Edited by Michele Faloci-Pulignani. *Archivio Storico per le Marche e per l'Umbria* 1 (1884): 557–625; 2 (1885): 193–266.

Berger, David, ed. *The Jewish-Christian Debate in the High Middle Ages: A Critical Edition of the Nizzahon Vetus*. Philadelphia: Jewish Publication Society of America, 1979.

Bernard of Clairvaux. *Apologia ad Guillelmum Abbatem*. In *Tractatus et opuscula*, edited by J. Leclercq and H. M. Rochais, vol. 3 of *S. Bernardi opera*, 81–108. Rome: Editiones Cistercienses, 1963.

———. *Bernard of Clairvaux on the Song of Songs, II*. Translated by Killian Walsh and Jean Leclercq. CF 7. Kalamazoo, Mich.: Cistercian Publications, 1983.

——. *Cistercians and Cluniacs: St Bernard's* Apologia *to Abbot William*. Translated by Michael Casey. Introduction by Jean Leclercq. CF 1. Kalamazoo, Mich.: Cistercian Publications, 1991.

——. *De moribus et officio episcoporum* (Epistola 42). In *Epistolae I. Corpus epistolarum 1–180*, edited by J. Leclercq and H. Rochais. Vol. 7 of *Sancti Bernardi opera*, 100–131. Rome: Editiones Cistercienses, 1974.

——. *Homilies in Praise of the Blessed Virgin Mary*. Translated by Marie-Bernard Saïd. Introduction by Chrysogonus Waddell. CF 18A. Kalamazoo, Mich.: Cistercian Publications, 1993.

——. *In laudibus virginis matris*. In *Sermones I*, edited by J. Leclercq and H. Rochais, 13–58.

——. *In Praise of the New Knighthood*. Translated by M. Conrad Greenia. Introduction by Malcolm Barber. CF 19B. Kalamazoo, Mich.: Cistercian Publications, 2000.

——. "In Vigilia Nativitatis, Sermo Tertius"; "In Nativitate, Sermo Tertius"; "In Epiphania, Sermo I"; "In Epiphania, Sermo III." In *Sermones I*, edited by J. Leclercq and H. Rochais, 211–19, 257–62, 291–300, 304–09.

——. *Liber ad milites de laude novae militiae*. In *Tractatus et opuscula*, edited by J. Leclercq and H. M. Rochais, 213–39. Rome: Editiones Cistercienses, 1963.

——. *On the Conduct and Office of Bishops*. In *Bernard of Clairvaux: On Baptism and the Office of Bishops*, translated by Pauline Matarasso, introductions by Martha G. Newman and Emero Stiegman, CF 67, 37–82. Kalamazoo, Mich.: Cistercian Publications, 2004.

——. *Sermones I*. Edited by J. Leclercq and H. Rochais. Vol. 4 of *Sancti Bernardi opera*. Rome: Editiones Cistercienses, 1966.

——. *Sermones super Cantica Canticorum 36–86*. Edited by J. Leclercq et al. Vol. 2 of *Sancti Bernardi opera*. Rome: Editiones Cistercienses, 1958.

——. *Sermons for Advent and the Christmas Season*. Edited by John Leinenweber. Translated by Irene Edmonds, Wendy M. Beckett, and Conrad Greenia. Introduction by Wim Verbaal. CF 51. Kalamazoo, Mich.: Cistercian Publications, 2007.

Bernardino of Siena. *S. Bernardini Senensis ordinis fratrum minorum opera omnia*. Vol. 2. Quaracchi, 1950.

Bertrand, Guy-M., ed. "Un office du XIIIᵉ siècle en l'honneur de Saint Joseph (Abbaye Saint-Laurent de Liège)." *Cahiers de Joséphologie* 2.1 (1954): 159–70; 289–322.

Bertrand of Pontigny. *Vita S. Edmundi Cantuariensis archiepiscopi et confessoris*. In *Thesaurus novus anecdotorum*, edited by E. Martène and U. Durand, vol. 3, cols. 1775–826. Paris: Delaulne, 1717.

Bevington, David, ed. and trans. *Medieval Drama*. Boston: Houghton Mifflin, 1975.

Beyers, Rita, ed. *Libellus de nativitate sanctae Mariae*. Vol. 2 of *Libri de nativitate Mariae*, CCSA 10. Turnhout: Brepols, 1997.

Birgitta of Sweden. *Birgitta of Sweden: Life and Selected Revelations*. Edited by Marguerite Tjader Harris. Translated by Albert Ryle Kezel. Introduction by Tore Nyberg. Mahwah, N.J.: Paulist Press, 1990.

——. *Den heliga Birgittas Reuelaciones extrauagantes*. Edited by Lennart Hollman. SFSS, ser. 2, Latinska skrifter 5. Uppsala: Almqvist & Wiksell, 1956.

——. *The Revelations of St. Birgitta of Sweden*. Vol. 1: *Liber Caelestis, Books I–III*. Translated by Denis Searby. Introduction and notes by Bridget Morris. Oxford: Oxford University Press, 2006.

————. *The Revelations of St. Birgitta of Sweden.* Vol. 2: *Liber Caelestis, Books IV–V.* Translated by Denis Searby. Introduction and notes by Bridget Morris. Oxford: Oxford University Press, 2008.

————. *The Revelations of St. Birgitta of Sweden.* Vol. 3: *Liber Caelestis, Books VI–VII.* Translated by Denis Searby. Introduction and notes by Bridget Morris. Oxford: Oxford University Press, 2012.

————. *The Revelations of St. Birgitta of Sweden.* Vol. 4: *The Heavenly Emperor's Book to Kings, The Rule, and Minor Works.* Translated by Denis Searby. Introduction and notes by Bridget Morris. Oxford: Oxford University Press, 2015. (*The Rule of the Savior*, 123–47; *The Angel's Discourse*, 159–91; *The Four Prayers*, 205–14; *Extravagant Revelations*, 229–317.)

————. *Sancta Birgitta: Opera minora I: Regula Salvatoris.* Edited by Sten Eklund. SFSS, ser. 2, Latinska skrifter 8:1. Stockholm: Almqvist & Wiksell, 1975.

————. *Sancta Birgitta: Opera minora II: Sermo angelicus.* Edited by Sten Eklund. SFSS, ser. 2, Latinska skrifter 8:2. Uppsala: Almqvist & Wiksell, 1972.

————. *Sancta Birgitta: Opera minora III: Quattuor oraciones.* Edited by Sten Eklund. SFSS, ser. 2, Latinska skrifter 8:3. Stockholm: Almqvist & Wiksell, 1991.

————. *Sancta Birgitta: Revelaciones: Book I.* Edited by Carl-Gustaf Undhagen. SFSS, ser. 2, Latinska skrifter 7:1. Stockholm: Almqvist & Wiksell, 1977.

————. *Sancta Birgitta: Revelaciones: Book II.* Edited by Carl-Gustaf Undhagen and Birger Bergh. SFSS, ser. 2, Latinska skrifter 7:2. Uppsala: Almqvist & Wiksell, 2001.

————. *Sancta Birgitta: Revelaciones: Book III.* Edited by Ann-Mari Jönsson. SFSS, ser. 2, Latinska skrifter 7:3. Stockholm: Almqvist & Wiksell, 1998.

————. *Sancta Birgitta: Revelaciones: Book IV.* Edited by Hans Aili. SFSS, ser. 2, Latinska skrifter 7:4. Stockholm: Almqvist & Wiksell, 1992.

————. *Sancta Birgitta: Revelaciones: Book V: Liber questionum.* Edited by Birger Bergh. SFSS, ser. 2, Latinska skrifter 7:5. Uppsala: Almqvist & Wiksell, 1971.

————. *Sancta Birgitta: Revelaciones: Book VI.* Edited by Birger Bergh. SFSS, ser. 2, Latinska skrifter 7:6. Stockholm: Almqvist & Wiksell, 1991.

————. *Den Heliga Birgittas Revelaciones: Bok VII.* Edited by Birger Bergh. SFSS, ser. 2, Latinska skrifter 7:7. Uppsala: Almqvist & Wiksell, 1967.

Blangez, Gérard, ed. *Ci nous dit: Recueil d'exemples moraux.* 2 vols. Paris: Société des Anciens Textes Français, 1979–1986.

Blunt, J. H., ed. *The Myroure of oure Ladye.* EETS e.s. 19. London: N. Trübner & Co., 1873.

Boccaccio, Giovanni. *The Decameron.* Edited by Jonathan Usher. Translated by Guido Waldman. Oxford: Oxford University Press, 2008.

Boethius. *Philosophiae consolatio.* Edited by L. Bieler. CCSL 94. Turnhout: Brepols, 1957.

Bonaventure. *Apologia pauperum.* In *Opera omnia*, vol. 8, 233–330.

————. *Bringing Forth Christ: Five Feasts of the Child Jesus.* Translated by Eric Doyle. Oxford: SLG Press, 1984.

————. *Commentarium in evangelium Lucae.* In *Opera omnia*, edited by the Collegium S. Bonaventurae. Vol. 7. Quaracchi, 1895.

————. *Commentary on the Gospel of Luke: Chapters 17–24.* Translated by Robert J. Karris. Vol. 8.3 of *Works of St. Bonaventure.* St. Bonaventure, N.Y.: Franciscan Institute Publications, 2004.

————. *Defense of the Mendicants.* Vol. 15 of *Works of St. Bonaventure.* Translated by José de Vinck and Robert J. Karris. St. Bonaventure, N.Y.: Franciscan Institute Publications, 2010.

———. *Itinerarium mentis in Deum*. Translated by Zachary Hayes. Commentary by Philotheus Boehner. Vol. 2 of *Works of St. Bonaventure*. St. Bonaventure, N.Y.: Franciscan Institute Publications, 2002.

———. *Legenda major*. In FF, 777–961.

———. *Lignum vitae*. In *Opera omnia*, vol. 8, 68–87.

———. *The Major Legend of Saint Francis*. In FAED, vol. 2: *The Founder*, 525–683.

———. *The Mystical Vine*. In *Mystical Opuscula*, vol. 1 of *The Works of Bonaventure*, translated by José de Vinck, 147–205. Paterson, N.J.: St. Anthony Guild Press, 1960.

———. *On the Perfection of Life Addressed to the Sisters*. Translated by Girard Etzkorn. In *Writings on the Spiritual Life*, introduction and notes by F. Edward Coughlin. Vol. 10 of *Works of St. Bonaventure*, 139–95. St. Bonaventure, N.Y.: Franciscan Institute Publications, 2006.

———. *Opuscula Varia ad Theologiam Mysticam*. Vol. 8 of *Opera omnia*. Edited by the Collegium S. Bonaventurae. Quaracchi, 1898.

———. *De perfectione vitae ad sorores*. In *Opera omnia*, vol. 8, 107–27.

———. *De quinque festivitatibus pueri Jesu*. In *Opera omnia*, vol. 8, 88–98.

———. *Saint Bonaventure's Disputed Questions on the Knowledge of Christ*. Translated by Zachary Hayes. St. Bonaventure, N.Y.: Franciscan Institute, 1992.

———. "The Tree of Life." In *Bonaventure: The Soul's Journey into God; The Tree of Life; The Life of St. Francis*, translated by Ewert Cousins, 119–75. Mahwah, N.J.: Paulist Press, 1978.

———. *Vitis mystica*. In *Opera omnia*, vol. 8, 159–229.

Boulton, Maureen B. M., trans. "The Childhood of Jesus Christ (*Les Enfaunces Jesu Crist*)." In *Piety and Persecution in the French Texts of England*, The French of England Translation Series 6, 97–123. Tempe: Arizona Center for Medieval and Renaissance Studies, 2013.

———. ed. *Les Enfaunces de Jesu Crist*. Anglo-Norman Text Society 43. London: Anglo-Norman Text Society, 1985.

———. *The Old French Évangile de l'enfance*. Studies and Texts 70. Toronto: Pontifical Institute of Mediaeval Studies, 1984.

Bradwardine, Thomas. *De causa Dei contra Pelagium et de virtute causarum*. Edited by Henry Savile. London, 1618. Reprint, Frankfurt am Main: Minerva, 1964.

Bromyard, John. *Summa praedicantium*. Venice, 1586.

Brown, Carleton, ed. *Religious Lyrics of the XVth Century*. Oxford: Clarendon Press, 1939.

Brown, Michelle P., ed. *The Holkham Bible: A Facsimile*. London: British Library, 2007.

Bunt, G. H. V., ed. *William of Palerne: An Alliterative Romance*. Groningen: Bouma's Boekhuis, 1985.

Burke, Tony, ed. *De infantia Iesu euangelium Thomae graece*. CCSA 17. Turnhout: Brepols, 2011.

Caesarius of Heisterbach. *Dialogus miraculorum*. Introduction by Horst Schneider, translation and commentary by Nikolaus Nösges and Horst Schneider. Vol. 2. Fontes Christiani 86.2. Turnhout: Brepols, 2009.

———. *Dialogus miraculorum*. Introduction by Horst Schneider, translation and commentary by Nikolaus Nösges and Horst Schneider. Vol. 4. Fontes Christiani 86.4. Turnhout: Brepols, 2009.

———. *Die Wundergeschichten des Caesarius von Heisterbach*. Edited by Alfons Hilka. Bonn: Peter Hanstein, 1937.

Capgrave, John. *Abbreuiacion of Cronicles*. Edited by Peter J. Lucas. EETS o.s. 285. Oxford: Oxford University Press, 1983.

————. *The Life of St. Katharine of Alexandria by John Capgrave*. Edited by Carl Horstmann. Forward by F. J. Furnivall. EETS o.s. 100. London: Kegan Paul, Trench, Trübner & Co., 1893.

Cawley, Martinus, trans. *Ida the Eager of Louvain*. Lafayette, Oreg.: Guadalupe Translations, 2000.

Caxton, William. *The Mirror of the World*. Edited by Oliver H. Prior. EETS e.s. 110. 1913. Reprint, London: Oxford University Press, 1996.

————. *W. Caxtons Infantia Salvatoris*. Edited by Ferdinand Holthausen. Halle: Niemeyer, 1891.

Chaucer, Geoffrey. *The Riverside Chaucer*. Edited by Larry D. Benson. 3rd ed. Oxford: Oxford University Press, 1988.

Chrysostom, John. *In Joannem homiliae*. PG 59:23–482. (Homilia 17: 107–14; Homilia 21: 127–34; Homilia 85: 459–468.)

————. *Saint John Chrysostom: Commentary on Saint John the Apostle and Evangelist: Homilies 1–47*. Translated by Sister Thomas Aquinas Goggin. FC 33. New York: Fathers of the Church, 1957. (Homily 17: 161–73; Homily 21: 201–12.)

————. *Saint John Chrysostom: Commentary on Saint John the Apostle and Evangelist: Homilies 48–88*. Translated by Sister Thomas Aquinas Goggin. FC 41. Washington, D.C.: Catholic University of America Press, 1959. (Homily 85: 427–45.)

————. *Saint John Chrysostom: Discourses against Judaizing Christians*. Translated by Paul W. Harkins. FC 68. Washington, D.C.: Catholic University of America Press, 1979.

Cicero. *Tusculan Disputations II & V, with a Summary of III & IV*. Edited and translated by A. E. Douglas. Warminster: Aris & Phillips, 1990.

Clare of Assisi. *Clare's Letters to Agnes: Texts and Sources*. Translated by Joan Mueller. St. Bonaventure, N.Y.: Franciscan Institute, 2001.

————. "Epistola ad sanctam Agnetem de Praga I"; "Epistola ad sanctam Agnetem de Praga IV." In FF, 2263–66, 2281–84.

————. "First Letter to Agnes"; "Fourth Letter to Agnes." In *The Lady: Clare of Assisi: Early Documents*, edited by Armstrong, 43–46, 54–58.

————. "The Form of Life of Saint Clare." In *The Lady: Clare of Assisi: Early Documents*, edited by Armstrong, 108–26.

————. *Regula*. In FF, 2290–307.

Clayton, Mary, ed. and trans. *Old English Poems of Christ and His Saints*. Cambridge, Mass.: Harvard University Press, 2013.

Clementines. In *Corpus iuris canonici*, edited by Emil Friedberg and Aemilius Ludwig Richter, vol. 2, cols. 1131–200. 2nd ed. Leipzig: B. Tauchnitz, 1879. Reprint, Graz: Akademische Druck - u. Verlagsanstalt, 1959.

Collijn, Isak, ed. *Acta et processus canonizacionis beate Birgitte*. SFSS, ser. 2, Latinska skrifter 1. Uppsala: Almqvist & Wiksell, 1924–1931.

Collins, A. Jefferies, ed. *The Bridgettine Breviary of Syon Abbey: from the ms. with English rubrics F.4.ii. at Magdalene College, Cambridge*. Henry Bradshaw Society 96. Worcester: Stanbrook Abbey Press, 1969.

Comestor, Peter. *Historia scholastica*. PL 198:1049–1722.

*Compilatio Assisiensis*. In FF, 1471–690.

Conlee, John W., ed. "A Disputacioun betwyx þe Body and Wormes." In *Middle English Debate Poetry: A Critical Anthology*, 50–62. East Lansing, Mich.: Colleagues Press, 1991.

Damascene, John. "Exact Exposition of the Orthodox Faith." In *Saint John of Damascus: Writings*, translated by Frederic H. Chase, Jr., FC 37, 165–406. New York: Fathers of the Church, 1958.

———. *De fide orthodoxa*. Edited by Eligius M. Buytaert. St. Bonaventure, N.Y.: Franciscan Institute, 1955.

Damian, Peter. "Sermo in natale domini sub persona Ariminensis episcopi" (Sermo 61). In *Sermones*, edited by Giovanni Lucchesi, CCCM 57, 358–60. Turnhout: Brepols, 1983.

Daniel, Walter. *The Life of Ailred of Rievaulx by Walter Daniel*. Edited and translated by F. M. Powicke. Oxford: Clarendon Press, 1950.

Davidson, Clifford, ed. *A Tretise of Miraclis Pleyinge*. With commentary on the dialect by Paul A. Johnston, Jr. Kalamazoo, Mich.: Medieval Institute Publications, 1984.

Davis, Norman, ed. "The Play of the Sacrament." In *Non-Cycle Plays and Fragments*, 58–89. EETS s.s. 1. London: Oxford University Press, 1970.

Dawood, N. J., trans. *The Koran*. London: Penguin, 2014.

Degenhart, Bernard, and Annegrit Schmitt, eds. *Evangelica Historia. Disegni trecenteschi del MS. L.58.Sup. della Biblioteca Ambrosiana*. Nota illustrativa, trascrizione e tradizione dei testi di Angelo Paredi. 2 vols. Milan: Electa Editrice, 1978.

Deitch, Judith, ed. *"Ypotis*: A Middle English Dialogue." In *Medieval Literature for Children*, edited by Daniel T. Kline, 227–48. New York: Routledge, 2003.

Delorme, Ferdinand M., ed. *Meditatio pauperis in solitudine*. Ad Claras Aquas, Florence (Quaracchi): Collegium S. Bonaventurae, 1929.

D'Evelyn, Charlotte, and Anna J. Mills, eds. *South English Legendary*. Vol. 2. EETS o.s. 236. London: Oxford University Press, 1956.

Dimier-Paupert, Catherine, ed. *Livre de l'Enfance du Sauveur: une version médiévale de l'Évangile de l'Enfance du Pseudo-Matthieu (XIIIᵉ siècle)*. Paris: Cerf, 2006.

Dobschütz, Ernst von, ed. *Christusbilder: Untersuchungen zur christlichen Legende*. Leipzig: J. C. Hinrichs, 1899.

———. *Das Decretum Gelasianum: De libris recipiendis et non recipiendis*. Texte und Untersuchungen zur Geschichte der altchristlichen Literatur 38. Leipzig: J. C. Hinrichs, 1912.

Dominici, Giovanni. *Regola del governo di cura familiare*. Edited by Donato Salvi. Florence: A. Garinei, 1860.

Dondaine, A., ed. "La Hiérarchie cathare en Italie, I: Le 'De heresi catharorum in Lombardia.'" *Archivum Fratrum Praedicatorum* 29 (1949): 306–12.

Donnelly, Linda Marie Asfodel, ed. and trans. "The Anonymous Fairy-Knight Lays: 'Tydorel,' 'Tyolet,' 'Doon,' and 'Espine.'" Unpublished MA thesis, University of Alberta, 1998.

Dove, Mary, ed. *The Earliest Advocates of the English Bible: The Texts of the Medieval Debate*. Exeter: University of Exeter Press, 2010.

Durandus, William. *Rationale divinorum officiorum I–IV*. Edited by A. Davril and T. M. Thibodeau. CCSL 140. Turnhout: Brepols, 1995.

———. *The Symbolism of Churches and Church Ornaments: A Translation of the First Book of the* Rationale Divinorum Officiorum. Translated by John Mason Neale and Benjamin Webb. London, 1843. Reprint, New York: AMS Press, 1973.

Dzon, Mary, ed. *Middle English Poems on the Apocryphal Childhood of Jesus*. Forthcoming.

Ebner, Christina. *Der Nonne von Engelthal Büchlein von der Genaden Überlast.* Edited by Karl Schröder. Bibliothek des Litterarischen Vereins in Stuttgart 108. Tübingen: Litterarischer Verein in Stuttgart, 1871.

Ebner, Margaret. *Margaret Ebner: Major Works.* Translated by Leonard P. Hindsley. New York: Paulist Press, 1993.

Ehrman, Bart D., and Zlatko Pleše, eds. *The Apocryphal Gospels: Texts and Translations.* Oxford: Oxford University Press, 2011.

Ekbert of Schönau. "Ninth Meditation: Of the Humanity of Christ." In *St. Anselm's Book of Meditations and Prayers,* translated by M.R., 101–32. London: Burns and Oates, 1872.

———. "Sermo de vita et passione Jesu Christi" (=Pseudo-Anselm, "Meditatio IX: De humanitate Christi"). PL 158:748–61.

Elliott, J. K., trans. *The Apocryphal New Testament: A Collection of Apocryphal Christian Literature in an English Translation.* Oxford: Clarendon Press, 2005.

———. *A Synopsis of the Apocryphal Nativity and Infancy Narratives.* New Testament Studies and Tools 34. Leiden: Brill, 2006.

Erasmus. "Homily on the Child Jesus" (*Concio de puero Jesu*). In *Collected Works of Erasmus: Literary and Educational Writings.* Edited by Elaine Fantham and Erika Rummell. Vol. 7. Toronto: University of Toronto Press, 1989.

Étienne de Bourbon. *Anecdotes historiques, légendes et apologues, tirés du recueil inédit d'Étienne de Bourbon.* Edited by A. Lecoy de La Marche. Paris: Librairie Renouard, 1877.

———. *Tractatus de diversis materiis praedicabilibus, Secunda pars, De dono pietatis.* Edited by Jacques Berlioz, Denise Ogilvie-David, and Colette Ribaucourt. CCCM 124A. Turnhout: Brepols, 2015.

Evagrius of Antioch. *Vita Beati Antonii Abbatis.* PL 73:126–70.

Fabri, Felix. *Fratris Felix Evagatorium in Terrae Sanctae, Arabiae, et Egyptii Peregrinationem.* Edited by Konrad D. Hassler. Vol. 1. Bibliothek des Literarischen Vereins in Stuttgart 2. Stuttgart: Societas Literaria Stuttgardiensis, 1843.

———. *The Wanderings of Felix Fabri (Part I).* Edited by Aubrey Stewart. Palestine Pilgrims' Text Society 7. New York: AMS Press, 1971.

Felix. *Felix's Life of Saint Guthlac.* Edited and translated by Bertram Colgrave. Cambridge: Cambridge University Press, 1985.

Ferrer, Vincent. *A Christology from the Sermons of St. Vincent Ferrer.* Translated by S.M.C. London: Blackfriars, 1954.

Fortunatus, Venantius. "Pange, lingua." In *One Hundred Latin Hymns: Ambrose to Aquinas,* translated by Peter G. Walsh, with Christopher Husch, 96–101. Cambridge, Mass.: Harvard University Press, 2012.

Fowler, Roger R., ed. *The Southern Version of* Cursor Mundi. Vol. 2: *Lines 9229–12712.* Ottawa: University of Ottawa Press, 1990.

Francis of Assisi. "The Admonitions." In FAED, vol. 1: *The Saint,* 128–37.

———. "Admonitiones." In FF, 25–36.

———. "Canticle of the Creatures." In FAED, vol. 1: *The Saint,* 113–14.

———. "Canticum fratris solis." In FF, 39–41.

———. "The Earlier Rule." In FAED, vol. 1: *The Saint,* 63–86.

———. *Epistola ad fideles (Recensio posterior).* In FF, 79–86.

———. "Later Admonition and Exhortation." In FAED, vol. 1: *The Saint,* 45–51.

————. "The Office of the Passion." In FAED, vol. 1: *The Saint,* 139–57.

————. *Officium passionis domini.* In FF, 145–63.

————. *Regula non bullata.* In FF, 185–212.

Froehlich, Karlfried, and Margaret Gibson, intro. *Biblia Latina cum Glossa Ordinaria. Facsimile of Strassborg 1480/81.* Vol. 4. Turnhout: Brepols, 1992.

Furnivall, Frederick J., ed., *The Minor Poems of the Vernon MS.: Part II.* EETS o.s. 117. London: Kegan Paul, Trench, Trübner & Co., 1901.

Gaucher, Élisabeth, ed. and trans. *Robert le Diable.* Paris: H. Champion, 2006.

Gautier de Coincy. *Miracles de la Sainte Vierge.* Edited by A. Poquet. 1857. Reprint, Geneva: Slatkine, 1972.

Geoffrey of Monmouth. *The History of the Kings of Britain: An Edition and Translation of* De gestis Britonum (Historia regum Britanniae). Edited by Michael D. Reeve. Translated by Neil Wright. Woodbridge: Boydell Press, 2007.

Gerald of Wales. *Gemma ecclesiastica.* Edited by J. S. Brewer. Vol. 2 of *Giraldi Cambrensis Opera.* RS 21. London: Longman, Green, Longman, and Roberts, 1862.

————. *The History and Topography of Ireland.* Translated by John J. O'Meara. Harmondsworth: Penguin, 1982.

————. *Speculum ecclesiae.* Edited by J. S. Brewer. Vol. 4 of *Giraldi Cambrensis Opera.* RS 21. London: Longman & Co., 1873.

————. *Topographia hibernica, et Expugnatio hibernica.* Edited by James F. Dimock. Vol. 5 of *Giraldi Cambrensis Opera.* RS 21. London: Longmans, Green, Reader, and Dyer, 1867.

Gerard of Frachet. *Vitae fratrum ordinis praedicatorum.* Edited by Benedictus Maria Reichert. Monumenta Ordinis Fratrum Praedicatorum Historica 1. Leuven: E. Charpentier & J. Schoonjans, 1896.

Germanus (?). *Historia Ecclesiastica, et Mystica Contemplatio.* PG 98:383–454.

Gerson, Jean. "Considérations sur Saint Joseph." In *Œuvres complètes,* vol. 7: *L'Œuvre française (292–339),* edited by Palémon Glorieux, 63–94. Paris: Desclée, 1966.

————. "Jacob autem." In *Œuvres complètes,* vol. 5: *L'Œuvre oratoire,* edited by Palémon Glorieux, 344–62. Paris: Desclée, 1963.

————. "Josephina." In *Œuvres complètes,* vol. 4: *L'Œuvre poétique,* edited by Palémon Glorieux, 31–100. Paris: Desclée, 1962.

Gervase of Tilbury. *Otia Imperialia: Recreation for an Emperor.* Edited and translated by S. E. Banks and J. W. Binns. Oxford: Clarendon Press, 2002.

Giannini, Gabriele, and Marianne Gasperoni, eds. *Vangeli occitani dell'infanzia di Gesù, edizione critica della versioni I e II.* Bologna: Pàtron, 2006.

Gijsel, Jan, ed. *Pseudo-Matthaei Evangelium.* Vol. 1 of *Libri de nativitate Mariae,* CCSA 9. Turnhout: Brepols, 1997.

Gollancz, Sir Israel, ed. *Cleanness.* Translated by D. S. Brewer. Cambridge: D. S. Brewer, 1974.

Gordon, E. V., ed. *Pearl.* 1953. Reprint, Oxford: Clarendon Press, 1980.

Goswin of Bossut. "The Life of Arnulf, Lay Brother of Villers." In *Send Me God: The Lives of Ida the Compassionate of Nivelles, Nun of La Ramée, Arnuf, Lay Brother of Villers, and Abundus, Monk of Villers, by Goswin of Bossut,* translated by Martinus Cawley, preface by Barbara Newman, 125–98. University Park: Penn State University Press, 2003.

————. *Vita b. Arnulfi Villariensis.* In AASS, Junii VII (30), 558–79. Paris: V. Palmé, 1867.

Gounelle, Rémi, and Zbigniew Izydorczyk, trans. *L'Évangile de Nicodème, ou, Les Actes faits sous Ponce Pilate (recension latine A): suivi de La Lettre de Pilate à l'empereur Claude.* Apocryphes 9. Turnhout: Brepols, 1997.

Gower, John. *Mirour de l'Omme*. In *The Complete Works of John Gower*, edited by G. C. Macaulay, vol. 1: *The French Works*, 2–334. Oxford: Clarendon Press, 1899.

———. *Mirour de l'Omme (The Mirror of Mankind)*. Translated by William Burton Wilson. Revised by Nancy Wilson Van Baak. Forward by R. F. Yeager. East Lansing, Mich.: Colleagues Press, 1992.

Gratian. *Decretum*. Vol. 1 of *Corpus iuris canonici*. Rome, 1582.

———. *Decretum*. In *Corpus iuris canonici*, edited by Emil Friedberg and Aemelius Ludwig Richter. Vol. 1. 2nd ed. Leipzig: B. Tauchnitz, 1879. Reprint, Graz: Akademische Druck - u. Verlagsanstalt, 1959.

———. *Gratian: The Treatise on Laws (Decretum DD. 1–20) with the Ordinary Gloss*. Translated by Augustine Thompson and James Gordley. Washington, D.C.: Catholic University of America Press, 1993.

Greene, Richard Leighton, ed. *The Early English Carols*. 2nd ed. Oxford: Clarendon Press, 1977.

Gregory the Great. *Dialogues*. Vol. 2: *Livres I–III*. Edited by Adalbert de Vogüé. Translated by Paul Antin. SC 260. Paris: Cerf, 1979.

———. *Gregory the Great: Forty Gospel Homilies*. Translated by David Hurst. CS 123. Kalamazoo, Mich.: Cistercian Publications, 1990.

———. *Homiliae in Evangelia*. Edited by Raymond Étaix. CCSL 141. Turnhout: Brepols, 1999.

———. *Homiliae in Hiezechihelem prophetam*. Edited by Marcus Adriaen. CCSL 142. Turnhout: Brepols, 1971. ("Book 1, Homily 2": 17–31.)

———. *The Life of Saint Benedict*. Commentary by Adalbert de Vogüé. Translated by Hilary Costello and Eoin de Bhaldaithe. Petersham, Mass.: St. Bede's Publications, 1993.

———. *Moral Reflections on the Book of Job*. Vol. 1: *Preface and Books 1–5*. Translated by Brian Kerns. Introduction by Mark DelCogliano. CS 249. Collegeville, Minn.: Liturgical Press, 2014.

———. *Moralia in Iob: Libri I–X*. Edited by Marcus Adriaen. CCSL 143. Turnhout: Brepols, 1979.

———. *Moralia in Iob: Libri XXIII–XXXV*. Edited by Marcus Adriaen. CCSL 143B. Turnhout: Brepols, 1985.

———. *Pastoral Care*. Translated by Henry Davis. Ancient Christian Writers 11. Westminster, Md.: Newman Press, 1955.

———. *Règle pastorale*. Edited by Floribert Rommel. Translated by Charles Morel. Introduction by Bruno Judic. Vol. 2. SC 382. Paris: Cerf, 1992.

Gregory of Nyssa. "Address on Religious Instruction." In *Christology of the Later Fathers*, edited by Edward R. Hardy, in collaboration with Cyril C. Richardson, 268–325. The Library of Christian Classics 3. Philadelphia: Westminster Press, 1954.

Gregory of Tours. *The Glory of the Martyrs*. Translated by Raymond Van Dam. Liverpool: Liverpool University Press, 1988.

Grosseteste, Robert. "De sanguine Christi." In *Matthaei Parisiensis Chronica majora*, edited by Henry Richards Luard, vol. 6: *Additamenta*, no. 72, 138–44. RS 57. London: Longman, 1882.

Guerric of Igny. *Guerric d'Igny: Sermons*. Vol. 1. Edited by John Morson and Hilary Costello. Translated by Placide Deseille. SC 166. Paris: Cerf, 1970.

———. *Liturgical Sermons: Book I*. Translated by the Monks of Mount Saint Bernard Abbey. CF 8. Kalamazoo, Mich.: Cistercian Publications, 1970.

Guillaume de Deguileville. *Le pelerinage de Jhesucrist de Guillaume de Deguileville.* Ed. J. J. Stürzinger. London: Nichols & Sons, 1897.

Guillaume de Lorris and Jean de Meun. *Le Roman de la rose.* Edited by Félix Lecoy. Vol. 3. Paris: Champion, 1970.

———. *The Romance of the Rose.* Translated by Frances Horgan. Oxford: Oxford University Press 1994.

Haleem, M. A. S. Abel, trans. *The Qur'an.* Oxford: Oxford University Press, 2004.

Hassall, W. O., ed. *The Holkham Bible Picture Book.* London: Dropmore Press, 1954.

Heffernan, Thomas J., ed. *The Passion of Perpetua and Felicity.* Oxford: Oxford University Press, 2012.

Henry of Lancaster. *Henry of Grosmont, First Duke of Lancaster,* Le Livre de Seyntz Medicines*: The Book of Holy Medicines.* Translated by Catherine Batt. The French of England Series 8. Tempe: Arizona Center for Medieval and Renaissance Studies, 2014.

———. *Le Livre de Seyntz Medicines: The Unpublished Devotional Treatise of Henry of Lancaster.* Edited by E. J. Arnould. Anglo-Norman Texts 2. Oxford: Blackwell, 1940.

Herman of Valenciennes. *La Bible von Herman de Valenciennes: Teil II (Von Josephs Ankunft in Ägypten bis zum Schluss des Alten Testamentes).* Edited by Otto Moldenhauer. Greifswald: H. Adler, 1914.

Hilary of Poitiers. *De trinitate: Praefatio, libri I–VII. Opera: Pars II, 1.* Edited by P. Smulders. CCSL 62. Turnhout: Brepols, 1979.

Hildegard of Bingen. "Berliner Fragment: Codex Berolin. Lat. Qu. 674." In *Physica: Liber subtilitatum diversarum naturarum creaturarum: Textkritische Ausgabe,* edited by Reiner Hildebrant and Thomas Gloning, 407–31. Berlin: Walter de Gruyter, 2010.

———. *Scivias.* Edited by A. Führkötter and A. Carlevaris. CCCM 43A. Turnhout: Brepols, 1978.

Hock, Ronald F., ed. and trans. *The Infancy Gospels of James and Thomas.* The Scholars Bible 2. Santa Rosa, Calif.: Polebridge Press, 1995.

*The Holy Bible Douay-Rheims.* 1899. Reprint, Rockford, Ill.: Tan Books, 1971.

Honorius of Augustodunensis. *Gemma animae.* PL 172:542–738.

Horace. *Horace: Satires, Epistles and Ars Poetica.* Edited and translated by H. Rushton Fairclough. Cambridge, Mass.: Harvard University Press/William Heinemann, 1942.

Horrall, Sarah, ed. *The Southern Version of* Cursor Mundi. Vol. 1: *Lines 1–9228.* Ottawa: University of Ottawa Press, 1978.

Horstmann, Carl, ed. "Kindheit Jesu." In *Altenglische Legenden: Kindheit Jesu, Geburt Jesu, Barlaam und Josaphat, St. Patrik's Fegefeuer,* 3–61. Paderborn: Ferdinand Schöningh, 1875.

———, ed. "Kindheit Jesu." In *Sammlung altenglischer Legenden,* 101–23. Heilbronn: Gebr. Henniger, 1878.

———, ed. "Nachträge zu den Legenden." *Archiv für das Studium der neueren Sprachen und Literaturen* 74 (1885): 327–39.

Hrotsvitha of Gandersheim. *Hrotsvit: Opera Omnia.* Edited by Walter Berschin. Munich: K. G. Saur, 2001.

Hudson, Anne, ed. *English Wycliffite Sermons.* Vol. 1. Oxford: Clarendon Press, 1983.

Hugh of Amiens. "Charta Hugonis." PL 192:1136–38.

Hugh of Saint-Cher. *In evangelium secundum Matthaeum, Lucam, Marcum, & Joannem.* Vol. 6 of *Opera omnia.* Venice, 1732.

Huguccio of Pisa. *Derivationes.* Edited by Enzo Cecchini. Florence: SISMEL, 2004.

———. *Summa Decretorum: Tom. I: Distinctiones I–XX.* Edited by Oldřich Přerovský. Monumenta Iuris Canonica, Series A 6/I. Città del Vaticano: Biblioteca Apostolica Vaticana, 2006.

Ignatius of Antioch. "Epistle to the Ephesians." In *Early Christian Writings: The Apostolic Fathers*, translated by Maxwell Staniforth, 75–84. Harmondsworth: Penguin, 1968.

Irenaeus of Lyons. *Contre les hérésies: Livre 1.* Edited by Adelin Rousseau and Louis Doutreleau. SC 264. Vol. 1.2. Paris: Cerf, 1979.

———. *Irenaeus against Heresies.* Translated by Alexander Roberts and W. H. Rambaut. Vol. 1 of *The Writings of Irenaeus.* Ante-Nicene Christian Library 5. Edinburgh: T. & T. Clark, 1868.

Isidore of Seville. *Etymologiae.* Edited by W. M. Lindsay. 2 vols. Oxford: Clarendon Press, 1911.

———. *The Etymologies of Isidore of Seville.* Translated by Stephen A. Barney et al. Cambridge: Cambridge University Press, 2006.

Jacobus de Lausanne. *Opus moralitatum.* Limoges: C. Garnier, 1528.

Jacobus de Voragine. *The Golden Legend: Readings on the Saints.* Translated by William Granger Ryan. 2 vols. Princeton: Princeton University Press, 1993.

———. *Legenda aurea.* 2 vols. Edited by Giovanni Paolo Maggioni. 2nd ed. Tavarnuzze: SISMEL, 1998.

———. *Legenda aurea vulgo Historia lombardica dicta.* Edited by J. G. Theodor Graesse. Breslau: Koebner, 1890.

———. *Sermones aurei de Maria Virgine.* Venice, 1590.

Jacopone da Todi. *Jacopone da Todi: The Lauds.* Translated by Serge Hughes and Elizabeth Hughes. New York: Paulist Press, 1982.

———. *Quelques poésies de Fra Jacopone da Todi.* Translated by Pierre Barbet. Paris: Desclée de Brouwer, 1935.

Jacques de Vitry. *The Exempla or Illustrative Stories from the Sermones Vulgares of Jacques de Vitry.* Edited by Thomas Frederick Crane. New York: Burton, 1971.

———. *Historia orientalis.* Edited by Jean Donnadieu. Turnhout: Brepols, 2008.

———. "The Life of Mary of Oignies by James of Vitry." Translated by Margot H. King. In *Mary of Oignies: Mother of Salvation*, edited by Anneke B. Mulder-Bakker, 39–127. Turnhout: Brepols, 2006.

———. *Vita Marie de Oegnies; Thomas Cantipratensis Supplementum.* Edited by R. B. C. Huygens. CCCM 252. Turnhout: Brepols, 2012.

James, M. R., ed. *Latin Infancy Gospels.* Cambridge: Cambridge University Press, 1927.

———, ed. *The New Testament Apocrypha.* 1924. Reprint, Berkeley, Calif.: Apocryphile Press, 2004.

Jean le Marchant. *Miracles de Notre-Dame de Chartres.* Edited by Pierre Kunstmann. Ottawa: Éditions de l'Université d'Ottawa, 1973.

Jerome. *Commentariorum in Esaiam libri I–XI. S. Hieronymi Presbyteri Opera, Pars I: Opera Exegetica.* Edited by M. Adriaen. CCSL 73. Turnhout: Brepols, 1963.

———. *Commentariorum in Matheum libri IV.* In *Opera exegetica: I.7*, edited by D. Hurst and M. Adriaen, CCSL 77. Turnhout: Brepols, 1969.

———. *Epistulae: Pars I: Epistulae I–LXX.* Edited by Isidore Hilberg, augmented by Conrad Smolak. 2nd edition. CCEL 54. Vienna: Österreichischen Akademie der Wissenschaften, 1996. (*Epistula 14*: 44–62; *Epistula 22*: 143–211; *Epistula 46*: 329–44; *Epistula 53*: 442–65.)

————. *Epistulae: Pars II: Epistulae LXXI–CXX*. Edited by Isidore Hilberg. 2nd ed. CSEL 55. Vienna: Österreichischen Akademie der Wissenschaften, 1996. (*Epistula 77*: 37–49, *Epistula 107*: 290–305, *Epistula 108*: 306–351.)

————. "Homilia de Nativitate Domini." In *S. Hieronymi Presbyteri Opera: Pars II: Opera Homiletica*, edited by D. G. Morin, CCSL 78, 524–29. Turnhout: Brepols, 1958.

————. "Homily 84." In *The Homilies of Saint Jerome*, trans. Sister Marie Liguori Ewald, vol. 2, 186–92. Washington, D.C.: Catholic University of America Press, 1965.

————. *Liber adversus Helvidium de perpetua virginitate B. Mariae*. PL 23:193–216.

————. "On the Perpetual Virginity of the Blessed Virgin Mary against Helvidius." In *Saint Jerome: Dogmatic and Polemical Works*, translated by John N. Hritzu, FC 53, 11–43. Washington, D.C.: Catholic University of America Press, 1965.

————. *St. Jerome: Letters and Select Works*. Translated by W. H. Fremantle et al. A Select Library of the Nicene and Post-Nicene Fathers of the Christian Church, 2nd ser., 6, edited by Henry Wace and Philip Schaff. 1893. Reprint, New York: Charles Scribner's Sons, 1912.

————. *Tractatus in Marci evangelium*. In *S. Hieronymi Presbyteri Opera, Pars II, Opera Homiletica*, ed. Morin, 451–500.

Jocelin of Furness. *Vita Waldevi*. In AASS, Augusti I (3), 240–77. Paris: V. Palmé, 1867.

John XXII. *Extravagantes Ioannis Papae XXII*. In *Corpus iuris canonici*, edited by Emil Friedberg and Aemilius Ludwig Richter, vol. 2, 1205–36. 2nd ed. Graz: Akademische Druck - u. Verlagsanstalt, 1959.

John of Cornwall. "The *Eulogium ad Alexandrum Papam tertium* of John of Cornwall." Edited by N. M. Haring. *Mediaeval Studies* 13 (1951): 253–300.

John the Deacon. *Descriptio Lateranensis Ecclesiae*. In *Codice Topografico della Città di Roma*, edited by Roberto Valentini and Giuseppe Zucchetti, vol. 3, 326–73. Rome: Tipografia del Senato, 1946.

Johnson, Holly, ed. and trans. *The Grammar of Good Friday: Macaronic Sermons of Late Medieval England*. Sermo 8. Turnhout: Brepols, 2012.

Josephus. *Flavius Josephus*. Edited by Steve Mason. Vol. 3: *Judean Antiquities 1–4*. Translated by Louis H. Feldman. Leiden: Brill, 2004.

Julian of Speyer. *The Divine Office of St. Francis*. In FAED, vol. 1: *The Saint*, 327–45.

————. *Officium S. Francisci*. In FF, 1105–21.

Justin Martyr. *St. Justin Martyr: Dialogue with Trypho*. Edited by Michael Slusser. Translated by Thomas B. Falls. Revised by Thomas B. Halton, Selections from the Fathers of the Church 3. Washington, D.C.: Catholic University of America Press, 2003.

Kellerman, James A., trans. *Incomplete Commentary on Matthew (Opus imperfectum)*. Edited by Thomas C. Oden. Vol. 1. Downers Grove, Ill.: IVP Academic, 2010.

Kempe, Margery. *The Book of Margery Kempe*. Edited by Barry Windeatt. Harlow: Longman, 2000.

Kim, H. C., ed. *The Gospel of Nicodemus*. Toronto: Pontifical Institute of Mediaeval Studies, 1973.

Labriola, Albert C., and John W. Smeltz, trans. *The Bible of the Poor (Biblia Pauperum): A Facsimile and Edition of the British Library Blockbook C.9 d.2*. Pittsburgh: Duquesne University Press, 1990.

Lactantius. *Lactantius: Divine Institutes*. Translated by Anthony Bowen and Peter Garnsey. Liverpool: Liverpool University Press, 2003.

Langland, William. *Piers Plowman: A New Annotated Edition of the C-Text*. Edited by Derek Pearsall. Exeter: University of Exeter Press, 2008.

————. *The Vision of Piers Plowman*. Edited by A. V. C. Schmidt. 2nd ed. London: J. M. Dent, 2000.

Leclercq, Jean, and Bernard Müller, eds. "Les méditations d'un moine au XII⁰ siècle." *Revue Mabillon* 34 (1944): 1–19.

*The Legend of Saint Clare*. In *The Lady: Clare of Assisi: Early Documents*, edited by Armstrong, 277–329.

*Legenda sanctae Clarae*. In FF, 2415–50.

Leo the Great. "The Letter of Pope Leo to Flavian, bishop of Constantinople, about Eutyches" (28). In *Decrees of the Ecumenical Councils*, translated by Tanner, 77–82.

————. *St. Leo the Great: Sermons*. Translated by Jane P. Freeland and Agnes J. Conway. FC 93. Washington, D.C.: Catholic University of America Press, 1996. (*Sermo 22*: 80–87; *Sermo 34*: 143–49; *Sermo 37*: 159–62; *Sermo 47*: 201–5.)

————. *Tractatus septem et nonaginta*. Edited by Anthony Chavasse. 2 vols. CCSL 138 and 138A. Turnhout: Brepols, 1973. (*Tractatus 22*: vol. 1, 90–101; *Tractatus 34*: vol. 1, 178–87; *Tractatus 37*: vol. 1, 200–204; *Tractatus 47*: vol. 2, 274–78.)

Le Palmer, James. *Omne Bonum: A Fourteenth-Century Encyclopedia of Universal Knowledge [British Library MSS Royal 6 E VI–6 E VII]*. Edited by Lucy Freeman Sandler. Vol. 1. London: Harvey Miller, 1996.

L'Hermite-Leclercq, Paulette, and Anne-Marie Legras, eds. *Vie de Christina de Markyate*. Vol. 1. Sources d'histoire médiévale publiées par l'Institut de Recherche et d'Histoire des Textes 35. Paris: CNRS Éditions, 2007.

Lombard, Peter. *Peter Lombard, The Sentences, Book 4: On the Doctrine of Signs*. Translated by Giulio Silano. Mediaeval Sources in Translation 48. Toronto: Pontifical Institute of Mediaeval Studies, 2010.

————. *Sententiae in IV libris distinctae*. Vol. 2. 3rd ed. Grottaferrata: Editiones Collegii S. Bonaventurae ad Claras Aquas, 1981.

Lotario di Segni. *De miseria condicionis humane*. Edited and translated by Robert E. Lewis. Athens, Ga.: University of Georgia Press, 1978.

Love, Nicholas. *The Mirror of the Blessed Life of Jesus Christ: A Full Critical Edition*. Edited by Michael G. Sargent. Exeter: University of Exeter Press, 2005.

Love, Rosalind C., ed. *Vita S. Rumwoldi*. In *Three Eleventh-Century Anglo-Latin Saints' Lives: Vita S. Birini, Vita et miracula S. Kenelmi, and Vita S. Rumwoldi*, 91–115. Oxford: Clarendon Press, 1996.

Luard, Henry Richards, ed. *Annales Monastici*. RS 36.3. London: Longman, Green, Reader and Dyer, 1866.

Ludolph of Saxony. *Vita Jesu Christi*. Edited by A.-C. Bolard, L. M. Rigollot, and J. Cardandet. Paris: V. Palmé, 1865. Reprinted as *Vita Christi*. Vols. 1 and 4. Analecta Cartusiana 241. Salzburg: Institut für Anglistik und Amerikanistik, 2006.

Lumby, J. Rawson, ed. Ratis Raving *and Other Moral and Religious Pieces in Prose and Verse*. EETS, o.s. 43. 1870. Reprint, New York: Greenwood Press, 2002.

Lumiansky, R. M., and David Mills, eds. *The Chester Mystery Cycle*. Vol. 1. EETS s.s. 3. London: Oxford University Press, 1974.

Lungarotti, Maria Cristiana, ed., intro. by Emore Paoli. *Le Legendae di Margherita da Città di Castello*. Spoleto: Centro Italiano di Studi sull'Alto Medioevo, 1994.

Macrobius. *Commentaire au Songe de Scipion*. Edited by Mireille Armisen-Marchetti. Vol. 1. Paris: Les Belles Lettres, 2003.

————. *Macrobius, Commentary on the Dream of Scipio.* Translated by William Harris Stahl. Records of Civilization, Sources and Studies 48. New York: Columbia University Press, 1952.

Mailly, Jean de. *Abbreviatio in gestis et miraculis sanctorum: Supplementum hagiographicum.* Edited by Giovanni Paolo Maggioni. Florence: Edizioni del Galluzzo, 2013.

Mandeville, Sir John. *The Book of John Mandeville with Related Texts.* Edited and translated by Iain Macleod Higgins. Indianapolis: Hackett, 2011.

————. *The Defective Version of Mandeville's Travels.* Edited by M. C. Seymour. EETS o.s. 312. Oxford: Oxford University Press, 2002.

————. *Le Livre des merveilles du monde.* Edited by Christiane Deluz. Sources d'Histoire Médiévale Publiées par l'Institut de Recherche et d'Histoire des Textes 31. Paris: CNRS Éditions, 2000.

————. *Mandeville's Travels.* Edited by M. C. Seymour. Oxford: Clarendon Press, 1967.

————. *Mandeville's Travels, Edited from MS. Cotton Titus c.XVI.* Edited by P. Hamelius. Vol. 1. EETS o.s. 153. London: Kegan Paul, Trench, Trübner & Co., 1919.

Map, Walter. *De nugis curialium: Courtiers' Trifles.* Edited and translated by M. R. James. Revised by C. N. L. Brooke and R. A. B. Mynors. Oxford: Clarendon Press, 1983.

Martin of Poland. *Chronicon pontificum et imperatorum.* Edited by Ludwig Weiland. In MGH Scriptores 22, edited by G. H. Pertz, 397–82. Hanover, 1872. Reprint, Stuttgart: Anton Hiersemann, 1976.

Martínez Díez, Gonzalo, and Félix Rodríguez, eds. *Concilium Laodicenum.* In *La Colección canónica hispana,* vol. 3: *Concilios Griegos et Africanos,* 153–72. Madrid: [Consejo Superior de Investigaciones Científicas, Instituto Enrique Flórez], 1982.

McNamara, Martin, et al., eds. *Apocrypha Hiberniae: I. Evangelia Infantiae.* 2 vols. CCSA 13 and 14. Turnhout: Brepols, 2001.

McNamer, Sarah, ed. *The Two Middle English Translations of the Revelations of St Elizabeth of Hungary.* Heidelberg: Universitätsverlag C. Winter, 1996.

Mechthild of Hackeborn. *The Booke of Gostlye Grace of Mechtild of Hackeborn.* Edited by Theresa A. Halligan. Toronto: Pontifical Institute of Mediaeval Studies, 1979.

————. *Liber specialis gratiae.* Edited by Ludwig Paquelin. Vol. 2 of *Revelationes Gertrudianae ac Mechthildianae.* Poitiers: Oudin, 1877.

Meiss, Millard, and Elizabeth H. Beatson, eds. *La Vie de nostre benoît Sauveur IhesusCrist and La Saincte vie de Nostre Dame.* New York: New York University Press, 1977.

Meiss, Millard, and Marcel Thomas, eds. *The Rohan Master: A Book of Hours: Bibliothèque nationale, Paris (M.S. Latin 9471).* New York: G. Braziller, 1973.

Millett, Bella, ed. *Ancrene Wisse: A Corrected Edition of the Text in Cambridge, Corpus Christi College, MS 402, with Variants from Other Manuscripts.* With glossary and additional notes by Richard Dance. 2 vols. EETS o.s. 325 and 326. Oxford: Oxford University Press, 2005/2006.

————, trans. *Ancrene Wisse: Guide for Anchoresses: A Translation Based on Cambridge, Corpus Christi College, MS 402.* Exeter: University of Exeter Press, 2009.

Mills, Maldwyn, ed. "Sir Gowther." In *Six Middle English Romances,* 148–68. London: J. M. Dent, 1973.

Milton, John. *Paradise Lost.* Edited by Alastair Fowler. 2nd ed. Harlow: Longman, 1998.

Mirk, John. *John Mirk's Festial.* Edited by Susan Powell. 2 vols. EETS o.s. 334 and 335. Oxford: Oxford University Press, 2009.

"Mirror of Perfection." In FAED, vol. 3: *The Prophet*, 214–54 ("Lemmens Edition").

*The Mirror of the Blessed Virgin Mary . . . and the Psalter of Our Lady*. Translated by Sr. Mary Emmanuel. St. Louis, Mo.: B. Herder, 1932.

Molanus, Johannes. *Traité des saintes images (Louvain 1570, Ingolstadt 1594)*. Edited by François Bœspflug, et al. 2 vols. Paris: Cerf, 1996.

More, Thomas. "The Confutation of Tyndale's Answer." In *The Complete Works of St. Thomas More*, vol. 8, part 1, edited by Louis A. Schuster et al. New Haven: Yale University Press, 1973.

Murray, Campion, trans. *A Meditation in Solitude of One Who is Poor*. Phoenix, Ariz.: Tau, 2012.

Nalgod. *Vita sancti Majoli abbati Cluniacensis in Gallia*. In AASS, Maii II (11), 656–66. Paris: V. Palmé, 1866.

Nazianzen, Gregory. "Select Orations of Saint Gregory Nazianzen." Translated by Charles Gordon Browne and James Edward Swallow. In *A Select Library of Nicene and Post-Nicene Fathers of the Christian Church*, 2nd ser., vol. 7, edited by Philip Schaff and Henry Wace, 203–434. 1890. Reprint, Grand Rapids, Mich.: Eerdmans, 1983.

*Opus imperfectum in Matthaeum*. PG 56:611–946.

Origen. *Origen: Homilies on Luke, Fragments on Luke*. Translated by Joseph T. Lienhard. FC 94. Washington, D.C.: Catholic University of America Press, 1996.

———. *Die Homilien zu Lukas in der Übersetzung des Hieronymus und die griechischen Reste der Homilien und des Lukas-Kommentars*. Edited by Max Rauer. Vol. 9 of *Origenes Werke*. Berlin: Akademie-Verlag, 1959.

———. *Origen: Contra Celsum*. Translated by Henry Chadwick. Cambridge: University Press, 1953.

Orme, Nicholas, trans. *Fleas, Flies, and Friars: Children's Poetry from the Middle Ages*. Ithaca, N.Y.: Cornell University Press, 2011.

Ovid. *Ovid's Metamorphoses, Books 6–10*. Edited by William S. Anderson. Norman: University of Oklahoma Press, 1972.

Paris, Matthew. *Chronica majora (The Creation to A.D. 1066)*. Edited by Henry Richards Luard. RS 57.1. London: Longman & Co., 1872.

———. *Chronica majora (1067–1216)*. Edited by Henry Richards Luard. RS 57.2. London: Longman & Co., 1874.

———. *Chronica majora (1248–1259)*. Edited by Henry Richards Luard. RS 57.5. London: Longman & Co., 1880.

———. *Flores historiarum*. Edited by Henry Richards Luard. Vol. 2. RS 95. London: Eyre and Spottiswoode, 1890.

Parker, Roscoe E., ed. *Middle English Stanzaic Versions of the Life of Saint Anne*. EETS o.s. 174. London: Oxford University Press, 1928. Corrigenda, 1930.

Patterson, Paul J., ed. *A Mirror to Devout People: Speculum devotorum*. EETS o.s. 346. Oxford: Oxford University Press, 2016.

Pecham, John. *Philomena*. In *Analecta Hymnica Medii Aevi*, vol. 50, edited by Clemens Blume and G. M. Dreves, 602–16. Leipzig, 1907. Reprint, New York: Johnson, 1961.

———. *Philomena: A Poem by John Peckham, O.F.M., Archbishop of Canterbury*. Translated by William Dobell. London: Burns Oates & Washbourne, 1924.

Peter the Florentine. "Concerning the Blessed Margarita of Faenza, Virgin and Abbess of the Vallombrosan Order Florence." Translated by Elizabeth Petroff. In *The Consolation of the Blessed*, 151–65. New York: Alta Gaia Society, 1979.

————. *Vita Margaritae Faventinae*. In AASS, Augustii V (26), 847–51. Paris: V. Palmé, 1868.

Peter the Venerable. *De miraculis libri duo*. Edited by Denise Bouthillier. CCCM 83. Turnhout: Brepols, 1988.

Peters, Edward, ed. *Heresy and Authority in Medieval Europe: Documents in Translation*. Philadelphia: University of Pennsylvania Press, 1908.

Pezzini, Domenico, ed. "Una 'Vita Beate Marie' tratta dalle 'Revelaciones' di santa Brigida di Svezia." *Hagiographica* 16 (2009): 167–30.

Piacenza Pilgrim. *Antonini Placentini Itinerarium*. Edited by P. Geyer. In *Itineraria et alia geographica*, CCSL 175, 129–74. Turnhout: Brepols, 1965.

————. "Travels from Piacenza." In *Jerusalem Pilgrims before the Crusades*, translated by John Wilkinson, 129–51. Warminster: Aris & Phillips, 2002.

Pickering, F. P., ed. *The Anglo-Norman Text of the Holkham Bible Picture Book*. Anglo-Norman Texts 23. Oxford: Basil Blackwell, 1971.

Pierre de Vaux. *Vie de soeur Colette*. Translated by Elisabeth Lopez. Travaux et Recherches 6. Saint-Etienne: Publications de l'Université de Saint-Etienne, 1994.

Plummer, John, ed. *The Hours of Catherine of Cleves*. New York: George Braziller, 1966.

Plutarch. *Plutarch's Lives*. Edited and translated by Bernadotte Perrin. Vol. 2. Cambridge, Mass.: Harvard University Press, 1948.

Porphyry. *Isagogue*. Translated by Edward W. Warren. Medieval Sources in Translation 16. Toronto: Pontifical Institute of Mediaeval Studies, 1975.

*Préparation à la vie religieuse*. Paris: Simeon Piget, 1664.

Prescott, Andrew, ed. *The Benedictional of St. Æthelwold: A Masterpiece of Anglo-Saxon Art: A Facsimile*. London: British Library, 2002.

*Il Processo di Canonizzazione di Santa Chiara d'Assisi*. In FF, 2455–507.

*Psalterium Beatae Mariae Virginis*. Basel, ca. 1473–75.

Pseudo-Anselm. *Dialogus beatae Mariae et Anselmi de passione Domini*. PL 159:271–90.

————. "Meditatio X: De passione Christi." PL 158:761–62.

————. "Tenth Meditation: Of the Passion of Christ." In *St. Anselm's Book of Meditations and Prayers*, translated by M.R., 133–35. London: Burns and Oates, 1872.

Pseudo-Bede. *De elementis philosophiae*. PL 90:1127–78.

Pseudo-Bonaventure. *Meditaciones vite Christi*. Edited by M. Stallings-Taney. CCCM 153. Turnhout: Brepols, 1997.

————. *Meditations on the Life of Christ*. Translated by Francis X. Taney, Anne Miller, and Mary Stallings-Taney. Asheville, N.C.: Pegasus Press, 2000.

————. *Meditations on the Life of Christ: An Illustrated Manuscript of the Fourteenth Century*. Translated by Isa Ragusa and Rosalie B. Green. Princeton: Princeton University Press, 1961.

Pseudo-Odoric. *De terra sancta*. In *Peregrinatores medii aevi quattuor*, edited by J. C. M. Laurent, 146–58. Leipzig: J. C. Hinrichs, 1864.

(Pseudo-)William of Tripoli. *De statu saracenorum*. In *Kulturgeschichte der Kreuzzüge*, ed. Hans Prutz, 573–98. 1883. Reprint, Hildesheim: Georg Olms, 1964.

Ralph of Coggeshall. *Chronicon anglicanum*. Edited by Joseph Stevenson. RS 66. London: Longman & Co., 1875.

Raymond of Capua. *Legenda beate Agnetis de Monte Policiano*. Edited by Silvia Nocentini. Florence: SISMEL, 2001.

————. *The Life of Catherine of Siena*. Translated by George Lamb. London: Harville Press, 1960.

————. *Vita s. Catharinae Senensis*. In AASS, Aprilis III (30), 862–967. Paris: V. Palmé, 1866.

*Register des Buchs der Croniken und Geschichten mit Figuren und Pildnussen von Anbeginn der Welt bis auf dise unnsere Zeit*. Nürmberg, 1493. Reprint, Munich: Kölbl, 1965.

Robert of Boron. *Merlin and the Grail: Joseph of Arimathea, Merlin, Percival: The Trilogy of Prose Romances Attributed to Robert of Boron*. Translated by Nigel Bryant. Cambridge: D. S. Brewer: 2003.

————. *Merlin: roman du XIII<sup>e</sup> siècle*. Edited by Alexandre Micha. Paris: Droz, 1980.

Robert of Torigni. *Chronique de Robert de Torigni*. Edited by Léopold Delisle. Vol. 1. Rouen: A. Le Brument, 1872.

Salimbene de Adam. *Cronica*. Edited by Giuseppe Scalia. Vol. 1. CCCM 125. Turnhout: Brepols, 1998.

Savage, Anne, and Nicholas Watson, trans. *Anchoritic Spirituality: Ancrene Wisse and Associated Works*. New York: Paulist Press, 1991.

Schaer, Frank, ed. *The Three Kings of Cologne, Edited from London, Lambeth Palace MS 491*. Middle English Texts 30. Heidelberg: Universitätsverlag C. Winter, 2000.

Schneemelcher, Wilhelm, and Edgar Hennecke, eds. *New Testament Apocrypha*. Translated by R. McL. Wilson. Vol. 1: *Gospels and Related Writings*. Louisville/London: Westminster John Knox Press/James Clarke & Co., 1991.

"Second Shepherds' Play." In *The Towneley Plays*, vol. 1, edited by Stevens and Cawley, 126–57.

Serranno, Arnaldo de. *Liber miraculorum S. Antonii*. In *"Liber miraculorum" e altri testi medievali*, Fonti Agiografische Antoniane 5, edited by Vergilio Gamboso, 152–407. Padua: Edizioni Messaggero, 1997.

Severus, Sulpicius. *Vie de Saint Martin*. Edited and translated by Jacques Fontaine. Vol. 1. SC 133. Paris: Cerf, 1967.

Shakespeare, William. *As You Like It*. Edited by Michael Hattaway. Updated ed. Cambridge: Cambridge University Press, 2009.

Sicard of Cremona. *Mitrale*. PL 213:13–434.

Smithers, G. V., ed. *Havelok*. Oxford: Clarendon Press, 1987.

Spector, Stephen, ed. *The N-Town Play: Cotton MS Vespasian D. 8*. Vol. 1. EETS s.s. 11. Oxford: Oxford University Press, 1991.

*Speculum perfectionis*. In FF, 1745–825.

Stephen of Sawley. "Les méditations d'Étienne de Salley sur les Joies de la Vierge Marie." In *Auteurs spirituels et textes dévots du moyen âge latin*, edited by André Wilmart, 317–60. Paris: Études Augustiniennes, 1971 [1932].

Stevens, Martin, and A. C. Cawley, eds. *The Towneley Plays*. Vol. 1. EETS s.s. 13. Oxford: Oxford University Press, 1994.

Suchier, Walther, ed. *L'Enfant Sage (Das Gespräch des Kaisers Hadrian mit dem klugen Kinde Epitus)*. Gesellschaft für Romanische Literatur 24. Dresden: M. Niemeyer, 1910.

Suso, Heinrich. *The Exemplar, with Two German Sermons*. Translated by Frank Tobin. New York: Paulist Press, 1989.

————. *Heinrich Seuse: Deutsche Schriften*. Edited by Karl Bihlmeyer. Stuttgart, 1907. Reprint, Frankfurt am Main: Minerva, 1961.

Swanton, Michael, ed. *The Dream of the Rood*. Revised ed. Exeter: Exeter University Press, 1996.

Talbot, C. H., trans. *The Life of Christina of Markyate*. Revised by Samuel Fanous and Henrietta Leyser. Oxford: Oxford University Press, 2008.

Tanner, Norman P., trans. *Decrees of the Ecumenical Councils*. With original texts edited by G. Alberigo et al. Vol. 1. London/Washington, D.C.: Sheed & Ward/Georgetown University Press, 1990.

Tatian. *The Diatessaron of Tatian*. Translated by Hope W. Hogg. In Ante-Nicene Fathers 9, 5th ed., 43–129. New York: Charles Scribner's Sons, 1925.

Terian, Abraham, trans. *The Armenian Gospel of the Infancy, with Three Early Versions of the Protevangelium of James*. Oxford: Oxford University Press, 2008.

Thérèse of Lisieux. *J'entre dans la vie: Derniers entretiens*. Paris: Éditions du Cerf/Desclée de Brouwer, 1973.

———. *St. Therese of Lisieux: Her Last Conversations*. Translated by John Clarke. Washington, D.C.: ICS Publications, 1977.

Thomas, à Kempis. *De imitatione Christi: libri quatuor*. Edited by Tiburzio Lupo. Storia e attualità 6. Città del Vaticano: Libreria Editrice Vaticana, 1982.

———. *The Imitation of Christ: A New Reading of the 1441 Latin Autograph Manuscript*. Translated by William C. Creasy. Macon, Ga.: Mercer University Press, 1989.

Thomas of Cantimpré. *Bonum universale de apibus*. Douai, 1627.

———. "The Life of Abbot John of Cantimpré." Translated by Barbara Newman. In *Thomas of Cantimpré: The Collected Saints' Lives: Abbot John of Cantimpré, Christina the Astonishing, Margaret of Ypres, Lutgard of Aywières*, edited with an introduction by Barbara Newman, translations by Margot H. King and Barbara Newman, Medieval Women: Texts and Contexts 19, 57–11. Turnhout: Brepols, 2008.

———. "Une oeuvre inédite de Thomas de Cantimpré. La 'Vita Ioannis Cantipratensis.'" Edited by Robert Godding. *Revue d'Histoire Ecclésiastique* 76 (1981): 241–316.

Thomas of Celano. "The Life of Saint Francis by Thomas of Celano (1228–1229)" (*Vita prima*). In FAED, vol. 1: *The Saint*, 180–309.

———. "The Remembrance of the Desire of a Soul" (*Vita secunda*). In FAED, vol. 2: *The Founder*, 239–393.

———. *Vita prima*. In FF, 275–424.

———. *Vita secunda*. In FF, 443–639.

Thomas of Hales. *The Lyf of Oure Lady: The ME Translation of Thomas of Hales' Vita Sancte Marie*. Edited by Sarah Horrall. Heidelberg: Carl Winter Universitätsverlag, 1985.

Thomas of Monmouth. *The Life and Miracles of St William of Norwich*. Edited and translated by Augustus Jessopp and M. R. James. Cambridge: Cambridge University Press, 1896.

———. *The Life and Passion of William of Norwich*. Translated by Miri Rubin. London: Penguin, 2014.

Thompson, W. Meredith, ed. *The Wohunge of Ure Lauerd*. EETS o.s. 241. London: Oxford University Press, 1958.

Tischendorf, Konstantin von, ed. *Evangelia apocrypha*. 2nd ed. Leipzig, 1876. Reprint Hildesheim: Georg Olms, 1987.

*Tractatus de poenitentia et tentationibus religiosorum*. PL 213:863–904.

Trevisa, John. *On the Properties of Things. John Trevisa's Translation of Bartholomaeus Anglicus De Proprietatibus Rerum*. Vol. 1. Edited by M. C. Seymour. Oxford: Clarendon Press, 1975.

Ubertino da Casale. *Arbor vitae crucifixae Jesu*. Introduction by Charles T. David. Venice, 1485. Reprint, Torino: Bottega d'Erasmo, 1961.

Ugolino Boniscambi of Montegiorgio (?). *Acta B. Francisci et sociorum eius.* In FF, 2085–2219.

———. *The Deeds of Blessed Francis and His Companions.* In FAED, vol. 3: *The Prophet,* 425–565.

Vincent of Beauvais. *Préface au Speculum Maius de Vincent de Beauvais: Réfraction et diffraction.* Edited by Serge Lusignan. Montréal: Bellarmin, 1979.

———. *Speculum historiale.* Vol. 4 of *Speculum quadruplex; sive speculum maius.* Douai, 1624. Reprint, Graz: Akademische Druck - u. Verlagsanstalt, 1965.

*Vita b. Benevenutae de Bojanis.* In AASS, Octobris XIII (29), 152–85. Paris: V. Palmé, 1883.

*Vita b. Coletae.* In AASS, Martii I (6), 538–86. Paris: V. Palmé, 1865.

*Vita b. Hermanni Josephi.* In AASS, Aprilis I (7), 683–707. Paris: V. Palmé, 1865.

*Vita II b. Osannae Mantuanae.* In AASS, Junii IV (18), 601–63. Paris: V. Palmé, 1867.

*Vita venerabilis Idae Lovaniensis.* AASS, Aprilis II (13), 158–89. Paris: V. Palmé, 1865.

Vito of Cortona. "The Life of Umiliana de' Cerchi by Vito of Cortona." Translated by Diana Webb. In *Saints and Cities in Medieval Italy,* 97–140. Manchester: Manchester University Press, 2007.

———. *Vita Æmilianae seu Humilianae, viduae Florentiae.* In AASS, Maii IV (19), 385–400. Paris: V. Palmé, 1866.

Vögtlin, Adolf, ed. *Vita beate virginis Marie et salvatoris rhythmica.* Bibliothek des Litterarischen Vereins in Stuttgart 180. Tübingen: Gedruckt für den litterarischen Verein in Stuttgart, 1888.

Walker, Alexander, trans. "The Arabic Gospel of the Infancy of the Saviour." In *Apocryphal Gospels, Acts and Revelations,* Ante-Nicene Fathers 8, 405–15. New York: Charles Scribner's Sons, 1926.

Walter of Wimborne. *The Poems of Walter of Wimborne.* Edited by A. G. Rigg. Studies and Texts 42. Toronto: Pontifical Institute of Mediaeval Studies, 1978.

Weber, R., ed. *Biblia sacra iuxta vulgatam versionem.* 4th ed. Stuttgart: Deutsche Bibelgesellschaft, 1994.

Wenzel, Siegfried, ed. *Fasciculus morum: A Fourteenth-Century Preacher's Handbook.* University Park: Penn State University Press, 1989.

Whalen, Brett E., ed. *Pilgrimage in the Middle Ages: A Reader.* Toronto: University of Toronto Press, 2011.

Wilde, Oscar. *The Complete Shorter Fiction of Oscar Wilde.* Edited by Isobel Murray. Oxford: Oxford University Press, 1979.

William of Auvergne. *De universo.* Vol. 1. Paris, 1674. Reprint, Frankfurt am Main: Minerva, 1963.

William of Conches. *A Dialogue of Natural Philosophy (Dragmaticon philosophiae).* Translated by Italo Ronca and Matthew Curr. Notre Dame, Ind.: University of Notre Dame Press, 1997.

William of Ockham. *Guillemi de Ockham Opera Politica.* Edited by J. G. Sikes. Vol. 2. Manchester: University Press, 1940.

———. *A Translation of William of Ockham's Work of Ninety Days.* Translated by John Kilcullen and John Scott. Vol. 2. Lewiston, N.Y.: Edwin Mellen Press, 2001.

William of St. Thierry, Arnold of Bonneval, and Geoffrey of Auxerre. *St. Bernard of Clairvaux: The Story of His Life as Recorded in the Vita Prima Bernardi by Certain of His Contemporaries.* Translated by Geoffrey Webb and Adrian Walker. Westminster, Md.: Newman Press, 1960.

———. *Vita prima s. Bernardi*. PL 185:225–454.

William of Tocco. *Ystoria sancti Thome de Aquino de Guillaume de Tocco (1323)*. Edited by Claire Le Brun-Gouanvic. Toronto: Pontifical Institute of Mediaeval Studies, 1996.

Wilson, R. McL., trans. *The Gospel of Philip*. London: A. R. Mowbray & Co., 1962.

Wright, Thomas, and J. O. Halliwell, eds. *Reliquiae Antiquae: Scraps from Ancient Manuscripts*. Vol. 2. 1843. Reprint, New York: AMS Press, 1966.

Wyclif, John. "Exposicio textus Matthei XXIII." In *Johannis Wyclif: Opera minora*, edited by Johann Loserth, 313–82. London: C. K. Paul & Co., 1913.

———. *De fundatione sectarum*. In *John Wiclif's Polemical Works in Latin*, edited by Rudolf Buddensieg, vol. 1.1, 13–80. London: Trübner & Co., 1883.

———. *Sermones*. Edited by Johann Loserth. Vol. 1: *Super Evangelia Dominicalia*. London, 1887. Reprint, New York: Johnson 1966.

Young, Karl, ed. *The Drama of the Medieval Church*. Vol. 2. Corrected ed. Oxford: Clarendon Press, 1962 [1933].

Zachary of Besançon (Zacharias Chrysopolitanus). *In unum ex quatuor*. PL 168:11–620.

## SECONDARY SOURCES

Aasgaard, Reidar. *The Childhood of Jesus: Decoding the Apocryphal Infancy Gospel of Thomas*. Eugene, Oreg.: Cascade Books, 2009.

Aasgaard, Reidar, and Cornelia B. Horn, eds. *Childhood in History: Perceptions of Children in the Ancient and Medieval Worlds*. Forthcoming.

Abate, Giuseppe. *La casa dove nacque S. Francesco d'Assisi nella sua nuova documentazione storica*. Gubbio: Oderisi, 1941.

Acres, Alfred. "Porous Subject Matter: Christ's Haunted Infancy." In *The Mind's Eye*, edited by Hamburger and Bouché, 241–62.

———. *Renaissance Invention and the Haunted Infancy*. Studies in Medieval and Early Renaissance Art History 67. Turnhout: Brepols, 2013.

Aers, David. "The Humanity of Christ: Reflections on Orthodox Late Medieval Representations." In David Aers and Lynn Staley, *The Powers of the Holy: Religion, Politics, and Gender in Late Medieval English Culture*, 15–42. University Park: Penn State University Press, 1996.

———. *Sanctifying Signs: Making Christian Tradition in Late Medieval England*. Notre Dame, Ind.: University of Notre Dame Press, 2004.

Ahl, Diane Cole. *Benozzo Gozzoli*. New Haven, Conn.: Yale University Press, 1996.

Alexandre-Bidon, Danièle. *L'Enfant à l'ombre des cathédrales*. Lyon: Presses Universitaires de Lyon, 1985.

———. "La Parure prophylactique de l'enfance à la fin du moyen-âge." *Razo* 7 (1987): 5–35.

Ali, Hans, and Jan Svanberg. *Imagines Sanctae Birgittae: The Earliest Illuminated Manuscripts and Panel Paintings Related to the Revelations of St. Birgitta of Sweden*. 2 vols. Stockholm: Royal Academy of Letters, History and Antiquities, 2003.

Almazán, Vicente. "Saint Birgitta on the Pilgrimage Route to Santiago." In *Scandinavia, Saint Birgitta and the Pilgrimage Route to Santiago de Compostela: Proceedings of the VIII Spain and Sweden Encounters throughout History, Santiago de Compostela, October, 18–20, 2000,* edited by Enrique Martínez Ruiz and Magdalena Pi Corrales, 13–20. Santiago de Compostela: Universidade de Santiago de Compostela, 2002.

Amann, Émile. *Le Protévangile de Jacques et ses remaniements latins*. Paris: Letouzey et Ané, 1910.

Anderson, Wendy Love. "The Real Presence of Mary: Eucharistic Disbelief and the Limits of Orthodoxy in Fourteenth-Century France." *Church History* 75.4 (2006): 748–67.

Andersson, Aron. *St. Birgitta and the Holy Land*. Translated by Louise Setterwall. Stockholm: Museum of National Antiquities, 1973.

Arad, Lily. "The Bathing of the Infant Jesus in the Jordan River and His Baptism in a Font: A Mutual Iconographic Borrowing in Medieval Art." *Miscellània Litúrgica Catalana* 11 (2003): 21–44.

Ariès, Philippe. *Centuries of Childhood: A Social History of Family Life*. Translated by Robert Baldick. New York: Alfred A. Knopf, 1962.

———. *L'Enfant et la vie familiale sous l'Ancien Régime*. Paris: Librairie Plon, 1960.

Armon, Chara. "Servus, Pater, Dominus: The Development of Devotion to Saint Joseph in Franciscan Thought." Unpublished PhD thesis, Cornell University, 2003.

Arnold, John N., ed. *The Oxford Handbook of Medieval Christianity*. Oxford: Oxford University Press, 2014.

Ashley, Kathleen M. "The Guiler Beguiled: Christ and Satan as Theological Tricksters in Medieval Religious Literature." *Criticism* 24 (1982): 126–37.

Astell, Ann W. *The Song of Songs in the Middle Ages*. Ithaca, N.Y.: Cornell University Press, 1990.

As-Vijvers, Anne Margreet W., et al., eds. *From the Hand of the Master:* The Hours of Catherine of Cleves. Translated by Kathryn M. Rudy. Antwerp: Ludion, 2009.

Atkinson, Clarissa W. "'Precious Balm in a Fragile Glass': The Ideology of Virginity in the Later Middle Ages." *Journal of Family History* 8 (1983): 131–43.

Auerbach, Erich. *Literary Language and Its Public in Late Latin Antiquity and in the Middle Ages*. Translated by Ralph Manheim. Bollingen Series 74. Princeton: Princeton University Press, 1993.

Baert, Barbara. "The Gaze in the Garden: Mary Magdalene in the *Noli Me Tangere*." Translated by Audrey van Tuyckom. In *Mary Magdalene, Iconographic Studies from the Middle Ages to the Baroque,* edited by Michelle A. Erhardt and Amy M. Morris, Studies in Religion and the Arts 7, 189–221. Leiden: Brill, 2012

Bagley, Ayers. "Jesus at School." *Journal of Psychohistory* 13 (1985): 13–31.

Bakke, O. M. *When Children Became People: The Birth of Childhood in Early Christianity*. Translated by Brian McNeil. Minneapolis: Fortress Press, 2005.

Bale, Anthony P. *Feeling Persecuted: Christians, Jews and Images of Violence in the Middle Ages*. London: Reaktion, 2010.

———. "Fictions of Judaism in England before 1290." In *The Jews in Medieval Britain: Historical, Literary and Archaeological Perspectives*, edited by Patricia Skinner, 129–44. Woodbridge: Boydell Press, 2003.

———. *The Jew in the Medieval Book: English Antisemitisms, 1350–1500*. Cambridge: Cambridge University Press, 2006.

Balint, Bridget K. "Envy in the Intellectual Discourse of the High Middle Ages." In *The Seven Deadly Sins from Communities to Individuals*, edited by Richard Newhauser, Studies in Medieval and Reformation Traditions 123, 41–55. Leiden: Brill, 2007.

Barnay, Sylvie. *Le Ciel sur la terre: Les apparitions de la Vierge au Moyen Âge*. Paris: Cerf, 1999.
———. "De l'Enfant-Jésus à l'enfance spirituelle, une relecture de l'histoire du Christianisme." *Transversalités* 115 (2010): 15–26.
Bartal, Renana. "Repetition, Opposition, and Invention in an Illuminated *Meditationes vitae Christi*: Oxford, Corpus Christi College, MS 410." *Gesta* 53.2 (2014): 155–74.
Bartlett, Anne Clark, and Thomas H. Bestul, eds. *Cultures of Piety: Medieval English Devotional Literature in Translation*. Ithaca, N.Y.: Cornell University Press, 1999.
Bates, Linda Rachel. "Christ's Birth and Infancy in Middle English." Unpublished PhD thesis, University of Cambridge, 2010.
Batt, Catherine. "Henry, Duke of Lancaster's *Book of Holy Medicines*: The Rhetoric of Knowledge and Devotion." *Leeds Studies in English*, n.s., 47 (2006): 407–14.
Batt, Catherine, Denis Renevey, and Christiana Whitehead. "Domesticity and Medieval Devotional Literature." *Leeds Studies in English*, n.s., 36 (2005): 195–250.
Baum, P. F. "The Mediæval Legend of Judas Iscariot." *PMLA* 31.3 (1916): 481–632.
Bayless, Martha. *Sin and Filth in Medieval Culture: The Devil in the Latrine*. London: Routledge, 2012.
Bejczy, István. "Jesus' Laughter and the Childhood Miracles: The *Vita rhythmica*." *South African Journal of Medieval and Renaissance Studies* 4 (1994): 50–61.
Belting, Hans. *Likeness and Presence: A History of the Image before the Era of Art*. Translated by Edmund Jephcott. Chicago: University of Chicago Press, 1994.
Beretta, Roberto. *San Francesco e la leggenda del presepio*. Milan: Medusa, 2003.
Beringer, Alison L. "Before the Betrayal: The Life of Judas in a Vernacular Fourteenth-Century Austrian Manuscript." In *Between the Picture and the Word: Manuscript Studies from the Index of Christian Art*, edited by Colum Hourihane, 151–60. Princeton/University Park: Index of Christian Art/Penn State University Press, 2005.
Bériou, Nicole. "Parler de Dieu en images: Le Christ Pèlerin au Moyen Âge." *Comptes rendus des séances de l'Académie des Inscriptions & Belles-Lettres* 1 (2008): 157–200.
Berliner, Rudolph. "The Origins of the Crèche." *Gazette des Beaux Arts* 30 (1946): 249–78.
Berrouard, Marie-François, François de Sainte-Marie, and Charles Bernard. "Enfance spirituelle." DS, vol. 4.1, 682–714.
Berthon, Éric. "Le Sourire aux anges: enfance et spiritualité au Moyen Âge (XIIᵉ–XVᵉ siècle)." *Médiévales* 25 (1993): 93–111.
Bestul, Thomas H. "Devotional and Mystical Literature." In *Medieval Latin: An Introduction and Bibliographical Guide*, edited by F. A. C. Mantello and A. G. Rigg, 694–701. Washington, D.C.: Catholic University of America Press, 1996.
———. "*Meditatio*/Meditation." In *The Cambridge Companion to Christian Mysticism*, edited by Amy Hollywood and Patricia Z. Beckman, 157–66. Cambridge: Cambridge University Press, 2012.
———. "The Passion Meditations of Richard Rolle: The Latin Meditative Tradition and Implications for Authenticity." *Mediaevalia* 27.1 (2006): 43–64.
———. *Texts of the Passion: Latin Devotional Literature and Medieval Society*. Philadelphia: University of Pennsylvania Press, 1996.
Bettini, Maurizio. *Women and Weasels: Mythologies of Birth in Ancient Greece and Rome*. Translated by Emlyn Eisenach. Chicago: University of Chicago Press, 2013.
Beyers, Rita. "Dans l'Atelier des compilateurs: remarques à propos de la *Compilation latine de l'enfance*." *Apocrypha* 16 (2005): 97–135.

————. "Introduction générale aux deux textes édités." In *Libri de nativitate Mariae*, vol. 1, 1–34.

————. "The Transmission of Marian Apocrypha in the Latin Middle Ages." *Apocrypha* 32 (2012): 117–40.

Biller, Peter. "Intellectuals and the Masses: Oxen and She-asses in the Medieval Church." In *The Oxford Handbook of Medieval Christianity*, edited by Arnold, 323–39.

Binski, Paul. "The Faces of Christ in Matthew Paris's *Chronica majora*." In *Tributes in Honor of James H. Marrow*, edited by Hamburger and Korteweg, 85–92.

Birenbaum, Maija. "Virtuous Vengeance: Anti-Judaism and Christian Piety in Medieval England." Unpublished PhD thesis, Fordham University, 2010.

Biscoglio, Frances M. "'Unspun' Heroes: Iconography of the Spinning Woman in the Middle Ages." *Journal of Medieval and Renaissance Studies* 25.2 (1995): 163–76; figs. 1–9.

Bloomfield, Morton W. *The Seven Deadly Sins: An Introduction to the History of a Religious Concept, with Special Reference to Medieval English Literature*. 1952. Reprint, [East Lansing]: Michigan State University Press, 1967.

Boenig, Robert. *Saint and Hero: Andreas and Medieval Doctrine*. Lewisburg: Bucknell University Press, 1991.

Booton, Diane E. "Variation on a Limbourg Theme: Saint Anastasia at the Nativity in a Getty Book of Hours and in French Medieval Literature." *Fifteenth-Century Studies* 29 (2004): 52–79.

Borenius, Tancred. *A Catalogue of the Pictures, etc., at 18 Kensington Palace Gardens, London*. Vol. 1. Oxford: University Press, 1923.

Børresen, Kari E. "Religious Feminism in the Middle Ages: Birgitta of Sweden." In *Maistresse of My Wit: Medieval Women, Modern Scholars*, edited by Louise D'Arcens and Juanita Feros Ruys, Making the Middle Ages 7, 295–312. Turnhout/Abingdon: Brepols/Marston, 2004.

Boss, Sarah Jane. "The Development of Mary's Immaculate Conception." In *Mary: The Complete Resource*, edited by Sarah Jane Boss, 207–35. Oxford: Oxford University Press, 2007.

Boswell, John. *Christianity, Social Tolerance, and Homosexuality: Gay People in Western Europe from the Beginning of the Christian Era to the Fourteenth Century*. Chicago: University of Chicago Press, 1980.

————. *The Kindness of Strangers: The Abandonment of Children in Western Europe from Late Antiquity to the Renaissance*. New York: Pantheon Books, 1988.

Bouhot, Jean-Paul. "Les traductions latines de Jean Chrysostome du Vᵉ au XVIᵉ siècle." In *Traduction et traducteurs au moyen âge: actes du colloque international du CNRS organisé à Paris, Institut de Recherche et d'Histoire des Textes, les 26–28 mai 1986*, edited by Geneviève Contamine, 31–39. Paris: Éditions du CNRS, 1989.

Boulton, Maureen. "The 'Evangile de l'Enfance': Text and Illustration in Oxford, Bodleian Library, MS Selden Supra 38." *Scriptorium* 37 (1983): 54–65.

————. *Sacred Fictions of Medieval France: Narrative Theology in the Lives of Christ and the Virgin, 1150–1500*. Gallica 38. Cambridge: D. S. Brewer, 2015.

————. "Telling the Story of the Christ Child: Text and Image in Two Fourteenth-Century Manuscripts." In *Telling the Story in the Middle Ages: Essays in Honor of Evelyn Birge Vitz*, edited by Kathryn A. Duys, Elizabeth Emery, and Laurie Postlewate, 123–40. Cambridge: D. S. Brewer, 2015.

————. "Transmission or Transformation: Scribal Intervention in French Apocryphal Texts (13–15th Centuries)." *Romance Languages Annual* 5 (1993): 14–18.

Boyer, Jean-Paul, and Gilles Dorival, eds. *La Nativité et le temps de Noël: Antiquité et Moyen Âge*. Aix-en-Provence: Publications de l'Université de Provence, 2003.

Boyle, Leonard E. "Popular Piety in the Middle Ages: What is Popular?" *Florilegium: Carleton University Papers on Classical Antiquity and the Middle Ages* 4 (1982): 184–93.

Boynton, Susan, and Isabelle Cochelin. "The Sociomusical Role of Child Oblates at the Abbey of Cluny in the Eleventh Century." In *Musical Childhoods and the Cultures of Youth*, edited by Susan Boynton and Roe-Min Kok, 3–24. Middletown, CT: Wesleyan University Press, 2006.

Brandenbarg, Ton. "Saint Anne: A Holy Grandmother and Her Children." In *Sanctity and Motherhood: Essays on Holy Mothers in the Middle Ages*, edited by Anneke B. Mulder-Bakker, 31–65. New York: Garland, 1995.

———. "St. Anne and Her Family: The Veneration of St. Anne in Connection with Concepts of Marriage and the Family in the Early Modern Period." In *Saints and She-devils: Images of Women in the 15th and 16th Centuries*, edited by Lène Dresen-Coenders, 101–27. London: Rubicon Press, 1987.

Breeze, Andrew. "The Instantaneous Harvest." *Ériu* 41 (1990): 81–93.

———. "The Virgin's Tears of Blood." *Celtica* 20 (1998): 110–22.

Briggs, Katharine. *The Fairies in English Literature and Tradition*. Chicago: University of Chicago Press, 1967.

Brock, Sebastian. "Clothing Metaphor as a Means of Theological Expression in Syriac Tradition." In *Studies in Syriac Christianity: History, Literature and Theology*, no. 11. Hampshire: Variorum, 1992.

Browe, Peter. *Die eucharistischen Wunder des Mittelalters*. Breslauer Studien zur historischen Theologie, neue Folge, Band 4. Breslau: Müller & Seiffert, 1938.

Brown, Elizabeth A. R., and Thomas Waldman. "Eudes de Deuil et la première ostension de la sainte tunique d'Argenteuil." In *La sainte tunique d'Argenteuil face à la science: Actes du colloque du 12 novembre 2006 à Argenteuil organisé par COSTA (UNEC)*, edited by Didier Huguet and Winfried Wuermeling, 67–69. Paris: François-Xavier de Guibert, 2007.

Brown, Raymond E. *The Birth of the Messiah: A Commentary on the Infancy Narratives of the Gospels of Matthew and Luke*. New, updated ed. New York: Doubleday, 1993.

Burns, E. Jane. "Saracen Silk and the Virgin's Chemise: Cultural Crossings in Cloth." *Speculum* 81.2 (2006): 366–96.

Burns, Paul C. "Child Sacrifice: A Polyvalent Story in Early Eucharistic Piety." In *Not Sparing the Child: Human Sacrifice in the Ancient World and Beyond*, edited by Daphna Arbel, Paul C. Burns, et al., 141–64. London: Bloomsbury, 2015.

Burr, David. *The Spiritual Franciscans: From Protest to Persecution in the Century after Saint Francis*. University Park: Penn State University Press, 2001.

Burrow, J. A. *The Ages of Man: A Study in Medieval Writing and Thought*. Oxford: Clarendon Press, 1986.

———. *Gestures and Looks in Medieval Narrative*. Cambridge: Cambridge University Press, 2002.

———. "God and the Fullness of Time in *Piers Plowman*." *Medium Ævum* 79.2 (2010): 300–305.

Bynum, Caroline W. "Bodily Miracles and the Resurrection of the Body in the High Middle Ages." In *Belief in History: Innovative Approaches to European and American Religion*, edited by Thomas Kselman, 68–106. Notre Dame, Ind.: University of Notre Dame Press, 1991.

————. "The Body of Christ in the Later Middle Ages: A Response to Leo Steinberg." In *Fragmentation and Redemption*, 79–117.

————. *Christian Materiality: An Essay on Religion in Late Medieval Europe.* New York: Zone Books, 2011.

————. "Did the Twelfth Century Discover the Individual?" In *Jesus as Mother*, 82–109.

————. "The Female Body and Religious Practice in the Later Middle Ages." In *Fragmentation and Redemption*, 181–238.

————. *Fragmentation and Redemption: Essays on Gender and the Human Body in Medieval Religion.* New York: Zone Books, 1992.

————. *Holy Feast and Holy Fast: The Religious Significance of Food to Medieval Women.* Berkeley: University of California Press, 1988.

————. "Jesus as Mother and Abbot as Mother: Some Themes in Twelfth-Century Cistercian Writing." In *Jesus as Mother*, 110–69.

————. *Jesus as Mother: Studies in the Spirituality of the High Middle Age*s. Berkeley: University of California Press, 1982.

————. "Mysticism and Asceticism of Medieval Women." In *Fragmentation and Redemption*, 53–78.

————. *The Resurrection of the Body in Western Christianity, 200–1336.* New York: Columbia University Press, 1995.

————. "Women Mystics and Eucharistic Devotion in the Thirteenth Century." In *Fragmentation and Redemption*, 119–50.

————. "Women's Stories, Women's Symbols: A Critique of Victor Turner's Theory of Liminality." In *Fragmentation and Redemption*, 27–51.

————. "Wonder." In *Metamorphosis and Identity*, 37–75. New York: Zone Books, 2001.

————. *Wonderful Blood: Theology and Practice in Late Medieval Northern Germany and Beyond.* Philadelphia: University of Pennsylvania Press, 2007.

Cain, Andrew. "Jerome's *Epitaphium Paulae*: Hagiography, Pilgrimage, and the Cult of Saint Paula." *Journal of Early Christian Studies* 18.1 (2010): 105–39.

Callisen, S. A. "The Evil Eye in Italian Art." *Art Bulletin* 19.3 (1937): 450–62.

Camille, Michael. "Seductions of the Flesh: Meister Francke's Female 'Man' of Sorrows." In *Frömmigkeit im Mittelalter: politisch-soziale Kontexte, visuelle Praxis, körperliche Ausdrucksformen*, edited by Klaus Schreiner, with Marc Müntz, 243–69. Munich: Fink, 2002.

Cannon, Joanna. "Dominic *alter Christus*? Representations of the Founder in and after the Arca di San Domenico." In *Christ among the Medieval Dominicans: Representations of Christ in the Texts and Images of the Order of Preachers*, edited by Kent Emery and Joseph P. Wawrykow, 26–48. Notre Dame, Ind.: University of Notre Dame Press, 1998.

————. "Kissing the Virgin's Foot: *Adoratio* before the Madonna and Child Enacted, Depicted, Imagined." *Studies in Iconography* 31 (2010): 1–50.

Canova, Giordana Mariana. "Contributo alla iconografia antoniana: antiche immagini minate di S. Antonio." *Il Santo*, ser. 2, 19/2–3 (1979): 473–50.

Cardile, Paul Y. "Mary as Priest: Mary's Sacerdotal Position in the Visual Arts." *Arte cristiana* 72 (1984): 199–208.

Carol, Juniper B. "Our Lady's Coredemption." In *Mariology*, vol. 2, edited by Juniper B. Carol, 377–425. Milkwaukee: Bruce Publishing Co., 1957.

Carr, Sherwyn T. "The Middle English Nativity Cherry Tree: The Dissemination of a Popular Motif." *Modern Language Quarterly* 36.2 (1975): 133–47.

Carruthers, Mary. *The Book of Memory: A Study of Memory in Medieval Culture*. 2nd ed. Cambridge: Cambridge University Press, 2008.
———. "Sweetness." *Speculum* 81.4 (2006): 999–1013.
Cartlidge, David R., and J. Keith Elliott. *Art and the Christian Apocrypha*. London: Routledge, 2001.
Casey, Mary. "Conversion as Depicted on the Fourteenth-Century Tring Tiles." In *Christianizing Peoples and Converting Individuals*, edited by Guyda Armstrong and Ian N. Wood, International Medieval Research 7, 339–46. Turnhout: Brepols, 2000.
Cattin, Giulio. *Musica e Liturgia a San Marco*. Vol. 1. Venezia: Edizioni Fondazioni Levi, 1990.
Chambers, E. K. *The Mediaeval Stage*. Vol. 2. London: Oxford University Press, 1903. Reprint, 1925.
Chareyron, Nicole. *Pilgrims to Jerusalem in the Middle Ages*. Translated by W. Donald Wilson. New York: Columbia University Press, 2005.
Châtillon, Jean. "*Nudum Christum Nudus Sequere*: A Note on the Origins and Meaning of the Theme of Spiritual Nakedness in the Writings of Bonaventure." Translated by Edward Hagman. *Greyfriars Review* 10.3 (1996): 293–340.
Chenu, M.-D. "Theology and the New Awareness of History." In *Nature, Man, and Society in the Twelfth Century: Essays on New Theological Perspectives in the Latin West*, edited and translated by Jerome Taylor and Lester K. Little, 162–201. Toronto: University of Toronto Press, 1997.
Chorpenning, Joseph F. "Icon of Family and Religious Life: The Historical Development of the Holy Family Devotion." In *The Holy Family as Prototype of the Civilization of Love: Images from the Viceregal Americas*, edited by Joseph F. Chorpenning, 3–40. Philadelphia: Saint Joseph's University Press, 1996.
Clanchy, Michael. "Did Mothers Teach Their Children to Read?" In *Motherhood, Religion, and Society in Medieval Europe, 400–1400: Essays Presented to Henrietta Leyser*, edited by Conrad Leyser and Lesley Smith, 129–53. Farnham: Ashgate, 2011.
Clark, Gillian. "The Fathers and the Children." In *The Church and Childhood*, edited by Wood, 1–27.
Clivaz, Claire, Andreas Dettwiler, Luc Devillers, and Enrico Norelli, eds. *Infancy Gospels: Stories and Identities*. Tübingen: Mohr Siebeck, 2011.
Cochelin, Isabelle. "Besides the Book: Using the Body to Mould the Mind: Cluny in the Tenth and Eleventh Centuries." In *Medieval Monastic Education*, edited by George Ferzocco and Carolyn Muessig, 21–34. London: Leicester University Press, 2000.
Cochelin, Isabelle, and Karen Smyth, eds. *Medieval Life Cycles: Continuity and Change*. International Medieval Research 18. Turnhout: Brepols, 2013.
Cockerell, Nina. "Nativity Group." In *Dictionary of Art*, edited by Jane Turner, vol. 22, 679–82. New York: Grove's Dictionaries, 1996.
Cohen, Esther. "The Meaning of the Head in High Medieval Culture." In *Disembodied Heads*, edited by Santing et al., 59–76.
———. *The Modulated Scream: Pain in Late Medieval Culture*. Chicago: University of Chicago Press, 2010.
Cohen, Jeremy. *Christ Killers: The Jews and the Passion from the Bible to the Big Screen*. Oxford: Oxford University Press, 2007.
———. "The Jews as the Killers of Christ in the Latin Tradition, from Augustine to the Friars." *Traditio* 39 (1983): 1–27.

Coletti, Theresa. "Devotional Iconography in the N-Town Marian Plays." *Comparative Drama* 11 (1977): 22–44.

Comet, Georges. 'L'Iconographie de la Nativité à l'époque médiévale." In *La Nativité et le temps de Noël*, edited by Boyer and Dorival, 203–11.

Constable, Giles. "Opposition to Pilgrimage in the Middle Ages." In *Mélanges G. Fransen*, edited by Stephan Kuttner and Alfons M. Stickler, vol. 1, Studia Gratiana 19, 123–46. Rome: Libreria Ateneo Salesiano, 1976.

———. *Three Studies in Medieval Religious and Social Thought: The Interpretation of Mary and Martha; The Ideal of the Imitation of Christ; The Orders of Society*. Cambridge: Cambridge University Press, 1998.

Cook, William R. *Images of St Francis of Assisi in Painting, Stone and Glass from the Earliest Images to ca. 1320: A Catalogue*. Italian Medieval and Renaissance Studies 7. Florence/ Perth: L. S. Olschki/University of W. Australia, 1999.

Cooper, Lisa H. *Artisans and Narrative Craft in Late Medieval England*. Cambridge: Cambridge University Press, 2011.

Cooper, Lisa H., and Andrea Denny-Brown, eds. *The* Arma Christi *in Medieval and Early Modern Material Culture, with a Critical Edition of "O Vernicle."* Farnham: Ashgate, 2014.

Cooper-Rompato, Christine F. *The Gift of Tongues: Women's Xenoglossia in the Later Middle Ages*. University Park: Penn State University Press, 2010.

Cornell, Henrik. *Biblia pauperum*. Stockholm: [Thule-tryck], 1925.

———. *The Iconography of the Nativity of Christ*. Uppsala: Lundquist, 1924.

Couch, Julie Nelson. "Apocryphal Romance in the London Thornton Manuscript." In *Robert Thornton and His Books: Essays on the Lincoln and London Thornton Manuscripts*, edited by Susanna Fein and Michael Johnston, 205–34. Cambridge: D. S. Brewer, 2014.

———. ' "Misbehaving God: The Case of the Christ Child in Laud Misc. 108 'Infancy of Jesus Christ.'" In *Mindful Spirit in Late Medieval Literature: Essays in Honor of Elizabeth D. Kirk*, edited by Bonnie Wheeler, 312–43. New York: Palgrave, 2006.

Cousins, Ewert. "Francis of Assisi: Christian Mysticism at the Crossroads." In *Mysticism and Religious Traditions*, edited by Steven T. Katz, 163–90. New York: Oxford University Press, 1983.

Cuffel, Alexandra. *Gendering Disgust in Medieval Religious Polemic*. Notre Dame, Ind.: University of Notre Dame Press, 2007.

Cullmann, Oscar. "Infancy Gospels." In *New Testament Apocrypha*, vol. 2, edited by Hennecke and Schneemelcher, 414–69.

Curley, Michael J. "Conjuring History: Mother, Nun, and Incubus in Geoffrey of Monmouth's *Historia Regum Britanniae*." *Journal of English and Germanic Philology* 114.2 (2015): 219–39.

d'Alverny, M.-Th. "Deux translations latines du Coran au Moyen Âge." *Archives d'histoire doctrinale et littéraire du Moyen Âge* 22/23 (1947–48): 69–131.

Davis, Stephen J. *Christ Child: Cultural Memories of a Young Jesus*. New Haven, Conn.: Yale University Press, 2014.

Deanesly, Margaret. *The Lollard Bible and Other Medieval Biblical Versions*. Cambridge: Cambridge University Press, 1920.

Debby, Nirit Ben-Aryeh. *The Cult of St Clare of Assisi in Early Modern Italy*. Farnham: Ashgate, 2014.

Delany, Sheila. " 'Phantom' and the *House of Fame*." *Chaucer Review* 2.2 (1967): 67–74.

Del Popolo, Concetto. "Anastasia levatrice di Maria." *Lettere Italiane* 57.2 (2005): 261–71.

Demaitre, Luke. "The Idea of Childhood and Child Care in Medical Writings of the Middle Ages." *Journal of Psychohistory* 4.4 (1977): 461–90.

Derbes, Anne. *Picturing the Passion in Late Medieval Italy: Narrative Painting, Franciscan Ideologies, and the Levant.* Cambridge: Cambridge University Press, 1996.

Despres, Denise L. "Adolescence and Interiority in Aelred's Lives of Christ." In *Devotional Culture in Late Medieval England and Europe,* edited by Kelly and Perry, 107–25.

———. "Cultic Anti-Judaism and Chaucer's Litel Clergeon." *Modern Philology* 91.4 (1994): 413–27.

———. "Mary of the Eucharist: Cultic Anti-Judaism in Some Fourteenth-Century English Devotional Manuscripts." In *From Witness to Witchcraft: Jews and Judaism in Medieval Christian Thought,* edited by Jeremy Cohen, Wolfenbütteler Mittelalter Studien 11, 375–41. Wiesbaden: Harrassowitz, 1996.

Dimmock, Matthew. "Mandeville on Muhammad: Texts, Contexts, and Influence." In *A Knight's Legacy: Mandeville and Mandevillian Lore in Early Modern England,* edited by Ladan Niayesh, 92–107. Manchester: Manchester University Press, 2011.

Dinzelbacher, Peter. "The Beginnings of Mysticism Experienced in Twelfth-Century England." In *The Medieval Mystical Tradition in England: Papers Read at Dartington Hall, July 1987,* edited by Marion Glasscoe, 111–31. Cambridge: D. S. Brewer, 1987.

Dodds, Michael J. "The Teaching of Thomas Aquinas on the Mysteries of the Life of Christ." In *Aquinas on Doctrine: A Critical Introduction,* edited by Thomas G. Weinandy et al., 91–115. London: T. & T. Clark, 2004.

Dor, Pierre. *La tunique d'Argenteuil et ses prétendues "rivales": Études historiques.* Paris: Éditions Hérault, 2002.

Douie, Decima L. *The Nature and the Effect of the Heresy of the Fraticelli.* Manchester: University Press, 1932.

Dove, Mary. *The Perfect Age of Man's Life.* Cambridge: Cambridge University Press, 1986.

Duffy, Eamon. "Mater Dolorosa, Mater Misericordiae." *New Blackfriars* 69 (1988): 210–27.

Dumont, Charles. "St. Aelred and the Assumption." *Life of the Spirit* 8 (1953): 205–10.

Duncan, Thomas G. " 'Quid Hinieldus cum Christo?' The Secular Expression of the Sacred in Old and Middle English Lyrics." In *The Sacred and the Secular in Medieval and Early Modern Cultures: New Essays,* edited by Lawrence L. Besserman, 29–46, 187–90. New York: Palgrave, 2006.

Durand, Jannic. "Byzantium and Beyond: Relics of the Infancy of Christ." In *Saints and Sacred Matter: The Cult of Relics in Byzantium and Beyond,* edited by Cynthia Hahn and Holger A. Klein, 253–88. Washington, D.C.: Dumbarton Oaks Research Library and Collection, 2015.

Dutton, Elisabeth. "Review of *The Christ Child in Medieval Culture: Alpha es et O!,* edited by Theresa M. Kenney and Mary Dzon (Toronto: University of Toronto Press, 2012)." *Speculum* 89.4 (2014): 1172–73.

Dutton, Marsha L. "Christ Our Mother: Aelred's Iconography for Contemplative Union." In *Goad and Nail,* edited by E. Rozanne Elder, CS 84, Studies in Medieval Cistercian History 10, 21–45. Kalamazoo, Mich.: Cistercian Publications, 1985.

———. "The Face and the Feet of God: The Humanity of Christ in Bernard of Clairvaux and Aelred of Rievaulx." In *Bernardus Magister: Papers Presented at the Nonacentenary Cele-*

*bration of the Birth of Bernard of Clairvaux, Kalamazoo, Michigan, 10–13 May 1990*, edited
by John R. Sommerfeldt, 203–23. Kalamazoo, Mich./Cîteaux: Cistercian Publications/
Commentarii Cistercienses, 1992.

———. "The Invented Sexual History of Aelred of Rievaulx; A Review Article." *American
Benedictine Review* 47 (1995): 414–32.

Dyas, Dee. *Pilgrimage in Medieval English Literature, 700–1500*. Woodbridge: D. S. Brewer, 2001.

Dzon, Mary. "Birgitta of Sweden and Christ's Clothing." In *The Christ Child in Medieval Culture*, edited by Dzon and Kenney, 117–44.

———. "'Bold in His Barnhoed': The Christ Child as Knight in *Piers Plowman*." Forthcoming.

———. "Boys Will Be Boys: The Physiology of Childhood and the Apocryphal Christ Child
in the Later Middle Ages." *Viator* 42.1 (2011): 179–225.

———. "Cecily Neville and the Apocryphal *Infantia Salvatoris* in the Middle Ages." *Mediaeval Studies* 71 (2009): 235–300.

———. "Conflicting Notions of *Pietas* in Walter of Wimborne's *Marie Carmina*." *Journal of
Medieval Latin* 15 (2005): 67–92.

———. "Jesus and the Birds in Medieval Abrahamic Traditions." *Traditio* 66 (2011): 189–230.

———. "Joseph and the Amazing Christ-Child of Late-Medieval Legend." In *Childhood in
the Middle Ages and the Renaissance: The Results of a Paradigm Shift in the History of Men-
tality*, edited by Albrecht Classen, 135–57. Berlin: de Gruyter, 2005.

———. "Margery Kempe's Ravishment into the Childhood of Christ." *Mediaevalia* 27.2
(2007): 27–57.

———. "Out of Egypt, Into England: Tales of the Good Thief for Medieval English Audiences." In *Devotional Culture in Late Medieval England and Europe*, edited by Kelly and
Perry, 147–241.

———. "Saintly and Other Children in the *Golden Legend* of Jacobus de Voragine." In *Childhood in History*, edited by Aasgaard and Horn, forthcoming.

———. "Wanton Boys in Middle English Texts and the Christ Child in Minneapolis, University of Minnesota, MS Z822 N81." In *Medieval Life Cycles*, edited by Cochelin and
Smyth, 81–145.

Dzon, Mary, and Theresa M. Kenney. "Introduction: The Infancy of Scholarship on the Medieval Christ Child." In *The Christ Child in Medieval Culture*, edited by Dzon and Kenney, xiii–xxii.

Dzon, Mary, and Theresa M. Kenney, eds. *The Christ Child in Medieval Culture: Alpha es et O!*
Toronto: University of Toronto Press, 2012.

Eames, Elizabeth S. *Catalogue of Medieval Lead-glazed Earthenware Tiles in the Department of
Medieval and Later British Antiquities, British Museum*. 2 vols. London: British Museum,
1980.

*Early Printed Books: Major Acquisitions of The Pierpont Morgan Library 1924–1974*. New York:
The Pierpont Morgan Library, 1974.

Edwards, Glenn M. "Canonistic Determinations of the Stages of Childhood." In *Aspectus et
Affectus: Essays and Editions in Grosseteste and Medieval Intellectual Life in Honor of Richard C. Dales*, edited by Gunar Freibergs, 67–75. New York: AMS Press, 1993.

Eisler, Colin. *Masterworks in Berlin: A City's Paintings Reunited: Painting in the Western World,
1300–1914*. Boston: Little, Brown, and Co., 1966.

Ellington, Donna Spivey. *From Sacred Body to Angelic Soul: Understanding Mary in Late Medieval and Early Modern Europe*. Washington, D.C.: Catholic University of America Press, 2001.

Elliott, Dyan. *Fallen Bodies: Pollution, Sexuality, and Demonology in the Middle Ages*. Philadelphia: University of Pennsylvania Press, 1998.

———. *Spiritual Marriage: Sexual Abstinence in Medieval Wedlock*. Princeton: Princeton University Press, 1993.

———. "True Presence/False Christ: The Antinomies of Embodiment in Medieval Spirituality." *Mediaeval Studies* 64 (2002): 241–65.

Erickson, Carolly. "Bartholomew of Pisa, Francis Exalted: *De conformitate*." *Mediaeval Studies* 34 (1972): 253–74.

Erlemann, Hildegard. *Die Heilige Familie: ein Tugendvorbild der Gegenreformation im Wandel der Zeit: Kult und Ideologie*. Münster: Ardey, 1993.

Evangelatou, Maria. "The Purple Thread of the Flesh: The Theological Connotations of a Narrative Iconographic Element in Byzantine Images of the Annunciation." In *Icon and Word: The Power of Images in Byzantium. Studies Presented to Robin Cormack*, edited by Antony Eastmond and Liz James, 261–79. Aldershot: Ashgate, 2003.

Falvay, Dávid. "St. Elizabeth of Hungary in Italian Vernacular Literature: *Vitae*, Miracles, Revelations and the *Meditations on the Life of Christ*." In *Promoting the Saints: Cults and Their Contexts from Late Antiquity until the Early Modern Period: Essays in Honor of Gábor Klaniczay for His 60th Birthday*, edited by Ottó Gecser et al., 137–50. Budapest: CEU Press, 2010.

Falvay, Dávid, and Peter Tóth. "New Light on the Date and Authorship of the *Meditationes vitae Christi*." In *Devotional Culture in Late Medieval England and Europe*, edited by Kelly and Perry, 17–104.

Farmer, David. *The Oxford Dictionary of Saints*. 5th ed. Oxford: Oxford University Press, 2004.

Ferreiro, Alberto. *Simon Magus in Patristic, Medieval and Early Modern Traditions*. Studies in the History of Christian Traditions 125. Leiden: Brill, 2005.

Filas, Francis L. *Joseph and Jesus: A Theological Study of Their Relationship*. Milwaukee: Bruce Publishing, 1952.

Flint, Valerie I. J. *The Rise of Magic in Early Medieval Europe*. Princeton: Princeton University Press, 1991.

Flora, Holly. *The Devout Belief of the Imagination: The Paris* Meditationes Vitae Christi *and Female Spirituality in Trecento Italy*. Disciplina Monastica 6. Turnhout: Brepols, 2009.

———. "Women Wielding Knives: The Circumcision of Christ by His Mother in an Illustrated Manuscript of the *Meditationes vitae Christi* (Paris, Bibliothèque Nationale de France, ital. 115)." In *The Christ Child in Medieval Culture*, edited by Dzon and Kenney, 145–66.

Flores, Deyanira. "The Nativity Scene in the 'Lives of Mary' in the Apocrypha (II.–IX. Cent.), the Byzantine 'Lives of the Virgin' (VII.–XI. Cent.), Medieval Women Mystics (XII.–XIV. Cent.), and Medieval 'Lives' of Jesus, Mary and Joseph (X.–XV. Cent.).'" *Marian Studies* 60 (2009): 51–128.

Fogelqvist, Ingvar. "The New Vineyard: St. Birgitta of Sweden's 'Regula Salvatoris' and the Monastic Tradition." In *In Quest of the Kingdom: Ten Papers on Medieval Monastic Spirituality*, edited by Alf Härdelin, 203–44. Stockholm: Almqvist & Wiksell, 1991.

Forsyth, Ilene H. "Children in Early Medieval Art: Ninth through Twelfth Centuries." *Journal of Psychohistory* 4.1 (1976): 31–70.

————. *The Throne of Wisdom: Wood Sculptures of the Madonna in Romanesque France*. Princeton: Princeton University Press, 1972.

Fortini, Arnaldo. *Francis of Assisi: A Translation of* Nova Vita di San Francesco. Translated by Helen Moak. New York: Crossroad, 1981.

Foulon, Jean-Hervé. "La Nativité dans la prédication de saint Bernard, abbé de Clairvaux." In *La Nativité et le temps de Noël*, edited by Boyer and Dorival, 213–23.

Frank, Jr., Robert Worth. "*Meditationes Vitae Christi*: The Logistics of Access to Divinity." In *Hermeneutics and Medieval Culture*, edited by Patrick J. Gallacher and Helen Damico, 39–50. Albany: State University of New York Press, 1989.

Freedberg, David. *The Power of Images: Studies in the History and Theory of Response*. Chicago: University of Chicago Press, 1989.

Friedman, John B. "Nicholas's 'Angelus ad Virginem' and the Mocking of Noah." *Yearbook of English Studies* 22 (1992): 168–80.

Frojmovic, Eva. "Taking Little Jesus to School in Two Thirteenth-Century Latin Psalters from South Germany." In *Beyond the Yellow Badge: Anti-Judaism and Antisemitism in Medieval and Early Modern Visual Culture*, edited by Mitchell B. Merback, 87–118, 454–62. Leiden: Brill, 2008.

Frugoni, Chiara. *Francis of Assisi: A Life*. Translated by John Bowden. New York: Continuum, 1999.

————. "Sui vari significati del Natale di Greccio, nei testi e nelle immagini." *Frate Francesco* 70.1 (2004): 35–147.

————. *Una solitudine abitata: Chiara d'Assisi*. Rome/Bari: Laterza, 2006.

Frye, Roland Mushat. *Milton's Imagery and the Visual Arts: Iconographic Tradition in the Epic Poems*. Princeton: Princeton University Press, 1978.

Fulton, Rachel. *From Judgment to Passion: Devotion to Christ and the Virgin Mary, 800–1200*. New York: Columbia University Press, 2002.

Gabra, Gawdat, ed. *Be Thou There: The Holy Family's Journey in Egypt*. Texts by William Lyster, Cornelis Hulsman, and Stephen J. Davis. Cairo: American University in Cairo Press, 2002.

Gaiffier, Baudoin de. "Le Diable, voleur d'enfants: à propos de la naissance des Saints Étienne, Laurent et Barthélemy." In *Études critiques d'hagiographie et d'iconologie*, Subsidia Hagiographica 43, 171–93. Brussels: Société des Bollandistes, 1967.

————. "L' 'Historia apocrypha' dans la Légende dorée." *Analecta Bollandiana* 91 (1973): 265–72.

Gambero, Luigi. *Mary in the Middle Ages: The Blessed Virgin Mary in the Thought of Medieval Latin Theologians*. Translated by Thomas Buffer. San Francisco: Ignatius Press, 2000.

Garcia, Hugues. "Les diverses dimensions d'apocryphité: le cas du cycle de la nativité de Jésus dans le plafond peint de l'église Saint-Martin de Zillis." *Apocrypha* 15 (2004): 201–34.

————. "L'enfant vieillard, l'enfant aux cheveux blancs et le Christ polymorphe." *Revue d'Histoire et de Philosophie Religieuses* 80.4 (2000): 479–501.

Garidis, Miltos. "Approche 'réaliste' dans la représentation du Mélismos." *Jahrbuch der österreichischen Byzantinistik* 32 (1982): 495–502.

Gaston, Robert W. "Affective Devotion and the Early Dominicans: The Case of Fra Angelico." In *Rituals, Images, and Words: Varieties of Cultural Expression in Late Medieval and Early Modern Europe*, edited by F. W. Kent and Charles Zika, 87–117. Late Medieval and Early Modern Studies 3. Turnhout: Brepols, 2005.

Geary, Patrick J. *Furta Sacra: Thefts of Relics in the Central Middle Ages*. Princeton: Princeton University Press, 1990.

Geiger, Gail L. "Filippino Lippi's *Triumph of Saint Thomas Aquinas*." In *Rome in the Renaissance: The City and the Myth*, edited by P. A. Ramsey, Medieval & Renaissance Texts & Studies 18, 223–36. Binghamton, N.Y.: Center for Medieval and Early Renaissance Studies, 1988.

Gero, Stephen. "The Infancy Gospel of Thomas: A Study of the Textual and Literary Problems." *Novum Testamentum* 13 (1971): 46–80.

Gerould, Gordon Hall. "The Ballad of *The Bitter Withy*." *PMLA* 23.1 (1908): 141–67.

Gertsman, Elina. *The Dance of Death in the Middle Ages: Image, Text, Performance*. Studies in the Visual Cultures of the Middle Ages 3. Turnhout: Brepols, 2010.

———. "Signs of Death: The Sacrificial Christ Child in Late Medieval Art." In *The Christ Child in Medieval Culture*, edited by Dzon and Kenney, 66–91.

———. *Worlds Within: Opening the Medieval Shrine Madonna*. University Park: Penn State University Press, 2015.

Giannarelli, Elena. "Infanzia e santità: un problema della biografia cristiana antica." In *Bambini santi: Rappresentazioni dell'infanzia e modelli agiografici*, edited by Elena Giannarelli and Anna Benvenuti Papi, 33–39. Turin: Rosenberg & Sellier, 1991.

Gianotto, Claudio. "L'origine de la fête de Noël au IV^e siècle." In *La Nativité et le temps de Noël*, edited by Boyer and Dorival, 65–79.

Gibson, Gail McMurray. "Swaddling Cloth and Shroud: The Symbolic Garment of the Incarnation in Medieval Literature and Art." Unpublished MA thesis, Duke University, 1972.

———. *The Theater of Devotion: East Anglian Drama and Society in the Late Middle Ages*. Chicago: University of Chicago Press, 1989.

———. "The Thread of Life in the Hand of the Virgin." In *Equally in God's Image: Women in the Middle Ages*, edited by Julian Bolton Holloway et al., 46–54. New York: Peter Lang, 1990.

Gilbank, Robin. "The Childhood of Christ and the Infancy of the Soul in Aelred's *De Iesu Puero Duodenni*." In *Rhetoric of the Anchorhold: Space, Place and Body within Discourses of Enclosure*, edited by Liz Herbert McAvoy, 173–87. Cardiff: University of Wales Press, 2008.

Gilbert, Creighton. "The Archbishop on the Painters of Florence, 1450." *Art Bulletin* 41.1 (1959): 75–87.

Gilchrist, Roberta. *Medieval Life: Archaeology and the Life Course*. Woodbridge: Boydell Press, 2012.

Glover, Sarah Rose. "Illustrations of the Miracles of the Virgin in English Books of Hours." Unpublished PhD thesis, University of Virginia, 2003.

Gnilka, Christian. *Aetas Spiritalis: die Überwindung der natürlichen Altersstufen als Ideal frühchristlichen Lebens*. Bonn: P. Hanstein, 1972.

Goldstein, Morris. *Jesus in the Jewish Tradition*. New York: Macmillan, 1950.

Gondreau, Paul. *The Passions of Christ's Soul in the Theology of St. Thomas Aquinas*. Scranton, Pa.: University of Scranton Press, 2009.

Goodey, C. F., and Tim Stainton. "Intellectual Disability and the Changeling Myth." *Journal of the History of the Behavioural Sciences* 37.3 (2001): 233–40.

Goodich, Michael. *From Birth to Old Age: The Human Life Cycle in Medieval Thought, 1250–1350*. Lanham, Md.: University Press of America, 1989.

————. *Miracles and Wonders: The Development of the Concept of Miracle, 1150–1350*. Aldershot: Ashgate, 2007.

Gounelle, Rémi. "Une Légende apocryphe relatant la rencontre du Bon Larron et de la Sainte Famille en Égypte (BHG 2119y)." *Analecta Bollandiana* 121 (2003): 241–72.

Graef, Hilda. *Mary: A History of Doctrine and Devotion*. London: Sheed & Ward, 1985.

Graves, Janet M. " 'The Holy Well': A Medieval Religious Ballad." *Western Folklore* 26.1 (1967): 13–26.

Greef, Lise de. "*Uterus Cordis*: Speerbildchen Featuring the Christ Child in the Wounded Heart." *Jaarboek van het Koninklijk Museum voor Schone Kunsten, Antwerpen* n.v. (2009): 52–97.

Green, Richard Firth. "Changing Chaucer." *Studies in the Age of Chaucer* 25 (2003): 27–52.

————. "Christ the Changeling." Unpublished paper delivered at the Medieval Academy of America Annual Meeting, Toronto, 12 April 2007.

————. *Elf Queens and Holy Friars: Fairy Beliefs and the Medieval Church*. Philadelphia: University of Pennsylvania Press, 2016.

Green, Rosalie. "The Missing Midwife." *Romanesque and Gothic: Essays for George Zarnecki*, edited by Neil Stratford, 103–5. Woodbridge: Boydell Press, 1987.

Greenspan, Kate. "Matre Donante: The Embrace of Christ as the Virgin's Gift in the Visions of 13th-century Italian Women." *Studia Mystica* 13.2/3 (1990): 26–37.

Gregory, Andrew, and Christopher Tuckett, eds. *The Oxford Handbook of Early Christian Apocrypha*. Oxford: Oxford University Press, 2015.

Greven, Joseph. *Die Anfänge der Beginen: ein Beitrag zur Geschichte der Volksfrömmigkeit und des Ordenswesens im Hochmittelalter*. Münster: Aschendorff, 1912.

Gribetz, Sarit Kattan. "Jesus and the Clay Birds: Reading *Toledot Yeshu* in Light of the Infancy Gospels." In *Envisioning Judaism: Studies in Honor of Peter Schäfer on the Occasion of His Seventieth Birthday*, vol. 2, edited by Ra'anan S. Boustan et al., 1021–48. Tübingen: Mohr Siebeck, 2013.

Gros, Gérard. "La *semblance* de la *verrine*: Description et interprétation d'une image mariale." *Le Moyen Âge* 97 (1991): 217–57.

Grousset, René. "Le boeuf et l'âne à la nativité du Christ." *Mélanges d'archéologie et d'histoire* 4 (1884): 334–44.

Grundmann, Herbert. *Religious Movements in the Middle Ages: The Historical Links between Heresy, the Mendicant Orders, and the Women's Religious Movement in the Twelfth and Thirteenth Century, with the Historical Foundations of German Mysticism*. Translated by Steven Rowan. Notre Dame, Ind.: University of Notre Dame Press, 1995.

Gudiol, Josep. *Pintura Gótica Catalana*. Barcelona: Ediciones Polígrafa, 1986.

Gurewich, Vladimir. "Observations on the Iconography of the Wound in Christ's Side, with Special Reference to Its Position." *Journal of the Warburg and Courtauld Institutes* 20 (1957): 358–62.

Hahn, Cynthia. "Joseph as Ambrose's 'Artisan of the Soul' in the Holy Family in Egypt by Albrecht Dürer." *Zeitschrift für Kunstgeschichte* 47.4 (1984): 515–22.

————. " 'Joseph Will Perfect, Mary Enlighten, and Jesus Save Thee': The Holy Family as Marriage Model in the Mérode Triptych." *Art Bulletin* 68.1 (1986): 54–66.

Hale, Rosemary Drage. "*Imitatio Mariae*: Motherhood Motifs in Devotional Memoirs." *Mystics Quarterly* 16 (1990): 193–203.

————. "Joseph as Mother: Adaptation and Appropriation in the Construction of Male Virtue." In *Medieval Mothering*, edited by John Carmi Parsons and Bonnie Wheeler, 101–13. New York: Garland, 1996.

———. "Rocking the Cradle: Margaretha Ebner (Be)Holds the Divine." In *Performance and Transformation: New Approaches to Late Medieval Spirituality*, edited by Mary A. Suydam and Joanna E. Ziegler, 211–39. New York: St. Martin's Press, 1999.

———. "The 'Silent' Virgin: Marian Imagery in the Sermons of Meister Eckhart and Johannes Tauler." In *Medieval Sermons and Society: Cloister, City, University*, edited by Jacqueline Hamesse et al., Fédération Internationale des Instituts d'Études Médiévales, Textes et Études du Moyen Âge 9, 77–94. Louvain-la-Neuve: Collège Cardinal Mercier, 1998.

Hall, Thomas N. "The Miracle of the Lengthened Beam in Apocryphal and Hagiographic Tradition." In *Marvels, Monsters, and Miracles: Studies in the Medieval and Early Modern Imaginations*, edited by Timothy S. Jones and David A. Sprunger, Studies in Medieval Culture 42, 109–39. Kalamazoo, Mich.: Medieval Institute Publications, 2002.

———. "The Portents at Christ's Birth in Vercelli Homilies V and VI: Some Analogues from Medieval Sermon Literature and Biblical Commentaries." In *New Readings on the Vercelli Book*, edited by Andy Orchard and Samantha Zacher, 62–97. Toronto: University of Toronto Press, 2009.

Hamburger, Jeffrey F., and Anne-Marie Bouché, eds. *The Mind's Eye: Art and Theological Argument in the Middle Ages*. Princeton: Princeton University Press, 2006.

Hamburger, Jeffrey F., and A. S. Korteweg, eds. *Tributes in Honor of James H. Marrow: Studies in Painting and Manuscript Illumination of the Late Middle Ages and Northern Renaissance*. London: Harvey Miller, 2006.

Hamilton, Marie P. "Echoes of Childermas in the Tale of the Prioress." *Modern Language Review* 34.1 (1939): 1–8.

Hamilton, Sarah. "The Virgin Mary in Cathar Thought." *Journal of Ecclesiastical History* 56.1 (2005): 24–49.

Hanawalt, Barbara A. *Growing up in Medieval London: The Experience of Childhood in History*. Oxford: Oxford University Press, 1993.

———. "Medievalists and the Study of Childhood." *Speculum* 77.2 (2002): 440–60.

———. *The Ties that Bound: Peasant Families in Medieval England*. Oxford: Oxford University Press, 1986.

Hanning, Robert W. *The Individual in Twelfth-Century Romance*. New Haven, Conn.: Yale University Press, 1977.

Hansen, Morten Steen. "The Infant Christ with the *arma Christi*: François Duquesnoy and the Typology of the Putto." *Zeitschrift für Kunstgeschichte* 71.1 (2008): 121–33.

Härdelin, Alf, and Mereth Lindgren, eds. *Heliga Birgitta, budskapet och förebilden: föredrag vid jubileumssymposiet i Vadstena 3–7 oktober 1991*. Stockholm: Almqvist & Wiksell, 1993.

Harf-Lancer, Laurence. "Fairies." In *Encyclopedia of the Middle Ages*, edited by André Vauchez et al., translated by Adrian Walford, vol. 1, 526. Chicago: Fitzroy Dearborn, 2000.

Harvey, E. Ruth. *The Inward Wits: Psychological Theory in the Middle Ages and the Renaissance*. London: Warburg Institute, 1975.

Haskins, C. H. "The Greek Element in the Renaissance of the Twelfth Century." *American Historical Review* 25.4 (1920): 603–15.

Hassig, Debra. *Medieval Bestiaries: Text, Image, Ideology*. Cambridge: Cambridge University Press, 1995.

Heck, Christian. *Le Ci nous dit: l'image médiévale et la culture des laïcs au XIV^e siècle: les enluminures du manuscrit de Chantilly*. Turnhout: Brepols, 2011.

Hennecke, Edgar, and Wilhelm Schneemelcher, eds. *New Testament Apocrypha*. Vol. 1: *Gospels and Related Writings*. Translated by R. McL. Wilson. Louisville/London: Westminster John Knox Press/James Clarke & Co., 1991.

Hennessy, Cecily. *Images of Children in Byzantium*. Farnham: Ashgate, 2008.

Herbert, J. A., ed. *Catalogue of Romances in the Department of Manuscripts in the British Museum*. Vol. 3. 1920. Reprint, London: British Museum, 1962.

Herlihy, David. "The Family and Religious Ideologies in Medieval Europe." In *Women, Family and Society in Medieval Europe*, 154–73.

———. "The Making of the Medieval Family: Symmetry, Structure, and Sentiment." In *Women, Family and Society in Medieval Europe*, 135–53.

———. "Medieval Children." In *Women, Family and Society in Medieval Europe*, 215–43.

———. *Medieval Households*. Cambridge, Mass.: Harvard University Press, 1985.

———. *Women, Family and Society in Medieval Europe: Historical Essays, 1978–1991*. Edited by A. Molho. Providence, R.I.: Berghahn Books, 1995.

Herlihy, David, and Christiane Klapisch-Zuber. *Les Toscans et leurs familles: une étude du catasto florentin de 1427*. Paris: Presses de la Fondation Nationale des Sciences Politiques, 1978.

Hervieux, Jacques. *The New Testament Apocrypha*. Translated by Dom Wulstan Hibberd. New York: Hawthorn Books, 1960.

Hill, Thomas D. "The Baby on the Stone: Nativity as Sacrifice (The Old English *Christ III*, 1414–1425)." In *Intertexts: Studies in Anglo-Saxon Culture Presented to Paul E. Szarmach*, edited by Virginia Blanton and Helene Scheck, 69–77. Tempe/Turnhout: Arizona Center for Medieval and Renaissance Studies/Brepols, 2008.

Hoffman, Werner J. "Vita Beatae Virginis Mariae et Salvatoris Rhythmica." In DS, vol. 16, 1025–29.

Holsinger, Bruce. *Music, Body, and Desire in Medieval Culture*. Stanford: Stanford University Press, 2001.

Homan, Richard L. "Two *Exempla*: Analogues to the *Play of the Sacrament* and *Dux Moraud*." In *Drama in the Middle Ages: Comparative and Critical Essays*, edited by Clifford Davidson and John H. Stroupe, 2nd series, 199–209. New York: AMS Press, 1990.

Hood, John Y. B. *Aquinas and the Jews*. Philadelphia: University of Pennsylvania Press, 1995.

Horn, Cornelia B., and John W. Martens. *"Let the Little Children Come to Me": Childhood and Children in Early Christianity*. Washington, D.C.: Catholic University of America Press, 2009.

Horton, Adey. *The Child Jesus*. New York: Dial Press, 1975.

Hourihane, Colum. "Defining Terms: Ecce Homo, Christ of Pity, Christ Mocked, and the Man of Sorrows." In *New Perspectives on the Man of Sorrows*, ed. Puglisi and Barcham, 19–47.

———, ed. *The Grove Encyclopedia of Medieval Art and Architecture*. 6 vols. New York: Oxford University Press, 2012.

Hout, Nico van. "*The Legend of St Christopher*: A Painting Attributed to Jan van Amstel Reexamined." *Simiolus* 33/1–2 (2007–2008): 43–52.

Hulbert, J. R. "Some Medieval Advertisements of Rome." *Modern Philology* 20.4 (1923): 403–24.

Hulst, Cesario van. "La storia della devozione a Gesù Bambino nelle immagini plastiche isolate." *Antonianum* 19 (1944): 35–54.

Hundersmarck, Lawrence F. "Reforming Life by Conforming It to the Life of Christ: Pseudo-Bonaventure's *Meditaciones Vite Christi*." In *Reform and Renewal in the Middle Ages and*

*Renaissance*, edited by Thomas M. Izbicki and Christopher M. Bellitto, Studies in the History of Christian Thought 96, 93–112. Leiden: Brill, 2000.

Izydorczyk, Zbigniew. "The *Evangelium Nicodemi* in the Latin Middle Ages." In *The Medieval Gospel of Nicodemus: Texts, Intertexts, and Contexts in Western Europe*, 43–101. Medieval & Renaissance Texts & Studies 158. Tempe, Ariz.: Medieval & Renaissance Texts & Studies, 1997.

Jacobs, Andrew S. *Christ Circumcised: A Study in Early Christian History and Difference*. Philadelphia: University of Pennsylvania Press, 2012.

Jager, Eric. *The Book of the Heart*. Chicago: University of Chicago Press, 2000.

James, M. R. "An English Bible-Picture Book of the Fourteenth Century (Holkham MS. 66)." *Walpole Society* 11 (1923): 3–17.

———. "Legends of St. Anne and St. Anastasia." *Proceedings of the Cambridge Antiquarian Society* 9, n.s., 3 (1894–98): 194–204.

———. "Rare Mediaeval Tiles and Their Story." With a note by R. L. Hobson. *The Burlington Magazine* 42 (1923): 32–37.

Jansen, Katherine Ludwig. *The Making of the Magdalen: Preaching and Popular Devotion in the Later Middle Ages*. Princeton: Princeton University Press, 2000.

Janson, Dora Jane. "Omega in Alpha: The Christ Child's Foreknowledge of His Fate." *Jahrbuch der Hamburger Kunstsammlungen* 18 (1973): 33–42.

Jászai, Géza. "Der Besuch der Engel: Zur Ikonographie eines Bildes in Meister Bertrams Buxtehuder Altar." *Westfalen. Hefte für Geschichte, Kunst, und Volkskunde* 55.1–2 (1977): 53–58.

Jensen, Robin Margaret. *Face to Face: Portraits of the Divine in Early Christianity*. Minneapolis: Fortress Press, 2005.

Johnson, Hannah R. *Blood Libel: The Ritual Murder Accusation at the Limit of Jewish History*. Ann Arbor: University of Michigan Press, 2012.

Johnson, Ian, and Allan F. Westphall, eds. *The Pseudo-Bonaventuran Lives of Christ: Exploring the Middle English Tradition*. Medieval Church Studies 24. Turnhout: Brepols, 2013.

Jørgensen, Johannes. *St. Francis of Assisi: A Biography*. Translated by T. O'Conor Sloane. New York: Doubleday, 1955.

Juhel, Vincent. "Le Bain de l'Enfant Jésus: des origines à la fin du douzième siècle." *Cahiers Archéologiques* 39 (1991): 111–32.

Jung, Jacqueline E. "The Tactile and the Visionary: Notes on the Place of the Sumptuous in the Medieval Religious Imagination." In *Looking Beyond: Visions, Dreams, and Insights in Medieval Art & History*, edited by Colum Hourihane, 202–40. Princeton/University Park: Index of Christian Art, Department of Art & Archaeology, Princeton University/Penn State University Press: 2010.

Justice, Steven. "Eucharistic Miracles and Eucharistic Doubt." *Journal of Medieval and Early Modern Studies* 42.2 (2012): 307–32.

Karnes, Michelle. *Imagination, Meditation, and Cognition in the Middle Ages*. Chicago: University of Chicago Press, 2011.

———. "Nicholas Love and Medieval Meditations on Christ." *Speculum* 82.2 (2007): 380–408.

Karras, Ruth Mazo. "The Aerial Battle in the *Toledot Yeshu* and Sodomy in the Late Middle Ages." *Medieval Encounters* 19 (2013): 493–533.

———. "'This Skill in a Woman Is By No Means to Be Despised': Weaving and the Gender Division of Labor in the Middle Ages." In *Medieval Fabrications: Dress, Textiles, Clothwork, and Other Cultural Imaginings*, edited by E. Jane Burns, 89–104. New York: Palgrave Macmillan, 2004.

Kauffmann, C. M. "Art and Popular Culture: New Themes in the Holkham Bible Picture Book." In *Studies in Medieval Art and Architecture Presented to Peter Lasko*, edited by David Buckton and T. A. Heslop, 46–69. Stroud: Allan Sutton 1994.

Keller, Peter. *Die Wiege des Christuskindes: Ein Haushaltsgerät in Kunst und Kult*. Worms: Wernersche Verlagsgesellschaft, 1998.

Kelly, Stephen, and Ryan Perry, eds. In *Devotional Culture in Late Medieval England and Europe: Diverse Imaginations of Christ's Life*. Medieval Church Studies 31. Turnhout: Brepols, 2014.

Kendall, Roy. *Christopher Marlowe and Richard Baines: Journeys through the Elizabethan Underground*. Madison, N.J./ Cranbury, N.J.: Fairleigh Dickinson University Press/Associated University Presses, 2003.

Kenney, Theresa M. "The Manger as Calvary and Altar in the Middle English Nativity Lyric." In *The Christ Child in Medieval Culture*, edited by Dzon and Kenney, 29–65.

Kessler, Herbert L."Gregory the Great and Image Theory in Northern Europe during the Twelfth and Thirteenth Centuries." In *A Companion to Medieval Art: Romanesque and Gothic in Northern Europe*, edited by Conrad Rudolph, 151–72. Malden, Mass./Oxford: Blackwell, 2006.

Kieckhefer, Richard. "*Ihesus ist unser*! The Christ Child in the German Sister Books." In *The Christ Child in Medieval Culture*, edited by Dzon and Kenney, 167–98.

———. *Magic in the Middle Ages*. Cambridge: Cambridge University Press, 2004.

———. *Unquiet Souls: Fourteenth-Century Saints and Their Religious Milieu*. Chicago: University of Chicago Press, 1984.

King, Andrew. "A Thematic Reconsideration of the Textual Ancestors of 'The Bitter Withy.'" In *Folk Song: Tradition, Revival, and Re-creation*, edited by Ian Russell and David Atkinson, 320–35. Aberdeen: Elphinstone Institute, University of Aberdeen, 2004.

Kiser, Lisa J. "Animals in Sacred Space: St. Francis and the Crib at Greccio." In *Speaking Images: Essays in Honor of V. A. Kolve*, edited by Charlotte Morse and Robert Yeager, 55–72. Asheville, N.C.: Pegasus Press, 2001.

Kittredge, George L. *Witchcraft in Old and New England*. 1929. Reprint, New York: Russell & Russell, 1954.

Klapisch-Zuber, Christiane. "Holy Dolls: Play and Piety in Florence in the Quattrocento." In *Women, Family, and Ritual in Renaissance Italy*, translated by Lydia Cochrane, 310–29. Chicago: University of Chicago Press, 1985.

———. *Le voleur de paradis: Le Bon Larron dans l'art et de la société (XIV<sup>e</sup>–XVI<sup>e</sup> siècles)*. Paris: Alma Éditeur, 2015.

Kline, Daniel T. "The Audience and Function of the Apocryphal *Infancy of Jesus Christ* in Oxford, Bodleian Library, MS. Laud Misc. 108." In *The Texts and Contexts of Oxford, Bodleian Library, MS Laud Misc. 108: The Shaping of English Vernacular Narrative*, edited by Kimberly K. Bell and Julie Nelson Couch, 137–55. Leiden: Brill, 2011.

———. "Resisting the Father in *Pearl*." In *Translating Desire in Medieval and Early Modern Literature*, edited by Craig A. Berry and Heather Richardson Hayton, Medieval &

Renaissance Texts & Studies 294, 1–29. Tempe: Arizona Center for Medieval and Renaissance Studies, 2005.

———. "Structure, Characterization, and the New Community in Four Plays of Jesus and the Doctors." *Comparative Drama* 26.4 (1993): 344–57.

Klockars, Birgit. "Giorni di festa e di lavoro nella vita di santa Brigida." In *Birgitta: una santa svedese: celebrazioni in occasione del sesto centenario della morte, 1373–1973*, 116–33. Rome: Bulzoni Editore, 1974.

Knipping, John B. *Iconography of the Counter Reformation in the Netherlands: Heaven on Earth.* Vol. 1. Nieuwkoop: De Graaf, 1974.

Kuczynski, Michael P. "An Unpublished Middle English Version of the *Epistola Lentuli*: Texts and Contexts." *The Mediaeval Journal* 2.1 (2012): 37–60.

Kuuliala, Jenni. "Sons of Demons? Children's Impairments and the Belief in Changelings in Medieval Europe (*c.* 1150–1400)." In *The Dark Side of Childhood in Late Antiquity and the Middle Ages*, edited by Katariina Mustakallio and Christian Laes, Childhood in the Past Monograph Series 2, 79–93. Oxford: Oxbow Books, 2011.

Lacroix, Benoît, and Albert-M. Landry. "Quelques thèmes de la religion populaire chez le théologien Thomas d'Aquin." In *La Culture populaire au moyen âge: études présentées au quatrième colloque de l'Institut d'études médiévales de l'Université de Montréal, 2–3 avril 1977*, edited by Pierre Boglioni, 165–81. Montréal: L'Aurore, 1979.

Ladis, Andrew, and Shelley E. Zuraw, eds. *Visions of Holiness: Art and Devotion in Renaissance Italy.* Athens: Georgia Museum of Art, 2001.

Lafontaine-Dosogne, Jacqueline. *Iconographie de l'enfance de la Vierge dans l'Empire byzantin et en Occident.* 2 vols. 2nd ed. Brussels: Académie Royale de Belgique, 1992.

Lagorio, Valerie M. "Variations on the Theme of God's Motherhood in Medieval English Mystical and Devotional Writings." *Studia Mystica* 8.2 (1985): 15–37.

Lambert, Malcolm. *Medieval Heresy: Popular Movements from Bogomil to Hus.* 3rd ed. New York: Holmes & Meier, 2002.

Lamy, Marielle. "Les Apocryphes dans les premiers chapitres des deux célèbres 'Vies du Christ' de la fin du Moyen Âge (Les *Meditationes vitae Christi* du Pseudo-Bonaventure et la *Vita Christi* de Ludolfe le Chartreux)." *Apocrypha* 20 (2009): 29–82.

———. *L'immaculée conception: étapes et enjeux d'une controverse au Moyen Âge, XII^e–XV^e siécles.* Paris: Institut d'Études Augustiniennes, 2000.

Landolt-Wegener, Elisabeth. "Darstellung der Kindheitslegenden Christi in Historienbibeln aus der Werkstatt Diebolt Laubers." *Zeitschrift für schweizerische Archäologie und Kunstgeschichte* 23 (1963/64): 212–25.

Lane, Barbara G. *The Altar and the Altarpiece: Sacramental Themes in Early Netherlandish Painting.* New York: Harper and Row, 1984.

———. "'Ecce Panis Angelorum': The Manger as Altar in Hugo's Berlin *Nativity*." *Art Bulletin* 57.4 (1975): 476–86.

Laneyrie-Dagen, Nadeije. "'Lorsque l'enfant paraît': La fin du Moyen Âge." In *L'enfant dans la peinture*, edited by Sébastian Allard, Nadeije Laneyrie-Dagen, and Emmanuel Pernoud, 26–52. Paris: Citadelles & Mazenod, 2011.

La Rocca, Sandra. *L'Enfant Jésus: histoire et anthropologie d'une dévotion dans l'Occident chrétien.* Toulouse: Presses Universitaires du Mirail, 2007.

La Roncière, Charles-M. de. "La Nativité dans la dévotion de saint François d'Assise." In *La Nativité et le temps de Noël*, edited by Boyer and Dorival, 231–43.

Larrington, Carolyne. "The Candlemas Vision and Marie d'Oignies's Role in Its Dissemination." In *New Trends in Feminine Spirituality: The Holy Women of Liège and Their Impact*, edited by Juliette Dor, Lesley Johnson, and Jocelyn Wogan-Browne, Medieval Women: Texts and Contexts 2, 195–214. Turnhout: Brepols, 1999.

Latham, R. E., ed. *Dictionary of Medieval Latin from British Sources*. 17 Vols. London: Oxford University Press, 1975–2013.

Laurentin, René. *Jésus au temple: Mystère de Paques et foi de Marie en Luc 2, 48–50*. Paris: Lecoffre, 1966.

Lavaure, Annik. *L'Image de Joseph au Moyen Âge*. Rennes: Presses Universitaires de Rennes, 2013.

Lavin, Marilyn Aronberg. "Giovannino Battista: A Study in Renaissance Religious Symbolism." *Art Bulletin* 37.2 (1955): 85–101.

———. "Giovannino Battista: A Supplement." *Art Bulletin* 43.4 (1961): 319–26.

Lawrence, C. H. *Medieval Monasticism: Forms of Religious Life in Western Europe in the Middle Ages*. 2nd ed. London: Longman, 1989.

Le Brun, Jacques. "La dévotion à l'Enfant Jésus au XVIIᵉ siècle." In *Histoire de l'enfance en Occident*, vol. 1: *De l'Antiquité au XVIIᵉ siècle*, edited by Egle Becchi and Dominique Julia, 427–57. Paris: Seuil, 1998.

———. "Jésus-Christ n'a jamais ri?: analyse d'un raisonnement théologique." In *Homo religiosus: Autour de Jean Delumeau*, 431–37. Paris: Fayard, 1997.

Leclercq, Jean. *Chances de la spiritualité occidentale*. Paris: Cerf, 1966.

Le Goff, Jacques. "Head or Heart? The Political Uses of Body Metaphors in the Middle Ages." In *Fragments for a History of the Human Body, Part Three*, edited by Michel Feher, Ramona Naddaff, and Nadia Tazi, 12–27. New York: Zone Books, 1989.

———. "Laughter in the Middle Ages." In *A Cultural History of Humour: From Antiquity to the Present Day*, edited by Jan N. Bremmer and Herman Roodenburg, 40–53, 245–7. Cambridge, Mass.: Polity Press, 1997.

L'Engle, Susan, and Robert Gibbs. *Illuminating the Law: Legal Manuscripts in Cambridge Collections*. London: Harvey Miller, 2001.

Levy, Bernard S. "The Annunciation in Thomas de Hales' 'Love Ron.'" *Mediaevalia* 6 (1980): 123–34.

Lewis, Charlton T., and Charles Short, eds. *A Latin Dictionary*. Oxford: Clarendon Press, 1996 [1879].

LeZotte, Annette. "Cradling Power: Female Devotions and Early Netherlandish Jésueaux." In *Push Me, Pull You: Physical and Spatial Interaction in Late Medieval and Renaissance Art*, edited by Sarah Blick and Laura D. Gelfand, vol. 2, 59–84. Leiden: Brill, 2011.

Lieberman, Max. "Saint Joseph, Jean Gerson et Pierre d'Ailly dans un manuscrit de 1464." *Cahiers de Joséphologie* 20 (1972): 5–110, 253–61.

Linardou, Kallirroe. "Depicting the Salvation: Typological Images of Mary in the Kokkinobaphos Manuscripts." In *The Cult of the Mother of God in Byzantium: Texts and Images*, edited by Leslie Brubaker and Mary Cunningham, 133–49. Farnham: Ashgate, 2011.

Lindquist, Sherry C. M., ed. *The Meanings of Nudity in Medieval Art*. Farnham: Ashgate, 2012.

Lipton, Sara. "'The Sweet Lean of His Head': Writing about Looking at the Crucifix in the High Middle Ages." *Speculum* 80.4 (2005): 1172–208.

Little, Lester K. *Benedictine Maledictions: Liturgical Cursing in Romanesque France*. Ithaca, N.Y.: Cornell University Press, 1993.

Loomis, C. Grant. *White Magic: An Introduction to the Folklore of Christian Legend*. Cambridge, Mass.: Mediaeval Academy of America, 1948.

Lubac, Henri de. *Medieval Exegesis*. Vol. 1.1: *The Four Senses of Scripture*. Translated by Marc Sebanc. Grand Rapids, Mich.: Eerdmans, 1998.

Lugt, Maaike van der. "The Incubus in Scholastic Debate: Medicine, Theology, and Popular Belief." In *Religion and Medicine in the Middle Ages*, edited by Peter Biller and Joseph Ziegler, York Studies in Medieval Theology 3, 175–200. York: York Medieval Press, 2001.

———. "La personne manquée: démons, cadavres et *opera vitae* du début du XIIᵉ siècle à Saint Thomas." *Micrologus* 7 (1999): 205–21.

———. *Le Ver, le démon et la vierge: les théories médiévales de la génération extraordinaire: une étude sur les rapports entre théologie, philosophie naturelle et médecine*. Paris: Les Belles Lettres, 2004.

Lunghi, Elvio. "Il presepe di Greccio nella pittura italiana dei secoli XIII–XIV." *Atti Accademia Properziana del Subasio*, ser. 7, no. 1 (1996): 109–24; figs. 1–15.

Luomanen, Petri. "Judaism and Anti-Judaism in Early Christian Apocrypha." In *The Oxford Handbook of Early Christian Apocrypha*, edited by Gregory and Tuckett, 319–42.

Lutton, Rob. "The Name of Jesus, Nicholas Love's *Mirror*, and Christocentric Devotion in Late Medieval England." In *The Pseudo-Bonaventuran Lives of Christ*, edited by Johnson and Westphall, 19–53.

MacLehose, William F. "Fear, Fantasy and Sleep in Medieval Medicine." In *Emotions and Health, 1200–1700*, edited by Elena Carrera, 67–94. Leiden: Brill, 2013.

———. "Health and Science." In *A Cultural History of Childhood and the Family in the Middle Ages*, edited by Louise J. Wilkinson, 161–78. Oxford/New York: Berg, 2010.

———. "The Holy Tooth: Dentition, Childhood Development, and the Cult of the Christ Child." In *The Christ Child in Medieval Culture*, edited by Dzon and Kenney, 201–23.

———. "Relics of the Christ Child." In *Encyclopedia of Medieval Pilgrimage*, edited by Larissa Taylor, 601–3. Leiden: Brill, 2010.

———. *"A Tender Age": Cultural Anxieties over the Child in the Twelfth and Thirteenth Centuries*. New York: Columbia University Press, 2008.

Madigan, Kevin. *The Passions of Christ in High-Medieval Thought: An Essay on Christological Development*. Oxford: Oxford University Press, 2006.

Magginis, Hayden B. J. "Images, Devotion, and the Beata Umiliana de' Cerchi." In *Visions of Holiness*, edited by Ladis and Zuraw, 13–20.

Maggioni, Giovanni Paolo. "La Littérature apocryphe dans le *Légende dorée* et dans ses sources immédiates." *Apocrypha* 19 (2008): 146–81.

Mâle, Émile. *L'Art religieux après le Concile de Trente: étude sur l'iconographie de la fin du XVIᵉ siècle, du XVIIᵉ siècle, du XVIIIᵉ siècle: Italie-France-Espagne-Flandres*. Paris: A. Colin, 1932.

———. *L'Art religieux du XIIIᵉ siècle en France: Étude sur l'iconographie du Moyen Age et sur ses sources d'inspiration*. 8th ed. Paris: A. Colin, 1948.

———. *L'Art religieux du XVIIᵉ siècle: Italie, France, Espagne, Flandres*. Edited by Gilles Chazal. Introduction by André Chastel. Paris: A. Colin, 1984.

———. *Religious Art in France: The Late Middle Ages: A Study of Medieval Iconography and Its Sources*. Edited by Harry Bober, translated by Marthiel Mathews. Bollingen Series 90.3. Princeton: Princeton University Press, 1986.

———. *Religious Art in France: The Thirteenth Century: A Study of Medieval Iconography and Its Sources*. [Edited by Harry Bober, translated by Marthiel Mathews.] Bollingen Series 90.2. Princeton: Princeton University Press, 1984.

Marcus, Leah [Sinanoglou]. *Childhood and Cultural Despair: A Theme and Variations in Seventeenth-Century Literature*. Pittsburgh: University of Pittsburgh Press, 1978.

————. "The Christ Child as Sacrifice: A Medieval Tradition and the English Cycle Plays." In *The Christ Child in Medieval Culture*, edited by Dzon and Kenney, 3–28.

Marrou, Henri-Irénée. "Saint Augustin et l'ange: une légende médiévale." In *L'homme devant Dieu: Mélanges offerts au Père Henri de Lubac*, vol. 2, 137–49. Paris: Aubier, 1964.

Marrow, James H. *Passion Iconography in Northern European Art of the Late Middle Ages and Early Renaissance: A Study of the Transformation of Sacred Metaphor into Descriptive Narrative*. Kortrijk, Belgium: Van Ghemmert, 1979.

Marx, C. W. *The Devil's Rights and the Redemption in the Literature of Medieval England*. Cambridge: D. S. Brewer, 1995.

Mathews, Thomas F. "The Chariot and the Donkey." In *The Clash of Gods*, 23–53.

————. *The Clash of Gods: A Reinterpretation of Early Christian Art*. Princeton: Princeton University Press, 1993.

————. "The Magician." In *The Clash of Gods*, 54–91.

Mauquoy-Hendrickx, Marie. *Les estampes des Wierix conservées au Cabinet des estampes de la Bibliothèque Royale Albert Iᵉʳ, Catalogue raisonné, Première partie*. Bruxelles: Bibliotheque Royale Albert Iᵉʳ, 1978.

Maxwell, Felicity Lyn. "Mapping the Meditations: A Survey of Recent Research on the Pseudo-Bonaventuran *Meditationes vitae Christi* and Nicholas Love's *Mirror of the Blessed Life of Jesus Christ*." *Bulletin of International Medieval Research* 13 (2007): 18–30.

McDevitt, Mary. " 'The Ink of Our Mortality': The Late-Medieval Image of the Writing Christ Child." In *The Christ Child in Medieval Culture*, edited by Dzon and Kenney, 224–53.

McDonnell, Ernest W. *The Beguines and Beghards in Medieval Culture with Special Emphasis on the Belgian Scene*. New Brunswick, N.J.: Rutgers University Press, 1954.

McGuire, Brian Patrick. "Becoming a Father and a Husband: St. Joseph in Bernard of Clairvaux and Jean Gerson." In *Joseph of Nazareth through the Centuries*, edited by Joseph Chorpenning, 49–61. Philadelphia: Saint Joseph's University Press, 2011.

————. *Brother and Lover: Aelred of Rievaulx*. New York: Crossroad, 1994.

————. "Children and Youth in Monastic Life: Western Europe 400–1250." In *Childhood in History*, edited by Aasgaard and Horn, forthcoming.

————. *Friendship and Community: The Monastic Experience, 350–1250*. CS 95. Kalamazoo, Mich.: Cistercian Publications, 1988.

————. *Jean Gerson and the Last Medieval Reformation*. University Park: Penn State University Press, 2005.

————. "Sexual Awareness and Identity in Aelred of Rievaulx (1110–67)." *American Benedictine Review* 45.2 (1994): 184–226.

————. "When Jesus Did the Dishes: The Transformation of Late Medieval Spirituality." In *The Making of Christian Communities in Late Antiquity and the Middle Ages*, edited by Mark F. Williams, 131–52, 188–93. London: Anthem Press, 2005.

McNamara, R. F. "Crib, Christmas." In NCE, vol. 4, 364.

McNamer, Sarah. *Affective Meditation and the Invention of Medieval Compassion*. Philadelphia: University of Pennsylvania Press, 2009.

————. "The Author of the Italian *Meditations on the Life of Christ*." In *New Directions in Medieval Manuscript Studies and Reading Practices: Essays in Honor of Derek Pearsall*, edited by Kathryn Kerby-Fulton, John J. Thompson, and Sarah Baechle, 119–37. Notre Dame, Ind.: University of Notre Dame Press, 2014.

————. "The Origins of the *Meditationes vitae Christi.*" *Speculum* 84.5 (2009): 905–55.

Mehl, Dieter. *The Middle English Romances of the Thirteenth and Fourteenth Centuries.* London: Routledge & Kegan Paul, 1968.

Meinardus, Otto F. A. "Zur 'Strickenden Madonna' oder 'Die Darbringung der Leidenswerkzeuge' des Meisters Bertram." *Idea: Jahrbuch der Hamburger Kunsthalle* 7 (1988): 15–22.

Mellinkoff, Ruth. *Outcasts: Signs of Otherness in Northern European Art of the Late Middle Ages.* 2 vols. Berkeley: University of California Press, 1993.

Metz. René. "L'Accession des mineurs à la cléricature et aux bénéfices ecclésiastiques dans le droit canonique médiéval." In *Mélanges Roger Aubenas*, Recueil de mémoires et travaux 9, 553–67. Montpellier: Faculté de droit et des sciences économiques de Montpellier, 1974.

Metzger, Bruce M. *The Canon of the New Testament: Its Origin, Development, and Significance.* Oxford: Clarendon Press, 1997.

Meurgey, Jacques. *Les Principaux manuscrits à peintures du Musée Condé à Chantilly.* Paris: Société française de reproductions de manuscrits à peintures, 1930.

Meyer, Paul. "*Chanjon*, Enfant changé en nourrice." *Romania* 32 (1903): 452–53.

Micha, Alexandre. "Robert de Boron's Merlin." Translated by Miren Lacassagne. In *Merlin: A Casebook*, edited by Peter H. Goodich and Raymond H. Thompson, 296–307. New York: Routledge, 2003.

Miles, Clement A. *Christmas in Ritual and Tradition.* London: Unwin, 1912.

Miles, Laura Saetveit. "The Origins and Development of the Virgin Mary's Book at the Annunciation." *Speculum* 89.3 (2014): 632–69.

Mills, Robert. "Jesus as Monster." In *The Monstrous Middle Ages*, edited by Bettina Bildhauer and Robert Mills, 28–54. Toronto: University of Toronto Press, 2003.

Mimouni, Simon C. "Les *Vies de la Vierge*: État de la question." *Apocrypha* 5 (1994): 211–48.

Minnis, A. J., and Eric J. Johnson. "Chaucer's Criseyde and Feminine Fear." In *Medieval Women: Texts and Contexts in Late-Medieval Britain: Essays for Felicity Riddy*, edited by Jocelyn Wogan-Browne et al., 199–216. Turnhout: Brepols, 2000.

Minty, Mary. "Kiddush Ha-shem in German Christian Eyes in the Middle Ages." *Zion* 59 (1994): 209–66 (in Hebrew; summary in English: xii–xiv).

————. "Responses to Medieval Ashkenazi Martyrdom (Kiddush-ha-Shem) in Late Medieval German Sources." *Jahrbuch für Antisemitismusforschung* 4 (1995): 13–38.

Mollat, G. *The Popes at Avignon, 1305–1378.* Translated by Janet Love. London: Thomas Nelson and Sons, 1963.

Morris, Bridget. "The Monk-on-the-ladder in Book V of St Birgitta's *Revelaciones.*" *Kyrkohistorisk årsskrift* (1982): 95–107.

————. *St Birgitta of Sweden.* Woodbridge: Boydell Press, 1999.

Morris, Colin. *The Discovery of the Individual, 1050–1200.* Toronto: University of Toronto Press, 1987.

Mossman, Stephen. *Marquard von Lindau and the Challenges of Religious Life in Late Medieval Germany: The Passion, the Eucharist, the Virgin Mary.* Oxford: Oxford University Press, 2010.

Mowbray, Donald. *Pain and Suffering in Medieval Theology.* Woodbridge: Boydell Press, 2009.

Muir, Carolyn Diskant. "Bride or Bridegroom? Masculine Identity in Mystic Marriages." In *Holiness and Masculinity in the Middle Ages*, edited by P. H. Cullum and Katherine J. Lewis, 58–78. Toronto: University of Toronto Press, 2005.

————. *Saintly Brides and Bridegrooms: The Mystic Marriage in Northern Renaissance Art.* London/Turnhout: Harvey Miller/Brepols, 2012.

Mulvaney, Beth A. "The Beholder as Witness: The 'Crib at Greccio' from the Upper Church of San Francesco, Assisi and Franciscan Influence on Late Medieval Art in Italy." In *The Art of the Franciscan Order in Italy*, edited by William R. Cook, 169–88. Leiden: Brill. 2005.

Murbach, Ernst, with illustrations by Peter Heman. *The Painted Romanesque Ceiling of St. Martin in Zillis.* Translated by Janet Seligman. New York: Praeger, 1967.

Mursell, Gordon. *English Spirituality from Earliest Times to 1700.* Louisville, K.Y.: Westminster John Knox Press, 2001.

Nagy, Piroska. "Religious Weeping as Ritual in the Medieval West." *Social Analysis* 48.2: *Ritual in Its Own Right: Exploring the Dynamics of Transformation* (2004): 119–37.

Neff, Amy. "The Pain of *Compassio*: Mary's Labor at the Foot of the Cross." *Art Bulletin* 80.2 (1998): 254–73.

Newhauser, Richard. "The Sin of Curiosity and the Cistercians." In *Erudition at God's Service*, edited by J. R. Sommerfeldt, Studies in Medieval Cistercian History 11, 71–95. CS 98. Kalamazoo, Mich.: Cistercian Publications, 1987.

Newman, Barbara. "'Crueel Corage': Child Sacrifice and the Maternal Martyr in Hagiography and Romance." In *From Virile Woman to WomanChrist*, 76–107. Philadelphia: University of Pennsylvania Press, 1995.

————. "Love's Arrows: Christ as Cupid in Late Medieval Art and Devotion." In *The Mind's Eye*, edited by Hamburger and Bouché, 263–86.

————. *Sister of Wisdom: St. Hildegard's Theology of the Feminine.* Berkeley: University of California Press, 1989.

————. "What Did It Mean to Say 'I Saw'?: The Clash between Theory and Practice in Medieval Visionary Culture." *Speculum* 80.1 (2005): 1–43.

Nicholson, R. H. "The Trial of Christ the Sorcerer in the York Cycle." *Journal of Medieval and Renaissance Studies* 16.2 (1986): 125–69.

Nilgen, Ursula. "The Epiphany and the Eucharist: On the Interpretation of Eucharistic Motifs in Medieval Epiphany Scenes." *Art Bulletin* 49.4 (1967): 311–16.

Nixon, Virginia. *Mary's Mother: Saint Anne in Late Medieval Europe.* University Park: Penn State University Press, 2004.

Nold, Patrick. "Pope John XXII, the Franciscan Order and Its *Rule*." In *The Cambridge Companion to Francis of Assisi*, edited by Michael J. P. Robson, 258–72. Cambridge: Cambridge University Press, 2012.

Noye, Irénée. "Enfance de Jésus." In DS, vol. 4.1, 652–82.

O'Connell, Patrick F. "Aelred of Rievaulx and the 'Lignum Vitae' of Bonaventure: A Reappraisal." *Franciscan Studies* 48 (1988): 53–80.

Ogle, Marbury Bladen. "The Discovery of the Wonder Child." *Transactions and Proceedings of the American Philological Association* 59 (1928): 179–204.

————. "The Orchard Scene in *Tydorel* and *Sir Gowther*." *Romanic Review* 13 (1922): 37–43.

Olsen, Ulla Sander. "Work and Work Ethics in the Nunnery of Syon Abbey in the Fifteenth Century." In *The Medieval Mystical Tradition in England; Exeter Symposium V; Papers Read at the Devon Centre, Dartington Hall, July 1992*, edited by Marion Glasscoe, 129–42. Woodbridge: D. S. Brewer, 1992.

Oosterwijk, Sophie. "'I cam but now, and now I go my wai': The Presentation of the Infant in the Medieval Danse Macabre." In *Essays on Medieval Childhood: Responses to Recent Debates*, edited by Joel T. Rosenthal, 124–50. Donington: Shaun Tyas, 2007.

———. "Swaddled or Shrouded? The Interpretation of 'Chrysom' Effigies on Late Medieval Tomb Monuments." In *Weaving, Veiling, and Dressing: Textiles and Their Metaphors in the Late Middle Ages*, edited by Kathryn M. Rudy and Barbara Baert, 307–48. Medieval Church Studies 12. Turnhout: Brepols, 2007.

———. "The Swaddling-Clothes of Christ: A Medieval Relic on Display." *Medieval Life* 13 (2000): 25–30.

Orme, Nicholas. *Medieval Children*. New Haven, Conn.: Yale University Press, 2001.

Os, Henk W. van. *The Art of Devotion in the Late Middle Ages in Europe, 1300–1500*. Translated by Michael Hoyle. Amsterdam: Merrell Holberton, 1994.

———. "The Discovery of an Early Man of Sorrows on a Dominican Triptych." *Journal of the Warburg and Courtauld Institutes* 41 (1978): 65–75 (plates 10–15).

———. "The Madonna and the Mystery Play." *Simiolus* 5.1/2 (1971): 5–19.

———. "Mary as Seamstress." In *Studies in Early Tuscan Painting*, 278–81. London: Pindar Press, 1992.

Osier, Jean-Pierre. *L'Evangile du ghetto*. Paris: Berg International, 1984.

Otter, Monika. *Inventiones: Fiction and Referentiality in Twelfth-Century English Historical Writing*. Chapel Hill: University of North Carolina Press, 1996.

Ozanam, Frédéric. *The Franciscan Poets in Italy of the Thirteenth Century*. London: D. Nutt, 1914.

Palazzo, Robert P. "The Veneration of the Sacred Foreskin(s) of Baby Jesus: A Documented Analysis." In *Multicultural Europe and Cultural Exchange in the Middle Ages and Renaissance*, edited by James P. Helfers, 155–76. Turnhout: Brepols, 2005.

Panofsky, Erwin. *Early Netherlandish Painting: Its Origin and Character*. 2 vols. Cambridge, Mass.: Harvard University Press, 1958.

Pareles, Mo. "Inhuman Infants and Pork Futures in *The King of Tars* and the Medieval English Children of the Oven Miracle." Unpublished conference paper presented at the Sewanee Medieval Colloquium, April 2, 2016.

Park, Katharine. "Impressed Images: Reproducing Wonders." In *Picturing Science, Producing Art*, edited by Caroline A. Jones and Peter L. Galison, 254–71. New York: Routledge, 1998.

Patterson, Lee. "'What Man Artow?': Authorial Self-Definition in *The Tale of Sir Thopas* and *The Tale of Melibee*." *Studies in the Age of Chaucer* 11 (1989): 117–75.

Payan, Paul. *Joseph: Une image de paternité dans l'Occident médiéval*. Paris: Aubier, 2006.

Pemberton, Elizabeth G. "The Seamless Garment: A Note on John 19:23–24." *Australian Biblical Review* 54 (2006): 50–55.

Perdrizet, Paul. *La Vierge de miséricorde: étude d'un thème iconographique*. Paris: A. Fontemoing, 1908.

Pérez-Higuera, Teresa. *La Nativité dans l'art médiéval*. Preface by Marie-Thérèse Camus, translated by Christiane de Montclos. Paris: Citadelles & Mazenod, 1996.

Petrén, Erik. *Kyrka och makt: Bilder ur svensk kyrkohistoria*. Lund: Signum, 1990.

Petrina, Alessandra. "Incubi and Nightmares in Middle-English Literature." *Atti dell'Istituto Veneto de Scienze, Lettere ed Arti* 152 (1993–1994): 391–422.

Phillips, Dianne. "The *Meditations on the Life of Christ*: An Illuminated Fourteenth-Century Italian Manuscript at the University of Notre Dame." In *The Text in the Community: Es-*

*says on Medieval Works, Manuscripts, Authors, and Readers*, edited by Jill Mann and Maura Nolan, 237–81. Notre Dame, Ind.: University of Notre Dame Press, 2006.

Phillips, Susan E. *Transforming Talk: The Problem with Gossip in Late Medieval England*. Philadelphia: University of Pennsylvania Press, 2007.

Poignet, Jean-François. "Recherches sur les récits de visions du Christ en Occident, jusqu'au XIII$^e$ siècle." Unpublished Thèse de troisième cycle, Université de Paris X, 1985.

Posset, Franz. "*Christi Dulcedo*: The 'Sweetness of Christ' in Western Christian Spirituality." *Cistercian Studies Quarterly* 80.3 (1995): 245–65.

Poulenc, Jérôme. "Saint François dans le 'vitrail des anges' de l'église supérieure de la basilique d'Assise." *Archivum Franciscanum Historicum* 76 (1983): 701–13.

Pringle, Denys. *The Churches of the Crusader Kingdom of Jerusalem: A Corpus*. Vol. 2. Cambridge: Cambridge University Press, 1998.

Puglisi, Catherine B., and William L. Barcham, eds. *New Perspectives on the Man of Sorrows*. Studies in Iconography: Themes and Variations. Kalamazoo, Mich.: Medieval Institute Publications, 2013.

Purkiss, Diane. *At the Bottom of the Garden: A Dark History of Fairies, Hobgoblins, and Other Troublesome Things*. Washington Square, N.Y.: New York University Press, 2000.

Purtle, Carol. "Le Sacerdoce de la Vierge et l'énigme d'un parti iconographique exceptionnel." *Revue du Louvre* 46.5/6 (1996): 54–65.

Quasten, Johannes. *Patrology: The Beginnings of Patristic Literature*. Vol. 1. Utrecht: Spectrum, 1966.

Raby, F. J. E. *A History of Christian-Latin Poetry from the Beginnings to the Close of the Middle Ages*. 2nd ed. Oxford: Clarendon Press, 1953.

Rahner, Karl. *Visions and Prophecies*. Translated by Charles Henkey and Richard Strachan. Freiburg: Herder, 1963.

Ratzinger, Joseph (Pope Benedict XVI). *Jesus of Nazareth: The Infancy Narratives*. Translated by Philip J. Whitmore. New York: Image, 2012.

Reed, Annette Yoshiko. "The Afterlives of New Testament Apocrypha." *Journal of Biblical Literature* 133.2 (2015): 402–25.

Reilly, Bernard F. "Santiago de Compostela." In *Medieval Iberia: An Encyclopedia*, edited by E. Michael Gerli, 733–37. New York: Routledge, 2003.

Reinsch, Robert. *Die Pseudo-Evangelien von Jesu und Maria's Kindheit in der romanischen und germanischen Literatur*. Halle: Max Niemeyer, 1879.

Remensnyder, Amy G. *Remembering Kings Past: Monastic Foundation Legends in Medieval Southern France*. Ithaca, N.Y.: Cornell University Press, 1995.

Resnick, Irven. *Marks of Distinction: Christian Perceptions of Jews in the High Middle Ages*. Washington, D.C.: Catholic University of America Press, 2012.

———. "Marriage in Medieval Culture: Consent Theory and the Case of Joseph and Mary." *Church History* 69 (2000): 350–71.

———. "Ps.-Albert the Great on the Physiognomy of Jesus and Mary." *Mediaeval Studies* 62 (2002): 217–40.

Reynolds, Brian K. *Gateway to Heaven: Marian Doctrine and Devotion, Image and Typology in the Patristic and Medieval Periods*. Vol. 1: *Doctrine and Devotion*. Hyde Park, N.Y.: New City Press, 2012.

Reynolds, Philip L. "Infants of Eden: Scholastic Theologians on Early Childhood and Cognitive Development." *Mediaeval Studies* 68 (2006): 89–132.

————. "Thomas Aquinas and the Paradigms of Childhood." In *The Vocation of the Child*, edited by Patrick McKinley Brennan, 154–188. Grand Rapids, Mich.: Eerdmans, 2008.

Riché, Pierre. "L'enfant dans la société chrétienne aux XI<sup>e</sup>–XII<sup>e</sup> siècles." In *La cristianità dei secoli XI e XII in Occidente: coscienza e strutture di una società*, 281–302. Milan: Vita e Pensiero, 1983.

Ringbom, Sixten. "Vision and Conversation in the Early Netherlandish Painting: The Delft Master's *Holy Family*." *Simiolus* 19.3 (1989): 181–90.

Robson, Janet. "Assisi, Rome and *The Miracle of the Crib at Greccio*." In *Image, Memory and Devotion, Liber Amicorum Paul Crossley, Studies in Gothic Art*, edited by Zoë Opačić and Achim Timmerman, Studies in Gothic Art 2, 145–55. Turnhout: Brepols, 2011.

Robson, Michael. *St. Francis of Assisi*. London: Geoffrey Chapman, 1997.

Rode, Rosemary. *Studien zu den mittelalterlichen Kind-Jesu-Visionen*. Published PhD thesis, Johann Wolfgang Goethe Universität, Frankfurt am Main, 1957.

Roelvink, Henrik. "Andlig släktskap mellan Franciskus och Birgitta." In *Heliga Birgitta, budskapet och förebilden*, edited by Härdelin and Lindgren, 99–122.

————. *Franciscans in Sweden: Medieval Remnants of Franciscan Activities*. Assen: Van Gorgum, 1998.

————. "Var den heliga Birgitta medlem i den franciskanska tredje orden?" *Signum* 13 (1987): 153–55.

Roisin, Simone. *L'Hagiographie cistercienne dans le diocèse de Liège au XIII<sup>e</sup> siècle*. Louvain: Bibliothèque de l'université, 1947.

Rooijen, Henri van. *Theodorus van Celles: Een tijds- en levensbeeld*. Cuyk: van Lindert, 1936.

Rosenthal, Erwin. "The Crib of Greccio and Franciscan Realism." *Art Bulletin* 36.1 (1954): 57–62.

Ross, Ellen M. *The Grief of God: Images of the Suffering Jesus in Late Medieval England*. Oxford: Oxford University Press, 1997.

Roth, Norman. "Ritual Murder." In *Medieval Jewish Civilization: An Encyclopedia*, edited by Norman Roth, 566–70. New York: Routledge, 2003.

Rowe, Nina. *The Jew, the Cathedral, and the Medieval City: Synagoga and Ecclesia in the Thirteenth Century*. Cambridge: Cambridge University Press, 2011.

Rubin, Miri. *Corpus Christi: The Eucharist in Late Medieval Culture*. Cambridge. Cambridge University Press, 1991.

————. "From 'Theotokos' to 'Mater Dolorosa': Continuity and Change in the Images of Mary." In *Resonances: Historical Essays on Continuity and Change*, edited by Nils Holger Petersen, Eyolf Østrem, and Andreas Bücker, 59–80. Turnhout: Brepols, 2011.

————. *Gentile Tales: The Narrative Assault on Late Medieval Jews*. Philadelphia: University of Pennsylvania Press, 1999.

————. *Mother of God: A History of the Virgin Mary*. New Haven, Conn.: Yale University Press, 2009.

————. "The Passion of Mary: The Virgin Mary and the Jews in Medieval Culture." In *The Passion Story: From Visual Representation to Social Drama*, edited by Marcia Kupfer, 53–66. University Park: Penn State University Press, 2008.

Rublack, Ulinka. "Female Spirituality and the Infant Jesus in Late Medieval Dominican Convents." In *Popular Religion in Germany and Central Europe, 1400–1800*, edited by Robert Scribner and Trevor Johnson, 16–37. New York: Macmillan, 1996.

Russell, Jeffrey Burton. *Witchcraft in the Middle Ages*. Ithaca, N.Y.: Cornell University Press, 1972.

Rutt, Richard. *A History of Hand Knitting*. Loveland, Colo.: Interweave Press, 1987.

Sabatier, Paul. *Vie de S. François d'Assise*. Paris: Fischbacher, 1894.

Sahlin, Claire L. "'His Heart Was My Heart': Birgitta of Sweden's Devotion to the Heart of Mary." In *Heliga Birgitta, budskapet och förebilden*, edited by Härdelin and Lindgren, 213–27.

———. "'A Marvelous and Great Exultation of the Heart': Mystical Pregnancy and Marian Devotion in Bridget of Sweden's *Revelations*." In *Studies in St. Birgitta and the Brigittine Order*, edited by James Hogg, vol. 1, 108–28. *Analecta Cartusiana* 35:19: Spiritualität Heute und Gestern 19, Institut für Anglistik und Amerikanistik. New York: Edwin Mellen Press, 1993.

Salmesvuori, Pävi. "Birgitta of Sweden and Her Pilgrimage to Santiago de Compostela." In *Women and Pilgrimage in Medieval Galicia*, edited by Carlos Andrés González-Paz, 113–21. Farnham: Ashgate, 2015.

Salter, Elizabeth. *Nicholas Love's "Myrrour of the Blessed Lyf of Jesu Christ."* Analecta Cartusiana 10. Salzburg: Institut für Englische Sprache und Literatur, 1974.

Santing, Catrien. "'And I Bear Your Beautiful Face Painted on My Chest': The Longevity of the Heart as the Primal Organ in the Late Middle Ages and Renaissance." In *Disembodied Heads*, edited by Santing et al., 270–306.

Santing, Catrien, Barbara Baert, and Anita Traninger, eds. *Disembodied Heads in Medieval and Early Modern Culture*. Leiden: Brill, 2013.

Saward, John. *Perfect Fools: Folly for Christ's Sake in Catholic and Orthodox Spirituality*. Oxford: Oxford University Press, 1980.

———. *Redeemer in the Womb: Jesus Living in Mary*. San Francisco: Ignatius Press, 1993.

Sawyer, John. "'A man of sorrows and acquainted with grief' (Isa. 53:3): The Biblical Text and Its Afterlife in Christian Tradition." In *New Perspectives on the Man of Sorrows*, ed. Puglisi and Barcham, 7–18.

Scarciglia, Alfredo. *Il Natale nella mistica domenicana*. Siena: Industria Grafica Pistolesi Editrice, 2007.

Scavone, Daniel. "Joseph of Arimathea, the Holy Grail, and the Edessa Icon." *Arthuriana* 9.4 (1999): 1–31.

Schapiro, Meyer. *Late Antique, Early Christian and Mediaeval Art: Selected Papers*. New York: George Braziller, 1979.

———. "'Muscipula Diaboli,' The Symbolism of The Mérode Altarpiece." *Art Bulletin* 27.3 (1945): 182–87. Reproduced in *Late Antique, Early Christian and Mediaeval Art*, 1–11.

———. "A Note on the Mérode Altarpiece." *Art Bulletin* 41.1 (1959): 327–28. Reproduced in *Late Antique, Early Christian and Mediaeval Art*, 12–15.

Schiller, Gertrud. *Iconography of Christian Art*. Translated by Janet Seligman. 2 vols. Greenwich, Conn.: New York Graphic Society, 1971/1972.

Schiwy, Günther. *Birgitta von Schweden: Mystikerin und Visionärin des späten Mittelalters: eine Biographie*. Munich: Beck, 2003.

Schlegel, Ursula. "The Christ Child as Devotional Image in Medieval Italian Sculpture: A Contribution to Ambrogio Lorenzetti Studies." *Art Bulletin* 52.1 (1970): 1–10.

Schmitt, Jean-Claude. *Ghosts in the Middle Ages: The Living and the Dead in Medieval Society*. Translated by Teresa Lavender Fagan. Chicago: University of Chicago Press, 1998.

———. *The Holy Greyhound: Guinefort, Healer of Children Since the Thirteenth Century.* Translated by Martin Thom. Cambridge: Cambridge University Press, 1983.

———. "'Unorthodox' Images? The 2006 Neal Lecture" (Followed by Robert Bartlett, "Comment on Jean-Claude Schmitt's Neale Lecture"). In *The Unorthodox Imagination in Late Medieval Britain*, edited by Sophie Page, 9–38, 39–44. Manchester: Manchester University Press, 2010.

Schneemelcher, Wilhem. "General Introduction." In *New Testament Apocrypha*, vol. 1, edited by Hennecke and Schneemelcher, 9–75.

Schreckenberg, Heinz. *The Jews in Christian Art*. New York: Continuum, 1996.

Schreiner, Klaus. "Marienverehrung, Lesekultur, Schriftlichkeit: Bildungs- und frömmigkeitsgeschichtliche Studien zur Auslegung und Darstellung von 'Mariä Verkündigung.'" *Frühmittelalterliche Studien* 24 (1990): 314–68.

Schuler, Carol M. "The Seven Sorrows of the Virgin: Popular Culture and Cultic Imagery in Pre-Reformation Europe." *Simiolus* 21/1–2 (1992): 5–28.

Schultz, James A. *The Knowledge of Childhood in the German Middle Ages, 1100–1350*. Philadelphia: University of Pennsylvania Press, 1995.

Sears, Elizabeth. *The Ages of Man: Medieval Interpretations of the Life Cycle*. Princeton: Princeton University Press, 1986.

Serra, Aristide. *Sapienza e contemplazione di Maria secondo Luca 2, 19.51b*. Rome: Edizioni Marianum, 1982.

Shahar, Shulamith. *Childhood in the Middle Ages*. Translated by Chaya Galai. London: Routledge, 1992.

Shaver-Crandell, Annie, and Paula Lieber Gerson. *The Pilgrim's Guide to Santiago de Compostela: A Gazetteer*. With the assistance of Alison Stones. London: Harvey Miller, 1995.

Sheingorn, Pamela. "Appropriating the Holy Kinship: Gender and Family History." In *Interpreting Cultural Symbols: St. Anne in Late Medieval Society*, edited by Kathleen Ashley and Pamela Sheingorn, 169–98. Athens: University of Georgia Press, 1990.

———. "'Illustrius patriarcha Joseph': Jean Gerson, Representations of Saint Joseph, and Imagining Community among Churchmen in the Fifteenth Century." In *Visions of Community in the Pre-modern World*, edited by Nicholas Howe, 75–108. Notre Dame, Ind.: University of Notre Dame Press, 2002.

———. "Joseph the Carpenter's Failure at Familial Discipline." In *Insights and Interpretations: Studies in Celebration of the Eighty-Fifth Anniversary of the Index of Christian Art*, edited by Colum Hourihane, 156–67. Princeton: Princeton University Press, 2002.

———. "Reshapings of the Childhood Miracles of Jesus." In *The Christ Child in Medieval Culture*, edited by Dzon and Kenney, 254–92.

Shoemaker, Stephen J. "Mary at the Cross, East and West: Maternal Compassion and Affective Piety in the Earliest *Life of the Virgin* and the High Middle Ages." *Journal of Theological Studies*, n.s., 62.2 (2011): 570–606.

Simons, Walter. *Cities of Ladies: Beguine Communities in Medieval Low Countries, 1200–1565*. Philadelphia: University of Pennsylvania Press, 2001.

Simons, W., and J. E. Ziegler. "Phenomenal Religion in the Thirteenth Century and Its Image: Elisabeth of Spalbeek and the Passion Cult." In *Women in the Church: Papers Read at the 1989 Summer Meeting and the 1990 Winter Meeting of the Ecclesiastical History Society*, edited by W. J. Sheils and Diana Wood, 117–26. Oxford: Basil Blackwell, 1990.

Smart, Alastair. *The Assisi Problem and the Art of Giotto: A Study of the Legend of St. Francis in the Upper Church of San Francesco, Assisi*. Oxford: Clarendon Press, 1971.

Smith, Katherine Allen. "Bodies of Unsurpassed Beauty: 'Living' Images of the Virgin in the High Middle Ages." *Viator* 37 (2006): 167–188.

Smith, Kathryn A. "Accident, Play, and Invention: Three Infancy Miracles in the Holkham Bible Picture Book." In *Tributes to Jonathan J. G. Alexander: The Making and Meaning of Illuminated Medieval & Renaissance Manuscripts, Art & Architecture*, edited by Susan L'Engle and Gerald B. Guest, 357–69. London: Harvey Miller, 2006.

———. *Art, Identity and Devotion in Fourteenth-Century England: Three Women and Their Books of Hours*. London/Toronto: British Library/University of Toronto Press, 2003.

———. "Canonizing the Apocryphal: London, British Library MS Egerton 2781 and Its Visual, Devotional and Social Contexts." 3 vols. Unpublished PhD thesis, New York University, 1996.

Smoller, Laura A. "'Popular' Religious Culture(s)." In *The Oxford Handbook of Medieval Christianity*, edited by Arnold, 340–56.

Sonne de Torrens, Harriet M. "*De fontibus salvatoris*: A Survey of Twelfth- and Thirteenth-Century Baptismal Fonts Ornamented with Events from the Childhood of Christ." In *Objects, Images, and the Word: Art in the Service of the Liturgy*, edited by Colum Hourihane, 105–37. Princeton: Princeton University Press, 2003.

Southern, Richard W. *The Making of the Middle Ages*. New Haven, Conn.: Yale University Press, 1953.

———. *Saint Anselm: A Portrait in a Landscape*. Cambridge: Cambridge University Press, 1990.

Spearing, A. C. *Medieval Dream-Poetry*. Cambridge: Cambridge University Press, 1976.

Spicq, Ceslas. *Ce que Jésus doit à sa mère selon la théologie biblique et d'après les théologiens médiévaux*. Montréal: Institut d'Études Médiévales, 1959.

Steel, Karl. *How to Make a Human: Animals and Violence in the Middle Ages*. Columbus: Ohio State University Press, 2011.

Steinberg, Leo. *The Sexuality of Christ in Renaissance Art and in Modern Oblivion*. Revised ed. Chicago: University of Chicago Press, 1996.

Steiner, Emily. *Documentary Culture and the Making of Medieval English Literature*. Cambridge: Cambridge University Press, 2003.

Stephens, Walter. *Demon Lovers: Witchcraft, Sex, and the Crisis of Belief*. Chicago: University of Chicago Press, 2002.

Sticca, Sandro. *The Planctus Mariae in the Dramatic Tradition of the Middle Ages*. Athens: University of Georgia Press, 1988.

Strickland, Debra Higgs. "Gazing into Bernhard Blumenkranz's *Mirror of Christian Art*: The Fourteenth-Century Tring Tiles and the Jewishness of Jesus in Post-Expulsion England." In *Jews and Christians in Medieval Europe: The Historiographical Legacy of Bernhard Blumenkranz*, edited by Philippe Buc, Martha Keil, and John V. Tolan, 149–87. Turnhout: Brepols, 2016.

Sumption, Jonathan. *The Age of Pilgrimage: The Medieval Journey to God*. Mahwah, N.J.: HiddenSpring, 2003.

Swanson, R. N. "Passion and Practice: the Social and Ecclesiastical Implications of Passion Devotion in the Late Middle Ages." In *The Broken Body: Passion Devotion in Late-Medieval Culture*, edited by A. A. MacDonald, Bernhard Ridderbos, and R. M. Schlusemann, 1–30. Groningen: Egbert Forsten, 1989.

Tasioulas, Jacqueline. "'Heaven and Earth in Little Space': The Foetal Existence of Christ in Medieval Literature and Thought." *Medium Ævum* 76.1 (2007): 24–48.

Tatlock, J. S. P. *The Legendary History of Britain: Geoffrey of Monmouth's* Historia Regum Brittaniae *and Its Early Vernacular Versions*. Berkeley: University of California Press, 1950.

Temporelli, Agostino. *Oratorio della Santissima Trinità*. Momo: Parrocchia della Natività di Maria Vergine, 2000.

Thompson, John J. "The *Cursor Mundi*, the 'Inglis tong,' and 'Romance.'" In *Readings in Middle English Romance*, edited by Carol M. Meale, 99–120. Woodbridge: D. S. Brewer, 1994.

———. *Robert Thornton and the London Thornton Manuscript: British Library MS Additional 31042*. Cambridge: D. S. Brewer, 1987.

Tolan, John. *Saint Francis and the Sultan: The Curious History of a Christian-Muslim Encounter*. Oxford: Oxford University Press, 2009.

Torrell, Jean-Pierre. *Aquinas's* Summa: *Background, Structure, & Reception*. Translated by Benedict M. Guevin. Washington, D.C.: Catholic University of America Press, 2005.

———. *Le Christ en ses mystères: la vie et l'œuvre de Jésus selon saint Thomas d'Aquin*. Vol. 1. Paris: Desclée, 1999.

———. *Saint Thomas Aquinas*. Vol. 1: *The Person and His Work*. Translated by Robert Royal. Washington, D.C.: Catholic University of America Press, 1996.

Toubert, Hélène. "La Vierge et les sages-femmes: un jeu iconographique entre les Évangiles apocryphes et le drame liturgique." In *Marie: Le culte de la Vierge dans la société médiévale*, edited by Dominique Iogna-Prat, Eric Palazzo and Daniel Russo, 327–60. Paris: Beauchesne, 1996.

Tozzi, Ileana. "L'iconografia della natività nei luoghi del primo Presepe." *Arte cristiana* 92 (2004): 463–65.

Trachtenberg, Joshua. *The Devil and the Jews: The Medieval Conception of the Jew and Its Relation to Modern Antisemitism*. New Haven, Conn.: Yale University Press, 1943.

Traina, Cristina L. H. "A Person in the Making: Thomas Aquinas on Children and Childhood." In *The Child in Christian Thought*, edited by Marcia Bunge, 103–33. Grand Rapids, Mich.: Eerdmans, 2001.

Tress, Daryl McGowan. "Aristotle's Children." In *The Philosopher's Child: Critical Perspectives in the Western Tradition*, edited by Susan M. Turner and Gareth B. Matthews, 19–44. Rochester, N.Y.: University of Rochester Press, 1988.

Twelftree, Graham H., ed. *The Cambridge Companion to Miracles*. Cambridge: Cambridge University Press, 2011.

Twomey, Michael W. "Christ's Leap and Mary's Clean Catch in *Piers Plowman* B.12.136–44a and C.14.81–88a." *YLS* 5 (1991): 165–74.

Twycross, Meg. "'As the Sun with His Beams When He Is Most Bright.'" *Medieval English Theatre* 12 (1990): 34–79.

Upson-Saia, Kristi. "Holy Child or Holy Terror? Understanding Jesus' Anger in the Infancy Gospel of Thomas." *Church History* 82.1 (2013): 1–39.

Urbach, Zsuzsa. "'Ego sum deus et homo': Eine seltene Darstellung der Infantia Christi auf einem Triptychon des Christlichen Museums in Esztergom (Gran)." *Acta Historiae Artium Academiae Scientiarum Hungaricae* 36 (1993): 57–76.

Ure, John. *Pilgrimages: The Great Adventure of the Middle Ages*. London: Constable, 2006.

Valensi, Lucette. *La Fuite en Égypte: histoires d'Orient et d'Occident: essai d'histoire comparée*. Paris: Seuil, 2002.

Van Banning, Joop. "Saint Thomas Aquinas et l'*Opus imperfectum in Matthaeum*." In *S. tommaso nella historia del pensiero*, Studi tomistici 17, 73–85. Vatican City: Editrice Vaticana, 1982.

Vaughn, Míceál F. "The Three Advents in the *Secunda Pastorum*." *Speculum* 55.3 (1980): 484–504.

Velu, Anne Marie. *La Visitation dans l'art: Orient et Occident, V<sup>e</sup>–XVI<sup>e</sup> siècle.* Preface by François Bœspflug. Paris: Cerf, 2012.

Vidal, Jaime. "The Infancy Narrative in Pseudo-Bonaventure's *Meditationes vitae Christi*: A Study in Medieval Franciscan Christ-Piety." Unpublished PhD thesis, Fordham University, 1984.

Vigneras, L.-A. "L'abbaye de Charroux et la légende du pèlerinage de Charlemagne." *Romanic Review* 32 (1941): 121–28.

Vincent, Nicholas. *The Holy Blood: King Henry III and the Westminster Blood Relic.* Cambridge: Cambridge University Press, 2001.

Vines, Amy N. "Lullaby as Lament: Learning to Mourn in Middle English Nativity Lyrics." In *Laments for the Lost in Medieval Literature*, edited by Jane Tolmie and M. J. Toswell, Medieval Texts and Cultures of Northern Europe 19, 201–23. Turnhout: Brepols, 2010.

Vitz, Evelyn Birge. "The Apocryphal and the Biblical, the Oral and the Written, in Medieval Legends of Christ's Childhood: The Old French *Évangile de l'Enfance*." In *Satura: Studies in Medieval Literature in Honour of Robert R. Raymo*, edited by Nancy M. Reale and Ruth E. Sternglantz, 124–149. Donington: Shaun Tyas, 2001.

Vloberg, Maurice. *L'Eucharistie dans l'art.* 2 vols. Grenoble/Paris: B. Arthaud, 1946.

Voicu, Sever J. "Notes sur l'histoire du texte de L'*Histoire de l'Enfance de Jésus*." *Apocrypha* 2 (1991): 191–32.

———. "La tradition latine des *Paidika*." *Bulletin de l'AELAC* 14 (2004): 13–24.

———. "Ways to Survive for the Infancy Apocrypha." In *Infancy Gospels*, edited by Clivaz et al., 401–17.

Wade, James. *Fairies in Medieval Romance.* New York: Palgrave Macmillan, 2001.

Ward, H. L. D. *Catalogue of Romances in the British Museum.* Vol. 2. London: British Museum, 1893.

Wareing, Gregory. "The Teaching of St. Ailred of Rievaulx on Poverty." *Citeaux Commentarii Cistercienses* 18 (1967): 342–52.

Wasyliw, Patricia Healy. *Martyrdom, Murder, and Magic: Child Saints and Their Cults in Medieval Europe.* Studies in Church History 2. New York: Peter Lang, 2010.

Watson, Nicholas. "Censorship and Cultural Change in Late-Medieval England: Vernacular Theology, the Oxford Translation Debate, and Arundel's Constitutions of 1409." *Speculum* 70.4 (1995): 822–64.

Webb, Diana. *Pilgrims and Pilgrimage in the Medieval West.* London: I. B. Taurus, 2001.

Webb, Heather. *The Medieval Heart.* New Haven, Conn.: Yale University Press, 2010.

Wee, David L. "The Temptation of Christ and the Motif of Divine Duplicity in the Corpus Christi Cycle Drama." *Modern Philology* 72.1 (1974): 1–16.

Wenzel, Siegfried. *Preachers, Poets, and the Early English Lyric.* Princeton: Princeton University Press, 1986.

Wilken, Robert L. *John Chrysostom and the Jews: Rhetoric and Reality in the Late 4th Century.* Berkeley: University of California Press, 1983.

Williams Boyarin, Adrienne. *Miracles of the Virgin in Medieval England: Law and Jewishness in Marian Legends*. Cambridge: D. S. Brewer, 2010.

Williamson, Joan B. "Enfances." In *Medieval France: An Encyclopedia*, edited by William W. Kibler and Grover Zinn, 319. New York: Garland, 1995.

Wilson, Adrian, and Joyce Lancaster Wilson. *A Medieval Mirror: Speculum Humanae Salvationis, 1324–1500*. Berkeley: University of California Press, 1984.

Wood, Diana, ed. *The Church and Childhood: Papers Read at the 1993 Summer Meeting and the 1994 Winter Meeting of the Ecclesiastical History Society*. Studies in Church History 31. Oxford: Blackwell, 1994.

Woolf, Rosemary. "The Effect of Typology on the English Medieval Plays of Abraham and Isaac." *Speculum* 32.4 (1957): 805–25.

Wyss, Robert L. "Die Handarbeiten der Maria: eine ikonographische Studie unter Berücksichtigung der textilen Techniken." In *Artes Minores: Dank an Werner Abegg*, edited by Michael Stettler and Mechthild Lemberg, 113–88. Bern: Stämpfli, 1973.

Youngs, Deborah. "Adulthood in Medieval Europe: The Prime of Life or Midlife Crisis?" In *Medieval Life Cycyles*, edited by Cochelin and Smyth, 239–64.

———. *The Life Cycle in Western Europe, c. 1300–c. 1500*. Manchester: Manchester University Press, 2006.

Zervou Tognazzi, Ioanna. *Teologia visiva*. Città di Castello: Edimond, 2003.

Ziolkowski, Eric. *Evil Children in Religion, Literature, and Art*. New York: Palgrave, 2001.

Zuffetti, Zaira. *Il bambino Gesù nell'arte*. Milan: Àncora, 2015.

# INDEX

## ACKNOWLEDGMENTS

When I was still a graduate student, I recall a younger friend of mine, an undergraduate, once asked me if I intended to make the Christ Child the main focus on my scholarly career. I quickly answered no to what I perceived as a fanciful idea. Yet now that I think back to that question, I realize there was much that could be said in its favor. I did not realize back then how much further work I would continue to do on the medieval Christ Child. At times I was propelled by new discoveries and at other times I was inspired by the realization that what I had earlier thought I had understood was actually much more complicated than I had originally imagined. I have very much enjoyed working on the medieval Christ Child over the years—a topic that, like the divine child himself, never seems to grow old. But at the same time, I am glad to shift my attention to different though related areas of medieval piety and culture.

It is much to my regret that my beloved mother, who for decades filled my life with joy and was always tremendously supportive in my education and career, passed away before I had fully completed this study. I dedicate this book to her, who, probably without ever fully understanding my fascination with the medieval Christ Child, always had a childlike heart and sense of wonder. Day after day, she taught me the meaning of a mother's love, and for that I am truly grateful, as well as for her unfailing belief in the value of my work.

Many people along the way have helped me in ways both great and small. This book began under the guidance of Joseph Goering and George Rigg, both of whom have provided wonderful examples of medieval scholarship and basic human kindness. Special thanks also go to Nicole Fallon, Theresa Kenney, William MacLehose, and David White, all of whom helped me substantially improve the manuscript. I am also deeply grateful for the support of other friends, colleagues, and scholars, including Suzanne C. Akbari, Ann Astell, Thomas Bestul, Paul Barrette, Winston Black, Tony Burke, Isabelle Cochelin, Bill Cook, Christopher Dodsworth, Holly Flora, Valerie Garver, Robert

Getz, Rachel Golden, Thomas Heffernan, Valerie Heuchan, Laura Howes, Zbigniew Izydorczyk, Fr. Andrew Jaspers, Richard Kieckhefer, Roy Liuzza, Camin Melton, Amy Neff, Richard Newhauser, Nicholas Orme, Emily Reiner, William Robins, Jay Rubenstein, Miri Rubin, Andrew Seeley, Pamela Sheingorn, and Donna Trembinski, as well as many other people who encouraged me in this project. I am also indebted to the anonymous reviewer of my manuscript and thankful for my very patient and exceptionally pleasant editor, Jerry Singerman. In addition, I am very appreciative of the assistance I have received from various librarians, especially those at the Pontifical Institute of Mediaeval Studies Library in Toronto and the Hodges Library at the University of Tennessee-Knoxville. At my home institution, Kathleen Bailey in the Interlibrary Loan Office and Leonard Houston at the front desk of the Hodges Library were extremely helpful, as were many other people in Knoxville and beyond. I must also acknowledge the crucial financial and research support I have received over the years from a number of sources, especially the Hodges Fund for Better English, the Marco Institute for Medieval and Renaissance Studies, and the Fox Center for Humanistic Inquiry at Emory University. Lastly, I am grateful to my family members, both human and feline, for never holding it against me that my book absorbed so much of my time, energy, and spirit over the years.

It is worth noting a few of the general principles that have guided my writing and use of sources. Throughout this book I have cited the Douay-Rheims translation of the Bible, as the most literal translation of the Vulgate available, given that the Vulgate was standard within the medieval West. I have aimed to cite consistently both the most up-to-date critical editions as well as reliable English translations of the medieval and other sources under consideration. In cases where I do not cite someone else's translation, I provide my own. Linguistic details are important to me, since I believe that specific words reveal much about an author's frame of mind and the presuppositions of his or her culture.

I look forward to seeing how other scholars will proceed in the quest for the Christ Child that I have engaged in here, in this wide-ranging study of medieval curiosity about the hidden life of Jesus and also of medieval perspectives on human life itself—birth, death, and the ages in-between. I am certain that my own desire to know more about the Christ Child and his family will continue throughout the years.